Julia
Kirkpatrick

Katherine=
Jane Batten

Sir John
Strachey,
1823–1907

Col. John   Sir Charles   Sir Arthur   Winifred=Sir Hugh Barnes

Sir John Peter Grant,
K.C.M.G.

Gen. Sir
Richard Strachey,
G.C.I.S., F.R.S.,
1817–1908   =   Jane Grant

James Strachey
Barnes

Mary=   John St John
Hutchinson

s

Major Bartle=Ethel McNeil
Grant

(2)
Jeremy=Dame = Sir
Peggy Rupert
Ashcroft Hart-
Davis

(1)

Duncan James
Corowr Grant
(see Stephen
genealogy)

(2)
Rex Warner = Barbara= Lord N. M. Victor
Rothschild,
G.M., F.R.S.

(1)

Lucy

Jacob   Miranda   Sarah

Philippa,
b. 1874

Pernel,
1876–1951

Marjorie,
1882

Giles Lytton,
1886–1932

(1)
Rubye Mayor=

Oliver,
b. 1874 =

(2)
Ray Costelloe

Alix Sargant=
Florence

James Beaumont,
b. 1887

Karin
Costelloe = Adrian Stephen

vrence= Julia=
(1)
Hon. Stephen
Tomlin

Barbara   Christopher

Ann   Judith

on,=   Charlotte
Houghton,
m. 1888

(1)
Dora Houghton,
1893–1932,
m. 1922

= R. Partridge,
d. 1960

(2)
= Frances Marshall,
b. 1900,
m. 1933

Noel Lewis,
b. 1894

= Catharine
Alexander,
m. 1925

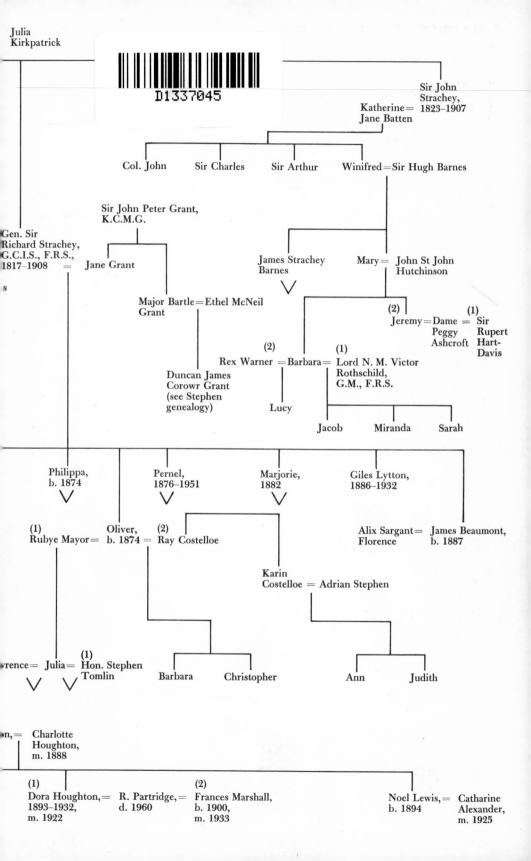

David Garnett has also edited
The Letters of T. E. Lawrence
and
The White/Garnett Letters

CARRINGTON

Letters and Extracts from her Diaries

CHOSEN AND WITH AN INTRODUCTION BY

David Garnett

WITH A BIOGRAPHICAL NOTE BY

Noel Carrington

JONATHAN CAPE
THIRTY BEDFORD SQUARE LONDON

First published 1970

© 1970 by David Garnett and The Sophie Partridge Trust

Jonathan Cape Ltd, 30 Bedford Square, London WC1

ISBN 0 224 61954 3

Printed and bound in Great Britain
by W & J Mackay & Co Ltd, Chatham

147,681

B/8730

Contents

Contents

Illustrations

Preface

The reader may ask: 'Who was this woman Carrington anyway?' And when I reply that he should read this book to find out—for all her qualities good and bad are revealed in these letters—he may be annoyed and ask: 'But to look at? Was she beautiful?'

To provoke him still further I will say that he probably wouldn't have thought so, but that I enjoyed looking at her.

Lady Ottoline Morrell called her 'a wild moorland pony'. Quite good. Aldous Huxley, whose characters are closely drawn from life as far as *appearances* go, wrote of 'the serious moonlike innocence of her childish face', and described her bobbed hair hanging 'in a bell of elastic gold about her cheeks' and her large china-blue eyes 'with an expression of ingenuous and often puzzled earnestness'. He remembered that she was often out of breath when she talked and that 'her words were punctuated with little gasps'.

Later he emphasized her childish appearance in a suit of mauve pyjamas—the pyjamas reappear in later pages and the reader will learn that they were drawn from life. But for private reasons Huxley made Mary Bracegirdle an exceedingly stupid girl, unable to decide whether he or Gertler would be a more suitable lover.

The book is *Crome Yellow* (1921); the setting is Philip and Lady Ottoline Morrell's beautiful country house Garsington Manor and they, Mark Gertler, Dorothy Brett and others are caricatured within its pages.

Carrington's 'little gasp' had already been noted by Gilbert Cannan in his novel *Mendel*, written five years earlier. It is the story of Gertler's early life and Carrington, who was a fellow-pupil of Gertler's at the Slade School of Art, is its heroine.

'Her voice rather irritated him [Gertler]. Her accent was rather mincing and precise and between her sentences she gave a little gasp which he took for an affectation.' Cannan gives no description of her appearance but refers several times to her shyness and 'very charming air of diffidence'. The reader is meant to think her very attractive and to fall under her spell, as Cannan seems to have done.

Aldous Huxley's description is too doll-like and Carrington did not have golden hair. It was the colour of weathered straw—very pale

brown with a glint of gold in it. Her complexion was pink and cream,
like apple blossom. She had a broken nose and the edges of her two
upper front teeth were not square but obliquely pointed, worn away at
the sides.

Tens of thousands of young women have china-blue eyes, talk in
little gasps and have sex trouble, but one does not want to wade through
their correspondence. Carrington would have always been attractive to
her friends; what makes her interesting and fascinating to subsequent
generations is her relationship with Lytton Strachey, the critic who
sprang into fame with *Eminent Victorians* and his biography of Queen
Victoria. Carrington devoted her life to Lytton, and after his death
from an undiagnosed cancer of the intestine decided that it was not
worth living, and shot herself.

The reader of these letters will find himself plunged into a part of the
social life of England during the First World War and the 1920s, and
will want a few clues to understand Carrington's place in it.

It was a world of distinguished intellectuals, writers, painters and
University men who were standing out against the war, often conscientious objectors. After the war it was reinforced by younger men who had
survived, or had been born too late to take part in it.

Scarcely any of them believed that war could come again in their
lifetime. It was a time of elation. The old barriers and conventions would
be swept away, and could be disregarded.

In *Eminent Victorians* and *Queen Victoria* Lytton Strachey had called
into question the credentials of the great men of the age which had made
that slaughter almost inevitable. He instantly became famous and a
leader of intellectual and pacifist dissent.

One corner of this critical British world which rejected Victorian
morality, art and conventional behaviour has since been called 'Bloomsbury', from the parish in central London where many of these free-
thinking heretics lived. The chief figures in this group were the sisters
Vanessa and Virginia Stephen, their husbands Clive Bell and Leonard
Woolf, with some of the Strachey family and the Stracheys' cousin
Duncan Grant. Also Roger Fry, the great art critic, and Maynard (afterwards Lord) Keynes, who revolutionized economics.

Carrington did not quite fit into this group and entered it more as an
appendage of Lytton Strachey's than in her own right. And when
famous hostesses such as Lady Cunard, Margot Asquith (afterwards
Lady Oxford) and Lady Colefax invited the literary lion Lytton Strachey
to their houses they would no more have thought of including Carring-

ton than of asking him to bring his housekeeper or his cook.

This did not apply to Lady Ottoline Morrell, who had got to know Carrington before the girl met Lytton Strachey and through whom she made friends with Bertrand Russell, Aldous Huxley, Katherine Mansfield, Middleton Murry and many of the intellectuals, artists and Bohemians whom Lady Ottoline delighted to entertain. Carrington was more at home in the world of Augustus John, Henry Lamb and the painters trained like her at the Slade School of Art than with the Bloomsbury painters Vanessa Bell, Duncan Grant and Roger Fry, who looked across the channel and were influenced by Cézanne, Matisse and Picasso. Carrington's painting remained insular. She was far more at home in Wiltshire, where she created Lytton Strachey's beautiful house Ham Spray and helped him to entertain large numbers of guests, than she was in Bloomsbury. Her husband Ralph Partridge fell in love with Frances Marshall and they lived together during the week in Bloomsbury from 1926 until Carrington's suicide, after which they married and lived at Ham Spray. But their week-ends were very often spent at Ham Spray which was always Ralph Partridge's country home.

Frances Marshall belonged far more to the Bloomsbury world than Carrington. She was very well educated, interested in abstract ideas and was more articulate and though younger more mature.

Lytton was homosexual, but he did not dislike women: quite the contrary. Some of his happiest relationships were with such women friends as Virginia Woolf, Dorelia John, Ottoline Morrell, his cousin Mary St John Hutchinson, and his sisters Dorothy Bussy and Pippa Strachey. By far the most important was his relationship with Carrington, with whom he fell in love in the spring and summer of 1916.

They became lovers, but physical love was made difficult and became impossible. The trouble on Lytton's side was his diffidence and feeling of inadequacy, and his being perpetually attracted by young men; and on Carrington's side her intense dislike of being a woman, which gave her a feeling of inferiority so that a normal and joyful relationship was next to impossible.

Yet for many years they were happy together. Like Matthew Arnold in Max Beerbohm's caricature, Lytton Strachey was never 'wholly serious'. Everything, including his own deep feeling and beliefs, was the subject of constant jokes and gay exaggerations. To take Lytton *au pied de la lettre* is to misunderstand him entirely. His humour appealed to Carrington and hers to him—and both did much to bind them 'indissoulubly' together. When sexual love became difficult each of them tried to compensate for what the other could not give in a series of love affairs. The first of Carrington's compensatory affairs was with Ralph Partridge, who forced her to marry him. It was not a success, but the link could not be broken.

The interest of these letters is, then, partly that of following a very complex and original character in a very intimate but strange situation. But many people will, I think, feel Carrington's fascination. Her husband, Ralph Partridge, said that once you got her into your blood it was for ever. Gerald Brenan, one of her lovers, wrote in his diary: 'Compared to her, other women seem vulgar and without taste. She has on them the same effect as Dorelia [Augustus John's wife] has . . . she does not make them seem less beautiful, not less intelligent but she deprives them of that intimate connection between beauty and intelligence which is taste . . .'

I, a casual intimate, would say that she had the strength of character that one finds in a child but that a girl often loses when she becomes a woman. When she talked to me she seemed to be confiding a secret, and I was flattered. She made me feel like a child and she was a child herself.

She had indeed many of the childish, or adolescent characteristics that afflict girls at puberty. She never overcame her shame at being a woman, and her letters are full of references to menstruation. Although her sexual desire had greatly increased between her affair with Mark Gertler and that with Gerald Brenan, and although she was in love with Brenan as she had never been with Gertler, they follow a curiously similar pattern: almost the same deceptions, excuses and self-accusations are repeated in each relationship. And in each it was the hatred of being a woman which poisoned it.

Like a child, she found it hateful to choose; and after breaking off a relationship for ever she would immediately set about starting it again.

Like a child, she would tell lies which were bound to be found out and her life was complicated by continual deceptions and imbroglios.

She is an almost textbook case of the girl who can only be happy with a 'father figure'. She loved her father, hated her mother and found her only lasting happy relationship with Lytton Strachey exaggerating their age difference.

When caught out, or in an emotional crisis, she often behaved like a child, confessing her guilt, telling more lies and appealing to Lytton for help and forgiveness.

Her sexual love was unconsciously directed to her brother Teddy, killed in 1916 in the war, who played a large part in her dream life. She thought of him always as a sailor and her last love affair was with a sailor whom she identified with Teddy and who had many of his attractive qualities.

She was uneducated, but appeared much more ignorant than she was because she misplaced the letters in spelling words: thus 'minute' is always 'minuet'.

Although she had no background of general knowledge she was a remarkably well-read young woman before she ever met Lytton, and had a very decided taste of her own in literature. She had a longing to make up for her ignorance and Lytton was an ideal teacher.

She was very secretive, and it was only to Lytton, and later to Julia Strachey, that she revealed herself almost completely; though she hid from them the romanticism which she displayed in her letters to Gerald Brenan—letters signed 'Queen of Georgia'. She was very fond of secret names. With Lytton she was at first 'votre grosse Bébé', then 'your niece' until she finally settled down as Mopsa. Charming variants are found in many of these letters. She hated her own name Dora and by 1915, when I first met her, had transformed it to Doric. Later she reversed this in letters to Gerald Brenan and it became Cirod. In his diaries Brenan almost always refers to her as C.R.D. The private name with which she signs a letter usually corresponds with the temper in which it was written.

There is an equal variety in the names she applied to those she loved. Among others Lytton is 'Grandpère', a 'Yahoo', 'A Toad In The Hole', 'Old Count Bumbel', her 'rat-husband' and a 'bugger-wug'.

Though her end was tragic, for she was totally committed to Lytton, I do not think of her as primarily a tragic figure. The greatest of her, or perhaps I should say of our, misfortunes was that the men she loved and lived with after her breach with Mark Gertler cared little for painting. It did not occur to Lytton Strachey, or to Ralph Partridge, that her painting should be put first. Gertler was too much of an egotist to encourage her and work with her. At the end of her life the only painters she saw much of, Augustus John and Henry Lamb, belonged to an older generation. There was nobody to work with her as Duncan Grant worked with Vanessa Bell. It is possible that if there had been such a companionship, her psychological blockage would have been overcome. But in her isolation it increased, and she became discouraged. I think that this was the greatest harm that Lytton did her, except by dying when he did.

DAVID GARNETT

Textual Note

Carrington was an extremely prolific letter-writer and fortunately much of her correspondence has been preserved. There are, inevitably, gaps. When she was living for weeks in the same house as Lytton Strachey she naturally did not write to him. Her letters to Ralph Partridge were not preserved, and those to Bernard Penrose have disappeared.

The chief collections which survive are to Mark Gertler, to Lytton Strachey, to Gerald Brenan, to Julia Strachey and to her brother Noel Carrington. Minor collections are those to Margaret Waley, to Christine Nash, to Barbara Bagenal, to Rosamond Lehmann, to Professor W. J. H. Sprott and to myself.

My chief difficulty has been that the early letters are less 'amusing' and, taken as a whole, less interesting than her later ones, so that there is a danger that the reader will dismiss her as a school-girlish and self-absorbed young woman before he finds himself fascinated and charmed by her original and complex character and by her wit.

The early letters are to some extent essential to understand her. I have left out those written before 1915—at the end of which year she first met Lytton Strachey—and have, rather reluctantly, kept those of the early period to a minimum.

The enormous volume of her correspondence has made the task of selection difficult and arbitrary, but my choice has been made with the following objects: first, to choose letters that tell the story of her personal life and principal love affairs; second, I have chosen those that illustrate her wit and charm—often revealed in the drawings in the text; third, I have chosen those that reveal her extremely complex character and for that reason have included passages from her diaries and her poems.

I have been able to check the text of the letters with the originals in the case of those to Lytton Strachey, Julia Strachey (Mrs Gowing), Rosamond Lehmann (Mrs Philipps), Christine Nash, Professor J. H. Sprott, Dorelia John and myself.

In all other cases I have worked from Xerox copies, except for those to Alix Strachey, where I was provided with typescripts checked by James Strachey.

Many letters are almost indecipherable; some water-stained, others faintly written in pencil. A large number are undated. Rather than omit a charming or revealing letter, I have sometimes placed it where it seemed to belong. Such letters are marked n.d. I have included many drawings, but I have usually shifted their position for the convenience of the printer. Carrington made a habit of inserting a small drawing instead of a name—particularly when referring to Henry Lamb. I have often been obliged to replace it with a name.

Carrington's spelling was wildly inaccurate. To follow its vagaries would have charmed a few but would have irritated a majority of readers, and would also have made the composition and proof-correcting vastly more expensive. I have therefore corrected her spelling, keeping only a few examples which add charm or meaning, as well as one or two words which are obscure.

Her spelling must sometimes have exasperated Lytton Strachey. He protested angrily at her early practice of spelling his brother Oliver's name Olivier—but after reading *Nuits sans Georges* for the wine I can hear him murmur delightedly: 'Who was Georges? Who indeed!' I have unfortunately not had space to include the letter in which it occurs, written when she was touring France with Dorelia John.

I wish to express my thinks for the help which has been given me by her brother Noel Carrington, who supplied the appendix on his sister's early life and made many of the Xerox copies; to Frances Partridge; to Julia Gowing; to Alix Strachey and to all the other recipients of the letters; to Doctor F. Warren Roberts of The Humanities Research Center, Austin, Texas; to Mrs Marjorie Gertler, who has allowed me to quote from letters written by Mark Gertler. Finally I wish to thank Michael Howard, my publisher, who has given me much help, support and advice, and my daughter Amaryllis Garnett, who has acted as my secretary. Professor Quentin Bell sent me the letter to Maynard (Lord) Keynes, and Mr Michael Holroyd that to Augustus John. I thank them both.

D.G.

1915

[The capitalized passages in the following letter were cut out of a letter from Gertler to Carrington and pasted on to her letter to him.]

To Mark Gertler

April 16th, 1915   *Ibthorpe House, Hurstbourne Tarrant,*
                                                        nr Andover, Hants

NEXT LETTER. WHEN YOU WRITE, WHENEVER YOU DO *DON'T* MENTION OUR SEX TROUBLE ETC ETC ETC: *AT ALL* I AM HEARTILY SICK OF IT—JUST WRITE AND TELL ME ABOUT YOURSELF THE COUNTRY AS USUAL. AND IF EVER I WRITE ABOUT IT TO YOU, *PLEASE* TAKE NO NOTICE.

OUR FRIENDSHIP IS NO WORSE OR BETTER THAN ANY OTHER FRIENDSHIP. AT ANY RATE WE ARE INTERESTED IN EACH OTHER —ENOUGH. WHY SHOULD WE FUSS?

I WANT *SIMPLY* YOUR *FRIENDSHIP* AND *COMPANY* MORE THAN ANYTHING IN THE WORLD.

You wrote these last lines only a week ago, and now you tell me you were '*hysterical and insincere*'. When you talked me about it at Gilbert's[1] and said you loved my friendship were you hysterical and insincere? Yes I know that your real love is 'beautiful and not low'. Do not think I ever doubted that.

Only I *cannot* love you as you want me to. You must know one could not do, what you ask, sexual intercourse, unless one does love a man's body. I have never felt any desire for that in my life: I wrote only four months ago and told you all this, you said you never wanted me to take any notice of you when you wrote again; if it was not that you just asked me to speak frankly and plainly I should not be writing. I do love you, but not in the way you want. Once, you made love to me in your studio, you remember, many years ago now. One thing I can never forget, it made me inside feel ashamed, unclean. Can I help it? I wish to God I could. Do not think I rejoice in being sexless, and am happy over this. It gives me pain also.

[1] Gilbert Cannan, the author whose home, Mill House, Cholesbury, Bucks, Gertler and Carrington often visited for week-ends.

Whenever you feel you want my friendship and company, it will *always* be here. You know that. This is all I can say.

REMEMBER THAT I WOULD SACRIFICE ALL FOR YOU, MY VERY LIFE IF YOU ASKED IT OF ME.

You write this—yet you cannot sacrifice something *less than your life* for me. I do not ask it of you. But it would make me happy if you could. Do not be angry with me for having written as I have. And please do not write back. There can be nothing more to say. Unless you can make this one sacrifice for me. I will do everything I can to be worthy of it.[1]

To Mark Gertler

Wednesday evening [May, 1915]   *Hurstbourne Tarrant*

I am writing again, as I promised I would. It has been a lovely day, a beautiful hot sun, and cobalt blue sky with passing clouds. I have been hard at work on my picture of saint John the Baptist it was good having a model this morning, as I got on much better with it. Mancini's[2] figure is quite good to draw. But his face fills me with depression. Curious how no models have good heads to draw. He comes again tomorrow and Friday. I am so glad all this wedding is over, you have no idea how terrible a real English wedding is.[3] Two people, with very ordinary minds want each other physically, at least the man does, the woman only wants to be married and have his possessions and position. To obtain all this they go through a service, which is comprised of worthy sentiments uttered by the old apostles and Christ! Many relatives come and friends all out of curiosity to see this presumably religious rite; afterwards they all adjourn to the house, and eat like animals and talk, and view each other's clothes and secretly criticise everyone and then return home. All this costs a great deal of money: a bouquet of flowers which the bride carries into the church for 15 mins, and afterwards leaves in the house behind her, which dies the next day as none of the flowers have stalks, costs £2. It seems curious. The dress she

---

[1] Carrington was just twenty-two when she wrote this letter. Gertler and she had been close friends for four years.

[2] A professional model.

[3] The marriage of Carrington's elder sister.

wears for about 1 hr. costs about £10. And yet this is a so called 'quiet' middle class wedding. But it astounds one, the ridiculous farce, the sham festivity. If only they all got merry and drunk, and danced: or if only they were all moved and religious it wouldn't matter. But to be nothing real. Thank god it cannot happen again now. I was almost glad it rained. I felt my sky and country here anyrate were not 'pretending' to shine and be happy.

It makes it much worse for me now, coming up to London. I long, and long for you to talk to. Everything they say jars so terribly. They are so commonplace and material. This morning I just longed to run away from them all, and escape to London. You can never know what it is to have a Mother and family, and surroundings like those people in 'the Way of all Flesh'. Like 'Anne Veronica's' parents. The only thing to do is to make up your mind not to be irritated by it all, but to love the country, the trees and the good hot sun. Soon I will pick you some flowers but there aren't many out just now. I had a long letter from both my brothers which made me happy. I have a beautiful little bantam cock and hen now of my own; a farmer gave them to me. They look like a lovely Chinese silk painting.

I hope you are keeping well. I am glad you are so happy working at your picture now. You will write again soon, will you not please! I am glad you like [Lytton] Strachey so much. Does he talk more when you get him alone? Thank you especially for the photograph of your cottage. I do like it very much. I expect you will have Brett back soon. She is with that terrible woman Zena in Paris.[1] How can she endure being with people like that. But she said she was going to see the Puvis de Chavannes which I would like to see. It's just like being in a bird cage here, one can see everything which one would love to enjoy and yet one cannot. My father is in another cage also, which my mother put him in, and he is too old to even chirp or sing. I am sorry to give you such an outburst of self-pity but I didn't quite realize until I saw you again how much I miss not being with you more. The little green stream still flows swiftly through the meadows.   My love to you, CARRINGTON

[1] The Hon. Dorothy Brett, daughter of Lord Esher, a fellow pupil at the Slade and close friend of Carrington's and Gertler's. Her brother had married Zena Dare.

To Mark Gertler

Wednesday [*1915*]   [*Hurstbourne Tarrant*]

When I saw your handwriting on the envelope, I was so excited I
hardly liked to open it.

I am going to be perfectly honest in this letter, as I hope always in
future to be with you, so I will not pretend to be reserved. I am so
terribly happy now that I want to rush right up to London at once and
see you. It is no kindness to you which makes me come back but pure
selfish reasons of my own! Because I am miserable when I am not your
friend. Do not be unhappy. Be very happy. Already I am far away,
planning everything. Cannot I come and stay in Miss Walker's cottage?[1]
If what I write is badly expressed it is only because of my extreme joy,
which I cannot contain. I dare scarcely believe your letter is really true.
I keep reading it over and over again. Lately I have hated this country
for being so beautiful, and all the birds for singing so brightly. Now it
has all become wonderful again. Do write me very long letters all about
your work and what you are painting now. Brett sent me last week such
a good phot. of your 'creation', and the portrait of her. You cannot think
how happy I am to have them. The 'creation' looks fine even although it
is so reduced in size.

I hope you are well, and enjoying this lovely weather in the evenings
on the Heath. I will try and come up soon, and see you and your new
picture. How is it coming out, the one with the triangles of bright
coloured fruit? I find it impossible to write about these matter-of-fact
things, when all the time I am only thinking: 'How good it all is.' It has
seemed such a long time.

                        Write very soon again please. CARRINGTON

To Mark Gertler

Tuesday [*December 1915*]   [*Hurstbourne Tarrant*]

God damme! But a man came round this morning and called to see my
mother about a letter! I thought it might be me—so I dashed in, and
just saved my mother from reading my letter to you!! And now I have to

---

[1] At Cholesbury, near Gilbert Cannan's house.

go to the bleeding court on Friday, to be a witness at Bow Street.[1] Christ! and you will be there also. I really am so excited and upset. This man asked me heaps of questions, which I'm sure I shall contradict. Isn't it all hellish. So I shall see you sooner than you thought. Before Graham Campbell we are to appear; that isn't your Campbell I suppose? It would be too much like a Cinema if it was. I shall be [at] Brett's studio *Thursday* evening now.   CARRINGTON

To Mark Gertler

Friday, December 1915   *87 Carlisle Road, Hove, Sussex*

Dear Mark, Thank you for your letter. How terrible! I feel nothing is safe now. Will my letter be read word for word in court! I wonder now what I did write in it.

I have just come back from spending three days on the Lewes downs with the Clive Bells, Duncan [Grant], Mrs Hutchinson[2] and Lytton Strachey. God knows why they asked me!! It was much happier than I expected. The house[3] was right in the middle of huge wild downs, four miles from Lewes, and surrounded by a high hill on both sides with trees. [Drawing omitted] We lived in the kitchen for meals, as there weren't any servants, so I helped Vanessa [Bell] cook. Lytton is rather curious. I got cold, and feel rather ill today. They had rum punch in the evenings which was good. Yesterday we went a fine walk over tremendous high downs. I walked with Lytton. I like Duncan, even if you don't! What traitors all these people are! They ridicule Ottoline![4] even Mary H[utchinson] laughs at the Cannans with them. It surprises me. I think it's beastly of them to enjoy Ottoline's kindnesses and then laugh at her.

I am sorry that you have been ill and worried lately. I am still amazed at them chucking your still life. I can see no reason for it.

[1] A postman had been arrested in Hampstead for stealing letters and was found to be carrying a letter from Carrington to Gertler. The police returned it to her and then called her as a witness for the prosecution. 'Your Campbell' was Gordon Campbell, later Lord Glenavy, a friend of Gertler's.

[2] Mrs (Mary) St John Hutchinson, wife of Jack St John Hutchinson, K.C., and cousin of the Stracheys.

[3] Vanessa Bell had borrowed her sister Virginia's house, Asheham, in the autumn and winter of 1915.

[4] Lady Ottoline Morrell, half-sister of the 6th Duke of Portland, who kept open house for writers and artists of talent at Garsington Manor. Lytton stayed there for long visits.

Except a personal dislike for you, because you do not pander, and pay them homage.

I got up every morning when I was with them very early at 8 o'ck and went long walks by myself over the downs. It was grand. The huge sun rising upon the edge of the down. So near and so powerful that one felt like a small moth compelled to draw near to it, blinking in its brilliant light. I have never been so near the sun before and then when one did reach the summit the wind was terrific, it shouted in one's very ears, and pushed and pushed till one was perforced to lie down on the wet morning grass, and then what a sight greeted the eye: way over to Lewes in the north with huge distant downs, and then Newhaven and the shining sea in the south, and far below behind in the deep deep basin, the little house surrounded by the trees and all the time the mighty rushing wind, and the glaring sun. They never got up till about ten o'ck, so when I returned they were still in bed.

I am going to get some job soon in London. And then I will come up and stay. Have you heard anything yet from Beecham? Don't you like Roderick Random very much. I am now reading Peregrine Pickle. What have you been doing, have you seen much of Brett?

Goodbye now for a little while. I will send you the end of Gilbert's [Cannan] book soon.   My love to you. CARRINGTON

[No letters from Carrington to Gilbert Cannan have survived. Her interest in him was probably literary. He had written a book about Samuel Butler, many of whose works she read with excitement and which she recommended to Gertler.

On his side Gilbert was writing his novel *Mendel*, in which the young Jewish genius (Gertler) is the hero, and Carrington is the heroine. *Mendel* is dedicated, with a poem, to D.C., and Cannan was obviously attracted by her, calling her his 'darling Daisy'. A year later she was ashamed of having let him kiss her and she referred to him unkindly when he had gone insane after the war.

She resented his having written *Mendel* and disliked the distorted portraits of Gertler and herself and of Gertler's friend Currie, who had murdered his mistress and committed suicide. *Mendel* is indeed a very bad novel.]

To Mark Gertler

Monday [December 1915]   *87 Carlisle Road, Hove*

Dear Mark, Thank you for your letter. But you really are annoyed without cause! For the Bells were only 8 miles from here, so naturally it wasn't very difficult to get over to them. Whereas London costs nearly 10/- to get up to. But I hope to come quite soon now. Possibly next week. Now will you be happy. But you make me unhappy, surely it was *you* who left me after this summer for nearly three months without a word. Why should I if I hadn't [words illegible] and be friends? You leave me alone, quite alone without a word, and then you reproach me for not seeing you now for a few weeks! I do not love you physically, that you know, but I care for you far more than I do for anyone else.

I have written about a job, and hope to hear this week. Probably it will mean working all day. But we can see each other in the evenings and at weekends. But it will be good to earn my own living at last! Your letters of course excited me terribly. I am still always excited about motor cars and duchesses!!! So you are famous, and *also* infamous to judge by the critics! I hope you will sell your pictures. That is most important when one has to do with these idle rich. We leave here on Friday I think, at least I hope so. Yes, I'll go with you to Gilbert's but it will be nearly Xmas by then. But I really will try and come.

What a damned mess I make of my life and the thing I want most to do, I never seem to bring off. My work disappoints me terribly. I feel so good, so powerful before I start and then when it's finished, I realise each time, it is nothing but a failure. If only I had any money I should not be obliged to stick at home like this. And to earn money every day, and paint what one wants to, seems almost impossible.

Yesterday I walked over to Rottingdean over the downs with Noel.[1] It was lovely country. I am afraid I shall never really get intimate with him; he is so governed by conventions, and accepts the 'public school' opinions. It's a pity, perhaps he will get out of it in time. You would like him, but it wouldn't be any use now because he's so patriotic, that I am sure you would hate him, and he you! It's a good thing Eddie [Marsh][2] doesn't know him, for he's almost as beautiful as Rupert Brooke. I wonder who all the Baronesses are who you are meeting? It

---

[1] Noel Carrington, her youngest brother, convalescing after wounds.

[2] Edward Marsh (later knighted), patron of poets and painters, then secretary to Winston Churchill. He had befriended Gertler.

wasn't Baroness D'Elanger was it? How pleased your people must be
with you at last!

Have the Lawrences[1] ever gone to Florida? Well when I really do
come up, I will tell you, and we'll have a party in Brett's studio. I hope
you are well, and taking care of yourself. Do not think of me bitterly;
rather be glad that you are of value to me because I am often so weak,
and need you. Goodbye, and soon I will see you now.   CARRINGTON

Do send me your newspaper cuttings to read about your pictures next
letter.

To Mark Gertler

Wednesday [*December 1915*]   *Hurstbourne Tarrant*

Dear Mark, Here is a letter, and a parcel of clothes! You do not mind
me sending them you. The only decent thing is a pair of black silk
socks, and two or three ties. So don't trouble to thank me. [Ten lines
omitted]

I am sorry I told you about Lytton, I did not mean to.[2] Only I would
rather you knew about it from me. Please don't ever mention it again, as
I am annoyed enough as it is because I let the fact make me so miserable.
As a man so contemptible[3] as that ought not ever to make one miserable
or happy. And so I shall try and forget it. I am going on Saturday to
Ottoline's with Brett so I don't expect I shall see you until I return on
Monday. I had a weary time hunting for a job. It's fearfully hard to get
anything. And they always keep me waiting 2 hours before they will
interview me. I do hate that Miss Mortimer, thank Goodness I won't see
much of her. She is one of the most revolting females I have ever come
across. But I quite see Brett's point that to live so cheaply is worth
anything in the shape of Miss Mortimer.

Write to me at 100 St Mary's Mansions, *Paddington*, as I shall have
left here on Friday. I did enjoy our evening so much at Brett's. I hope
you are better now—I am sorry you have been so ill lately. CARRINGTON

Do not think I did not want to see you this last week! but honestly I
spent all my time rushing round after this job. Write me about Gilbert.

---

[1] D. H. Lawrence had planned to found a community in Florida.

[2] There had been a curious passage between Carrington and Lytton Strachey at
Asheham. Lytton went for a walk with Carrington and kissed her, to her surprise. Next
morning she stole into his bedroom very early with a pair of scissors, intending to cut off
his beard. But as she bent over him, he opened his eyes and she was fascinated.

[3] i.e. a homosexual.

1916

To Mark Gertler

April 1916   *16 Yeoman's Row [Brompton Road, London]*

Dear Mark, I have just written a long letter and torn it up. Because I found it so difficult to write what I really meant.

Please do not be unhappy: mentally at any rate there are happy times before us—

I will not come down to Gilbert's. Although I would like to.

I think it best if I do not see you for a bit. As it nearly sends me mad with grief, at seeing you so miserable.—I will write when you come back from Cholesbury. When we are both calmer we will talk it over. Please let me be alone for a little while, as I cannot bear it—and my Mother is here now which fills me with despair. But dear if only *you* will be happy, it will make me happier also.   CARRINGTON

To Lytton Strachey

[April 20th, 1916]   *Hurstbourne Tarrant*

Perhaps on Euston platform at 10 o'clock on Saturday.
You might keep one blearly eye open on the off chance.
Incredible internal excitement.   BÉBÉ C.

To Mark Gertler

Saturday [April 22nd, 1916]   *Hurstbourne Tarrant*

Dear Mark, I was sorry to desert you when you went to Cholesbury. But as I had to leave London for here on Thursday at one o'ck it was hardly worth coming down for the evening. I hope you enjoyed yourself. It is lovely down here, wonderful woods full of primroses, and white anemones, and blue flowers. And the tulips are all coming out I planted in my garden. And some marvellous red flowers in the garden which I am going to bring back to paint like this. And bright orange [drawing of flower omitted] red. I shall do a big painting when I come back of them. I shall see you on Wednesday night at Brett's. How good it is that everything is alright again. I am longing to see you again. Like a hungry person who has been waiting for [a] meal a long time.

I went a long walk on Thursday onto the wild common. It was such a perfect evening. What a rotten system it is that you should not be down here with me.

I am reading Emerson's Essays at present they are very interesting. —It's rather a relief getting away, and having things done for one. Instead of cooking and washing up oneself. I get cursed tired always being tidy and clean! We will see a great deal of each other now.

So goodbye. CARRINGTON

To Lytton Strachey

Sunday evening [June 1916]   *16 Yeoman's Row, Brompton Road*

Mon chère grand-père Lytton, Your letter was a great comfort to me as I, even without the old Paget,[1] sank into the depths of the deepest depression soon after my arrival in London. What shall I write to you about? I will start by using violent language so that you do not show my letter, as is your wont, to the whole of the company at the Breakfast table, or will you promise to refrain from such practices otherwise I will write no more. Send me the frantic Rimbaud poem even in pencil. I am even more excited now over him . . . Yesterday I spent the afternoon reading a life of Musset with Noel. So that soon I shall be able to read Rimbaud myself.[2] I have a wonderful idea about it all. I will show you perhaps one day—a picture.

But you did not enclose 'another work of your hands', unless you mean the drawing of the Garsington Manor roof with emblems?

Have you recovered from your greyest gloom yet? Indeed I sympathise with you. It seems long ages since we were at Garsington, everything seemed bare, and so chilly here and then I hate more and more

[1] Miss Paget, 'Vernon Lee', the authoress, was a fellow guest at the Morrell's house, Garsington Manor, where Lytton Strachey was staying.

[2] On June 7th Lytton sent Carrington his translation of Rimbaud's 'Le Bateau Ivre', with a note ending: 'Hope to see you tomorrow. Off to le beau Peter [Warren] in a minute or two. Yrs Lytton.'

having to go to the mouldy museum everyday. My greatest pleasure is a
motor bike which I am going to learn, and then all England is within
my grasp. Will you meet me at Newbury and then away to the Inkpen
Hills, and Combe? I had tea alone with Alerick[1] on Saturday. He is never
allowed a newspaper to read. So I told him as much as I could remember
about what went on in this world—He is so beautiful—Barbara[2] came
to supper on Friday with me. I am miserable over my work just now. All
grey stones compared to what I want to paint. What do you do all day
now? I still am writing this letter with a censor inside. I trust you so
little sometimes. Are you still starved? I shall send you like a poor
soldier biscuits and bully-beef?

No, I cannot write you anything, and I thought I had so much to
say . . . But send me the Rimbaud poem.

My studio is incredibly dirty and I sit knee-deep in crockery, and old
letters, and everywhere drooping flowers, with pools of deep-red petals
and on the mantel shelf long spines with vertebras hanging brown and
musty by little threads. These were once lupins.

The buses and tubes disappoint me, only aged hags, and men with
yellow teeth sit and chuckle, and the soldiers have pink raw faces with
boils.

Will you write a tale about the grove on the little hills at Wittenham.
Surely, you cannot but do so. The deaf lady [Dorothy Brett] sends you
her greetings. Write a long letter again soon. I send you a small brown
paper parcel and remain.

Votre grosse bébé CARRINGTON

[Pug dogs were a great feature of life at Garsington Manor.]

[1] Alaric, to whom Carrington was giving lessons in painting, was the son of the Belgian
Baron de Forest.
[2] Barbara Hiles, Carrington's close friend, and like Brett and Gertler a fellow student
at the Slade.

To Lytton Strachey

Tuesday morning [June 13th, 1916]   *16 Yeoman's Row, Brompton*
                                                                      Road

Chère grand-père, It was indeed ungrateful of me not to write before,
and thank you for the amazing poem.[1]

But so many things happened at once, and I got frantically depressed,
and so it was no use trying to write. You will believe me I know when I
tell you, that the poem made me ill with excitement. I cannot understand how all these people go on so calmly. And when it becomes too
much, and one tells them, how little are they astounded. I will ask you,
because I care so much that I do not mind even if it is a nuisance to you.
But you *must* send the poems about the dove-cot and the Brown sky
and the ladies with the silver finger-nails searching for bugs, almost
immediately. Are you coming with Lady Ottoline this week to London?
We have just been down to Wittering for Whitsun.[2] It was an exciting
place, but the company, repeat it not was dull. I had a wonderful walk
from Chichester late at night there, with only a half sucked acid-drop
of a moon for company. I like Mary H[utchinson] so much. The conversation was merely lewd without being amusing, and a dreadful domestic
couple called [name omitted] made everything dismal for me. Do not you
hate united pairs. [One line omitted] But is not the shore with the long
flat stretches of mud, and sea grass beautiful and a wild black horse
which frolicked madly on the grass. I came back in a motor car with
Shearman[3] and Mark. Yellow wine, and purette de Foie Gras on the top
of High hills near Arundel for lunch. Do you know I can ride the motor
bicycle now all round Regent's Park before breakfast tearing quicker and
quicker leaving gaping faces of city clerks behind on either side. Next
week end I go to Hampshire, and Combe ['you may get a letter' crossed
out] n'importe! Last Thursday the arch-bugger Lou Lou Harcourt[4]
came to supper with us at Brett's studio, a terrible long creature tightly
buttoned in a frock coat all the way up, and then a face bulging out all
pink, and very tight above his collar. Really a night-mare of a face.

---

[1] The translation of 'Le Bateau Ivre'.

[2] Eleanor, West Wittering, was the St John Hutchinsons' house in the country.

[3] Montague Shearman, son of the judge of the same name, who collected Gertler's
paintings.

[4] The Rt Hon. Lewis Harcourt ('Lulu') was created Viscount the following year. For
his appearance see Max Beerbohm's caricatures.

Of course my grievance is purely personal for he dared to say to Mark outside afterwards that I was 'a nice plump little thing'. But you are laughing. I will spoil his tight pink face for him one day. He made up to Mark with great rapidity outside. His conversation was as bombastic as Philip's![1] Now this letter cannot be published at breakfast. Are you writing your Clump story? do not be so carelessly lazy. What sort of gossip do you want? But Faith[2] will have told you everything at the week-end. She came to tea with me last Friday and had a curious conversation. Brett told me afterwards it was with a purpose. I do hate having conversations with good motives behind them. Are you still crouching over the fire reading life upon life of Rimbaud?

I was severely reprimanded by the Baron for imparting to Alerick news of the war, and the outside world. But we still have tea alone together. He loves the early Italians. But I am sure it will end disasterously. I wish I wasn't so ancient!

Tomorrow Ottoline comes to dinner with us at Brett's studio—a wonderful picture is in the making—which you will like also I think ...and next week I shall see Combe again. But you would never get as far as Newbury alone. Some motor bus on the way would devour you. I shall wait and only strands of your red beard would be blown up to me from the valley of Newbury. And to wait with only a red beard for company under the gibbet on Inkpen Hill—too much. This is no letter. But you know how much I loved Rimbaud.

votre Bébé CARRINGTON

To Lytton Strachey

Monday evening [June 19th, 1916]   *Hurstbourne Tarrant*

Promise you will *not* show my letter to a Wissett[3] breakfast or I will *never never* write to you again quickly. Promise.

Chère grand-père Lytton, I can hardly believe it is true. For it has just

---

[1] Philip Morrell.

[2] Faith, sister of Nicholas Bagenal, had married Hubert Henderson (later knighted) the previous year.

[3] Lytton was staying at Wissett Lodge, at Wissett in Suffolk, with Vanessa Bell. Duncan Grant and David Garnett were living there. Harry Norton was a fellow guest.

happened. It seemed like some vile nightmare. You must realize it; and
yet you never can because you never went there.

I went out to tea with a neighbour. Canny Scotch farmers [the
Mackilligans]. When suddenly the old lady, curse her yellow face and
grey hair, told me with much malice glee (for she had long past known of
my great love) that Combe House had been taken by some woman and was
now under repair. You can imagine what this meant. Taken! By whom?
what repairs? At last I managed to escape and rushed away on my bicycle
to The House. Never had the landscape appeared more lovely; as if to
flaunt, it showed its very best, because it was no more. Do you know the
feeling of running vainly for a train which has gone. How the faces of
the children, even the rabbits and plovers, laugh and shriek in one's face
in derision and yet one must go on. How I cursed myself for being so
foolish as to believe that no one but I could ever live there. It only
seemed a long while to wait; always a certainty. And now it had suddenly been snatched clean away one day I will show you the beauty of
the valley with the steep down along the side covered with high trees.
And the hard bare round downs in the distance so enormous, and perfectly rigid. When at last I was near I hardly dared to venture into the
garden and The House. What repairs! But it had to be. The grass was
all cut in the garden. The orchard pruned, walls mended, and neat.
Little violas with pert yellow faces and geraniums sniggered round the
foot of the house in newly made beds. Think! Violas, in such a garden!

I found the master builder in an undignified position behind the
wall, round the corner. He retreated before me, abashed, doing up many
buttons. The painters in the house smiled. But I persuaded him to
forgive me, and went over the house with him. Lytton it was more
amazing that I had ever seen it before and one room upstairs had a
black-lead wall painted all over with a pattern of white flowers by hand!
They discovered this under an old wall paper. Traces of red walls with
yellow patterns were found in all the other rooms, but distempered
over! The dining room was entirely panelled with Jacobean oak. Thank
God the woman does not seem to be so bad. But the spirit has been
driven out by distemper, and white paint everywhere. It will never be
what it was. A huge chunk of me is cut away, so many dreams. It all
seems impossible. What right had they to come and steal it? Oh,
Lytton why is one so small against these creatures. No more.

Lady Ottoline had dinner with us all last Wednesday and after went
to the Palladium where we heard the incomparable song: 'I'm Burlington Bertie of Bow'. She was very lively, with a tall purple ostrich

feather, no doubt purloined from Lulu's estate. Poor Faith came in for
much criticism, and you were not entirely exempted! It was a plan that
we should go to the Garsington Pub in July. But now that July is so
close upon me I feel I do not want to go. I will make up my mind this
week when I return to London. Probably the last fortnight of July.
Perhaps three weeks.

The prospect of learning French, down to Low Dutch with you
certainly is enticing. But what of Philip the King and the Pugs? also
now I know from Brett *what was said* when I sat enthralled beside you
on the lawn. And when we came back glowing with inspired eyes from
The Clumps! Wissett sounds a long way off. It will need much persuasion to make me walk so far I fear. Besides you are not very kind,
are you? You laugh much and often. Yesterday I bicycled to Hungerford. Truly most excellent downs just before Shalbourne with groves
of beeches like those on the Clumps, on their summits. And what good
towns Hungerford and Newbury! We returned by Highclere, and
Kingsclere far east of Newbury. Last week we had dinner at the
Hutchinsons'. Mary read one of her stories, which was good. I liked it
very much. [Two lines omitted] Faith thinks that you have degenerated
and have become spoilt!!! We passed a heavy vote of censure on you. I
sat this morning under gooseberry bushes on hard grey earth picking
fruit to fill Hutchinson's belly—as they are coming to dinner with me
tomorrow. But his digestive apparatus and the prickles made the whole
thing rather revolting. What did you talk to Norton about under your
laurel bushes? Have you heard a nightingale yet? Hell upon you, hoary
old villian but why could you not take Rimbaud with you away—and
you have, but you are lazy. Do not try and deceive me. Next week I shall
love you no more, for I shall have a Rimbaud of my own all the way from
France! Farewell. Dans un misère gris je reste votre bèbè

CARRINGTON

[On July 28th, 1916, Lytton wrote to Carrington on Savile Club notepaper: 'I hope you will have seen Barbara and heard from her about
Wales. Do you think you could come? It sounds as if it might be
pleasant. From about Aug. 12th I gather, for a fortnight or so ... In
case you don't see Barbara, I'd better add that the place is a cottage
belonging to her people in the region of Llandudno, and that the company will be she, Nich [Bagenal] and your grandpapa...It seems to
me so appallingly hot that a walking expedition would hardly be suitable.
I think I should crumple into tissue paper. What do you fancy? Perhaps

we might walk back to England through Wales? It would then be
September...Write, write, write for Jesus' sake! You *must* come to
Wales. Your utterly dissolved Missionary.' (The tail of the Y is pro-
longed into a phallic drawing.)

Barbara was to marry Nicholas Bagenal, who had just come out of
hospital after a wound on the hip. She had invited Lytton, as a chaperon,
and Carrington. This holiday was only realized after 'the mass of
intrigue' referred to in Carrington's letter of August 5th.]

To Lytton Strachey

Sunday afternoon, July 30th, 1916   *Shandygaff Hall*
                                             [Garsington Manor], Oxford

Reverend Sir, It is all very complicated! Jack Hutch has just written to
me, a long letter *insisting* that I go on the 15th to Eleanor! Mark's affection has increased in my absence.

And I want so much to go to this land of mountains and (since this
disgusting cult of truth has begun) so much to be with you again. Did
you ask Mary [Hutchinson]? Tell me exactly what she said when you
asked her? Then how much do you all really want me to come? It would
be awful to walk so far, and then be met with the chilly eye of criticism!
You had better write here. I do not feel sufficiently energetic to think
out any complicated method of transport. And I go no more to London
as the Baron and his offspring have gone away to Cornwall. If Ottoline
asks to read it I will damn her eyes, and answer nay. No one is here this
weekend except Gilbert [Cannan] and Eva-Red-Tent, and Mark. Will
you write outrageous verse for the 'Garsington Chronicle'? Ottoline
has already written a personal review of her visitors. But so dull. Because she said nothing of them she has not told us all before. It was
strange meeting Norton the day after you left. I wanted so much to
know his last day at Wissett!! Ottoline insists on trying her best to get
my state of virginity reduced, and made me practically share a bedroom
with Norton!! And Poor Brett got sent out four times in one morning
with Bertie [Bertrand Russell] for long walks across remote fields by her
Ladyship!! So you betrayed me to Maynard [Keynes]! But he is much
more truthful than you only rather cryptic. I read John Donne all day
now. A lovely poem about Fair ships in harbours. But what will ever

be written as wonderful as Rimbaud's 'libarians'.[1] Her ladyship has now taken on your duties as educator to the young, and reads us the Irish and English poets during the long evenings. Even Philip plays the missionary and recites Shelley through his hairy nostrils. This is a poor letter but I lie exhausted, in the sun after swimming in that cess-pool of slime.

Monday morning in bed. 5 o'ck.

I spent a wretched time here since I wrote this letter to you. I was dismal enough about Mark and then suddenly without any warning Philip after dinner asked me to walk round the pond with him and started without any preface, to say, how disappointed he had been to hear I was a virgin! How wrong I was in my attitude to Mark and then proceeded to give me a lecture for quarter of an hour! Winding up by a gloomy story of his brother who committed suicide. Ottoline then seized me on my return to the house and talked for one hour and a half in the asparagrass bed, on the subject, far into the dark night. Only she was human and did see something of what I meant. And also suddenly forgot herself, and told me truthfully about herself and Bertie. But this attack on the virgins is like the worst Verdun on-slaughter and really I do not see why it matters so much to them all. Mark suddenly announced that he is leaving today (yesterday), and complicated feelings immediately come up inside me.

Brett sold her big pictures of Black Widows to Lady Hamilton. So she is happy. I leave here about Friday probably. Il y en a qui m'enseignent à vivre—et d'autres qui m'enseignent à mourir—Maintes et maintes fois I look at the hills. On these hot days they once again seem very near.

I am glad you are working hard, and eating vigorously. Ici il fait de plus en plus chaud chaque jour! Goodbye. Votre bébé très triste.

I heard a [picture of bird omitted] nightingale last night!!! It sang outside my window in the starlight.

---

[1] Is this perhaps *Illuminations*? The word is clear in the MS.

To Lytton Strachey

Tuesday [August 1st, 1916]   *Garsington Manor, Oxford*

All is saved, Mary has written and asked me to go *next* week end. The
Lord be praised! or is it my uncle who deserves the hymn of thanks-
giving?

   Beautiful pictures of Jimmy [Wilde, featherweight boxer] in today's
Sketch! Did you see them?

   I leave here on Friday evening—and go home to Hampshire from
Wittering the following Tuesday. Farewell.

To Lytton Strachey

Saturday, 8 o'ck [August 5th, 1916]   *London*

Write me another letter soon please.

   At last I have left! It seems strange to be out of that mass of intrigue.
You have no idea how *incredibly* complicated it became just before I
left. But isn't it wonderful about going to Wittering *and* Wales!
Ottoline in one of the many farewell interviews that I had with her
yesterday morning, asked me if I was really a fraud. All very embarrass-
ing.

                                                        Wittering, 7.30

It is Sunday now, and I write sitting up in bed in the big barn with
shrieking birds all round, and a wonderful picture of green grey mud,
and little grey blue distances outside. I have read Donne's poems continuously the last week. They surprised me more, and more with great
wonder. Il Seraglio was not performed on Friday when I was in London,
so I could not see it. I loved your little poem! Thank you so much. I am
still half asleep so pardon the gross lack of intelligence displayed in this
letter. Then the suddenness of finding oneself here is rather confusing.
Have you heard from Barbara, as to when she will expect us? I think I
shall go by train as far as Gloucestershire and then bicycle up through
Wales. But all this will depend on how soon I can escape from my
parental home. It is wonderful here we walked from Bosham, and had
lunch in yellow cornfields with Jack and Mary, and then sailed down
the river, in a big ship with a bulging white sail, and pale yellow mast.
It was exciting, riding up and down, with smacks on the green waves.
A curious sailor creature called Whiney. [One line omitted] He is as

stupid as a hen. Showed us warts on his hand, one had the top taken off, and bubbled thick red blood all over his horny hand. The wart conversation went on a long time.

He seemed strangely undisturbed at it having no connection with us. Then we had tea at Eleanor, and swam in the warm sea. Even Mark came in. Looking very absurd, in a bathing dress! I liked Aldous Huxley at Garsington. We used to sleep on the roof together, as it became so unbearably hot in those attics. Strange adventures with birds, and peacocks, and hordes of bees. Shooting stars, other things. But I am still too sleepy to write about all this: later on the high mountains. I like Mary very much. It is extraordinary the feeling of space here—after only looking at near objects, the pond, and ilex tree at Lollipop Hall.[1] I felt almost light headed with joy gazing over miles of empty flat land yesterday! we lit candles up the ilex tree one night. Great black shadows  on the reptile branches. I was worn almost thin trying to capture my letters before Ottoline saw who they were from. Your first note which only arrived on Friday nearly brought about the fall or decline of Doric,[2] especially as her Ladyship was in high wrath because you had written curtly demanding some books, and told her no scandal! She makes me steeped in debt by giving me *all* her letters to read. And then has long jabberfications about people deceiving her and being reserved! But I did enjoy it very much in between all these confusions. I did a Goyaesque portrait of our Lady of mystery which gave me some pleasure. But as I made her look like a pole-cat it had to be suppressed from the public eye.

Of course I can hardly agree with you about the Garsington chronicle as I invented the idea! Lytton:—'To hell with that girl.' But probably it would be too difficult to do it the way I meant. But as it will be plentifully filled with a long discourse by her Ladyship and essays by Mademoiselle [Juliette Baillot] and Maria [Nys][3] your valuable services will be easily dispensed with! Very hot this morning—how the gulls

shriek and yell. But all is heaven sans les s

Goodbye chère grandpère   votre grosse bébé CARRINGTON

[1] Garsington Manor.
[2] Carrington, who hated her name Dora, had changed it to Doric.
[3] They married Julian Huxley and Aldous Huxley respectively.

To Mark Gertler

Monday, August 1916   *c/o Mrs Hiles, Llanbedr, Taly-cafn S.O.,*
                                                    N. Wales

I arrived here on Saturday evening. After a terrible, one of the most terrible, journeys I have ever undergone. Crowds of horrible sticky sweating people.

I am most happy here. Just Lytton, Barbara and Nicholas. We go out most of the day for long walks, and bathe in a wonderful pool with waterfalls. The mountains are quite high, and one gets Cézanne landscapes of mountains with dull green trees, and ugly white cottages with Slate roofs. Lytton has brought John Donne so I read him in the garden. He seems to me one of the most marvellous poets! How vividly he felt everything. He once had a Great Love for a little girl of 15 years and wrote the most violent outbursts of passion every anniversary of her death. But such comparisons. It is very long or I would copy it out for you. Barbara's cottage is very small, all white outside with a small garden filled with flowers. And all round these huge mountains and a big river in a flat valley below. I hope you are enjoying yourself at Cholesbury. What are you painting now? Give Gilbert and Mary my love. What happened to Gilbert at his tribunal in the end? The Weather is wet here, and quite cold. Horrible after the heat of the south! and those hot sands. What a perfect time we had at Wittering. It amazed me afterwards when I thought it over. Have you heard anything of Brett? She hasn't written to me since Garsington. This country is really very fine.

But so different from Hampshire that I find it hard to get my eye ranged properly. It is all so big, and there is no crisis like one has in England. By a big hill and the rest of the country flat and one sees everything planed out so as to speak, leading up to the centre. Here it vastly big and no order. Donne is so wonderful, you must have a book. I will give you one myself. Also Shakespear's sonnets I am reading. I have not heard from you since Wittering do you realize that? Willain. The people all speak Welsh here and But little English. I miss you. The intimacy we got at lately makes other relationships with people strangely vacant, and dull. Are you writing any more Philosophy? Again I laugh at Gilbert's remark on the top of the bus. How annoying it is to be able to write so little of what I want to you. But it always seems rather false directly I put it down. But you must believe much more now by what I have felt with you.

Yours with love   friend CARRINGTON

[From Wales Lytton and Carrington set off on a surreptitious little tour together, staying at Bath and Wells. From the letter to Lytton on September 1st it is clear that they were already looking for a cottage.

Lytton was at this period—and indeed until the publication of *Eminent Victorians*—a very poor man.]

[The following page from an incomplete letter from Carrington to Keynes, with lines in Lytton Strachey's handwriting, was found among Vanessa Bell's papers.]

To Maynard Keynes

August 29th, 1916   *The George Hotel, Glastonbury, Somerset*

Dear Maynard, We are staying here. A very Christian atmosphere prevails, which Lytton is enjoying incredibly. Also a miller's lad. I doubt if Lytton will ever return. He wanders day after day with a guidebook on architecture in his lean hand gazing at ancient ruins.

[The rest of the letter is missing. On the opposite page in Lytton Strachey's handwriting is:]

> When I'm winding up the toy
> Of a pretty little boy,
> —Thank you, I can manage pretty well;
> But how to set about
> To make a pussy pout
> —*That* is more than I can tell.[1]

[1] I suspect that Lytton sent these lines to Maynard to conceal that he was having physical relations with Carrington.

To Lytton Strachey

Friday evening [September 1st, 1916]   *Hurstbourne Tarrant*

Dear Uncle Lytton, I feel burdened with so much affection and gratitude towards you tonight that I will pen you a letter whilst the inclination is heavy upon me. What a journey! That train was *more than one
hour* late at Templecombe so I did not get here until six o'ck. But I had
a happy time however exploring the village in the hot sun. It possessed
many excellent houses and buildings and one worthy inn, built thus
as every good inn should be—with outside steps running up to
an upper door. There are some charming little villages beyond Glastonbury with green orchards, Cole and Bruton by name, if I remember
arightly. Which you might explore.

Home. No discoveries! As I expected, the most utter boredom and
peevishness. They suspected I was in London, and sent wires up there
on Wednesday! Masses of letters: a long one from Alaric, and some
beautiful landscapes of Cornwall which they had painted for me. Black
abuses, and threats from Percy Young![1] which threw me back again
into despair. BUT—an aged doctor of 92 years who died at Bath, left me
a legacy of £20! My Father just told me as I was bolting down some
kedgeree. For I was ravenous. So it does not matter how extravagant
we have been! The downs round Salisbury are lovely. It was wonderful
to see them again. You are lying on your couch now, with its crochet
background reading Gardiner. Will you truly write a poem on Widcomb House and the two old Ladies? only seriously. It is not a subject
to treat lightly. I did enjoy myself so much with you, you do not know
how happy I have been, everywhere, each day so crowded with wonders.
Thank you indeed. It is melancholy here, their heavy dullness, and this
dimly lit room burdened with dreary furniture.

Il faut que vous boutonniez vos boutons des mouches (tous les)
chacun nuit! (s) n'oubliez-pas mon ami! Go to bed at 10.30 and take
your Gregory pills. Write to me sometimes, and tell me of your travels,
perhaps Rimbaud. Thank you so much for giving me Dr Donne, dear
Lytton. I have been so happy, incred i a b l y [going up a musical scale]
happy! Quelque fois je voudrais être un garçon de moulin!

                                        votre nièce CARRINGTON

[1] Who kept a shop of artists' materials.

To Lytton Strachey

Wednesday morning [September 6th, 1916]   *Shandygaff Hall!!*
                                                       [Garsington Manor]

Well may you be surprised at my being here chère Grandpère! quite
suddenly yesterday morning I bicycled over—as I had to see Brett
(who is still here) about the London House. An Excellent arrangement
is now made. Maynard [Keynes] and Sheppard[1] are to live in Clive's
[Bell] house and we take 3 Gower Street for nine months. Katherine
[Mansfield] and [Middleton] Murry will live in the Bottom floor, Brett
on the second, and I in the attics. But my rent will only be nine pounds
a year!!! So what affluence I shall have for Hotel life!!!! I shall like
living with Katherine I am sure—Murry has a job at the W.O. [War
Office]. It was strange arriving here again. Maria—Clive. The old
Professor. Brett. Mademoiselle, Pipsie [Philip Morrell] and Ottoline
seated at tea in the dining room! Numerous questions at once from
Clive about you, and Wales. I restrained from all enthusiasm—which
you will hardly believe, and created no mysteries. Ottoline dislikes me!
Rather plainly. Had a long talk with Katherine in bed this morning, she
and Murry have been here for weeks. A concert is in preparation for
this evening. Great confusion. Like Clapham Junction, chairs and
tables being shunted about everywhere. The performers and Pipsie at
the Pianola! What an evening last night. Philip reading Boswell's life of
Johnson with his own remarks freely strewn in between the passages.
'That's good excellent', 'all this part is very dull I'll leave it out'. Clive
cackling in the comfortable chair, your chair, pugs snoring, Ottoline
yawning, Maria, Mademoiselle and even Katherine knitting woollen
counterpanes. Brett with her telephone.[2] What a scene! I thought of
you, and longed to transport it all to you, lying on your sofa with its
crochet background. 12 o'ck Ottoline has just taken me round the
garden, but all conversation absolutely failed. I suddenly realized I did
not want to talk to her in the least. It is extraordinary being here again.
They all seemed enchanted. I cannot explain it. I think I shall not wait

---

[1] Maynard Keynes and John Tressider Sheppard (afterwards knighted, and Provost
of King's College Cambridge), who was working at the War Office, went to live in Clive's
house at 46 Gordon Square, and Maynard let his house at 3 Gower Street to a group
including Carrington, Katherine Mansfield and John Middleton Murry.
[2] Her ear-trumpet.

for the concert tonight, but bicycle home after lunch. I feel so desperately lonely. Your letters gave me much pleasure. [Seventeen lines omitted]

I am writing not in the monastic Building, for the house is in an uproar with Eranees [the violinists Jelly and Adila d'Aranyi] squeaking and scratching on their instruments, and tuning and retuning!

To Lytton Strachey

Friday morning [*September 8th, 1916*]   *Hurstbourne Tarrant*

I am not certain whether I am not becoming rather like Maria [Nys] with my letter writing! But have patience.

Tomorrow I am going to look at a house near Hungerford for you. I boldly went into all the estate agents in Newbury yesterday, and enquired about houses. This house is only £32 with a huge orchard four miles from Hungerford. But more anon when I have seen it. Clive is writing to you. He will share if its near Newbury, so that he can come over from Oxford.[1] Will you like this? Brett has taken your Garsington house. ('Her great leap.' 'The great plunge.' They are merely trying to excite our curiosity with those letters!) If you were here, and could see these downs. So lovely, you would tremble with excitement at the prospect of your little cottage. I have maps of every square inch of the country now! And correspondence with every auctioneer in Newbury, Marlborough, and Reading! There is an amazing house to let in the middle of Savernake Forest. But £70 a year! Lytton, *all* the books arrived yesterday! I was so thrilled at having John Donne again last night. Thank you very much. And for Tom Jones also.

Katherine [Mansfield] is writing to you a description of the concert so I will refrain. It was full of comic incidents, and humour abounded. We wished you had been there.

Never have I seen the garden look so wonderful. A moon shining on the pond, covered with warm slime, bubbling, and fermenting underneath and great black shadows cast from the trees over it all. And inside, music and these strange villagers with their babies, and young men in hard white collars and thick serge suits. Clive sitting lost in thought on

---

[1] Clive Bell was working, as a conscientious objector, on Philip Morrell's farm at Garsington.

the steps. Maria in her yellow trowsers, lying, covered in a black cloak in the passage, distractedly in love with Ottoline. We acted a play. Katherine sang some songs and danced ragtimes. We talked late into the night together after it was all over in bed.

What fun we will have in Gower Street. She will play all the games I love best. Pretending to be other people and dressing up and parties! What weather. I am so full of energy that I cannot concentrate on this letter. I long to rush off and be on the downs.

Here are some photographs. I loved your long letter about your walk, and Westbury. There is great indignation at Garsington because I refrained from any excitement about our journey and merely gave a short description of the landscape! To hell with them! If one is ecstatic they accuse one of being superior and uplifted. If one is silent, and tempered, of being cryptic and exclusive! What news from Barbara about her pursuit of the cottage?

Thank you again very much for John Donne.—Iris [Tree, who had been a fellow student at the Slade] is back again. What excitements in store for us all. I have just found an amazing history book of Noel's which gives me from the beginning, the histories of every country, all at the same time in comparison. I am just coming to Egypt, and Greece. Also a table of all the men of importance, writers etc. in the different countries in the corresponding centuries.

My Love to you CARRINGTON

To David Garnett

Saturday [Postmarked September 14th, 1916]   *Hurstbourne Tarrant*

Dear Bunny, I am sorry to have taken such a long time in answering your letter.

Will you when we come to London come to dinner with me? I made a muddle about sending your letter to some wrong address and sat waiting for you to come to tea with a clean table cloth and new buns, and no Bunny. Your letter amused me, I remember, especially the description of the Laird [Duncan Grant] entertaining the Americans and Clive and Vanessa. Barbara has told you all the news of Wales. So what have I to write? Then I think you are all too critical, and letter writing reaches such a high mountain pitch with you! It's almost as bad as writing a letter to the Times.

I bicycled over to Garsington for the day on Wednesday and heard from Ottoline that the old Pelham[1] might not let you stay on at your farm. I do hope it will come alright. Maynard must shut the P.M. in Margot's[2] wardrobe and keep him there until he signs a document allowing you to stay on at Wissett. Such an evening at Garsington. The Eranees [d'Aranyis] gave a concert to all the village people. In the hall a gathering of nearly a hundred aged mothers with babies and children in red flannel dresses and white pinafores all the labourers in those thick grey serge suits and white washed collars. It was a strange assembly to see standing round the table in that shiny red panelled room eating rock cakes!

May I come and see you in the winter with Barbara if you still stay at Wissett? We, (Brett, the Murrys and I) are going to live in Maynard's house in Gower Street, the end of this month. I shall be rather glad to live in a civilized house again; the mice, and general dirt of that studio of mine in Yeoman's Row rather suffocated one. I have fine days here wandering over these downs. They are terrifyingly big, but it's rather lonely after living with such excellent company for so long. How did your poem end about the Bubble? I think I shall go back to London next week to do some work for Roger[3] restoring Mantegna frescoes at Hampton Court and move in Gower Street afterwards.

My love to Duncan and Vanessa and you   CARRINGTON

To Lytton Strachey

Saturday afternoon [September 16th, 1916]   *Hurstbourne Tarrant*

I was just flying into a tangent at not hearing from you. Considering I had sent you a map of the best land in Europe, and plans and diagrams worthy of Inigo Jones! But I might have known that, (without that treasure of a niece) you would leave no address behind. Fool. Oh aged Fool! I think however that you must live at Ashford Hill, (that which I sent you the photograph of) near Kingsclere and only 4 miles from Midgham Station on the Newbury line to London line. It is vastly

---

[1] An appeal committee for allotting work of national importance to conscientious objectors.

[2] Maynard Keynes was a friend of the Prime Minister and Mrs Asquith.

[3] Roger Fry employed Carrington as his assistant in this work.

superior I am sure to Hemel Hempstead. If you had any power of guiding your directory senses you would go back to London *via* Newbury, and get out at Midgham Station, and go and see the cottage at Ashford. *But*, doubtless master Siddons[1] has seized my letter and has stolen the map and alluring drawings, and ground plans of the houses.

And I feel too enraged at the present moment to write it all again! And the energy lost! 40 miles in one morning did I bicycle for your sake revered uncle! Searching the highways and hedges, for your blasted house! 40 miles!! And then he leaves no address behind. You must know that all this is provoking, Natalia my dear. I am going to London on Tuesday morning so may D.V. see you. Do not flatter yourself, vile man, for one moment that it is in anyway to oblige you as I had arranged to do so two days ago.

I have to go in to Newbury for the day on Monday to see an erstwhile friend, so if you have the energy to come this way back to London, I would meet you at the station, and show you Ashford and then you could depart on your way rejoicing to London. There is a train 11.42 Oxford, Newbury 1.28. or 2.49—3.59. I will meet both in case you come. It won't make any difference to me, as I shall have nothing in particular to do all day. I swear I have no Christian feelings towards you! only a desire to live at Ashford sometimes!

I am just going up to Combe to pay a call. But the courage it will require to ring *this* bell. Widcomb? In anger I remain your niece DORIC. Severe style architecture. And I told Ottoline I was vague as to *your* future plans. And you tell her I am busy with Barbara finding you a house???

[Duncan Grant and David Garnett had been refused permission to continue working on the Wissett Lodge fruit farm by the Pelham Committee. Vanessa Bell, who knew and liked that part of Sussex, visited Lewes on market day and found employment for both young men and an unused farmhouse, Charleston, on the Firle estate from which she rented it. Charleston was to become the home of the Bell family for the next half century. Duncan Grant and David Garnett lived there for the rest of the war, and Duncan lives there today.

Their employer, Mr Hecks, wanted a labourer urgently, so David Garnett went on ahead, while Vanessa and Duncan organized the move from Wissett to Charleston. In London he met Barbara Hiles and

[1] The son of the landlady at Tor House, Wells, where Lytton was lodging after his tour with Carrington.

Carrington and persuaded them to accompany him to Sussex for the
week-end before he started his job. They took bicycles and rode out
from Lewes to Firle, where they left them at the Ram Inn. They then
walked over the shoulder of the downs to Leonard and Virginia Woolf's
house, Asheham. They believed they would find them there and hoped
that they would put them up for the night, or at least let them sleep in
a barn. Asheham was locked up and it was already evening when they
reached it. It was cold, and they had no sleeping bags or blankets.
However, they noticed that one of the upstairs windows at the back of
the house was open, so David Garnett climbed up a drainpipe, got in
and let in his companions. They found some apples, but the bedding
was locked up. There was, however, one bed with a blanket or two, so
the three slept on that, going to bed in the dark, for they were afraid to
show a light. Next morning they left soon after dawn and climbed the
down behind Asheham, and walked along the ridge to Firle Beacon,
where they saw Charleston below them. They descended and inspected
the house and garden, though without breaking in. They must somehow have got food—perhaps they stole some from the Woolfs. In the
afternoon they walked back across Firle Park to Firle and had a good tea
at the Ram, where Bunny had taken a room until Charleston should be
habitable. In the evening the two girls bicycled back to Lewes and
Bunny started work pulling mangolds the next morning.

The cowboy is a joking reference to Lytton whom I had called a
cowboy because of his sombrero hat.]

To David Garnett

Tuesday evening [October 11th, 1916]   *3 Gower Street, London*

Dear Bunny, It was a good time, and it was with sorrow that Barbary
and I parted from you, although we mangled you heavily all the way to
Lewes! We slept in a Commercial Hotel in the High Street, kept by
excellent old people and the next morning had breakfast with a large
assembly of elderly commercial travellers who took the greatest of
interest in us, so we had to invent a kind of story about a walking tour
over the downs. We ate an enormous breakfast; Barbara's mushrooms,
bacon, 3 slices of bread and butter each and marmalade, and our bedroom all for 3/6 each!!! Unfortunately I met one of the aged C. Travellers in the Post Office later with our bicycles, which caused him some

uneasiness and many enquiries followed as to our walking tour!

We found some wonderful houses in Ickford. The cursed luck was that one which was absolutely perfect had just been taken 2 weeks ago. The other was about £300 a year with 8 acres, another furnished vicarage 5 gns a week with a most saintly atmosphere which we feared would quite annihilate poor Uncle Lytton.

I am glad you enjoyed our company. I am sorry to be so solidly virtuous. But I still maintain it is quite impossible to talk seriously, or make love with another person in the same bed. Perhaps I'm wrong, probably romantic. Not that it matters. I like you very much, although you aggravate me terribly sometimes. The cowboy has, I fear, banished you temporally from my body. And perhaps you others from my mind. But he was most divinely beautiful. And I am here, and you are there. A curse on it all! We came back Friday evening and got out at London Bridge in our eagerness to arrive here, instead of Victoria. On Saturday evening Lytton came to dinner with us here.

It was very difficult not to tell him about Asheham and Charleston in detail. And other things!! Bunny you *must not* tell anyone about Asheham, promise truly. Because you see Vanessa will get all the blame and dishonour thrown on her and as we did succeed in doing it so well, why should they ever know and cause confusion and desolation in the camp? Lytton saw Virginia on Saturday at Richmond, actually. I nearly said 'Had she found out?' quickly. I am glad you like Mr Hecks but won't it be wonderful when Vanessa comes and you can go home every night to Charleston and wake up early and see the pond below and the shining willow tree—and boys whistling driving cows up the Lane. Curse you!!! I did like your letter.

My love CARRINGTON

To David Garnett

Friday

All is discovered Bunny, I saw Roger [Fry] on Thursday (yesterday) and he asked me if we stayed there as Virginia was in rather a panic as strange people had broken in, eaten all the food and *moved the beds*!!!! some old hag had written a wild letter telling of our outrageous frightfulness. 'Of course I knew at once it was a fabrication about the beds being moved and the furniture. But told Virginia you had possibly just got in to look at it' said the worthy Roger. So I told him to confess to Virginia about the apples being eaten and us looking at the house and agreed with him that the other rumours must be an invention of the heated brain of the old hag!! But I saw Vanessa and Duncan, so lovely in a new suit, last night and confessed the truth and my mistrust to Roger, which Vanessa promised to keep up as Roger said he really thought they would be angry if we had broken in for the night. 'But of course that idea was preposterous!!!!' But *How* did they find out?? You must put that book back. Can you in the dead of night quietly without any commotion? It is all very exciting!! I was very tempted out of wickedness to make a mystery of it and deny everything just to aggravate the wolf. No news of any house, wretched! And I still long for my beautiful cowboy, a curse on everybody because I shall never see him again.

Vanessa thinks it will be alright and will pacify Virginia about it. In a terrific hurry, so cannot write properly.   Love CARRINGTON

To David Garnett

[*Postmarked October 17th, 1916*]   *3 Gower Street, London*

Dear Bunny, *What* have you written to Virginia? Everything is in such a blasted muddle now and I have to go to dinner with Virginia and her wolf on Thursday to 'explain about Asheham'—so for god's sake write *by return* and tell me exactly what you have told Virginia. Roger thought it was a mistake writing at all, because since Virginia had taken the whole thing so calmly and it was all settled, it was a pity to rake it all up again and perhaps make the he-wolf furious. But no matter, and of no avail if you have already written. Only I do not want to contradict your letter (*and put that book back sometime*) which I certainly shall do if I do not know what you wrote!!

How do you fare?   In haste CARRINGTON

[*Postscript*]

Poor Carrington has to face the he-wolf all alone to dinner she is dreading it and I don't envy her.

Are you in Charleston yet?   Yours BARBARA

To David Garnett

Wednesday [October 25th, 1916]   *3 Gower Street, London*

Dear Bunny, I am afraid I cannot come down this next Sunday as I think in every probability I shall have to go home to my people, as my brother [Teddy] has been reported missing. But I will come another day and eat sandwiches with you and disagree and argue frantically. I am just going in a few minutes with grandfather Lytton to the Wolves den. And make a hash of it for you, as I do not feel in a untruthful diplomatic mood tonight! But I will try my best. Goodbye.

Yrs affectionately CARRINGTON

To Lytton Strachey

[November 6th, 1916]   *3 Gower Street, London*

Will you come on *Wednesday morning* at 10.30, and then you can stay rather longer than usual, and go straight up to Faith's, or is that too much for your constitution for one day?

I just had an inspiration over your picture—another foot higher and wider! But such a good design. I am excited. You must know it will be really a good picture. Do not forget your essay on M. Julie [de l'Espinasse]. I dare not telephone, so resort to this laborious method of transacting conversation.

The photographs of the Plumpton House came this morning The revd sir said the photographs did not show it off to its full advantage!!!

Pergular (?) walks, and *masses* of greenhouses much worse than the erections near to Roger's house—so I re-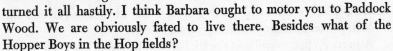turned it all hastily. I think Barbara ought to motor you to Paddock Wood. We are obviously fated to live there. Besides what of the Hopper Boys in the Hop fields?

CARRINGTON

To David Garnett

[About the last week November 1916]

[Map omitted] Bunny, be an [drawing of an angel omitted] and go on your bicycle next Sunday morning and look at a Farm house called Hay Reed near Wilmington. I have marked it on the map for you. It's in between Arlington and Wilmington which is Vacant and write immediately and tell me what it is like and whether suitable and then we will rush down with all speed and take it. I have written to the owner, but he will only tell me the sanitation is out of doors and the number of rooms. Make a small drawing of it and particularly notice the country round and the garden. Do, be kind, and run down the red road for me, and look at it as soon as you can.

Thank you but I know all I want to now since the ancient Bard told me *all* your conversation! I did enjoy my morning with you. I was so distracted on leaving you *and* that conversation that I left that canvas on the bus and arrived without it! I am [so] excited at the prospect of at last finding a farm house that I cannot write you a proper letter! Go almost immediately!! Promise you will and I will be your willing slave. Tomorrow I am going away to Hampshire. We are leaving our house there on Tuesday next for ever which fills me with distress as I love that country better than any in all the south.

Write me another long letter when you have time, about what you do. I am working very hard now, painting.

Oh it's a good game Bunny. But rather obvious!!!

Love CARRINGTON

To Lytton Strachey

December 8th, 1916

Chère Oncle, Here are two oldish gloves, if they fit you, and an odd one. Will you sit tomorrow morning please? Early.

A party on Sat. evening at the Richardson woman.[1] I am taking Alix. Will you come also?

---

[1] Dorothy Richardson, the 'stream of consciousness' novelist.

1 Dora Carrington, *c.* 1910, at the time of her entry to the Slade School of Art. There are no good photographs of Carrington in later years. This was taken before she bobbed her hair and broke her nose

2 Lytton Strachey, painted in the autumn and winter of 1916. This portrait is referred to in the letter of November 16th, 1916, and in the Diary, January 1st, 1917

3 The Mill, Tidmarsh *c.* 1918.
The Mill House is on the left.
The black swans are imaginary

4 David Garnett. See letters of
December 8th, 1918, and
January 22nd, 1919

5 E. M. Forster, painted at Tidmarsh, *c.* 1920

6 View from near Yegen, Spain, *c.* January 1924. See letter of January 1924 to Frances Marshall. When he first came to Yegen Gerald Brenan wrote to Carrington (November 29th, 1919): 'But the chief charm of both Mecina and Yegen is the view—perhaps the most beautiful in the world—at one's feet in the "plain", or rather basin, of Ugijar are row after row of desert hills, rounded, carved out and shaped by wind and water, covered with little bushes or else with almond trees.

'Beyond is the coast range, through a broad gap in which one sees the sea—some 40 miles away. The sun rises out of it every morning. The mountains are completely bare, but are not steep or jagged. They are wonderfully modelled by a network of gullies and ravines . . . which, if I could draw, I should like to draw all day long.'

It was fun that party on Wednesday. Barbara and I slept there, in crêpe de chine nightgowns with pink rosebuds round the neck. I ravished votre petit [Geoffrey] Nelson for you.

Dinner tonight with Virginia tout seul. Pray for me.

Yours, CARRINGTON

[Carrington's habit of giving her friends old clothes later infuriated Gerald Brenan. He believed it was due to a wish to patronize. But the gift of an odd glove to Lytton Strachey is difficult to construe as an act of patronage. I always thought these acts of benevolence were due to a wish not to waste anything which might be useful.]

To Lytton Strachey

Sunday [December 10th, 1916]   *3 Gower Street, London*

I rang up this morning to enquire after your lordship's health, but found from Pippa, that you are still lying on your couch of death. I am grieved, and hope you will soon be better.

Next week I am going to stay with the Jew [Gertler] at Cholesbury. Gilbert has lent him his castle for a week. He is going to ask you to come down on Wednesday or Thursday for a day or so. You will come? I promise you vast quantities of food and drink, and raiment for the night season. A fire in your bedroom and our love shall out-heat the very fires and be hotter than the very soups and curries, as Ottoline would write no doubt.

I have to come up to teach on Wednesday so I could come to Faith's and fetch you, and take you back with me about 5.30. So do get well again. It was just as well you did not come to that party. For assuredly you would be dead by now, had you gone. Henry's [Lamb] exwife [Euphemia] played the most prominent part in all proceedings. C'était enffet une scene qui aurait pu charmer un esprit beaucoup mouns réfléchi que celui auquel elle s'offrait! Seldom have I seen such a debauche of white arms and bosoms. It was indeed a sight to see— everyone trying to outrival their companions in viciousness. Beauty was absent. It was no wonder that the female element turned to their own species for les embrasures. When the males consisted of Horace Cole, Boris [Anrep], the Armenian [John], Rodker, and even more degraded specimens. You should have seen the little miss who came to Garsington last summer, to teach those children dancing! But it was the journey to that Place and back which would have annihilated you!—But *that* cannot be written in a few lines. Le livre—Marlowe—m'a plu. Will you telephone me some time tomorrow. Fear the mad women too much to venture again. I am not going away till after tea. My Love to you, do get well soon.   CARRINGTON

[From the following two letters it becomes clear that during her stay alone with Gertler at Gilbert Cannan's 'castle', actually a windmill and millhouse, Carrington had given way to Gertler's persistence and sexual intercourse had taken place. But she had annoyed him by her 'inability to really get interested'. Subsequent letters show that sexual relations with Gertler were, for Carrington, always a wretched failure.

Lytton told me at the time that it was due to Gertler's violence and Carrington's worry and disgust over contraceptives. The real reason was that she was not in love with him, but with Lytton. Blaming herself did not improve matters.]

To Mark Gertler

Saturday, December 1916   *3 Gower Street, London*

Dear Mark, I am going home after all this afternoon so I shall not be at Gordon's [Campbell] tomorrow night. Will you tell them how sorry I am. Do you miss me very much already? Meet me here on Tuesday evening at 7.30 unless I wire to the contrary and make any other arrangement. I read Marlowe again last night and knew what one thing meant more than I did last week! It certainly is a necessity if one wants to understand the best poets. No she's not going on to say that is *why* she takes sugar in her coffee now. But taking sugar incidentally does make one appreciate those poets more fully. But I only like sugar some times, not every week and every day in my coffee. I think you would like it so much and take it so often in your coffee that you wouldn't taste anything in time, and miss the taste of the coffee. But darling I shall look after that alright and only allow you three lumps a month. You've had more than three for this month. So no more till next year, you sugar-eater you!

    Goodbye then till Tuesday evening   Yr PERIWINKLE
                                               CRINKLE CRINKLE

To Mark Gertler

Saturday [December 1916]   *Hurstbourne Tarrant*

Dear Mark, This to cheer you in my absence, or have not you noticed
it yet? I will come next Wednesday evening to Monty's [Shearman] if I
am back by then. I came down last night here. It was fearfully cold
travelling down. Today it is snowing white, and a piercing wind. But
I love the hugeness of it. The great space between one and the hills
opposite, after the houses in Gower Street which press against my very
nose, on every side. The irregular shapes of the sky and hills are a joy
after the square shapes of London houses and square slits of sky. I am
sorry if I have annoyed you lately about that business and making such
a fuss. It is only my inability to really get interested I am afraid and
really I did try that thing. Only it was much too big, and wouldn't go
inside no matter what way I used it! But I won't be so childish any
longer. I wonder what you will talk about at the Campbells' on Sunday?
Remember to tell Monty to send out his invitations to his party. Are
you working again yet? I am so excited about my painting now. I want
to do nothing else all day long. Today I shall go for a long walk over the
Downs. But it is cold. Almost too cold out to be really happy.

Again I repeat

I am sorry lately if I've been tiresome and in bad humours, but the
difficulties that go on inside me, in spite of my fat exterior. I envy often
amiable people who can love more simply, and get on. I suppose they
aren't so selfish as we are, or do not care so much about their own ideas
and can part with them more easily. I want to come and see your
sculpture again when I come back. I am going to do some work for Miss
Berry here. But heavens! how dull it is compared to a minute's painting,
or even reading is a greater joy to me. But she is so good that I mustn't
disappoint her. I will try and come in to Monty's on Wednesday about
9 o'ck if I can.

1917

Carrington's thoughts after painting
Lytton's portrait (facing p. 48)

[From an entry in her diary dated January 1st, 1916[1]]

I wonder what you will think of it when you see it. I sit here, almost
every night it sometimes seems, looking at your picture, now tonight it
looks wonderfully good, and I am happy. But then I dread showing it.
I should like to go on always painting you every week, wasting the afternoon loitering, and never never showing you what I paint. It's marvellous having it all to oneself. No agony of the soul. Is it vanity? No
because I don't care for what they say. I hate only the indecency of
showing them what I have loved. It's been a happy day today. I wonder
what you think when you go away. Very different from what I do. That
much I know. Did you like the Lettercase—You do not lavish your
appreciation I must tell you—If I was a man I should heap you with
presents, bags of soft something, until you *had* to cry out thanks
because they overflowed on top of you, and weighed you down. I would
love to explore your mind behind your finely skinned forehead. You
seem so wise and very coldly old. Yet in spite of this what a peace to be
with you, and how happy I was today.

To bed now, and have you sitting in your green armchair staring at
the impossible book, all night and I shall find you there in the morning.
So goodnight. What dreams in store? Who can tell—

To Mark Gertler

Friday January 5th, 1916 [*January 1917*]   *3 Gower Street, London*

Dear Mark, I could hardly sleep last night through wretchedness because
I am so miserable at making you unhappy. And how to explain it? I
came last Sunday to the Campbells hoping it would be alright. But it
wasn't. Am I very different or are you suddenly? I want frightfully to
get on with you but I feel so wretched when I am with you now. I am
sure it is some rotten nerves. You weren't right when you said I wasn't

[1] Actually 1917. Carrington wrote the wrong year.

depressed because I am nearly all day. Only it makes me a thousand times more frantically wretched to know you are also sad, and I am the cause of it all. But you must know it is not that I dislike you. It's something in between us—that is hateful. Really inside me. I am going to think seriously and simply find out what it is—and then I will come back to you. I am going away on Saturday for a week. but I want to see you just once before I go. Will you meet me on Friday afternoon only Hampstead is so far to go to and I shall be ill, and it makes me rather tired. Could we go to Monty's rooms, as you have the key? Or would you rather I came up to your studio? Dear, please for heaven's sake forgive me this wrong I am doing you.   Yrs CARRINGTON

To Mark Gertler

Monday [*January 1917*]   *3 Gower Street, London*

It was kind of you to be so patient last night with me. You cannot think how I hate myself sometimes—often. I will try and get over this soon and will come and see you then. But at present I am in a vile mood, and it's not fair to either of us when I am possessed of a devil to come together and be miserable or else curse each other. Just think I have gone to the country and then when I come back it will be alright again. I've no more to say to you now. Except do not be unhappy. To be fair I don't think I will see you until next week. I am going to work hard and get all these vile jobs finished, clear everything off. It's the only use this miserable devil is to me, to do my duty jobs—Honestly I think my nerves are a bit tied up and Jangled. Tell Monty I am working hard so that is why I will not come down and see him at Adam Street.

But please be very happy it's really alright and I get much more depressed if I think you are sad.   Yrs CARRINGTON

[Virginia and Leonard Woolf had lent Asheham House to their old friend Saxon Sydney-Turner who had recently fallen in love with Barbara Hiles. Carrington and Lytton were invited to accompany them but Lytton decided not to go on account of the very severe weather. There was a bitter frost and the downs were covered in snow, which is the reason for the teasing tone of the following letter. She shows a certain youthful impatience with Lytton's debilitated state. Tobogganing on tea-trays was a great feature of the visit to Asheham.]

To Lytton Strachey

January 29th, 1917   *Asheham House, Rodmell, Sussex*

Asheham as you perceive is surrounded by sunshine, and smoke surges
from every chimney in dense volumes. Should you for a moment contemplate coming, do I beg you bring only the lightest of summer under-
clothing and some antidote for mosquitos and gnats which invest the
garden in the evenings.

We arrived here after a long and dusty Journey on Saturday evening.
Fortunately the old hag had some iced drinks prepared for us in the
kitchen, for Saxon was nearly dropping from the heat. Um-ah-well,
Thank you for a pocket handkerchief—admit my Mercy is everlasting
and my goodness endureth for ever, for sparing you from the jeers of
James and the scorn of servants!

Well, and how is my aged grandad. I trust he is looking after himself, and not sliding on the ponds in the Parks with the lads of the city.
It often worries me that you are so careless over your health, and appetite. I should be so much happier if I could only think you were well looked
after—But you were always reckless even as a boy. One day perhaps
you will realise how much you have made your poor aunt suffer—We
are all very happy here, and actually warm. I plastered all the windows
and the bottoms of the doors up with brown paper. And we have terrific
fires in all the rooms. Saxon is as I suspected a lunatic. He spent the
whole of Saturday night and all Sunday breaking the ice in the cistern,
and putting his arm down pipes and then drying his wet shirt *on* his

arm in front of the fire. He insisted on getting up at eight o'ck and
lighting the fires. It is impossible to have any control over his actions.
But he seems fairly well in spite of his strange habits. Barbara is cheerful, and full of industry.

Yesterday we had a tea party. Bunny, Duncan, Adrian and Karin
[Stephen] walked over from Charleston. They ate the most tremendous
tea. Like starving stags, and brought a dog. Saxon read Swinburne to
us in the evening. I loved so much the poem about the Nightingale and
the man.

Did you go to the Sale or did greed overcome you at Simpsons?

It's lovely here, we walked this morning to Glynde, it was truly
quite hot in the sun, and the downs exquisitely beautiful, with patches
of sunlight and olive green shadows running about over them. We had a
ride back in a cart, which we stopped on the road.

Every delight seems to have congregated here to rejoice us, sun in
the day season and a moon by night. It is strange living here again when
I remember how amazed I was with you all round the fire that evening I
first came.   My love CARRINGTON

To Lytton Strachey

Sunday [February 4th, 1917]   *Asheham House, Rodmell, Sussex*

What a juggernaut you were not to come here. It was been very hot every day and no rains or winds. But still;—Sit in your beastly Jaeger pants and grouse over your fire. Who cares? Voltaire wrote your poetry, or else you did. (This is not designated for a compliment merely a slight insult.)

I come back to-morrow. I am already miserable for I love living here so much. It has been rarely beautiful. Last night the moon was so brilliant that the trees cast shadows, like they do in the early spring across the road, and the sky was graduated like a Franchesca painting very transparent and speckled with stars, and a huge moon in the middle, all the downs have been sprinkled with Cerebros (finely powdered salt used in the XX century) showing the indentations, like an engraving. I want frightfully to come and stay here again, and paint.

Saxon has been reading us a latin story about Psyche and Venus whose conduct greatly resembled Ottoline I thought, in Apuleius—I liked the way the poet rebuked the lamp for the part he played!! I have just been reading the life of Thomas Beddoes who I found on the bottom of the bookshelf. I thought he sounded very interesting. You never told me of him, why didn't you? We had a party on Friday evening, Vanessa, Duncan and Bunny, and the beautiful Maynard—Bull-boy. Such a dinner. Soups, Beef sausages and Leeks, Plum Pudding, Lemon Jellies,

and Punches afterwards!!!—The conversation was instructive and serious. Maynard stayed the night, and Barbara and I walked over to Charleston yesterday with him across the downs and had slides on the pond and played with my beautiful cowboy, who had grown even more entrancing since I last saw him! Saxon is really better I think. Virginia wrote today and said you were going skating with her, a comic sight, I

trow. I wish I could have seen the fun! I am much better in health and spirits who could fail to be in such a place as this.

We have all just been writing long poems to Nick [Bagenal]. Saxon's was best, and he brought in a reference to Pegasus and his wings. But I brought in some even more remarkable references of a less classical order. Barbara's was of a lower order still. When will [you] come and sit for me? Tuesday? Telephone me on Tuesday morning. Barbara greatly appreciated your telegram yesterday. Saxon read us Atlanta. I did like it very much. Some of the choruses are wonderful. A charming creature, with rather decayed teeth, called Willie waits on us night and day. He calls Saxon in the morning and has long conversations with him, but Saxon never seems to know what they are about. Saxon is now as I write wandering disconsolately in the garden with a Badmington racket and B[attle] D[ore] and S[huttle] Cock. But the ladies have taken to the pen and there is no one for him to play with. I think there can be few people with such natures as he possesses, or it would be different. I slid all the way down the Firle Beacon on Maynard's despatch case. A terrific rate. Yesterday when we went to Charleston, it was a great game. What can I draw you pictures of? Cowboys and cowbulls on the downs by moonlight? [Illustration omitted]

There is a lovely yellow owl which flies round the house in the evening. Yesterday I saw him quite close as I walked along the road!

We have been in to Lewes twice. It is a wonderful town—One house near the lodge, do you remember, a double faced house with a sundial and moulding on the wood like this at the side of the windows which is a rare [two illustrations omitted] pattern. Now I must stop burbling as Saxon and Barbara are going to the post. I wish you were here.

Love from CARRINGTON

Monday morning

Abandoned idea of returning today such lovely snow on the downs, and then tea-trays, so we stay on—and on—and on so pay no attention re Tuesday etc.

[Lytton had written in a letter headed *Lunacy Lodge February 9th* that there was no coal and there would be no fires in his mother's house in Belsize Park Gardens and that 'It seems improbable that we shall meet until my coffin passes down Gower Street on its way to the Paupers' Cemetery.']

To Lytton Strachey

Saturday [February 10th, 1917]   *3 Gower Street, London*

I am grieved to hear of your sad state and the near approach of

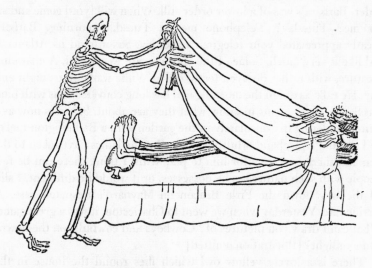

Try no more to elude his boney figures. They will be warmer far than those you sit round in the padded room lighted by that perfidious gas fire. [Illustration omitted]

We returned on Thursday evening. Saxon put us in a first Pullman Car from Brighton!!!! That's the *only* decent way to travel. The waiters, and French actresses seemed slightly amazed at us and Barbara pinched a pocketful of lump sugar when they weren't looking and I stole the

French actress's papers Tatler etc when she was out of the apartment.

It was pretty dismal getting back again, carrying armfuls of bay-trees to console us for the absence of Asheham. But last night Nelson called for me and we went tobogganning on Parliament Hill by moonlight till nearly 12 o'ck. It was rather wonderful. We picked up two charming youths, who came on our sledge and carried it up to the top of the hill everytime, and held my coat for me and then dragged our sledge home! I am going skating this morning with Alix [Sargant-Florence][1] and le petit Geoff [Nelson] tonight on Hampstead. Alix is going to live here when Katherine and Jack Murry leave, which they do next week.

I went and found her in a sad plight yesterday sitting fully dressed in outdoor clothes on a bed, with a gas fire roaring in a tiny room, remains of 12 days' meals, for she hadn't left the room for that number of days! Her face was pale grey with deep red rims round her eyes. She admitted all the females in the houses were now raving lunatics and she likewise insane. Chappers [Miss Chapman, the housekeeper] obtained by means of much wile and guile two tons of coal yesterday. I have now commanded her to marry the wretched colonel and to make him into a footman, and to attend to all our wants in the lower regions. This she readily complied to, and they are to be married next Tuesday. May they perish in the night! (Maynard is to be best-man with maidenhair fern and a chrysanthemum in his button-hole).[2]

We did have fun tobogganing before we left Asheham and Saxon really became much better if one can judge at all from activity as a sign of health. Here are some wood cuts for you. Not very good. But it was rather difficult as I only had one tool. Now I have some more I will do some better ones. Do get well soon and join us in these festive sports on land and water. I am truly sorry you have been so ill. If it were not for the crowd of jibbering inmates at the Lodge and the denseness of their volume I would come and sit by your bedside, read Beddoes, and bring you a wreath of Bayleaves for your burial.

Later

I have just been skating on Regents Park with Brett. It was hardly successful as I had no boots, and my ankles leant upon the ground heavily. You were utterly mistaken to think the comforts of London were greater than those of Asheham, we had hot water all day. No wet dung heaps, as here, to sit on and masses of coal and food! Please do not die for indeed I should miss you.   CARRINGTON

[1] Alix Sargant-Florence, who was to marry James Strachey.
[2] This marriage did in fact take place.

To Lytton Strachey

February 21st [*1917*]

[Illustration omitted] NOT tomorrow morning as Brett has gone away
and I am painting in her room as the light is so good down there.
Friday perhaps or Saturday. But please recover your-self. You were in
no fit state for human intercourse the other day! [Augustus] John came
to tea yesterday so I asked if one might go on Sunday to tea there. David
[John] will play Bach to us. I had such an exciting evening yesterday
drawing in little French cafes in Fitzroy St, wonderful French people
who danced and sang bawdy, from the laughter, French songs.

Farewell old hermit.   Yr CARRINGTON

To Lytton Strachey

Monday [*February 26th, 1917*]

Thank you so much for being so kind to me yesterday. I was rather heavy
with depression inside and when I lay in bed, I realized how you had comforted me. It was his birthday yesterday,[1] and David [John] with his
black hair, and sullen face reminded me so much of him years ago. You
will not mind if I want to see you often, for it's wretched being alone and
knowing how he went, without ever being seen or loved. He had the
independence of a child like Poppet [John], all his joys contained inside
himself, made by himself.

Forgive me for writing. Only I think you would have loved him too,
as you did that little Poppet.   Yr CARRINGTON

[Early in March 1917 Dorelia John invited Lytton Strachey to stay at
Alderney Manor, Parkstone. He understood the invitation to be for a
week or so. Dorelia only stayed the week-end, but suggested Lytton
should stay on, which he did for a week, being looked after by the housekeeper. During this solitary week he wrote four letters to Carrington
asking her to join him.

The following letter is in reply to the first of his.]

[1] Carrington's favourite brother Teddy, who had joined the army after a time at sea in
a minesweeper, had been reported missing on the Somme.

To Lytton Strachey

Thursday [March 8th, 1917]   *3 Gower Street, London*

Chère Grandpère, Not that your miserly letter deserved any reply.
After our long discourse on the value of letter writing at lunch the
other day I at least expected something more than a page of Hums, ahs
intermitted with Ho, Ho's. I laughed softly to myself when Il Maestro
[Augustus John] told me on Sunday that Dorelia was returning on
Monday!

I had tea with him, and then we went to all those Belgian cafés in
Fitzroy City. He was almost interesting, as he gave me a complete
history of his life, and parents, the mysterious sister [Gwen John the
painter] who lives in Paris, a brother, and yet another sister. You know
it wasn't the Strand where he met Dorelia. I have, ever since you told
me (walking across N. Wales from the Dante Lake) thought when I was
in the Strand, near Adelphi, of John looking back at Dorelia in a Black
Hat, and now it was all a false vision, as he met her in Holborn.

I wish I was with you in the country. It must be pleasant to be away
from all these confusions, and to have real wood fires. But do not return,
for cold weather, like unto no cold weather that one has before witnessed in intensity now rushes round corners of the streets, up the
stairs, into the innermost chambers, and perishes one in one's very bed.
Truly, the cold is awful and the discomfort more than exceeding
great. Saxon has at last disappeared to Bexhill. Rather to the relief of his
guardians! The Mill is only for sale, £1000 premium and £30 a year rent
for 17 years!!!! So that's that. But, still, hold your ear close to my lips
and I will disclose that in the same village there are two smaller cottages
of rare beauty to let furnished, one 30/- a week which I am making in-
vestigations about. My leg is much better than you in health. Last night I
had a wonderful dream about a Russian soldier, who was dying on a
battlefield. But alas Alix could give me no explanation!! Barbara and
Faith [Henderson] toil day and night making dresses for the John
Beauty Chorus.[1] On Sunday Saxon took Barbara and I to Queens Hall to

---

[1] Part of a charity matinée in aid of the Lena Ashwell concerts for troops. There were
songs and dances by Slade students:

> John, John, how he's got on
> He owes it, he owes it to me
> Brass earrings I wear and I don't do my hair
> And my feet are as bare as can be.

Carrington's mother was horrified at her having taken part in a performance which
resulted in such vulgar publicity. Jacob Epstein scented in it a conspiracy against himself.

hear Schubert's unfinished Symphony. Entrancing in its loveliness.

Leonora No 1 on Saturday afternoon, but you won't be back in time. Marjorie [Olivier] has been removed now to her family which is a great relief.[1]

This cold has frozen my inside, so that I cannot even think of anything to write to you about.

Will you telephone me one morning when you return to Belsize?

And what of Antony and Cleopatra? You never telephoned me from Bournemouth as you promised! I have missed you rather. Does that please you vain wretch?

My Love CARRINGTON

[Lytton's invitations asking Carrington to join him at Alderney Manor became warmer as the week went on. He wrote: 'You could hardly find it colder than London and much less confusing, also one bed is warmer than two.']

To Lytton Strachey

Thursday evening [March 22nd, 1917]   *3 Gower Street, London*

I didn't go after all today. The snow and acute cold and then I could not bring my brain to bear on deciding what train to take and the mode of travelling when I arrived in the country. Now tomorrow early I shall post off on a bicycle and so defy the motorcars and agitation of my mad mother.

I missed you horribly today, and felt slightly angry for having confessed to you that I did care so much.

How loveable you are sometimes. Like the horse often I would tear you to pieces, and eat you up, as it seems too slow. You must write me very long letters in the country.

Yr loving CARRINGTON

[Lytton on March 23rd responded to Carrington's declaration of the 22nd with the words: 'I miss you too, you know. That was such a divine hour—why regret any of it? A great deal of a great many kinds of love.']

---

[1] She had been suffering from delusions.

From Carrington's Diary

Monday, April 13th, 1917

Awoke after a horrible dream. Mrs G. Jones was lying on the grass and showed me some photographs of three boys in vests and sailors' breeches, one was Teddy. Then she said they had been lost. Presently Teddy came in himself and I remember rushing at him, telling him how I had thought he was dead and how I closed my fingers into his hard fat cheeks. Very brown and kissed him and hugged till I nearly crushed him to atoms. After all this I awoke and felt rather miserable, as I remembered soon I should have to see Mark. Talked to Alix and Brett to while away the time; spoke to Lytton on the telephone and arranged to see him after supper. Talked to Brett. At last Mark telephoned not angrily as I expected; went up on the 24 Bus at Penn Studio. He was very calm. Looked at his pictures first and talked about the copy of the Cézanne he was doing and his big merry go round. Then he said: 'what are you going to do with it?' His calmness amazed me and his complete unselfishness and generosity. I became more and more wretched and wept. It seemed like leaving the warm sun in the fields and going into a dark and cold wood surrounded by trees which were strangers. I suddenly looked back at the long life we had had between us of mixed emotions. But always warm because of his intense love and now I had to leave it all and go away. Then suddenly he saw it also: the end of all this closeness, the final goodbye, the separation of two brothers, with a life between them, and he broke down and sobbed, and then it was agony. For he wanted to die and I thought how much this love mattered to him, and yet in spite [of] its greatness I could not keep it, and must leave. His loneliness was awful. We left the studio and had tea in a Suisse cafe in a dark back room. He didn't talk much, hardly at all about Lytton; only—'Will you live with him?' 'No.' 'But he may love you.' 'No he will not.' That I thought made it easier a little. He begged to still be friends and see me. But we both knew it could not be so and it was separation. I felt for another country—America. How very much I cared for him suddenly came upon me. The unreality, and coldness of Lytton. Then we went inside a bus, for it rained, to Tottenham Ct Rd. We laughed sometimes on the way.

Bitterly—when we thought of Kot[eliansky] went to B. Museum shops and chose a Giotto and Mark a Velazquez to copy. I left frightfully

ill with a bad pain in my side. Had a bath. When I found Lytton was
after all having tea with Alix and Mrs S[argent]-F[lorence] went in. But
felt too ill to even listen to the conversation and Lytton sat there quite
calmly, quibbling and playing lightly with his words. We went out to
dinner. I was glad to have to talk of other things. Virginia and himself,
Ray [Oliver Strachey's wife], Mrs S.-F. who we met at the Mont Blanc.
Peter Warren. His diseases, and Maynard. The time they took over
dinner was appalling. Shall I wait until I got home was my main thought.
Fortunately soon after we had sat down in front of the fire he asked me.

(C) I thought I had better tell Mark, as it was so difficult going on.

(L) Tell him what?

(C) That it couldn't go on. So I just wrote and said it.

(L) What did you say in your letter?

(C) I thought you knew.

(L) What do you mean?

(C) I said that I was in love with you. I hope you don't mind very much.

(L) But aren't you being rather Romantic and are you certain?

(C) There's nothing romantic about it.

(L) What did Mark say?

(C) He was terribly upset.

(L) Did he seem angry with me?

(C) No. He didn't mention you.

(L) But it's too incongruous. I'm so old and diseased. I wish I was more
able.

(C) That doesn't matter.

(L) What do you mean. What do you think we had better do about the
physical?

(C) Oh I don't mind about that.

(L) That's rather bad. You should. I thought you did care. What about
those boys, when you were young.

(C) Oh that was just being young. Nothing.

(L) But do you mind me being rather physically attracted.

(C) I don't think you are really.

(L) Why? Because of your sex.

(C) Yes partly. I don't blame you. I knew it long ago and went into it
deliberately.

(L) They will think I am to blame.

(C) They needn't know.

(L) Mark will tell them.

(C) No he won't.

(L) But my dear aren't you being rather romantic. You see I'm so very ancient, and well—

(C) It's all right. It was my fault. I knew what I was doing.

(L) I wish I was rich and then I could keep you as my mistress.

(C) (I was angry then inside) It would not make any difference.

(L) No it wouldn't, true. What about Abingdon? That day.

Then I told him the story of the letter from Mark in the morning, walking round the Pond with Brett. The hot sun on our heads. Mark's awful sorrow and anger and suddenly how my conscience smote me because I had let Gilbert [Cannan] kiss me.

And on your Birthday?

At the Mont Blanc. Mark's great rage and misery. How he came back here, his helplessness and all the time I knew that I should have one day to tell him and all the time these words came through my head, and I could *not* bring myself to say them.

Then he sat on the floor with me and clasped my hands in his and let me kiss his mouth, all enmeshed in the brittle beard and my inside was as heavy as lead, as I knew how miserable it was going to be.

You will not mind spoiling me? Just this once tonight.

Why are you so chaste?

And then I knew he would soon go.

Suddenly he said: 'What about Madame Florence is she sleeping here?' And I leapt inside and hoped he meant to stay and sleep on Brett's sofa. But he said he must go home after talking about Mrs S.-F. for a little while. The misery at parting and my hatred of myself for caring so much. And at his callousness. He was so wise and Just. Then he left and I went down later and talked long into the night with Alix. But there was no consolation. Still it was good to be able to talk of it.

Tuesday, April 14th

All day I wonder how it is this has happened to me. Why for the first time I have acted myself, and decided what to do of my own accord. I would do nothing but wander vaguely all day. Then I went at 7.30 o'ck to The Tour Eiffel to meet Mark. He was a little late. For a brief moment we talked of pleasantries. Then suddenly I said 'We had better now I think [not] see each other any more.'

(G) Yes I had come to that conclusion also.

(C) What did you do last night?

(G) I saw Kot at the Farmers and then went into the Campbells and talked Philosophy with Gordon Campbell. [Six lines omitted] What did you do?

(C) I went home and had a bath and then found Alix had her Mother and Lytton at tea. So I went out to dinner with Lytton.

(G) Yes. How did that go off?

(C) All right.

(G) Then what did you do.

(C) Went to my rooms. I told Lytton then.

(G) And what did he say?

(C) He was sorry.

(G) Was that all he said? Mark laughed curiously.

(C) Well. It wasn't his fault. What more could he say?

(G) Fancy just saying that. Nothing more.

(C) No.

(G) Good God. And he doesn't care?

(C) No, I knew he did not.

(G) I never want to see you again. So will you mind if I leave you directly after dinner?

(C) No.

(G) To think after all these years in 3 months you should love a man like Strachey twice your age (36) and emaciated and old. As I always said life is a crooked business.

I don't blame you.

Only I admit I'm disappointed that it should be Strachey. Don't you see how young and beautiful you are? I can't see you again. Unless you ever change and love me then I could of course. Don't spoil what has passed. It was good. It's better to stop now than to become enemies, and curse.

I don't blame you.

Long silences. Drank some coffee.

I waited outside and thought here in Percy Street it ends at last, on a night such as it is:—grey. And watched the woman give him the change with her blue rimmed eyes and pink face, inside. I thought he'd walk towards Tottenham Court Rd. But he didn't, he came and said quickly 'Don't think I'm angry with you. As I'm not. Goodbye.'

Goodbye. And left down Charlotte Street and I walked back to Gower St and Mrs R[eckes the housekeeper] opened the door, and Alix talked to me, and they did not know what a difference there was, as if my nose had been cut away.

And so it all ends like this about as crooked as it could be.

[Carrington found it impossible ever to be 'off with the old love'. For the old love always became more precious to her after the arrival of the new. This is shown clearly in her letters to Mark Gertler—and later in letters to Gerald Brenan.]

To Mark Gertler

Tuesday night [April 14th, 1917]   *3 Gower Street, London*

Thank you very much for treating it as you have. And for your very great love in the past few years I thank you. I shall never forget it.

Would you mind not telling anyone (except your friend Monty [Montague Shearman], or Kot if you so wish to) about it, anyway for the present. As it was too great a thing to let them know about, and jeer.

I will return your El Greco very soon and any other books, if I have them. I hope you will soon be happy again. And forgive, for causing you so much sorrow,   Your friend CARRINGTON

To Mark Gertler

Monday [May 1917]   *3 Gower Street, London*

Dear Mark, I am sorry, I am afraid I rather messed things last night for you and made you tired and depressed today. Monty did not say anything about it. So I left it as it was, and said nothing. But I've a shrewd idea he knows. But I rather think he was grateful, instead of angry with me, for he thought it made you happier perhaps. He little knew. I will lunch with you 1.30 Tour Eiffel. I am sorry to have vexed you by not answering at once this morning about seeing you. But it did rather depend on which evening Lytton could see me. That was why and I thought you would understand.

I feel rather dejected today. Probably because I hardly slept the whole night. I hope you feel better now—What pleasure is there compared in the walk we had together in the morning. You must admit. It has done you no good. Made you tired ill, and mentally miserable and for me the same. Do be happy though. I will see as much of you as I can.

You are not right [Page torn and piece of letter missing] in theory—
Although I think your song was
I *don't* want to live with him [Lytton]. Honestly [I don't] want to. But
I only said if he [wanted me to I would not] oppose him. There was no
about me seeing that poem. I know that what you say is comic about
Lytton. But no more comic than your lack of response to Monty. It is a
mystery to me that my bulk and size should ever move anyone to a flux!!

I suppose by this time I've enraged you But it wasn't my intention.
This was meant for a nice letter to make you happier.

Yr loving CARRINGTON

To Mark Gertler

Wednesday [May 1917]

I am sorry to have made such a commotion about it. But what really
upset me was:
(1) That you had not been *quite* honest in not telling me. Everything.
(2) That seeing that you did not know whether it might not by chance
have gone right up, that you took any risk. Through (I still maintain)
selfish and lazy motives. That was really what upset me so much. I care
so much for living. That the prospect of that [pregnancy] fills me
with, for a moment even with absolute horror. If you ever lie to me
again, even a fraction of a lie, no matter what your motives are, I shall
not forgive you.

But talk about it no more and I will come tomorrow at five.

Yrs CARRINGTON

To Mark Gertler

Wednesday [May 1917]

Dearest Mark, I am afraid I've deserted you rather badly. But you will
forgive me or must.

I shall be back from Cambridge next weekend. But I'll write to you
from there and tell you for certain and see you the second I am back
again. By the way: merely out of interest as I do not very much care—
Did you tell Mary [Hutchinson] about what happened between us. Or

Monty tell Jack [Hutchinson]? Because *Clive* [Bell] knew everything
last weekend at Garsington! I should just like to know—I am not
annoyed, only I prefer if possible—evidently impossible, all those fly
catchers at Garsington should [not] know what goes on inside one!!

I had a lovely time in the country; bicycled 52 miles on Monday over
into Wiltshire from Marlborough. It was wonderful. The downs and
hedges all covered with scented blossom. Did you enjoy Wittering? My
Love to you. Please write to me they will forward it from here. I did care
so much for your big picture. And your tulips are the best still life
you've ever done. But I think that big picture will be tremendous when
it's completed. How proud I felt of you!

Yr loving CARRINGTON

[Lytton was appearing before a tribunal at Hampstead which would
decide whether he was to be exempted from military service.]

To Lytton Strachey

Tuesday [*May 22nd, 1917*]   *3 Gower Street, London*

I saw Maynard [Keynes] this morning. He said the reason why he did
not offer to appear as witness for you was because he appeared for James
and he thought it might not be well to repeat it. But he would write a
letter willingly of course. He seemed against Philip [Morrell, M.P.] who
he said was very blundering and said St Loe S[trachey] was much
better. What about Saxon or Norton? Anyway he said Philip need *not*
come tomorrow since it was only your health, and not conscience that
was to be tried. And you could have time to rake up someone better
than Philip, if they referred you back to your conscience court. You
will not forget to telephone.

And your parrifin tonight! Most important.

Maynard was très agréable, as you would say, and I let him tell me
the whole history of his weekend with *Mrs* G. Keppel etc. all over again!
You might telephone tomorrow morning and tell me what Maynard's
doctor said. What about Roger [Fry] as a witness? Or Charlie Sanger?
Maynard thought Desmond MacC[arthy] would be rather impressive.
But I put my trust on your protruding ribs and your fleshless shanks. It
is a case indeed of Thank God! bare bones!

My LOVE CARRINGTON

[Lytton learned on June 9th that he was given exemption for six months, after which he would have to be examined again. He immediately telegraphed the news to Carrington and wrote a letter explaining.]

To Noel Carrington

1917   *3 Gower Street, London*

Dearest Noel, I am up a gum tree as the debts close in about me. And next week on the 14 we have to move from here and I have no wherewithal. Dear Brother hearken unto my prayer. Lest I be utterly consumed. I swear Faithfully I am making earnest attempts now to earn the bright sovereigns and give up my profligate life. Oh Saint Lewis hearken upon my supplications. The nett amount of Bills is £8.10. But I swear the golden day will come when all will be returned to you.

Miserably your sister DORA

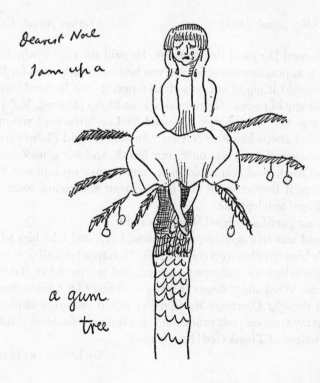

To Noel Carrington

[*1917*]

Dear Noel, Bless you. And thank you. Alas!
The gum tree was not 'fruitful' *but* by a miracle
has now grown fruit even 5 large pears!

My love, will write soon   Yrs D.C.

To Mark Gertler

[*July, 1917*]   *60 Frith Street, Soho*

Dearest Mark, I was coming to lunch with you today. But one thing
after another went wrong, and got complicated until it was much too
late, and yesterday I had to go to the British Museum to look at prints.
So that was frustrated and Alix is arriving suddenly this afternoon, so
tea is off today. In fact frustration on every side! Tonight I might come
in to Monty's. But then there is still yet one further complication;
Lytton is staying here with me since Belsize Park is shut up and I don't
know if you'll like it if I come with him to Monty's. Although he wants
to see you again badly. How I loved your letters; they did so please me,
especially the descriptions of Evan's [Morgan] party. I was glad not to
go. Just to have that description from you! Also it was kind of you to
write to comfort me, and be so very sympathetic. Do be happy. I shall
see such a lot of you soon, as after Sat. I shall [be] quite alone up here.
Yes I say it frankly, Lytton will be away for two months. So you will have
no more reason to curse him or me. For you will have me every night
you want to. What confessions we honest people make! Monty is a dear,
very dear creature. Bless him! He bought a wood block I did. Did you
like it? A Black Swan. I thought of you when I did it; once you loved
swans so much. And my wood blocks in Virginia's book?[1] Did you like
them? I am almost rich now. What a temptation it is *not* to pay one's
debts! Who do you think I met this morning at the Omega[2] and spoke to
through forwardness without an introduction and then found it was
your petit admirer Karline [Richard Carline, the painter]. But he was not
so beautiful as I had imagined. Not my type of good looks I am afraid.

[1] Three of these blocks are reproduced on pp. 72, 94, 240.
[2] Roger Fry's Omega Workshops.

Still we had a long conversation. He seemed pleasantly simple and easy to get on with. Rather like my brother Noel.

I will send you a wire when I shall see you tomorrow morning. Again I am frank and say it depends on Lytton what meals he wants here. His cynical frigidity and discipline keeps one pleasantly cool on a hot day like this, as Brett would say. So good for Carrington. I am doing you some photo prints. Bless you for your long letters. My Love to you dear. And a wire tomorrow from me.   Yr CARRINGTON

THE MARK ON THE WALL
By
VIRGINIA WOOLF
Woodcut illustration by Carrington for *Two Stories*,
by Leonard and Virginia Woolf (Hogarth Press, 1917).

To Barbara Bagenal

1917   [*60 Frith Street, Soho*]

[Extract]

... The sun is shining, and has even pierced the pickle Jammy gloom that hangs over SoHo.[1] So it *must* be divinely lovely where you are. Hot and Bright. Alix enjoyed Charleston. But more of that anon.

> The gas stove roars. The pickled air
> steals through the cracks in the windows
> The green Paint hangs heavily on the louse ridden walls
> I sit in despair before an Italian Tin Box[2]

[1] Crosse and Blackwell's factory was then at the top of Charing Cross Road and a smell of pickles often pervaded Soho. One of her letters to Lytton Strachey is addressed from 60 Pickle Lane.

[2] Carrington had been commissioned to decorate a metal trunk. She was still engaged on it over two years later.

And wish and wish life was different
That there was no such things as lumbago and Tin Boxes
And that I could be with my Barbary horse
on the ridge of Downs above Asheham.

Karin[1] allowed a motor car to run over my beautiful dog Jasper. Curses on her deaf ears and Jasper's inattentive mind. Bless you and your husbands   Yrs CARRYBUG [drawing of insect omitted]

To Lytton Strachey

Wednesday morning [*July 25th, 1917*]   *60 Frith Street, Soho*

Très Chère Monstratos,[2] Another letter! I conclude life is dealing hardly with you since you have no better occupation—Than to write letters— Gadding? Mon Dieu. En cette été. La chaleur est trop grande, pour qu'ils, qui habite dans Soho la puissent supporter. Il est bon que vous le sachez, monsieur! The cats drink water in the gutters of the Square. The hair falls out from the backs of the dogs, and lies on the footway. The very pavements are greasy with sweat which oozes from the holes in the boots of the passers. Steam rises up from the rotten fruit on the barrows and mingles with the dark grey air which hangs heavily over the city. Yes, and many worse things could I relate to you, Sir.

Life here is dominated by the insect world, flies cover the jam laden faces of the children, and nest in the thick warm powder on the prostitutes. Till one might well be living in a populace of negroes. So seldom does one see any white skinned creatures.

And then you write from your loggia of gadding! I went to the Magic Flute with Monty on Sunday. It was too amazing. But I got dreadfully exhausted long before the end. Miss Clampsaw Dudley [Helen Dudley of Chicago] was there, a lonely figure leaning against the balustrade. But the populace. Some thing must be done about it. It ought to be stopped.

They might reserve one gallery for the lower classes, and *un*-intelligentsia. It was monstrous. The company behind us, talked well into every scene, and then: 'I don't like those long waists, do you ma, so

[1] Karin, wife of Adrian Stephen, was deaf.
[2] Presumably Monostatus the 'villain' in *The Magic Flute*.

unbecoming. Besides it don't suit her a bit. Aren't those Birdie creatures lovely. I wish they'd come on again.' and Father: 'No my dear. It is the general style of the thing that makes it first rate. It has a certain style. It's not the songs that make an opera, but style.' Then also reading the life of Mozart from the programme all the overture, and looking for ma's spectacles which fell under our seats most of the last act. I could cry with rage.

Tuesday morning a letter from [Augustus] John and Geoffrey [Nelson] asking me to a party in the evening. Finished Roger's [Fry] blasted woodcut in the morning. Lunch with squash Pat at Shearns. She is going to Derbyshire for two months. Went to Percy Young [who ran the artists' materials shop] and got thoroughly miserable and savage over the war. His son and two nephews had been killed, and his fury against the government was great. Do you know they actually sent his nephew out with a *wooden* foot again, and he is in the Flying Corps and has to drive a machine!!

Boris [Anrep] and Faith [Henderson] called about ten o'ck for me in a cab for the Party. It had been given in honour of a favourite bar-maid of the Pub in Chelsea, near Mallord St, as she was leaving. She looked a charming character, very solid, with bosoms, and a fat pouting face. It was great fun.

Joseph, a splendid man from one of those cafés in Fitzroy St., played a concertina, and another man a mandoline. John drunk as a King Fisher. Many dreadfully worn characters, moth eaten and decrepit who I gathered were artists of Chelsea.

Nina [Hamnett]. MacEvoy. Evan [Morgan]. Beerbohm female. Geoffrey [Nelson]. Un petit garçon from Slade, who would have laid *you* low!! But he seemed without intelligence. Some Russians and upper class females in evening dresses. Some appalling pimps of the military and Naval tribe. Dorothy Warren, and a few more fitchews unknown.

I had a grand scene with Geoffrey in the kitchen eating chunks of meat pie. He made passionate declarations of his most serious and ever-lasting Love for me. Whereupon I played the Strachey god, and said 'Aren't you being a *little* hysterical. You see I know really what you are like and what is going on inside you,' and delivered a long lecture on being insincere, and inventing crises, so he frowned desperately, assured me I completely misunderstood him and then was more humble in the dust, than it is fit for man to be. Whereupon I pounced on him heartily and kissed him violently which made him very awkward and embarrassed!!!

John made many serious attempts to wrest my virginity from me. But he was too mangy to tempt Me even for a second. 'Twenty years ago would have been a very different matter my dear sir.' Still the barmaid, and other strumpets obliged, so n'importe. There was one magnificent scene when a presentation watch was given the barmaid, John drest in a top hat, walking the whole length of that polished floor to the Barmaid sitting on the sofa by the fireplace, incredibly shy and embarrassed over the whole business, and giggling with delight. John swaggering with his bum lurching behind from side to side. Then kneeling down in the most gallant attitude with the watch on a cushion. Then they danced in the middle of the room, and every one rushed round in a circle shouting. Afterwards, it was wonderful to see John kissing this fat Pussycat, and diving his hand down her bodice. Lying with his legs apart on a divan in the most affected melodramatic attitudes!!
[Illustration omitted]

Soon it became rather boring, as the moth eaten carpets woke up and did stunts which consisted of singing cockney songs without any end or point to them. One after another these old gentlemen revived and upped and croaked. Dorothy Warren was the comble. So Evan and I made so much noise with our conversation that the spirits of Chelsea were subdued. Boris then became aware of my charms, and started some very heavy and moist amours. But it was too hot. More attempts by John who could hardly stand by now. It is always rather amusing watching a party die, and to see the pairing off. Faith quite exhausted, being caressed by the most degraded old sand Bag. MacEvoy and Nina. John and the Barmaid. Then joy! the car came at three and we whisked off. Anrep doing as much heavy work as a hand from the opposite side of a taxi will permit.

A long letter from Noel this morning. He is going to get leave with luck the end of this month, and wants me to organize a week's holiday for him either (1) a walking tour (2) bicycling expedition (3) cottage by the sea (4) Farm house (5) or the caravan in Somerset. My head reels. The difficulty of arranging it. I think a cottage in Dorset and get Barbara to come and then I might find a farm house at the same time. But it will be decent seeing him again.

[Arthur] Waley today lunch, and British Museum. I am going to look at Italian woodcuts if I can find any.

Mark this evening. Next Sunday I am going down to Kent for the day to see a Mrs. Wadsworth who has a cottage there. Waley is going to be in a inn there also. The rapidity of this young chinaman is almost

alarming!! This morning—I am just off to Chelsea to paint—Très. Très.
Chère. I am still so happy.

You never told me about that luncheon with the Female Homer
Pigeon. Do you remember? I am glad Gordon goes well. I should never-
theless like a little poetry to be written. *I hope you are keeping well.* It is
good news that your mother is mending. I am glad. Alix has been staying
with Majorie O[livier] in the country.

Dearest old Fakeer I love you so much.

Je pouverais t'embrass an millemille des temps.

Yr. CARRINGTON

To Lytton Strachey

Friday afternoon [August 3rd, 1917]   *60 Frith Street, Soho*
                                                          Chelsea. Studio

Will there be a letter from you tomorrow? If not there *will* be visited
on your old head a thousand furies. Yes, even your retreat at Guildford
will not save you, twenty harpies with jagged teeth will oust you from
your hiding place e'n though it be the W.C. and will then tear every
hair off your head, and chin and pour maggots down your bare throat.
So sir, Even so. Sir. What is there to write about? Alix arrived yesterday
morning. Then I toiled to Chelsea, and worked all day till 7 o'ck. Then
to Hampstead, and dinner with Saxon who seemed to be crumbling in
the head, as bulges of bone and matter had started to protrude from
various places on his head, and neck. I urged him to take measures to
have the before mentioned bulges pressed back again by the physician
to their original dwellings—but the Saxon will not go until Saturday—
rash man. By that time the protrudances may have complete control,
unlike Haig [C.-in-C. of the British army], of the situation.

After dinner I forced the poor man to read two gentlemen of Verona.
I taking all the best parts to read myself, Launce and Speed and Lucetta.

Friday

Went to London Library with Alix after breakfast this morning.
Found a brilliant new game, completely shutting my eyes and being a
blind girl led by Alix. I did it without opening them once from Piccadilly
to the Library, amid the most sympathetic glances of the onlookers!

But the rest. Do you know one could live 15 more years if one never had to look at vehicles, and faces, and bad architecture. But I will not deprive you of your one pleasure in life sir. Do not fear.

Had absurd lunch in A.B.C. at 12 o'ck. But also invented which was more important a new manner of speech with Alix. It needs great concentration but the effect is tremendous! Difficulties are arising over the picture of Les Beaus in shop—dans Boutique—as you will, sir. But I have hopes of carrying it through. Alix went away this afternoon. James is coming to dinner with GEORGE [Reeves] next Wednesday. Don't you dare to come up on Wednesday, sir. A completely new turn of events has occurred. James told Alix that George, last time he saw him, drew him aside, and with tears in his eyes confessed that—married life was a mistake he was *not* happy. He found she was dull, and unintelligent after all and he could not see his old friends as he used to, and, in short, he greatly regretted the whole business. So sir. What do you think of *that* sir? I rang Leonard [Woolf] up. Lost my head, and merely asked him the size of his paper, and the type! Instead of the main issue—Asheham —Proof of Lucretius and Death at last. But will Roger [Fry] have further inspirations, and insist on an entirely new Block? There seems no limit to his inventions!

A letter from the middy Geoff [Nelson] today, in the wilds of Westmorland, snaring rabbits with a young brother, and catching trout. He is coming to spend Sunday with me. Shall I draw his fair form, for the pupil of the Centaur?[1] Here is a letter from that Cottle woman. What do you think of it? Don't lose it anyway, as it might be of some use. No news yet from the Dorset Post offices. Barbara has found a small cottage under Firle Beacon for 3/- a week. I enclose a sheet of her letter about it. Would not it be good to take it? The emptiness of this city is amazing. Old Saxon the only other inhabitant except myself. But personally I could [do] with that old gentleman Giles Lytton Strachey. Does the General Progress? Time's winged chariots. Do not gather flowers by the roadside, or you will be too late. Will you not? Now I have imparted to you the new method. Do you grasp it? More beloved than any creature, please come next week again. I could kill you dead with my hugs today, Shall I bring Geoffrey down on Sunday and take you for a walk by the canal? It would be charming, would it not?

All my love to you.   Your CARRINGTON XXXXX

1 Carrington cut a bookplate for Lytton of Cheiron and a pupil, reproduced on p. 330.

[George Reeves the pianist was an old friend of Lytton's. 'A completely new turn of events has occurred ...' This is a typical Carrington practical joke and took Lytton in. He replied next day: 'The George story amazes me. I really can hardly believe it. Are you going to strike in? I think it *most* odd. Almost as odd, if not odder than Saxon's love affair.'

On the 7th he wrote: 'I seem to gather that the George story was a flam. Petite diablesse!']

To Virginia Woolf

Wednesday [August 1917]   *60 Frith Street, Soho*

Dear Virginia, This is really an answer to Leonard's letter, only addressed to you because I want to ask you if I might come a day or two, just before the 23rd to stay with you, or in the cottage with Willie, or the hay rick, if your house is overcrowded? as I am going to stay with the Charleston People on the 23rd. But it does not matter really. Thank Leonard for his instructions re the Lettering. I will try some soon. The man Lawrence who cuts my wood will get the size exact. Alix has just been in here on her way to you today—I have been painting hard all this week in Chelsea and not seen anything of the world. Except on Bank holiday when I went on the Heath, and rushed up and down in swing boats and round on the whili-gigs.

Next week my brother is getting leave, so I am going on a walking expedition with him, we are rather vague as to what part of England to explore. I am in favour of the Berkshire Downs. Barbara is just back from Charleston. I am going to cut you some paper covers designs on linoleum, which is easy to cut, and cheap. Don't you miss your printing very much? There is a press just opposite us in Frith Street. I love watching the men and small boy apprentices setting up the type, and printing off with marvellously rapidity on the sheets of paper. I hope you are well. Please remember me to Leonard.

Yrs affec CARRINGTON

[The beginning of the following letter is a good example of Carrington's facetious family style—so different from the humour in letters to Lytton.]

To Noel Carrington

Sunday afternoon tout seul!   *3 Gower Street, London*

Dearest Noel, I am indeed sorry to have incurred your displeasure by not writing sooner. The why, and wherefore you shall soon be acquainted with my dear Brother. Wouldst thou have a brief summary of my daily deeds since I last wrote to you? That I trow would take too long besides sore trying your patience. [Three pages omitted]

Last Monday Augustus John gave a party. We all went. It was great fun. And I enjoyed myself very much. Dancing vigorously. Last Wed. Mrs Gough gave another party. And it was even better. Alix S.-Florence (who I've painted a portrait of) lent me a topping Cossack dress and I was the Belle of the Ball! Had great fun with Augustus John who fell completely to my charms. Also the great Horace Cole, of London fame [as a practical joker]. Besides lesser members of the army! I wish the dress belonged to me. I think I shall make myself one, si possible.

Last Wed. Lytton's little nephew and niece came up to London. So I had them to lunch here, and then we went to Maskelyne and Cook's Mystery show. It was rather good. Some fearfully comic conjuring, and some wily young officers went up out of the audience to try and explore his horrid mystery—But with all their wiliness they were 'done'—

Do write to me soon again please. I should like an engraving of Molière if you see one, or Madame du Chatalet in particular, Voltaire's friend. Please.

I will write again soon.

Yrs affec. DORIC

[Lytton had planned a walking tour with Carrington dressed in boy's clothes.]

To Lytton Strachey

Friday [August 10th, 1917]   *60 Frith Street*

Dearest Lytton, This in the letter box! Nearly melted me to tears when I returned. How blessed it was to see you again yesterday. I woke up this morning and found it difficult to believe I *was* grieved about the Spectacles and now I feel it will always happen until in the end you will forbid all advances![1] Hours were spent in front of the glass last night strapping the locks back, and trying to persuade myself that two cheeks like turnips on the top of a hoe bore some resemblance to a very well nourished youth of sixteen. It's an alarming spectacle seeing one's self side view. I hardly ever have before. But, dear, promise you'll come

a vision

[1] Marjorie Strachey planned to write a pamphlet on 'The management of spectacles and pince-nez while making love'.

even with a female Page for a companion. I think those cursed military authorities make the other rather more difficult, as the life of a village policeman is so dreary, that the sight of a fat cheeked Boy and German Bearded spy would throw him into a spasm of alertness and bring up all this stupidity surging into his gullet.

I hope you were not wrecked after yesterday's exertions. [Fifteen lines omitted.]

James stayed, and conversed into the late night. He is your only serious rival you must know!

But the probability of us both being arrested the first night, *you*, for the *offence* that I am not a disguised female, and me for the offence that I *am*! But one might find out first whether it is a criminal offence!

My love to you and write today please.

Yr Loving CARRINGTON

To Lytton Strachey

Thursday, 6 o'ck [*October 18th, 1917*]   *Hurstbourne Tarrant*

And you are sitting in your room, toasting your feet in front of an empty grate, surrounded by your legions of paper knights and horsemen. Oh it's wretched having lost you and not to have you tonight to talk to. Dearest Lytton I can never thank you enough for these weeks. I did not realize how happy I had been until this evening. It's strangely beautiful here with the drooping beech trees and apples lying in the wet grass— But more melancholy and autumnal than a grave yard. If you were only here and so many wishes. You have spoilt me far too long and now I feel as if suddenly I had walked into a greenhouse in the winter. For in the paper I saw the first thing on the red clothed table when I came in, Teddy's death. It was a year ago and now they announce it officially. It's rather worse being here with all his books and things about, and where I saw him last and the remoteness of my parents. Forgive me for writing but I wanted you so badly. One is not even left alone to cry. Dearest Lytton I love you so much.   CARRINGTON

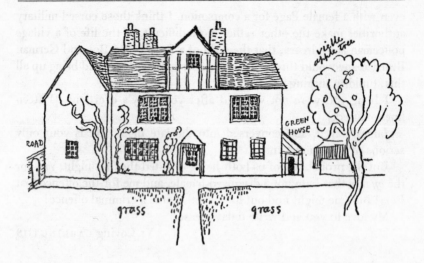

To Lytton Strachey

Friday morning [October 19th, 1917]   *Hurstbourne Tarrant*
1 mile from Pangbourne

THE MILL HOUSE, TIDMARSH

Old fashioned House.
    grounds over 1 acre small orchard.
    Hall, 3 recpt rooms, kitchen etc.
    Electric Light. 6 bedrooms, box
    room. *Bath H & C.*
    Rent £52   3 years lease.
    Nr. Church & P.O.   London 65 mins.

Mother gave it to me with an order to view which she had received. I've
just telephoned the agents and it's still to let, so will go over tomorrow
and see it. Sounds too good to be alright! will look at Peasemore and
Stanmore en route.

    No more news. Amazing sun and this country looks very lovely.

    Just entrapped into a tea with old Mère Merritt as I was waiting for
the telephone call in P.O.

    Please write soon.

                                          MOPSA

To Lytton Strachey

Friday, 3 o'ck [Saturday, October 20th, 1917]   *Tea shop, Newbury*

Dear, I've just been to all three houses. But Tidmarsh Mill it is to be.
It's very romantic and lovely.

Vast Big rooms, 3 in number,
2 Very big bedrooms and 4 others,
Bathroom; water closet;
very good garden and a shady grass lawn
with river running through it.

The house is very old with gables and some lattice windows. It is
joining on to the Mill. A charming Miller showed me over it. Very well
built in good condition. The miller said one could get people, old Hags
from village [Illustration omitted]. More apple trees fruit trees vegetables.
2 miles from Theale St. 1 mile Pangbourne. *Oliver must see it.*
Peasemore was rather good but in village opposite church. Stanmore a
wash out, no garden to speak of. Oliver etc must go and see Tidmarsh
on Tuesday. Electric light in every room. I'm wildly excited. Hooray!

Will write again in detail   CARRINGTON

[Oliver Strachey had to see the Mill House, Tidmarsh, as one of the
syndicate who were putting up money to rent a cottage for Lytton. The
other members were Maynard Keynes, Harry Norton and Saxon
Sydney-Turner.]

*Back view of Mill
from orchard garden*

To Mark Gertler

Thursday [November, 1917]   *60 Frith Street, Soho*

I was glad to hear from you. Last night I had dinner with Monty and had a long talk with him. And he told me about your pictures, and now that you were happier. [D.H.] Lawrence and Koteliansky came in also later. Good old Kot! How charming he is. Lawrence was in a great state at being expelled from Cornwall, and obviously could think and talk of nothing else and had a great contempt for Monty and the world in general. Afterwards I went back to Gordon Square where I am staying as Frith Street is too awful and Alix was in occupation in my room. But she didn't like being there alone because of the raids, so came to Gordon Square also. At 11.30 a raid started, and went on till 2.30. We sat downstairs with the maids. Alix's heart is so bad, I was rather nervous about her. She was obviously very ill, and frightened. Maynard lay in bed upstairs, and went to sleep and never moved! An extraordinary man!

I will stay in London till Wed. next as I want to see you and Brett. So may I come to tea on *Monday* afternoon, or won't you be up by then? Perhaps Tuesday. Write and tell me which day. I am quite well. Only feeling rather tired today as I never slept last night. But London's a beastly place after the country, crowded with hideous people, prostitutes, and debased soldiers, and so grey and gloomy, and then the beauty of the night torn to pieces by these guns and bombs. I long to rush away! And envy you your retreat, and good Brett by your side. Ruth [Selby-Bigge][1] is in London, but so occupied I can't get her although I telephone 6 times a day! Thus is one treated by one's ancient loves! Poor Monty was very sad without you, and glad to have me to talk to I think about you. What a nice person he is. I can't write you a long letter about myself for I've such a bad head and feel so sleepy, and in a few minutes I've got to go, and teach that little brute of a Joan Laking. But dear I'm so glad to know you are friendly. Of course I am!

love CARRINGTON

---

[1] As Ruth Humphries, she was a friend and fellow student at the Slade.

To Mark Gertler

Sunday afternoon [November, 1917]   *Hurstbourne Tarrant, Andover*

Dearest Mark, I reached here yesterday afternoon. Just in time for tea. Dear, I was sorry to be rather estranged in the morning. But I had not slept much, and I was feeling very depressed. But I *did* think your still life very good and the charcoal of those women. That will be a tremendous picture I am sure. What fun it was on Friday going to the Cinema with you. We must go again when I come back. Alix told me she was going, on your suggestion, to ask you and Monty to stay at Lord's Wood[1] some weekend!

[Twenty lines omitted] No, I'm not going away with Lytton! But my people are leaving Hampshire, and are going to live in a town, Cheltenham. So I've got to go home for a little while, when they move to help them and take away my goods and furniture.

Then I'll be back again in London all the winter I expect. It will be good to see you tomorrow. I am going to do Jack Hutchinson a wood block now. Ruth is impossible to see. Is not it maddening, a whole week and she can't find a minute to come to me! UGH! as the book says. The devil take her relations and Government work which she does in her folly.   CARRINGTON

To Lytton Strachey

Thursday 6 o'ck [November 8th, 1917]   *Frith Lane*

HAVE you taken your sana-to-GIN, if not will you please do so at ONCE without further delay. If I find on investigation you have dared to DISOBEY my commands. Henceforth be gone. I have done with you.

I find from Brett that Ottoline is coming up to London tomorrow and to the best of Brett's belief is not returning to Garsington till Saturday. But I shall telephone her tomorrow and find out for certain at 9 o'ck. I will then communicate with your Lordship. Brett has also given me for Tidmarsh 1 Big chest of Drawers. All right I'll stop now, but there was no need for you to be so testy. Two tables for wash stands,

---

[1] Mrs Sargent-Florence's house at Marlow.

one easy chair, 1 sofa 1 electric light lamp (reading), 1 mattress, 1 coffer, 1 big desk writing table AND one COAL-BOX Which is very cheerful— And excessively kind of her—Her big picture from a photograph looked very good—She said she liked my work, especially the Beeny Dogs on the shelf. But well I am glad you are better today. I shall never part with your

It is now mine. I feel like strong man with electric sparks flying out. But really I shall see you tonight at old Pozzo[1]—you wretch! Of course you'll be there, curvetting on the High Toe. Did you get the socks this morning at old Madame White-Fuz-Bush? Dearest Yahoo, Good morning.   Your MOPSA

[In theory, Tidmarsh was to be a house where Lytton could live with Carrington economically and which members of the syndicate could visit whenever they wished.

In practice it was Lytton's house.

Furnishing it was a problem—but fortunately Carrington's family were moving from Hurstbourne Tarrant to a smaller house and she was able to filch a good many household goods for Tidmarsh.

It will have been noted that she had lied to Gertler on the subject of living with Lytton.]

---

[1] Pozzo de Bongo, nickname given to Maynard Keynes by Lytton.

To Lytton Strachey

[November 1917]   *Monty's room*

Lytton Dear, I hope you are better now. I have just had dinner with
Mark. He is so charming and gay. Full of news of Shandy gaff [Garsing-
ton]—What a day! Alix with the winds of Charleston. Then teaching
that petite bête—Brett to tea at Frith Street shrieking at the tops of our
voices, a thousand accusations!!! But she too is delightful. Then I went
in to Tilney Street for a brief while. And found Ottoline talking to a
professional pearl-stringer. The gossip!!! 'But surely the duchess of
Ripon had black pearls?' 'But Lady Meux she had the finest pearls I ever
strung ... she said as how she'd leave me her money. But she didn't.
Her maid had forty thousand pounds ... Her name was the same as
mine. Barnes ... She came off the streets before she married Lord
Meux!!!' Ottoline absorbed in the pearly stories of all these old hags,
and their past histories.—But she looked very wonderful. Ottoline in
various huge hats which she tried on to show me.

I told her about Tidmarsh vaguely—But put my foot in it slightly
over a trivial matter as usual!

Monty is playing Beethoven so I must stop and listen.

I may be rather late tomorrow, so will you start tea without me if I'm
not at B[elsize] P[ark] G[ardens] by 4.30 and if you're not well enough.
Telephone and tell me. I send you all my Love again—a whole day and
no work. But you mustn't scold. 15 only this week.

Dear dear old yahoo I wish I could have you here now xxxxxxx

Love from your MOPSA

To Lytton Strachey

Friday, 1 o'ck [November 9th, 1917]   *60 Frith Street*

Dearest Lytton, They tell me you are to be in bed all today. Oh wretched
day! most vile day! Now everything is ruined. The gay clouds in the
blue sky which I thought we would be under on the Heath this afternoon. May they turn to rain and keep me company in my gloom.

Never again are you going to behave like this! After November you
will start a regular life at Tidmarsh, supported by glasses of milk, and
vigorous walks.

Did not you smile faintly when you got my letter with the Big Print after the conversation last night on code letters? It was a brilliant evening!! And you excelled them all in your remark about Mr. Lewis. After you left the conversation became lurid with abortions and limbless Bodies. The ten month versus nine month birth case, and menstruations were discussed. Then the horrid murder of the Bloomsbury Belgian, and how one would dispose of a body if one committed a murder. In the end it was decided Roger would embalm it, fake a mummy case and sell it as an antique at the OMEGA! I am just going out with Oliver to lunch now. If you are not well enough you won't travel tomorrow and get worse will you? And *your* SANATOGEN if you please at once.

I've caught your COLD you wretch. But the diseases are so manifold that attack this poor human frame, that this latest acquisition almost passes unnoticed. Just had lunch with Oliver at his club.[1] Very ormolu. Beautiful curry. Surrounded by generals and vice-roys of India on the walls. Took him to Omega and London Group afterwards.

Faith has promised us two BEDS for Tid*der*Mar*sh, and we are going to buy up all the Omega club crockery and chairs and Oliver has signed the lease!!!!!

Do get spritly SOON and appear before me clad in your gay new clothes with your beard, waving like an aspen in the Breeze

Your POLLYPUSS MOPSA

waving like
an aspen in the
Beeze
Your PoLLYPUSS MOPSA

[1] The Oriental Club, Hanover Square. Lytton was also a member.

To Lytton Strachey

Alix has burnt the bottom out of the geyser. So life and my neck are
both very grey.

[*November 14th, 1917*]   *60 Frith Street, London*

Well, you are a wretch, and no mistake.
And there will be four empty stalls in the front row.
The lives of two persons who might otherwise have been united in holy
matrimony, a plain young man and longing spinster, prevented owing
to four empty seats.

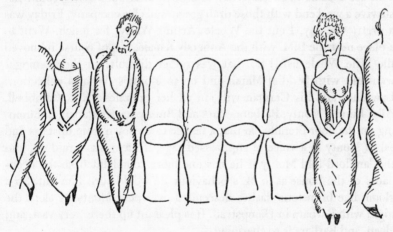

Four people (unknown) rendered unhappy by being refused seats.
They had travelled from Burnley to witness the performance, two
sisters, and a mother of a Mr Brown (spottist painter) a vast sum of
money which might have been devoted to Tidmarsh flung to the winds,
and much hair and rage.

Alix and Sheppard who might have become friends for life refused
the opportunity AND ALL BECAUSE Giles Lytton Strachey is a man of
loose morals and uncertain purpose.

Tomorrow. D.V. and *G.L.S.V.* at one o'ck.

I was sorry about lunch today. But Ruth [Selby-Bigge] was bringing
a north country man with whom she works to lunch, in the City, and it
might have been distressing if we *both* disliked him for poor Ruth—

I am glad you are better.

Last night I heard some good Bach. Tonight I go to the Magic Flute. I have asked Faith if I can come in tomorrow after dinner because if you go on Friday, and stay until Xmas at Garsington, it will [be] rather a long time before I see you again.

I send you all my Love, in spite of your wickednesses

Your Loving MOPSA

To Lytton Strachey

Sunday morning [*November 18th, 1917*]   *Hurstbourne Tarrant*

You see I came back yesterday afternoon after all. I felt I could not survive a weekend with those drab green walls for company. Friday was a pretty vile day. I cut the Whale [Arthur Waley] for lunch. Went to a place near the B.M. with the Annersly female, and of course in moved the little Whale fish!! So that was rather difficult! In the evening I went out with [Eddie] Marsh and on to Monty's. What a collection! Lawrence and his German wife, in all her grossness, Kot, Campbell, Alix, Bunny, Monty, Barbara. Mark and Bunny started dancing, thumping on the floor literally, so that a female came down from upstairs and asked Monty in a voice of suppressed rage, if there was a raid on, and the landlord told Monty if he has one more complaint from the occupants of the house as to M.'s behaviour he would turn him out. So a gloom like brimstone dashes descended over poor Monty—I slept the night with Barbara in Hampstead. It is pleasant up there, very vast, and clean, and Barbara is so charming—

This country is looking divine now. I saw a Heron standing by a lonely pond, as I came along the road, and the Downs stood up terrific-(k)ly high enveloped in mists in the distance. I've been wandering about the house and garden on a grand looting expedition all the morning. I think by Wednesday a fair collection of Balbage [? salvage] ought to be amassed!

My mother is of course frightfully stingy when it comes to the point of giving me anything useful. And she sold to a dealer the only two things I really cared for. A very old Japanese china candlestick 14 *cent.* and a 18 cent English silk embroidered picture of a bird.

I found in a stable some water-cans and jugs which will be useful. And I've got free permission to devastate the garden and green house of trees and plants—But it's rather sad leaving this place. The view from the window now that the trees are bare, is lovely. One can see right up the valley and the ridge of the hill opposite stands up hard and sharp like the back bone of a whale. But one day when we are old, and very rich I shall bring you here to live. I enclose two cuttings the one refers to a past conversation at beeny—the other to the future! Will you write me a long letter about Garsington, and the conversations and your gallivantings in London? Will you ask Ruth to dinner one night with you at Commercio? Mrs John Selby-Bigge, 7 Wilbraham Place, w. I told her you might. I see by the smoke from the thatched chimney that the old man is making malt in the brewhouse just outside the back gate, so I shall go, and toast over his furnace, and gossip about the village with him.

Mr Bound[1] sent me a big bag nuts, and walnuts. Everything is just the same, even to the conversations of my parents. Even the apples lie on the grass only they are decayed, dark brown, like garrulous old men, and only a few virgin green maidens lie at their sides. The paths are thick with leaves. A few gnats in the air. Not a sign of a bird or a sound from the hills—I perceive this letter is verging towards the sentimental. New paragraph.

How is your system? If I had the courage I would ask my mother for a number of bed pans and a commode which lie in the box room upstairs. But perhaps it would hardly be tactful. It is exciting about your Book of Lives.[2] Will the Preface be finished by the time I come back? May I have you next Sat. and Sunday? Please start taking your sanatogen instantly. I will send the grey muffler tomorrow and please get well soon. How I wish I could transport you here now and this second, to take you with me for a walk over the hill. Dearest Lytton. You ought to be a little happy, as I love you so entirely.

Your MOPSA xxxxxx

PS *Monday morning*
The looting expedition progresses with unexpected success. An oak coffer and small gate legged table has been added to the collection, and a camp-bed! I have dug up a great many bulbs and roots to put in the garden. Did you see Brett's big picture! Please tell me what you thought of it. I shall go over on Thursday to Tiddermarsh and try and interview the old hag, and Percy or Patrick as you will.

More Love MOPSA

[1] Owner of Ibthorpe House, and a farmer.
[2] *Eminent Victorians.*

To Lytton Strachey

Tuesday afternoon [November 20th, 1917]   *Hurstbourne Tarrant*

Quelle Juar! At last it is all packed. Without the heavy looting having
been discovered. But the escapes have been as narrow as the way to
Heaven. Everything is packed with apples artichokes and potatoes,
instead of straw and paper! This method will probably insure all the
china being smashed. But anyway the food supply is guaranteed for
some months!!

I have been given as a present a big wheel-back chair. But you hate
those articles I remember. I have also a huge sack of plants, and bulbs
for the garden and some carnations in pots for the greenery-house. Pots
of jam, and a big bottle of cherry brandy! Are you getting a little cheerful now old Yahoo at the prospect of Tidmarsh complete with potatoes
on the hob by Christmas? Here is the grey muffler. I will write again
on Thursday evening after I have seen Patrick Stone and the old hag.

Please write to me soon. It seems a desperately long time since I last
saw you. The collection of baggage even includes malt extract for you—
and mosquito lotion for when you sit with Patrick conversing over
Egyptian Flour Mills under the Yew Tree next summer—also a Gurkha
dagger to keep hostile forces at bay. It's dreadfully exciting really after
these years of conversation, moving at last! Probably I shall find on
Thursday the Mill was a mirage and the evil faced carrier will be sitting
there in the road on my boxes eating the apples and drinking the malt
extract. I hope you are keeping well.

Dear, I send you my Love   Yr. MOPSA

To Lytton Strachey

Thursday evening, 6.30 [November 22nd, 1917]   Hurstbourne Tarrant

Dearest Lytton, Well if you don't propose honourable marriage after
you have read this letter, I've done with you!

This morning I rose from my bed of nightmares, not slumbers, drest,
and after a hurried breakfast set off at 7 o'ck on my iron steed in the
grey light for Tidmarsh. Reached Tidmarsh by ten o'ck. Greeted by the
dear Patrick (and oh Lytton a miller's boy, un peu George et John

Bigge. But so lovely, driving Patrick's cart) with the greatest cordiality. He is charming really. The furniture was all there installed. So I unpacked all the potatoes and apples and put them on the shelves. Nothing broken. But it looked a very small pile! Planted bulbs in the garden. Crown Imperials, Pinks and Sweet Williams. Then interviewed three old hags. Mrs. Justice was 'Willing' but had a baby and can only come in and light the fires and make the early breakfast at seven o'ck and perhaps in the evenings at six. But she seemed vague because of the child. Mrs Bushel has a goitre and cannot move with rapidity. But the goitre under the black lace collar upset me too much. [Forty lines omitted]

I return Sat. morning at 1.30 Waterloo. Will you call for me after lunch at Frith Street 2.15? As I write this it is almost too much. Do you believe me? To have you tight, and bodily next Sat. in less than two days. I am glad you thought Brett's picture so good.[1] From the photograph I thought the Aldous [Huxley] part of the composition looked a bit feeble. But it was hard to tell. Who can have sent the little book from Paris? *Surely* Madame B. Alix has now added to her crimes, and has broken down with the help of Bunny the entire door of my bedroom, panelling and all and the glass globe above it!! Auld Reekie lost her temper at last and went for Alix! I am hardly surprised. She wrote me a very indiscreet, and amusing account of her week end with Bunny at Lord's Wood. [Ten lines omitted] I looted 1 lb of sugar also, many cakes of soap 2 bath towels. My mother suspected the worst and actually came out into the garden and inspected each baggage as it was carried into the van!!!!!

Fortunately the sacks of vegetables passed for roots of plants! Did you write and ask Ruth to dinner. She wants to meet you so much.

Well, and will I have a formal proposal after today's work? I can write no more. My eyes are dim with fatigue. I wonder if 'Everything', as the great poet says 'will become as clear as clear someday or other'.

'In the meantime' well ... we shall see.

Lytton you have all my Love Bless you.

Your MOPSA xxxxxxxxxx

Saturday 2.15 and afterwards the Gallerie-Walleries and tea at no —not the Camp Hut ...

HOW MUCH SANATOGEN DOES YOUR SYSTEM NEED?[2]

---

[1] A Conversation Piece on Garsington Lawn.
[2] These words are cut out of an advertisement.

To Mark Gertler

[After Christmas, 1917]   *The Mill House, Tidmarsh, Pangbourne*

Dearest Mark, I was glad of your letter. I could not come up for Gilbert's party. Was it fun? Do write me a long description of it. And how you behaved? Was Monty depraved? Did Jack let off air? Was Gwennie [Gwendoline Wilson] half-bare? I am going to Cheltenham tomorrow to my people for a week. So write to 'Tatchley' Prestbury—near Cheltenham. Not a P.C. for my mother to read. What have you been doing? I confess I long to be back and see you again. I will after Cheltenham. I find being Mary, and looking after a house a confounded bore. Thank goodness it's all over now. I shall not bother any more about the old house and the furniture, but start painting. There are most wonderful Cézanne views from the garden of the river and trees, and a big quarry near with a brick-kiln. You will love this place. I shall ask you to stay here when none of [the] others are here to annoy you. What are you painting now? I wish you weren't sometimes my enemy, I could tell you so much more and frankly. But your moods terrify me into silence and discretion. Have you seen anything of Alix? She's staying at 45 Downshire Hill. God. It will be dreary going home again and listening to the endless conversations of my mother and meeting relations who are detestable as yours in their way. So respectable and Christian. Barbara has gone to Charleston. Lytton's new book [*Eminent Victorians*] has been accepted by the publishers, and will come out in the spring. Dear Mark this letter is a offer of greater friendliness because I miss you. After next week I'll come and stay in London in B[rett]'s studio and see more of you. How is Monty? The beauty of these winter mornings with the orange sun shining in the river and lighting up the tall Cézanne trees.

My Love to you and Best wishes CARRINGTON

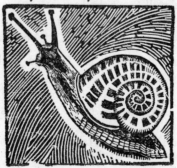

Woodcut (reduced) by Carrington for *Two Stories*, by Leonard and Virginia Woolf (Hogarth Press, 1917).

1918

To Lytton Strachey

Sunday evening 6 o'ck [January 20th, 1918]   The Mill House, Tidmarsh

Not a sign of a human being! Alix is pretty well damned now. To have
enough energy to go to Lord's Wood with Bunny and not enough
imagination or curiosity to come here. She's a dull green toad! The havoc
wrought in my loneliness is great. The entire house now resembles a
painting by Barbara Strachey.[1] Even Legget has given up her compliments. There *is* a post on Sunday! I send on one letter for you and the
pants. The Nation and N[ew] S[tatesman] have arrived. I wonder if you
want them. I shall bring them up (and dispatch them to Noel, if you've
read them already at B[elsize] P[ark] G[ardens]). I sleep worse and worse.
It must be a disease. I got up this morning at 7 o'ck and gardened from
sheer boredom of lying in bed. Another electric light globe shattered.
Can you abstract a few from some ODD rooms in Belsize? as it's getting
a little tedious having to carry a globe in one's pocket to fit on each
time one enters a room. I've rigged up my studio in that tank room. It
will make a very good work place as there are so many shelves to spread
the litter out on. And the lighting is good. Did you go tobogganning
with le petit Geoffry? I wonder. Donald now cuts up our wood and Mrs
Legg says he'll come and work in the garden under my supervision.
From conversations I gather Mr Legg is rather severe and un peu
difficile so Donald flees from his wrath and prefers the Labours of our
domicile to sitting alone with the horrid stepfather. I've thought of a
brilliant idea to subdue the Buzzards.[2] Purchase a ferret or a mongoose,
and put it at night under the floors and in the attics, et voila! EXIT
[Drawing of a mongoose chasing a boot omitted] la bottine de monsieur
Wellington! I suppose you will promptly put forward some absurd
objection. God! Which Group is Mr Hogben[3] going to join and not of

[1] Oliver Strachey's daughter, then aged 5.
[2] Lytton had been disturbed by noises overhead in the night. The intruders (no doubt
rats from the cornmill) were called 'Buzzards in Wellington Boots' by Carrington.
[3] Lancelot Hogben, zoologist and science popularizer, who was then a conscientious
objector.

course that it will make any difference to whether you will. I shall be sorry to leave here. London sounds pretty deadly and I've but little hope of pulling off the Monty business, especially as the bridge is finally broken between Mark and me, Well. [Drawing of bridge omitted]

Next Sat. we shall meet no doubt at Paddington and tramp the long long platform of Reading side by side. Shaw's view of Lister was very different from what you told me returning that day from Sulham.

My love dearest Lytton, CARRINGTON XXXXXXXXXXXXX

[After their guests were moving away from a party given by Jack and Mary St John Hutchinson on St Valentine's Day, 1918, at their London home in Hammersmith, Gertler, rather drunk, assaulted Lytton who was walking away with Carrington.

Maynard Keynes, Harry Norton and Sheppard intervened, Maynard leading off Gertler, Sheppard going off with Carrington and Norton with Lytton. Gertler came up and apologized to Lytton the following evening when I was dining with him at the Eiffel Tower restaurant.]

To Lytton Strachey

Friday morning [February 15th, 1918]

Dearest Lytton, In case you are not in when I telephone, Faith asked you to go up to Downshire Hill after supper tonight *Frid.* I forgot the message last night. I am so sorry about that scene. It was rather my fault for not being more careful. I hope only you were not in any way upset by it. Maynard will go down Sat about 5 o'ck train. I do not know quite what I shall do. But I'll phone you after breakfast tomorrow and say which train definitely.   CARRINGTON

To Mark Gertler

[February 15th, 1918]   *46 Gordon Square*

Please do not worry about last night. I am only *very* sorry if I gave you the cause for your distress. It was quite unintentional. You must know. But I have forgotten it all this morning. Thank you for your letter. Do always write when you feel inclined to do so. I like so much hearing from you. I leave London today.   My love to you CARRINGTON

To Mark Gertler

[February 28th, 1918]   The Mill House, Tidmarsh

I will come, *if you want to see me*, when I am in London. But I hardly see
the use of corresponding when you are so antagonistic towards me.
When I said I wanted to tell you more about myself, I did not mean to
make that crude statement, which I knew you already knew, but it is
clear I cannot really help you, and after all it is a little discouraging and
exhausting to have feelings for a person, and to know one day they care
for you and the next day to receive an entirely contradictory letter
saying there is no connection between the two persons. When you do
make up your mind for any decent length of time that I can be of use
to you, I will gladly. But otherwise I would rather leave it. Evidently
from your last letter *We think so very differently about relative values of
everything now.* Yet it is impossible for me not to care every time I see
you. Very much. This letter is not bitter; only I feel rather tired, and
perhaps disappointed about it. But *don't* write any more. I would rather
not start it again. And you also feel that, I know, permanently inside.
My best wishes for your work.   D.C.
There is no answer to this letter.

To Mark Gertler

Friday morning [early March 1918]   The Mill House, Tidmarsh

Dearest Mark, I have just heard about you being called up. I am dreadfully sorry and so worried. *Please*, will you write and tell me as soon
as you know anything definite. I should be glad if you could spare time
to write by return and tell me exactly what happened, and what line
you are going to adopt, and what the chances are? It is frightful. But I
have such confidence in Fortune protecting you as she has in the past,
that I refuse to believe the worst will happen and you will get put in the
army. Do not get too unhappy. Remember things have always turned
out better than you expected in previous calamities. I will come up to
London if you would like me to do so. Dear, I fear I was unkind in my
last letter perhaps, and rebuked you and perhaps it came at the same time
as this bad news. If so please forgive me.

I shall be so worried until I hear news of your state. Please write as soon as you can and let it be at length, with every detail. For the moment let us forget all that has just past. The sorrows of today being yours are mine also.   My affectionate love CARRINGTON
If there is anything I can do to make you happy do not fail to ask me.

To Lytton Strachey

[*March 19th, 1918*]   *5 Phene Street, Chelsea*

Dearest Lytton, I am still so happy about your complete and entire exemption, that you shall have a letter this morning. I shall be glad to be back with you tomorrow. Barbara seems better today. I spent the morning up there. Now I am waiting for Ruth and tea. But no sign of either, and it's five o'ck. The meeting I knew would be too crushing, so did not go. No more excursions to London for a long while!—There is no knowing what train we will come by tomorrow. But I will send a wire from Paddington and do all the ordering in Pangbourne as we come through.

> Think I come back Ptolemny CaT
> To kiss your cheecks sleek and FaT?
> Oh NO! Oh NO! Its old CounT BummbeL
> A Pollypuss kiss, and NoT one GrumbeL.

Dearest Lytton, Hurray I am glad you're free. Let's go off for the week end and make long noses at the Lord Mayor of Hartland.
[Drawing omitted]   Many xxxx from your MOPSA

[Noel Carrington and his friend and fellow officer Major ('Rex') Partridge were on leave, and Noel had arranged for a trip to Scotland with Carrington, Partridge and the daughter of a Scottish friend of Partridge's. Partridge later adopted the name 'Ralph' to please Lytton.]

To Lytton Strachey

8.30 [*July 4th, 1918*]   *In train to Kingussie*

Well, what a lot can happen in a day! I met Noel at 12 o'ck. We then shopped, and talked in St. James Park till 1.30. Went to the Automobile

Club for lunch. The young man Partridge had just come back from
Italy, the one I was telling you about the other evening, so he and
another young Oxford man who was A.D.C. to Robertson—had lunch
with us. The A.D.C. was very attractive but obviously rather alarmed by
my appearance and manners! A pity, he was so charming with a beautiful head. After tea he left us, so we went down the Strand and sat in the
Embankment Gardens and talked. I found Partridge shared all the best
views of democracy and social reform, wine and good cheer and operas.
He adores the Italians and wants after the war to sail in a schooner to
the Mediterranean Islands and Italy, and trade in wine without taking
much money and to dress like a brigand. I am so elated and happy. It is
so good to find someone who one can rush on and on with, quickly. He
sang Italian songs to us on the platforms and was in such gay spirits—and
used his hands gesticulating. But the important thing was he seemed so
enthusiastic over reconstruction after the war and free thinking.
Fortunately he is to be in England 3 months. So I hope I shall see him
again. Not very attractive to look at. Immensely big. But full of wit and
reckless. And he was in London last night and we never knew and so one
must never give up hope that there are none left. He is sending me a
book by Anatole France to read—Angels—I cannot remember the name.
We are travelling 1st class by ourselves in a splendid carriage! Noel is
reading your book. He is very nice. But one felt so much the difference
between Partridge, a bond of dreams and worldly things. He adores eating and drinking and said as we sat on high chairs in the buffet at
Euston: 'I always feel sorry for women that they don't know what it is to
appreciate food. In Italy we had such amazing dishes and the wines!!'
Noel just told me the father of a College friend of his was vicar at the
Vicarage where Keble was. Southrop the name. He had been there.
And you are sitting with John and Ruth in front of a not too bright fire,
rather bored? I wonder, I have no idea how you will get on.
    And next weekend at Tidmarsh what of that? Write to me soon. I'll
send a PC with address tomorrow. How I loved our few days in London and the operas. Dear. Thank you so much. I wished you had stayed
today and met the young man. He deplored the English women and their
stodgy characters. The Italians he said walked so well and dressed all in
unity, which was indeed a true observation as we watched those drabs
slouching and stumping past us on the Embankment. The train rushes
too fast to write properly. We are nearing Crewe now. And have
fastened the door with a strap inside so the mob cannot enter. Noel
travels in full military attire ornamented with red tapes and braids so I

hope the Grants[1] or Glases will be pleased with us!

I hope you'll control Legg and get her to look after you properly—Noel just said he thought the sarcasm in your book so gentlemanly that Mary might not see it and might miss the point. So I told him the story of Claudius Clear.[2] But I am really wondering if we will go in the ship with this young man to those Islands. He is going to learn the mandolin to play on the SHIP, he said. Or whether, like all visions. Dear, if it is at all feasible I will certainly try to induce you to come to the Peaks and crags.

I am so excited now about going to Kingussie and your country. What a difference it does make, it being *your* place. I loved you so much last night. Please take great care of yourself for me, until I come home.

Yr CARRINGTON XXX

To Lytton Strachey

Monday morning [*July 8th, 1918*]   *Roy Bridge Hotel*

Very dearest Lytton, Yesterday we walked from Loch Laggan here 18 miles. I was almost sorry to leave Loch Laggan it was such a good hotel, and the mountains behind inviting. But dear one:—one adventure on the way was worth any mountain or stream—Oh, but why weren't you there to enjoy it with me to the full? They are just appreciative these two, and see nothing with their eyes. It was Wuthering Heights and Wordsworth, about one o'ck, and the rain had been pouring down steadily since we left Laggan and we were very wet and cold. I suggested forcing an entry into a bleak farm house on the high Banks. A woman came to the door; she was tall but had one of the most inspired faces I've ever seen on female shoulders, so sensitively chiselled, pale, and ill—with wild excited eyes and surmounting this extraordinary head was a high headdress, a kerchief of a greyish flannel tying up her matted brown hair. I longed to draw her. But there was no chance. So I drew quickly the

---

[1] Carrington planned to visit Rothiemurchus, the home of Lytton's Grant cousins, where he had often stayed as a young man.

[2] The Rev. Dr Robertson Nicoll who spoke for the Nonconformist conscience in a regular article in the *British Weekly*. He wrote a full-page article on *Eminent Victorians* in two successive numbers, the second on Dr Arnold, without recognizing Lytton's irony, but saying that Mr Strachey did not sufficiently recognize Arnold's great work of purification of English schools from hideous vice, a subject on which it was difficult to write in a family paper.

eldest boy, Donald, for her to send the father in France. She had been in bed 3 weeks ill with poisoning from the bread, and lived all alone on the mountains there, keeping a small farm with her four small children. There was an old party, the image of Mrs [Sargent-] Florence, who had come to help her while she was ill. The old woman was extraordinary also. Such character, with an old blue cap on her head from the holes in which tufts of hair protruded, like grass from the chinks in an old wall. They lit a fire in an empty room for us, and brought us huge oatcakes, curds and whey, new butter and glasses of milch. This stupid scotch girl made all conversation nearly impossible as she sat down also by the kitchen fire and asked Mrs MacDonald questions, such as Inez would ask. 'Now tell me abute Bonnie Prince Charlie'—'will your little girl sing us some Gaelic songs', till I could have cried with rage. She spoke Gaelic, and a Scotch in a lovely voice. She would always put us up if we wanted to stay there. We had to leave her about three, and move on to this place. Oh dearest, I longed for you to be with me then.

This place is much more fertile, and wooded with great water falls, and ferns on the rocks. We move this morning to Arisaig—and tomorrow to Skye with the unknown MacDonnell as a guide and make for your hotel in the centre. After Wednesday the Bouncing Lass goes back to her parents and we go straight on to Aviemore. I find Noel is very interesting to talk to, although he fairly worsted me in an argument last night. I wonder if you will like Partridge. Noel said he would probably like to come to Tidmarsh very much if we asked him. I hope to God there will be a letter for me from you at Arisaig tonight when we reach there!

Do you know Glasgowers don't even eat their porritch properly! Your weekend is just over. I wonder who came in the end to torment you. It seems a thousand years since I left you at Paddington. And one doubts at moments whether England and Tidmarsh ever existed, or will again! But of course I am really enjoying myself very much, you know that!

If you do come up to Scotland remember to bring my galoshes—and a pair of brown leather gaiters from the oak chest—Breakfast has appeared, so farewell.

Oh Lytton I do love you frightfully. So much Love and Lust from
Your MOPSA XXXXX

To Lytton Strachey

Saturday evening, 9.30, July 13th, 1918   Frasers Cottage, Rothiemurchus

Dear, Your letter has only just arrived posted last Wednesday Tidmarsh. It's mostly my fault for always moving about and the Scotch for only running one mail train a day to the Highlands.

By now you will doubtless have received post cards at Tidmarsh, and wires referring to my life here and inviting you to partake of it. But it's quite clear if Wolves come next week 20th and Charleston is 26th, it's not very possible. Also the expense, I clean forgot that, Noel's such a treasure that he pays for everything, so it hardly occurred to me to come here might be rather ruinous, until you mentioned it! All your news (especially as I've *not* received the 3rd letter yet written to Arisaig!) is a little confusing.

But that letter will probably arrive tomorrow as I told them to send on letters to Newtonmore from Arisaig. I must say I went clean off my head with joy to hear from [you] again. Dear, how much I love you. Do you know? When I saw your handwriting I had to laugh, even although Noel was with me. Frazer's son—the postmaster, brought them in this evening and the poor earthenware pot that I bought in Banbury! But worst of all those little peas that I've reared so lovingly for you! Dashed to the ground in a whirlwind! The rest of your letter staggers my brain. Ray [wife of Oliver Strachey] weekend with the Duchess, Tidmarsh? And my frantic wires. Will you, I wonder, start off for Scotland as I leave it. Shall we spend the rest of [our] lives in Highland expresses— trying to write letters and catch posts. What a nightmare! We walked to Loch Eunach this morning. What a very wonderful place it is. I am so happy here, almost completely so. Noel is rather charming now we are alone. He loves the little cottage and wins the hearts of all the Scotch rustics. I made a rhubarb tart tonight, and Noel said the pastry was so good that he would give me full marks. And I've never made it before and just invented the quantities. Mrs Cameron makes us lovely scones every day for our tea. You would love our kitchen! Brass candles, with sweet williams, roses, pinks and pansies in a bowl on the deal table. Noel reading Florence Nightingale, by the huge peat and wood fire. We looted it from the Laird's wood this afternoon on the way back from lake Eunach. The doors are all painted a lovely Prussian blue, did I tell

you, with yellow ochre wood work and pale pink-cream walls. I think
Duncan [Grant, who was born at Rothiemurchus] must have had a
hand in it. Upstairs all the doors are a lovely dark yellow. But I'm being
good, and not badgering you to come, which is truly virtuous, as I can
hardly bear to leave it all. Yet it would be reckless I know. Next year we
two will come here for a whole month. And afterwards go to Sligachan.
I will arrive Tues. morning 8.20 London Euston station. I'll ring up 96
South Hill Park [Oliver Strachey's house in Hampstead] and find out
where you are. Noel wants me to be in London on Wed evening to see
him off and have dinner with the nice creature Partridge. But if I find
you are at Tidmarsh I shall come down Tues. morning straight. So expect me if you are there by the morning train. If you're in London—I
shall see you at Hampstead.

All my love CARRINGTON

Arriving Tues. morning Euston 8.20 will ring up South Hill Park re
your location.

To Virginia Woolf

August 21st, 1918   *Tatchley, Prestbury, nr Cheltenham, Glos.*

My Dear Virginia, I did enjoy that weekend with you so very much, that
I must try and write a letter now to thank you and Leonard for having
me. I tackled Lytton about the James's[1] letters. You were quite wrong.
He was strongly in favour of them being brought to light and refuted
any idea of intrigues on his part. There was a vast gathering at Gordon
Square in the evening: Clive and Mary, and all the others. Sheppard
came in very decrepit and broken about 10 o'ck, and gave a ghastly
account of his medical Board at Cambridge. He's been classified Grade 1.
But it was impossible to gather whether the danger of Karkhi really
is as great as he made out it was—I saw Lytton off as the cock crew
nine at Kings X. H.B. Irving got in the same train, with an actor manager. Lytton was certain they also were destined for the party at Headlong Hall!![2] Jack Hutchinson who wrote to Mary from some other castle
in Northumberland said that Heinemann, and many other Jews and

---

[1] Henry James.
[2] Lytton was going to stay with Edward N. Hudson, founder and proprietor of
Country Life and friend of Madame Suggia, at Lindisfarne. In Peacock's novel a mis-
cellaneous party of guests are invited to stay at Headlong Hall.

dagoes were staying at Lindisfarne, and that all the food one could get there was bad crab, and foul lobster. So what has become of our Marquis of Tidmarsh amidst such spiritual and corporeal horrors? I dread to think.

I have been so excited ever since I saw those artists at Charleston,[1] and their work. I would not have missed that one day for any attractions you literary people could offer me!

It's extraordinary to be back here with my people again and the old mahogany furniture of my earliest youth. So respectable, and so highly polished. My mother's long conversation about dividends, and relations, which has gone on without a pause, since I first entered the house yesterday afternoon. But I've a great deal of work to do, and there are Cotswold Hills just across the lane to explore. So I expect I shall hold out for a week. We are going to Wooler [in Northumberland] first. I'll write you a long letter from there. And when we come back in September I'll come down, and dig the garden for Leonard like an old Mole. Virginia, I did enjoy staying with you so much. Please give Leonard my love.   Yrs CARRINGTON

PS I was crimson with shame on the way to the station over that biscuit box. It was worse than a Ferguson. So I'll make you another. The coal cart man drove me the whole way to the station on Monday morning. He's a good man.

To David Garnett

Tuesday evening [October 2nd, 1918]   *The Mill House, Tidmarsh*

Dear Bunny, You wrote such an amusing letter from the Globe, Exeter, that I am sorry not to have answered it before. But when we returned from Gordon Square here, Mrs Legg announced brightly that she was going away the next day for a week's holiday. As if I hadn't enough already of looking after the old gentleman in London! So nearly all my time has been taken up preparing food for human consumption and cleaning rooms which I with much greater speed make dirty again. Then last Wed. Clive and Mary [Hutchinson] were to have come so there was great commotion. Pies were baked, partridges roasted (which to

---

[1] Duncan Grant and Vanessa Bell.

give Clive his due, he sent). Then they played us false two days and then went to Roger's [Fry] instead. They said the trains weren't running because of the strike. But it was truly incompetence on Clive's part, as we found out the trains did run. Anyway, it wasted the devil of a time. Last weekend Madame Bussy [Lytton's sister Dorothy] came. I like her. She is so sympathetic and very entertaining. Mrs Legg is worse than a traitor as she promised to be back last Thursday and now it's nearly Wednesday and there is no sign of her. Lytton went up to London this morning to attend to his various Affaires. So I am all alone today and have quickly become a slut. I am writing to you in the kitchen with a black cat purring on the table. And I've just eaten a huge supper of coffee and marrow jam tartlets. Now how do you enjoy yourself? Please write me a letter about the Boxes [farmers at Welcombe] and the country. How happy I was there last summer. The Doe [rabbit] is going to have a family next week. We have started eating the cockerels as they consumed such vast quantities of food. I shall have 7 hens this winter. Last Friday I went up to London and Mr Partridge took me to the Ballet and we saw 'the good Humoured Ladies'. It was good. I had seen it before with Alix but right from the back of the upper regions and Mr P. had seats in the front of the stalls. It was too exciting seeing their faces so close—and every gesture. [Gerald] Brenan had been in London with him the last week. Mr P. asked me if I had read 'Despised and Rejected' and also made a louche joke about Lytton and Buggery. But I don't think all the same there is anything between him and Brenan. By the way, the man who wrote Despised and Rejected is being prosecuted by the Censor of morals!!! I just had a long letter from Alix this morning—seemed very happy. This is a dull letter but I feel like you do after a hard day's work at Charleston, as stupid as a cow and quite as boring. Please give Jenny and Rebecca Ann and Mrs B[ox] my love and a more intime variety of the same to you.   Yrs affec CARRINGTON

To Virginia Woolf

Tuesday [*October 1918*]   *The Mill House, Tidmarsh*

Dear Virginia, Lytton, (like some King whose name I forget, but I learnt a long poem about him when I was a child) went to bed and never smiled again until your letter came. Then he laughed outright very loud five times. And the second time he read it, ten minutes later he laughed seven times.

So will you write again? If you only knew his state of *complete* despair, as only a Strachey can despair, and utter misery, your pen would not remain idle. His hand is a little better today. But much too swollen to write with yet. Where did Goldie[1] have his shingles? My conversation now is entirely on that subject. Unfortunately to Lytton's chagrin, only innkeepers, charwomen and chemists' assistants seem liable to the foul disease. So your news of Goldie's suffering raised his spirits a little. For horrid thought; he believed it was a complaint of the lower classes. He is going to Glottenham to stay with Mary next Monday. D.V. Your words indeed came true, for this morning hardly had the loathsome shingles quitted its hold on his frame, when a bilious attack seized the stomach and now he cannot even eat his meals which up to now had been his one form of recreation and amusement. And you say the mange will follow? Well. I only hope it will attack him when he is at Mary's, not here. But to come to business. How can I do woodblocks when for the last month, ever since in fact we left Northumberland, I've been a ministering angel, hewer of wood and drawer of water? Honestly Virginia since I came here I've only been able to finish a picture which I sent Monty Shearman. Yes my ewe lambs are now in the market place and so one small woodblock. So you mustn't bully me. I go to Chelten-ham next Monday for a week. And I'll work very hard down there. By the end of this month I will try and send you some. Roger I hear is cutting wood all over the carpets in Gordon Square. What fun life in London seems, parties, Ottoline, and feathers flying. Here it is over-flowing jordans, milk puddings, poultices and then, overflowing jordans again the next morning.

My love to Leonard and please write to Lytton again. If you had heard the torrent of affection and admiration which flowed over your letter, well, you would write again.   Yrs affec CARRINGTON

To Virginia Woolf

Thursday [October, 1918]   *The Mill House, Tidmarsh*

Dear Virginia, You are as bad as Duncan who when we asked him to come here for a weekend wrote some ten days later to say he thought

[1] Goldsworthy Lowes Dickinson.

Vanessa had answered for him, but had just found out that she hadn't. What are we to do? One may come, both may come, and again we are not to count on either coming. No. You *must both* come. Lytton's been very ill. For nights his life was despaired of, and yet on his return to life his old friends treat him like this. He is in the depths of gloom. And all the books are too heavy for him to hold. I will kill our one and only cock the pride of the village, cockerel then, as you will have such an obscene mind, and a bottle of sloe gin will be opened for your pleasure over a vast wood fire at night. I appeal to Leonard who *has* a little real affection in him for his old friend. Please write a PC and say when we may expect you. And if you dare refuse I shall pray to God to send the shingles upon your heads and I'll never cut a blasted wood block for you again. Truly.   Yrs CARRINGTON

To Lytton Strachey

Thursday night, 10 o'ck [October 31st, 1918]   *Tatchley, Prestbury*

Not that there is anything to write about to night dearest.—But that I am thinking of you, and wondering how you passed your day and seeing the old hand as I last saw it, and speculating if any more wrinkles can now be seen on those two fingers. I don't think I shall ever forget the vision of that hand! And when I write your life as an old lady, I shall draw for the preface a shingled hand. [Fifty-four lines omitted] I can't help feeling it's wretched to touch the money he [her brother Teddy] saved probably through being a soldier in this war. You know it was just two years ago this October. At the very place where they are shooting now. I hate coming home because everywhere in the house I see his things and in my rooms all his school books, the queer boxes, and carved things he made, old chemistry jars, boats, and in the drawers his note books, drawings of engines, and frigates. You remember in that poem the room with the quick silver. It was all so like him. He wasn't a bit intellectual, only so charming. Really like one of those south country people, or a sailor. But mostly I think I loved him for his exquisite beauty and strength. I cannot forget one of the last days he was at Hurstbourne. In the afternoon I found him fast asleep on the sofa, curled up. His dark brown face, and broad neck, the thick black shiny hair and the modelling on his face, like some chiselled bronze head.

You don't mind me talking now. But it's been so heavy inside lately.

Those leaves lying on the lawn at Tidmarsh, and the cold smells made me remember Hurstbourne so vividly. And here, with all his things, I cannot forget hardly for a moment in this house.

When we passed Box Hill an incident came back. How up a certain white quarry he slipped down backwards down the loose clay and hurt his side. We ran on, and left him behind and afterwards he came running up very red and crying. And then long after when he rowed at school, he told me how the ribs were bent, and it still hurt. You comforted me once when we came back from tea at Dorelia's. So I write now. You would have loved him if you had seen him. It is blessed to know you. Such a comfort. Take great care of yourself and if you want me to take you to London and do anything, you will write?

My love, goodnight. CARRINGTON

To Lytton Strachey

Thursday night, 9.30 [November 7th, 1918]   *Tatchley*

Pray worthy Poet do not laugh at this somewhat curious scarf

PRay worthy Poet do not laugh
at this somewhat curious scarf

... For with Loving hands I made it, and even if it's not successful as a sling, it will, to use my favourite phrase, 'come in' for something else. I couldn't write this morning, there was so much packing to do. And this afternoon I accompanied my mother to a concert. Mark Hambourg, at the piano. There was one good piece by Bach, but for the rest, Il ne me plaisait pas. Chopin, and numerous minor exercises to show off his great skill at playing trills. But next to my mother sat *the* most exquisite creature that my eyes have yet lighted upon. He had the loveliness of a Boticcelli angel. I should think he was sixteen, slightly of the lower classes, with masses of black hair, and a very narrow fragile face—with dark brown eyes and a short curling upper lip, altogether more romantic and Italian than one could conceive possible. What he was doing in that congregation, God knows. For it might otherwise have been a Kensington High Church assembly. There were a few odd characters like Saxon, enthralled by every note. But for the most part they were the dullest most provincial, ill mannered people I've ever seen. Mark Hambourg was rather interesting. So very like another Mark in his movements, and mannerisms. I wonder how you are today and what you have decided about the future. I go to London tomorrow at cock crow. 8.30. Oh I *shall* be glad to leave this house. It's a pretty bad nightmare. And I could write several pages on the state of mind of the provincial young Lady of the present day. I tried to reform, or at anyrate unseat, one of them on the top of the Hill last night. But she triumphed and entirely ignored, in fact did not listen to a word I said. This hasn't been a good looting visit. Only one small silver cream jug, and some vegetables, and eggs for Alix!

But the fur coat this morning was the greatest comfort. For it's icy cold in these regions now. I've not had a word from Legg re that empty envelope which arrived and about the ration book which did not come. Rather a nuisance. I only hope you've got yours alright.

Dearest, I shall be glad when you can write again. Perhaps the wine cups and Geoffrey's arms will make me forget a little how much I miss you and your letters. You can't deny you aren't excited about Peace now. I say, you must come up to London and make merry, shingles or no shingles, next week. Dear Lytton I send you all my love tonight and remain   Votre jamais charmant maîtress MOPSA

[The following letter was written on Armistice Day 1918. Millions were reprieved from death. But though a pacifist Carrington was spiritually insulated from the war—a failure to connect.]

To Lytton Strachey

Monday morning, 9 o'ck [November 11th, 1918]
45 Downshire Hill, Hampstead

What an angel you are! I was never so glad of a letter before! You need never write again (not to be taken literally) for I shall remain happy for weeks because you tell me you are better and, oh Lytton, it is too good to believe that the old hand can write again. It's just as good as Peace, only I wish I could hug you hard this morning because I love you so much. And Jack can, that's the peculiar thing about life.[1] Well there's Sunday to describe. I had lunch with A. Waley again, at the Isolabella and oh joy a brimming cup of Zambalaoni! He was rather amusing, and talked a great deal; also read me some Piers Ploughman which I liked immensely. After, in Shaftesbury's Avenue, we saw Dorelia looking amazingly beautiful. She asked after 'Strachey' which she says in a curious voice which sounds as if it must be Strakey but just avoids it at the last moment. She leaves London next Tuesday for Dorset. Boris [Anrep] is going to decorate their walls in Chelsea with a fresco of The first women taking their seats in the Houses of Parliament! Waley tells me he [Boris] has a theory now that all art should have a great underlying motive, and at present the greatest symbolic movement to him is the freedom of women! Then we moved to the Arblemarble (?) Club in Dover Street. That struck me as very curious that Waley should for six years have sat in such a club. I think the S. Kensington gentry went away wiser than they came and many I fear with (Damn I can't remember the word) suppressed fixations. For Waley never alters the pitch [of] his voice for any company. Then tea at Gordon Square. Only Harry [Norton] visible when I arrived. He appeared in excellent spirits, and asked with great feeling after your condition. Then, my dear, who should come in, but Bluff Major Bell [Clive Bell's brother] just home on leave from France, thinking to find Clive at Gordon Square. You

[1] One of Carrington's wild jokes. Lytton was staying with Jack and Mary Hutchinson.

couldn't imagine the scene. It was too extraordinary. He evidently had
no idea of what Harry was like and roared with laughter like a Bull at
every remark Harry made! 'Well *I* can't say *I* think much of this
armistice now we have them on the run. I think we might as well finish
the job and enter Berlin.' 'Of course I wouldn't trust a Bosch. But I
suppose they'll take care he isn't allowed to have the chance of turning,'
and many more appalling statements. Harry was a perfect gentleman,
and never even looked as is his wont.

Then Sheppard entered and the Major roared even louder. I thought
it would never end. Finally Alix appeared, very stiff, and immensely
solemn. That was too much. I think it flashed across him, we must be
the young ladies of these curious friends of Clive. Anyway with a great
bellow of laughter he left the room!—But it was exceedingly strange.
Then until 7 o'ck we discussed: what else can one discuss in Gordon
Square, Maynard and his table manners! And a forthcoming party to
celebrate Peace. Harry had a great scheme for the party of a charade of
Pozzo's life—all at the table—beginning with Mrs Keynes trying to
teach him not to dip his bread in the soup. But Sheppard's more
gentlemanly instincts suppressed the motion—Then little [Edward]
Wolfe and oh—Geoffrey [Nelson] arrived. Geoffrey was too pathetic,
rather fat and lumpish and began: 'It's wonderful to be back. The sky
was all white when I left Ireland and the sea a bright blue.' I think he
must have arranged the speech. It was exactly like his letters. But as no
one answered him, his voice gradually died away and one heard murmurs about 'lovely yellow shore', 'tubs of salted fish which the fishermen'. Fortunately Harry broke it up by taking us all off to the Café
Royal for a great dinner. I walked ahead with le petit Loup—a splendid
dinner, and beakers of wine.—Geoffrey bored me dreadfully with more
Irish stories. Alix rapidly became very drunk and Sheppard took the
conversation into his own hands by relating all his love affaires since he
was four years old. Then Harry talked bawdy—and rather upset little
Wolfe. Gilbert Cannan and little Gwen [Wilson, who later married Lord
Melchett] who sat at the next table became correspondingly gloomier,
as our spirits rose. And there was cherry brandy and sloe gin to finish
up with! Back to Gordon Square—Alix so drunk that she had to leave
the company and was violently sick outside. I left her lying on Sheppard's bed groaning with mortification and anguish. Geoffrey to my
horror I find lives *exactly* opposite this house in Downshire Hill with his
aunt, Mrs Vessey. He's alright, but oh Lytton such a bore. Bunny is
Virginia in brilliance compared to him! Harry asks me to tell you that

next Thursday evening there will be crackers and squibs at Gordon
Square and if you are well enough your company would greatly add to
the pleasure of all concerned! Perhaps Mary will come up with Clive. I
doubt it being a good party. But I always think after talking a whole
Sunday afternoon about a party and the guests, one can't believe it will
[be] anything but a funeral feast. I am very well and so happy Lytton
this morning because you are better. Barbara, they say, is going on as
well as can be expected, and is quite cheerful. I enclose a letter from
Dorothy [Bussy]. Tonight I believe Monty gives a party, but I don't
know if I shall be allowed to go yet. I see him at lunch. They say there
was a great one there last Saturday with Lala [Mrs Vandervelde] and the
Russians.[1] I am sure there is a great deal more to tell you but I forget it.
Such a dull letter from the Partridge this morning. It says Brenan is
going to be married soon. Geoffrey tells me that [Horace] Cole is now
settled in Ireland with his bride and has become a respectable landed
gentleman.

   I love you so much Lytton. Only sometimes it's hellish to have you
so far away.   All my love CARRINGTON
W[aley] told me that the Jones[2] sat in consultation for a whole day
gathered round the round table discussing whether they should call at
the Mill House. In the end they decided it would be kinder not to do so.
—Thank God!

To Lytton Strachey

Thursday morning, 9 o'ck [November 14th, 1918]   *45 Downshire Hill,*
                                                              Hampstead

Lytton, it was good to see you again on Monday and I am so happy
because you are really better. But I felt in a bad mood, the last two days,
I think really because you vanished so suddenly, so I waited till I had
ceased to be peevish. You are too good a friend, to me, to inflict with
tedious letters about a hysterical mind. I read a letter to you in the
underground last night and actually had to laugh at myself for being
such an ass!

On Tuesday night we went to Gordon Square. Clive has already I

---

[1] Dancers in the Diaghileff ballets.
[2] The family of E. B. C. Jones, later Mrs Peter Lucas, lived at Pangbourne.

expect written a long account of it to Mary [Hutchinson]. It was one of the most exciting evenings I have ever spent. I suppose if one had been a man, with Cambridge behind, it wouldn't have astounded one quite so much. The only conclusion however arrived upon by everyone was that French letters must be more advertised to reduce the population, and that all the black races must be castrated. But it was astonishing apart from the arguments to see the characters of all those people, their faces, and attitudes. Yesterday I went to tea with Mark, to see his work, and met there a Miss Ruch, a pupil of Bertie and Moore. Mark was very charming and interesting. I liked a new painting of his of a Harlequinade and some pen and ink drawings. He had some singular stories about Roger [Fry] and himself and Bertie [Russell].

Then the evening I spent here with Alix. Today I paint Mrs Bridgeman. With a golden crown on her head as Queen Elizabeth!—Oh I know what I did on Tuesday, which I forgot, had lunch with Aldous [Huxley] and then went to tea with Osbert [Sitwell]. He had bought two African figures of wood which excited me very much.

His appearance was too wonderful! Lying on two chairs, surrounded by silk shawls and cushions, writing poetry on a large sheet of paper. His collar turned up straight against his cheeks, like Byron, with a black tie wound round. His hair brushed like those consort people from the back forwards and the front backwards like this,

 and the most lovely striped silk vest underneath which he showed us, and striped drawers, the circles running round like a football jersey. He gave a very good account of his father appearing suddenly to see him and the way he ordered the servants to pretend he was just living in lodgings in the house. He then crept into his bed, and interviewed his father, who was so charmed with the rest of [the] house that he almost took the first floor for himself. Osbert now lives in terror of his appearing again. Aldous told me that he took the Sitwells to see Mr [name omitted] of Chelsea, who instantly, when alone, tried to rape them, separately! Also that the Prince of Wales has now taken Mr——'s house as a pied de terre!

Now I must stop as I have got to go and see Barbara in her nursing home. Oliver gives a party next Monday. Perhaps you'll rise from the dead for it. My love to you dear Lytton.   Yrs very loving CARRINGTON

To Lytton Strachey

Friday morning [*November 15th, 1918*]   *45 Downshire Hill, Hampstead*

Dearest Lytton, I see yesterday's letter isn't posted yet. But never mind.
How are you?—I saw Barbara yesterday morning she looked surpris-
ingly well and a Japanese grub in the cot beside her. What is the female
body made of? For she told me it took nearly 24 hours coming out with
acute pain *all* the time. In the end they had to pull with pincers. The
next morning she woke up and had coffee, and eggs for breakfast, and
now feels quite well! [Twelve lines omitted] I saw some good Cretan
Figures in the Museum and, oh Lytton, Antinous! What a Catamite to
possess!

The evening I spent here drawing. This morning I paint La Bridgeman, lunch with Monty, afternoon to Barbara again and at 6 o'ck
George [Reeves] is going to take me to his place to play to me. He said
on the 'phone that Suggia is not well and the Doctor wants her to play
as little as possible. But next week perhaps she would be practising,
and he would take me to hear her. [Eight lines omitted] Give Mary
[Hutchinson] my love please. What a stupid letter this has become. And
oh Lytton I do love you so very much. I can't say this idle life of distractions makes it easier not to miss you.   Yr MOPSA

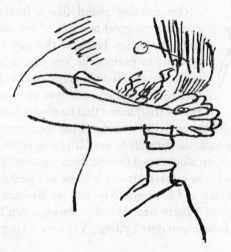

she squeezed so hard that his head broke off IBID. Ecce Homo!

To Lytton Strachey

Monday, 12 o'ck [November 18th, 1918] 45 Downshire Hill, Hampstead

Tibberations I see I am doomed. You'll put violets on my grave in
Golders Green Cemetery sometimes? I've left you all my possessions in
case they 'may come in useful'. Thank you for bearing with me so long.

HER

LOVE WAS UNREQUITED

Goodbye yr CARRINGTON

[In a letter of November 18th, 1918, from the St John Hutchinsons'
house, Glottenham, where Lytton was recovering from shingles, he
wrote of a visit from George Reeves who had 'a touch almost, I thought,
of Voltaire', and of that of Madame Vandervelde who was rushing off
to Belgium, 'where she hopes to make a triumphal entry in a day or two,
whether as a supporter of King Albert, or leader of the Bolshevists, she
seemed to be uncertain'. He said also, 'I shall be here a week longer at
any rate, and I hope a little longer; there seems no point in leaving this
field of clover until one is obliged.']

To Lytton Strachey

Tuesday night, 8 o'ck [November 19th, 1918]   45 Downshire Hill,
Hampstead

Well dearest here is a faithful portrait of your Mopsa. Except for the
Red Beard, a very good imitation of her Holy Ghost! Yellow jersey,
shawl, and medicines to boot. Yes, even bread and milk in the bowl!
Yesterday, since you never wrote, I have every hope that I should pass
away before the clock struck twelve. But God who seeth all things, one
too many peutêtre? saw the boney fingers of my well beloved scratching
feebly with a goose's feather, and spared my life until tonight, when
behold dear Alix brought me a letter from you. Oh dearest it has made
me so happy that I have sat up for the first time today, and have forgotten the horrors of this loathsome disease. Mrs Bridgman [the house-
keeper] has just brought me in my bowl of bread and milk, made very
differently I confess to your Tidmarsh brew! And now, oh dear dear

one, I am happy. I confess to day I felt wickedly towards you and cursed God for not letting me die. You hate me writing neither one way or the other. So I will be serious when I mean to be serious, and tell you that your letter only just came in time. All day I've been reading Sense and Sensibility and when Marianne received no letter from Willoughby I could have cried in sympathy for her. You will see by this letter that I still have a temperature and am not yet normal. Oh God! I've just upset the whole of the inkpot over my sheep skin coat, the sheets and blankets. I see any reunion with Alix is fatal! For the other night she and James upset an inkpot over Faith's best Persian mat and James used my new bath sponge to mop it up with. Last night Alix who is slightly ill, also taking her temperature in the bath room, started brushing her hair with the thermometer in her mouth, hit it with the brush, broke the tube and swallowed a considerable amount of the mercury!

Disaster follows disaster—and La Bridgeman groans. Well I've not written to you properly since Sunday afternoon. Well that evening after supper the priggishness of that young cherub annoyed me.

On Saturday night I alarmed them considerably by starting a conversation on Freud, and complexes of children. Howard [Hannay] admitted he was very interested in the theories of Freud but knew if he once started reading those sort of books it would become an obsession with him. His wife said 'you remember Howard it very nearly did once.' He: 'Yes and I felt I should be seeing all sorts of queer things in my friends.' C. 'It's astonishing the number of perverts one does discover.' Howard with absolute horror. 'Oh I'd never go as far as saying *that*,' and instantly turned the conversation. So on Sunday night we talked of Bolshevism and in the end I got onto my pet theme of the prevention of prostitution, and suggested that if decent intelligent females lived with young men, prostitutes would considerably diminish. I saw Howard and his wife getting more and more uneasy, till at length he said, 'Personally I cannot understand the feelings of a young man who can "go" with any woman. I should have thought it essential to feel love towards a woman to get over the repugnance and disgust of the act!!' The obvious reply of referring him to other methods with another sex I left unsaid—as he seemed so upset. The next morning they said at breakfast that neither of them had slept all night as they had talked so much! I would have given a good deal to hear that conversation! But really, Lytton, can you believe such a young man could exist? And his intentions are, to teach Philosophy after the war, at Oxford to undergraduates! There was a great deal more conversation of great import, and bearing on their states of mind. But I will tell you of it later. I was glad to see however when the small boys were given a lump of dough by the cook to play with, they insisted on making very prolonged no I don't know the plural COCKS. But I spared the already perturbed parents any allusion to the fact. I went to bed when I got back here yesterday morning, as it was so bleak and cold outside and all today I stayed in bed. You were mistaken about Alix, for she is the best of nurses. Most reassuring. And has never yet asked me how I feel! I regretted missing my lunch with Phillis and Edgar. But everything can reoccur in this life.

Maynard takes me to dine at Kettners on Thursday, and the new ballet afterwards! I shall go to Tidmarsh to recover next weekend, and stay there I expect indefinitely unless London offers any inducement to return. But these plagues hardly make existence worth living here. Dear Lytton, I am glad you are so happy and well cared for. Do you know, I wonder, how much I care? So much, that to know you are getting better and happy, makes it possible for me to bear your absence. Dennis wrote to me from the Hague where he has been a prisoner of war and said he would soon be in London. You forget who he is. He was at school with Noel and I used to paint him. He used to be as lovely as a Norwegian sailor. Yes, Voltaire. I remember a little engraving I had, the same sunken eye, and nose.[1] What I can't get over is his seriousness about music, and his great sensitiveness—combined with that extraordinary character, and the ginger waved hair.

Really Lalla [Vandervelde] is une grande aussi grosse Dame sans merci. I like to picture her riding behind [King] Albert, on a white palfrey waving a union Jack above his head.

Give Mary my love please. Don't forget. Oh the horror of this winter. My hands have become icicles, it is as if I was lying on the pier at Brighton. Yet every window, and crack is sealed! Dearest. I love you oh so much tonight.   Your ever devoted CARRINGTON

To Mark Gertler

[December 8th, 1918]   *The Mill House, Tidmarsh*

Dearest Mark, Thank you so much for your letter. It's very odd how natural it seemed to see a letter in your writing again, and after a whole year! This weekend David Garnett came. I know you dislike him, well, well. Anyway he was very kind to me, and sat for a painting,[2] and one evening in contortionist positions without his clothes, so I am full of gratitude as it means I can now get on with some compositions. He also cut up a lot of wood and was an obedient slave in the house. How exciting it is to draw nudes. Really I wish one could have a person to sit every day, as the excitement of drawing always upsets me rather. NO not the excitement of beholding a rather over fat young man! [Nine lines omitted] I am glad Roger [Fry] liked your work so much. He is one of the *best* people I think. As he really cares so much for good work. And is aloof from criticising people for their personal weaknesses and characters. I've been reading a History of the Popes by Macaulay which I liked very much. But most of this week has been spent getting my studio ready and setting the old house straight. I grudge every $\frac{1}{2}$ hour spent on such things. But my nature is so dreadfully untidy that unless I start 'straight', in a week I should not be able to move because of the mess.

[1] Lytton had compared George Reeves to Voltaire in appearance.
[2] Now in my possession.

And with painting that would be impossible as you know. I like looking back on my visit to London because I saw you. What I always feel is we are meant to persevere through this somewhat awkward time because later things will be better for us. Yes when we are very old with grey hair we will live in a little cottage, probably Miss Walker's at Cholesbury and you will hold my withered old hands in yours. Well, well. [Twenty lines omitted]   Yrs affectionate CARRINGTON

[Carrington's father, who had been partially paralysed for ten years, died in late December 1918.]

To Lytton Strachey

Sunday [*December 1918*]   *Tatchley, Prestbury*

Dearest, You were so good to me all yesterday. I must thank you at once—Well it was absolutely different from anything I had imagined. But the daughter of Lear has come down for breakfast, so I must stop for the moment: well that's over. Last night to judge from every appearance nothing might have happened. The conversation at dinner was too horrible. My sister sat there in a black evening dress, with her pale fat face as hard as a block of steel. When my mother said: 'We had to go to Davis the local undertaker; it will be just plain wood, not oak, with a cross on top of the coffin. There is such a shortage of wood you see', the sister replied: 'Naturally at a time like this with a great shortage of materials, wood is required by the Government for purposes of greater National Importance'. And so it went on from coffins, to wills and deeds of settlements. My sister's toneless voice discussing strokes, and other cases of death through paralysis she had known. Her character is such that my mother was completely dominated by it and I saw her becoming less and less human. I didn't want them to weep, but at least they might not have taken such a cold hellish interest over his relics. I couldn't help remembering all the time that a dead body lay in the next room, across the passage, instead of that human being in the bath chair in front of the fire. You are right: there's nothing so crushing and wretched as hard human beings without feelings. They were simply like two pieces of furniture conversing. The piano, and the marble mantelpiece could not have felt less. They say the funeral will not be until

Thursday so I suppose I shall have to stay till then. If I was a little braver I would run out of this house.

I don't believe they can [have] felt physical affection for a person.

It used to be so different when I came home, and went into the dining room. He used to hug me and almost cry because he was so glad to see me. They sat eating cold turkey, and made some polite address, and then discussed my clothes and what I must buy. The little cook with her wizened face feels more grief.

Dear one. I felt some more love grow to you today. I hope you'll look after yourself properly and do ask someone if you find it lonely. I shall come back Thurs. evening if I can. But I'll write again, and let you know for certain.

Do you know they sent a wire to me on Saturday which never reached Tidmarsh. How little one knows what the last state will be. As a little boy running in these lanes of Prestbury, my father little guessed he would die amongst those women folk, in such captivity in the same village. Dearest, your friendship means so much that I must just thank you. Because today more than most days I feel the importance of knowing you, my very dearest friend.   YOUR CARRINGTON

1919

To Lytton Strachey

Wednesday morning [*January 1st, 1919*]   *Tatchley, Prestbury*

Dearest Lytton, It was good to get two letters from you this morning
and so full of Tidmarsh and that little painted room of many colours.
I don't believe if I lived alone at the Mill, small boys would cut up logs
of wood for me. No, it requires a beard and long white fingers to be
served like that in this world. But you must have been far more tired
than I was, by the time you reached home. Let's make a vow here, and
forever, never to go to Reading again.

May I write you a really grim letter. It's pure selfishness because I
can't bear it going round and round in my brain.

It seemed like Sunday all yesterday for the blinds were all drawn. In
the morning I had to go to the town with my mother, and be fitted by
incomparably grand young Ladies at some female shop. They couldn't
see that it's not very interesting choosing stockings and black coats. My
mother seemed entirely engrossed and talked continuously about the
'correctness' of certain things. I couldn't see what on earth all this had
to do with my father being dead. All lunch the conversation was on
clothes, my sister is unparalleled in her stoniness. I bought a pair of
black boy's boots when I was left alone, which enraged my sister and
mother when they saw them. My spirits by the afternoon had become so
depressed that at last I couldn't bear it any longer. I hated them for
being so indecently interested in his death and my mother went on
talking about his peculiarities to my sister who was so bored that she
merely said 'Yars' 'Yars' [one line omitted]. The rooms are so arranged
that to go to the lavatory one has to pass my father's bedroom, which
rooms are both at the end of a long passage on the ground floor.

I went in to see him for all day I keep wondering how he lay. It was
so different from anything I had imagined. I thought he would have
been on his bed, as he used to lie in the mornings. But there was a long
narrow coffin covered by a white sheet and the bed stood there by itself
so big and empty.

When I lifted a napkin, oh Lytton, there was not his face, but a face

very small, and pale yellow. So dim and icy cold. Then I knew how very
much I loved him and now how lost it all was. That cragged hoary old
man with his bright eyes, and huge helpless body but so big always, now
lay in this narrow box in white linen and it was a ghost compared to
that man, that lay there. And then a vision of all those people whose
faces I have loved came. Teddy too, must have gone all pale like that—

I could not believe the change would be so horrible. I hated something for making his face so smooth. Yes it was saint like, like the marble
bishops in the cathedrals. Oh Lytton why didn't I love him more when
he could feel. I might have fought for him; he was too helpless himself.
I knew what he cared for; how my mother tormented him, and how he
suffered, and yet I did so little. I read yesterday Tolstoy's Ivan Ilyitch.
My father hadn't even Geriasim to comfort him. I miss him so dreadfully this time, here. He was so like me, that I felt always he understood
and was on my side. Now I am all alone with these two. I know my
mother cared and is unhappy. But I can't forgive her for taming him as
she did, and for regarding all his independence and wildness as 'peculiarities' and just making out he was a sentimental good husband. Then
can she really care, when she talks as she does, knowing that pale ghost
lies in that other room. I hate my sister seeing me. It's so beastly not
even to be allowed to cry without my mother calling for me to go with
her to some infernal shop. And when my mother leaves the room, my
sister speaks in such a way that my blood rushes hot into my head.

But I am glad he has escaped from it all. I like to think of him wandering vaguely in India in that bright light, really loved by people and
perfectly happy. But instead I see him captive in all these houses, in the
cold grey winters always being worried by domestic details, scolded like
a child, restricted, wretched. And I knew, and never told him. Ten
years must have been a long time for him.

Dearest, I am glad that there is you for me to love. I knew you care:
you did not have to tell me so. I shall beg my mother to let me leave on
Thursday. You'll forgive me for writing so. But it makes it better to
know I can talk to you.

Oh, I wish I could forget that ghostly face and in this little bedroom,
on every side I see Teddy's things. His books, and photographs. Your
letters comforted me so much this morning. Dearest Lytton, you've
meant more to me these last few days than ever before.

Yr loving CARRINGTON

PS My mother has just been in the room and wants me to stay on with
her, I gather indefinitely, when I said I really couldn't she accused me

of being selfish, and said she couldn't bear being left alone. I wish you were here to advise me, I can't believe I can do any good, as I feel too wretched to cheer her up, which is what she says she wants. I thought I could come back, and stay. Or is it really selfish of me to go away because I can't bear this?

To Mark Gertler

Tuesday [January, 1919]   *The Mill House, Tidmarsh*

Dearest Mark, It was good of you to write so kindly. I am much happier now. It was the reproach of a thousand memories which every piece of furniture in that house brought me, reproaches for not having been kinder to him when he could feel. Directly I knew that little yellow face was hidden under the ground I felt more happy. I don't feel any link with them—my mother and sister. Every time I see them they are more remote; with him I did feel connected. He was so like me in many ways. Sometimes I feel almost glad he has gone off this planet, and that I am now not joined by that curious link. But how irritating all these petty material issues are. I am now offending my mother and everyone mortally because I won't go home and live with her. 'Cheer her up.' How illogical. How can one cheer a person with whom one has no sympathy, and no affection. She feels miserable for the death of a Christian husband and for the loss of an occupation, because every day she spent looking after him like a nurse to a little child. She grumbled and pretended to hate it, but now that she has nothing to do she cries because she says she can't think how she will spend her day. We both loved a totally different person. I loved my father for his rough big character. His rustic simplicity and the great way he lived inside himself and never altered his life to please the conventions, or people of this century. He would have been exactly the same if he had lived under Elizabeth. My mother hated all this and even admitted to me she married him out of pity, because he wanted looking after. She has a character like Mary Cannan; she adores making a martyr of herself, toiling unnecessarily—and working off her sensual side in religious outbursts. But it all has a dreadfully unsettling effect on one. I knew you would understand, because you love your mother probably in much the same way as I did my father.

I've done no work at all today. I seem to have stuck somehow. I wish
I could have some more people to paint portraits of. Do you know that
feeling when one wishes to have quite straight forward work all ready
arranged as it were, to make one work. Directly the brushes start one
gets inspired and ideas rush in. But the blankness sometimes is appalling.
When literally one can't think of any thing to paint!! Ideas come only
too vaguely to be of use. Yesterday those little boys came and I worked
all the afternoon on them, and got on fairly well with it. They are so
charming. I quite love their fat shining faces and droll naive characters.
It's wonderfully quiet down here. Today the sunshine was so lovely
that I went out into the garden and dug and felt like one does when the
spring first comes, very new, and young. And full of energies. Tell me
how are you now? If it was flu you must be very careful. And not go out
too soon or you will get ill again. I am sorry you are lonely. You were
down at Garsington when I came up to London 2 days after Xmas. So I
couldn't see you!! But next time I come, I will arrange an assignation
with you at the National Gallery. And we'll go to a ballet afterwards.
Brett wrote from Scotland yesterday. A very chaotic letter. But apparently she was very happy. [Two lines omitted] What have you been reading
lately? I have French lessons also, but I am awfully slow and stupid.
We have been reading Molière. I've just started that new book by
Berty [Russell] about the Ideal State and Socialism.—It looks as if it
will be interesting from the preface. Have you seen much of Berty
lately? This letter isn't very comforting when you are ill. But I wrote
at once to tell you how much your letter pleased me and to beg you to
take care of your health. Write again soon, please. And tell me how your
work goes. Do the people—like Roger [Fry] etc like your Circus, or
haven't you shown it yet? With love to you dear friend.

Yr CARRINGTON

To Mark Gertler

Friday [January 1919]   *The Mill House, Tidmarsh*

Dear Mark, Thank you for your long letter. Tonight I feel infinitely
lonely, and rather depressed. Partly because I am alone and then I
suddenly realized a few moments ago what a beastly ungenerous nature
I had created inside my frame. Yet, you realize all my letters to you are
like woodcuts, limited in their technique, and that certain elements, as

colour, will never be able to be shown. My brother has been spending the last two days with me here. Yesterday a friend of his [R. S. Partridge] came down to stay—I had been reading Berty's new book on the reform of the state, and foolishly fell into the belief that it was all very possible. That except for a few bloated capitalists, and politicians *everyone* really wanted to see such a life of freedom, and happiness. And when this young man and my brother started talking together after dinner, I woke up into realizing how hopeless, and distant such ideals are; that the educated people make the blockade which prevents revolutions, and progress. This young man thought himself very advanced and yet was so self satisfied, and narrow minded, as to simply dismiss with a few cynical phrases any variety of mankind who he didn't agree with. A certain callousness, and lack of reverence for life, and death appalled me. They neither of them felt any passion or interest in things like we do. They discussed their futures and weighed the advantages and disadvantages of certain professions. But there was no desire to do any creative work of their own. What a gulf this fixes between one and such people. My brother is so charming that it hurted to hear him becoming intolerant, and complicatedly conventional. Today was [so] beautiful, that I forgot, when I woke up and saw a golden moon disappearing like a guilty orange cat from the larder, down below the trees, and barns and the sun shone out.

And Noel was so gay and happy, [after] all the disappointments and problems of life of last night. We borrowed a little pony trap from the blacksmith, and drove to some enchanted woods where Monkey Puzzler trees and great dark yews, and conifers grow and had lunch in a little inn. And then drove home in the afternoon. Now they have gone. And I feel depressed because I feel I may have hurt them, and spoilt their pleasure by being standoffish and superior. Noel looked so beautiful out in the garden that I really felt after all if he had such a good nature, his views and prejudices didn't much matter. This is contrary to anything Berty would say. But I confess at that moment I felt it!!! I suspect this intolerance of young boisterous men is really old age on my part!

To David Garnett

[January 22nd, 1919]   *Tatchley, Prestbury*

Dear David, The last of the mohicans [Lytton] will arrive shortly. I
hope you appreciate my mother's kindness to this phantom country
boy,[1] 'all rags and tatters' as Sheppard used to sing—I say, you *are* a
Juggernaught. Why didn't you come down on Friday evening for the
weekend? Lytton suggested that you thought I didn't want you. I
really couldn't have you when those young men were with me. I am sure
you wouldn't like the Partridge—My brother Noel is charming so you
will meet him later doubtless—But you must have known I would have
liked your coming. All preparations had been made for your portrait and
you failed me! Villian! I hope these thick wool garments will be of use.
My mother tells me they are very warm and so I take her word for it.
The pyjamas seem without coats, but as I saw last time you were at
Tidmarsh you were addicted to the habit of sleeping 'odd', I thought it
wouldn't matter. I just started saying to the little madame: 'Oh it
won't matter as I know he sleeps with odd coats and pyjama trowsers'
when I stopped at 'matter' and thus saved my reputation. But it is
difficult to become a perfectly innocent daughter at five minutes' notice.
God the boredom of this house! I hope to escape next Saturday. Give
Duncan [Grant] my love. Tell him I liked his drawing in the Burlington
Magazine very much indeed. And reverence him for drawing it. My love
to Vanessa also. Don't forget.   Yrs DORIC

By train so go to the station *Berwick* and fetch it.

To Lytton Strachey

Wednesday [January 22nd, 1919]   *Tatchley, Prestbury*

Dearest one, Well here I am, and you are pavement tapping, boy accosting [in the] streets of London. I don't foresee much of interest happening to me here. So I am contenting myself with organizing a grand
Trunk to Trunk Loot indoors. You groan. No I promise I won't bring
back a single Benares Brass Bowl, or one carved Bracket. Haydn's

---

[1] Carrington had told her mother I was a poor farm boy deserving of charity and had
sent me some clothes belonging to her brother Teddy which did not fit me.

dictionary, a rattle to keep the birds from our cherries, some chintz to cover a chair, and an eiderdown quilt also some new pyjamas which I suppose I shall have to give up to Le grand signor! My parent was of course perfectly well, having recovered the day of my arrival. What a waste of time all this business is. You see I am bad tempered already. You will write and tell me your plans? I gather she won't go away till next week. So if you want the house for any lofty, or base purposes I can easily stay here till Monday. But if you would like my company to assist at cutting the cottage pie, I will come back on Saturday. I saw George's [Reeves] name looming large on the Telegraph front sheet this morning! Even at the risk of driving you mad with my incessant repetition, I whisper very softly, not to disturb your siesta, that you have made me so happy lately, and I have loved the evenings, and you become more precious to me every day.

Such a nightmare last night, with Aldous in bed. Everything went wrong, I couldn't lock the door; all the bolts were crooked. At last, I chained it with a watch chain to two nails. Then I had a new pair of thick pyjamas on and he got so cross because I wouldn't take them off and they were all scratchy. Everything got in a mess, and he got so angry, and kept on trying to find me in the bed by peering with his eyeglass, and I thought all the time how I could account to my mother for the mess on my pyjamas!

Now for the Promenade, and the Colonels with their ladies. Tell me how everything fares with you and the adventures. Launce and his dog. 'Cock' George, and the Black Mortimer.

All my love from your MOPSA

To Lytton Strachey

Friday [*January 24th, 1919*]   *Tatchley, Prestbury*

Presentiment, that dark Hag, whispers in my morning ear that Prince Harry [Norton] will carry the field, and you, to Cambridge. I shall await a wire from Marjorie to seal my doom. Good bie ... Good ... bie the maiden cried
We'll not see HIM again.

The moment I read, 'We will treat your word of honour as a gentleman later' I felt certain the good old Buggery ghost was about to enter

the court. What Hell fiends they are those smug Judges![1]
Scene—Heinemann's [William Heinemann the publisher] House. Next
week. E[minent] V[ictorian] 'I believe we have a friend in common ...
your accompanist ... Mr George Reeves.'
P. Donna Claire [?Clara Butt] languidly but with great volume. 'Have
I an accompanist? I really forget. I suppose someone *does* play the
piano. I never thought about it, one might enquire.'
Exit G.R. under the tablecloth.

Scene—Heinnemann's House. Next week.

Give dear George my love when you see him. I am glad you are
enjoying yourself. But perhaps after all I shall see you tomorrow. I shall
certainly go back for the weekend, if there is any prospect of seeing your
dear face! [Drawing omitted] And Willie Burton? Will one ever see
him again? Imagine the scene if I meet him down town this morning,
when I am with la mère C!!! His naivety is such he wouldn't I believe
suspect anything.

What news of Irene Vanbrugh and your play?

Good-bie Good-bie.   from your forsaken MOPSA XXXXXX

[1] The inquest on Billie Carleton the actress who died of an overdose of cocaine after
the Victory Ball on November 27th, 1918, was reported in *The Times* of January 24th,
1919. In cross-examination Reggie de Veulle, asked if he had given Miss Carleton cocaine,
replied: 'On my honour, no.' Mr Hayes, cross-examining: 'I will deal with your honour
later on.' He then blackened de Veulle's reputation in the minds of the jury by suggesting
that he had had lucrative friendships with older men and that he was a transvestite. At the
end of the inquest de Veulle was arrested and accused of manslaughter for supplying
Billie Carleton with drugs.

[The following extract from Carrington's Diary seems to me to show an accurate picture of Lytton's life and character at this period. It contrasts strongly with the teasing picture she gives of him in her letters to him, as she thought he might like to imagine himself—as 'a pavement tapping, boy accosting' adventurous pervert.]

From Carrington's Diary

[February 14th, 1919]

Talking about Lytton, if one did try and write what happened to him every day, what a grim failure it would be. All his adventures and experiences are mental, and only enjoyed by himself. Outwardly it's like the life of one of the hens. Meals dividing up the day, books read in morning, siesta, walk to Pangbourne, more books. A French lesson with me, perhaps dinner. Reading aloud. Bed and hot water bottles, and every day the same apparently. But inside, what a variety, and what fantastic doings. And great schemes I suspect. Sometimes internal ragings which never come out. And plans for a future which I could never guess. I wonder how much his appearance captivates me. One learns very little of his inside. Some things one knew from the beginning. That his conversation is always fascinating, and instructive. He is kind and sympathetic, intolerant, and prejudiced to a degree sometimes. Obstinate and with a grandness and aloofness I've never met before. But everything very sudden, like a bird flashes across the sky on a walk. I mean his angers, and laughter. Painted too vilely today. I give up the nude bathers with disgust and turn to something new tomorrow. A long walk, and talk about the Georges before tea.

[February 18th, 1919]

Today mother sent me Teddie's sailor clothes. How awful it is to realize how little I knew, or appreciated him—Yet one's senses become hardened by space of time. A year ago would I not have cried? And now I just felt dully miserable. Bones in some cloggy wet clay now, which used to fill those trowsers so tightly. How I loved him at Hurstbourne when he came on leave carrying his sack on his back. And in London at the Garnes'[1] flat when Nellie the servant showed him into my

[1] Possibly Dr William Garnett's.

bedroom and he sat on the bed, so brown with his black shining eyes
and hair. No there will never be such a face again. His beauty was so
immense and solid. Why need he have died? one feels [he] was a soldier.
And never cared for life. He had seen so little of this life. And even if he
[had] never would have cared for this. I selfishly wanted him. Little
Roy, that child, reminds me of him, his grunts, and fat cheeks and
smiles. And a little packet of sailor clothes in my bedroom is all that he
has left me. Cruel hateful war. That such loveliness should have been
destroyed. There is no one to tell. They are old, and after all how can
they feel when they never saw him. Yet Lytton has taught me how to
feel as I do tonight.

To Lytton Strachey

Monday [March 3rd, 1919]   *The Mill House, Tidmarsh*

Dearest, The post hasn't come yet, although I hardly expect I shall get
one from you. The beauty of the day yesterday! I could have cried to
see it passing before my eyes besmirched by soots in this vile plague-
stricken city.

We *could* have gone to Newbury. That was curious:—that spring
should have returned again. Just as it did last year.

Everything rolls on much the same, only the faces differ and the
conversations vary. I mean I'm not really interested in any of it. Because
you are not here with me. Well—well. Breakfast has just come and gone.
Too much has been eaten and oh ever so much too quickly. Because I
read the Browning love letters. It's difficult to believe they were posted
in pillar boxes. They have just both been writing to each other about the
spring! There, there *was* a letter! Dear little Nero; anyrate we shall now
be able to lay claim to half the exquisite kittens that old cat Ottoline
produces. You can tell your story to Percy!! After all it's monstrous that
little Nero should get nothing for all his pains. Yesterday Noel turned
up for breakfast suddenly. He was staying at the Tour Eiffel with the
Bird Partridge for the week end. He seemed in very gay spirits.

He and Partridge are going to the south of Spain on a tramp steamer
next month.

I incline rather to forcing myself on them. What do [you] think?
Madrid, and Bil Bayo? (or however it *is* spelt) of course one might have
better company. But on the other hand will one ever get the chance to

go again? I thought anyway I might see if I could get a passport; that, they say, is the chief difficulty. I went by myself to a wonderful concert in the afternoon at the Aeoilean Hall. Bach sonatas with flute and piano. All the Stracheys were there and poor Monty found himself next to me. He was with Mark's successor [name omitted]. I thought an impossibly vulgar young man.

Keep a little beef for me on Wednesday. [One line omitted]

Love dearest one.   Yr CARRINGTON

To Mark Gertler

[March 1919]   *1917 Club, 4 Gerrard Street, London W.1*
                                       write to *c/o Thomas Cook, Madrid, Spain*

Dearest Mark, Thank you so much for your letter—Yes it was unfortunate that I couldn't come to Garsington. But this Spanish business made everything so rushed that I hadn't time to stay with Ottoline. But it was just good to see you for that little while. I enjoyed the dance. The young men were so lovely. But God how dreary, ordinary and stupid! They would make good bedding plants but not for use in the daytime. As they thought I was 16, and a nice young lady I didn't have even any consolation in any direction! We sail tomorrow morning early. It sounds too extraordinary. I can hardly believe it. I wish I had other company. I don't take much to the young man, and his sister is still worse. Noel is all right, but completely influenced by the young man. Still if I see some El Grecos and Goyas I shall be quite contented, and really one always enjoys these holidays in spite of people I find. I hope you'll feel better after Brighton, and be able to get back to your work. I hope Brett's scheme of your living with her at night, may make things rather happier for you. I've got a confounded swollen neck which doesn't make me feel very cheerful today. But the doctor said it wasn't serious [drawing omitted], only I am so vain, that I hate being hideous [one line omitted] I cover it with scarfs and that nearly stifles one. It also is rather painful. I expect Spain will set one up in health again. You'll write to me? And I'll send you post cards, and a letter. It will be exciting coming back again. I'll come and see you directly I get back to London. Be kind to Brett.

My love to you dear friend.   Yr CARRINGTON

[Carrington left for a walking tour in Spain with her brother Noel, Partridge and his sister Dorothy.

I have omitted a number of very long descriptive letters to Lytton about her impressions of that country.]

To Lytton Strachey

[*April 15th, 1919*]   *Madrid*

My dearest Lytton, I got your letter this morning. I was overjoyed to hear from you. And to know you were with Alix and James, and so happy. How we'll talk when we get back:— Lyme Regis, Castro del Rey, Regis Lyme, Rey de Castro and ad finitum (?). This morning I spent in the Prado. How can one say what one feels when all the air has been pressed out of one's lungs through the sheer exhaustion of marvelling.

The portraits of Goya perhaps delighted me as much as anything. Especially the reposing lady draped. I forget her name. El Greco is quite, quite different from what you would imagine. The pictures are so large, and the colour incredibly beautiful. Then there was Velasquez which I looked at with you. Several which were quite new to me. Then I saw some wonderful Titians. And other Italians. But one can't look at them when one knows there are Goyas to feast upon.

Downstairs there were great rooms filled with decorations by Goya and pen and ink, and red chalk drawings, sketches for the etchings and some new ones. Many very bawdy. But marvellously drawn. He had such wit, compared to most painters. But it nearly killed one with fatigue. Especially as I never slept at all last night in that 3rd class wooden seated train from Sevilla. There are disputes going on with Thomas Cook about a passage back, which may be difficult to arrange. Noel unfortunately is obliged to be back on the 25th, I would give much to linger a little longer in this country. What a statement to make to you. But oh Lytton, Lytton, Lytton, I am so happy here, and the sun is so good and hot.

Your letter and the Prado have made this day one complete day of pleasure for me. I feel it is like some dream. Once one wakes up and comes back to England, it will never come again. Tomorrow I hope to go to the Prado all the morning by myself, and on Thursday to Toledo for the day. On Friday we shall have to leave for BilBayo: spelt wrong Bil Bao. When shall I see you, Where shall I see you, again?

Madrid is very stuffy after those mountain towns and the people almost as hideous as the wanderers of Tottenham Court Road. Yes, would you believe it?

I send you all my love and xxxxxxxxxxx Oh I wish you could only be here to make it quite perfect.   Your CARRINGTON

To Lytton Strachey

[*April 18th, 1919*]   *Bilbao*

My dearest Lytton, It's over. We now stand at the gate of this paradise Spain, waiting for the keeper to open the gates, and push us out. The only curious thing in this analogy being however that although the time is up, and the Park closed, no keeper will open the port of Bilbao. We arrived here yesterday morning after a perfectly appalling journey all night in the train from Madrid. In the end I abandoned the idea of trying to sleep, and gave up my body for the use of others. Noel went to sleep in my lap, and R.P. rested his enormous bulk on my shoulder. But it rather devastated the moral and wears out the buttocks! I had imagined Bilbao was a place full of lovely sailors and ships, but in case any misguided person should in future console themselves during a night journey from Madrid with equally Castilian imaginings, I will here record in cold ink that of all ports on God's earth it is the vilest. Even the Spaniards are debased, and so hideous that I believe they must really be French. They all wear the most stupid clothes and are rude and ungracious. The town is unredeemed by a single building which one could call architecture. In short it is very like what one conceives a south American port run up in 2 weeks by a cinema firm would be. We went with an introduction to the Consul. Because his name was Innes I imagined he'd be rather like Augustus' friend [the painter]. That one would promptly find one a boat to sail on. I even envisaged a lunch at a little house belonging to Innes with engravings of Spanish ships on the wall. After walking through this disgusting place for nearly half an hour, (It was Good Friday so everything was shut) we found the Consulate. Noel walked in with his Andalusian hat on the back of his head, and asked a great fat bulky man who appeared, whether we could see Mr Innes. The Bulk drew himself up, and said in a Scotch accent: 'I am he' and looked at us all with great severity. Noel kept his face, and asked if he could tell us of any boats sailing for England. He said he knew of none, and thought it improbable we could ever get any captain to take us. [Three pages omitted]

Wednesday night was curious. R.P. saw an advertisement for dancing at some club outside Madrid, so he, N.L.C. [Noel Carrington] and I went on a tram after dinner at 10 o'ck, the tram went at least 8 miles, and finally landed us in a suburb in the country,where were found a very smart Casino, and club. Of course when we got inside we saw we had made a mistake. Two officials rushed up to us, looked us up and down in absolute horror and some young Madrid rakes gazed up from their tables, in full evening dress, with a look of great coldness of their faces. One official then firmly indicated that owing to our singular appearance he couldn't let us in. The other porter however took us across to a little café on the other side of the road, and said the next tram would be 20 minutes, so we had better have some coffee. A most singular conversation then took place. He first asked what hotel we were staying at in Madrid, then how much we paid. R.P. got very nettled and I thought we were in for a dust-up. He was the most shady looking cadger you could conceive. Then he suggested we stayed the night at the suburb with him and said: 'you come from Chicago?' In bad English 'you are acrobats? Did you come here tonight for a job?' all of which R.P. answered in the affirmative.

So suddenly we became a troupe and a long story which the little porter supplied by asking the questions came out about our lives. He was evidently very anxious to persuade us to stay and to try and get us to show him our turns. I must say R.P. was rather good at lying. It turned out he was French and a deserter. Having escaped with some Australians from a Greek Hospital in Egypt. It was the kind of thing Katherine [Mansfield] and Murry would have enjoyed. I only regretted I wasn't an acrobat! It was all very Fantastic because one believed it oneself in a curious way. We parted very good friends and returned on the tram at 1 o'ck to Madrid.

[Rest of letter missing]

To Mark Gertler

Saturday [April 1919]   *The Mill House, Tidmarsh*

Dearest Mark, I came back here this morning early, so I shall not see you
until next week. Directly I know which day I shall come up to London, I
will send you a post card, so that I can be sure of seeing you. What a
boost Clive gave you in the Athenaeum! Not that it matters much, but
it's always a pleasure added to having done something good, if people
who really understand about painting like Roger [Fry] appreciate one's
work so highly. We'll have a regular El Greco afternoon when I come
back. I will be able to tell you the colours of all those pictures, and also
the Goyas. I hadn't any money, or I would have bought you some
reproductions in Madrid. It's nice to be back here in the country, and
see all the flowers in the garden. I found London rather appalling those
two days. Living quite vaguely, and wild for more than a month makes
the narrow street life, and hideousness of civilization, jar on one rather
acutely. I hope you enjoyed your visit to Garsington. One comes back
so full of enthusiasm about Spain, and those pictures, and longing to, in
some way, convey the pleasures one has had to other people, only to
find no one wants to hear a damn word on Spain! I have seen sights one
hardly dreamt of and people so beautiful that one quivered to look at
them, and then those El Grecos at Madrid and Toledo, yet one has to
keep it all inside. I feel so strong just now—and savage. But I see it will
wear off in this cold climate before many days. I am again sorry to have
been so stupid as not to have seen you in London. My love to you. Do
keep well.   Yr CARRINGTON

To Mark Gertler

Sunday [May 1919]   *4 Verulam Buildings, London*

I hope you didn't take my behaviour ill last night. But honestly I do
think when I see you so seldom you might, when you know how much I
dislike it, not get drunk when you go out with me. I don't care what you
say but I simply think it's very boring. And I also protest against you
having quarrels and arguing with me in public:- before people like

Nelson and Chili [Alvaro Guevara the painter] I think it's much better in future to see you alone as we never get on when we are with other people. I wasn't well enough to go out tonight. And tomorrow I am going back to the country. But I will come up again next week end probably and come to tea again.

I don't want to quarrel with you and I thought I had better explain why I left you last night.

My love to you.   CARRINGTON

I forgot to post this so have opened it to add

PS Monday evening

I didn't go after all this morning so I wired to you—as I wanted to be nice because I had been beastly the other night. But I know now from little Nelson that you were with Kot. My love to you again.

Yr CARRINGTON

To Lytton Strachey

Wednesday [*May 21st, 1919*]   *1917 Club, 4 Gerrard Street, London*

Dearest, [Three lines omitted] What fun the party sounded last night! Remember it all to tell me next week. I loved seeing you so much on Monday night. Do you know how very much I care for you? And it's a better sort of affection than it used to be, because now I am not so impatient to be always with you. Because I know always you are here. How badly one always writes these mental feelings. It's so easy to give an exact description of Clive's [Bell] hair, and the cushions at the club. But so hard to say what I want to tell you about my love for you. But this isn't a place inducive to writing such letters. I am taking that large cat into the country for Waley. He saw it was such a trouble to keep in London. And I really get so much pleasure from having many cats to look at on the lawn. Really they are very like the Russians [ballet dancers]. They move so beautifully I am almost certain to see you at Garsington on Saturday. [Five lines omitted] Clive was so charming to me this morning I believe he's starting to treat me as a female—not as a hybrid!

You won't go and get ill, will you. I am only afraid you'll get too tired rushing about. I'll write from Pangbourne. I am so happy at going back. The beauty of that garden fills me more and more, and tomorrow I start my painting—and you say you'll start your writing. Well—we shall see? Dear. Dear. Why are all the inhabitants of this place like frogs and lizards from the underworld. One might write a Greek play especially for this club with a great chorus of monsters and insects!

Promise me a letter tomorrow. Lytton I must tell you what a difference just knowing you makes. But it will be good to have you next week ... an if the High Ladies of the Court grant me my wish. Hugger me, and Bugger me and cover me with Kisses   Yr CARRINGTON

From Carrington's Diary

Sunday

Bathed in my bath.[1] A letter from bank, shoe maker, and Brett. Painted La Major [Partridge] and I think improved it. Bathed again at 12.30, and read the Young Visiters in the sun in the orchard. I envy that book. How good, firstly to be able to create so detached from this world, and then to live such a life, a life without accounts, parents, and these Russian situations! I saw Lytton writing on the lawn and out of sheer reverence did not dare disturb him so sent back the dinner three times. Finally cut mine off, and started eating it as I was so hungry. Lytton came laughing in and said 'I have been waiting for you to call me'—and I had thought he was having inspirations and had not dared interrupt him! We roared with laughter most of lunch over it. Minnie was absolutely awed by reverence for the great author! And asked what time he would take tea! I painted most of afternoon. Interesting conversation at tea about Peterloo, Trades Unions, and Cooperation. Lytton has promised to read me the first part of Victoria tonight—I am excited.

To Lytton Strachey

Wednesday [June 18th, 1919]   *The Mill House, Tidmarsh*

Dearest Lytton, You know Sunday was one of the most perfect days! It was Marlow in its beauty. Thank you so much for taking me. Alix went to her home yesterday to stay with her mother a few days. I wish you hadn't to be away in this marvellous weather. I find it hard to believe

[1] The outdoor 'Roman Bath' at the Mill House, Tidmarsh.

that it's as hot, or lovely anywhere as in this garden. I prayed earnestly
for your welfare last night. I hope it wasn't as bad as you anticipated.[1]
I feel the meeting with Shaw may slightly sugar the quinine. Partridge
came over today after breakfast on his bicycle. He has just gone away.
He of course didn't give me any account of your essay club. Partly
perhaps because I didn't ask him. He said you were a great success. But
confessed regret that you didn't like him personally. Will you write me a
detailed account of it? Was Dunlop to your taste?

I fear I shall not see you perhaps on Saturday, as Noel wants me to go
to a Ball with him in the evening which means staying in Oxford the
night. I'll come back Sunday morning as the cock crows eight.
N.B. James proposed himself for the week end with his second wife.[2] As
he will have told you.

Drawing the bud Partridge in my studio was not without its bass
accompaniament this afternoon. It was slightly Russian, like a short
story. He is so naive and young. I felt like some mature hag boosted
up with a complete knowledge of mankind!! All the while Mrs Mason
sang below, and churned her plates, the Mill creaked round and at
intervals the water came crashing into the tank from the pump below.
He is so accomplished, and as smooth as any ebony table. Perhaps
painted black, and upright he would answer better than a door for
Lady T. that really it's rather, in fact, very enjoyable.

But gordie, gordie, when he talks about Oxford and the doings of
those young men, UGH! I see it means a large bed in that cottage at
Marsland if one is to put up with him for a fortnight.[3] And painting all
day long so that one doesn't have to talk.

Tell me about your luncheons, the gossip of Lindisfarne and Bernard [Shaw]. Last night I taught those children to swim in the Bath
before supper. Little Roy was like a frog in one's arms, kicking right and
left with his sturdy legs.

Mrs Legg has tea with Mrs Mason today. Good Heavens, Mason
talked to me last night for a little whilst she was picking gooseberries.
It's too horrible the life of a woman like that. And when she said in a
voice like stone 'I've given up enjoying myself now, or expecting to, I've
been disappointed too often in my life.' And the account of her husband
she gave and her rage, absolute rage against him and her life. Now I
must rush with this to the post.

[1] Lytton was reading a paper on Shakespeare to the Christchurch Essay Club. It is
published in *Books and Characters* (Chatto, 1922).

[2] i.e. Alix Sargant-Florence and not Noel Olivier.

[3] She was planning a holiday at Welcombe with her brother Noel and Partridge.

Lytton every time you come back I love you more. Something new which escaped me before, in you completely surprises me. Do you know when I think of missing a day with you it gives me proper pain inside. I can't help saying this at a risk of boring you.

Goodbye CARRINGTON

To Lytton Strachey

Monday [July 14th, 1919]   *West Mill Cottage, Welcombe, Bude*

Dearest, Twenty times a day I wish you were here! One can't tell ever what would have happened. But I feel now it would have been worth while almost to engage this cottage for three months just on the chance of being able to come with you!

Well you shall know what I've done since Friday. On Saturday we went to shop and bought food. That took most of the morning, walking up and down innumerable valleys. One's memory fails one horribly remembering these depths. Such a lunch at the Bush Inn, Morwenstow, for 1/3, cream, saffron buns, and black-a-berrie jam. Then I went after tea to see the Boxes. On the path down the hill Mrs Box appeared driving the cows; she held up both her arms and waved them, with a stick in one hand. And then ran towards me! It was delightful to see her again. She is still full of vigour and every day she fetches the cows from the marshes by the cottage and takes them back to the farm! And *she* is 72!

Then we called on Jenny and Rebecca Ann. They of course thought the Major the most lovely young man they'd ever seen and inwardly thought what a nice pair we made!

The evening was spent quarrelling vigorously over the war and C.O.s till I became so tired and angry that I gave it up. The night was pleasant but oh dearie, I see God has devised matters so that there can be no pleasures without sorrows in this damned life. I hope for the best. But there is no doubt a teapot and a tube of macaroni aren't very efficient syringes, and that Lysol mixed in equal quantities with water produces great pain. Quoth the Raven Never More. The entire story is too humiliating and Rabelaisian to be written to such an indiscreet old gentleman as you are. So you must wait until we are again hob-nobbing over our winter blaze.

Noel came late on Sunday afternoon. It was such a perfect day. We went and swam in the sea and lay in the hot sun on the rocks. He read me the beginning of Cézanne which I enjoyed enormously. Noel seems very happy and gay. I gathered from his account of a dinner that the Wolves had been playing with him unmercifully. I could hear Virginia plying and probing him with questions. Even *he* seemed a little perturbed by her curiosity! The major remains exactly the same. I'm afraid there's no chance of his ever becoming less dull. His extreme kindness however makes him fairly easy to get on with. This afternoon we took a long walk over Hartland way and missed our tea. Called in on Box who had roasted us a cold fowl and a huge bag of scones and reached the cottage at eight o'ck.

It's been too cold today to paint. A cold wind blows from the sea: up till today it's been baking hot. I hope this isn't going to continue. But it's very warm inside this little cabin and there are a great many blankets, besides a perpetual hotwaterbottle for chilly nights. Did the old sea salt ever roll up upon you? And Anurepina?[1] I await news anxiously. There's no doubt that eventually in our old age we shall both have to come and live here in Cornwall just because the people are so kind and sympathetic.

I wish I had been at the poetry reading of that great poet G.L.S. which took place one evening. And now I wish that when I come back I'd find a new poem to read by him. I've Wordsworth here and Blake and three new wood blocks, so I ought to be happy. We live like Princes with masses of good food and cream every day. And tomorrow we have eel-pie! All the same, all the same, it doesn't prevent one wishing that a certain young gentleman (as Mrs Box called you today) was here with your   MOPSA XXXXX

---

[1] A mountainously tall village woman at Tidmarsh who looked after Lytton.

To Lytton Strachey

Sunday morning [*July 20th, 1919*]   *West Mill Cottage, Welcombe, Bude*

I am sitting down in that little ravine you remember, just before you turn down to the sea. Do you remember the day you sat with me in the sun? Oh—I tried to paint but the wind blew my easel down, so I've been forced to retreat to this little valley. It's baking hot here lying on the greenery out of the wind. And more divinely beautiful with the waters babbling over the grey rocks beneath me, and above the high cliffs great white balloons of clouds racing across a cerulean sky. The young men are trout fishing. So far they have only caught eels! So much to write about. And everything is so distracting. Buzzards, grasshoppers. —One of those birds has just flown down, is now perched on the rock above me. There is *no* bird so grand, and elegant! It looks completely artificial sitting on a great stone under a little cavity in the sun. Which just shows how clever the stuff Bird man is when he puts in natural surroundings in the glass case. Your letter delighted me, oh ever so much. Was there ever such a kind Fakir? It only makes me unhappy a little not to have you here. Then I wanted so much to see Forster. You know you have spoilt me horribly—really it's difficult to put up with such dull conversations day after day. The George weekend alarms *me* also a little. Tell me quickly perhaps you'd rather I didn't come back till Monday, I don't mind a bit if you would rather have him alone. Then is Suggia coming, and Maynard? The Buzzard is simply fast asleep in the sun, standing up too. I am glad Anurpina looks after you so kindly. Do you talk about her lover the fishmonger in the evenings, or do you read E[lizabeth] and E[ssex] to her? [Sixty-eight lines omitted] The major is so sympathetic that if he was only silent I might unbend considerably more to him. I'll be back D.V. on Friday night or Saturday.

To Lytton Strachey

Friday [*August 29th, 1919*]   *Railway Hotel, Oxford*

Dearest, It's awful I've not heard from you once yet, because I left Tidmarsh on Wednesday, and have had no letters forwarded. It seems disconnected, when I can't imagine at any time of the day, a picture of you and what you are doing. [Three lines omitted]

But I seized the opportunity of rushing off on Wednesday morning with Majorio [Partridge] to Cirencester. Brenan met us. I am still baffled by his character. At moments one thinks he's only an energetic talkative Bunny. He seems so vague mentally, and talks about himself and his plans about as persistently. But then unlike Bunny he is much more obstinate, and not in the least influenced by people evidently. He goes to Spain next month with over a ton of books. He had just spent £50 on books in London, and with £150 in his pocket, which he has saved and intends to live by himself in a cottage in the south. His father is a typical crusty retired major, the Irish and Indian combination, who refuses to allow him a penny unless he settles down to a respectable occupation. But Brenan himself is so curiously self centred and detached it's hard to find out very much about him. He liked your book tremendously, E[minent] V[ictorians] and said he would like to come to Tidmarsh before he left England. Do you know you simply must come with me for a walk from Cirencester to Stroud through Lord Bathurst's Park. Never have I seen such Avenues, such terrific trees and little arbours where Pope wrote and some temples of stone in groves of cypresses. Then after one emerges from this enormous forest and Park one comes into amazing valleys, with wooded sides. We went over a wonderful 12 cent. Cotswold House called Daneways which is used as a sort of show house, to exhibit the furniture and iron work made by one Gimson. The house itself had lovely ceilings, and was a feat of architecture and beauty. We walked on to a village called Bisley and spent the night in an excellent little house, very cheap only 10/- for the three of us, with a big supper and breakfast. Brenan insisted on us getting up at six o'ck in order to walk to Chedworth. But as it was pouring gallons, we only got half a mile before we were forced to take refuge in a minute shed with a cart in it, into which we clambered. There we sat till half past eleven! The rain and mist never stopped once! We returned to Bisley and chartered a high stepping dogcart. Brenan went back across the valleys to his home and we drove into Stroud. After lunch of course it came out gloriously hot. On Stroud station I recognized, simply by their features, Brenan's father and young brother. The brother is much more interesting to look at, more sensitive. He goes to Oxford next term. I got on splendidly with the crusty major of course because I praised his Cotswold country which he seemed to think he was personally responsible for. Then we trained to Oxford as the Majorio had

to get his clothes for Spain.[1] In the High I saw Noel on a bicycle, who
had ridden over from the east on the vague chance of meeting us. We
had a great supper and then retreated to our hotel. The major left at
2 o'ck this morning for Liverpool, and to Spain this afternoon. I really
am sorry for him. He seems so unhappy and lost. N.L.C. and I will go
back to Tidmarsh today. Oh to wake up and look at those magic words
in gold: COOPER'S MARMALADE out of my Hotel window. Breakfast
with Noel and the Commercial Travellers. They are surely that which
makes our England, the country that it is. What a sentence, sorry! We
walked over at 9.30 to dear Garsington. As I wanted to see Brett about
the furniture. There they were:—all the troupe with their Queen in
their midst. Toronto [the Canadian poet Frank Prewett] was back
again, looking strangely lovely on a great sienna horse, he and Noel
went off riding together before lunch. I sat in the red room with Mark,
Brett, Julian,[2] and the Frog more or less in complete silence for almost
one hour. Then I had a conversation with Ottoline, which was interesting from a great many points of view. I think Mark's work is very good.
It has improved enormously. The colour is so charming, and delicate
in his landscapes. Ottoline actually asked me, but no, you're such a
traitor you'll tell Charleston and I shall be disgraced. But you may guess
it relates to a barmacide lunch.[3] Ethel Sandys [Sands] turned up after
lunch. So Noel and I beat a retreat to Oxford. Mark and Ottoline walked
half the way with us along the road. Mark related to Noel, I suppose one
of the few people who haven't heard it, the entire history of his life.
Which, strangely, delighted Noel, who was very impressed by him.
Ottoline regaled me with grim stories of Katherine and Murry and our
other mutual friends. She goes off next Monday to Ireland with Minnie
[Ottoline's maid] and Julian. She intends to drive in a gig accompanied
by Minnie alone, to Galway and Donegal. [15 lines omitted]

   I loved your letter. I send you a kiss and all my love. No. I didn't
like Forster's novel very much. It seemed all the time as if it hadn't
quite come off.

Hugs to the Bugger-wug   from XXXX MOPSA

---

[1] Major Partridge was going on a holiday to north Spain.
[2] The Morrell's daughter.
[3] Lytton and Clive Bell used to complain of the insubstantial food offered at Garsington,
here compared with that in the *Arabian Nights*.

To Lytton Strachey

Tuesday night [October 28th, 1919]   *chez Box*

Dearest, We have just come in after a long walk to Hartland Point. The valleys, and cliffs are very lovely past the quay and Hotel, but I still think Speke's Mill valley, and the waterfall, are far the most beautiful. Then we walked back across fields, and through lanes to Stoke, and looked at the church. Then we had tea in a little cottage with three grey tabby cats and an old lady. I heard Saxon murmuring once to one of the cats 'but why aren't you a Christian?' The old lady clearly thought he was mad. We reached Boxina's at 7.30. She gives us beautiful suppers, tartlets, and cream, and tea afterwards. This evening I have been cutting a wood block. I found after the walk today the situation a slight strain. It seems absurd to try and talk to someone who clearly doesn't want to reply, or listen—Yet a silence sometimes for more than [an] hour is difficult. You were right of course as you always are. A gloomy letter from La Major. I think I had better abandon that business. I confess my incompetence to deal with him. But you have no interest in it. It now seems fairly clear that unless Barbara wires to Saxon that she is coming here, he will return with me on Saturday evening. But I think he will probably depart on Sunday. Still I shouldn't pay any attention to it, as it's quite clear everything hinges on Barbara, about the movements of whom he really knows nothing. I confess at this point I look forward to next Monday with raptures! There are masses of sloes on the hedges here so I will bring a big bag full back with me. I found a partridge today in a trap with its leg broken, and bleeding to death. I killed it. But what brutes these people are. Saxon at this point brings out once again the Bradshaw and starts writing to Barbara! If after all this, Saxon-and-me returning on Saturday is fatal to your peace of mind, if you have uttered one groan, it's easy enough to send me a mysterious wire, and I'll import Saxon straight to Banbury and spend the week myself there or at Oxford with Ruth. I rely on your honesty. Dear, I miss you so much. I hope you are keeping well. My love, and I am sorry this letter is so dull, But I am a little tired.

MOPSA XXXX

To Lytton Strachey

Friday [*November 21st, 1919*]   *20 Springfield Road, London*[1]

Dearest Lytton, Pretty grim. Pretty grim. But the good things of London have slightly compensated. A nigger orchestra on Wednesday night. More pleasing visually than orally to me. Yesterday morning was wasted up here. She [Carrington's mother] is impossibly mad and I with difficulty kept my senses till after lunch. Then I called on Alix who was out. Went down Charing X Road, and tried to find a book to send to Noel for Christmas. Without any success. Then I went into the Leicester Galleries. Duncan was there with Maynard. And later Vanessa and Virginia joined us. Do you know I recognized the Arnold Foster from that painting and from Mark! What a horror. Ugh, as you say. I must tell you the Matisses are very good. They vary enormously obviously being relics which he hasn't sold for the last ten years. There was a curious scene, Duncan trying to persuade Maynard to buy a picture. Maynard quibbling between one £500, and one 170 guineas! He admitted he had had a very good day on his telephone.[2] We all set on him finally, and insisted on his buying a lovely little picture of a negligée girl in a chair, very good colour, and much more solid, and carried out than the other paintings. Really I think it was quite the best of all the pictures there. Virginia of course was amazingly witty, creating a great uproar in the heads of the elegant ladies by her observations. Then I cut off and went to Suggia's concert. Coming out to get his tea, I met George [Reeves]. Rongé with disease and spots. Well, well. He shrieked, and asked after you and giggled and shrieked again and vanished. On the platform at the end of the concert he waved his hand. Suggia was superb, and played a lovely Bach Sonata. With the most beautiful gavotte at the end of it. Our Major who of course accompanied me, was completely overcome by her charm. Poor young man. Things might have been so different for him, if only *he* had been a little different.

Then the Spanish Restaurant with our old friends [E. J.] Dent & Co. Then Parade, The Good Humoured Ladies, and Les Sylphides. A perfect programme. The new ballet is very exquisite. I think you will love the tumblers. Iris [Tree] was there with her muff.[3] Henry [Lamb]

---

[1] Carrington's mother had taken a house in London.

[2] i.e. on the stock market.

[3] Iris Tree had married Curtis Moffat.

in the Heights. And many other old friends. I'll be back tomorrow morning to lunch. And then solitude and a house where the female tongue wags no more.

My love to you.   Yr CARRINGTON

To Gerald Brenan

[*November 21st, 1919*]   *20 Springfield Road, London*

[Eighteen lines omitted] I can't discuss Philosophy any more than R.P [artridge] can. So you must have a selection of my days at random after all. First let me say how much I would like to come and make jam for you. Really I think there is quite a chance of persuading Lytton to come out to Spain in March if only he finishes his new book and the faithful R.P. as 'courier' and possibly other companions. Then I might drift down, as they would certainly live in towns, and see you for a little.

You must know I was horribly untruthful to you in London. But it causes one curious pain raking up truths nakedly. Also I didn't know you well enough. But in Spain why should everything not be told? You are rather like me you know, I am sorry to say it. But you lied slightly about la Egyptienne; your assumed indifference. It wasn't an exact revelation. Still I did enjoy those days in London with you. By the way R.P. tells me you put on your accounts £1.8. to my name. Really I am sorry. I will bring you some salt butter, and a pot of marmalade when I come out. I've lived almost entirely at Tidmarsh since I returned from St Malo.[1] I enjoyed that in a way. The country was so exquisite. And the house we lived in amazingly beautiful. I've only been over to Oxford twice. But the young man [Partridge] comes over most weekends to Tidmarsh. He is studying English Literature now. Which of course he finds exciting. I think it's a very good thing for him that he's given up that law. He may get a job as a traveller in foreign books for the Clarendon Press. I like him more than I did. It's difficult not to when anyone is so excessively kind and digs my potato patch and sits for my pictures. [Twenty-one lines omitted] ... tell me about the people you know. And your truthful, *and un*truthful adventures.

You ought to get Virginia Woolf's new novel 'Night and Day'. It's

---

[1] Carrington had stayed with Margaret Waley near St Malo.

very interesting. I will tell you [of] any new books on Psychology which I come across but probably J[ohn] H[ope]-J[ohnstone] will supply all these sort of needs for you.

Still tell me when I can do anything for you. And for god's sake don't go and be reckless, and get ill, or you'll be able to eat no jam.

Lytton asked me to send you his love, last time when I told him I was going to write.

She [Carrington's mother] has started: Discussing my clothes. I am sorry but I see there is nothing for it but to end this distinctly boring and degraded epistle and go to bed. Again, take care of yourself please.

I send my love   Yr CARRINGTON

To Lytton Strachey

Thursday [December 11th, 1919]   *20 Springfield Road, London*

Dearest Old Egotistical HumBuG, So *you've* caught the humility disease? I don't believe it. You're as vainglorious as ever, and just pretend not to be laughing at the young mules who kneel at the foot of the mountain of iniquity. Your letter delighted me so much. And made my mother's horror fade away almost into limbo. Yesterday morning I went to la femme de trunc eternal.[1] She was most charming and forgave me everything instantly. Those houses are lovely in York terrace. They have such a superb view from the back. She must be enormously rich I've come to the conclusion. The sumptuousness of the house was great. The French XVIII style, mixed with Italian and rococo English. Many of the pictures, and objects in themselves were lovely, but the total effect indescribable—! I paint up in her bedroom, warmed [by] four amazing electric bulbs—elongated in full erection on the floor. The trunk really looks rather pleasant now, with sportive youths, and pages with greyhounds in the arches. I had lunch at Canuto's in Baker Street avec nos roi[2] [Rex Partridge]. He was very charming, but you know all that I expect he has written to you. Then back to the old tin box. Till five o'ck. Then a meeting with le Roi again to fix up about the evening. He wanted to take me to a dance, but his mother positively forbids him to bring me to their flat! She doesn't realize how really safe I am, for I

---

[1] See letter to Barbara Bagenal, July 1917, p. 72.

[2] He had not yet been re-named Ralph by Lytton. See Letter to Alix Strachey of April 15th, 1921, p. 173.

positively don't want to marry her cherished lamb. But it's really a relief as I hate being involved with families, and being led into fast deceits. Back to this benighted hole to tell my mother I was going out to dinner with Brett. Really it's incredible the way she treats me. Conversation: D.C. 'I am going out to dinner with Brett' M.C. 'Well that *is* disappointing, And I was having a joint of lamb, *now* I shan't eat it. *You've spoilt* my dinner. And I *was* so looking forward to having an evening with you, and there *was* to have been a sweet omelette for dinner too. Well you *must* be back early. *Have* you got your purse alright, *do* you want some pennies for a bus? I've just had a letter from the agents at Andover.' etc.

The horror of her situation is appalling. But I look the other way and try not to see it. I fear I can't get back till Saturday morning. Literally it's impossible to do anything with her *and* the trunk all day. I suggested R. might go down on Friday to keep you company, and stay the weekend, if nobody is coming, as he doesn't go to Barbara until Monday now. I shall try and come as early as I can on Saturday. There was such a fracas when I suggested going on Friday night. And as it's the last visit for I hope, some months, I gave in.

I shall try and go and see Alix after breakfast this morning for a few minutes. My only consolation out of these wasted days is the thought of a bundle of banknotes from the Duchess of York.[1] Lytton, you give me such a happy life. One day I really hope I shall be an artist, and then you'll see my affection. We went to a concert at Queen's Hall last night, and heard a Beethoven No. 5 which I knew well, so enjoyed. Then we walked vaguely through the streets looking [at] the faces of the whores and jam tartlets in Regent Street. Peered in le Café Royal, but the general spectacle of bloated kippers and their Queens with [Augustus] John like a diseased Fish King in the middle with a white cod faced Chili [Guevara] at his side made me fly. Finally we went into a glittering Lyons in Shaftesbury Avenue, and sipped chocolate. Then back to my mother and your letter. I have risen at 7.30 this morning to write to you! Otherwise it's impossible to be alone, and without conversations about house agents!

Dearest. I send you my love. Si vous plaîts prends mes lettres dans un coin, as I don't like that young man reading all my letters to you!

Goodbye, and take care of yourself   Yrs CARRINGTON

---

[1] Duchess of York because she lived in York Terrace; the owner of the trunk.

To Gerald Brenan

[*December 15th, 1919*]   *The Mill House, Tidmarsh*

Dear Muchacho,[1] I was delighted to get your long letter. It was so full of
variety, as long as a month, with all its varying days. Lytton enjoyed it
too, and now the wretch R.P. has taken it off with him. So you have the
choice of a vague answer, or waiting at least a week before I get hold of
it and write you a proper reply. This much I remember. R.P. says it's
no good sending you skis as they will get broken and also stolen en
route and they are at least 6 foot high. So he recommends you making
some yourself out there!! Typical of this prudent man. He even
enjoined me not to send you a plum pudding because he says it will get
stolen also! But I'll defy him and we shall see. If it vanishes somebody
is the happier. If it's never sent, nothing good can possibly come of it.
The recipes I will copy out tonight, before I close this letter, if I can
find them. Your letter moved me so much. I didn't realize how passionately I love Spain till you conjured up those images of the hills before
we reached Sedella near Burgo. Lytton favours Italy for the spring, and
Scilly [Sicily], but I will if you are still in Spain, do my best to get him to
change his mind, and to come your way with R.P. and I. Oh a great deal
has happened in this Mill since you last set foot in it! What fun to
write a letter which would incriminate everyone, and be a lasting testi-
mony to these strange times and the nakedness of a female's mind. But
I can't. Simply because the world isn't made up of such simple people as we
are. Later perhaps I'll be able to write ALL to you. I find everything so
interesting. But this isn't fair so I won't go on. I've become much
fonder of R.P. He has become so much more charming and has given
up his slightly moral character which used to tire me. So we never
quarrel now, and have become a perfect pair of pigeons in our affections.
I certainly will never love him but I am extremely fond of him—I
believe if one wasn't reserved, and hadn't a sense of 'what is possible'
one could be *very* fond of certainly two or three people at a time.

To know a human being intimately, to feel their affection, to have their
confidences is so absorbing that it's clearly absurd to think one only
has the inclination for one variety. The very contrast of a double relation is fascinating. But the days are too short. And then one has work to

---

[1] *Muchacho*=boy.

do. So one has to abandon some people and the difficulty of choosing
is great. Don't you find it so? Honestly when I get to London, and meet
old loves, and friends I can hardly bear the feeling of being away from
them. Yet when I am here again, with Lytton ... [The rest of this letter
is missing]

Woodcut by Carrington.

1920

To Gerald Brenan

[*January 12th, 1920*]   *The Mill House, Tidmarsh*

Dear Muchacho, A letter for Partridge has just come five minutes ago.
But he is in London, so I impatiently opened it, to know your news. How
sad it all sounds. I am upset by it. I know it all so well. The difficulties
of moving in a house; the expenses and feeling ill. And Malaga with its
Victorias. How that one day we spent in Malaga comes back to me. I had
ten blisters on one foot and six on the other. The agony was exquisite.
The roads hard and hot. Then I was too hot to eat the lunch they gave
us, and the afternoon burnt one's face and made me hungry. Then we
walked along that long road to Velez Malaga. It got darker and darker
and I was so hungry and my feet hurt so I nearly cried. Then all we
could find was a little fishermen's Inn for the night. And the people
were hostile and pressed on us and smelling children crowded round
and still we had to sit waiting for a dinner; 10 o'ck at night, and trying
to be amiable. Then R.P. started wrangling with his sister. Noel became
gloomy and I hoped the end of the world would come, as you did. Never
have I felt quite so wretched as that night. Oh Brenan I wish I could be
out with you to make things better. One can get faint amusement out of
such despairing situations when one has another with one. But I hope
now it's passed, and you are installed with books in your cottage and
happy. I think the lack of money is perhaps more sordidly grim than
anything. I've known it in London, walking from Waterloo to Hampstead because I hadn't a penny. Eating twopenny soup packets, meal after
meal, in a smelling studio in Brompton Rd—and for you, removed even
from the chances of meeting people to lend you money, really it must
have been despairing.

Dear Brenan, I am so sorry about Ball.[1] But you have P[artridge] and I
now, always I hope for friends. I have every hope we shall come out at
the end of March—(only don't tell J. H[ope]-J[ohnstone] as it will be
important that my people don't get suspicious before I leave England—).

Lytton I found this morning in bed, studying a Spanish Grammar.

[1] Reynolds Ball, a friend of Brenan's and of mine, had died of typhus in Poland, while
working for famine relief.

Which I took for a hopeful sign. I shall bring some money for you in case you are very poor. Tonight I've got a vile throat, all thick with horrid blisters and boils inside. It makes me feel rather cheerless but I cannot go to bed for that would upset Lytton. R.P. has been down in Devonshire with his father since last Thursday. Do you mind these vague remarks. Yet I am not wholly material. I should like to know more about your imaginings, and mental travels. Sometimes with Lytton I have amazing conversations. I mean not to do with this world, but about attitudes and states of mind, and the purpose of living. That is what I care for most in him. In the evenings suddenly one soars without corporeal bodies on these planes of thought. And I forget how dull and stupid I am and travel on also. It's rather a responsibility having someone in love with one. One's behaviour becomes so much more important and it ties one to the earth in a curious way. But the interest is enormous. Do you know even at the most intimate moments, I never get the feeling of being submerged in it. I find myself outside, watching also myself and my workings as well as his from the detached point of view. I confess it has made me much happier his affection. For owing to the fact that I deserted almost everyone, except Alix, for Lytton, there were moments when Lytton did not want me, when I recognized the isolation of it all, when one turned in despair for some relation with a mortal to assure one, that one wasn't entirely cut off. Now it is good to tell one's feelings, and feel his fondness at such times. I hope you got the plum pudding I sent. I am slightly doubtful, I had to fill in so many forms and I could only think of 'La Fruita Pan' to express the contents of the parcel. But we'll bring you stores with us in March. Lytton won't walk, so that we can bring baggage. Perhaps you'll meet us at Seville, or Cordova and so have a change of scene. But if we set foot in Spain I promise you we shall see you. I write tonight because I feel too degraded to do anything else; my throat aches worse and worse. The thought of eating is agony. Yet if I don't, Lytton will notice and tomorrow R.P. will be here, and I shall have more than ever to conceal it. Clive Bell and Mrs Hutchinson came here last weekend. They aren't my style. Too elegant and 18 cent. French; for that's what they try and be. I felt my solidity made them dislike me. Then I had to make their beds, and empty chamber pots because our poor cook Mrs Legg can't do everything and that made me hate them, because in order they should talk so elegantly, I couldn't for a whole weekend do any painting and yet they scorned my useful grimy hands. [Twenty-six lines omitted]

My love to you   CARRINGTON

[While Carrington was in London, Lytton had attended a local sale and bought a four-poster bed.]

To Lytton Strachey

Thursday [January 20th, 1920]   *41 Gordon Square, London*

And shall we really find you listening to the birds under the moon, or the morning sun in the Great Four Poster
[*Over the page, from Ralph Partridge*]
What a triumph about the bed. You might of course just leave it in the garden and build the New Wing round it. Tchekhov[1] is all finished now and being taken to the printers to-day. I shall be ready for some typing during the week-end. My love to you   RALPH
[*From Carrington*]
Don't wait dinner on Friday as [Ralph] will not get away in time to catch the six so we'll have dinner before we come down. What a triumph! What a triumph! What a triumphant girl is your   CARRINGTON
Good Mr Auctioneer how I love you.

[1] *The Notebooks of Anton Tchekhov* (The Hogarth Press where R.P. was working) was not published till 1921.

To Lytton Strachey

Tuesday, 10 o'ck [February 10th, 1920]   St Mildred's Hall, Turl Street,
Oxford

'She stitched and stitched until her eyes were red', *Mansfield* never had
she such a joy before neddle upon neddle, reel upon reel, and even in
the dim recesses of time paper she found. Oh tell it not in Gath.
BUTTONS I only hope you secure and some more equally repugnant
to you gifts for me. I see I should have adored that House of Loot. The
button boxes, the minor cabinets the pieces of stuff which 'would have
come in useful.'[1] But I must not torture myself with such tantalizing
thoughts. What a pity you didn't come to that tea party of generalisers
yesterday. It was such a nice one. I liked Michael Davies.[2] He looked
more interesting than the average young man up here. But unhappy and
moody. Perhaps that is just the gloom of finding Barrie one's keeper for
life. Then Russell a cousin of Bertie. He says B.R. has gone back to
Cambridge again. And Neil Little, rather vain-glorious, and a superb
generaliser! But they all agreed that Imperialism was monstrous and we
ought to give up India and felt very fine gentlemen at having discovered
this all in one afternoon over tea. Then a supper with a bottle and a pork
pie—and a dance at 8. No new young men. All rather dreary Etonians.
Perhaps they aren't underneath but it's damned hard work turning the
sods to discover the body. (This is only to be read as a figurative speech!)
Lovely Alan [MacIver] glanced in for a brief moment in the evening,
with a shining wet face after rowing. I thought he looked, again, very
beautiful. I danced most of the evening with our Ralph, and in between
dances we retreated up here and ate cakes and pies and sat over the fire.
The 'missies' were incredibly dull. Really it's difficult to see how
mother nature could with lumps of dough, and a carving knife, have
contrived such heights of perfect dullness in their faces. Lust hid her
face in her orange mantle, and withdrew after the first ten bars of music
and a respectable two headed middle aged muse called 'Healthy and
Jolly' appeared, and sat with us solidly for the evening. One young man
a Jew called Baring discussed Psycho-analysis with me and dreams! but
managed very skilfully to steer off P's and C's! I have lunch with him

---

[1] Lytton had been choosing unwanted articles from a family cottage at Ledbury.
[2] Michael Davies and his brother had been adopted by Sir James Barrie.

today, and a tea party patter with Ralph, at Neil Little's rooms. One
watches lovely red headed, curly headed, striped headed youths gliding
down the street below. How far away! Now we are going to look at the
library, and the Ashmolean till lunch. What a damn'd muggy place this
is. Tidmarsh is a Brighton in comparison. This is also a dull letter, but
that can't be helped. I loved your present. And he was so delighted over
the books, which I am now going to arrange for him. In fact don't you
think the pug dogs might be removed—and perhaps given to Ottoline—
But *did* you notice them? An absurd notice in the Times today on
Duncan saying that the painting of the open window was the best
picture in the show. And even more stupid things about his vagueness
and lack of intention. My love to you dear.   Your MOPSA

To Lytton Strachey

10 o'ck [February 13th, 1920]   In train to Oxford, approaching Bletchley

My Dearest Friend, The pleasure of coming back to you tomorrow
almost makes it worth while going away. Really it is the best possible of
lives in the best possible of worlds—ours at Tidmarsh. And lately it
has seemed happier each day. I am now in a slow crawling microbe
moving towards Oxford. Yesterday morning was simply Milton in its
fairness. Ralph loved your Cambridge, and confessed he found it
more sympathetic than Oxford! I saw your Willow Tree by Kings
Bridge and thought of you. He was full of appreciation over Trinity. It
certainly looked its very best with the willow pale green, and so new, and
the sun shining cleanly on the pinkish stone library. But there wasn't
really time to linger and many colleges, and gates we never saw, as his
train went at 4 o'ck. I went in after seeing him off at the station and saw
Sheppard. There were two young men there, [T. H.] Marshall,[1] and
[Patrick] Blackett.[2] The former looked rather intelligent and dominating.
Mr Blackett an uncouth Bedalian perhaps, shy creature. Sheppard is
producing the White Devil on the 9th March. Don't you think you, and
your children might have a prolonged birthday treat and go there for it?
After the beauty of the music, and the songs had faded from my mind, I
reviewed the Fairy Queen less enthusiastically in bed yesterday morning.

[1] Elder brother of Frances Marshall.
[2] Later president of the Royal Society.

The scenery was really rather unpleasant, arty, and all pale purple and green like some Suffrage tea-room. But I forgive even the most mincing young lady because of the loveliness of that music. Sheppard was delighted because the Newnham Authorities have forbidden the young ladies to act in Webster, so that the female parts can now all be taken by the young men! The young men I thought however, didn't show the same enthusiasm at the abolition. Fredegond[1] [Shove] came in yesterday evening. And was very entertaining. Full of whimsical bawdy and scandal. And gave me an amazing description of Virginia and Vanessa when they were young. James, I gather, isn't going there for the Fairy Queen as he remains in Paris. And Alix alone has returned. So shall I write a review for the Athenaeum instead? Ralph is incredibly happy to have shaken off those Oxford Eight people finally.[2] It was a dreadful scene, when that enthusiastic blue came into his rooms and appealed to his sporting honour and vanity. I really thought he was very good the way he politely but with great firmness stuck to his lie and got out of it. Sheppard sent you his love. I thought he seemed rather subdued and worn.

I will get the food for the week end as I come through Pangbourne. And I've sent a P.C. to Saunders ordering some chunks of beef and fisherie. And we will be back very early tomorrow.   Yr loving MOPSA

[Late in March 1920 Lytton with Ralph Partridge and Carrington set off for Portugal and Spain. They took a boat to Lisbon and proceeded by train to Seville, Cordoba and Granada.

From there they made a most exhausting journey by motor-bus, horse carriage and mule to Yegen, the tiny mountain village where Gerald Brenan had leased the upper floors of a beautiful house. The journey took three days. On the last day they were travelling for twelve hours and Lytton was exhausted. To add to their troubles Partridge and Carrington were constantly bickering and Brenan was dismayed by what he had let himself in for.]

---

[1] Fredegond, cousin of Vanessa Bell and Virginia Woolf, married Gerald Shove.
[2] Ralph Partridge had refused to train for the Oxford and Cambridge boat race.

To Gerald Brenan

Sunday [April 18th, 1920]   *Hotel Terminus, Madrid*

Dear Geraldo, At last I have time to write you a letter, so warm of
thanks that your fingers would get burnt, if you knew how much I loved
the Yegen life, those four days. I shall always look back on them as some
of the best visionary days I have ever spent. And in a curious way so
interesting, combining so many delights of which your company was
one of the greatest. It's strange but I feel like apologising because I feel
I didn't 'show up' very well. I was rather tired, and anxious, and selfish.
I am afraid you didn't enjoy our visit as much as we did. I shall I
promise you, if it is possible, come out with our dear R.P. next September, in a different frame of mind armed with pots and paints, and no
griefs. But you will keep well till then? And eat properly. I know it's a
dreadful nuisance, but truly you know you weren't looking very well
in spite of your red face and you shouldn't get boils on your feet in good
health. Please take care of yourself. It would be such a pity if you were
to get weak; or lose a foot! What a nice ride that was from Berja in the
motor bus. One road really seemed to me an illustration of Russell's
theory of infinity. And the driver drove like one possessed. But that
village we changed at :- I forget the name with the nice market place
with arches? Delighted me very much. I should have liked to have
lingered there longer. Almeria itself was very much to my taste.
Sailors, ships, barrels of Malaga wine, and a market, full of coloured
humanity, eggs and oranges; a good town for painting in. Then a
splendid train ride to Granada with tremendous mountains, the back
side of your great range with groves of vines, and cave dwellings. And
the vastest of blue grey mountains with cruel hard profiles and as
desolate as grave yards. We saw one amazing town from the train called
Guadix, with a whole settlement of cave dwellers. We didn't reach the
blasted Granada till nearly 10 o'ck. And spent the next morning in those
good gardens of the Generalife. Then caught a train at 1.30 and
reached the Gardens of the Aranjuez at 6.30 after rather a grim night
lying on the orange be-peeled floor of a third [class] carriage. We, by
greater cunning managed to get in the Gardens at 7 o'ck and spent two
lovely hours wandering under plane trees, and through lilac groves before
the dew and rain had dried. The air was full of good smells and not a soul

in the gardens. We caught a train at 9.30 and reached Toledo at about 12 o'ck. The Hotels are ruinous at Toledo otherwise it is a perfect city. I think we saw every El Greco that it was possible to see and most of the town. El Greco filled me with such amazement, that I can think of nothing else. The beauty of the death of the knight in that church. I agree with you in thinking the composition of the upper part magnificent. We also saw very fine ones in St Vincent's church and a portrait of a cardinal in a convent outside the central city. This morning we spent in the Prado. Almost too much to see: Goya, El Greco, and Velasquez. One gets torn literally inside. Tomorrow we go to the Escorial, and then on Wednesday I shall see the Prado again. These pictures make me want to give up everything and become an artist entirely. The importance of their work seems above everything else. How El Greco sweated with agony over each picture one feels. He never attacked anything that was not as hard as granite to hew. I cannot bear to think of leaving these pictures.

R.P. I think is enjoying himself. I was sorry you saw his sorrow. I wanted our visit to be entirely happy with you. But it is a great thing that the beauty of your landscape, and your life sent us all away purified from cares.

Your honey still graces our breakfasts. And your figs are yet with us. It was such a good time. Thank you so much. I send my love.

Yr CARRINGTON

To Gerald Brenan

Started on May 5th, 1920   *The Mill House, Tidmarsh*

Dearest Gerald, At last I am back in this valley of green grass, and a wilderness of weeds. How much has happened since I left you. But what a difference it makes writing to you now, when I know the face of the postman who will leave your letter (this very letter at the door), and *your* library. I believe if you were to cross-examine me when I was 80, I should remember every detail of Yegen and your kitchen! So much did I love even the smallest details. What shall I tell you of first? But please be very lenient to my shortcomings as a writer. I've even a greater respect now than I had before I came to see you, for your character, therefore I'd like to please you with my letters, since I can no longer charm your stomach with delicacies. (PS By the way was that a good marmalade pie I made you.) First perhaps you'd like to hear about J. H[ope]-J[ohnstone] which is going backwards as that's the most recent event almost. I went and visited him last Saturday at 6.30. First of all I shall tell you how much I liked him. That I completely withdraw any statement I made about him being affected. And also a statement I thought, but didn't make, that he didn't sufficiently appreciate you, or your friendship. Gerald, I really think he'll come out in September for a month! I pleaded so eloquently and described the beauties of Yegen with so great incoherence and confusion at the same time with much feeling that I believe he will go to you in September. The great drawback was his finance but finally I told him that he could easily earn his keep with his flute playing in inns and on streets and really the whole journey could with *his* economy be done for £20. (N.B. R.P. upheld this when I discussed it later.) I went then at 6.15 and stayed till after 11 o'ck talking about you, and Spain and listening to his flute.

He has probably written a contrary letter telling how I bored him, but that doesn't matter. I shall visit him again soon in case his practical business nature sees some reasons for not going in September! In fact I shall, like an inopportune widow give him no rest, till he sets sail in despair. Oh Gerald I wish you were here, such afflictions have fallen upon us. And Ralph would give a good deal I think to have you with him. There is nothing new. It is only he is very unhappy which makes me in despair also. And as far as I can see there is no solution. It seems appalling that in this world when one gets on with so few people, when one does care for someone as much as I do for him, and he does me, one must part because of these difficulties. It is impossible to go on being perpetually unhappy and worried which is what he is doing now. Yet I know, even if I did not think of myself, to marry him, would not make it any better. Because one cannot change a spirit inside one. And it is that he cannot possess. But I will not burden you with all this. I think it is aggravated by his being at Oxford, with no real interests to occupy his time when he is away from me.

Lytton came back to Tidmarsh yesterday. We spent the evening reading poetry. But it was rather depressing because one missed Ralph and I cannot bear to know such good people are miserable.

Friday
I write now in a train to Oxford.

It's delightful being back at Tidmarsh. We have a new housekeeper which is rather tiresome. But otherwise the joy, after so much travelling and beastly Hotels, and finally LONDON, of waking up in that big bedroom and seeing the sun outside shining on the grass and to hear cuckoos in the fields beyond is very great. The beginning of this sentence is so removed that I've underlined it. It appears that the root of all my diseases: throats and colds—is a defective nose. I went to a specialist in London, who discovered I had bent the cartilage in the centre, and that until it was straight I would never get better. So next week I have to go into a hospital in LONDON and have it cut out. I confess I am not looking forward to it. As it will make one rather weak and also increase, and ruin, my already too large nose. But if it really does rid me of these infernal throats I shall not complain. I betrayed you to J[ohn] H[ope]-J[ohnstone] and told him you were not well and didn't eat proper food, so he will shortly write you a lecture. Which perhaps you'll pay more attention to than you do to mine. Lytton will write to you soon. He loved Yegen so much you know. It was a pity he got so tired at the beginning of the visit. But in spite of that he said he would be always glad he undertook, for him, such an amazing experience.

Do you know sometimes I almost feel like flying with my paint boxes and leaving all these complications and simply changing my life and settling at Yegen. But I suppose it would [be] fantastic! From the train now I can see the Wantage downs and the tops of those woods where we picnicked last summer. [The rest of this letter is missing]

To Lytton Strachey

2 o'ck [*May 7th, 1920*]   *St Mildred's Hall, Oxford*

My Dearest Lytton, He [Partridge] has just gone off to row. He is *quite* happy again. I just teased him about being unhappy, and behaving so badly, and he was charming, and didn't talk about it any more and said: 'Do you know for a moment I was so cross, that I nearly kept Lytton here last night, as I didn't want him to go. And I wanted for a moment to make you suffer because I was cross with you. But then when I thought how you would miss him not coming I let him go. Because I wanted after all to make you happy.' I am going up to Ruth [Selby-Bigge] whilst he rows this afternoon and we dine with them tonight. Dear one, I dare not say it hardly. But I think it may come alright. He is so friendly. And

7 Lady Strachey (Lytton Strachey's mother), November 1920. Now in the National Gallery of Scotland, Edinburgh (see letter on page 170)

8 Mrs Box of Welcombe, *c.* 1919. See letters of July 14th and 20th, 1919

quite happy and talking about Tidmarsh and you. I think yesterday must
have been a pent up outburst. Oh I am so sorry you were so unhappy.
I think it best to stay here the weekend. I will come back early on Monday.
I only hope James will come and that you won't get depressed. Everything today seems to have disappeared. I expect that in spite of everything you said, you really comforted him a great deal. I have every hope
by next week we will have him back at Tidmarsh. Will you accept my
insurance on it? For—thirty pounds?

Please dear, will you burn this letter? As he reads everything he can
find when he comes to Tidmarsh. And we will remember these days
without reminders.

I want to buy either a little fox, or a snake which I saw in an arcade
this morning.

Would you mind a little dear fox?

I am just going to send you a wire and go up to Ruth's. I thank you so
much.   Yr most loving CARRINGTON

To Lytton Strachey

Saturday, 6 o'ck [May 8th, 1920]   *St Mildred's Hall, Oxford*

Dearest Lytton, I was so glad of your letter this morning. [One line
omitted] My dear one, all is for the best, not a trace of unhappiness in
him today. I think you must be responsible for it because he is so happy
now and never refers to anything, or makes those announcements about
the future. We had tea with Ruth yesterday and then went a long walk
in the country. And talked about things. But he was perfectly calm, and
happy. I told him that I wanted him to realize when I gave you affection
it didn't rob him of any, and that one ought not to give affection to him,
at the expense of making other people unhappy. When really one had so
much love inside and enough to give to so many people. (But it's
impossible to explain now in this letter.) I think he saw how fond I was
of him and that it was important to concentrate on the happiness we
had, instead of all the time aiming for something we hadn't. [Three
lines omitted] And coming back across the fields by Marston at seven
o'ck he said shyly 'Do you know I thought it might be rather nice to go
to Tidmarsh this weekend perhaps', 'or even if we can't this weekend
perhaps next week.' I could have cried for pleasure at hearing him say it.
But as he had to row this evening till 7 o'ck, and as your letter said you

had asked someone else and Ottoline had asked us out tomorrow, I thought it might be better for him to come over one day next week. But it's such a great relief to have him as he used to be, perfectly happy, and so charming all day long. [Thirty lines omitted] I shall bring you back a little surprise on Monday.

Lytton screams 'A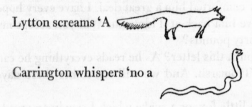

Carrington whispers 'no a

Yr most loving CARRINGTON

To Lytton Strachey

[*May 21st, 1920*]   *Royal Free Hospital, London*

Dearest Lytton, I was never more delighted than yesterday when the door opened and an elderly spruce bearded gentleman entered. Now today I wonder if he really did come:—or was it a vision. [Twenty-eight lines omitted] Side view I look rather like this [illustration omitted]. I can't believe I shall ever look the beauty I did before! [Five lines omitted] But it was so kind of you to come yesterday. And I loved seeing you so much. Give Ottoline my love.

Yr most loving MOPSA

To Lytton Strachey

Saturday morning, 7.30 [*May 22nd, 1920*] *Royal Free Hospital, London*

Very dear Lytton, I am feeling much better today but I've not been allowed to get up yet. Unfortunately one has now perceived the routine of the day so that it seems longer and with fewer hopes and surprises than it did before. Noel[1] was allowed in yesterday, and Margaret [Waley] so I was well off. Then dear Alix sent me a big bag of fruit,

---

[1] Noel Olivier. She was a qualified doctor.

marmalade, oh Alix! Golden shred! That was not worthy of your
epicurean mind! blackberry jelly, and two novels by Forster. I read
Howards End all yesterday and finished it. Really I shall insist on an
explanation from Forster. Why must Leonard fall down dead with the
books on top of him? And the grimness of his men and women. I think
perhaps they get too grim even for him and that is why he kills them
off. Does he really live with such horrid creatures at Weymouth,[1] or is
it because he's deaf, and imagines the world like his books. Let us
shout together at him at Tidmarsh and tell him nobody really ever gets
killed. But of course our cats do. I forgot black Agrippa is to be drowned
this very Sunday with innocent child in his black arms. But we could
keep that from Forster. Really I felt quite upset last night about it. I find
the worst feature now is I get such headaches in the back of my head
always lying on a pillow. I dare not complain, as I don't think soft
pillows in the sense we understand soft, exist in this Hospital. Today
I've got the other disease so I am more complacent lying in bed. I am
thinking over everything very seriously and when I get back I'll give
you six ultimatums and then off with your head! Like the King I sit on
horseback reviewing my past life and the future. Today I decided it was
a very happy one and mostly, can you guess why, because of a friend I
have? And you'll be going off to Oxford very soon and sporting yourself, perhaps in white flannels, and a Trinity blazer, along the tow path
arm in arm with Alan. I suspect you [of] the vilest vanities when my
back's turned!

The nosey is recovering its shape to my infinite relief. But do you
know I weighed myself this morning and I was only 8 stone 8 lbs.
Which pleases me. It looks as if it will be divinely fine this weekend at
Oxford, I am glad. Write me a letter from Garsington dear, as I gather
from a remark I overheard, my escape will be more like Wednesday
morning than Tuesday. Give Ottoline my love please. Soon the news-
paper-girl will come in which is the one excitement of the morning for
me. It's awful to think of whirligigs and fun, and fields of buttercups in
the sun (but I will spare you a poem entitled 'Whitsun in a Hospital'
which I will send to Gerald instead) going on this weekend. Perhaps
they aren't as nice as I imagine. I suppose there are fishmongers on the
merry go rounds who would spit [down] one's neck, and pugs in the
buttercup fields that Brown the Brown [bread and] Butter. And really I
suppose young men aren't as nice as one imagines they are, lying in a

---

[1] E. M. Forster was living at Weybridge.

sage green ward. Positively my heart leapt up to see a man in trowsers yesterday enter the ward, although he was a miserable spotty doctor. But to think of a world of females as one lives in here, chills the blood. I think I shall draw today. I see rather good compositions lying in bed of white nurses and bedclothes, and green green walls. I wish I could have seen Virginia. Did you tell her how sorry I was it couldn't be arranged? How nice it is to think of the summer coming, and no more cold and rain. But of course you are hardly the person to write that to! I am much happier today and feel ever so much better. But what a long time it seems since Thursday. My first sneeze has just taken place. Very extraordinary sensation!

Now goodbye and my dear one   Yr MOPSA

To Lytton Strachey

Friday, 12 o'ck [September 3rd, 1920]   *The Mill House, Tidmarsh*

Don't leave my letters lying about. It may be childish but I rather hate those grown up people knowing how much I care for my

Dearest Lytton, Such a busy morning, one of those grand clearance mornings that I love. Wilfully destroying vast masses of horrors. No nothing of yours, only pollypusses. A telegram from Ralph to say he hasn't got the car so I expect we'll spend a quiet weekend here. It's so hot now. Blazing. No really, and no mists, just because my Dear one has gone away. I've invited the Nashes over for the weekend rather vaguely. His wife is attractive, German. It's a pity we haven't a piano she plays so well. But I hardly think somehow they will come. All this decision business has upset me. I feel rather unhinged by it. I hate so much (a) to be responsible, and make any decision in any direction (b) perhaps even more to hurt a human being and make anyone unhappy. It seems wrong that with a surplus of affections for so many human beings that there can't be combined happiness for more than two people at a time. But I shall leave it now, and see how things work out. Do you know how extraordinarily happy that conversation you had with me on Wednesday evening has made me? I care so much. I hope you'll get really rested down in Sussex and quite forget that old Hag Victoria. I wish I could be with you in spirit, sitting invisibly by the fire tonight watching you talk, and listening to all the fun. Perhaps I shall be there, so you had better be careful. No, really it's lovely here now so hot that one can sit with pleasure out of doors and birds chirping, just because you've gone away. What a damned cynic this old clerk of the weather must be. How I miss you already. The last few days were such good ones.

Did you hear anything of Doggie[1] and his fair Inez. Please write to me Driftway, Middle Wallop, Nr Stockbridge, Wilts.[2] Oh Hell. I wish there was no such place on the map. Lytton dear, do you know what comfort you are to me. I feel as long as you live on this earth I can never mind anything.   Yr most loving MOPSA

[Carrington was doubtful whether to agree to go and live for an experimental period with Ralph Partridge at 41 Gordon Square. Her letter brought the following reply from Lytton:]

September 4th, 1920   *Charleston, Firle, Sussex*

My dearest, I am sure that all is really well between us, which is the great thing. Some devil of embarrassment chokes me sometimes, and prevents me expressing what I feel. You have made me so happy during the last 3 years, and you have created Tidmarsh, as no one else could have—and I seem hardly to have said thank you. But you must believe that I value you and your love more than I can ever say. It seems to me that your trying the G. Square experiment is probably right. But whatever happens you must rely on my affection.

Let me hear from you again. I am writing this on my bed in an attic. I send you a great deal of love—and won't leave your letters about!

[He was staying with the Bells and describes how Maynard Keynes had been converted to the idea of summer time and had insisted on adopting it: so all the clocks were an hour fast. 'Vanessa is too feeble to put him down, and Clive too tetchy to grin and bear it. Luckily the atmosphere is entirely comic instead of being fundamentally tragic as in Tchekhoff. Everyone laughs and screams and passes on.']

[1] James Doggart.
[2] Carrington's mother had gone to live there.

To Lytton Strachey

[*October 25th, 1920*]   *41 Gordon Square, London*

My Dearest Lytton, I feel dreadfully depressed now, installed high up in this gloomy grey Square. The beauty of that walk made me long to be in the country again. To sit on the edge of the river and paint those barns against the red stained woods. But all these thoughts are backsliding—and Bull of Bashanish. I love the smell of fallen poplar leaves and the loveliness of the coloured trees and Tidmarsh so passionately: I can't write what I feel. Because I cannot trust you to tear up my letters, and Ralph will read them. Will you burn this one? I won't write another one ever again like it. Perhaps you thought I didn't care leaving you this morning, and when you told me you were depressed last week and had not written Victoria, that I did not mind. Oh God. *You* said the middle of the week would go so quickly, but the weekends, they go quicker far. And I saw so little of you ... Yet I must try honestly to forget now that I have given my promise to stay here with him. Perhaps in a few weeks I will either numb some senses or realize I cannot bear it. He is so good to me. He tries to make me happy. But I have to hide my pain, which makes it harder. For I do miss you so frightfully. Promise this, dear to me, if you feel it matters to you, my being away, if you feel ill, and worried to write and tell me ... I shall not tell you this again, because if he knew it would only make him wretched so please directly you have read this *burn it in the fire*. It is just an omission [?admission] that I feel I must make to you, and that it can be the secret of an afternoon between us ... The secret of my grief at leaving—. Next weekend we will talk a little together. You will tell me how you feel. Oh wasn't it a wonderful talk this morning. I see you now crawling under the fence on your hands and knees like a mild red bear in spectacles, in the orange leaves.[1]

You mustn't think I am not happy here. It's only I had to tell you and you alone, how much I cared. Oh Lytton, why should it be so difficult? Write to me, but say nothing of this.

My dear one goodbye. This week I will come on Friday afternoon. Tell me if the Dog [James Doggart] is coming.

Yr most loving CARRINGTON

---

[1] So that they could be alone together.

To Lytton Strachey

Tuesday [*November 2nd, 1920*]

Dearest Lytton, What a perfect day! The sun even penetrates old London, and now shines in my window. What a number of curious things seem to have happened since yesterday. Perhaps just as many have happened to you! Hope-Johnstone arrived to tea yesterday with an invitation to a party at his studio in the evening. He is a regular kiosk of gossip. Roger's [Fry] success in Paris, intrigues, and rumours. But I dislike him, and his methods. Nothing he tells one seems genuine. I think he is a very affected bore. I suspect he has qualities which he only shows Gerald. I can't believe Gerald would tolerate him as he is in London. Ralph was very cheerful, and worked away for Leonard. At eight o'ck we went into Karin's [Stephen]. We started at once discussing psycho-analysis and the topic never varied once! Ralph got on very well with them. Adrian is certainly less grim than he used to be. Whether it's the result of psycho-analysis or not I don't know. They both swear Mr Glover (the doctor who anylises them PS I have a complex about spelling this word) has improved their characters enormously, their memories, and spirits. I almost believed them. They have rather nice rooms. Also an early Duncan which interested me, of boys on horse back, a decorative painting in monochrome. I quite enjoyed the evening, a good deal of wild gossip passed, concerning the mad and the semi-mad.

Then at 10.30, after we had dressed up, Ralph in a blue French blouse and his cords looking very charming, your Mopsa in blue silk pyjama trousers, and a frock affaire on top with a shawl, we went to J.H.-J. How it brought back another world! These familiar Bohemian figures. Some new ones, but mostly acting the traditional parts. John very drunk, lurching about like a cossack in Petruschka, from woman to woman. Two Bohemian Fitzroy artists playing guitars and pipes in the corner, a mêlée of dancing people, little syphilitic harlots from the Café Royal, with faces like chewed india rubber, when you looked at them closely. [Lillian] Shelley, a little older but much the same.

She sang some strange songs and recited some moving blood curdling romantic poems, during the evening. Dorelia like some Sibyl sitting in a corner with a Basque cap on her head and her cloak swept round her in great folds, smiling mysteriously, talking to everyone, unperturbed

watching the dancers. I wondered what went on in her head. I fell very
much in love with her. She was so amazingly beautiful. It's something
to have seen such a vision as she looked last night. And 'How is Strachey?
Is Victoria nearly finished? Tell him I really will come and see him in
the country ... yes quite soon ... I'll bring some food with me ...'
Then a mysterious smile. Ralph also fell in love with her. But was too
shy to approach the Deity. Then Sylvia Gough completely drunk
looking more vicious that it is possible to conceive. Dancing recklessly with her thin loose legs flying like a marionette figure in every direction. A great many revolting Café Royal girls, who made one almost sick.
A group of dingy artists from Fitzroy Street who looked like road
sweepers. Evan Morgan, who I saw in an interval whilst Shelley was
singing, eyeing Ralph. Chili [Alvaro Guevara] who actually, so Ralph said,
accosted him! A very perfect tart of a young man who you would have
loved, very slim, one of those fair semi-Greek Henryesque faces, but
probably riddled with disease. He came with Lords Berners and Chili.
We danced all the time, and quite enjoyed it. I had some very entertaining
dialogues with John, who was like some old salt in his transparent drunk-
enness.

'I say old chap will you come away with me.'
DC But you know what they call that?
'Oh I forgot you were a boy.'
DC Well don't forget it or you'll get 2 years hard.
'I say are you insinuating', drawing himself up and flashing his
eyes in mock indignation, 'That I am a Bugger.'
DC My brother is the chief inspector of Scotland Yard
'Oh I'm not afraid of him.' But in a whisper. 'Will you come to
Spain with me? I'd love to go to Spain with *you*'.
DC This year, next year, sometime.
John 'Never.' Then we both laughed in a roar together.

Ralph was very entertained. He hadn't met John before. We left
with the musicians, who packed up their instruments, at 1.30. Some more
horrid upper class whores came in and I saw it would become a vast
party of slobbers, and as I was tired, I hardly thought it worth while to
linger. I thought we had what little cream there was off the top of the
jug.

This morning we got up un peu tard. A parcel of woollens from my
demented mother which I am wearing now. Then a journey to Birrell
and Garnett to get some addresses of book shops. I was looking in the
shelves whilst Frankie [Birrell] and Ralph were talking shop. Suddenly I

smelt something very vile, turned round to discover the armchair in
flames. Frankie suddenly saw it, looked very surprised, and just gave it a
kick or two expecting it to go out. In the end I had to smother it with
gloved hands. The cover was completely ruined, and most of the chair
burnt.[1] What a character Frankie is! Then glory be to God R.P. went
down to Hendersons and managed to sell 125 copies of the Hogarth
productions! He was wildly delighted, as it was his first venture into a
bookshop as a pedlar.

Would you like 2 vols of memoirs of Marguerite de Valois from B.
and Garnett's shop as a little present? They were rather charming
books. I am just going to tea with Faith [Henderson] today, and later to
Brett's for dinner.

To Lytton Strachey

November 24th, 1920   *41 Gordon Square, London*

Dearest Lytton, A properly dated letter! I hope you are keeping well,
and that *Victoria* goes well also. [Eight lines omitted] Alan [MacIver] gave
us a super dinner at the Café Royal upstairs. Really when the food is so
good and rich I unfortunately always feel rather sick. I suppose it's a protest from the outraged brown bread and marmalade at seeing strangers
enter their sacred Halls! But I like cocktails very much; of that I am
certain. Also ices with different layers, and nuts on the top. Afterwards
we went to what is called a musical comedy at a theatre in Drury Lane.
It was interesting. The herd instinct of the sham-upper-class audiences
and the tendency of modern humour. A young man called Leslie
Henson was the chief actor in the play. He was a very skilful combination of George Robey, little Tich, and almost every comedian on the
Musical Halls, including Charlie Chaplin. In painting, such a wilful
'crib' of artists, blatantly mixed up on a canvas would produce an out-
cry. I don't think anyone notices the lack of originality in a comedian.
There was one French actor in the play. And it was amazing the difference. He only had the part of a waiter.

But the point he gave to his acting, the completeness of it, was

---

[1] This happened *twice* owing to Frankie's leaving a lighted pipe in an armchair. On
the second occasion he was sitting in it when a passer-by observed flames through the
window and raised the alarm.

astonishing. It was a play adapted from the French. One saw the indecent situations, the indecent suggestions, and yet they had so covered
it up, that all South Kensington could watch without a blush. Really I do
think the English are appalling stupid to laugh at such jokes and
applaud such hideous vulgar scenes. This morning I went at eleven o'ck
to paint Her Ladyship [Lytton's mother]. She is superb. It's rather
stupid to tell *you* this. But I was completely overcome by her grandeur,
and wit. I am painting her against the bookcase sitting full length in a
chair, in a wonderful robe which goes into great El Greco folds. It is
lined with orange. So the effect is a very sombre picture with a black
dress, and mottled cloak, and then brilliant orange edges down the front
of her dress. She looks like the Queen of China, or one of El Greco's
Inquisitors. Pippa was superb. For, do you know, when they heard I had
captured her as a model, Roger, Duncan, and Vanessa then stormed the
castle, and asked her to sit for them. Pippa valiantly pleaded that as I
had asked first I must be allowed to paint her first, and alone. They had
suggested my joining them in a quartet! It's all very well for a nude
model as a back is as good as a front. But I didn't like the idea of painting her Ladyship back view in a confusion of easels and conversation!
[Eighteen lines omitted]

Gerald [Brenan] wrote me such a long letter on Monday. I am still
trying to digest it. I wish he wouldn't write a letter continuously for
two weeks as its volume quite overpowers one when it does arrive! Six
pages were devoted to you, and a criticism of your work. And I thought
Gerald showed remarkable intelligence in his remarks. But as he has
asked me not to show it to you I don't very well think I can. There was
one remark however which Ralph must have found difficult to swallow.

'As to his being a master of English prose there is no possible
question. Gibbon cuts a small figure beside him, in spite of the greater
"weight" of the Decline.'

I will bring you, however, the letter and his poems to read next
weekend. [Ten lines omitted] I cannot but help being lonely without
seeing you, and I feel so often perhaps you miss me, and that you aren't
comfortable. Victoria matters so much to me. That['s] what Ralph doesn't
feel. The importance above everything [that] a work of art, and a creator
of such works, has for me. And yet do you know, this morning I felt
these conflicting emotions are destroying my purpose for painting.
That perhaps that feeling which I have had ever since I came to London
years ago now, that I am not strong enough to live in this world of
people, and paint, is a feeling which has complete truth in it. And yet

when I envision leaving you and going like Gerald into isolation, I feel I should be so wretched that I should never have the spirit to work. But this must sound childish to you. Did you ever see in the hall of Bunny's house [the bookshop in Taviton Street] a picture belonging to Miss Bulley, of a groom with a horse and a dog? It is a terrific masterpiece, belonging to that late 18th cent. school of English sign painters. Dearest be happy till I come back. And write to me sometimes.

Yr loving CARRINGTON

To Lytton Strachey

[December 1920]   *41 Gordon Square, London*

If you'd like to lunch chez moi, will you come? You might telephone about 11.30 or leave a line so that I can tell the hags. Otherwise Ralph will meet us, if he can, at a quarter past three, at the 1917 Club, to proceed afterwards to Mark's show. But what a day to see pictures! What a soup to live in!

and cold soup too!

Last night I dreamt of Queen Victoria!   DC

1921

To Lytton Strachey

[*January 3rd, 1921*]   *41 Gordon Square, London*

Dearest Lytton, Yesterday I went with Brett to the Burlington Fine
Arts and saw, what I still even on cool reflection, think the best picture
I ever have seen. By Piero di Cosimo—a picture completely of wild
animals, and the most beautiful birds, in a landscape of bushes, and a
distant sea. I shall go again tomorrow to amaze over it. Really in these
famished days of pleasure, it was a joy to see such a picture. You I am
sure will adore it also. Afterwards we went to the New English. It was
too awful and depressing to describe. Even Chili's pictures were a disgrace. Brett spent the entire day with me. In the evening we both drew
Ralph. Brett was so excited however, that she said she couldn't draw
properly!

Thursday

Yesterday Barbara arrived at lunch time very delighted to be back in
London. In the afternoon we talked, and at six o'ck Faith and Hubert
[Henderson] came in to see Barbara, and a few minutes later Leonard
[Woolf]. Then we had the greatest of dinner parties. Virginia clothed
in gold brocade and scarlet as an Eastern Prince. Looking very beautiful
and tremendously gay, and lively. Saxon, Leonard, and us three. Mrs
Sneddon produced a four course dinner, ending with an additional
course of cheese straws! Then at 9 o'ck we went to the party at Bunny's
shop.[1] The Anreps came, and a young lady of Bunny's from the floor
above.[2] And Oliver and Inez. Most of the company spent the time reading books from the shelves! And discussing business, and printing. After
the Wolves left, we danced, listened to the gramophone, and played
hunt the slipper, which old Anrep and Ralph enjoyed naturally, pinch-
ing the ladies' legs looking for the shoe. On the whole I think it went off

---

[1] Then on the ground floor of 19 Taviton Street, Gordon Square.
[2] Ray Marshall, Frances Marshall's elder sister, later Mrs David Garnett.

alright and Barbara enjoyed it very much. Now I must go to the post as I am going to paint Margaret Waley at 11 o'ck.

[From Ralph Partridge]
Thank you so much for the shaving implements. Ralph sends you his love, and thanks.   RALPH

I will come down on Friday evening. Barbara, Saxon and Ralph are coming down on Saturday. No more news.

[From Ralph Partridge]
Have to dance among the fishes on Friday—will be down as early on Sat. as I can. Fond love R. D.C. has broken my nose. SHAME.

To Alix Strachey

April 15th, 1921   *The Mill House, Tidmarsh*

At last I've an evening completely to myself, dearest Alix, so I'll commemorate it with a letter to you. The Major and Lytton both went back to London this morning and left me here alone. I started a still-life yesterday of tulips, and I was so pleased with it that I stay here alone to finish it. After *all* London's a slight fraud! Lytton is now on the crest of his wave and lunches and dines with the shipowner's wife 'Maud' [Cunard] and Chelsea pseudo aristocracy, daily. So I hardly ever see him except in the evenings when he totters into 41, almost dead with exhaustion and high society. Partridge, christian-named Ralph now, is on the crest of the Woolf's back, or the Hogarth [Press] wave. They have just produced Tchekhov's note-books which are very masterly and amusing. Short stories of the East by Leonard ... which I've not and never will read although wood cut cover by yours humbly. R[alph] P[artridge] is so busy tying up these books and typewriting that I get rather merged into it and find it interrupts my painting. Also my enthusiasm for tying up books was rather curbed as all the parcels I did tie up were returned to Leonard disintegrated in a pulpy mass. I heard rumours that the Woolf growling was fearsome, so I hid from his wrath. [Forty-three lines omitted]
Lytton's 'Victoria' has been a great success in every periodical and paper in England and Scotland. Even the 'Times' and 'Daily Mail'

bow before him! Many say it can't be so good as E[minent] V[ictorians] to receive this adulation. But it is I think, much better. His fortune will soon be immense, if a revolution does not come and cut short his life. For he is definitely joining the Upper Classes I regret to say. He's charming to me. I think he is walking on air for the moment and can't be disagreeable!! Last Tuesday he hired a private motor and took Ralph and me to Hampton Court. It was fun whirling through London, pretending to be one of the idle rich. Hampton Court is an amazing place. I much prefer it to Versailles. I think it is probably the greatest achievement of architecture in England. The colour is so remarkable.

We had lunch in an inn over-lapping the river, and then motored back to London, dropping the private secretary at the Woolves' Lair on the way back. I've never been to see your mother yet. I think I won't until you come back. I am so frightened of becoming drawn into her colour scheming.[1]

You might spend part of your summer when you return at Tidmarsh, it's neither as bad as [word illegible] or Gordon Square, and we now boast of a cellar containing rare port and wines and Tiptree jams. Write to me again soon. Did I tell you at Easter Bunny and Mrs Bunny turned up here for one day on a walk they were making to Goring. She is— Heavens, what a face. What a character DOUR and SILENT. No one can understand it. R.P. thought her breasts rather attractive but that was all he could see in her favour. Perhaps Bunny is losing his eyesight, as well as his wits. Francis [Birrell] is distinctly cut up about it and weeps on one's neck whenever one goes to the shop. [Twenty-six lines omitted]

I have hopes of going to Italy with Lytton, but I see the finances are rather black for me. Lytton goes on the 7 May to La Berenson in Florence for 2 weeks. Then, D.V., I may go out with R.P. and Pippa and join him. But it's rather vague as R.P. may not escape from the Wolves. [Six lines omitted]

My love dear one,   Yr CARRINGTON
PS My beautiful friend Phyllis [Boyd] is shortly to marry a French Vicomte [de Janzé], a farmer in Normandy.

[1] Mrs Sargant-Florence held eccentric views on music and painting.

To Lytton Strachey

Saturday morning, 12 o'ck [May 14th, 1921] The Mill House, Tidmarsh

My dearest Lytton, There is a great deal to say and I feel very incompetent to write it today. Last night I composed a great many letters to you, almost till three in the morning. I then wrote an imaginary letter and bared my very soul to you. This morning I don't feel so intimate. *You* mayn't value my pent up feelings and a tearful letter. *I* rather object to them not being properly received and left about. Well there was more of a crisis than I thought when I wrote to you on Thursday. Ralph had one of his break downs and completely collapsed. He threw himself in the Woolves' arms and asked their sympathy and advice. Leonard and Virginia both said it was hopeless for him to go on as he was, that he must either marry me, or leave me completely. He came down to Reading yesterday and met me at the Coffee tea shop. He looked dreadfully ill and his mouth twitched. I'd really made my mind up some time ago that if it came to the ultimate point, I would give in. Only typically I preferred to defer it indefinitely and avoid it if possible. You see I knew there was nothing really to hope for from you—Well ever since the beginning. Then Alix told me last spring what you told James. That you were slightly terrified of my becoming dependent on you, and a permanent limpet and other things. I didn't tell you, because after all, it is no use having scenes. But you must know Ralph repeated every word you once told him in bed; that night when we were all three together. The next day we went for a walk on the Swindon downs. Perhaps you remember. I shall never forget that spot of ground, just outside Chiseldon, at the foot of the downs, when he repeated every word you had said. He told me of course because he was jealous and wanted to hurt me. But it altered things, because ever after that I had a terror of being physically on your nerves and revolting you. I never came again to your bedroom. Why am I raking all this up now? Only to tell you that all these years I have known all along that my life with you was limited. I could never hope for it to become permanent. After all Lytton, you are the only person who I have ever had an all absorbing passion for. I shall never have another. I couldn't now. I had one of the most self abasing loves that a person can have. You could throw me into transports of happiness and dash me into deluges of tears and despair, all by a few words. But these aren't reproaches. For after all it's getting on for 6 years since I first met you at Asheham; and that's a long time to be happy. And I know we shall always be friends now until I die. Of course these years of Tidmarsh when we were quite alone will always be the happiest I ever spent. And I've such a store of good things which I've saved up, that I feel I could never be lonely again now. Still it's too much of a strain to be quite alone here waiting to see you or craning my nose and eyes out of the top window at 41 Gordon Square to see if you are coming down the street, when I know we'll be better friends, if you aren't haunted by the idea that I am sitting depressed in some corner of the world waiting for your footstep. It's slightly mythical of course. I can pull myself together if I want to and I am more aware than you think, the moment I am getting on your nerves and when I am not wanted. I saw the relief you felt at Ralph taking me away, so to speak, off your hands. I think he'll make me happier, than I should be entirely by myself and it certainly prevents me becoming morbid about you. And as Ralph said last night you'll never leave us. Because in spite of our dullnesses, nobody loves you nearly as much as we do. So in the café in that vile city of Reading, I said I'd marry him. And now he's written to his father and told him. After all I don't believe it will make much difference and to see him so happy is a rather definite thing. I'd probably never marry anyone else and I doubt if a kinder creature exists on this earth. Last night in bed he told me everything Virginia and Leonard had told him. Again a conversation you had with them was repeated to me. Ralph was so happy he didn't hear me gasp and as it was dark he didn't see the tears run down my cheeks. Virginia told him that you had told them you didn't intend to come to Tidmarsh much after Italy and you were nervous lest I'd feel I had a sort of claim on you if I lived with [you] for a long time, ten years and that they all wondered how you could have stood me so long and how on earth we lived together alone here, as I didn't understand a word of literature and we had nothing in common intellectually or physically. That was wrong. For nobody I think could have loved the Ballades, Donne, and Macaulay's Essays and best of all, Lytton's Essays, as much as I. Virginia then told him that she thought I was still in love with you. Ralph asked me if I was. I said I didn't think perhaps I was as much as I used to be. So now I shall never tell *you* I do care again. It goes after today somewhere deep down inside me and I'll not resurrect it to hurt either, you, or Ralph. Never again. He knows I am not in love with him. But he feels my affections are great enough to make him happy if I live with him. I cried last night Lytton, whilst he slept by my side sleeping happily. I cried to think of a savage cynical fate which had made it impossible for my love ever to be used by you. You never knew, or never will know the very big and devastating love I had for you. How I adored every hair, every curl on your beard. How I devoured you whilst you read to me at night. How I loved the smell of your face in your sponge.[1] Then the ivory skin on your hands, your voice, and your hat when I saw it coming along the top of the garden wall from my window. Say you will remember it, that it wasn't all lost and that you'll forgive me for this out burst, and always be my friend. Just thinking of you now makes me cry so I can't see this paper, and yet so happy that the next moment I am calm. I shall be with you in Italy in two weeks, how lovely that will be. And this summer we shall all be very happy together. Please never show this letter to anyone. Ralph is such a dear, I don't feel I'll ever regret marrying him. Though I never will change my maiden name that I have kept so long—so you mayn't ever call me anything but Carrington.

I am not going to tell my mother till the day before, so she can't make a fuss, or come up to London. I think we'll probably get united by Saint Pancras next Saturday and then drift over to Paris and see Valentine [Dobrée]. If my Fiend comes on I'll linger there for 2 days and then Italie. I've suggested Mousie and her Dan coming here for the month. And I hope I'll coerce them into it. Then we won't have to worry about the garden and the dampnesses. Nick and Barbara are still here, and this weekend Saxon, and Alan [MacIver] and Michael [Davies] come this evening. We'll pay off all the books before we leave. Now I must leave you, and paint the other side of the grey hound.[2]

Later.

Nick has just mown the lawn and it is now as smooth and short as a field of green plush.

All the ducks and chickens survive and Ralph spends his time lying in the sun on the lawn trying to persuade them to swim in a pan of water. I thought you had been clever to escape the thunder storms and rains, but today the heat is more wonderful than anything in your land of the Romans. Saxon is an extraordinary character!! I am telling no one what I've told you. It will remain a confession to a priest in a box in an Italian church. I saw in a London Group catalogue a picture by Walter Taylor called 'Reading Lytton Strachey's Victoria'—such is fame. I shall do a

---

[1] In an earlier letter she had asked him to leave it behind.

[2] Carrington was painting an inn sign for the Greyhound. See letter to Noel Carrington of July 15th, 1921, p. 188.

still life of a dozen Victoria's arranged in a phalanx for the next London Group. My dear I am sorry to leave you. I'll write again tomorrow. It's such a comfort having you to talk to.

My love for a dear one   Yr CARRINGTON

3 o'ck Saturday,
PS I've just read this letter again. You mustn't think I was hurt by hearing what you said to Virginia and Leonard and *that* made me cry. For I'd faced that long ago with Alix in the first years of my love for you. You gave me a much longer life than I ever deserved or hoped for and I love you for it terribly. I only cried last night at realising I never could have my Moon, that some times I must pain you, and often bore you. You who I would have given the world to have made happier than any person could be, to give you all you wanted. But dearest, this isn't a break in our affections. I'll always care as much, only now it will never burden you and we'll never discuss it again, as there will be nothing to discuss. I see I've told you very little of what I feel. But I keep on crying, if I stop and think about you. Outside the sun is baking and they all chatter, and laugh. It's cynical, this world in its opposites. Once you said to me, that Wednesday afternoon in the sitting room, you loved me as a friend. Could you tell it to me again?

                                                              Yrs CARRINGTON

To Lytton Strachey

Thursday, May 19th, 1921 Driftway, Middle Wallop, Stockbridge, Hants

Dearest Lytton, I am staying down here for two days before we whisk over to Paris. My mother bore the shock very well, and is fortunately making no fuss over it. So little fuss indeed one is apt to think perhaps she has known all along my wicked ways! She is mercifully not coming up to London which is a great relief. Dear, I've had it on my conscience that I wrote you rather a horrid letter last Sunday from Tidmarsh, but I was rather 'beside' myself, as they say. I hardly saw, or knew what I was writing. Now I am quite happy again and calm and I love my Lytton. Ralph is such a dear and somehow so childishly happy that I don't feel it's a plunge in any direction. In fact I suspect it will make practically no difference. Ralph is coming down here today to be inspected. Then we'll glide off tomorrow to London, have a joy day looking at Max's

[Beerbohm] pictures (I see they charge 5/- entrance today! Private view was yesterday.) The nameless show and in the evening 'Bulldog Drummond' with Alan, and Marjorie [Strachey]. Saturday 10 o'ck St Pancras' Registered altar, then your 11 o'ck train, and Paris. I have asked Valentine to get me rooms at her hotel, and perhaps will stay till Monday before we move on to Italy. I believe I feel all these proceedings very little because I am so excited about ITALY! It's almost too exciting sometimes, and already I am depressed about coming back, and the end of the month being up! It's wonderful to be in Wiltshire again, and see the downs and the juniper bushes, and the rings of beech trees on the tops of the hills. The cuckoos are cuckooing to despair almost. Bees buzz in the garden which is full of big poppies, and flags. Italy will have to be in fine trim to equal the beauty of Middle Wallop. So tell her to muster up her birds and flowers to greet Queen Mopsa next week. I've just been reading the History of Vanessa and Swift and their letters.

I didn't know it was like that. It touched me strangely. How lovable was Vanessa, rather like Alix I thought. On Tuesday evening we went into 51 G[ordon] S[quare] after dinner, and talked to the [Strachey] family. Simon and Janie [Bussy] were there, the latter I thought very attractive. Marjorie was in one of her most hectic moods. Rae [Oliver Strachey's wife] was there also and her ladyship. We played bridge afterwards, and gossiped with Rae, and Marjorie. I had an awful time over my passport signing 'D. Partridge' on every line, and making a thousand mistakes. I got Noel Olivier to sign for me as she is a doctor. She thought Mrs P. was an excellent joke and fairly roared over it! I didn't tell her it was nearly or would soon be a grim truth. Unfortunately in her merriment she signed it wrong so I had to forge her name. Which may yet land me in jail instead of in Paris! But I trust they'll not discover it. I am bringing my spy glasses, an air cushion, and a camera, and a drawing book. C'est tout. Here's a little blue flower for you. I'll write if I can tomorrow.

Dearest Lytton, love me always as much as you do now and I'll be happy.   Yr CARRINGTON

To Lytton Strachey

Friday, May 20th, 1921   *41 Gordon Square, London*

Dearest Lytton, Your letters have all arrived. They are such a joy to us.
Everything is so happy now and Ralph is charming. So you mustn't be
worried about your children. We start tomorrow evening. There has
been a bloody hitch about the passports, or rather mine. Noel Olivier
like an idiot, went and signed her married name on my passport, when
she is registered as a doctor under the name of Olivier. So it was refused.
We then had a fearful hunt to find anyone, Monty was out of London,
my brother in law out, my bank shut, so in the end, we dashed off to
Charlie Sanger. He was simply charming and so kind he melted me
completely. The Americans will try and get them visaed by 1 o'ck
tomorrow but it means we miss the 11 o'ck train and won't get off till
the evening, isn't it infuriating? Still we try and bear up. But to wait a
whole day in London is too stupid. Then I don't think we'll leave Paris
until Monday as I have a Fiend on Sunday, D.V. Then 2 days' journey
to Pisa. We'll send you a post card to Venice from Pisa and say when we
shall join you. I am so very happy dear. I am glad you thought of Tidmarsh so affectionately. But sorry Florence has not been more pleasant.
We saw Max's picture of you today, and thought it not very good.
We had dreadful news in the paper this morning. It is too awful.
Michael [Davies] was drowned yesterday, with Noel Buxton's nephew,
in Sandford Pool outside Oxford. It was only last weekend he was at
Tidmarsh. We both feel dreadfully upset. He was so lovable and
rather a rare character and enjoyed his life so much. It's cast rather a
cloud over us today. Alan comes up tonight and we go out with
Marjorie.

I saw her ladyship this morning and took her some flowers from
Wiltshire. She seemed very well and gay.

We are taking very little, as if it's not too hot we shall walk.

You can't think how happy your letters made us both. You really
never will realise how much we both in our separate ways love you.
[Seven lines omitted] My love dear and Ralph's xxxxxx CARRINGTON
[*From Ralph Partridge*]
Ever so happy now.   RALPH

To Gerald Brenan

May 21st, 1921

Next Saturday morning at 10 o'ck at St Pancras's shrine I shall change
my beloved name of Carrington to a less noble one of Partridge. You
smile and say 'how are the stiff-necked fallen', 'where are her grand
principles!' They are *still* here, young man, locked in my Amazon
breast. 'I never will change my maiden name that I have kept so long',
rings a good song. To you I shall ever be Carrington *and* to myself. I
sent you some books as a present did you ever get them? And I sent
your letter to Lytton to Italy. Oh, I am very glad you think so highly of
E[minent] V[ictorians]. Lytton has not received such high praise, as
that, from anyone. No one comes to the occasion, except Lytton's wild
Russian sister Marjorie and MacIver, Ralph's friend. And we then leave
for Paris [one line omitted] two days, and then go to Italy, and join
Lytton in Venice. Do you feel it is desertion? No, it is not, truly. It was
decided so suddenly and I wanted to see the Giotto frescoes in Assisi
and Ravenna and then Lytton gave us both tickets to go to Italy as a
present! That alone made it possible. Isn't he a proper friend? I wish
badly you could be with us. Then it would be perfect. Ralph was given
a month's holiday as a gift from his worthy employer. Do not hurry
with your letter. but send it to c/o Thomas Cook, Venice, Italy, as soon
as you can. Is this an action of folly? It hardly seems 'an action' at
present, only something which means nothing to me, but apparently
something to him. Does going to Italy count? May I have one small good
mark. We shall not be dull, and I will climb the Apennines. I will join
your society, if you think me worthy. I am going to send you a little
money only a few little Spanish notes as a present. You will see why I do
it, and why they are so few. No I fear you'll destroy the Irish paper, if
you have it back and I still believe I can get it printed. And then like
Shelley I will distribute it from the tops of the buses. But I forgot I was
telling you news, *not* answering your letter. The reason? Ralph was very
unhappy, and said if I didn't, he couldn't bear it.—He is too good a
man for a little wretch like me to make unhappy.

Besides I had inward reasons. A devil, a plague to destroy inside me,
he will help in the destruction. And he makes me very happy and helps
me bear the brunt of this tiresome world. It won't make any difference,
for we'll not 'set up' in a house with a neat maid in black and white and

have napkin rings. We'll live at the good Mill and keep a little room in Gordon Square and always a bed for Geraldo. He is so charming, such a good companion, I couldn't have married anyone else, unless perhaps ... But you shall never know that perhaps. G.B. Perhaps? or perhaps not!

You were right. The hint has soaked in, one should not treat nature as 'a little habit'. It should occur at rare intervals, when it forces itself on us and not be reduced to terms of the weather. 'The weather is very hot here now' or cold, or wet. Yet I tell you, that this Wiltshire air is echoing with cuckoos' whistles. They give the air, a sense of great perspective.

I hear them almost as far as Salisbury which is ten miles away, and west to Selborne. I am so sorry the neuralgia plagues you, I will send you some excellent flat tablets for the same, 3 of which hurt no man or woman. I read Vanessa's letters to Swift. It almost makes me weep. I understand it so well. Dear Geraldo never cease to remember I am still your friend Carrington, and you can rely on my help if ever you want it.

My love to you, D.C.

[While in Italy she continued writing to Gerald Brenan and a long letter contains the following:

'Now I've read your letter again to the bitter end. Ralph nearly always seizes my letters so if you wish to write a particularly passionate one put a red stamp on the outside upside down, then the faithless wife can conceal it before he reads it.'

Carrington's letter of May 14th took six days to reach Lytton. He replied as follows:]

Lytton Strachey to Carrington

Friday night, May 20th, 1921   *I Tatti, Settignano, Florence*

My dearest and best, Pippa [Lytton's sister] came this evening with your letter of last Saturday. She was rather a long time on the journey, so it took more time to come than it need have, and now I'm afraid that this may not be able to reach England before you start—in which case you might not get it till you reached Venice, and in the interval be uncertain as to what I was thinking. So I am sending you a wire tomorrow morning

to ask you to let me have your Paris address, in order that I may send
this there. I hope by this time you will have had my other letters—
though I am afraid they may have seemed a little inadequate—I was
writing more or less in the dark. But I hope that in any case you never
doubted of my love for you. Do you know how difficult I find it to
express my feelings either in letters or talk? It is sometimes terrible—
and I don't understand why it should be so; and sometimes it seems to
me that you underrate what I feel. You realise that I have varying moods,
but my fundamental feelings you perhaps don't realise so well. Probably
it is my fault. It is perhaps much easier to show one's peevishness than
one's affection and admiration! Oh my dear, do you really want me to
tell you that I love you as a friend!—But of course that is absurd, and
you *do* know very well that I love you as something more than a friend,
you angelic creature, whose goodness to me has made me happy for
years, and whose presence in my life has been, and always will be, one
of the most important things in it. Your letter made me cry, I feel a poor
old miserable creature, and I may have brought more unhappiness to
you than anything else. I only pray that it is not so, and that my love
for you, even though it is not what you desire, may make our relationship a blessing to you—as it has been to me.

Remember that I too have never had my moon! We are all helpless in
these things—dreadfully helpless. I am lonely and I am all too truly
growing old, and if there was a chance that your decision meant that I
should somehow or other lose you, I don't think I could bear it. You
and Ralph and our life at Tidmarsh are what I care for most in the
world—almost (apart from my work and some few people) the *only*
things I care for. It would be horrible if that were to vanish. You must
not believe, too readily, repeated conversations. I think that possibly
some bitterness of disappointment makes you tend to exaggerate the
black side of what you're told. I cannot be certain—but I think you
exaggerate. Certainly, I thought it was generally agreed that one didn't
believe quite everything that came through Virginia! As for the physical
part, I really think you exaggerate that too. I find that in those things I
differ curiously at different times, and what I said to Ralph on that
occasion I can't remember, and I think it may have been a passing
phase.

Perhaps all this isn't very important; but you seemed in your letter
to suggest that my love for you has diminished as time has gone on: that
is not so. I am sure it has increased. It is true that the first excitement,
which I always (and I suppose most people) have at the beginning of an

affair, has gone off; but something much deeper has grown up instead.

So far as I can judge, I believe you are right, and that if Ralph wants marriage it is best for you and for him that it should be so. But I hope that (apart from his happiness) it *won't* make much difference to anybody! I do so long to see you and talk to you both. I don't quite understand how you propose to get married so quickly—I thought that sort of abrupt business was hideously expensive. But perhaps the father Partridge will stump up! It is infuriating to hear no details. Well, at any rate, I hope you will get off to Paris, and have an enchanting holiday. That wretch Ralph has not written me a word! What is to be done with him?

It continues to be pretty dreary here, but on Monday Pippa and I depart for Siena, which will be a great relief—especially if by that time the weather takes it into its head to clear up. Thunder and oppression continue day after day. The visit to the Sitwell Castle of Monteguffone was most entertaining—a truly astounding place—but too much for me to describe now—it is fearfully late, and I am dropping.

Oh! My dearest dear, I send you so very much love! I feel happier now that I have written, and I hope what I have written will seem as it should be to you. There is much more to say, but that must be for talking.

Give my love and kisses to the wretch.   From your own LYTTON

Sunday morning
Your wire has just come, and I am sending this to Pippa, as I calculate that it will get there before you. Go and look at Byron's palazzo there on the Arno—where he wrote some of Don Juan—and I think you will like the Campo Santo etc. and the whole dead town. Pippa and I leave here tomorrow, probably for Bologna—then, via Ravenna, to Venice.

                                                   Much love from LYTTON
PS If you wrote to Poste Restante, Ravenna, we should probably be there in about a week.

HONEYMOON

[In a pencil diary Carrington has recorded her movements from May 21st, 1921, when she married Ralph Partridge, until June 6th, when they set off to Venice and met Lytton.

They spent two days in Paris and then took the train, reaching Siena in the evening. They stayed some days and made an excursion to

San Gimignano, and after returning to Siena left by train for Perugia. There 'We got rather drunk and had one of our brawls, I suspect in loud voices!'

Later things went better as they set off on long walks, climbing a mountain on June 2nd. 'A young huntsman with a gun joined us, he was going to shoot wolves which live in the woods on the mountains. A charming young man with a handsome face and merry eyes. Half way up he carried my pack which was a relief as it [was] rather heavy climbing. Ate cherries on the way at halts. At 11 o'clock we were over the highest top of the mountain 4500 feet high. After showing us the way he left us ... Had a superb lunch under some beech bushes. Radishes, an omelette with ham, chocolate to drink, bread and butter and honey, cherries. Walked on. Discovered I had lost my gold ring. Rather a cloud on the day. It was to my taste narrow, and plain.'

They spent three days walking and climbing from Tuscany into the Romagna, picnicking, arriving late in mountain villages and finding beds with difficulty and it is clear that they were happy together. Ralph was an ideal companion for such an adventure.]

To Lytton Strachey

Tuesday, 4.30 [June 28th, 1921]   *The Mill House, Tidmarsh*

Here you are. I hope you will receive it in time.
Dearest Lytton, What a silly a certain lion was to leave this pretty Mill this morning! The sun is shining particularly warmly today and the garden abounds in delights.

You know I love you very much. That letter made me so happy. So happy, that I must just tell you once more, that I shall never, never desert you and always be   Your loving CARRINGTON

To Lytton Strachey

Thursday [July 13th, 1921]   *The Mill House, Tidmarsh*

Dearest Lytoff, I sent you a dismal postcard this morning.—I mean a dismal picture, but I rushed down in my pyjamas before the postman came and it was the only card I could see 'lying about.'

We reached the Woolfs rather late for tea but of course they are so charming they never really mind and the tea was delicious. Really Virginia does make heavenly jams. Then, after tea, Leonard went for a walk over the downs with Ralph, and Virginia and I trailed behind gossiping and croaking. Mary [Hutchinson], you and your writing (of which I knew nothing), Vanessa and Mary, Ralph and THE SITUATION, the merits of Rodmell against Asheham, composed our conversation. I came back filled with enthusiasm for Virginia. It's impossible not to fall in love with her I find. She was so friendly to me I couldn't help collapsing completely. Dinner. Then a sogjourn—which I know is spelt wrong but I can't make it look better—to the summer house. Leonard very grave after a terrible silence. 'Well I think we had better perhaps discuss the Situation.'[1] Then he started. Really he is superb: so logical, fair, and intelligent. Then Virginia gave her point of view. Then Ralph rather tentatively returned the fire. And I summed up the proceedings at the tail end of everything. Ralph is writing to you and will talk it all over when we meet again. Leonard and Virginia will also talk it over. So I will not now repeat it. We slept like logs on the Rockeries but I doubt if *your* back bone will hold out! Really Tidmarsh is the Carlton in its comforts. Why do we ever fuss? The next day Wednesday was divine wasn't it? So lovely at Rodmell I longed to stay on. It was terrible to have to leave. Leonard gave us masses of apples and pears to take back with us. We spent most of the morning picking pears for him at the top of a ladder. Then we raced off before lunch as La grand Loup et fille[2] were appearing in fact did appear at a quarter to one? to John's [Selby-Bigge] at Chiddingly. We found him and Vincent seul about to eat a lunch of chops and treacle tart. So in we swooped like buzzards and ate exactly half of all they had. We saw their vast chicken farm. They get 300 dozen eggs every week and have over 3,000 hens! John obviously has a genius for carpentering and building. Vincent looked very romantic and beautiful but curiously vague and detached. They rather revive my enthusiasm for building a new wing at Tidmarsh! They have, in 2 months, built a long wing to their house and really it's very good. One long big room and a big bedroom facing south, with a huge fireplace. John looked very well and was most friendly. He couldn't ask us to stay as Ruth was at Kingston and there was only one maid in the place. We went over to Kingston at 3 o'ck and saw Ruth just for one hour. Ralph

---

[1] i.e. whether Ralph Partridge should continue to work at the Hogarth Press.
[2] Leonard Woolf's mother and sister.

was captured by Sir Amherst S.-Bigge and spend a solid hour walking round the garden with him whilst I chattered to Ruth. Then we left and started back home at 4 o'ck. We had a lovely run across new country to Guildford and reached Tidmarsh and an omelette at 8 o'ck. Will you tell us dear if Wittering is possible? I say, Chisenbury Priory is for sale again in today's Times!!! Do let's go and see it one day soon. Lytton dear, I love you so much today. We talked for a long time over the fire last night and a great deal about you. I feel much happier today. Ralph is so fond of you and Tidmarsh. Bless you my dearest one. I hope the good weather will go on, and that you will enjoy Rodmell. It's perfect here today. This morning Mrs Wright united two families of bees with great success. I wasn't stung and I had no glove on one hand.

I wish dreadfully you were here just because it's so warm and beautiful.   Your loving MOPSA

Two sweet ducks passed away today; one will soon fly to Rodmell. The other we feast off tomorrow. I send the only letters. The others I'll forward to Rodmell.

To Noel Carrington

Sunday [July 15th, 1921]   *The Mill House, Tidmarsh*

Dearest Noel, As this elegant figure below, which some old gentlemen at St Pancras tell me is my husband, clad in a familiar and dirty pair of white shorts and a rowing vest is writing you a letter by my side I feel I cannot do less than imitate his excellent Sunday example.

But what can I tell you? Life is happy. The sun is as hot as India now in England. R.P. works hard now all day at the Hogarth Press and returns ravenous and wolfish at 7 o'ck for his evening meal. Lytton comes down every weekend and often Oliver and Inez and sometimes good people like Brenan, who is back from Spain on a holiday and various friends. Tidmarsh is still a communal nest for breakers of the law so the Partridges escape having a home to ask in-laws to stay in and refrain from silver teapots and cradles.

I've become signboard painter to the county of Berkshire. I've done and finished one signboard for the Tidmarsh Inn and now I've three other commissions given me on the strength of it. If the Brewery will stump up £10 a sign I'll be content to be their painter for the rest of my life, and when you come back my humble efforts will greet your eye at every pub you tarry at! I will do the Phoenix bookplate and one for you very soon, tell Cumberledge. Tidmarsh is so lovely this summer, full of charming animals, geese, ducks and hens and a yellow cat and such good company. We have a gramophone now and it [is] really getting quite a vast library as Lytton is becoming reckless with his wealth in buying books. [Fourteen lines omitted]

I had one long day on those Wantage Downs alone with Brenan a week ago, very near where we three spent a day with Brenan just before you set off to India. It is baking hot and we cooked our lunch under a beechwood and basked on the downs and talked about Spain and people we knew. I think you must get out at Gib. on your way back from India and we'll meet you and then go and stay with Gerald in his cottage in the mountains.

You know of course mother has left and sold Driftway ... [Twenty-four lines omitted] It's good to think you'll be with us in the spring and the daffodils.   Your loving sister D.C.

[After the picnic alone with Carrington described in the foregoing letter and a visit to Tidmarsh, Gerald Brenan fell violently in love with Carrington.

He had planned to leave for Spain but delayed his departure.]

To Gerald Brenan

Friday morning, 8 o'ck [August 5th, 1921]   41 Gordon Square, London

It's just eight o'ck and I have packed up my clothes and look out on a grey sky with plane trees waving, and lurching in a cold wind. I've rather a hollow sort of feeling inside about going away for the Lakes. Already I see the rain, uncomfortable wicker chairs, a linoleum table-cloth and discomforts on every side—and I am so sorry to leave you.

But perhaps it wouldn't have gone on being so very happy if we had lingered! Thank you again for the Clare, and the Ingres although at the same time I must reprove you severely. Grrrr. One day in Yegen with nothing but some dry peas to eat, like the unfortunate Mr Blanco last night, you will realize the wisdom of my reproval. And God won't send pages of Clare and Ingres disguised as an omelette from the clouds. But how very perfect it is that we have with so little restraint been able to understand, to a hair's breadth, our fondness for each other.

Please keep very well in Yegen, and don't get ill or I shall worry.

If you ever did and wanted someone, if J.H.-J. doesn't go out, you must always wire, R.P. and I would come at once. Please remember this.

This letter is dull, and explains nothing but how can one write? I think you know that the discovery of a person, of an affection, of a new emotion, is to me next to my painting, the greatest thing I care about. I shall think of you very often dear. Please say nothing in your letters. I shall know in spite of their nothingness. G-rrrrrrrrrr 'how difficult life is.' Yet G-rrrrrrrrrr how exceedingly and excessively happy the same life can be.

You've not got the camera! I'll leave it wrapt up and addressed to you on the hall at 41 G.S. Please call for it today, or some day, and do go and see Birrell. A chemist photographer will explain the camera to you.

My love my very dear one. Goodbye till the spring.   D.C.

[While Lytton, James Strachey, and Carrington settled in for their holiday at Watendlath Farm, Cumberland, Ralph Partridge visited his friends the MacIvers who lived a few miles away.]

To Gerald Brenan

Sunday [August 7th, 1921]   *c/o Mrs Wilson, Watendlath Farm,*
                                               nr Keswick, Cumberland

Well, two days have past, as the postman only calls once a day for letters, and as my letter is seldom ready when he does call I will start one now to you, with an exquisite fountainpen belonging to Alix and try and get it finished by tomorrow afternoon. A scene of our sitting room in the farm house. Our daily life is dominated by Mr Wordsworth as we call the amiable stuffed ram who is attached to the wall above the window.

Lytton sits muffled in overcoats reading 'Family Life' by C.F. Benson looking infinitely depressed, Alix plays chess with an invisible James, who has crept out of the picture. They take twenty minutes over every move, and never speak, and I sit as you see at the corner of the table. It is black night outside and rains. On my right twenty photograph frames face me, north country rustics in their hideous Sunday clothes.

The two most cherished relatives have mats of sheep's wool to perch upon. They really deserve a still life or a sonnet to themselves. I would like to, if I could, write a novel introducing these twenty human beings, with their portraits, as they appeared in my novel. Still Mr Wordsworth glares down on me with his glassy yellow eye and moth eaten countenance. Yesterday I went a long walk with Lytton, some 10 miles, before supper.

Alix and James arrived at 8.30 in the evening. It's delightful to have
Alix with me again. I love her very much. She is so unlike other women,
so impersonal more like a man. This morning we went a walk by ourselves to Rosthwaite, and talked of everything that had happened since
we parted last September. They give one the most stupendous meals
here. So big that I've ruined my digestion with sheer greed ... [Remain-
der of letter omitted]

[Ralph joined them and shortly afterwards Brenan arrived. Carrington
painted his portrait in a barn and they made surreptitious love while
Ralph spent his time fishing.

The strain however became too much and Carrington asked Gerald
to leave.]

To Gerald Brenan

August 25th, 1921

His sunburnt face all wet with rain
Was laid upon the bracken brown,
(Yet why was our love all tinged with pain?)
He said he loved my grass green gown
Yet it was grey, I still persist.
We peered out from the open door
And watched for one in rain and mist,
Then threw back on our bracken floor
Hugging and tossing as before.
The yew tree barn I guess is there
An empty bottle in the wall,
The bracken still smells sweet and rare
The river crashes down the fall.
But where can I find his streaked wet hair,
Oh where can I press a hot cheek bare,
Oh could I have you Love with me,
Just once again at our green yew tree
I should NOT peer out from an open door
For that phantom cross the rainy moor

[Drawing omitted] Goodbye. This letter is without interest. But you
aren't far enough away yet in my head for me to write nicely. I read

Lady Hester's life at lunch again today. Isn't she superb? I send you my
love. Write for Fordie's same *very* soon.

> I want some more
> Some more she cried
> You may mean some more is the *place*
> And then you give her some more kisses on her face.
> Some more some more some more
> She cried kisses on the coral[1] shore.

To Gerald Brenan

Tuesday evening [August 30th, 1921]   *Watendlath Farm, nr Keswick*

Dear, You can't think how I minded sending you away. But I felt a
shiver when R[alph] suddenly came over that mound. It might have
been different. It seemed a warning from the heights. I think one can't
keep things at a certain pressure indefinitely. I felt you were becoming
slightly strained, was I right? The whole relation was shifting to one
of trying escaping alone. Yet you must know my heart was almost
breaking and my eyes crying when you left. Ralph unfortunately made
it worse. He became instantly very depressed, you wronged him when
you said he did not care very much. He clung to me and burst out 'I
always feel something may happen to Gerald, and perhaps we will never
see him again.' I think he thought of Michael Davies, who was drowned.
He became suddenly so sweet, and lonely and talked of no one but you,
and how he cared for you all the way back. Then he turned on me, and
said it was *my* fault because I had made you go, by not persuading you
to stay, and if anything happened to you he would never forgive me,
and said it was my selfishness that made you go. It was dreadful because
I couldn't tell him anything and I couldn't tell him I cared fifty times
more than he did, that you should have gone. Yet, I feel now it was best.
All the same I think it is about as fine a torture as could be invented to
force a loved one to leave one when there was no necessity for a departure.

The beauty of Watendlath is the same as last night. I have just been
a walk with Lytton and Ralph round the tarn, right round the end of

---

[1] Spelled 'choral' in the original.

9 Gerald Brenan, *c.* 1921

10 Hurstbourne Tarrant, the view from Carrington's studio. Watercolour, 1916
(see letter on page 57)

[the] tarn. But its loveliness made me sad. Lytton also is going tomorrow. Maynard Keynes wants him in Sussex on Friday. This adds to our gloom. We both miss you so much, very much. You know Gerald you mustn't pay too much attention to our wrangling, and disputes.

Really I love Ralph so very much. That is why I am a little discontented he isn't rather more to me. I would so like to find all I want in him. I fear you thought we were rather a disagreeable couple. But really I think he is very happy with me and I with him. What a wonderful time we had. I also go over all the pleasures we enjoyed with our eyes, and our other sensibilities. I could not suddenly bear to hazard such pleasures for a few moments more, which might have marred everything. Ralph loves you so much, he would have been wretched even if he had only dimly guessed we cared a little more than ordinary friends. Now, we neither of us feel any guilt. And who can tell what may not have happened by next spring? But we will have the pleasure always now of remembering this short very perfect span in our lives. And we will write conscious of it, all this long winter—Promise you believe me when I tell you I did want you to stay?

You mustn't think I ever do not care as much as you do. I believe I know your feelings to a hair's breadth—Write to me from the Pyrenees. I shall give Lytton this letter to post tomorrow, and I hope you will get it before you leave London, otherwise I trust God it will be sent to you unopened. [One line omitted] I've given up my painting this evening to write to you. Alix told me she saw you in Keswick and she took my breath out of my cheeks by saying you all but ran into a big motor bus in Keswick street. *Please* be *very* careful. What can I tie on your finger to make you remember not to run into motors, or sit on railway lines? It seems gloomy without you. Ralph is fishing before dinner. And I've fetched your picture from the barn. Now there is no reason to ever go there again. I was sorry not to show it you. I don't want you to see my work unless it's to *my* satisfaction. I am rather vain after all I find, to have your good opinion.

Your train will soon be rushing into London.

Please write to me very often Gerald we leave here on Friday. Write to Tidmarsh always please; not 41 Gordon Square.

Now you are gone I remember all the times I might have been more friendly. I pour coals of contempt on my head for not taking more risks, for not being more adventurous, for not spending more time with you alone. Grrrrr. But this always happens. Why have we these predestined lives of inaction?

Gerald your sympathy, and friendliness made me happier than I can ever tell you. Don't let [name omitted] and her coal black charms quite obliterate Watendlath and   Your DORIC xxxxxx

To Gerald Brenan

Tuesday, September 14th, 1921   *The Mill House, Tidmarsh*

Dearest Gerald, Here are the photographs. [Twenty-four lines omitted] On Monday we had a perfect day at Newbury. We walked to Theale and took a sluggish little train to Newbury. We went at once to our treasured book shop. Which I am sure I must have often told you about. It is kept by a most remarkable man Mr Jarvis, who collects musical instruments, books, china, glass, and a great many curious objects. His wife keeps a little draper's shop next to his shop. Mr Jarvis is very learned, but slightly queer. All his violins he believes to be Strads, or partly Strads. He often draws me aside and says 'This is a charming little Rembrandt I picked up last week. You recognise the master hand in the drapery?' He is so courteous and refined I have never once corrected him. All my most treasured possessions come from his shop. The delft dishes, my Spanish book of woodcuts, Lytton's snuff box, and at least 20 of Lytton's books. We rashly told Garnett of this shop last spring and he found a first edition of Pliny, and 1st ed. of Bacon besides many other rare books. To continue our adventures: on Monday we reached the shop and found it closed, so I asked at the draper's shop next door, a young woman in charge said bleakly 'Mr Jarvis is very ill, they don't think he'll recover.' 'The shop is closed, and is probably all going to be sold up'—imagine our feelings, or rather mine, as the others waited outside. I pressed the woman for news. She was indifferent. At last I said desperately, 'I suppose it's pleurisy?' 'No, it's not *that*, it's a stroke, and they don't think he'll recover.' 'Anyhow it's no good trying to buy any books, because the shop is shut.' We all fell into a deep despair. I most deep, for I secretly was very attached to this long bird like man with the charming voice and handwriting and noble character. Lytton in misery because he would not be able to look at the books any more. Ralph indignant because he'd told us before we set out that the shop would certainly be closed (Jarvis often went off for days at a time to sales) and there was no point in Newbury. We had a wretched lunch at the White Hart which sad meal, a fiendish waitress rendered more hideous, by her vile manners and bad attentions. Then Lytton resolved to go back and see if we could speak to Mrs Jarvis, the wife. Fortunately she *was* there in the draper's shop, and most sympathetic. She let us go into the curiosity room and choose some china. I selected 5 exquisite old coffee cups, of finest china, with saucers, all sprigged and different. Three without handles. Then we found two large decanters square shaped, which cost 6s each; very old glass. A deep Spanish bowl for salad and 8 very old liqueur glasses of great beauty and I am sure of much value, which only cost 3/6 each. And 3 very heavy glass drinking tumblers for 4/- each, one which was dated 1720.

Mrs Jarvis was delighted at selling them, and carried them to Mr Jarvis's bedside in a inner room so that he might price them. He is able to talk, and she says there *is* hope of his recovery. You, do not, I know think much of glass, but when you see these you will agree with me in praising their exquisite beauty. We shall drink old white port from them. We then, elated at our good purchases, and the news that Mr Jarvis might get well, bought 3 buns, and set out to walk home along the side of the canal. It was a perfect hot afternoon and the beauty of the long diminishing canal was amazing. We passed locks and mills, groves of willows, old red barns and flat fields of grazing cattle. At Midgham we took train back to Theale.

All Tuesday (yesterday, when I started this letter to you) I had to spend bottling green greens for the winter and apples and more apple jelly. Now my domestic labours are all done, and I shall fill the store cupboards no more. Ralph exchanged your aunt's glass jordan for 6 large casseroles, and an iron saucepan and 6 earthenware dishes for eggs! Pray God the truth will never leak out. The rooks are building again in our elm trees. Their voices have a melancholy autumnal note. There is arrant bilge written in this week's Nation and Athenaeum on the 'Bat Russians',[1] and even worse bilge by Murry on the Russian Ballet. What a pass things have come to! No one can just enjoy with their eyes simply, they must argue and reason and criticise. Leonard wrote yesterday telling Ralph that he must start work again this week. Poor Ralph hoped his holiday might continue until October, so is rather downcast. Our garden is full of huge sunflowers. They are magnificent plants. Last night the box came from Gordon Square, so I quickly unpacked, and drew out your herb book. Lytton was delighted with it

---

[1] La Chauve-Souris, cabaret turns compèred by Balaieff.

also. It's most interesting, and the plates improve on being looked at more closely. Now I must leave you until the afternoon.

Lunch is over and I am back with you. I hope tomorrow very much you will have written to me. The heat of the summer is gone. Winds, and rain ever since Monday beat down upon the Mill. And the lawn is covered with apples. I will start 'my life' next week after I have spent a few days with my mother. She will be able to tell me some dates, and names I am a little vague about. Do you know she is going out to Spain in October to my brother's farm near Gibraltar?[1]

Ralph is very happy, and I am a 'gud woman' again, as Kot would say.

Now the question is shall this letter go to the Pyrenees or Spain? I will toss up for it. Bless you Gerald. I still care a great deal, and miss you so often.   With love DORIC

PS I will ask Blair [Brenan's younger brother] over soon here. My love again xxx

To Lytton Strachey

Monday 11 o'ck [October 3rd, 1921]   *The Mill House, Tidmarsh*

Dearest Lytton, I must thank you once more for yesterday. You cannot think how I loved every moment of that ride. To you the hedges the little commons, and the faces of the cottages didn't mean very much perhaps. To me they were friends. I didn't realize until I approached Hurstbourne how much I loved that country and that house. It was so lovely that I longed to go slower to show you the little walks, the best views, and to tell you absurd things that would probably have bored you. But I owed all my pleasures yesterday to you and perhaps the Duchess of Kent.[2] Sometimes I feel so happy that I could almost wish it could stop now, because it will be terrible to change ever to a less happy state. I hope you are very happy also. Wasn't it a gay weekend in spite of the two 'solemns'? I must admit also to a dim liking for the dog's face! The house seems very empty now you have all gone. In a few minutes I will retreat to my studio upstairs. The beauty of the day outside is doing

---

[1] This was Carrington's eldest brother, Sam, who having married and left the army had set up a farm in Spain. It failed.

[2] Who gave birth to Queen Victoria and thus enabled Lytton to hire the car.

its best to tempt me into lazinesses, but I am carefully not looking out of [the] window. Do you know that *same* butterfly is still glued to the *same* sunflower! Yes, really, I have examined him very carefully. There he sits in the sun probing and probing into the bags of honey.

Will you look for some braid for me?

My love to you CARRINGTON

To Lytton Strachey

2 o'ck [*October 3rd, 1921*]   *The Mill House, Tidmarsh*

Dear, I only had time to scribble a very horrible horrid letter this morning. Now I write more leisuredly to say I have heard from Harris [dentist] and my appointment is 12 o'ck on Friday. So Ralph will probably come up with me, and we can spend a day together in frivolity if you can escape. If not 'Bats' [La Chauve-Souris] in the evening. If Ray is away I thought perhaps Oliver might smuggle us into 41 G.S. otherwise Brett, or the Ivanhoe. Today is marvellous! Why, why aren't you here? I am reading a life of A Bee which I found in one of your Edinburgh Reviews by Dr Shipley. The horrid influation for the bee world has begun I perceive. Yesterday the scones reached even greater heights of perfection for tea. We meant to go and look at Stoke but the beauty of the garden was so great, we couldn't tear ourselves away. Are any three people so happy in this world as???? I think it's almost dangerous. I feel the elm trees will collapse on our little home one fine morning just to put us in our places, and rooks will consume the fragments of our broken bones.

We will call on Friday as soon as our train arrives, at 51 Gordon Square for orders.

There is nothing to say since I wrote this morning. I feel for no reason almost too absurdly happy today. What a lovely poem that was on the sunflower. I think of it every time I go into the garden.

Bless you my dear one. Do you know how much you are loved by two people? I was so happy with you this weekend. I wish I could build you a tabernacle of honeysuckle to show you how fond I am of a wurzle bruzle curly burly bearded gomonster.

Later, 5 o'ck.

PS Don't get any braid because I think I'll make them without any embellishments. There was only just enough material. It made me gasp it was so near and Venice so far. How charming to have such a good excuse to make a journey back to Venice next week!

I hope, and pray Elizabeth [Bibesco née Asquith] won't come curvetting over here this week when you are away. She is equal to it, I am sure. Bees in the drain, bees in my hair, bees everywhere but where they should be, in the garden. [Six lines omitted]

My love again MOPSA MOPPING

To Gerald Brenan

December 18th, 1921   *The Mill House, Tidmarsh*

An old variety of handwriting born of a new china inkpot and a new Ladies' nib. A Happy Xmas [Drawing of plum pudding and mince pies omitted] and a Happy New Year.

It's a pity that after three years that mellow plum pudding should have been devoured by the heathens of Malaga! Now I'll answer your letter. What fun it sounds, masons, masons everywhere. *I* have built 2 new fire places since you visited Tidmarsh, and I have a big box of cement in my larder with which every day I bung a hole to keep the rats out. I was born on the ... hardly had I started this sentence when a great black cat, a strange cat leapt upon the table seized the pen from my hand, threw the pen on the floor stamped on it, and uttering a low moan vanished up the chimney. Can I now after such a menace, such a black threat, tell you? My hand quakes now, and although you may not believe me, that pen was red hot when I picked it up, and across my palm is burnt a Ram's Horn. Oh gordie, gordie what *can* have happened to those books, they were sent off by Birrell and Garnett on May 19th about, not registered (God rot them for I am sure I told them to do so) and they were such splendid books. Beg the post office at Granada to search their secret recesses, and the post office at Madrid. Also cannot (Maria or) the postman remember if he brought a parcel to your house in May? I suspect you must have just left for England and somehow they were not delivered because you weren't at Yegen. Anyway let's give it up after this final attempt, and curse B. and G. for ever. By the way have you read Lytton's 'Victoria'? Has Hope-Johnstone brought it out, as I think, if not, I might get Lytton to give me an American edition to give you. I sent you a rather drab looking Defoe novel from B. and Garnett's shop the other day. It's rather a dull gift. But I couldn't see anything else. Pearls. Pearls. But why should I send my pearls to the swine at Yegen, for them to spoil with their foul beshitting?

Ha! Ha! I kept *that* secret from you well, that I had in Regent Street, a great House of Pearls! You little knew of *that* secret retreat. And that many an evening I graced the ballrooms of Piccadilly clad only in a vestment of pearls. But it's all over now. All gone. Partridge and Cooper, Stationers in Fleet Street. So if you want any MSS paper, or pens, or pen wipers I can let you have some on approval. *We* also are preparing for Xmas, and for the great Shah of Persia, Maynard Keynes and his attendant slave, Sebastian Sprott. Yes that is really his name! Boxes arrive, not on mules, it is true, but on a carrier's cart from the station, by every train. Boxes from Fortnum and Mason, a large bacon from the Jew Waleys of Essex, crates of rare wines from Soho, and vast cheeses from Jermyn Street. I have just made two silk dressing gowns, one for myself and one for Ralph. Mine is speckled like an eastern sky and Ralph's deep sea green. Then he is also having a pair of yellow silk pyjamas. By the way you never sent me a pattern of your silk. I can easily get it for you at Liberty's. For it is awful to think of you night after night lying naked from the knee to the toe! I saw some superb handkerchiefs in Liberty's. What a mixture of horror, and taste is mingled together in that shop. I went up to London last Thursday. Had tea with my super-refined sister in Finchley Road. No, you couldn't imagine such a perfect specimen of horror if you thought for 20 years. She talks disparangingly of the whole world. She is very refined and superior and constantly says 'I can't think why she married him, he only has £700 a year.' 'They must have come in for some money lately they have 2 cars now.' It was the most hideous house I've ever seen. Such good drab taste. Two footmen like the footmen one sees in West End plays. In fact she looked very like Irene Vanburgh sitting at her writing table when I entered the room. She gave me a petticoat for a Xmas present and a pair of stockings. As they also have a house in Portland Place and a car, I expect they must have £3,000 a year. Her saggy discontented face still haunts me and to think for at least 10 years we lived side by side and slept in the same room together. Now I feel she is more removed from me than Mrs Lloyd George, or Princess Mary. In the evening Lytton, R[alph], Alan MacIver and I went to a play, Charles Hawtrey. It had a curious merit. One had to laugh all the time. It combined the pleasures of Gilbert and Sullivan and a music hall melodrama. I slept at the MacIvers house in Kensington. They are marvellous those respectable houses. One ought to be preserved intact every 10 years to show to future generations. They should be on view. How lovely it would be to spend a day in one, when we are about sixty. I always fear some ghastly revolution will sweep them all away from us, as they were swept in Russia. How nice it is when the year is nearly over. Already I am tired of these grey drawn out days, the stale memories of this year. I long for a new blank year, with no regrets, no sentiments. Clean, and entire with 365 days to spend.

Tragedy. An unknown friend sent me a lovely Treacle Print. Prudence and Justice. It arrived in a paper parcel completely smashed. I pieced it, tearfully, together only to see it had been one of the best Treacle Prints ever made. I have not the heart to throw this broken image of loveliness into the dust bin, and yet it is impossible to stick a thousand pieces of glass together. And all my life I have longed to possess a Treacle Print. What irony! Death haunts me, I think of it at least three times a day and last night I dreamt of the dead. It is menacing but I hope if I put off writing my will, God out of decency will wait till I have done so. Of course one of these days out of sheer idleness I shall make a will, and then He will have no excuse for delaying. I hope you will write to me soon and tell me about your visitor. Is Hope Johnstone as good at Spanish as you are now? Lytton bought on my advice a most lovely bedspread, Queen Anne embroidery with a big sun flower in the middle, very pale colours, with flowers embroidered all over it. It is a vision of delight. *You* will be envious! I will write to you after Christmas and tell you of our feasting, and the conversations. There are so many things for me to do. A lampshade to design, a dresser to paint yellow; Lytton's bed also to paint. Two wood cuts to make and at least forty letters to write before Christmas. I am old fashioned enough to love writing letters at Xmas. I suppose it's a complex because I really love getting them back. Not a complex to investigate certainly. My poor mother hates Spain. It rains; it is cold; and my brother and sister in law are unkind to her. So the poor woman returns again next month. Bringing an Andalusian hen and cock for our establishment.

Ralph has become a hen-maniac and secretly I have a complex against them. Because I don't like the taste of eggs. If you had read Mr Aldous Huxley's latest book [*Crome Yellow*] you would realize that a certain young lady called Mary Bracegirdle always talks about complexes. But it's a book which makes one feel very very ill. I don't advise you [to] read it.

Annie has taken a turn for the good, and now makes us delicious bread, suet puddings and other inventions. Morally she has taken a turn for the bad; lies, and loafs about with young boys. But I've decided now to interest myself in her morals no more, only in her cooking.

This is a dull letter, but I am hors-de-combat. Lytton is reading us a fine play out of Dodsley's Plays called 'A Wife Killed by Kindness'. I think it's by Heydon.[1] We now have some lovely Handel songs on the gramophone and many new Mozarts. I wish that silly fellow R[alph] would learn the flute.

> In May we'll sail away
> On a fine day in May.
> ... Whither away?

Now I must send you my love and a blessing for Christmas.

Please don't write anything in your letters, as it's not so easy as it was to get them from the postman and Ralph always wants to read your news.

Give J.H.-J. my love.   Yr DORIC XXX

To Gerald Brenan

> A BaD, CoLd
> DuLL letter
> But we live in a
> BaD DuLL coLD
> climate
> and I've a cold, Bad, DuLL character
>
> oh to be my Persian cat
> lying snug upon the mat

---

[1] *A Woman Killed by Kindness* by Thomas Heywood.

1922

[Clive Bell had criticized Bernard Shaw in the *New Republic* in a way Carrington thought unjustified. She therefore got Ralph to type the following letter which she signed.]

To Clive Bell

10 Adelphi Terrace, London

Dear Clive Bell, Thank you for the numerous compliments you have paid me in this week's New Republic. I am sorry I cannot return the compliment that I think you, or your prose, 'Perfectly respectable'.

In my young days a 'taxicab' was a name given only to aged whores, ugly as Shaftesbury Avenue.

You do not, it would appear, lead a very enviable aesthetic life; to me it seems dull.   Yours BERNARD SHAW

[Clive was completely taken in although a moment's reflection would have shown him that taxicabs were unknown in Bernard Shaw's young days. He therefore wrote a letter to Shaw getting in reply a postcard saying he had never written to him.]

To Lytton Strachey

February 15th, 1922   *The Mill House, Tidmarsh*

Dearest Lytton, Thank you so much for your letter. We shrieked with laughter under our canopy of blue very often as we read it...Especially about Clive and Shaw's letters. Really he *was* a greenhorn. Did it never occur to him Bernard Shaw wasn't likely to type the address on his note paper? Perhaps he does. Perhaps God inspired me, and the first letter was the image of the second! Poor Shaw I wonder what he thought of Clive's apologies! 'Clive Bell completely ga-ga. Never wrote him a letter in my life.' I see a new aspect: a new avenue in life now! Forgery between lovers, enemies, dukes and duchesses. Yesterday was

a perfect day. Ralph telephoned to Leonard and found out he hadn't
any work for him. Then we went to Englefield Park and skated on the
big lake. It was wonderful. Fortunately Mr Tidbury's brother was
skating and told Ralph the hunchback of Pangbourne lent skates, so
R[alph] rushed back on his bicycle and borrowed some. The fallow deer
stood all round amazed to see humans walking on their water. And
strange geese with black necks and white faces gazed at us in dismay.
There were only five other people besides us skating. Unfortunately the
sun was so hot it thawed and about 12 o'ck became rather unsafe; one
man fell in. But it wasn't deep. I wish it would freeze more often, now
that we have discovered this perfect skating lake so near us. I sit
writing to you like Nelson's Column with lions on every side, with a cat

on either arm of my chair with an untasted tea before me on a chair.
Little Walton keeps on crawling on to the letter and begging for milk
so to end your letter I've been forced to pour them out some.

Such a calamity this morning. R[alph] came rushing in to breakfast aghast. I said: 'Has the broody smashed her eggs?' 'No, but the cock is nearly dead.' The old cock flew at him in the run. Ralph (less patient than his women folk) flew into a rage, and hit the cock on the head with a saucepan. Unhappily it cut the cock's comb nearly in two, and he, the cock, nearly fainted with the shock and was soon a mess of blood. I rushed out, and saw it was hopeless. One would never be able (unless one sewed it with silk) to mend it and I had no medical silk or needle to do it with, so his poor neck was gently wrung. And next Saturday evening ⟨signboard⟩ Alas Poor Yorick. Which is a sad warning to fighting cocks! All the little chickens are very well except one which passed away the day you left. It was one of the new Rhode Islanders brought from Hampstead Norris. [Three lines omitted] No black cloth yet. I feel sure he [the local parson] will come on Saturday when we've got our dimities spread out before the fire and ludo on the floor. Blankets arrived they look superb. What *can* we want at Tidmarsh? I can only think of the Oxford Dictionary! [Fourteen lines omitted]

I painted my roebuck[1] all today. I want to get rid of it and start some serious work. I've put him in the snow one side with a dutch snow landscape in the background. It's simply pouring with rain now I write very quickly because it's nearly six o'ck. I hope you haven't been forced into Bunny's shop yet. Can't you get Pippa to be a little more precise and if she will come, what will she like to do? Did you take Aldous's book of poems to Davis?[2] I see [Alec] Penrose has been decorating an opera at Cambridge. The Ibsen play sounds rather good at Oxford. I suppose you wouldn't like a matinee with R. and me on Saturday afternoon? I didn't know Mark's pictures were so dear. No don't buy one unless you like them. He might do something more lively this year. £40 is too much to spend unless one really likes a picture very much.

My love dear,   Yr devoted CARRINGTON

[1] An inn signboard.
[2] Irving Davis the bookseller, partner of G. Orioli.

To Lytton Strachey

February 28th, 1922   *Hotel Hammerand, Wien*
                        Later: Pension Franz, Wahringerstrasse 12, Wien 1

Dearest Lytton, I will just start a letter to you whilst R[alph] is paying
the bill. We couldn't go to Pension Franz until Uncle Willie Sargant
left which he did yesterday evening. First I will tell you about Alix. You
know it was the *most* serious operation. I hadn't grasped that, when we
left England. They had to cut a big piece of rib away to clean out the
lungs and she can use only one lung to breathe with now. But ever since
the operation she has been getting a little better. The temperature has
been more steady and lower. Poor James is very exhausted and I think
was very glad to have us. For ever since Alix entered the nursing home
he has never left his room except for a few hours and until Sunday he
had not seen Alix for 8 days. She must have changed terribly for he
could hardly tell me of her appearance. [Twenty-three lines omitted]

I have not written to you since a postcard at Nuremberg. I put on the
postcard that I thought all the architecture in Germany hideous. But
later I retracted just as I was posting the postcard, so I rubbed it out
with a wet finger as a false statement! For the old part of Nuremberg is
indeed very remarkable. The houses are immensely tall, ten or 12 stories
high, with tall very steep sloping roofs. Red tiled. Many half-timbered
Elizabethan, some older, and some late 17 cent. We climbed a high tower
and looked over the town. The effect was very lovely, like some Cana-
letto painting. We inspected Dürer's house on Sunday morning. It gave
me a complete vision of mediaeval life, or perhaps it's the middle ages I
mean, (or perhaps they are the same!) We did enjoy Nuremberg, it was
so wonderfully cheap. We bought you some dozen sheets of book
binding paper for less than 1/-! We bought a lovely pocket case for 4/-
and all our expenses came to under £1, for hotel and meals, and two
cinemas, and a Dancing Hell, which was a very naive affair. What
charming people the Germans are! They enjoy their life so tremendously.
Their plainness, their stoutness never depresses them. They all sat
drinking weak wine, laughing and smiling at each other. The little
girls danced with gauche young men, with beaming hot faces. I made one
conquest: a fair German youth came and asked with a click of his heels
and a stiff bow, if he might have 'the honour'. Unfortunately I was so

hot I really couldn't, but I appreciated the compliment. We were sorry
to leave such a clean, sunny town. Vienna is indeed the grimmest city
I've ever been in. Much, much worse than Madrid, worse than Manchester. Everything is a deep grey. All the houses are either old and
crumbling, or new and cemented Baroque. The roads are grey and cold
with slimy mud.

Heaps of grey snow piled up on the sides of the roads. The plaster
peels off the houses. Nobody smiles. All the faces are grey and the boots
covered in mud. We nearly burst into tears on Monday. We both
became so depressed in this fearful prison of a town. At first I was
surprised why James never stirred outside his nursing home. Now I do
not wonder. Life here is just as expensive as England and the food is
horrible. Everything has an overcoat of batter. The meat often wears
two waistcoats and 2 mackintoshes to conceal its identity. The very
cakes wear masks. The butter is ashy pale and tasteless. I had chicken
last night that tasted of fried mongoose and then one's lunch costs 4/-,
each bed and breakfast 5/- each, and the room had stained glass
windows, and was practically a dentist's consulting room. The Pension
Franz is *much* better. The rooms are light, and James and Alix's
untidiness is human and the sight of books makes one happier. Madame
Philip Florence has one room and we share the other. She is very
pleasant and we all get on quite well together. We always see James
after breakfast, and again for tea. The nursing home is a most extraordinary place. Nuns in sweeping dresses with flowing head dresses are
nurses. For it is an R.C. institute. Baroque dominates, and sham
tapestries. The appearance of cleanliness, James says, is only super-
ficial. He lives in a little white bedroom, just opposite Alix's door.
Nobody but James could have borne living in that bedroom for 2 weeks
day after day! If you could only see the vision that greets my eye as I
write to you now. What can I compare it to and make you see it?
Perhaps a flat in a high building in the Strand, near Waterloo Bridge.
Only it is greyer and trams run below! But let us leave the Pension
Franz and go to the gallery together. This morning we were happy for
the first time. Two divine Giorgiones; one of those Three Men and the
big rock and landscape, a tremendous picture. Then the head of a boy
also Giorgione. Too divine. A superb Raphael, of a Madonna and children with landscape, a lovely nude by Bellini. At least 20 Canalettos,
so amazing you ought to come to Vienna just to see them. A superb
Tintoretto of Suzanna and the Elders, perhaps the most remarkable
picture in the Gallery. A great number of Breughels, only one good one,

the famous Snow Scene with Dogs. Two good Cranachs. At his worst
he is awful. Some lovely Rembrandts and some Italian pictures. I shall
go back again tomorrow and make a more thorough inspection. There
is a riding school which James says I shall like, and tomorrow we see
Figaro together. Unfortunately the good music season seems to be over.
Really I am amazed every hour how James and Alix could stand life in
this Pension and this city! The hideousness of the rooms is not to be
imagined. We travelled on the train with Mrs Riviere, who made
friends with us. R[alph] rather succumbed to her charms. We also fell
in with a dreadful Englishman who I called the Jabberwock and an
Armenian travelling to Constantinople. It was rather fascinating
talking to them in the most degraded way. Fortunately we escaped
from them after Nuremberg. And we've not met them since. But R[alph]
will tell you all our adventures. James says he is fairly well. I think
Alix's recovery will make him better faster than anything. I thank you
darling Lytton for making it possible for us to come. Keep well till
R[alph] gets home to you.   My love MOPSA

To Gerald Brenan

[*March 22nd, 1922*]

This to catch you before you leave Yegen. We leave England on the
30th of March. We will stay two days, or three in Paris looking at
pictures, till the 2nd of April. Then travel slowly to Bordeaux looking
at old towns on the way. [Twelve lines omitted]
    Aren't you glad you are going to see us so soon???? And I am
secretly bringing enough money for you to come back to England with.
Only that must be kept very dark. So you have secrets with Ralph do
you? It was very cunning, because now he can't read my letters any
more and I know really you must have written a very indifferent secret
to him. I think he feels it was a bad exchange; virtue for vice. As he
suspects rightly that my letters are more fascinating than his, and because he refused to show me yours, mine are now always refused him on
the highest principles. Lytton is so delightful. This time I insist on your
knowing him better. He said he wished you could persuade Robin
John to come. All the accounts [three words omitted] of the horrors of

the journey only heightened Old Birrell's[1] enthusiasm to see Yegen and you. Will you [be] there to receive them? Perhaps you will just see them for a few days before you start.

Now I must leave you for other matters.

I do not write fully because you may never get this letter. I'll bring tea in any case for you [two words omitted]. My love to J.H.J. if he would like it " " " " " G.B. " " "
" "
                                                    from CARRINGTON
[Some lines missing] My throat is getting bad again so I hope the south will set me up. I bring you a hot water bottle, and I'll try and buy the K. scope next week. Alix is improving in health very gradually but it's dreadfully slow. She still has fever. Do you know Francis Birrell and Père Birrell started today for YEGEN. Nothing will stop them. Bring me £5 worth of dishes, and pots, and stuffs. Lytton will buy them for Tidmarsh and you can make a handsome profit regard it as *business*. [One line omitted]

---

[1] Francis Birrell and his father Augustine were visiting Spain and Carrington had encouraged Francis to make the journey to Yegen.

To Lytton Strachey

[*April 29th, 1922*]

Oh why are you not here to enjoy the loveliness

oF The Mill House,
Tidmarsh,
Pangbourne?

Really to day saturday its beauty is unparelled.

are out

also

never

before

seen at

Tidmarsh

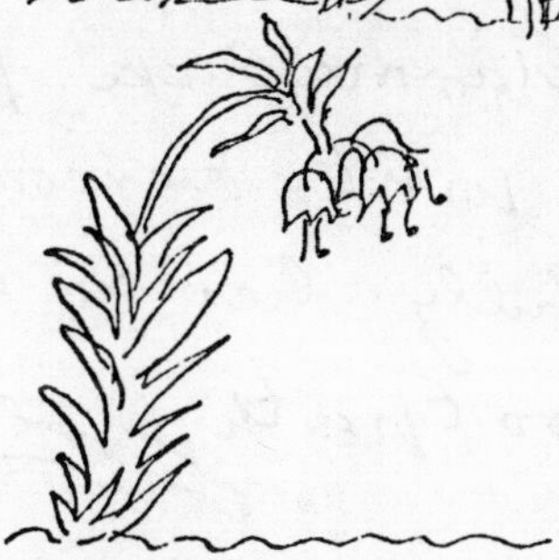

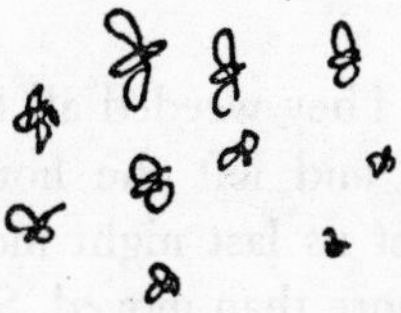

fly laden with honey

little

gambol about in the green orchard

and the Black cat in the wildess state of spring Lust

Careers about the garden after Ralph crying out be rape d!

Really she is unabashed her attentions

old Marmaduke feels the weight of his winter overcoat & rather fretfully lies in the sun on the footpath.

The Charltons[1] really are amazing occupiers! They weeded all the footpaths, cut the hedges, cut the box hedges and left the house shining with cleanliness! Annie was here to greet us last night more exquisite and seductive than ever. R[alph] was more than moved. She *is* a coquette. Fires crackled on brick hearths. The wallflower's sweet scent pervaded every room. Tulips shone on a clean yellow cloth in the dining room. An exquisite French dinner à la Tidmarsh greeted us on the table.

We are overpowered by eggs. Two huge buckets in the larder already.

[1] George Charlton and his wife had rented The Mill House, Tidmarsh.

The little ducks are monsters, all the chickens alive and a garage complete in the paddock! Thousands of letters, bills, papers, and packages of books for you! All is very beautiful, and I've come to the conclusion we must never never leave this earthly Paradise. Really I think Annie was very clever to keep the live stock so superbly when we were away. I've given her a new print dress as a reward.

Please bring back a Duncan [Grant] for our walls.

The heat is really almost too much today in the garden. Ralph has a great deal of news about the Hogarth Press to tell you, so do hurry back. Dear Lytton I hope Pippa will bring us good news, and that I shall see you on Monday.

There are so many Country Lifes to look at, I feel almost bored with old houses. Our sitting room resembles a dentist's waiting room today.

My fondest love,   Yr CARRINGTON

[From Ralph Partridge]
I love you so much, do come down like the wind, the wonderful Charlton aftermath will all too soon disappear. The Hogarth is in the clouds, to rise or fall!   Your RALPH

To Gerald Brenan

Tuesday, May 2nd, 1922   *The Mill House, Tidmarsh*

Kunak, Which in Georgian means a superb and superior kind of friend, in fact a friend who has reached planes of friendship and love, *only* reached in Georgia. How can I thank you enough for the plates and the rug-ery?? They are so lovely I rush into the dining room every five minutes to gaze on their beauty, ranged in rows on the yellow dresser. (You ought to get our village carpenter to paint you some furniture I am sure he would.) Oh but Gerald the weight of that china! You really carried it on your back all those miles over those Pyrenees? Do you know I could hardly stagger with it from the station *on my bicycle* to the Mill House, and you carried tents, sleeping bags, and personal baggage as well. If you had known of my joy over the plates your burdens would have seemed feather bags. I feel I wasn't half grateful enough, but you never told me how terribly heavy they were. Bless you. Bless you. Bless you. Lytton is in almost equal raptures and even the stoical Ralph is moved into frenzies of delight. They were only both very sorry not to see you. But I felt for you in your 'cold' distress so acutely that I thought it sheer selfishness to ask you to stay when you sniffed so wretchedly. You only seemed fit, to tell you the blunt truth, for your parental closes, and I hope they will soon restore you to a presentable condition. I've written to my mother to ask her how long she stays with my aunt in the Cotswolds. When I hear from her I may be able to make some plans. xxx Ralph was so sorry to miss you last night and hopes you will come back here soon. Here is a letter from Clare, full of affection, and so many apologies I am sure, that you will soon be in love with her again. Please write me a detailed account of your family life to amuse me. Lytton thought the photographs even from a photography point of view very very good. No one else will ever see them.

Mais il est un très exquise jeune homme, et, je suis très ronche avec la desire pour lui. Hélas. Je voudrais que j'étais un jeune et jolli fille aussi. Hélas I've nothing to tell you. We simply eat tremendous meals, talk like kings, and laugh like jesters. Lytton has brought some amazing books from London. A novel by Middleton Murry and a superb book of some aged Victorian peer, which is simply an attack on Victoria. But what an attack! The old peer triumphs over Lytton by sheer brilliance of sentiments. It will delight you beyond any book at Tidmarsh. I am so happy. I feel filled with Russian feelings of goodness and love for everyone. I could kiss the old butcher who brings the meat to the door, I feel so spiritually light hearted. Gerald dear, I was glad to see you again. Only your collar slightly abashed me. I believe collars are the mainstay of virginity. Clare once told me a story of a young woman she knew who always wore stick-up-white-stiff collars. One day she accidentally left them off. The change was extraordinary, she suddenly felt very randy, rushed off, started a new life, had lovers, even Sapphic affaires, took to drink, drugs, and never returned to the path of virtue! Which a white collar had supported for nearly 30 years unimpeached. Now I must stop. I've so many things to do. The tapestry you brought looks lovely on a bed in a pink room. I do hope your cold is better. I love the plates very much indeed. They are almost too lovely to be possessed by such a creature as your D.C.

Dear Gerald if I have moods of being tiresome do not despair. I am so fond of you. I value friendship higher than anything. That is why I am sometimes a little nervous of in any way threatening our present very happy relation. Burn this letter, or all may one day be in the kettle of fish. Here's a pretty kettle of fish! Bless you again. Your most loving   DORIC

To Gerald Brenan

Wednesday [May 3rd, 1922]   *The Mill House, Tidmarsh*

Kunak, I am sorry the cold is still so bad. The birds here sing divinely
also and a cuckoo wakes *me* also through my blue chintz curtains!
I've gotten your cold! Fiend! So now through the impenetrable mists,
and shloses that bedim our ears, our noses and affections, also my
spelling let us between these gigantic invulnerable forests fogs. Let
us hold discourse. I've got ever such a throat and a weeping nose. 'How
can that be?' said the husband. 'From whom my dear can you have
caught this unpleasant cold?' Who, indeed? [Eighteen lines omitted]
R[alph] doesn't see my letters. I always get them in the morning before
he comes down. He has been so friendly and charming since France.
Perhaps that is partly why I've had this reaction of virtue!

No, but really all I meant was: please don't dwell on it, and please
don't expect anything from me. I can't give you anything worth much,
except my friendship. Don't let us spoil the pleasure we get from being
friends by having complications and too many secrets from Ralph. But
we'll talk about it sometime. It's not very important in any case. What
would be fun would be to walk from Swindon to Pewsey and take a
train back here. I promise you'll be very happy with me because I am so
fond of you; so don't feel gloomy. It will be lovely to have you here.
We'll go long walks, and we'll out talk these birds. And Wednesdays
we'll make expeditions to London on cheap tickets, and see the great
world, and the intelligentsia of Richmond and Hampstead.

Please write to me often. I've an aching back, a sore throat and a cold
so [you] must forgive this diseased letter. Don't quarrel with your
father.

Grrrrrrrrrrrr Bless you.   Your loving COLDRINDA

To Gerald Brenan

5 o'ck [early June 1922]   *The Mill House, Tidmarsh*

I have reached Tidmarsh and now tea is over and we sit on the lawn
where for nearly a month every afternoon you have sat with me. Lunch

was awful: the weather had turned everything bad. My most lovely
steak and kidney pie had to be given to the hens

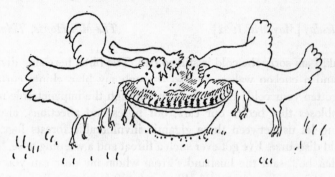

and it was such a delicious pie full of eggs, rare spices, kidneys and
steak. Then Lytton thought the cockerel which we had the minute the
pie vanished from the table, was bad, so that had to [be] whisked away.
Then we felt so exhausted and our noses so weakened by smells that we
could only just face two eggs, and a little salad. Then Pippa arrived and
for hours I sat on the lawn and talked to her of Alix and Vienna. I miss
Annie almost more than Ralph! I never realized how much work she
must do every day, until today I had to do it myself. Lytton is reading a
big book on Mount Everest and the expedition. Some of the photographs
are marvellous. It makes one almost want to rush off there. It's almost
worth your while coming back here to see this book. The Tibetans look
the most intelligent people. You are rather Tibetan you must know at
moments. Ha! Ha! what a subtle compliment. Lytton likes you. He
talked of you a long time. I forgot all about your cheque, and in the
morning I looked out of a window and saw a rook carrying it off to its
nest, I suppose for bumphf, so that's that, a complete rookery on your
part. Rooked by rooks for rook shit. They have expensive taste in
Bromo, as I told them this morning when one fluttered onto the lawn. I
love the animal book so much. Too much. I will give it back to you, as
really I am not a fit person to possess such a rare treasure. Even Lytton
was delighted with [it]. Bradfield College acts 'Antigone' in the open
Theatre this month on the 24th. I was so excited.

I wish Lytton could have been here to go with me. The wind was
awful last night. I couldn't sleep, so today I feel just as tired again. I
wonder what has happened to R[alph] since I last saw him at 6.30
yesterday. [Six lines omitted] Unless one is uncritical and allow[s] affections to overlook the follies of one['s] friends *no* friendships can survive.

No, you aren't a load round my neck, or if you are, I miss my load and would be glad of it soon again. Bless you. I agree, confusions when one is with other people made intimacies difficult. Believe me I shall manoeuvre the ∽ [1] all right. I have written today to Ruth Selby-Bigge. Tomorrow or very soon I will make plans, and give you more positive days. Be frightfully careful of my letters. You must burn these. Don't leave them in your pockets at Rodmell, as V[irginia] reads letters recklessly and she is the worst possible person to know anything. Now I must leave you and rush for the post. You see by my writing I write tearing like a may-fly up and down the pages.

I've so many letters to write before the post. Gerald you mustn't think I don't care. But I have lost something which seems to prevent me giving myself away completely ever again. But in some ways I can give you everything and I do give you a great deal of love.

Your DORIC

To Gerald Brenan

[*June 5th, 1922*] [*Extract*]

Must I shout my remarks in the evening to Lytton on the lawn for you to hear.

I LOVE GERALD VERY MUCH, AS MUCH as prunes, as roast duck and peas, as Venice, as crown imperials, as tulips, as Devonshire cream and raspberries, as walking on Combe Downs, as Padua, more MORE MORE MORE than all these things do I love Gerald.

How happy your letters make me! Very, very, happy. I sing like Annie as I brush the rooms this morning, for has not my Charlie a nice face? I would I could write to you, all day, but breakfasts must be cooked, hens fed and a hundred and one other things done. I say when do you leave the Cotwolds????? 'Cos could I not cram in a day, a pure day, just this week? It seems rather a pity if you pass this way to London not to have one day this week together, if you don't go to Sussex after all.

Darling Gerald I'll never call you Kunak again if you dislike it.

KANUK or Kobjek or KOTNOB.   Yr DORIC XXXXXX

---

[1] Carrington used this sign ∽ in letters to Gerald Brenan to mean sexual intercourse.

[A full account of the part played by Clare Bollard in the emotional entanglement is given in Holroyd's *Lytton Strachey*, vol. 2 (Heinemann, London, 1968), pp. 451–6. It is perhaps worth pointing out that Mrs Bollard never passed periods in an asylum as there stated, and that the portrait of her husband is a caricature and not a very good one.

The explosion came when Ralph discovered from her that Gerald was in love with Carrington and that he had asked Clare to have a flirtation with Ralph in order to enjoy Carrington more easily. Any normal man would have felt bitter resentment at such deception, and Ralph had a violently jealous disposition. His rage and violence were hysterical. According to Barbara Bagenal, he told Leonard Woolf that he felt bound to kill Gerald and, more abnormally, he went to see Mark Gertler and demanded particulars of his sexual relations with Carrington. This may have been because Clare was a friend of Gertler's and that she had passed on some of his confidences. But it is easy to exaggerate the influence of Clare. For Ralph's discovery of Carrington's love affair with Gerald was inevitable. Indeed the fact that Carrington— and later Ralph—could regard Clare as a scapegoat helped somewhat in the uneasy reconciliation which followed—though their relations were never the same again.]

To Gerald Brenan

Friday morning, 7 o'ck in bed, June 10th, 1922   *The Mill House,*
                                                                      Tidmarsh

Dearest Gerald, Do not think I shall write anything that can matter to any of us or R[alph] now. It is simply I cannot bear having these conversations in my head any longer with you. I have resisted a hundred times since you left, the impulse to go to Cirencester and see you. But I know it will only make it worse for us both if I did. Yesterday I hardly looked once at your face or your body because I did not feel strong enough. Now since you have left I have only thought of you. Lytton was so kind when I told him of all your misery. You mustn't think for a moment [he] was against you. He said he was so touched by the way you behaved in coming to Tidmarsh, and your gentleness, only he thought perhaps after all this may have been inevitable. That you could not have lived always, as we have lately lived, in a strain, deceiving Ralph—But that the cruelty of it ending, so appalled him that he could hardly bear to think of you separated from us. He says he is sure when R[alph] gets over the shock of it, he will not wish never to hear or see you again. His affection for you will return, and he will let me write. But *we* know somehow that something is lost that cannot be altered now. I did *not* discuss *anything else* with Lytton. He was terribly shattered. He has had to bear everybody's unhappiness. Last night he read me Hardy's Poems. Some of them are almost too real for one to bear. Ever since you left the house I have thought of nothing else. Oh Gerald please please remember how I cared, and still care. That you alone acted just as in the worst moments I knew and wished you would act, has been my only happiness in this nightmare. You alone did think of me, and remember that a friendship was more worth than anything else. I never until and then only for an awful moment, when Lytton said (after he saw Ralph yesterday morning), believed you could forget my affection and my feelings, and everything we had said to each other.

It was trusting you in that one thing that kept me from breaking down, from rushing away wildly and at moments from ending my life. If when I first saw you I was cold it was not from ill feeling. The second I saw [you] in Pangbourne I knew *you* were my friend. Oh Gerald I moon in the orchard looking at the seat where we two sat, at the flattened grass where you lay. And I wish I could have told you then how I cared, how great my misery was when I knew I should not see you again, I could not simply trust myself to speak. I knew it would hurt you more to see me cry. I longed to have your affection to cling close to you and tell you all my thoughts and talk to you only of yourself, but I dared not. It was only the most dreadful strain to talk of [Clare] and R[alph] as I did, and not to talk to you of what I minded most and felt so cruelly. But I could not bear our last meeting should be one of senseless grief. Yet it was best so. And I feel, you must have, even if I behaved coldly, you *must* have felt my pent up love go out to you with every sudden look, whilst we sat on the grass. You will care for the little picture; I gave you so much more, as I gave you that.

I am crying now again. I cannot see the paper. Oh I have cried since you left until my eyes ache. Even Annie knows I am unhappy and tries to be kind to me. She speaks so gently, and I saw last night she had cried also. The last straw was when I was trying to plant some lettuces in a Despair of wretchedness, the cats both came and sat beside me, and rubbed my hands with their faces. Lytton's pale face, and affection makes me break down every moment. Gerald, my dearest friend you

mustn't think it wasn't worth while, for you know it was. That I mind
so terribly is awful. That you care even more is worse still. The irony,
the superb irony, was that no good could come of it. I was tied, I could
not leave with you. I should have felt for ever an exile, with a ghost
between us. I couldn't have left with the memory of that face in the
orchard distorted with rage, and horrid threats of murder. *Our* relation
was so very perfect. It was never marred by callousness, or too much
intimacy. It never faded into something casual. Every day I learnt more
to be fond of you, found new pleasures. That no one now will notice
what I wear, or how I feel, that I shall no longer rush down to get letters
from the post, that no longer I can plan to see you in Spain is more
awful to me, than anything else. If this had happened with anyone else,
if only I had had the outlet of being able to write to you my feelings, my
griefs, and my happinesses I could have borne it. One never knows until
one loses a person exactly how much they mattered to one. You may
think (you are so humble in remembering I care for you) I could decide
easily to live this altered life here? Do you not know it would have been
far easier to rush off with you? Not to endure this pain? But I could not.
One does owe something more than the enjoyment of life to a person
like Ralph. How superb he has been, only Lytton knows. You will forget
me, you will in time simply look back on me as something that was very
good, and perfect for a few short years. It would *have been different for
Ralph.* Do not ever quite forget me however. For Gerald should anything ever happen, I shall not have made new friends to turn to. I should
still remember you. My dear, there is one thing I shall thank you for
always. I think you will see in time it was the greatest thing you could
do, and the kindest—You MUST burn this letter, dear please. I have
said more in it than I meant to when I first started to write, but the
agony I have been through since you left has left me less brave.

Please remember my last wish and your promise to me. *Do* not see
R[alph] or [Clare] before you leave England. Will you send Lytton the
postcard. I shall wait for that. You must remember that cheque is torn
up. If I may sometimes write to you, and if R[alph] does not mind you
writing back, I will tell you. But it will not be for a little time. It is the
swiftness of this death to our friendship that I find hardest to bear. A
little warning, if we could have talked alone one day together, would
have made it so much easier.

Do do please not think anything you ever gave me was wasted. Oh I
cry again. I weep to think, I must not write any more.

I remember everything. You must also. Your friendship was one of the most perfect I ever had. We never once quarrelled. And I never liked you less; only more, as we knew each other better. Remember that. You mustn't please tell J[ohn] H[ope]-J[ohnstone] about this, for if he comes back to England he will tell others, and it may make it harder for me.

Remember dear I gave you a great deal, for I loved you, for that remember if you can, not to talk of this to anyone. I think the Woolfs will still go to Yegen. And Forster would also. I am sure of that. You must write to Virginia please from Spain. I will give you Forster's address at the bottom of this letter; if I don't you can always write to his publishers.

Every word now recalls a joke, a happier mood when [we] were such friends only a week ago. Tidmarsh pervaded with you, memories.

Do not hate [Clare]. I think she did it unconsciously she [did] not mean all this pain. But I never think of her now. It is better not to, otherwise one gets thoughts which hurt one's head to contain. And *you* mustn't rebuke yourself for anything you did or said. Because I've never once rebuked you. I forgive everything. It was simply misfortune. Gerald I've never once turned against you. And I still care as much as I did a week ago.

Do not write back, but I know you will not do that. I am the weaker ship to write as I write now. But I hope it will make you a little happier to know I still love you. Gerald I still don't realize quite what I've lost in you; my one happiness is that *you* never deserted me, or thought ill of me, and our affection wasn't killed, only forcibly divided. Forgive me this letter, I write in such misery. I only hope you will soon forget, and please never reproach me. I could not bear that last blow. Will you try and write again. Remember I think more of your writing than of anybody's but Lytton's and could you send Lytton sometimes the things you write, for judgement? Then I can read them also. I shall think of you not only today but for weeks and weeks and only with love. Goodbye. If you knew how brave I am at not asking to see you again, you would be happier. Bless you, my very dear friend.   Your KUNAK

To Gerald Brenan

Sunday morning, 9 o'ck [June 11th, 1922]

Gerald, I see R[alph] has written to you. Please even if he begs you, do *not* see him again. I will some day send you a letter telling you every thing that happened since you left. R[alph] has now been hardened and is cynical. I am treated rather like a peculiar variety of imbecile! It may be too difficult, but Lytton begs me to be patient for a little. He says Ralph's hardness is just the reaction after all this.

I only hope *you* will not find J. H[ope]-J[ohnstone] cynical if you go back to Yegen. If I knew a little about you I should be happier. But you mustn't write, and I won't, not for some time. Remember the postcard to Lytton. Lytton is so very just. He understands both sides. I can't write more now. Gertler once said that [Clare] did everything she touched with a touch of genius. I agree. This is altogether too masterly. I only hope you will think it was worth it all. My dearest Gerald. Bless you. Goodbye again.   Your KUNAK

Later. 5 o'ck Sunday

I did not mean to write another time, but now I must.

Ralph has today for the first time talked to me. He admitted he nearly didn't come back because I hadn't told him everything at first on Wed. morning. When I told him the reason I think he believed me. But I see [Clare] is determined to push matters as far as she can, even now. Really the things she told him, unnecessary things she had heard from Gertler. And when I asked him how I had behaved 'treacherously' to her to deserve such treatment, the *only* treachery she could produce was my questioning her motives about her telling me not to see Gertler. Now everyone is against me. You are let off as being 'vague', and well inten-tioned. I am a deliberate villain! Yet I can see R[alph] really believes me a little, and when [Clare] leaves he will grasp we were fond of him, and we didn't behave quite so elaborately as he now believes. The sordid-ness of it all and the lack of necessity for all this, wearies me. I feel per-haps more than anything the hardness of [Clare's] heart. The meanness of all this conduct. You will go away soon please? I want to think of you away from all this. Lytton is superb. Today I am perhaps less unhappy than yesterday, that is all. You must always let me know where you are in case I want to write.

The uttermost indifference is shown to all my actions now. But R[alph] is so unhappy I don't think he realizes quite how I feel. Gerald dear, you must forgive me for having made all this bother and having caused you pain. What a misfortune it has turned out! You mustn't regret anything you did, nothing matters now. I shall never regret knowing you. I will tell you later how everything goes. Please remember not to tell J.H.-J. very much for my sake. I hate it all so much. I'd like to feel it wasn't going on any longer. Again goodbye. I am going to try and be an artist and paint very hard this summer. But I will write to you sometimes unless you would rather I did not. Only you must not write until I tell you. My love dear from your   KUNAK

Gerald Brenan to Carrington

June 11th, 1922

I do not understand the possessive instinct and I do not share it: it is part of my philosophy that love is free and unrestricted and is increased by being divided.

I never never thought of myself as his rival or as his wife's lover. You, he and to some extent Lytton formed with myself a closed circle. I thought of other people as outsiders. In one fatal case I gave them my garrulity, I never gave any of them (except H[ope]-J[ohnstone]) my confidence as I gave it, yes, to Ralph.

The famous plot! That was childish. As you know it was not very serious. I thought that if Clare and R[alph] went about together, we should sometimes be alone. My worst plot did not go beyond that.

[On June 13th Brenan wrote a letter imploring Carrington to come to London for a last meeting before he went to Spain. Every line of his letter is alive with passion and despair.]

To Gerald Brenan

Wednesday afternoon, 3 o'ck, June 14th, 1922. Written in my bedroom

Gerald, I simply couldn't come up to London today. You needn't think I didn't want to come, for I did. For some half hour I thought I would,

that I would simply tell no one and come tomorrow. Then Lytton called
me in his room and gave me your long letter. He was so kind, and so
completely honest with me, I felt a wretch for having a deceit already in
my head, when he and R[alph] were trying to believe me again. So I
told Lytton you wanted me to go to London. He was against it. He said
it could do no good. He did understand your feelings, and mine but he
said it would only make it harder if we saw each other again. You would
suffer more. I would be wretched all over again. Then R[alph] would
have to know and he would suspect perhaps, or be unhappy. Lytton
wanted to go instead of me but I knew unless you wired for him you
would probably prefer to be alone. Oh Gerald if you only knew how
your letter tore me inside, for it *is* true I am immoral or I shouldn't be
writing to you now, a letter which perhaps I shall not confess to having
written. Perhaps because I act on my affections and my desires and not
on principles I am not fit companion for such people. Yes I feel that
sometimes. In that we are alike. R[alph] has been kinder to me. But
he looks so ill and upset it makes it very difficult to forget anything for a
moment. I write every day to you a long account of my feelings and of
everything that happened since you left last Thursday afternoon nearly
a week ago now. But I shall not send it you for, perhaps, a whole year.
I could not come and see you without telling Lytton. For I had *promised*
to do nothing without telling him. Also the certainty of meeting someone like Duncan Grant, or 'an enemy' made it absolutely impossible even
if one had been completely unmoral, and rash.

Then I could not bear to be with you again. To see you, and hear
your voice, and to see you wretched, I felt was more than I could stand.
Your long letter has made me realize a hundred times today what I am
losing in your friendship. I felt I couldn't stand seeing you again even if
Lytton and Ralph had begged me to go and yet how much I longed to
see you. I was torn backwards and forwards by longing to go, and
wretchednesses. I am glad these hot days stifling with the memories of
the last month are gone. A howling wind tears the elms and the rain
beats against my window pane. Now the organgrinder has just been
playing in the village. Do you remember it on a Wednesday, two weeks
ago now?

I shall not write again. You must *not* write either please, I mean this.
But I want you to know I *don't* believe C[lare]'s word against yours. I
knew even in my worst moments you couldn't have said the things you
were reputed to have said. I felt you couldn't have. Anything that you
said foolishly I've forgiven, after all it didn't matter. We ought to have

been *entirely* wise and it was no use unless we both were. Well we weren't. And now we have plenty of time to go over everything and see how unwise we were. We've forty years probably to think it all over! R[alph] still sees C[lare] although he never tells me he does. But he isn't coming back tonight or tomorrow night. I shall be here quite alone till Saturday, as Lytton goes away tomorrow for 2 days. I am going to change my bedroom into a studio. For now I shall have a great deal of time to paint. Lytton will tell you if I am ill, or if I die. I hate myself for being so strong. I wished many days last week that I could get ill to feel things less acutely. You will write to Lytton sometimes? Just tell him you are in Yegen and if you move tell him your address. For sometimes I may want to write. Lytton loves the Thompsons and I pretended the book on English houses was really meant for me. We are all so tired and unhappy, and yet we can't go away, because where can one go to? I think Lytton must long for next week when he can get away from us all, and be in Venice. He hates these sordid 'repeatings' as much as we do.

Let us forget all that part of it, and this last week. And think of a friendship which, while it lasted, no one but we two knew the texture of it. How far C[lare] was from ever understanding us. I am glad that the intimacy of our friendship wasn't dragged out into this shattering daylight. The *most* important thing to us both they never bothered to ask about! I alternate between despair and hatred of myself and my character, and a hatred against the irony of the whole situation.

I shall read your letter very often. It was dear of you to write me such a long one. And one which gave me so much pleasure. You are right it wasn't 'inevitable' until [Clare] knew. Then it was. And perhaps if I had been wiser, and less fond of her I would have seen it. I repeat what you say: 'I cannot regret having known you.' But you must tell Lytton what you do, and sometimes send him your writings. I shall write a life of myself at intervals in the form of letters to you, which perhaps on the 7th of June next year I will send you. That memorial day. The day my parents married incidentally. Yes I remembered the National Gallery. But I couldn't go. I feel a captive now. My spirit has gone. When one is forced to choose one can't go back and face the torment of choosing all over again, or tempt oneself. I feel very altered, so tired. Thank goodness our friendship was never sordid, that while we lived we were so superbly happy. I feel as if I am in a tomb today. I hear the wind, and the rain but I can't move. I wonder what you are doing? I spend my afternoon in the Mews with you. And are you listening to the organ grinder at this moment? I verge between a hundred moods of sentiment,

grief, moments of rage, but mostly gloomy unhappiness. My one comfort is you never turned on me. You weren't cynical. Tear this letter up.
Don't tell John or J. H[ope]-J[ohnstone] I wrote this letter today. I can
bear no more reproofs, no more concealments. You will have forgiven
me by now for not coming today. I was too worn out. I haven't a
particle of rashness left in me. In a few years I suppose I'll be tamed. I
am more aware of everything than you suppose, or anyone supposes.
Oh I wish I could have prevented a little you being unhappy. I wish
you could have left before all this happened. Could J.H.-J. one day
send me a photograph of you, with some other photographs? No one
can mind that? I would give a good deal to be you leaving this country
today. It will be better soon I know, but one thing won't get better ever
and nobody but you and I see that: that is the loss of our friendship.
This is goodbye. I am firmer than you think. Nothing will make me
write again. But I wanted you to know why I couldn't bear meeting you
today. It wasn't I didn't care just as much as you did. I simply couldn't
stand any more unhappiness, for I also want to be now removed from
all these scenes, and scandals. My dear Kunak goodbye. I tell you very
little but I cannot. Besides there is no use in it now. Your loving DORIC

FINIS

A little later [*June 15th, 1922*]
Gerald, You see I am completely unmoral still. I say I won't write
another line, then I open the envelope again, and write line after line ...
I want to rewrite all I have written but if I do you will never get it. I
mustn't write any more. One must remember the play is over, the
audience has left; the epilogue has been said. The tailpiece and FINIS
written on the last page. These are just fly leaves, blanks, then the solid
Morocco cover and the book is shut and is put on its shelf. In secret we
may write a second volume. But we must not read it until we are very
old, and hideous and impotent. Please remember dear it was harder for
me not to see you yesterday than you can possibly imagine.

It wasn't until I went to bed last night and I knew you had sailed I
could stop longing to go to the mews to see you again. My one comfort is
my imaginary letter which I write every day to you.

You will write sometimes to Lytton. He will I am sure show me your
letters.

He was never against us. He was on our side. He does understand
friendships such as we had. But I mustn't write another word. The

imaginary letter must hear the rest. Everything seems extraordinarily
unreal now you have gone. I wish I could tell you all I think but there
is no use now in telling you. If I become a very good painter no one can
take that from me and today I feel rather proud, rather moved from
everyone, even cynical about myself, except that I wish to paint very
well. But remember I never thought differently of you to what I always
thought. And I think you knew pretty exactly what I did feel. Well.

Goodbye now. Grrrrrr.

[The following letter is a remarkable example of Carrington's habit of
writing in a style acceptable to her correspondant, suppressing one side,
and exposing another, of the truth.]

To Alix Strachey

(Only for one day in London) June 19th, 1922   *59 Finchley Road*

Dearest Alix, Your post-card came this morning. It was exactly as I had
conjured, your superb sanatorium. No it's not true. I am NOT interested
in the tubes, only you mustn't take the breath out of my lungs by
descriptions of operations which are not going to take place.

Great excitement at Tidmarsh as Lytton felt sure the 'Pension Kranz'
was really 'Franz' mentioned in the capture of Gerrard Lee Bevan,[1] and

[1] Gerrard Lee Bevan, chairman of The City Equitable Fire Insurance Co., absconded
to France in an aeroplane after embezzling his company's funds. He dyed his hair and grew
a beard but after staying at the Hotel Franz in Vienna was arrested and at first feigned
madness.

that James was really the Lee Bevan captured, and that he could end by tearing his beard out in the cells of some castle dungeon, and no one could prove that James was James and not Mr. Lee Bevan. However to-day we are reassured, the papers say he owns to his name and his beard is dyed and he also a dyed villain of deepest German dye. Truly the reaction to 'dyed bearded Lee Bevan' came out the very next day in 'Is Germany Capturing the Dye Trade!'

Oh! Alix dear, would you were in England now that Despair is here. Never, never have I been more wretched and less able to know the truth, or my mind or anybody's mind. R[alph] now says I am so incor-rigible in my lies, deceits and delusions, he will gladly pay for me to go to Freud to be cured. Lytton will give a rather cynical story I expect when he sees you in the Lakes. I am so worn out with scenes, explosions and tears that I can only give you the serial headings without com-ments. Only the bleakest serial sketch because I still doubt if anything is true or if I am capable of speaking the truth. At Watendlath perhaps you observed Gerald Brenan conceived a passion for me. It had started before Watendlath really. However we both knew it was hopeless be-cause (a) I wasn't in love with him and (b) because R[alph] would be in a state if we went to bed together. So nothing happened except embra-sades. Then he went off to Spain and it all faded away. He admitted himself it faded rather when he left me, and he really only enjoyed writing me long letters and being friends. [Twenty-seven lines omit-ted] They [Ralph and Clare] wanted to spend Whitsun at Tidmarsh. Annie was away. Pippa was coming and I honestly could not face cooking for 5 people for 3 days and having to see R[alph] making love under my nose. [Ten lines omitted] Lytton was superb and tried to smooth it out. I am afraid he must have found it terribly boring and nervy work. I made a great many miscalculations and errors of course. Gerald went off to Spain and I am never to write or see him again. I didn't care for him sufficiently to go off with him. I wish I could have to get away from it all. Lytton says R[alph]'s complex about my virtue is almost insane. It has made him dreadfully wretched and reduced him to a man of nerves. You of course, will be cynical and say 'why do I put up with it?'. Well, I suppose it's because I care a great deal more for living with Lytton and R[alph] and Tidmarsh, than I do for occasional affaires and Gerald's friendship, and I really am very fond of R[alph]. Incidentally I must add I had begged [Clare] never to tell R[alph] about this absurd affaire with G[erald] because it would so upset him, so she knew quite well what she was doing. I like to see other people live with honest relations to each other—this has reduced us all pretty completely. R[alph] now says he can't face living with me at moments because I am such a fraud etc. Lytton thinks it will be alright in time, [One line omitted] but that I mustn't if I am going to live with R[alph] have any more affaires. As they were not even affaires, romances I suppose is the only word for this one and as I have had no others, it isn't much of a sacrifice to give up this imaginary life of rouée. I am now feeling as you'll see rather grim—I mean now to paint and become very serious. So perhaps the end of this rather wretched business will be I'll paint and be some good as an artist. But it means Alix, unless the explosives become too much for me, I'll not be able to come off to the Lakes and see you. It was always rather dim and now it's dimmer. You must understand—should I get too much for R[alph]'s nerves and he for mine then I'll fly to you in Italy. [Four lines omitted] Lytton was an angel—my only support—really I could not have survived these scenes without him. But to you who haven't seen and heard this, you must find it I suppose like every other domestic quarrel. [One line omitted]

Forgive this tedious letter but I wanted to tell you a little and I promise you if I am not happy I will come to you and James. I shall try to find you a cottage in Dorset, Devon or Cornwall for August. Lytton goes to Venice today so I feel rather sad. You mustn't think I am in despair. It's only I've been sleeping badly and feel rather ill and Lytton's going makes it rather worse today. *How* I look forward to you two coming back to England.

Bless you, my fondest love,   Yr CARRINGTON
PS Only for you and James, this letter and don't write back a hymn of hate against R.P.—in fact don't mention it. But tell me about yourself.

[Lytton had done everything he could to allay Ralph's fury and to console Carrington. He was however on the point of leaving for Venice on a holiday with W. J. H. ('Sebastian') Sprott. He was afraid of leaving Carrington alone and invited Barbara Bagenal to stay at Tidmarsh during his absence. He could not have made a better choice.]

To Lytton Strachey

Wednesday morning [June 21st, 1922]   *59 Finchley Road, London*

Dearest, You will be in Paris exactly the same half hour that I write this
letter to you. For it is just eight o'ck before breakfast—Oh you will
never know how miserable I was when you left last night in the train.
How much I longed to beg Sebastian to let me go instead, and leave all
this. Ralph would not talk to me and left me almost at once to go and
have dinner with [Clare]. Yes, it was a curious experience to be deserted
in London for a whole evening. I walked about in the squares of Bloomsbury to while away the time till 1 o'ck. When I went back to bed. And
you are no longer in England! That's what I keep on saying to myself.
But dearest one, I did not mean to say a word to you of my unhappiness,
because already you are so far away and I promised not to send it even
on paper to Venice to pursue you and pest you. But I must, (since now
it seems almost impossible to speak on what one most feels) thank you
Lytton, for all you have done for me, and for him, trying to make us
both happy. You alone prevented me many days from committing acts
of madness and flying away somewhere. And when you said even if he
left me you would still be my friend, that has made me, in the worst
moments lying in bed going over it all happy, or a little happy. I am
going to try and be brave, and not to be defeated. I so sincerely believe
there is enough still between us below this mug-mire to make it worth
while going on with it. I know how good he has been and how hard it is
for him, but it's very hard to have patience to wait till things get better,
at moments. Blessed one, you mustn't think of us again. And I'll not
worry you with any letters. Oh Lytton dear if you only knew how I love
you, and how I cried inside at you going away last night. But it must be
as happy a Venice as last time and just send me post cards sometimes
with your news.

Last night although I went to sleep in tears I had a most lovely
dream with the Prince of Wales in the country on some downs. But we
found great difficulty in getting away from the courtiers, and equerries!
In fact the end was never accomplished as I woke up just as it was about
to happen. I go this morning to the National Gallery, and to the Burlington, lunch with Alan. Then South Kensington Museum till tea, then
Virginia and Leonard at Richmond. Dear, I am going to try and be very

good. You know I was ashamed of my deceits and faults, but you must remember that would have been far worse if it wasn't for your kindly tuition all these years. How I wish now I had told you everything at [word omitted]. I came so near to doing it once and then the moment past.

I read the account of Sotheby's sale today in the Times! '£2,025 only gentlemen for this book, only £2,025 ... ?' The Bunyan. Mine cost 7/- at Newbury, *nearly* a 1st edition. '18/- for this book gentlemen. Mr Strachey has it.' Thank goodness I leave here tomorrow at cockcrow. It's too much of a nightmare. Even I in my despair, am in Paradise compared to these snobbish slugs. Bless you again and again.

Yr CARRINGTON

To John Hope-Johnstone

[June 21st, 1922]

Dear J.H.-J. I expect Gerald has told you some of the volcano we've all become involved in.

I've promised not to write to him again. So I must just ask you to do something for me.

Please tell Gerald he must not for any reason write to me again. If he wants to write he must write to Lytton. Really it is rather important. I liked those photographs very much that G[erald] showed me. I think if you come back to London I would rather not see you. As it's better to make a clean sweep of all this. I wouldn't have written to you but I am so afraid G[erald] may write sometimes. One rather loses one's nerve at moments.

And may I ask you to tell as few people as possible whatever G[erald] may tell you? There's no reason why you should do anything I ask you, I know. But I thought perhaps you would.   Yrs CARRINGTON

To Lytton Strachey

Tuesday [June 27th, 1922]   *The Mill House, Tidmarsh*

Darling Lytton, The state of your patients? Monday was a black day. Even bright little Barbara collapsed under the gloom. He went off unhappy, and returned even more silent. He was friendly to Barbara, and markedly hostile I thought, to me, so all my feelings of thinking things were progressing fell with a thud. After dinner I went upstairs and painted as the light was still good and R[alph] went out for a walk with Barbara. Suddenly he came into my room after I had gone to bed and talked to me. I tried to tell him things he wanted to know and told him frankly of my affection for Gerald and what our relations had been. Ralph after this talk became infinitely happier and remained so this morning until he went off to London. Whether this change means anything, or not, it's difficult to say, but I felt this morning he had shaken off something, perhaps his pride and that things were changed in a way they hadn't been since the crash. I must tell you just these feelings because I know you care. Barbara is really very understanding and I think her calmness and simple affection has a wonderful influence. A sinister budget again from Paris this morning.[1] So I said 'wouldn't it be a good thing not to read it until you get in the train.' To my surprise he said 'Yes I think it would' and put it away in his case. Barbara thinks if once he gets fond of me again, and Tidmarsh, he will see things more in perspective and will turn against the 'repeatings' and intrigues. Anyhow today is happy and that is all one is certain about. Bless you. I forget when I last wrote. Did I tell you Alix and James wrote to me? There is real friendship! Their portraits [will] be framed and hung on the wall as the perfect example of 'Good Friends'. [Thirty-seven lines omitted]

Bless you my dearest my love and love to Sebastian. Yr CARRINGTON

To Lytton Strachey

Wednesday, 5 o'ck [July 12th, 1922]   *The Mill House, Tidmarsh*

Darling Lytton, I do hope you'll enjoy London very much, I miss you today ... although I talk such a little I do love being with you and it makes me happy in a very real way. I wish I could forget everything. I try to, but some things it's difficult to get over. It isn't easy to lose a friend. I miss Gerald's letters, and his friendship more than I ever thought, in my wildest moments I should; and when one mustn't talk of it, it keeps on tormenting one's head. But I won't talk of him because it only makes me remember him more; then, after all, no one else can mind except me. Only if I am grousy, and sullen you mustn't think me

[1] From Clare.

altogether selfish. I've read 'the Watsons'[1] today with my meals. It
wasn't very good. But perhaps it was because it didn't end and one felt
rather angry at being defrauded. I haven't kept my Reform Bill. Today
I've not yet, and it's nearly 5 o'ck painted a stroke. But there are two
sweet boys mending something in the bath room, a senior builder for-
bade me to forth in any W.C. except the garden, the bricklayer crashed
broken glass on the wall with all violence possible 2 men repaired
drains outside, Mrs Stiles whisked and broomed about inside, so I
became restless and rushed off into the orchard and bashed, and nailed
away at the fence. Now it's all repaired and set up again on its feet until
the next storm. An organ grinder played this afternoon and brought
melancholy to me. It plays the gayest of tunes but I always feel like
crying when I hear it. It has played every afternoon that I have been
particularly unhappy here. The day I wrote to you when you were in
Florence and told you I should marry R[alph]. The day I wrote my last
letter to G[erald] and many other days, all Black days. So today which
was so lovely, and smelt so good, suddenly by an organ grinder made me
all despair.

I shall open Dora's[2] letter and if the news is too devastating I'll
wire it to you at 51 Gordon Square and then you can ring up R[alph] at
Richmond. Remember everything you see and do. I wish I could hear
Suggia tonight. Lytton dear, I loved my walk with you so much yesterday in the fields. You are more to me than I can ever express to you. I
wish I could make you as happy as you can make me. I write in an
absurd humour, so forgive the stupidity of this letter. My fondest love,

Yr MOPSA

To Lytton Strachey

Tuesday, 5 o'ck [September 25th, 1922]   *The Mill House, Tidmarsh*

Darling Lytton, *I* am still at Tidmarsh, and *you* will read this in Berlin!
You can't think how sorry I am that we can't be with you. You must
forget nothing and you must come back laden with surprises: German
sweets, post cards of Russian actresses, boots lined with fur, cigars for
the Majora, and German picture books and honey cake! That is the

---

[1] Jane Austen's unfinished novel.
[2] Unidentified.

most lovely cake in the world! Beg James to find you some. I felt very
inadequate in my thanks this morning dear one. But you must know
behind my trivial verses I meant a good deal. I knew how awful it would
be, even for a few minutes last night facing that sort of conversation.
But I am so glad you craved it. I almost thought perhaps you thought I
had been nonsensical to be so alarmed since when you talked to him you
found him so calm. But you know he does change very rapidly, and
partly because of my position, and partly because I dislike these scenes,
I know and ask very little of his present feelings now, and of what has
happened since she [Clare] came back. But I do know a great deal of his
past feelings, and her conduct. So my moments of alarm aren't quite
groundless. But Lytton how can I ever thank you for all your support
and your conversations? When you are here a creeping paralysis seems
to come over me and I can say nothing of what I feel. But when you
leave me I want to rush after you and hug you for all your goodness.
You are almost *too* good you know. Sometimes I feel almost embarrassed.
You must always tell me if you aren't quite happy, and if I could make
anything more comfortable in any way. I think Ralph is immensely
relieved at having talked to you. I think he felt there was rather a gulf
growing up because she was never mentioned. And yet, up till now, I
think he would have resented any approaches from you; I believe you
chose the one and perfect moment to speak to him. Later perhaps he will
be able to tell me more of his feelings. I am only so glad that you are
happy. I rely so entirely on your judgement. I haven't painted today as
I am rather stuck until the chair arrives. So I tidied up my room, and
arranged my paints and cleaned my palettes. It's even a dirtier business
than your book cleaning!

I do hope you didn't have a very 'ruff' crossing. It thundered here
this afternoon. The house seemed very dismal and sad without you. No
more jaunts when you come back. Promise? I hope Alix will come on
Friday. Perhaps James will come down here with you and then will go
back with Alix to Lord's Wood the next day. Already I am making plans
for your return you see. This is a stupid letter but I write very quickly
to catch the post, only I felt you hardly knew how much I loved you this
morning and I want you to know.

Bless you und der Gut Gott nach Du etwas sehen. Euer Liebe

MOPSA

To David Garnett

Friday, October 26th, 1922   *The Mill House, Tidmarsh*

Dear Bunny, I must write and tell you how much I enjoyed your book
[*Lady Into Fox*] last night. I read it breathlessly at a sitting in about 3
hours! Really I believe you must have written it especially for me it
pleased me so much! Lytton says the style is superb and I agree with
him, as in all things but *I* think *the story* is so beautiful and fascinating.

Ralph was reading a story by Beckford last night at the same time in
which the gentleman became a bear and some ladies swans, woolves
and various other birds, eagles I think, so somehow we all became raised
into a most beautiful world of animals through our various books.
Lytton was reading Vathek most of the time, and it was a cruel blow for
me to have to retire to bed with a mere man. But I mean to tell you
about your book. I suppose you will soon be worn out with flattery and
praise if you are not already. But I doubt if any can be as genuine as
mine because I am sure no one except a few people could like your book
as much as I did. Once I had a lovely dream about a fox and very often
buzzards are my night companions. But it is a rare pleasure to find a
book to read *by day* so entirely to one's taste. The people in England will
be idiots if they don't all read it as quickly as they can, for it makes one
so happy. Will you tell Rachel [Ray Garnett] how much I liked some of
her woodcuts. The very small one on the front page of the Reluctant
Mrs Fox behind the bush with her husband I think I liked best. I am just
going to write and tell Alix what a good book it is. Will you please send G.
Brenan a copy. *Reg: post. And put it down to my account* as soon as you
can. G. Brenan. YEGEN, Ugijar, Prov. de Granada, SPAIN in case you
have lost his address.

I am sorry to write such a bad letter, but this is the first one I have
ever, (except last week to Virginia), written an author in praise of his
book.

You must be very excited and proud to have made such a book! I
feel now one has mismanaged life. Surely nothing could be nicer than that
life in the woods with Madame FOX. I am sorry [W.H.] Hudson died before he could read it. But I can't help being very glad I am alive to have
read it. You mustn't think because I am rather a flatterer I say all this

without meaning it. Because really I do love your book so much and not simply because you wrote it.

Please remember me to that exquisite sister in law Frances [Marshall]. Perhaps if one can't hope to have tea at Tidmarsh with a Fox, sometimes a Rabbit will grace our board?

Your affectionate and most admiring   CARRINGTON

[Leonard Woolf had made it plain that there was no future for Ralph Partridge in the Hogarth Press.]

To Lytton Strachey

Monday afternoon [*November 6th, 1922*]   *The Mill House, Tidmarsh*

Dear, I posted your letters which I found on the table.

I feel very vacant headed today after all those arguments of yesterday. I do so want Ralph to keep in the [Hogarth] Press if possible because in so many ways it is such a good job for him. On the other hand it's intolerable if he really doesn't suit them, from both points of view. [Nine lines omitted] I wish you weren't in London. After all these mental crises one longs to sit over the fire, and read Shandy, and shut out this world of activity and crises. I wish my telling would have some effect on making you believe how good those dialogues were. But I know it doesn't! But all the same you might believe how very much we both liked them. Lytton dear I get blockades in the head when you are here, for such absurd reasons, so that I always feel you must think I'm very tiresome. I do love you so much. And you make my life a very happy one. I am feeling rather extremely today in my solitude how much *you* matter. Ralph agreed yesterday that nothing mattered compared to our Triangular Trinity of Happiness. Even expulsion from the Garden of Paradise Road[1] is nothing if we three are together. My dear, you are so good to us, and I love you terribly sometimes. Please take great care and don't get any colds. I am looking forward to Suggia!

Yr most loving   CARRINGTON

---

[1] The address of the Hogarth Press was then Paradise Road, Richmond.

To Gerald Brenan

Monday, November 14th, 1922   *The Mill House, Tidmarsh*

Kunak, Your letter has just come. I feel I deserve your reproaches. One does get into states of mind similar to those of scullery maids over this business. It's true what *is* this absurd frankness which we all talk about, and do not keep! How can we tell what our feelings will be when we see each other?

Oh Gerald you will never know what it was to be on the battlefield. If *you* have a nausea for these past events you can guess a little what I feel. But mercifully *you* aren't associated in my head with all these nightmare days and nights. I never connect you with them. Thank God I never saw you except once under those hideous clouds. Ralph has been the person who has in a way ruined himself for me in some curious way by being associated with all that ugliness. I learnt to dread him, and to fear him. Which are rather difficult sensations to recover from even in six months. My God, you know I *do* sometimes blast and curse Clare for all this havoc!

To Gerald Brenan

December 20th, 1922   *The Mill House, Tidmarsh*

Dearest Gerald, I am so old fashioned that I keep Christmas almost as seriously as Annie does. So I must write and wish you a Happy Christmas and a Gay New Year. I have nothing to send you. I meant to paint you a little picture, but it was never done. Perhaps I will think of some book that will please you when I will send it to you. I had a wonderful visit to Normandy. The beauty of the country still makes me a little discontented with our flat marshes, and these insignificant hills. I saw the forests of Eure (probably spelt wrong) that Ralph knew when he was in Normandy. Did you ever go there with him? It was fascinating living with people so strangely different from oneself. I only wish I could remember all the stories Phyllis told me. A wonderful account of Lady Munster her grandmother who lived at Brighton and had 40 clocks all going at the same time in her bedroom. But of course

you with aunt Tiz[1] will not think much of such tales. I left just a week
ago today on December 13th. The sea was very rough, and a French
woman vomitted all over my luggage. A just reward for my selfishness,
as although I knew she wanted a basin I refused to go and get it for her.
However I had some slight revenge when a custom's officer at Newhaven
insisted on opening my suitcases 'something damp in this case mam',
suspecting brandy or scent leaking over my clothes. 'Yes, a woman was
sick on my box'. He shut it up very quickly and gave me a look of rage.
Ralph met me at Victoria. We had so much to say, after a week, we
talked until we became tired with talking. And soon forgot all we had
important to say and talked absurdities. We had dinner at Ralph's
mother's flat, in Francis Street. I wish you could see them and the flat.
For pure Anglo-Indian plus sham Jacobean taste it is unrivalled. Mrs P.
is a pretty good example of a provincial missionary's daughter, full of
false pride and ignorance.

Dorothy is much more human. She sings so beautifully and has
learnt many lovely songs simply to please R[alph] and me, Mozart and
the Ganges song and many other good old English songs. Mrs P[art-
ridge] I think thinks we are very heathen not to like the Italian songs
that Dorothy used to sing in Milan. After dinner we rushed off to a
lecture by Roger Fry. He is giving a whole series of lectures. Tracing
the development of design, and 'significant form' in painting. He has
amazing slides, Giotto, and the Sienese school. He always shows one a
great many that one has never seen before. The last lecture brought one
up to Uccello. Tout le monde is at these lectures. The females are
characterised by their plainness and serious countenances, and males
by their long hair and pasty spotty faces. Everybody knows everybody
so before the lecture begins, the babble of conversation is not to be
described in words. Chelsea meets Bloomsbury, Hampstead bows to
Richmond and even ladies from Mayfair talk graciously to Logan Pear-
sall-Smith and Mr Tatlock.[2] If J.H.-J. was only there nobody you could
possibly think of is not there! After the lecture, Barbara, Ralph and I
went to Duncan's [Grant] studio above J.H.-J.'s old room, to a sort of
informal party. It was rather a classical party, with an air of a French
studio in 1889. Arthur Waley's mistress Miss De Z[oete] played Bach
on a harpsichord; the room was lit by candles, young earnest Cambridge
men twisted and twirled on their toes and shrieked in high nasal voices.

[1] Gerald Brenan's great-aunt.
[2] Editor of the *Burlington Magazine of Fine Art*.

Vanessa drooped like a flower with a too heavy head over some coffee boiling on a stove. Duncan moved about with sprightly steps with trays of biscuits and beer in glasses. I talked to Miss Margery Fry about Vienna and the poverty of the Germans and behind me I heard Ralph discussing Spain with Arthur Waley. The next day Thursday we came down here. Tidmarsh looked wonderfully beautiful after an absence of a week. It is so snug and warm, lined with its walls of coloured books. In the winter when it's so dark one can't see the rat holes and the dust; one curls up in it like a fox in its hole, contented. We had a very social weekend, Sebastian Sprott, a young lecturer in psychology at Cambridge, Morgan Forster, and Roger Fry.

So you didn't like 'Lady in Fox'. Morgan told me he had heard from you and repeated everything you wrote to him! And I liked it so much. Ralph is more on your side than on mine. He didn't care nearly so much for it as I did. But then again, *Lytton* likes it! Morgan is a charming character. He is so amusing and has good ideas when he is serious. Roger's vitality never fails. He talks from the moment he appears at breakfast till he goes to sleep murmuring his Coué chant. For he is a devoted disciple of that French Christ. They all left us on Monday. Tomorrow Ralph's holidays begin. I am glad, secretly I admit, because I want to finish a picture of him.

The yellow cat has passed away. Dead as a ducat. Maynard Keynes, and Lydia Lopokova come here for Christmas. I hardly know Lydia; opinions seem to differ very much about her character. After Xmas I will tell you what I think of her. Ralph will write and tell you all the Hogarth Press developments. I will not encroach on his domain. Roger's lectures (on the Italian pictures) have inspired me to start some big compositions. Suddenly reviewing my last year's work it seems disgracefully amateurish and 'little'. So I shall now start this Xmas after they have all gone a composition of an interior scene in this kitchen. Only I shall paint it very big. I do not want to tackle anything too difficult, or I know I shall then despair and give up the composition before it is finished. J.H.-J. hasn't sent our photographs yet. I hope he won't abandon them when he reaches his island friends. Ralph gave me your last letter to read.

I am so sorry you have not been well. What is the matter with you? If it is serious and continuous, do go to Seville and see an English or a German doctor. Please don't get decrepid like J.H.-J. and all those Fitzroy people. I have the greatest contempt for people like Middleton Murry and Katherine Murry who think it is 'interesting' to be ill and who sniff up their noses at any writer who hasn't cancer in the stomach, or violent consumption.

I've got such a good book on Rousseau. But I refrain from sending you any book, picture, verse, or prose after your severe 'Vixenish' rebuke.

My mother has just bought another house, this time at Minchinhampton. Poor woman she already writes, even before she has moved in and asks me if I know of anyone who would like to buy it! The shady eldest brother has returned from Spain bankrupt, and now lives fast and loose sponging on my sister in London. Mercifully I have not yet seen him. Do write to Ralph soon and send him some MSS. This was meant to be an interesting letter to cheer your Christmas feast. It seems to me on rereading it to be about as stale as that Christmas pudding must be which probably still sits in the poste restante at Granada. Would you like the New Statesman and Nation every week or do you take them yourself? Answer N. or M. Now I must stop, as the paper is all used up. I send my love and best wishes that next year we may all be happier: bless you.   Yr KUNAK
I'll try and write a more interesting letter after Christmas.

To Virginia Woolf

Thursday, December 21st, 1922   *The Mill House, Tidmarsh*

Dearest Virginia, I send you this little casket of sweetness as a token of my affection for you and Leonard. Please honour me by accepting it with my best wishes for a Happy Christmas, and successful New Year. Well, well. So now it's all over.

I thank you for trying so valiantly at Tidmarsh to come to a happy ending. But perhaps reviewing everything now it will all turn out for the best. Ralph is rather disconsolate at the moment but I expect his feelings will soon revive. I am sorry of course, because I cared so much for the Press that I couldn't help wishing Ralph to be in it also. But that's not quite a good enough reason for his staying in it when there are so many complications on both sides. But we are still all friends. I must say that seems to me a most important issue. In January I will come and see you again at Hogarth. We had a very gay and talkative weekend last Saturday, Sebastian, Morgan, and Roger. On Saturday

Maynard and Loppy arrive. We are all slightly trembling at their approach. Today we went to Reading. The male element were very crabbid and wouldn't let me spend any money on Christmas presents, so I am busy making toffee, and converting bromo boxes into Italian letter cases this evening.

I have never seen you since I went to Normandy but I will keep my adventures as a bribe so you may ask me to tea in January. I heard awful accounts of poor Lottie.[1] I think I am suffering from her disease. My cushions have become racked with cramps, and pains, these last few days.

I hope you and Leonard will enjoy Rodmell. Ralph sends you his love and best wishes. Lytton also sends his.

CARRINGTON sends even more.

Illustration from School edition of *Don Quixote*
(Oxford University Press, 1922).

---

[1] The Woolfs' servant.

Woodcut by Carrington for *Two Stories*.

1923

To Gerald Brenan

[*January 1st, 1923*]   *The Mill House, Tidmarsh*

Kunak, Write please to me soon. Now that it is all over, and we are free again, are we so chicken-spirited that we have no affections left?

I tell you Ralph has completely altered. I told him both times I wrote to you, and asked him if he would like to read my letters to you. He never bothered to, and then simply laughed at me when I said I had posted them two days later. Is all this to have a Tchekov ending? 'That after months of self denial, and anguish, when they could write they found all desire had vanished.' Or you may be ill? Or perhaps on a ship bound to Buenos Aires, or the West Indies? I send you all my love for this New Year. Lately, because perhaps I have nothing of you now, I have been living in a ghostly world of memories. I can't help being very fond. I am now so grateful that I had the little of you that I did have. It might have been even less. Here is a book on El Greco. I don't know if you have one on him already. He is almost my favourite artist. I am reading Hogg's life of Shelley now by myself in the evenings. Please, unless you feel disinclined write to me, or Ralph soon, if that (disinclined) I can wait. My dear, I wish I could see you again soon. I send all the love you want, and my best wishes for your work. Your loving DORIC

[In March 1923 Lytton, Ralph and Carrington visited Tunis, sailing from Marseilles on March 21st. They had planned to meet James and Alix Strachey who had been travelling from Algiers. But James wired to say that Alix had been taken ill at Hammam-Meskoutine. They therefore changed their plans and set off to meet them there.]

To Gerald Brenan

[*About March 23rd, 1923*]   *Written in the train between Tunis and*
Constantine

Last night after tea which I now brew in the Hotel on a spirit lamp,
Ralph and I went for an exploration into the Jewish quarter of Tunis.
At first we only saw the curious Yiddish eating houses and souks; there
seemed no very definite distinction between the Moslem quarters and
those of the Jewish people. Suddenly we came to a very narrow little
alley with only room for two people to walk abreast. In front of us
walked a little girl of ten, very gaily dressed, a short frock above her
knees, white socks, enormous fat pink legs, walking in little wooden
pattens very slowly, picking her way through puddles, as it had been
raining all day. Her hair was short, yellow tied with a big bow. We felt
we had reached the 'nymphs' quarter!

Suddenly she turned round. Her face was that of a hideous harlot old
and jaded, covered with thick paint, terribly made up. Then we saw more
and more of these horrible F A T creatures, the alley grew narrower. Some
in chemises just below their parts, *all* with bare legs, except for the low
white socks. They lay on little benches at the door of their little houses,
which seemed to consist of a single room, and hung about in groups at
the doors. They shrieked at us. I couldn't make out if they were French
or Jewesses. I think French. But you can't conceive the effect it had on
one, seeing these creatures, touching them, for the alley was so narrow.
They were painted as pantomime girls are painted for the stage and all
in these ridiculous 'little girl' dresses with fat doll-like legs. Ralph was
excited at these apparitions. I confess I was filled with a curious terror.
One awful thing was that the men, some Moslems, some French, walking
down the alley looked at them perfectly calmly and cynically. We saw
some amazing scenes in other alleys. Bake houses; a huge negro with a
great tray of little cakes which he was putting in a huge oven. His face
and bare top of his body lit up by the red furnace. Little coffee houses
with Moslems sitting round on high shelves against the walls, cross-
legged and smoking. Basket and rope shops with huge monster moham-
madans lying on heaps of plaited rushes, like great sheiks in some
Arabian Nights Dream. One in a little eating house suddenly leered and
made a most dreadful face at me like one of those lecherous Chinese
masks. As a rule they hardly look at one, or if they do, scowl.

Coming back we came across another Jewish quarter, with dark olive skinned women all painted and bedecked with earrings, long greasy black hair and Eastern trowsers and shawls. They were obviously harlots; one saw inside little rooms with divans, and old hags equally painted.

It's queer leaving these little alleys and souks to come out through a big archway and find trams, civilized French women and men in Paris clothes. Bon marchés and post offices. [Eight pages omitted]

[On the way they visited the ruins of Timgad and saw the Roman mosaics, 'finer than Ravenna'. It was a cold wet day and Carrington had been feeling ill with a pain in her chest. She caught a feverish chill. She had to go to bed when they arrived at Hammam-Meskoutine and was not allowed to see Alix Strachey before her departure with James, in case she should communicate infection. She was quite ill.]

To Gerald Brenan

April 27th, 1923   [*? Kairouan*]

I will write a more orderly letter soon. I hope you keep well. I long to have news of you, and hear all about the Woolfs [who were visiting Yegen]. You can't be too enthusiastic, to please me, over Virginia! I always feel she is one of the few people it has actually been tremendously good fortune to have known in this life. I am sure few women since the beginning of the world have equalled her for wit and charm, and a special rare kind of beauty.

This will be one of the longest holidays we have ever made. I doubt if we will be back in ENGLAND until the middle of May now. We spent a whole month at that curious place Hammam-Meskoutine. I don't regret it. For one never really enjoys a place utterly to its fullest until one has been there a long time. The last evening there was perhaps the most perfect. I had not been outside in the fields for nearly a week as I had been in bed. Everything had a peculiar vividness for this reason. I fell in love with olive trees again. The blue borage, orange marigolds, yellow daisies, and purple gladiolas seemed to me more brilliant and wonderful than I had thought before. We sat in a little grass valley, looking down a steep bank on to a little stream, which ran dark, and cold like some black snake beneath the oleanders, heavy palm trees, and tropical oaks. The gnats flew from flower to flower shining in the sun which was just sinking behind the great mountains. The asphodels looked ghostly pale and transparent and their stalks were invisible against the green grass, only their pink-grey flowers were lighted by the sun. Lytton read us Keats: Endymion and the Nightingale. The air was very still and hot, and I thought Keats and this world had never been so exquisitely beautiful before. The sun sank and we walked along the ridge of the hill through the olive trees, and asphodels listening to the nightingales and croaking frogs. To feel such ecstasy seems to me to make life, even if all the other days were dull and tiresome in the year, worth living. Someday you must go to Meskoutine. I am sure nowhere so much pure beauty is contained. I cannot forget those fields of flowers, and the amazing beauty of the mountains.

Monday, April 23rd [28th], 1923   *Kairouan*

This is a superb town! The raging wind has gone down, and the sky is completely blue. We have just seen the great mosque. One is allowed inside, for in 1840, the French stabled their horses inside, and so defiled the mosque for good. It is far more beautiful than Cordova, with a vast marble courtyard outside surrounded by a colonnade of marble pillars, which I think were taken from Carthage. Lytton has been buying leather morocco skins in the souks this morning. They are absurdly cheap, even although we are swindled, I expect, by these crafty Moslems. Yesterday we had coffee outside a little Moorish coffee house, and watched the sun go down. The good Moslems eat nothing from sunrise to sunset now for 40 days. It's very simple and rather extraordinary to see them sitting in rows outside the eating houses with oranges and cakes in their hands waiting until the muezzin from the minaret cries out. Then they all fall on their food, and drink up their cups of coffee. Kairouan is far more Eastern than Biskra. There are only 500 Europeans in the whole population, and no French buildings, and only this one hotel.

[Some words missing] are rather worm eaten and poxmarked. One sees no great sheiks or chieftains or Arab horses. Do write to me. We won't leave Rome c/o Thomas Cook until the 12th of May about and then Tidmarsh. My fondest love.   DORIC

To Virginia Woolf

Sunday, May 20th, 1923   *The Mill House, Tidmarsh*

Dearest Virginia, We are back again ... One expected a crowd of enthusiastic friends at Victoria, a budget of letters at Tidmarsh. There was nothing! Then I read last night your account of Spain and I felt you were the only person who understood the immensity of travelling to Timgad and Segesta and returning to England. Perhaps Hogarth [House] didn't disappoint you. I confess I was depressed the moment we climbed on board our ship at Boulogne (yesterday afternoon), and saw Bonar Law's dreary yellow face on the deck, and the crowds of dull English travellers. I even turned traitor to Kent and Sussex and despised them. The Clapham back gardens with the hens. But still I felt we were travelling to Tidmarsh and that the moment I saw its beauties my spirits would revive. Do you know for the first time in my life I turned against our Mill? I suddenly felt, as I suspect all our visitors feel, how very flat, and provincial it was and that the ducks, and chickens were just as dull as those in the Clapham back gardens. My mother was here and had put new covers on all the chairs and made the insides of all the rooms look completely hideous. But even she did not entirely account for my depression. One didn't realize what an exciting and beautiful life one had led these last two months until last night. You will suspect me imitating your travels in Spain if I tell you of all our adventures in Italy in this letter. And although I *know* you will accuse me of flattery I must tell you I thought your essay[1] was amazing! Everything came back to me. Every word you wrote gave me a vision of scenes I had quite forgotten and I loved you for writing it. This letter is all a prologue to a cadge for an invitation to Hogarth. Will you ask me to tea with you. So that I can talk to you *alone*, of all your adventures, and Gerald? I can easily come up for a day, or will you both visit this rather despondent Mill? Gerald alone did not play me false, last night and wrote me a long letter. But he simply omitted to tell me one word about the last month because he said you would tell me everything.

This is such a stupid letter. But I feel so excited and at the same time depressed that I can do nothing sensibly.

The cold here is dreadful after Rome and I can hardly bear the way

[1] Possibly 'To Spain'; Virginia Woolf, *Collected Essays*, 4 vols. (Hogarth Press, 1966, 1967), vol. 4, p. 188.

the elms seem to press against the windows, after living in an Archbishop's Palace at Ravello that looked across the Bay to Paestum. Lytton comes back tomorrow and then perhaps by murmuring the mystic word Segusta ... and removing the chair covers one will gain a little of one's lost happiness. Dear Virginia, I do so long to see you again. Please give Leonard my love. I send you a little present which I brought you in Rome. Perhaps round your garden hat?

My fondest love   Yr old CARRINGTON

To Gerald Brenan

Sunday, May 28th, 1923   *The Mill House, Tidmarsh*

Amigo, I put off writing the long letter that had been fermenting in my head since we left Italy because it is so difficult to write letters off hand, and then when I got back to England I felt the most violent depression which has only just left me. We have now been exactly a week in England. It was madness to return. Rome is a far better place in which to live than this flat greenery. The cold is awful in England. I was going to write to you this long letter after I had seen Virginia but then something she told me when I went to tea with her last Wednesday made everything vanish out of my head.

I wanted to go to tea with her alone, but that wasn't possible, as R[alph] was in London with me. Still it didn't make any difference really. Virginia said just as I was putting a piece of stale iced cake into my mouth, 'You know Gerald is going to get married; he has just written and told Leonard that he is engaged to that American girl.' I think it was the word 'engaged' that made me feel it wasn't true and then made me rather angry. I felt Virginia couldn't know you very well to use such a word in reference to you, or perhaps everything had changed. I quickly argued that my feelings were absurd, all words are absurd and 'engaged' is just as good a word as 'bedding'. Then she said: 'I thought he probably would get married very soon, but of course it may be one of his jokes.'

I wish I could have the definite feelings that Ralph has, he was plunged into a profound gloom, and felt he must go out and see you at once.

All the way back from Richmond, he talked about you and saw all the horrors of marriage, the end of our friendship and every possible disaster. If it is true that E. is going to live with you, or marry you, Gerald, I am so very glad. Because at any rate for a certain time, a few years, you will be happy, or happier than you have been this last year. No one but a fool imagines that he can be certain of achieving happiness for more than a few months. If it was only one of your passing jokes to Leonard which he misunderstood, then all I have written is unnecessary. But I wanted to tell you, because I think I probably care more for your happiness than anyone else, that I am very glad if you are going to [be] happy with E.

Will you please write, and tell me soon. It does in a curious way make rather a difference. I am not going to write a long letter today. In a few days I will.

In any case I refuse to believe our friendship was so ordinary that if you take a new friend, or a wife, to yourself, our relation ends. Ralph couldn't understand why I wasn't 'hurt'. Really he understands very little my feelings for you. Perhaps I shall be more contented if you remove finally all possibility of my ever coming to Spain alone. In spite of growing older I still find I have lapses. I am often very stupid. I hate facing certain things as impossibilities and seeing the limitations of our life.

Your letter is in my hand. It is not true [that] R[alph] is more human than I am and has no feelings about classes. You only know such a small portion of my life. You do not know the number of 'ordinary' friendships I make and my attachments for such people.

I told Virginia I wasn't surprised and that I guessed you would soon marry E. It was only half true. I wanted to gain a little time to hide my feelings from her. Then it is partly true for ever since you first told me about E. I had faced this as a probability.

Perhaps if you have her with you, you will be able to regard me more easily as a 'neuter' friend. It's pretty depressing what a mess I made of your feelings and of mine this last year. I always thank you for not reviling me.

Virginia was so charming. But it was a slight nightmare. I longed to talk to her about you, ask her hundreds of questions.

But I felt as if there was a glass window between us and that she couldn't hear what I was saying.

The flowered cottons were lovely. They looked so beautiful in the sitting room at Hogarth. Ralph's without a job. I hardly think we will ever get a Press. There seems no money to start it with. Perhaps something will turn up soon. Gerald, I am so glad about the money from your father. I do hope [Tiz] doesn't withdraw her allowance. Your poverty really was tedious. Why on earth couldn't your father have done it years ago? You must have been very diplomatic to bring off the allowance coup. This letter is incoherent, and stupid, but I only write with half of my brain. Do not because I am D.C. think you cannot write to me about my feelings, or I shall *despise* you.

If you are happy, or unhappy it matters to me. It will be a relief if for a change *I* am not responsible.

I think Ralph is writing to you. His agitation over your fate shows how deeply he cares. I have seldom seen him so upset. In a few days I will write sensibly of other matters. Even if you become a Moslem and marry four wives I am damned if I will stop writing to you.

Gerald dear I send you my love.

I can hardly bear Barbara going out to you. It's intolerable. Why do you allow it! Why can everyone go to Spain and stay with you except your rejected, and deserted   QUEEN OF NOTHING
PS Tidmarsh seems incredibly squalid and cramped after Ravello. And I hate these backyard hens and ducks. Ugh! Perhaps we will leave it soon. It is too green and stuffy.

Note by Gerald Brenan

This story of my engagement to an American girl must have been one of Virginia's inventions. When staying at Granada I had gone about with and flirted with an American girl who was engaged to a dentist in Buffalo. I never felt anything at all about her and when I made some physical advances to her one evening in the Alhambra Gardens I was repulsed. She believed in purity.

She of course never came to Yegen.

To Gerald Brenan

May 31st, 1923   *The Mill House, Tidmarsh*

Amigo, I will make some attempt to fill in the gaps now, the interval
between Rome (two weeks now) and Tidmarsh. But it shows how dreary
everything is, travelling, London, gossip, all dreary compared to friendship. Because in spite of my head being fuller than it's ever been full
before of things I want to tell you, I can only remember Virginia
saying: 'Gerald has just told Leonard that he is engaged.' I remember so
accurately what happened exactly a year ago today. You probably can't
remember. The gloomy days of despair didn't begin until June 7th
for us. How I sympathise with those aged women who suddenly say
over the cold mutton on Sunday evening: 'exactly twenty years ago, I
and my dear husband ... ' 'It was just this time of the year, I remember
the apple blossom on the grass, and the organ grinder ... ' I used to
wonder how my mother remembered. I see really it's one of the forms of
masturbation, a self indulgence. One doesn't want to forget. I went up to
London yesterday. I telephoned Virginia. I wanted to go and see her
alone. I wanted to hear more about you. But she was away from Richmond. You can't tell me anything. So don't bother to write me a sermon
of reproaches or explanations. If you tell me anything at all, I shall
understand. I know you couldn't have remained a hermit for ever and I
have said every time I read a letter from you that I didn't deserve such
luck to have your letters. And when you said our friendship was futile
and probably doomed because of all the circumstances, I knew you were
right. But I thought perhaps since nothing ever happens as I expect it
will happen, that perhaps we might always be friends. Perhaps you were
really as curious as I thought you were. What I regret, and always will
regret, is I didn't know you better when I might have known you. And
you never knew how fond I was. I concealed that. I can't think why I
did now. At the time there seemed some reason for it.

But I will refrain from more masturbation of the spirit. And I will
go back to my old philosophy that one need never be gloomy about the
future, since it is never what one thinks it will be. I wish, so very much,
I could come out with Barbara to Yegen. I find one doesn't care for new
people. And when I hear news of you indirectly, all my old impatience
to see you again and laugh and joke, comes back to me. I am going to do

my best to prevent Ralph getting involved in a business which prevents him having holidays. Then unless you lose all your money, or become a hopeless family man, we may meet more often. Shall I tell you what comes into my head. I don't really see that it matters. The difficulty is, without making a letter as bulky as the Bible, to describe one's *exact* feelings. The reason why your friendship matters is because you are nearer to me in spirit than anyone else. I agree so very closely with your views on life. It gives me a support, and a self respect for myself. Lytton has the effect of making me feel so stupid and hopeless about myself that I wish to avoid the world and retreat. It isn't that *he* thinks this about me, it is grasping his standards and preciseness, his truth and the way he is 'himself' so entirely. Ralph has the opposite effect. I feel it isn't a very serious matter after all and that one had better face oneself and then leave it alone. When I talk to you, I am not conscious of all these struggles. I feel clearer when I read your letters but not gloomy. How badly I express this. It seems complete balderdash when I read it over. And yet when it came to the point I couldn't face giving up Ralph and Lytton for you. All I want to put forward to you is my point of view. I can't give you my reasons for caring for you. Although it's illogical and impossible I do still care. Your letters and the knowledge that you think of me with affection matter very much to me. If you write back and say you have changed now and unfortunately you don't care so much for me, I don't really see it matters. It will just be a new fact to grasp. Only I think the truth is more interesting than a lie. I can quite see if I met someone new, Mr Ramsey,[1] of Cambridge, perhaps who they all say is a paragon of intellect and beauty, I should, if he fascinated me and begged me to write to him every week, write probably less to you. One can't repeat all one['s] emotions to two people every week. And it's affectation to pretend one does not adore the novelty of a new friendship. So I am quite prepared if you tell me that you have made new friends, so that it's rather difficult to keep up our old habits. But since I am imaginative will you tell me instead of letting my internal feelings stray about in this chaotic fashion?

If it's become rather a drudge to you, tell me. Later I daresay we will start it again. But I am the soul of discretion Gerald. I almost enjoy this virtue I possess. I'll even abandon my letter writing, until you restart it. It's curious but no matter what you do, or say, I never for a moment feel angry or criticise you. If you marry: in *you* I see it's

---

[1] Frank Ramsey, mathematician and philosopher.

perfectly sensible and even courageous. If you don't marry I think you are equally original. Alix would say I've a complex about you. Probably, I often suspected it. I am in love with Shelley and so I pretend Shelley lives in you and you can never do wrong for me. In any case I should make the most of your rare advantages, and trounce me and bounce me since you cannot turn me into a vixen!

Harry Norton agrees with you over 'Lady into Fox'. He said: 'I can't see any point in the book, why should a lady turn into a fox!'? Alix spent last weekend with the Nortons.—Yesterday I went up to London to my dentist again. I spent all the rest of the day with Alix. She is amazing. She never disappoints me. She always has some amusing new mood. Yesterday she had developed an aesthetic mood, and bought two carpets of great beauty for her rooms and told me the Cambridge gossip. Morgan Forster spent last weekend with us. I always feel I know him so well before he comes, but when he is actually here, I feel rather shy with him. He was very amusing about Mr 'Dunning' the great seer of Middleton Murry's group. On Monday I went into Reading with him. I found a superb book for 2/- of botanical prints. I love it so much. I can't part with it yet. Perhaps if you wrote to me before Barbara started for Yegen, it might start with Barbara. But I did buy expressly for you this 'Journal from High Latitudes' by Dufferin. Perhaps you have got it already. In that case you had better give it to Saxon, or Barbara. I read it in the train on the way back from Rome. It filled me with a great longing to go to Iceland. I think the illustrations are good, especially the drawing of Wilson. Don't thank me, it was such a cheap book.

I hated Switzerland. We passed through the Simplon tunnel and saw all the grand mountains, and lakes, complete with sunset, Swiss cows, chalets, and glaciers. It seemed to me a monument of all that was pretentious, and vulgar in the Victorian epoch. The country between Naples and Rome was lovely. Wonderful fields of corn, and vineyards, with distant blue mountains. It reminded me of that lovely picture by Poussin in the Louvre, 'Ruth and Boaz'. Beautiful women with bare legs and feet, broad straw hats and blue pinafores were heaping hay on to great carts in the fields.

They looked so gay, but at the same time classical. One returns to England and finds wet green fields, cold winds, and perpetual rain and females in the fields wearing artificial silk jerseys, with hideous young men in navy blue serge Sunday clothes. You have no idea how I hated Tidmarsh when we came back. I felt pretty gloomy when the hideous Switzerland blotted out Italy. And then when one reached Boulogne and

saw the groups of dull pink faced English ranged up in rows on the tiny
steamers and saw a condensed vision of English life with its conventions and dullness and felt all was ashes and brimstone. But I kept
murmuring 'Tidmarsh will be good and beautiful'. When we reached it
I saw it was just the same as the back gardens of Clapham which I had
despised from the train from Dover. I saw why you thought the ducks
and the bees so tedious, and boring last year! I owe you an apology for
my denseness in that direction. My mother had covered all the chairs
in neat holland and rearranged the furniture. The inside had become
surburban also. When I thought of Ravello and the great courtyard
with its marble staircase, I suffered terribly. It's better now. Two weeks
have dulled my sensations. I still hate the ducks and the bees, but I no
longer think of Ravello, and Rome.

I am contemplating buying a studio, and putting it up in the garden.
I find the room-space is too cramped. But perhaps we shall leave Tidmarsh next year; then it won't be worth while. I want to find a house on
the Lambourn Downs. I think it's a mistake to become sentimental over
any place and I can't quite get over my hatred for this garden and the
dull green fields since our return from Rome. [Seventeen lines omitted]

I advise you to take a ship to Naples and inspect Amalfi and Ravello.
All the country from Amalfi to Calva seemed to me very good. My
mother now lives near Newbury in an old Georgian cottage. Ralph and I
go over and see her once a week and loot her house of eatables and clothes.
Today Ralph found in the old cellars beneath her house 8 very old glass
wine flasks. They must be some 300 years old. I have washed them and
put them on the dresser. They are amazingly beautiful. Dark olive
green. One has a glass seal on it with 3 wild geese, and a hand rampant.
Next week we will see Duse act in 'Ghosts'. Lytton has just read the
play to us. We are now reading Othello in the evenings. Lytton acts the
Moor superbly whilst he reads. I am sending you Middleton Murry's
new magazine. It really is *very* good reading!

Can you imagine a man of education *could* sink so low? You must
read the story of Mr Joiner and Rosie. It is thought Middleton Murry
himself wrote it. It should be called 'The Servant Maid's Adelphi.' I am
going to write them a little story about a charwoman and a lost hairpin
in a drain. I promise you it will be accepted. Let us lower the 'Adelphi'
until ever [even] the scullery maids reject it!

Friday, June 1st, 1923
Lytton finished reading Othello last night. It is almost too moving. One

suffers so many emotions that one can hardly listen to the words. We go to Barbara this weekend. It think it would be more sensible not to see her before she goes to Spain. I mind so much. But then one isn't very sensible. Ralph has written you a long letter I see it lying on the window sill downstairs. His gloom about your intentions and your destination almost affect *me*! Will you write to me soon and tell me you are happy. Then I won't think about you any more if you would rather I did not. I long to know E. and yet I know, and understand your feelings so much and my own, that I shall probably never meet her. Could you send me a photograph of her? I will send it back to you. It is rather too mathematical, and intellectual to conceive 'E' being a human being. I am now definitely reconciled to you as a married man, a sort of D.H. Lawrence travelling about in Italy and Mexico with an amiable wife and family in a second class railway carriage. So don't write to me next week and tell me you will [be] coming back to England in July and that E. returns to America to marry an engineer in Boston. It was with great self restraint I refrained from sending you a long letter on the subject of marriage, the horror of its intimacy, the tediousness of domestic life, and the Siamese-twin relation. I suddenly at Palermo saw life and marriage so clearly that if it had not been for our swift movements since I should have written you a really Russian confession on the subject.

I get on so well with Ralph now. We scarcely ever quarrel. For there is nothing to quarrel about. After all we have been married four years now. And I am thirty years old. That's a pretty depressing fact to get accustomed to. It amazes me how easily people take decay, and corruption. I find it difficult to gauge whether one's brain isn't decaying with one's face. I am going to, do not smile cynically, give up the next three years to painting—if I fail to make any progress by the end of that time I shall abandon the occupation. But how ridiculous to say what one will do in three years. How pretentious one becomes when one is thirty! I think Ralph may become a bookbinder. It's a good honest trade, one isn't in a competition, one doesn't depend on other people's caprices, and one isn't tied like a house maid to a business firm. [Twenty-eight lines omitted]

There are so many books to read, new books. I have some six pictures which I drew at Hammam-Meskoutine to finish. So now I feel rather happy that everything is so dull and green. I can see no interruptions no excitements greater than bees swarming until next winter.

Fra Angelico's frescoes in the Sistine Chapel[1] seemed to me almost the perfection of painting—Do you remember a year ago that I promised I would send you this year a journal I kept? Well I break that promise.

Reading 'Othello' made me realize last night that a year is not long enough to forget some things. Ten years is a more suitable interval. Bless you. I send you my love. Don't answer this letter. I write it in a particular mood. By the time your answer would reach me, I should feel differently. I think I only just want to hear about you. For the moment I am bored by myself. I will send you some photographs soon. Perhaps Barbara will take them to you.   Your loving DORIC

Reading this over before I post it, it seems to [be] rather a dismal wail from a cast-off mistress! But I didn't mean it to be that. I merely want to ask you to write to me, since no matter what the news was that I received through Virginia, if you were ill, if you were going to America, becoming a sailor, marrying an American, I should at once want to hear more about it from you. Virginia, I saw, thought I didn't deserve to hear very much news about you. Anyway she told me nothing except extolling your virtues, which after all I knew about better than she did. I really only want to have a letter from you. Nothing more. I've long realized my life will never change much. If you marry, *you* will join the fixtures, fixed gas brackets. I would persuade you eloquently against marriage, yet what is there on the other side? I myself could not stand the few years of loneliness and isolation that I lived through after I left the Slade. The great thing I am sure is to realize the *grotesque* mixture of life. The pleasures of being loved and loving and having friends and the pains and sordidness of the same relations. The pleasures of freedom, and isolation, and the despairs at the same time which beset one in that state. One year I would like to take an average of the days one is happy against the wretched days. Perhaps it's absurd ever to think about it. If one painted pictures it wouldn't matter and one probably wouldn't think about it. But I can't see the use of painting pictures 'as good as' those at the London Group. I think except for a few French artists, and perhaps two English artists there are NO important LIVING artists. Painting hasn't advanced, there are very few inventors and original artists alive now. They reduce painting to the same culture as architecture, and furniture, always reviving some style and trying to build up a mixture with dead brains. The French cover their tracks better

[1] There are no frescoes by Fra Angelico in the Sistine Chapel. She probably means the Michelangelos. There are decorations by Fra Angelico in the chapel of Pope Nicholas V in the Vatican.

[than] the English do. But really I don't think much of this revival of Rembrandt, nudes à la Rubens, imitations of the naive artists, Poussin. Matisse seems to me one of the most definitely original artists alive now. I think all this 'culture', and 'groups' system perhaps is partly the reason of the awful paintings produced. Then the intelligence of most English painters is so low. They are only fit to be house decorators. Do you know, plain and aged that I am, I made a conquest just before I left England, at a party given by David Garnett? An American girl. I only know her name is Henrietta.[1] She has the face of a Giotto Madonna. She sang exquisite songs with a mandoline, southern state revivalist nigger songs. She made such wonderful cocktails that I became completely drunk and almost made love to her in public. To my great joy Garnett told me the other day she continually asks after me and wants me to go and see her. I am sure she is far more beautiful than your E.! And if you think I am imitating you I tell [you] I am not. Ralph cut my hair too short last week. When it has grown longer and my beauty restored, I shall visit the lovely Henrietta and revive our drunken passion. Gerald dear I care so much for you. Forgive me for whining and write to me soon.   D.C.

PS I saw George Hope-Johnstone aged 41, was in the courts last week with two other 'Morphia Fiends', completely wretched in health and arrested for forging prescriptions.

To Lytton Strachey

Monday evening [June 5th, 1923]   *The Mill House, Tidmarsh*

The close of the coldest day in the year.

Dearest Lytton, Isn't it awful poor Barbara has scarlet fever, I've just heard from Nick. They have taken her to a fever hospital for 6 weeks. I've written to Saxon and asked him here for the weekend. It must be rather bleak for him after he had arranged his holiday and made all the arrangements for Spain, now to be cut off, especially as he won't be able to see Barbara. Ralph has just been reading to me his favourite poem. Kubla Khan. Perhaps you will see Saxon? It would cheer him

---

[1] Henrietta Bingham, daughter of Judge Robert Bingham who was later U.S. Ambassador to Britain.

up. But perhaps you won't, since he will probably cheer you down. Dan has just cut our front lawns. The bees spent their day over their fires inside their hives, we did the same. Forty-eight eggs dispatched to the Woolves this morning.

We are just going to bed. Ralph sips lemonade over the fire. What do you sip I wonder at this mystic hour of eleven?

A new hen house arrived this afternoon from the Beenham zone, fortunately no mother hen inside it!

No more news. So good night. It will be nice to see you back on Wednesday. Please make every enquiry from James re Miss Milva.[1] Perhaps you will visit the Milva in person. The only bad news is: we had the Lear. It was combined with the 'Nonsense Book'. 'Nonsense Book and More Nonsense' our book was called. What shall we do. Sell our new acquisition to B[irrell] and G[arnett] for twelve pounds with a forged signature 'from the author'?

Bless you,   Your CARRINGTON

To Lytton Strachey

Wednesday evening [June 14th, 1923]   *The Mill House, Tidmarsh*

Darling Lytton, How can I thank you for taking me to la Duse? I never never enjoyed seeing anyone act so much before. I can't forget her face, and those hands. But you must know what it means to me and how I loved you for letting me see her?

We tottered back completely exhausted this evening by the 6.5. Not having sat down once 'since breakfast' as my mother so often says to me. We saw Max.[2] It's *not* good of you. Really very bad. But then I'm not a fair judge. I liked the imagining pictures best I think. Aldous was good. And the dreadful creator of Utopia and Mr Bennett. And Maurice Hewlett was superb in his back garden! James was there with us. We then moved to Duncan's show. I think Simon [Bussy] is quite right in everything he says in his review. And your picture is *far* and away the best. I had forgotten, a little, how good it was. James was rather depressed over them also. Uncle Charlie et femme were there! And

---

[1] This lady was concerned in importing objects from Berlin or Vienna for Carrington who shared expenses.

[2] An exhibition of caricatures by Max Beerbohm, with one of Lytton.

[Arundel] D'El Rey! Then we staggered to Stewarts for ices. Tea with Alix and James. Just as we were leaving Sebastian [Sprott], [Frank] Ramsey came in. I was completely captivated by the Ramsey Island. Even Ralph was moved! He is so charming to look at and very friendly. All you said of him was true. We left fortunately before his devastating intellect began, as I expect it did, to wreck the party. Sebastian [Sprott] was very sweet but he looked such a reed in the water's edge by the side [of] the great ox Ramsey. To go backwards: we had lunch at the club and met Leonard there. He was so amusing and very friendly. For five minutes, alone with him, I succumbed to his charms and we almost had an affaire, but of course Francis Birrell interrupted us. Leonard was very charming to Ralph who joined us later.

I took your book back to the 'Times' library. I thought 'Dolores'[1] was looking very melancholy—Ralph spent his morning with Noel at the Oxford Press. But he didn't see very much of the actual binding. I think Noel is going to show him more next week. He is going over to Oxford with him tomorrow.

I spent last night with Inez in her new flat. But that I must reserve until Saturday ... !!! Tidmarsh was very sympathetic. So clean and sweet smelling after London. The irises are just coming out, the poppies look too splendid. We voted after our visit to London, that Alix and James were the most friendly people, and Leonard second prize, Lydia a dull third and Frankie the greatest bore in Europe! Mr Lytton Strachey is not allowed to compete in the competition.

I heard rumours that your night didn't *end* in arms of Maud [Cunard] ...

We love you so much Lytton. You can't think what emotions we both felt at leaving you in Torrington Square that afternoon. It will be lovely to see you again on Saturday. The new Marvell, Nonesuch Press, is very beautiful. But I expect you have seen it.

I dreamt of Mrs Ball last night. She was so sympathetic in my dream! The curé of Sulham called this afternoon!! No letters. Not even a post card from Sibbie [Lady Colefax]. What can the matter be! What can the matter be! Forgive this tired letter but I am almost asleep and a flea bit my leg in the train.   My fondest love MOPSA

---

[1] An assistant at The Times Book Club.

To Lytton Strachey

Tuesday, 5 o'ck [July 10th, 1923]   *41 Gordon Square, London*

Dearest Lytton, Shattered by cocktails, late hours, thunderstorms heatwaves, and the discomforts of 41 G[ordon] S[quare] I take up my pen to write to you. I feel almost too weak to stir, far far too weak to reach Tidmarsh. Ralph sits almost nude on the sofa reading the Higher Literature of James's library. I wonder if you suffered from ce terrible thunder storm last night? It lasted here in London for 7 hours without an interval and it poured tubsfull the whole time. I can hardly tell you about the party, my hand sticks to the sheet of paper, my eyes close with sleep. It was a great success however and everyone seemed to enjoy it. R[alph] was the success of the evening and was in the wildest spirits. O[liver] S[trachey] was very far gone, and rather morose. Alan [MacIver] exquisite as ever, Byam Shaw as pink as a rosebud toujours. The youngest Davidson or Davison[1] came with one of the American beauties. Mrs Joad came, and was set upon by all the young men. My heart remained intact. I can't confess I enjoy London. The heat and hardness of the pavements reduce one's spirits after a few minutes. The car came beautifully up to London, passport photographs were taken this morning. All the negotiations will we hope be through by tomorrow morning. Do you see [W. H.] Hudson's books are for sale next Friday at Hodgson's. I would like to have seen them. Oh the heat! I long for Tidmarsh and our cold bath. I never never hated leaving you so much before. It was such fun talking to you about Blenheim. I hope Annie supports you with attentions. We will come down very early Thursday from London unless you wire and say you are coming back that day, after a Holford lunch the hand sticks, the brain sleeps. Goodbye d ... st My love to Pippa   Yr MOPSA
PS Two carpenters bang and clang upstairs here from 9 o'ck till 7.30 all day putting up bookshelves!

[Lytton had been invited to the annual gathering of French intellectuals at the Abbey of Pontigny in which Charles du Bos and André Gide were leading figures. Lytton was unhappy there and did not shine. Carrington and Barbara Bagenal and Sebastian Sprott accompanied him to France. Sebastian left them at Beaune and after Lytton went to Pontigny, Carrington and Barbara spent a holiday at Vermenton on the Yonne.]

[1] Douglas Davidson.

To Lytton Strachey

Monday [*August 27th, 1923*]   *Hôtel du Commerce, Vermenton, Yonne*

Dearest Lytton, Your letter was given me by Madame this morning, at
breakfast. I laughed so much.

But WHAT FIENDS! Mania, is too mild a word for deliberate torture.
How can you discuss translation for ten afternoons from half past two
until half past four? It just shows what the Frogs are to choose the
dullest and stoggiest, the most unsympathetic hours of the day to try
and shine in intelligence. I *should* make a speech if I was you. But not
on translation. I should make a speech on 'Imbecility in the Lower
Animals, the Frogs' In the style of Swift, (or perhaps Strachey), I
should give the habits of the toads and frogs who congregated in an
Abbaye. Mercifully I am spared my speech!

I regretted when I saw those lovely gardens and visions of curious
human beings that I was not an 'intellectual'. When I read your letter
today I was for the first time positively delighted to be spared such
tortures! How cruel of Blaise to dislike you. Did he tell M. who told N.
who told Dorothy [Bussy] that he disliked you? How did you find out?
Or did he spit in your face like a true Frog? If the American charmer
does a really good picture of you, mind you buy it. But I suspect she
won't somehow. I think the Jane [Harrison]–Hope [Mirrlees] liaison
interests me most. Win their confidences. I am sure they are a fascinating couple. [Boris] Anrep once gave me such an interesting account of
them. Was Mon. Mark Wardell there? And Petit Mark?

Yesterday evening after tea we climbed our hill behind the town,
and painted. I was so excited at painting again. Do you know I am never
quite so happy as when I can paint. Everything else seems to fade
miraculously. We painted till 7 o'ck, then the sun went down, so we came
back. A divine dinner again. Madame is a charmer, although she looks
rather like Nina Hamnett, thin, and pinched in the face. I couldn't face
'Les Deux Columbines' which had just begun as we finished dinner.
[Two lines omitted] So we went a long walk along the road in the moonlight. The country looked so exquisite and the sky was flecked with
silver-green clouds and covered with stars. Outside a cottage, on the
edge of the village, we heard a flute being played in the garden. A
magical tune, with trills, and variations. We couldn't see over the wall,

and everything was very quiet, only a chorus of grasshoppers and frogs
in the ditches. We walked for at least 3 miles until the distant songs of
some drunks at a bridge turned us back. [Thirty-six lines omitted]

I've thought over Spain. I think it's best to write to Gerald quite
frankly and tell him what I feel and the difficulties from my point of view.
I think it's rather wrong to pretend there are other reasons for not going
out to him. When the main one, is the one we discussed.

But I'll not send my letter for another week. Not that anything can
alter the difficulties you explained to me. But there is no immediate
hurry. I'll just write today and tell Gerald I can't tell him definitely
until another few weeks. Then we will discuss it with Ralph when he
comes back. You are so kind Lytton to care enough to bother over anyone so tiresome as ... There is a house to let in this village but not quite
grand enough for us I fear. There are TWO weather cocks on the house
opposite, one at each corner of the roof. [Picture omitted] I watch the
cupid turn in the wind as I lie in bed. Really I repeat six times a day,
how happy I am. Just because this village is so beautiful, the grocer is
huge and black and the hills so green, and striped. It's a very quiet
town and infinitely pale and delicate in colour. Now I must stop or I
I shall miss the post. What do you mean by saying you lost the post so a
letter 'has vanished'. I'll *not* have letters vanishing! The sun is coming
out again and the black boy turns south.

You are the dearest person in the world. But you must never laugh at
me for telling you so.   Your MOPSA XXXXXX
If only there weren't so many pictures to paint so many hills to climb,
rivers to explore, letters to write, I might learn how to cook an omelette.
I am sure he would teach me. Today looks divine. Daws fly in and out
of the Romanesque church tower, the black boy and his hoop, whirls in
the breeze. I think we shall go to Auxerre by train for the morning and
collect Barbara's letters and come back after lunch. My fondest love to
you.   Your CARRINGTON

To Lytton Strachey

Thursday morning [September 1923]   *Cofton, Star Cross, Exeter*

Dearest Rat-Husband, I wish you'd play your pipes and lure your two
Mopsämen home again. The cold here is terrible. LISTEN, with all this
wealth we have NO FIRES in any rooms in this house. I was simply

frozen to a block of salt last night sitting round a table in a large dining room with the rain and wind beating against the window pane, and NO FIRE. Give me our poverty stricken life with the rats, and a FIRE. The conversation is entirely about money and investments. Poor Mrs P[artridge] is in a great flutter because she saw Mr Sparke's estate announced in the Times and she realized her estate will have to be exposed to every curious eye. She is terrified someone will snatch her money if they know how much she has. Really it's Tchekhov it's so mad. Père Perdrix left over £38,000 in England, the India estate isn't settled yet. And yet they are too poor to have FIRES. GRRRRR. We only just bear up. Thank goodness escape will soon be here. The port was superb last night. But the females hardly sipped it. It might have been medicine. Cider is 1910, and more delicious than any cider I've ever tasted. A dreadful poor relation is staying in the house with a face like the fish footman in Alice in Wonderland. She sews curtains, and occasionally murmurs 'in Cornwall I've often noticed ...' But no one ever listens, so she never finishes her sentence.

Do you know one gets the most divine lunch on the express EXETER train! Real cold tongue (not tinned) and coffee that was far better than French coffee.

It would be almost be worth your comin' to Commins just to have the lunch on the train. Ralph looks very beautiful in his velvet jacket. It will be good to get back to our Lytton again and a fire. I hope darling your cold is better, and you aren't feeling depressed. A new essay when we come back on Harrington? And in exchange we will bring you anything from Curtis' Botanical library to a pot of Devonshire cream. The weather is *quite* as FOUL here as at Tidmarsh. My very fondest love and a kiss from the   MOPSA

[PS] There is a little robin that comes into the house quite bravely to pick up crumbs after lunch every day. The servants chase it from the kitchen because: 'A robin brings death.' It's dreadfully Ibsen. In fact there is a greenhouse leading out of the dining room, through which 'Robin enters on the left'. I wish a Rat wife would appear and lure the whole caboodle into the sea.

She's been at it, while I was shaving and now it's breakfast fondest love and many kisses from the   MOPSEMAN

To Gerald Brenan

Sunday evening [September 15th, 1923]   *The Mill House, Tidmarsh*

It's all settled dearest, we BOTH *will* come !!!!!! Ralph has written you a letter swearing *he* will come. Today he had a talk with Lytton on a walk and told me afterwards that Lytton relents and so *I* shall come. So WE BOTH *will come* some time the end of November and stay at least a decent lengthed month with you at Yegen. [Four pages omitted]

Virginia and Leonard are really superb people. We visited them on our way back. I always choose the Newhaven crossing, it's such a good place to see England at its best. We drove straight to the Woolves in the car. They are only a few miles from Newhaven; Sussex *is* a wonderful county! That part round Newhaven is filled with queer memories for me. We always went to Seaford or Brighton every year. And as I hated the sea, and bathing with family groups I used to walk on the Lewes downs, and paint. Within a stone's throw of the Woolves' old house. Little did she think that L[ytton] S[trachey] would kiss her on those downs. And turn her into a poetical dormouse. But that's a long story. Picture of young lady in a grass green dress musing at her letter. (I actually am wearing the g.g. dress at this moment.) [One page omitted]

I like the Woolves far more than they like me. Ugh. I have a queer love for Virginia which fills me with emotion when I see her. They talk better than any people I know. How quickly the conversation becomes intelligent and amusing when Virginia talks! We slept at Lewes in a superb old English Inn. The beauty of England, even although it is so vulgar after France, makes one's heart warm with an inside joy. It soon vanishes, but the first two days are always remarkable to me for their vividness.

Tidmarsh was exquisite with its rows of shining books, and the dresser with your plates.

Again I thank you for those plates. It's an achievement to have given me two presents which I literally look at every day and then think of you. The little picture on my mantelpiece and the plates. I wrote this morning a frantic letter telling you we are coming in December. It's true unless I commit some incredible act of folly, or unless Ralph changes his mind ... We are now on the most amiable terms. And I can't see any reason why we shouldn't go on being sensible like this, at any rate until December.

Ralph's carrying on some intrigue in London at the moment, so I sit alone in the dining room. Looking out not on anything as poetical as your mountains and blue skies, but on dark sombre elms and privet hedges. [Twenty-one lines omitted] Don't get ill on your travels. I dread these months before November. My dear I am so happy.

Your, elated   PRINCESS OF GEORGIA

[On November 4th, 1922, Gerald Brenan had defined Georgia as 'a country which, we are told, is not to be surpassed anywhere for the beauty of its scenery, the freedom of its manners and the purity of its ancient race.

'Georgians believe naturally in what is called free love between the sexes. Until lately I had never thought about this, but now I see I could never have believed in anything else. It is just because I have no totemic superstitions and because I share none of the usual feelings of men about private possessions that such an attitude is reasonable and possible for me. I do not distinguish sharply between love and friendship.']

To Gerald Brenan

Tuesday afternoon [about October 8th, 1923]   In the top attic, Tidmarsh

My dear, I can't write you letters when I don't know if you are at Yegen. Then I keep on saying one more month and *I* will be at Yegen. That makes it seem absurd to tell you what I am thinking in a letter, when we will talk to each [other] so soon. You can't think with what restraint I behave. I hardly ever mention Spain, even to Ralph. I feel if I pretend outwardly that it is very improbable I shall go, God with His white beard who dominates our lives from the top of the apple tree won't be able to frustrate us.

Are you really excited, as excited as I am? [Sixty-two lines omitted] Ralph has the character of Saint Francis, and simply refuses to squabble with his mother. I wish some malignant disease only to be contracted by middle aged middle class parents would sweep through England ... and swallow them all up. I would only allow one exception to be made and that couple to be preserved in the B.M. in a special gallery.

I shall buy painting materials at Granada. I know where there is quite a good shop, on the hill, on the left hand side. We won't stop at a single place on the way until we reach Granada. I long to come by Lanhiron [Lanjarón], you know what I mean, the way we came with Lytton, or will the river be too full? Ralph is up in London today book binding. He leads a very gay life with intrigues, and love affairs, after his book bindings shuts up. He is much happier now he is working for himself, and not under Leonard. [Eight lines omitted]

Do you allow me to admire Mr Norman Douglas? Lytton was so taken with 'Alone' he bought an entire set of all his books. I was very delighted with 'South Wind'. It seemed to me so interesting. But after that Fox into Lady faux pas I hardly dare venture an opinion.

Just to annoy you, I tell you Garnett has been awarded two of the grandest prizes in literature this year amounting to several hundreds.[1]

And that Middleton Murry shares *your* opinion in the Adelphi: 'I will have none of "Lady into Fox".' I have two very good numbers of that singular yellow magazine for you. I send this letter to Yegen, but I suppose it's hopeless to expect you will ever get it.

The photographs were very [illustration omitted].

Does that tempt you to write back? I think of you more than anybody else, but that's because you are the one person I love who I don't see. Take care of yourself please.

My fondest love. The restored   PRINCESS OF GEORGIA

To Lytton Strachey

Saturday [*November 17th, 1923*]   *102 Ridgemount Gardens, London*

Lying low, very low, very low indeed.

Darling Lytton, I lie low with the fiend, and lower still after an entire glass of sherry. So forgive my wandering wits. I hope you reached Cambridge safely. Do you know we reached the Edgware Road by 12 o'ck. So you would have reached London *quicker* if you [had] come with us and not by train. A curious evening here last night, Marjorie S. your sister, Frances Marshall your niece in law,[2] and Missie Partridge. Marjorie S. was at her wildest. She sang us song after song. Dorothy P[artridge] who had never heard, or *seen* anything like Marjorie before was completely bowled over! It was an extraordinary merry evening. Missie sang Mozart most beautifully. Even Marjorie was very pleased I

[1] £225 all told.
[2] Frances Marshall's elder sister Judy was married to Lytton Strachey's nephew, Colonel Dick Rendel.

think with her voice. Sweet Frances sang Purcell. Ralph sang Spanish songs, and only the Monster Mopsa was silent ... [Fourteen lines omitted]

I saw James yesterday. I lunch with them today. James says we must get Ham Spray and supports every extravagance! But then he is already bankrupt. What are we to do? I feel in terrible despair! I can hardly bear to let it fade, and yet it seems impossible unless the other client turns out to be a straw scare-crow. Lytton you are a darling. Perhaps I might see you next Tuesday for a moment. I will telephone you on the off chance, if I don't see you when I bring the post round in the morning after breakfast. I am completely boozed so I can't write sensibly. Give dear Sebastian my fondest love and tell him I will eventually send him a cat, by post and that I love him very much. I love you Lytton more and more, and you can't think how much I miss you although it's only yesterday that we parted. Noel has been asked to Suggia's party next Monday evening at Hudson's.[1] Mais you are certainly out of favour now. I saw Hudson at the Country Life office, on the stairs. He gave me the cold shudders. He *is* a gargoyle of a monstrosity. I hope you will enjoy yourself very much. The car is a great boon in London. We went for a drive in it this morning. It is such fun. Bless you a thousand times for being such an angel to me and to us.

Your loving and most intoxicated   MOPSA

To Lytton Strachey

Monday morning [*November 19th, 1923*]   *The Mill House, Tidmarsh*

Dearest Lytton, No letters for you of any interest. Another copy of La Reine Victoria from Paris. I wish you were here. You can't think how I miss you. I think you had better, unless you have anything very agreeable to do next week-end, come back here for Madame Stiles comes in every day and washes up and lights fires. The wretch Ralph deserted me last night and went up to Edward II. So I read Miss Mitford's life from cover to cover in that degraded book by Mr Roberts. As a life it seemed to me terribly provincial and English. The dreadful description, perhaps it was slightly invented, of the first night of her play when she bought an orange turban marked 'very chaste 5/6' pinned on to the back

---

[1] Proprietor and founder of *Country Life*.

and sat unconscious of the shrieks, in a box trying to look stately and dignified. It was certainly a very gloomy 'life'. But I think she and her mother deserved it. They ought to have deserted the awful old father when they won the lottery.

The party was rather amusing. I made a conquest of Mr [Raymond] Mortimer, and considerably agitated Mr Ritchie by telling him Dede had left a long correspondence by him, in our fire place when he stayed with us. Poor Mr Ritchie was in a great tremble. Master Mortimer was delighted of course. I thought he was rather gay and charming. Then there was a terrible funeste group of young men, friends of Julia and Hester [Chapman]. A very tall, monstrously fat Jew, a Beardsley character, you remember the drawing of the fop in Under the Hill by Beardsley. Unfortunately I found he was merely John Strachey [Lytton's cousin]. Then John Rothenstein [two lines omitted] and another very Balliol snobbish young man who I didn't know. They pretended they were very superior and upper class and stood in a group and sneered at the rest of the party. Hope-Johnstone was there. Arthur Waley, and his dark lady, the female Anreps. Oliver was in the highest spirits, completely intoxicated by the end of the evening. Poor Noel came but was so chrushed and mumble, he hardly spoke to anyone. I hope you enjoyed Cambridge. I had lunch with Alix and James on Saturday. They are the most charming people and the most curious.

Not a single word from Ham Spray and I expect we had better follow their example and never mention it again. It seems rather a tragic end. I felt my Ham Heart inside give a crack when it found the letter box empty. If only the walls of Tidmarsh weren't built of ice! Do not fear however that I will make your life a burden any more with my wailings. There are some griefs too great to speak about and Ham Spray is one.

You are always my dearest Lytton and I am your   CARRINGTON

To Lytton Strachey

Saturday [December 23rd, 1923]   *Yegen, Ugijar, Prov. de Granada,*
Spain

A week ago and we were shivering at Tidmarsh. Will you believe me when I tell you we had breakfast this morning out of doors in G[erald]'s open granary in the hot sun!!! I can get two witnesses to testify to this

statement. Oh Lytton dearest it was a thousand pities you came when
you did to Yegen, in all that discomfort, and not now, when everything
is so perfect, and the weather so hot. Really the sun was so hot that my
back and head got *un*comfortably warm and I moved into the shade
after breakfast! But I must tell you first of the most magnificent walk
we had from Orgeva here. We came a completely new route, walking
on the spine of a high range of mountains in view of the sea the whole
time. And do you know I SAW the mountains of AFRICA. It was so
clear. We walked through the most marvellous cork forests. Huge
twisted trees, some deep siena stripped of their bark and some grey
and twisted with the thick cracked-bark of cork. The country was
extremely varied, sometimes bleak, and arid and sometimes covered with
wild herbs and bushes. (A mule carried all our baggage by a shorter
route (the way we came before) by the river-bed). It was so hot I had
to shed my coat and Ralph complained bitterly of the heat! We had
fascinating conversations ranging on every subject. A lunch of cold eggs,
and pâté, and hot coffee from a Thermos G[erald] carried in his sack.
The country after lunch became far wilder, ravines and great rocks,
with the sea behind us, the sun casting fascinating shadows on the
rocks, and making the mountains, when it set, a ravishing Poussin pinkish brown. We had tea in a little house, given us by a deaf old witch and
a small boy. Real tea, which we made over the fire and lovely bread and
honey supplied by the ancient hag.

Our muleteer met us at this hut and the moon had come out by the
time we left as it was six o'ck. I rode the mule, and R[alph] and G[erald]
walked. G. was as usual rather vague about the way and hazarded that
we might reach Yegen at half past seven or possibly eight, and later,
'certainly not later than half past nine.' I was so happy on my mule that
I wasn't very concerned. The landscape looked astonishing. The moon
shone in a sky of stars, the air was quite warm and the mountains became more and more fantastic every moment. Doré, or Blake could
hardly have conceived anything more frenzied. It was completely silent,
except for a single owl that hooted like a cow down in the dark abyss.
We reached the house at half past nine, or a little later. Before, we were
surprised at the beauty of the house, but it was nothing to our surprise
this time. You would hardly know it. The new room, where we have
meals and sit in the evenings is really the most lovely room I have ever
seen. There is an enormous fire place where huge logs burn and half
across the room at night, a great curtain is drawn so one sits in a small
alcove over the fire. In the day time a window is open and one gazes

right out on to the mountains, as the window is very large. The establishment is completely different. Maria is now an accomplished cook and house keeper. You smile cynically. Do you know we sat on our first evening at a round table over the fire and were waited on by two servant girls, aged 17 and 12 years old? An omelette appeared, wine in lovely wine glasses, and then a delicious chicken cooked with rice and vegetables, the maids waiting on us like Elizabethan pages. They appear from behind the great red curtain and silently remove each course. This delicious feast ended by a large basket of most varied and bright coloured fruits being brought to us. Persimmons, grapes, oranges, figs, apples, pears, and chestnuts and almonds and the most wonderful nougat sweets.

Oh why, why, can't you be whisked here on a magical carpet?

The next morning we had our breakfast in the sun as I told you before, on the roof. It is Sunday today, and I write at 8.30 in the morning in the sun, waiting for breakfast in a thin *silk* dress, because it is so warm. How happy you would be with us! We all long that you could be here. We were a little tired after our walk (which was about 20 miles Ralph said) so we spent yesterday morning talking in chairs in the sun. Lunch was brought to us in another sitting room, Gerald's old study with the books. Again marvellous cooking. After lunch we went for a walk along the road and sat on the rocks. The sun is so hot it might be June in England. Tea over a big fire, and then more hectic conversations. Gerald's rage against 'Lady into Fox' is terrible!! He only allows 'Victoria', Tom Eliot, and Yeats and some of Virginia's work to be permissible. My attempt to convert him to Norman Douglas was a failure. He objects to N.D.'s style. This I feel almost personally, my passion for 'Together' is so deep. Perhaps it wasn't a good example of Norman Douglas to start Gerald with. [Forty-four lines omitted]

My dearest I love you so much. My only complaint is that I should be so happy here without you. It seems monstrous that anything should be so perfect and you in England. Gerald talks a great deal about you, and asked me to send you his love. My very fondest love. Your most loving

CARRINGTON

Ralph sends his love. He will write soon.

To Lytton Strachey

December 28th, 1923   *Yegen, Ugíjar, Prov. de Granada*

Oh Lytton, how we wished that you were with us last night! We had the most beautiful party. Three musicians, singers, and dancers. Two guitars and a lutta. They sat round the fire and the audience sat in long rows receding in the darkness at the end of the room. Curiously enough they *were* beautiful and not monkey-faced. The chief musician, the lutta, spelt in Spanish laud, had a face like an El Greco angel.

December 29th, 1923

They looked so wonderful with the lamplight on their faces and the deep shadows. At first they were rather shy and refused to sing. Presently a shepherd boy of about 15 opened his mouth, and sang a sad wailing copla. He reminded me of Michael Davies. He had a strange character: he hardly expanded even when the whole party became wild and tipsy. He was very anxious to be thought a man and put on a charming expression trying to look severe and unconcerned. Gerald took round drinks between the songs. As he is blind and the light was rather dim, he invariably over filled the glass, or poured the aniseed on to the floor and not into [the] tumbler! He is evidently adored by the villagers. They laugh at him whatever he does and Maria, and the girls spent their time trying to make him dance, or sing. After about an hour a new group of young men appeared and the great circle became elongated and dense with faces. Then a young man with a face so beautiful that it is imprinted on my memory so that I could draw every feature. He was slightly like Angus Davidson, only with a passionate rather conceited look instead of the Angus softness. The men all wore their hats. His hat was tilted back from his face and showed his rather bulging forehead with a shining highlight on it. He had a most amazing mouth a short upper lip with a slight curl. He sat between me and the lamp so I saw his profile silhouetted against the light. Suddenly the profile altered, the eyes glittered wildly the mouth opened, the forehead puckered. A strange wailing song came out and his whole body shook and the face became contorted with sadness and passion. It was a most moving song. The guitars and lutta played beside him as he sang. Then the song stopped, they all laughed clapped and he became the proud and randy creature again. He sat on the young men's knees making jokes and shrieking with laughter. The men and women keep very severely apart. The women sitting in a little group always on the worst chairs or on the floor. The men are very eastern the way they treat the women. I must say I suspected unconscious B—y amongst my proud faced seraphim and the musicians and amongst the groups of young men with arms round each other's necks. But Gerald assured us it was not so. By the way he has a fascinating story of Tetuan. Really very amusing. But Gerald must tell you himself sometime. After the singing, couples danced, rather stiff country dances. Maria, Gerald's housekeeper, although she is a garngarled old witch became very gay, and leapt about in a frenzied way, like a bobbing cork on waves. A young man with a comic face danced exactly like Duncan, leaping and crossing his legs in the air, which excited the audience to frenzy; clapping, and shouting an accompaniment to the dancers. Ralph and I were then forced to dance alone. Rather agitating, a group of sapphic little girls fell on my neck afterwards and Ralph was surrounded by admiring young men. Do you know I can hardly write to you because I am *uncomfortably hot*. I've moved three times since I began, to try and get into the shade. Oh Lytton, I wish a thousand times a day you were here with us!!

Yesterday afternoon we had a most frenzied afternoon at Mechina (that village we once walked to to look at a house.) We've bought masses of china. Huge plates, small plates, jugs, and Kashmir shawl, a table cloth, 2 striped rugs and a carpet. And in dead secrecy, no plate cost more than 2½ pesetas. The shawl which is very exquisite for a covering for a bed only cost 20 pesetas. And the carpets were 10 p. each. We now contemplate *a crate* of china from Almeria to Tidmarsh! It was a wonderful scene, old hags, young women, fat monsters, old men half witted men, all running out of their dens, and houses laden with jugs, plates, shawls and carpets and surrounding us with shrieks in the street. The bargaining was terrible. Gerald and Ralph of course were masters at it and we retreated a hundred times, to be entreated back again and then compromises, and arguments!

I think you will be equally enraptured when you see some of the jugs! One could buy lovely tables and chairs for 3p. each, Gerald says. But we can't face the business of packing them. Ralph is writing so I must stop. I've made three pictures, and I am just going to do another today. I'd like to paint the Seraphim to convince you toute les Spaniards ne sont pas singes! Life is very happy here. The perpetual heat, the delicious meals, the amusing talks, and the exquisite scenery day after day. Last night Gerald read Crashaw and Collins, and then Eliot, and Joyce to me, whilst Ralph slept in the rocking chair over the fire. My very very fondest love to you. Please keep well, and do send us a wire if the snows become too cold because really the heat is almost *too* intense here! All my love to the most charming of all creatures.

Your loving MOPSA XXXXXXX

1924

To Frances Marshall

Monday [January, 1924]   *Yegen, Ugijar, Prov. de Granada*

Dearest Frances, So many letters seem to have been written to you that I can't think of anything to tell you. I do wish you were a little rasher. Why didn't you abandon all and follow us? The sun alone would have been worth it, and who would live on coffee in Gerrard Street[1] when (he or she) could eat persimmons, grapes, oranges and turkey stuffed with chestnuts? And why do people eat breakfast in the cold shades of Brunswick when they might bask in the sun, munch toast and cherry jam on a roof gazing on the sea and the green mountains of Africa? And who would go to parties in Fulham Road when (he or she) could sit over a log fire and watch the dancers of the Alpujarras and hear exquisite shepherds sing ravishing coplas?

I have seldom been so happy continuously day after day. In the afternoon I generally go out with a little village girl of 12 and paint the mountains. She talks to me the whole time in Spanish. To everything I reply 'si, si' occasionally I vary it with 'no intendo'. She sits beside me and holds my paint box for me. R.P. spends most of his day arguing with Gerald. Yesterday we spent an entire day in a village haggling over jugs, and dishes. You would have laughed to have seen the finale: a small upper room in an inn, with about 80 females, children, weeping babies, crowded round us, every few minutes a new person pressed in with a plate. Sometimes terrible little Victorian rosebud horrors, which they were amazed when we refused. At last a small girl brought a broken china duck! The bargaining was terrible. Gerald and Ralph are the most adamant characters. We feel in despair at the thought of ever packing up these objects and getting them to Almeria and then England. I fell off a cliff yesterday into a ditch full of Spanish chestnuts so my hands are engrained with prickles today which is an excuse for writing so badly.

---

[1] Frances Marshall was an assistant in Birrell and Garnett's bookshop in Gerrard Street almost opposite Legrain's coffee shop. She lived in her mother's house, 27 Brunswick Square.

I hope in secret you will escape your overseers and come to Paris. Partly I confess because I would like to linger in that town and I know I shall have very little chance unless the Gerrard Street siren is there. Another time Frances you must come to Yegen. It is a unique Arcadia. I am always so fond of you. I was sorry at Tidmarsh I was so distracted with packing, but you will come again when we come back and admire sympathetically all our carpets, and dishes?

My fondest love   CARRINGTON

To Lytton Strachey

Before breakfast on the roof, 8 o'ck, January 2nd, 1924
Yegen, Ugíjar, Prov. de Granada

Dearest, Do you know we nearly sent you a wire yesterday 'Silence is brutal.' If only you knew how I am tormented in my dreams. Last night a letter came from you saying you had bought Ham Spray for £2000 and were moving in next week! My only correspondents since I left England have been one letter from N[oel] L. C[arrington], and Mr [Raymond] Mortimer and one from you. Ralph is in a dungeon because his young lady [Frances Marshall] has only written once. *Your* fate hangs on today's post. SHOULD the postman NOT bring a letter with the Tidmarsh mark we have resolved NEVER to return, but to live for ever in this TROPICAL heat eating persimmons and listening to the sweet guitars. We had another party the night before last, not quite such a large assembly. But some new characters which made it interesting. A lovely shepherd boy with a much better voice than any we heard before. To make our presence less royal Gerald asked the young man to dance with me. I had one exquisite dancer he was so pink, and beautifully mannered. I really believe he was at Oxford! The young men are far better looking than the females in this particular village. [Twelve lines omitted] Today is a great 'fiesta'. Already a brass band and a procession has been twice, or even thrice, round the walls of Yegen. Last night they carried, with lanterns and torches, the Holy Virgin round the village. All the windows of the houses were lighted with candles. We watched from our roof. Spanish fire works were sent off. Those that reached the stars were very gorgeous, but far more never left the earth. We live like princes, eating cold turkey and ham every day and drinking Spanish wine.

Yesterday we all walked to Valor and had lunch lying in a grassy grove under some slim grey poplars. How I longed to have you with me lying on the hot bank, gazing up at these exquisite bare poplars against the most delicate of blue skies. A butterfly flew above my head and bumble bees searched for flowers. In the bank we found wild smelling violets. Ralph and Gerald on the way back from Valor after 'tea', i.e. black coffee, bathed in a mountain stream. We then climbed some mountains and came back to Yegen by another way. Gerald reads early Spanish poetry to me and one evening I had a French lesson and read Baudelaire. He has far more books on Verlaine and Rimbaud than you have, with a great many new portraits. He has one book with a facsimile of Rimbaud's poems in manuscript. Have you ever seen it? Ralph is reading the Arabian Nights and Proust. I suddenly have a mania for building a new house. There is so much to be said for these high long rooms with paved floors. Gerald is visibly weakening towards Norman Douglas. The chapter on the idiots wrung a little praise from him, But he still complains of his style.

However since he never stops praising a certain English writer I can forgive his coldness towards N.D. Oh Lytton, so often I have longed to have you here, to share all these delights with me. You could not feel Spain was 'antipathetico' in this weather and with such material pleasures. We have all been very well ever since we came. I do hope Tidmarsh is not uncomfortable for you in any way. I now have a great many new plans for furnishing H[am] S[pray]. All hideous furniture is to be sold and there are to be far fewer objects in the rooms. The pleasure of having so much space and so many rooms is very great here.

We lead very idle lives here. It is almost impossible to get over the continual pleasure of lying in the sun. But now I (will) go, and paint my landscape.

must
shall
ought

My love and xxx from your very happy   MOPSA
[Ten lines omitted]

[Gerald Brenan accompanied his guests to Granada, where they stayed in the same hotel.]

To Gerald Brenan

January 8th, 1924   *Granada*

Dear, I am so sorry about this morning. But I was cowardly. I couldn't face an argument with Ralph. He was quite happy but I knew if I said I wanted to [go] downstairs to you, he would feel hurt and complain.

Please forgive me. If you only knew how I minded, you wouldn't reproach me.

It was bound, as you said, to be a little difficult in this town. But please don't make it difficult by reproaching me. I think Ralph will certainly write some letters. Then we will go for a walk.

To me it is worth a good deal to be with you. But do not make me feel miserable, because I know it was my fault for being so selfish and asking you to come with us.

I will not neglect any opportunities to be with you and if they do not occur, I will ask you to come for a walk with me. It is only I dread having any 'feelings' before we go. I care so much. You ought to know there is only one reason which ever makes it difficult for me to be with you alone. Please smile at me so I shall know you understand that I also am unhappy.

I can't write properly.   DORIC

[On their arrival at Madrid Carrington and Ralph learned that Lytton had bought a lease of Ham Spray House for about £2,100.]

To Lytton Strachey

[*January 10th, 1924*]   *Hotel de Cataluña, Madrid*

My very dearest Lytton, Your letter has just been given to us by the chief cook [of Thomas Cook & Son]. You [are] too good, too kind. What can we do? You can't think how moved we were. How terrible the agitation must have been for you all alone. But a triumph I think, for after all we did bring old P. down a little. We must hope that the perfection of our lives will be so great in the sun and on the Downs that we will never regret it. I feel certain myself that we will master the situation.

The real thing that matters is the indissoulubility of our affections. The addition of hot sun, a verandah and the most beautiful country can only add to an already existing state of perfection. We love you *so* much. I do not know what to write to you. The past, the present, or the future. I can't also remember how much I told you at Granada. Already I've planned all the rooms at H[am] S[pray], painted them a hundred times, planted the garden, and cut down the fir trees. You were the dearest person in the world Lytton to send that telegram. Please don't be despondent, we will be back very soon now. Did it look lovely in 'Country Life'? I always feared the cunning Mrs P. would do something to finally break down our spirits. Never have I been so full of sensations. They rush through my head like flames up a chimney. But my predominant feeling after reading your letter is to be with you. I will tell you the future before I do anything else.

Today is the (Jan) 10th we are fixed here.

           11th we take train to Paris at 10 o'ck night.

           12th in train.

D.V. Sunday 13th at 6 o'ck we reach Paris, and go to Pas de Calais [Hôtel].

A little explanation. Ralph told Frances M[arshall] before he left England that he would be returning via Paris and if she cared to join us for a few days we would be very pleased. (She thought it doubtful so nothing was fixed.) She has just written to Thomas Cook saying that she has been able to get a holiday for a week and will come over next Saturday the 12th. Now the alternatives are

(1) *That you will come* over and join us for a few days or a week after Clive and Mary have left you on the Monday or Tuesday. In which case a wire from you would summon your faithful attendant spirit to the station to meet you in Paris.

(2) *That you won't come* because of the storms and beastly weather. In which case, I will (if F.M. does not object to my departure) come over on the Wednesday by myself and reach you and Tidmarsh as soon as possible. R[alph] is compromised, and will have to stay until the end of the week, but he has been such a dear he really deserves a little rest from the fatigues of looking after me, and the crates of china. You know we would love to have you in Paris, but on the other hand Madrid in pouring rain makes one hesitate to entreat you to come. The Sol says the Seine is rising daily, so visiting the Louvre in boats might be rather dreary. But you know *our feelings* and will come if you feel inclined. N.B. *Will* you if you do feel you would like to come, and the weather is more cheerful by the 13th, *send a* WIRE to the Pas de Calais (Rue de

Saint Pères) in which case I won't cross on the Wednesday—

The Louvre will be shut on Monday, so I would like to spend Tuesday in Paris. So that unless a wire comes, (and unless F.M. objects in which case I will of course wire) I will come over on Wednesday. If a wire comes, we will meet you at the station. I so fear the cold will wreck your health that I do not put my real feelings foremost.

The damned crate of china from Granada failed to arrive today by the goods train, so we have to wait here until tomorrow. We found to our horror at the last moment in Granada, that they refused to let china go as personal luggage in the luggage van with us! So it had to be dispatched by goods train. After this rebuff we rather regret we didn't send it by Almeria in the crate. As it is we shall have to part with our personal effects in the rucksacks, put them in the van, and carry the china on our laps in the carriage. Otherwise we should never reach Tidmarsh. Since goods trains apparently take 3 days to move anywhere. Do not mention chests of drawers and wardrobes. IF you only knew the agonies we have been through!

Another time we will manage better. But when one is abroad the expense of everything makes one try these curious methods of transport. Ralph has been terribly heroic and sympathetic over it all. We bought 2 lovely chintzes in Granada. If we want more, Gerald promises to buy them for us in April and bring them back with him. He *was* so good to us Lytton. Really, next to you, he is the kindest person I've ever known. He simply heaped presents on us at Yegen. And refused to take any money for our stay with him. He gave us all his most beautiful plates, and jugs. His kindness on the journey to Granada was typical of him. [Twenty-four lines omitted] I don't think I've ever been quite so gloomy in my life as on our second day at Granada. The mud in the streets was indescribable and it poured all day. Gerald of course after his gay spirits on the motor bus journey, collapsed into the deepest sadness. Ralph was rather gloomy; but calm. I felt the change from the beauty of Yegen and the perpetual sun almost as if I had entered a grave in Finland. The journey yesterday from Granada wasn't nearly as bad as we expected. Gerald saw us off in the pelting rain and then we settled down to our books and ate up the rich warm air of 60 humans in our elongated carriage.

I read Grimms' Fairy Tales. Gerald lent them me. They were very perfect as I at once became transported into a world of cats, toads, and golden birds. We reached Madrid at 10.30. Gerald had told us of an hotel, but as we always rather suspect his information, we allowed ourselves to be conducted by a charming porter who seized upon us into a

cab, and very slowly along the streets of Madrid. The pleasure of going
to an unknown hotel struck us as suddenly fascinating. To our amusement it turned out to be the exact hotel G[erald] had recommended to
us! It really is very good, only 12 p[esetas] a day with all our meals. Near
the P[uerto] del Sol and very clean. This morning we went to the goods
office to try and get our crate of china, but it won't be here until tomorrow so we must stay here till tomorrow night now! Ugh. [Twenty-
two lines omitted] I hope you have kept well all the time we have been
away, since you say nothing I hope you are well. You can't think how I
long to see you again. I think of you very often. My dearest you are
almost too kind to us. I only hope you are as happy, as you have made
us. Bless you. Un mille baisseurs.

                                                              your MOPSA
Later
     I can't tell you how good Ralph has been to me. He is the most per-
fect creature in the world. I don't think, (although I always do think I
know,) I ever realized before quite how unselfish, and charming he could
be until on this journey. He is writing to you today, so he will tell you
all his news.
     It's wonderful Lytton to have Ralph and you, and H[am] S[pray]
altogether to enjoy this year! Bless you. My love.   MOPSA
PS I think under the circumstances it would be a good thing if you put
mes lettres dans un lieu sur ou Mademoiselle S. n'pouvais pas lire les
lettres parceque la maison Jambon [Ham Spray].

To Gerald Brenan

Sunday 3 o'ck, January 13th, 1924   *Hôtel Pas de Calais, Paris*

My very dear Gerald, I am alone at last so I will write to you again. All
over again I must thank you for Yegen. Why are you so kind? Even the
hardest third class seats, and the foulest smells had no power of [word
illegible] on the magician? I believe it now. You made the journey purposely easy, and 'charmed' all the porters, the travellers and the customs
officers and my inside. You made [me] so happy that I simply find it impossible to be melancholy. I feel as if I never really cared for you before.
And you will only write me back letters to tell me Maria still smells.
Whilst I tell you nakedly so much?

Quickly, before the other two come back, I will tell you everything
that has happened since Madrid. The fatal crate did arrive that afternoon and in the evening we set off. Ralph's luggage and the rugs went
in the van and we took all the other objects on the rack with us. I had a
terrible dream, I thought I was fainting and couldn't touch Ralph who I
knew was sitting opposite in the carriage to wake him up. I really think
it was the heat, I suddenly forced myself to wake up, and touched him,
but the nightmare was so horrible I didn't sleep again. I loved watching
the country from the windows when the sun rose and then I read
Grimms' Fairy Tales when the windows got covered with steam. I love
those stories more and more. I will send you another copy when I get
back to England marked with my favourites, added to yours. Everything
worked perfectly at the frontier, *nothing* was examined, we passed
through the customs in 3 minutes, and then leapt into a train to Bordeaux. But I was very good, I did not taunt Ralph. The relief was
tremendous, for as you can imagine he was prepared to have every plate
examined! At Bordeaux we waited two hours in the station. We had a
carriage to ourselves except for two soldiers, so we lay down until Paris
this morning and I slept much better.

We reached Paris at 6 o'ck. After breakfast we found Frances Marshall at this hotel so we stay here with her. I really wanted to go back
tomorrow to Lytton, but I see it is a little difficult. Partly travelling with
half the luggage alone, and secondly leaving Frances here alone with
Ralph. She is obviously rather agitated lest her people should discover.
So I've given way and unless Lytton wires that he wants me very much
I shall stay here till next Saturday, reaching Tidmarsh on Sunday. I
went to the Louvre this morning and looked at the Italians. On Tuesday
I shall spend all day there, since R. and F. will be quite happy by
themselves I shall go to galleries all day by myself. She is very charming
and looked exquisite in her red shawl. And yet how curious it is. Ralph
said to me: 'Of course I would rather be alone in Paris with Frances,
but I see she half wants you to stay here because of her people, so you
had better stay, only I must see her alone. You weren't very tactful this
morning. Perhaps I'll take her to a play this evening.' The mystic S is
Silence you understand. It is only how easy it is for him and what a long
time it was before we were alone together at Yegen. Yet I do not mind.
I think my new philosophy it's perhaps why I do remember everything
you say, and what we do together, so vividly. Because I can never be
casual over you. You are far too rare.

Why did you despise the poems you gave me. You can't think how

much I love them. I will write of them and the sonnets in my next letter.
I want to read them again. May I say I loved you more for them?
Gerald does it make you happier if I tell you that your kindness and great
affection made me care far far more than I ever did before for you.
Everything, the beauty of your mountains, the singers, the poplars
all seem to me [to] have been [made] by you. You will always put my
letters very carefully away? And please never write before April anything that it would be difficult for me to read, unless I tell you before
hand that it is possible. If I am a 'governess' sometimes you will forgive
me. You know I [hate] that part even more than you do. I will write a
letter tomorrow with the more ordinary details of our lives. So that I
need have no fear [of] Ralph asking to read it. Suddenly everything is
exquisitely happy for me. Lytton wrote us a most sympathetic letter
today. You must know him better Gerald when you come to England. I
write very quickly because I haven't much time.

> It is decreed by all the Fates
> That gifts of iron forks,[1] and plates
> Should be these lovers' token.
> Painted plates may be broken,
> The fairest iron forks may rust,
> But our love last until we're dust.

Dear, I love you so very much. I can tell you nothing. Yet if you were
only here how much I could say. Please write to me often. Even if you
can't say very much. Goodbye. You were too kind to me at Yegen, but I
love you for it.   Your QUEEN OF GEORGIA

To Frances Marshall

[*January 23rd, 1924*]   *The Mill House, Tidmarsh*
Dearest Frances, It was charming of you to think of writing to me. I
must confess at once that you are one of the very few young ladies I
would ever again chaperone because your behaviour was so perfect! In
short you required no chaperoning! I am only sorry I was such a decayed pumpkin the whole of our jaunt in Paris. I now feel rather more
decayed, in fact I doubt if I shall survive, my headache grows worse and

---

[1] Gerald Brenan had given Carrington some ornamental iron toasting-forks.

worse, although I drink purge after purge and drug after drug. I expect every moment Lytton and Ralph in a rage will drive me out of the front door with the cats (who were both sick yesterday) and then throw me and them into the stream. I am sorry to hear you also are ill. I wonder whether it was the poisonous 'Mothersill'? I have a theory it was the poison added to an already fermenting inside that did the mischief and cut short the already slightly passé life of Madame P[artridge]. But the case of Missie M[arshall] is even harder. She a young bud with the dew hardly dry, laid in the cold tomb of Brunswick's church. [Four lines omitted] You see I am still very ill or I wouldn't be writing so feebly. Any bad spelling is due to my terrible headache, and aching teeth.

Really Frances, I was a little afraid you might have thought me churlish and green tempered in Paris. But I promise all my glooms and despairs were entirely within myself. I felt far iller than I dared confess because I didn't (a) want to bother Ralph and (b) to bother Lytton after he so nobly came over. I had a suspicion Ralph thought I hadn't been as friendly as I might have been to you. But I really felt too dim to show any signs of life except killing both the Madames at the hotel.

Nothing is unpacked except 12 large completely broken plates. After that incident I left the grand trunk and all the baskets unopened. I pieced a few together yesterday afternoon with some cement but I fear it's lunacy, and the pastime of Ophelia. Do get well soon. I am so sorry you have to go to work every day. And you will come and visit me here in my swamps and bogs one weekend? For I see I shall never reach London. Give my love to yourself.   Your CARRINGTON

To Gerald Brenan

[February 3rd, 1924]   *The Mill House, Tidmarsh*

Dear, Oh, why did you write that letter to me? Do you want deliberately to end everything and make things difficult? I have told you in every letter I write that I may always be asked by Ralph, that he may read your letters. If you write as you did yesterday you make it impossible for me to show him your letters.

He did ask, I refused, and said I was sure you would prefer, and so did I, that he should not read it. He at once became suspicious.

So I showed it him. Minus two pages which I was able to extract. He then said 'No wonder you don't want me to read Gerald's letters to you, because he is obviously in love with you, otherwise why should he be in this state ... '

The whole morning has been given up now, to what I most wish to avoid, discussing *our* relations. Dear, I am not angry, only I feel rather hopeless. Is it not possible for you to realize how difficult it is for me to read your letters in private? That we can only be intimate in our conversations? If you admit you are in love with me Ralph then says he knows it will end in my either giving way to you, or suppressing feelings, or making you very unhappy. So that if you write letters showing your feelings nakedly, it only makes more suspicions aroused and Ralph will feel there is danger or will be danger in our relations. I can't discuss this with length with you in a letter, because I *dread* your indiscretion replying to me. You *must* please Gerald wait until you see me again. And why should you write as you have done? You know my affection for you. I know your affection for me. Since we are not free at the moment to express our feelings need we agitate each other by these added difficulties? You need not think I am altogether stupid, I do understand. I know how hateful it is not to write everything you want to write. If you must at any time write something indiscreet although I beg you not to, *please put it in a small PS* so I can show Ralph half the letter.

Yesterday you wrote me a huge package, with *one* sheet which it was possible to show, and a PS eight pages long. How could I conceal it all, or pretend your envelope contained one sheet? If all this is too tiresome, I sometimes feel it may be for you, tell me. *I can't alter it at present.* After the spring we will devise a better plan of writing. You know our friendship is in your hands. You can end it in one line if it is too tedious for you. I write another letter now, quite honestly, but you will understand it is one I may show, therefore I do not say everything in it that I say on this sheet. Dear, I was wretched to have hurt your feelings, you will see in my letter how it must have happened. Please remember that I *always* care for you as much as I told you I did and that if I do not write it is *not* because I am not thinking of you. But I *will* write more often. I cannot bear your unhappiness; only since a kind of silence is enforced on us, you must believe me. And please I beg you do not make it difficult for me to have your letters. Ralph is very friendly, but I saw he was alarmed by your outburst and these arguments are unwise. One day I shall be forced to tell Ralph simply in self defence, more than I want to tell him. Please wait until April. I will send your memoirs, letters every day, if only you will not make our friendship impossible. I am to blame I know. I am terribly sorry. Please forgive me. I write *on Tuesday* next intimately. My very fondest love.

                                              Your most loving DORIC

PS Let us forget this misunderstanding and don't mention it again. I hate myself for having given you cause to be unhappy.

PS Dear, I will answer your letter, and your adventure, and write at length next Tuesday. That is in two days.

Private PS written in great haste

Private

added PS

Later

You mustn't dearest amigo, think I was angry. I couldn't be with you. Also no great harm was done, Ralph was slightly agitated but nothing more only please do not make your letters a source of agitation to me directly I see the outsides of the envelopes!

I must tell you the riveter at Reading has mended the plate so perfectly, not a trace of the breakages remains. So our weeping was imaginary. Your lovely pink primitive house dish stands on the dresser. I do love you for giving it me. We go tomorrow to see Ham Spray House. I write the day after. Please write to me very often, only no gloomy-emotions. Tomorrow I am sending you a little rivet to mend this slight breakage. It cost me nothing, for it was one of my possessions.

I love you very dearly.   Your DORIC

To Gerald Brenan

Tuesday morning, 11 o'ck, March 4th, 1924 The Mill House, Tidmarsh

Dearest Gerald, I hope you will soon write to me. If it wasn't that there is a decree out against protestations and scenes, I could tell you, that I almost wrote off a frenzied appeal for a letter yesterday when no letter came from you.

The last letter you wrote me reached me on Thursday and today is Tuesday.

I feel very gloomy, so do not expect anything but wails, and dismal howls and mia–owls. We went up to London on Saturday morning leaving Lytton fairly well. He has had slight lumbago in his back all this week, but I thought he had practically recovered from the influenza. When I got back on Sunday morning I found he was much worse. Mercifully his sister Pippa was here with him on Saturday, and sent for the doctor. The doctor says it is a relapse after the influenza and that he has fever and must stay in bed some time until he is quite strong. You can think of my feelings when Pippa said: 'thought it was pleurisy from all the symptoms, but the doctor assures me it is not.' Last night Lytton was worse, and felt new pains in his side. Soon the doctor will be here again, and then I shall know what these pains mean. Although I suspect the doctor is rather an owl, and probably isn't very expert. What a curse diseases are! I feel exhausted with rage against a universe that seems designed to torment people with fevers, or whole people with agitations over sick friends and now of course this train of thought has led me to think of what I have been trying to avoid thinking about, that *you* may be ill and perhaps that is why you haven't written. I won't let you spend another winter out of my reach.

The Yegen 'landscape' has been held up again by Lytton falling ill. But I am going to start painting again directly I have finished this letter to you. I send you £2 inside it. I hope you received £2 in my last letter. That is £4 from me altogether, and the crazy £10 cheque from Mrs P[artridge]. Bunny is determined to take Yegen for 6 months. Ralph says he ought to pay at least 30/- a week, if not more. So don't give it him for some absurd sum. I have not seen J. H[ope]-J[ohnstone] since I came back, but then as I've only been to London twice, for a day, it was improbable that I should. I hear he has gone to France. St Malo. But I saw on Saturday afternoon D.H. Lawrence and his fat German spouse Frieda and the great decaying mushroom Middleton Murry and an attendant toadstool called Dr Young at Brett's house in Hampstead. I went up there to say goodbye to Brett, but found to my dismay this dreadful assembly of Adelphites. Lawrence was very rude to me of course, and held forth to the assembly as if he was a lecturer to minor university students. Apparently he came back this winter expecting to be greeted as the new messiah. Unfortunately very few saw his divination. The great Dunning almost denied it. A few critics called him a genius but that wasn't enough. 'England is rotten, its inhabitants corrupt.' Mexico is the only country where prophets, and great writers are appreciated. So tomorrow Lawrence, and Frieda and Brett set off in an ocean liner for Mexico.

Of course on examination it comes out it is New Mexico that they go to, which is a state of U.S.A. But they speak about it as 'Mexico'. 'We lead a very primitive life, we cut our own wood, and cook our own food' 'and Lawrence makes the mo-ost beau-ti-ful bread'. Frieda always comes in like a Greek chorus, the moment D.H.L. has stopped speaking. I nearly said he could come to Tidmarsh if that was all he wanted by 'Primitive'.

'And here is Carrington, not very much changed, lost a little of her "ingenue" perhaps, still going to parties, still exactly the same, except I hear you are very rich now, and live in a grand country house.'

I took the shine off his Northampton noise and his whining 'ingenue' accent. I told him I had £130 a year which I had always had. 'Ah but yer married a rich husband!'—'He has £80 a year.'

'And yer don't mind the change, that's very fortunate.' I report this conversation so you can have an idea of the greatness of our present day geniuses.

He then gave a description of Mexico, with some fine literary passages at which all the assembly looked up and took notes in invisible note books. My brother Noel was at this strange tea party and of course was delighted at talking to the great D. H. Lawrence. Whenever D.H.L. talked about the Mexican Indians, Noel made some absolutely boring remark about Hindus. If D.H.L. described the Rockies and vegetation of the desert in Mexico, Noel at once described the Himalayas!!

The decayed Murry sat on a sofa and said nothing; he swayed backwards and forwards like a mandarin, with hollow eyes, toothless gums, a vacant smile and watery eyes. Only once he spoke. 'Say, Brett your butter's bad. It's not good.' (D.H.L. 'They've scalded it Brett, butter should'na be scalded. They've boiled the milk.') Otherwise the great Murry never spoke. It is reported he has given up the Adelphi and is, in a few months, going to follow the Messiah, Frau Messiah, and Brett to Mexico. He said, when asked what it all meant, and what would happen to the Adelphi, 'Oh, that's the last of my little hypocrisies.'

Inez's party was very like most parties for me. I was rather bored by it to tell you the secret truth. I had moments of enjoying myself but they weren't connected with the party. Alix was there, and was so gay and amusing that I loved seeing her again. Ralph was the Don Juan of the gathering and flew from flower to flower. Mrs Joad was there looking very much a femme fatal, but her taste is really too vulgar. One can put up with some things. The Princess Frances looked ravishing, she really is a charmer from her appearance and I expect from inside also.

Barbara was there 'leaping from rock to rock', looking about 16 years old and very pretty. But after a little, watching these people became rather tedious and they dance very monotonously. Snow covers the ground once more and the cold is still intense. I've bought a new Leary [Edward Lear] for you. (A very cheap book, so no complaints.) But I'll not give it you until we meet on Victoria's platform. No more news about the future, except that I look forward perhaps xxxx a little xxx to the arrival of the Grand Llama of Yegen.

[Augustus] John hasn't sailed for America yet. So we've put off the sale of his picture [belonging to Gerald Brenan] until after he has gone!

Later, 3 o'ck

The doctor thinks Lytton is going on alright. So my agitations are over. But I expect he will be in bed all this week. I've exhausted all my Yegen memories, so it is time you came back soon, and gave me some new ones.

I cannot write letters any more because the brain has become permanently dulled by this vile cold outside. When will you ride a white horse over the sea? As we passed down Knightsbridge on Saturday, I looked vaguely in the shops: I saw one called 'the Knightsbridge Kennels'. In the window were little kennels with small toy dogs and bigger dogs, asleep on straw. Ushering a doggie lady of 60 out of the shop was a red faced young man, with a yellow waistcoat and a neat navy blue suit and spats. It was my brother Sam.

I felt the gulf was a sea between us, so I did not stop. Mercifully he didn't see us.

I hope to go to Ham Spray on Friday to see the gardener. We are all going to plant trees. Lytton plants a mulberry, Ralph a medlar, and I shall buy a tulip tree. Will you bring me a small dragon's blood tree from Cadiz, and plant [it] in a corner of the garden?

Please write to me soon. Throw this dull mutton chop of a letter into the cat's plate, but put the £2 in your pocket. If by any chance you could buy two chintzes, of *the same design*, I would be grateful, as I want to make curtains for my four poster bed.

You are very dear to me. Bless you.   Your Princess DORIC

To Gerald Brenan

Tuesday, the Birth of the Virgin, March 25th, 1924 *The Mill House,*
Tidmarsh

Two letters from Granada have arrived with innumerable post scripts.
You are worse than an owl, dearer than a nightjar, wicked as a jay.
Sweeter than the nightingale. How can I blame ⎱
     thank   ⎰ you sufficiently.
     reproach
     love

But why did you stop short at four chairs? What only *four* chairs? Why
not Maria, her daughter, the round table, the large bed, the curtains,
several chests, and two cats? You are the dearest person in the world.
May I say that? I love your letters. I am glad it rains at Granada, as you
will hurry back all the quicker. You are a merchant of the first order to
buy everything so cheaply and to defraud le mère Perdrix so superbly.[1]
Try and arrive in London on a Wednesday or Friday morning, *not* on a
Tuesday or *Thursday* because those two days Ralph works in London
and it is possible I shouldn't be able to go and meet you at Victoria. I
think it would be best, just to meet you, then leave you for two days
with Tizzie [Brenan's great-aunt] and then come up again for another
2 or three days. Remember to wire for money if you fall short, but put
clearly where it is to be sent.

I am so happy today. I have two long letters to read and a great deal
to look forward to. Shall we ever be unhappy again? No more, or I shall
miss you in Paris with this letter. My very fondest love.

  O doski, doski   Your CIROD

[Carrington met Gerald Brenan at Victoria Station on his return to
England.]

To Gerald Brenan

Thursday, April 3rd, 1924
Dear, I simply can't tell you how happy you made me yesterday. I am
only sorry I was so agitated and rather tiresome over the telephoning.

---

[1] Ralph's mother had commissioned Gerald Brenan to buy a Spanish shawl for £10.

But that was not our fault. It didn't really matter. I only feared this morning, in the cold light of the Belgravia Hotel, you might think I was rather boring with my perpetual telephones!! Ralph quite understood, and didn't mind of course in the least. The truth was, I was rather tired and exhausted. I only saw, and felt, when I met you, how very much I had been looking forward to yesterday. It made me so happy, that really I minded nothing, not even the post office, or the Belgravia Hotel.

I hope you are not too exhausted today. I could hardly bear to think, as the train sped me away from you, of your exhaustion and weariness. Today is quite unreal. I can hardly believe that yesterday *we* talked to each other. I can remember nothing of what we said. And that at half past four you will see Ralph and talk to him. Already I long to come up to London again!

How very fond I am of you.

This morning I looked at all our treasures. I love my white shawl. You will see this summer how beautiful I will look in it, for you. I will see a little figure walking down the Inkpen Beacon; I will then rush into the house, and in a moment, a Botticelli nymph, in a flowered shawl will fly across hedges and dew ponds and treading softly on gentians will meet you. You were disappointed about the gentians? xx But all our promises must be 'possible' mustn't they? To me, if a gentian persuaded you to live in Marlborough Forest, it would not have grown in vain. xxx I feel light headed today. I can think of nothing but yesterday. The seriousness of life has departed. Do you know you were very charming, and looked, to me, beautiful.

I may say all this, but *you* must not reply! The little brocade bodice delights me. All my future dresses will be made with relation to my shawls and waistcoats. Isn't that a good idea? To keep certain valuable garments, as a basis for all one's other dresses? No dress will ever be made now, that does not harmonize with your shawl. xxxx Ralph took the three shawls to Missie P[artridge] this morning. I really don't mind which they choose. I will be delighted with either.

xxx

Lytton thought the chintzes were very beautiful. Is it absurd to be in such ecstasies over inanimate objects? Yet it is easier to show it over two tigers in a jungle on a blue background than over one tiger in a Belgravia Hotel. Tell me why is that?

I have talked so much yesterday to you, to Ralph last night till one o'ck, this morning from half past six till 8 o'ck, that I am tired. Oh I wish I was going to see you before Tuesday. But the next time, there will be no stations, no telephones, no trains to Tidmarsh. I have an idea, it was stoopid of Miss Moffat not to think of it before xxx all day until six o'ck, we can sit in Hampstead in my brother's house. (i.e. Brett's old house which he now rents.) So we can make our lunch, and tea over a gas fire in peace. Now I must be sensible and get some lunch ready for Lytton.

I could write to you all day. xxxx Don't for mercy's and Miss Moffat's sake write back anything that my mother couldn't read! You are too kind, too kind, she murmured.

PS Oh how happy I am! xxxxxxx
I would like to write you a poem, to show how much I love you this morning. Did you like the Pink Leary Book? Bless you a thousand times. xxxxxx I am so jealous I can hardly bear to think that by tonight, other people will have seen, and heard you, yet at the same time I would like you to be seen. Contrarie Miss Moffat! You aren't to [be] so nice to anybody else, until you see next Tuesday your   CIROD XXXX

To Gerald Brenan

Monday, 12 o'ck, May 5th, 1924   *In the garden [The Mill House,*
Tidmarsh]

Amigo mio, I doubt if I shall send you my rigmarole of Saturday after all. I have just had an absurd accident that has unhinged my, as you say my weak spot, mind. I, after breakfast, was walking over the bridge across the little duck stream, in rather a bad temper and vague mood and walked off the edge and fell with my bucket of duck's food into the stream. This for some reason drove me into such a rage that I ran into the hen's house and cried and in my rage tried to hit a hen on the head with a wooden spoon. I could blame no one. It was entirely my own fault and so I could only cry against myself. I wasn't even hurt, only rather wet, but the sudden fall has made my head feel light and empty. And fits of temper I find really make me feel ill for nearly the rest of the day. So my discourse on life, you, and your writing etc etc will not be sent till tomorrow. I sit in the sun surrounded by dandelions with shining yellow faces, buzzing bees, and heavy trees of cherry blossom. How could one be in a bad temper on such a day! How indeed? I ran to the post very early before anyone was awake this morning with a letter for

11 Watendlath Farm, Cumberland, August 1921. See letters of that period

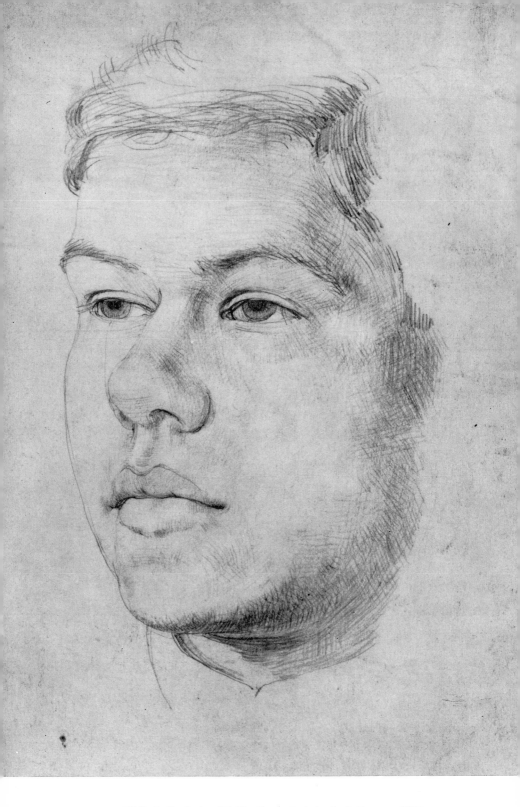

12 E. A. Carrington (Teddy, Carrington's brother). Drawn *c.* 1912

you. You ought to get it tonight. Do we write every day to each other? I forgot to ask you? I see it's important not to 'feel' life too much. Not to examine every blade of grass. It's better to take a general view of things otherwise, the moral may be, one falls into duck streams in despair. A certain laisser faire is to be cultivated je pense. I shall take some aspirins. I ought to have thought of it before. Yet how pleasant it is to have a friend to whom one can write everything. To whom I can tell my most absurd moods and all my pleasures. I shall start painting tomorrow. Because I give you such fine lectures on finishing your writing I am going to give myself a lecture. Tomorrow I shall finish two pictures although I would rather leave them alone. The Woolves come here next week end. I look forward to seeing them again. Please write me a very friendly letter. Don't reprimand me. I know I've been tiresome never finishing my proper letters, and sending you these scrawls instead. But we must, since we are no ordinary friends, forgive each other *all* our faults.

You will remember to be infinitely discreet with J.H.-J.? He is rather a gossip and I don't think has enough affection for me, not to perhaps, sometimes, throw out a word. I hope your eyes are better.

How very good it will be to see you again. Sometimes it seems impossible to write letters. Everything is too frail, and intangeable to put in paper. I confess my head aches so I *will* go indoors and take an aspirin. But you must never never worry about me dearest. Because truly I am the strongest of humans, and I am never ill. It's all a slight imitation of you, you will perceive. I see why people become naturalists, because it's the most lazy occupation. Shall I tell you in 20 minutes a dandelion on my left has been visited twice by a bee, and each time the bees stayed 58 seconds and carried away .008 grains of pollen. This is the 5 of May, 1924. One could sit here listening to birds, bees, and blue bottles and recording it all in a diary, or a letter, without using for one moment one's brain, or a monucle [? minuscule or molecule] of emotion.

You see I really ought to go indoors ... But I love the sun so much and then when this letter is over and put in its envelope, you will leave me. I can't bear to leave you just yet ...

xxxxx Dear Sweegie. How charming you are.

Hurrzi Hurrzi Dziomal Hji!

Which is the song of the road breakers in Kairouan and at the moment my song.

My love most dear one.   Yr CIROD

To Gerald Brenan

Saturday, 8 o'ck, May 17th, 1924   *The Mill House, Tidmarsh*

No letter. Written very quickly

Amigo mio, I have just read your letter. How dear you are. I shall be
happy all today. I felt a little dull also, but I knew you saw with your
eyes how lovely the world was and so you forgave your nightjar for
not singing a more lively song. Great beauty nearly always makes me
rather sober. But I have seldom enjoyed a day more. You know that?
And we have only to murmur those words: fair mile,[1] and we will be
happy! I am much better in health, my sore throat has vanished. I will
write tonight a long letter. I meant to write yesterday, but we went over
to Ham Spray and lingered there so late that the post had gone when I
returned. Bless you. I write feeling so very fond of you, and gay,
because for the first time for a very long time I feel the future will be
happy and without alarms. My fondest love dear Sweegie.

                                                         Yr CIROD

To Gerald Brenan

Monday afternoon, May 26th, 1924   *The Mill House, Tidmarsh*

Dear Sweggie, Thank you for your poem. It pleased me more than a
stupid letter from Mr B. this morning.

> An if Wednesday be fine
> In Chelsea we'll repine
> Bask amidst the tulips red
> Squeeze the drooping poppie's head.
> How nice t'will be to see
> My botanical Mr B.
>
> An if Thursday be fine
> We'll examine at Kew the pine
> Admire the cactus' penis pricky

---

[1] The Fair Mile where Carrington and Brenan had their first walk alone runs from
Moulsford to Blewbury Downs over the downs and is about seven miles from Tidmarsh
by road.

> Lick honey drops off creepers sticky
> How nice t'will be to see
> My botanical Mr B.

Sweggie dear I may be in London tomorrow but as I fear you will be engulfed in your parents, I shall give up my day to seeing Alix, Virginia and my mother-in-law (oh! and my Mr [Alec] Penrose of course.) But on Wednesday I will call at 10 Millman Street at 10 o'ck or let us say *10.15*, in case I am a little late in getting up, dressed very prettily in a sprigged muslin with roses in my bonnet. Barbara and Nick will be at the flower show, so I thought we might have lunch together afterwards. But that's as *you* please. In the afternoon I am given up to business. You to your parents? On Thursday *all is ours*. We will decide our fates on Wednesday. Bless you. I'll bring the picture. I can't write a proper letter. And then I must not tell you all my news or I'll have nothing to talk to you about on Thursday. My very fondest love. Bless you again,

XXX   your CIROD

To Gerald Brenan

Sunday, June 8th, 1924   *The Mill House, Tidmarsh*

My dear, I've no time as usual for a letter. Except that the reasons are not my usual reasons! I've a great deal to tell you. Yes, even I in my marsh have adventures. But I shall not tell you till Wednesday! I will meet you at the *ABC shop* in Tottenham Ct Road and Maple Street at *4.30* on *Wednesday* and I shall spend the whole evening with you. I had my Fiend yesterday! So that will not (be) there next week to ruin our afternoon.

I long to see you again.

Thank you a thousand times for all your letters. You have been a dear writing to me so often. Forgive me for not writing today. But I can't. I will tomorrow. So on Tuesday you will get a letter. Except that these posts are all queer because of Whitsun. Oh amigo mio, how fond I am of you. You are the most dear friend one could ever have. I shall have some money next week. So all our adventures on Wednesday will be mine, not yours. How maddening about the noises. I curse myself for dissuading you about that back bedroom. I am so sorry now. I never felt so happy before, since you came back from Spain, at the thought of seeing you again!

Bless you, my dearest amigo, and Wednesday 4.30 and tomorrow a letter so long, so affectionate, so amusing that you will forgive all these enforced silences.   My love yr CIROD xxxxxxx

To Gerald Brenan

Wednesday, 8 o'ck [June, 1924]   *[The Mill House, Tidmarsh]*

Amigo mio, Well shall I give you [a] dissertation on writing; how to construct a biography of your Saintess?[1] No, I will merely wish you good morning. I am truthful. What I mean is, that although new distractions always whirl me into the air and intoxicate me with a kind of curious excitement your power is so great you have only to murmur one word of disapproval, or hint that you are unhappy and I am instantly sobered.

What is true, is that I pay no attention unless I am spoken to, I always, if you say you will be generous, exploit your unselfishness. But that you know.

You know my secret life is with you. I doubt if I shall ever meet anyone again who will exercise the special magic that you are capable of, over me. I feel very intimate with you. I do not quite know why. I think I have lost that possessive feeling which I once had. I feel a certainty over our relation, that makes me no longer want to conceal my less virtuous side from you. Also you are so frank over your weaknesses, I should be a hypocrite if I tried to be better than I am to any one so honest.

This letter is written very quickly, just after breakfast. In a moment I shall run on my wheels to the post office and send you your flowers. You are good to write to me so often. You must tell me when I hurt your feelings, or offend you. I *never* mind being told things by you. In fact I would like to be taught other things, besides French. (Why don't you write to Alix, or leave a note first, then you could go and sit in those charming gardens[2] with her, and talk. She would be sorry to think she missed you.)

---

[1] Gerald Brenan was writing a life of St Teresa.
[2] Gordon Square Gardens.

Bless you amigo mio. This is no letter, I will write this evening again.

If only I could tell you a tenth of my feelings for you. You would see that my letters are no flattery. But who can judge emotions and affections in others? After all these descriptions of our feelings are really not the actual notes or actual colours. They are vaguely near to what we mean but I often feel the mere words themselves are full of complexes, and associations so that I long to invent new and special words to describe my exact feelings.

My love very dear Gerald   Your CIROD

To Gerald Brenan

Friday morning 10 o'ck, June 13th, 1924   [*The Mill House, Tidmarsh*]

I want a superlative of Amigo mio. I wish I could conjure up one word to tell you how much I care.

Dear. And now I would write no more. Do you see that in 'dear' I say all I can.

I thought as I lay in bed alone this morning, that perfection would be attained if you could have written, if when I ran downstairs I should find a letter from you. How well you know what pleases me! I feel rather stupid with you also. It is true when I am here alone I have a thousand interesting conversations with your Tibetan Ghost. But certain images will always remain. I almost feel at the moment I would like no image to ever approach that again, to encroach on a perfection of beauty, that contained all the senses. I remember nothing of yesterday morning. I believe you spent it with me. I only remember a dark hall, and the shutting of a door. I woke up and found myself in a barber's shop with a female hairdresser washing my hair with a strange smelling verbena hair wash. Alix didn't notice my hair, but Henrietta [Bingham] did! And then of course you must realize I wasn't quite truthful. I said Alix, but it was only half Alix, it was also for Henrietta I wanted it washed. We had a perfect lunch Alix, James and I. They were so amusing. Alix sold all her old clothes after lunch to a Jew with greasy curls in her bedroom, whilst we sat below. She came running in with £8 notes after he had left, shrieking with laughter. And then we all three leant out of the window and watched a discreet 'old-clothes' van move up to the front of the house and the old Jew and his companion, put in the baggage and drive off!

Then I rushed off to Knightsbridge to Henrietta's secret house. A house which nobody knew of except us. She had taken it for her friend who arrives tomorrow. But not a soul knew of it. We had a lovely tea in the kitchen, of biscuits and garlic sausage and tea with lemon. Then she drove me across the Park to Paddington. It is nice of you to be pleased because I am happy. I hope you will meet her soon. Perhaps it's all a delusion, she may of course be quite uninteresting inside. I hardly ever speak to her. We are the most silent of friends! But I feel sure she is very like her early Italian exterior. She also has a goodness that is unusual.

I will tell you when I will be in London again. I find your new rooms so sympathetic. I loved all your arrangements. You remembered everything I loved best: the peppermints I shall eat today. Did you notice what superb coffee Alix made? I think we ought to get Kenya coffee. I wonder if you enjoyed your evening with them? Do you know James saw you and Frances at Wembley. Alix said 'Is that an affair now?' James said 'No, I am sure it's not, from their backs, as they got out of the train, I saw it was no affair!' I have discovered the name of the mystic deadly nightshade plant that grows in the greenhouse at Ham Spray. It is called 'Solanum Aviculare, a native of New Zealand.' I wrote to Kew, and asked them for its name. Ralph said that proved I was getting very old, as only his father, or Saxon sent specimens to Kew and asked curators for the names of strange plants! What a happy evening I spent with you. I shall never forget it.

But I have already forgotten the name of the French poet and the name of the poem. I only remember 'the neck of a Queen bruised with kisses.' I spent half last night trying to remember it. Tell me, Sweggie, what was the name of it?

I telephoned Noel but I couldn't get him. His number was engaged. So will you ring him up? You had better ask him to leave the John at Fitzroy Street on his way to his office in his motor car. He wrote to me yesterday and said he and Edwards had tried *very* hard to sell it. So do not be too churlish to him, if you see him over it. (I say this, but of course you never are churlish!) I can hardly bear to give up writing to you! I can't bear to think of doing anything so dreary as feeding ducks and hens, on this particular morning. Ralph will be back at lunch today. I love you so much dear. I have every feeling for you, serious feelings intermingled with extreme gaiety.

I am so happy to think of you in those very charming rooms. Go and see Virginia and Leonard again. No I shall never have lunch with F[rancis] B[irrell] unless you are occupied. That was a good instance of my sham generosity, my attempt to gain affection and a good opinion by fraudulent means! Bless you, most dear amigo.

Your Princess of Georgia. CIROD

PS I write this in haste because I would like you to get it very soon. Bless you. Yr CIROD.

PS Please write rather ordinary letters, not even with PSs. This morning's letter will last me for many days. I will tell you then if I think it is prudent or imprudent about letters. Do you understand?

To Gerald Brenan

Sunday morning, June 22nd, 1924

Dearest amigo, XXXXXXXXXXX—

I have hardly any time to write to you. But I remember everything. You mustn't think I don't realize how good you are to me. I do see it. And then I behave badly. I get carried away by Kentucky Princesses who after all compared to my Amigo are not worth one half minute's thought. You were so dear to run after us. I knew you (or was that my vanity) really came to tell me, silently, you were sorry I was going. I did love being with you. I think of you very often. Will you forget my wickednesses, and remember a little, my affections? If only the John could be sold! Write me a long letter please. I am never quite certain of your affections, so the slightest silence on your side can always make me feel you have turned against me. I wish I could write a long letter. But we are starting for Ham Spray in 5 mins. My head is full of images, so strange and unexpected I can hardly believe they are real. I shall be more controlled and less thoughtless the next time we meet. I love you so much dearest Gerald. Remember nothing you do can ever offend me and I forgive you for any of your vaguenesses long before you have committed them. My dear dear amigo bless you.   Yr CIROD

PS I write tomorrow a long letter. That is a promise.

[Gerald Brenan, who had written on June 11th, 1922, 'I do not understand the possessive instinct ... it is part of my philosophy that love is free and unrestricted and is increased by being divided. I never thought of myself as his [Ralph's] rival or his wife's lover,' felt very differently when Carrington wrote that she was coming to stay in London with

Ralph and would not be able to see him. He replied: 'You have hardly any of the feelings or sensibilities of human beings. Do you really think to behave like this is nothing? ... If I could make you unhappy I would; I should be dishonest if I pretended to any good wishes or gratitude. I simply see in you an object which (for motives I don't understand) causes me the most elaborate suffering.']

To Gerald Brenan

Friday morning [July 25th, 1924]

I would rather know you didn't come because you didn't care for me, than you were prevented because you hadn't enough money. The fare is 10/3 return weekend. But I am glad at any rate you have told me you were poor. I should not have taken your present. The little right I had to ask you to do anything to please me vanished last Wednesday. So I shall not ask you to come again. I am only sorry I wrote those plaintive and rather unnecessary letters. You had much better conduct your life in the future without considering me. I agree with you entirely. I am impossible. I say this in no particular mood of deprecation, but the result of a week's thinking alone. The solution to all my difficulties lies up stairs in my studio. Henrietta repays my affection almost as negatively as you find I do yours. In the end I expect you will find Saint Teresa your best and most faithful mistress. I feel rather tired and dispirited and perhaps I shall not write for a little. Bless you. I love you.   Yr CIROD

[Lytton went on a visit to France while Ralph and Carrington moved into Ham Spray and made it habitable.]

To Lytton Strachey

Wednesday [July 30th, 1924]   *Ham Spray House, Hungerford, Berks*

Darling Lytton, [Twenty-five lines omitted] I go on with the painting day by day. But it's rather slow work; the effect however repays the boredom. For the house internally is now becoming really exquisite. The white wood work makes such a difference. Your carpets look *too* exquisite! They are very lovely. I've painted your bookshelves and Mrs Turner, who improves every day in charm and industry, has cleaned the woodwork and windows. I spent the last weekend away. I stayed Saturday night with Alix and James. They took Marjorie [Strachey] and me to Shepherds Bush Empire to see Little Tich, who was *perfect*. He is one of the few English geniuses. Unfortunately I got colly-wobbles inside. Poisoned fish I suspect [three words omitted] for dinner and had to retire. But I recovered by the time Little Tich appeared. Alix and James were charming. I love Alix more and more when I see her. I've asked them both to a house warming party on the 9th August to celebrate your return. Was that right? and Morgan. But Morgan hasn't replied yet. We are very, very happy here, the birds and the country seem to fill one's life with an external pleasure that seems perpetually new. I went down on Sunday to poor Barbara in Kent. Nick wrote me a letter imploring me to go and see her. She has been in bed one month now with a temp: sub-acute rheumatism. She seemed rather low. But didn't look as bad as I thought she would. Saxon was there, sleeping in a tent in the pouring rain! Noel, and his new young lady came into tea. She is very lovely, a Perugino angel with a wide forehead and golden hair. If Noel is wise he will not bring her down to Ham Spray before he has secured her! I had lunch with Sebastian, Gerald and Alix on Monday on my way back. Sebastian sent you his love.

Oh Lytton darling I *shall* be glad to have you home again. I can hardly bear enjoying so much loveliness without you. Forgive this dull letter, but I put so much energy into the vanished letter of yesterday. I can remember nothing today. I have just looked up Vannes on the map. How far away you are! In great haste, as the post will go unless I stop. My fondest love to Pippa and everything to you.

Your MOPSA

[The following letter was written after Carrington learned that Boris Anrep had asked Gerald to live for the months of August and September at New Romney giving lessons to his children Igor and Anastasia, and that he had accepted and was giving up his rooms in London.]

To Gerald Brenan

Monday, 8 o'ck [August 4th, 1924]   *[Ham Spray House, Hungerford]*

It is a lie, I am not very happy because of your good fortune. I am very
depressed. To begin with I felt enraged that the Marshall [Frances]
knew more about you and your plans than I did. And even Tommy
[Stephen Tomlin] knew. I was too proud to ask questions. I even pretended I wasn't surprised, as I knew of the possibility of it happening.
It means I see that I shall not see you for 2 months at least. Of course
it's just what we've been saying these last weeks would be a good thing.
But since last weekend I mysteriously changed. I gained a liberty. You
were quite right to persuade me to come up to London as you did. It
freed my inside, I discovered, from a complex. Tommy is staying here
till tonight. But perhaps you knew that? Everything suddenly seems
rather dreary, because I see now how much I secretly had been looking
forward to you staying near me this summer. I know I oughtn't to say
that now, but what does it matter. Yet I am glad querido mio that you
are happy. Perhaps you aren't particularly?

    Only if you had written.   Goodbye my love yr CIROD

To Gerald Brenan

Wednesday [August 6th, 1924]   *Ham Spray House, Hungerford*

Amigo mio, Here are the photographs of the sign boards.[1] It was *very*
kind of you to think of asking Mr Mills about it. I find it difficult to give
up at a moment's notice, my affection for you. I think too much about
you. I can't tell you as I have a horror of writing to you, if you are in
another mood. On Monday morning Ralph found me crying at breakfast alone. He was very sympathetic. But I couldn't bear to talk about
you at that moment, so I said I would talk about it later. Yesterday I saw
from something he said about you, he hadn't in the least grasped what I
was unhappy about and really had quite forgotten about it. This
morning he said, 'We must have missed one of Gerald's letters. He
never said anything to me about giving back the keys.' Then I saw it was

---

[1] Inn signboards Carrington had painted.

too late. I couldn't tell Ralph about your letter. It would mean endless conversations about you and our relations and then on Thursday Frances would hear it all and I should be treated 'sympathetically' by Ralph. So I said nothing. Now I shall never say anything. I don't really suppose Ralph will notice until a few months have elapsed that we aren't writing to each other! I prefer really to think of you alone inside myself, than to have you discussed, even with Ralph. His relations are so easy, he never finds Frances lacking in any quality. He can't understand our difficulties and if he does he simply thinks either you are mad, or that I deserve what I get because I behave so badly. Henrietta came on Monday night with Mina [Kirstein] and picked Tommy up, and carried him back to London. It was such a confusion I hardly had time to speak to her alone. She goes to Scotland for a month now and is engulfed in her father and brothers. So it's better to put her out of my head.

I am glad I knew her, as I did know her. It was an experience and I feel I have known the strange possibilities that some women are capable of. Alix was the only other woman who ever surpassed H[enrietta] in a peculiar variety of magical charm. I think Dorelia has it, but then I never felt it myself, for I never knew her. Lytton is still in Brittany but I hope he will come back soon, perhaps the end of this week. It was kind of you to lend R[alph] your rooms. He is very glad to have them. I shall do my best to beg him to leave them tidy. Ralph is binding some books for Boris. I have chosen the colours, and leathers very carefully, so I hope B[oris] and H[elen] will like them when they are finished. I am glad that I went that day to Helen's cottage by the sea, because I can imagine you in the evenings over the fire. Aren't the candlesticks beautiful? And the table Captivitch made? It makes all other furniture very shoddy I think. Ever since your letter came I have been *tormented* by trying to remember the name of the cottage at Romney. The awful thing was I knew Tommy knew the name, but I couldn't bear to ask him. As I knew he would then know why I wanted to know it. Thinking it over, it was a stupid letter to write. I am very happy in a quiet way here. I spend all my day painting by myself the woodwork and putting my rooms in order. Next Monday I shall start a painting—I don't quite know why I ramble on to you about my life here. It's partly because I can't bear to stop writing to you and there will not be another excuse tomorrow, as I shall have sent the photographs. On last Tuesday evening Ralph and I made a compact that we wouldn't quarrel, or argue, again. And that if we did the person who *first* made the quarrel would be to blame. This was because we both became instantaneously bored and disgusted by our habit of wrangling.

And, will you believe it, that we have not bickered once since this magic compact was made. It is a great improvement. You are not allowed to be cynical amigo, because it is really quite difficult to break bad habits. Perhaps by October I shall be such a transformed CIROD that you will forgive me. But I oughtn't to say that, I am sorry. If you change your mind and would like me to come for a day secretly to Canterbury, or the Romney marshes, or London, will you tell me? It is true, I am trying a little to persuade you. I confess my thoughts nakedly. But I also know you are capable of doing what you like and that is how I prefer you to behave. Please give Helen my love. Thinking of you, I see what a dear friend you have been to me. There will never be anyone quite so perfect in some peculiar ways. My rages against myself are almost unendurable.

In that we have something in common. Bless you. This letter is purposely flat. There is no point in writing anything else. And I shall not write again unless you expressly ask me. I'll be your ghost, you can conjure me to appear, or leave me in a grave, as you wish.

My love, dearest Gerald.   Your CIROD
And yet one has another self that shrieks GRRRRR half the day.
My love. C.
PS *Later*
After all I can only find these three photographs. I remember Noel borrowed the others. I will ask him to send the better one of the Grey Hound to you. So put off sending them to Mills. Till he sends it you, please.

To Gerald Brenan

[*September 26th, 1924*]   *Ham Spray House, Hungerford*

[First sheet missing; ten lines omitted] Then I went very fast on a bus from Hampstead to the bookshop; telephoned Henrietta [Bingham]. Her voice of course melted me and drove away all my humours which had accumulated against her. Then I had lunch with Frankie Birrell, Arthur Waley and Bunny. The latter was so friendly and simple I take back any of the absurd things I said about him. Then I dashed to your rooms collected my things, and tore to Paddington. H[enrietta] said on the telephone she would come and see me off. So I dashed up and down the platform looking for her. No sign of her and one minute for my train to start, all the windows blocked with beastly little school girls saying goodbye to parents, the platform crowded. I felt it was some terrible dream and that I would go mad. Suddenly in the distance I saw H[enrietta] walking down the platform very slowly with that enigmatic smile on her face. I pushed the school girls from the carriage door brushed through the parents and dashed towards her. The smoothness of her cheeks again returned and I remembered nothing but that she is more lovely to me that any other woman. We talked for one minute. I leap into the train. She kissed me fondly, and the train moved away.

She cannot come this weekend. But seeing her again just for that moment removed all my feelings against her.

James arrived today. Sebastian is still here. It pelts with rain and thunders. I feel much more contented than I have been for some time with life.

To Lytton Strachey

Monday [September 29th, 1924]   *Ham Spray House, Hungerford*

Very dearest Lytton, We had your wire this morning. I *am* glad you will be back tomorrow. Nothing in the way of news here. James is a very delightful companion. We play knave collecting in the evenings and all day James searches for indecent words in vast dictionaries crouching over the fire. Ralph worked the entire day yesterday, book binding and made some exquisite little books. Today le grand verte morocco is being tooled very chastely, in the style of Roger P[ayne]. I think it will be his masterpiece. I made a lovely owl kite this morning but the wind was almost too terrific and dashed the kite to the ground with such violence that it had to be repaired. Yesterday afternoon I went blackberrying with Annie on Sheepless Down. [Fifteen lines omitted] My love dearest Lytton   **Your MOPSA**

What can this be?
cried the rook in the tree
An owl in broad light
or is it a kite?

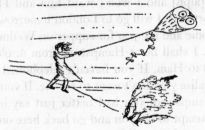

To Gerald Brenan

Tuesday [October 7th, 1924]   *Ham Spray House, Hungerford*

Well this is a bad beginning to our compact. I am undecided whether to simply abandon London altogether I now have so little taste for it.

You little realize how much you resemble your father when you write as you do.

I won't send telegrams and I won't enter into these arguments. If I say I want to sleep at Hampstead you ought to be fond enough of me to see that it is important I should be allowed to do so if I say I want to. If you say you don't want to see me unless I sleep at Fitzroy Street, I respect your peculiarities, and leave the decision to you. I hate sleeping at Fitzroy because it is so dirty and smells. That has nothing to do with you. You can't alter the texture of Fitzroy Street, or the noises in the streets. If I was coming to London by myself I would rather sleep at Hampstead. Now you see I have blurted out all my supreme hatred of smells, and dirt and your W.C. If I came and saw you I had resolved to spend the days and long evenings with you, but to sleep at Hampstead. This is against your feelings. I am sorry. I see we are both rather obstinate. You have your ideas on perfection and won't relent and I have mine.

But I *refuse* to be drawn into a controversy on it. I know you can point out very quickly how selfish I am and how you put up with heaps of things you don't like at H[am] S[pray] for me and so I should etc etc. But it is your attitude I can't bear. I won't now (even although I've really got over, by telling you, my hatred for that smelling street and W.C.) come and stay with you simply because you didn't care about having 2 days with me unless it was exactly as you liked it.

So let us abandon it. Don't send any wires or I shall be forced to tell R[alph] and I won't want him and F[rances] to revel in all our misfortunes. I will go to London tomorrow and if you want to see me I will come and see you for supper on Wednesday. If you don't I shall accept it. I shall be at Hampstead from 6. o'ck till 6.30. At the telephone is 2140 Ham. If you haven't telephoned me between those times I shall realize you don't want to see me. If you want to wire, it is 6 Pond Street Hampstead, you had better just say impossible and then I'll make no attempt to see you and go back here on Thursday. Really I hardly care now I feel so dishearted.   Yr D.C

To Gerald Brenan

Sunday [October 19th, 1924]   *Ham Spray House, Hungerford*

Oh but you did enrage me yesterday. Or rather I raged against Fate, and glue, and thick envelopes and curious amazon post mistresses and sensibilities and everything I could rage against. You posted your last *letter* to me *unsealed*. Really it was never glued, because when I examined it most carefully I saw the glue was virgin—unlicked. The post mistress gave it me breathless with agitation and confusion. 'I promise you it arrived in this condition. *I* never touched it Mrs Partridge, *I* hand it you just as it was handed to me,' etc etc. In a terrific loud voice so that R[alph] outside in the car, heard every word. Imagine my feelings all the way back in the car to Ham Spray. Can you? or does that mean very little to you? I was so sick with agitation, that by the time I reached my room I could hardly read what was inside. Please, please give up thick envelopes. They are fatal to keeping stuck even if licked and please remember to seal your letters, or I really shall go mad. Don't think me absurd. But it really is hideous to get letters, especially yours, after the whole village has read them. Now I have over boiled like the stew in the kitchen, and the whole letter smells of burnt onions and fat and am myself again, and quite merry.

My call on the Miss Woodmans was fascinating. They are most peculiar old ladies of about 63 and 66 years old. Do you know they were born in *this* house, Ham Spray. Isn't that extraordinary. Their father built this house and made the garden, when he was a young man of 21. They had lived at Ham ever since they were born. They were full of information on every subject. They are so poor they have no servants, but do all their own work and the garden. They were very outspoken and natural because they had sunk below all pretentions.

The fair at Newbury was wonderful. Annie and I went by ourselves and met R[alph] at the Newbury station. The streets were crammed with farmers, boys and girls. You never saw such a gay scene. Flare lights with cheapjacks, illuminating every face in the crowd. Boys stuffing confetti down the blouses of giggling girls. Strange leering faces pressed against each other. Stalls selling ginger snaps, and sweets. Amazing gypsies telling fortunes. The pressure of the crowd was terrific. For the stalls went down the street on both sides. Then in the square there were

huge merry-go-rounds, swing boats, lottery booths, quacks and astrologers. We went on a lovely swing merry-go-round, that whirled one
round very fast so one flew out into the dark sky like a revolving bird on
wings, higher than the houses, above the top of the shrieking merry-go-
round and below one saw, tearing round and round, the crowd and the
flaring lights. I could have stayed for ever. On this swinging-go-round
one saw life in such a fascinating way. We met the charming bee keeper,
or curiosity shop man, from Ramsbury. He was bursting over with
merriment, and good spirits. I felt so fond of him, although we had very
little to say to each other. I hit twice some dancing balls with a rifle on a
fountain and we lost some money throwing rings and arrows at targets.
I think all that is best in English life congregates at a fair. All the farm
boys looked so gay and beautiful and once I saw, for a second, a face
that was worth going to fifty fairs to see: a very pale young girl, with
black eyes like sloes dressed rather respectably in tailor made clothes
leaning on the arm of another girl, whose face was shrouded by a
drooping veil. As they passed me, the pale girl turned round and made
a most lascivious leering smile at some farm boys who were passing. I
looked at them, they were bewildered by her beauty and excited, but
couldn't make out evidently what she meant by her strange passionate
look. Then she laughed in their faces twisted round and rushed off on
the arm of her friend into the crowd and was lost from view. (If ever you
saw Birdie Jones, Schwabes's wife, in Chelsea, you would know a little
what she was like.) I wonder who they were. Perhaps shop girls in
Newbury. But she looked too refined and yet: but how can one tell
anything? But it was her face that made my evening happy.

Your letter now I am no longer angry, was so charming. You are a
dear to write to me Gerald so often. I have been painting very hard on
my decoration for the cellar door. I don't know yet if it's any good. I
worked the whole of yesterday morning from 10 o'ck till one o'ck. After
supper I made Ralph sit for me, and drew him. Today I will work again.
It alters one's whole attitude to life, working hard, I find. I mind none
of the vexations of life when I am painting. Yesterday afternoon R[alph]
and I went to a concert at Newbury. Some lovely Scarlatti music pleased
me and some Brahms quartettes, but of them I am not so certain. The
rest of the music was awful. Why do musicians have no taste in their
choice of music? Helen sent me a big basket of fruit as a present, with
a very strange fruit, like a green scaled lizard! Now I must write to your
mother before the post goes. Lytton comes back today. I will write *on
Monday* about coming to London. When I am working I feel so anxious

to get on with my painting I can hardly bear to go away. Yet xxx it is true one can't always, or one doesn't always, work.

Amigo most dear. I don't turn against you. You know I am far fonder of you than I ever admit. Why don't I admit it? I can't ever discover that. Perhaps you wouldn't be so nice to me if I did. I still care for you very very much. You see, I wasn't angry with you. I knew you couldn't help leaving your letter open, only I was angry with the post mistress, and everyone who read what was only meant for your Princess. Would you like some apples?

My very fondest love amigo most dear.   xxxxxxx Your CIROD

To Frances Marshall

Thursday [October 1924] [Ham Spray House, Hungerford]

Dear lady, I am glad to hear you are still very lovely and beautifully good inside. Do you know I am very fond of you? You didn't know. But I am. We had a very gay time at the fair last night and I hit two balls with a rifle! Whose balls? Whose indeed. My love   Yr CARRINGTON

To Gerald Brenan

Thursday 10 o'ck [October 30th, 1924]

I came back. But you were out. I think it's rather gloomy but I feel too depressed to say anything. I mean I've been thinking about it ever since Monday and felt underneath it was in some way hopeless. I get on your nerves. No one else does. You can talk and be happy with other people far more easily than with me. It is not ever your fault. In spite of our great affection for each other, there is something that produces an unhappiness between us. I think what you say is true. I mean it is, that I do not care enough. It has been *my* fault for continuing against your wishes with our relation. I can't bear to see you always so unhappy through me. Don't let us ever feel embittered. But no one has a right to make anyone wretched, and I least of anyone to you who never did anything but care for my happiness.

You have been dearer to me Gerald than you know.

For a little perhaps we had better not see each other. I shall leave it
to you. If you change your feelings and would like to see me again, you
know I have no feelings that would be against you ever. But if we part
let us say goodbye without any hostility and don't let us hurt ourselves
by saying anything to wound. I shall not try and influence you against
your judgements. Perhaps it was wrong of me to prevent you stopping
it before you went to Warren End [the Anreps' cottage]. Today perhaps I see you are right. You can't think how depressed I feel with
myself. I don't think it's any use writing to each other for a little, only
please don't turn against me. Even if I don't see you for some time I
could not bear to think you were against me. I can't write what I want
to say. Except that I would have you forgive me for all the wretchedness
I have caused you and remember that the happiness you gave me wasn't
wasted. My love   Yr C.
It's entirely my fault you couldn't help it you must remember that
always.

To Gerald Brenan

Thursday morning [*November 6th, 1924*]   [*Ham Spray House,*
                                                                Hungerford]

Dearest Amigo Mio, Your letter came this morning. You cannot think
how quickly it made me happy, for I had spent a bad night without
sleeping. Partly because I was cold and then I was worried and rather
unhappy. From pride I never mentioned your name once to R[alph]
since I left London. He was very sympathetic but often I think he forgot
I was not quite happy. I regretted my outburst to Helen. It is a fault,
this pride, yet I cannot help it. I longed to write to you. I longed to
come and see you again, but I felt it was an admission of failure. You
are more sensible, dearest amigo. It was good of you to write. I am
already so happy. I feel a different human being. I never knew how
much I minded till Thursday, when suddenly the whole point of being
in London vanished and all Friday was dust and ashes, as I had no one
to go about with. And in spite of one thinking one could see endless
people, in reality I found Ralph and Frances my only companions! And
even the party was rather dreary, and sombre for me. I cannot write
sensibly now. I feel too lightheaded and happy. The dreariness of
thinking I was not going to hear or see you till perhaps next year de-

pressed me terribly. I was foolish enough to believe it *completely*. I never for a moment believed you would write again. My dearest love, how quickly you have made me happy! I will write tomorrow a long letter. I agree with everything you say except that in any way anything is your fault.

I write in haste to catch the first post as I am just going to Hungerford.

My love dear dear Gerald   Your most loving CIROD

To Gerald Brenan

Friday morning, 10.30 [November 7th, 1924]   *Ham Spray House,*
                                                      Hungerford

Amigo, I have written you two long letters—one last night immediately after you telephoned and another this morning. I thought about our relation and you continuously all last night. I feel rather tired in consequence this morning. Nothing has really altered I see since last Thursday evening. Your telephone message last night confirmed that it was madness to believe the calmness of your letter in the morning. I get on your nerves you yourself admit, and you are constantly filled with suspicions. I can't help feeling our relation is in a bad state. I care, passionately, for a better relation. If it's impossible I would rather have no relation than these agitations, and unhappinesses. *You* can't be unhappy without affecting *me*. I have come to the conclusion after thinking very hard that it is best to keep to the conclusion we came to last Thursday. Not to see, or write to each [other] for some months until we both feel quite tranquil and altered and that you are working again and without nervous agitations.

Forgive the incoherence of this letter, but I am as tired of writing as I am of thinking about it. I have written two long letters already. The real truth is I know I can't make you happy in the way you want, and I can't bear to be the person who makes you unhappy, so I want to go away from everything for a time.

I won't see you again, and I rely on you to promise to tell me when you want to see me again later. I shall never stop caring for you. I hate myself for making you a single hour unhappy.

Let us remember last Thursday evening and write no more—That was a perfect momentary parting.

It mattered, and still matters that you care for me.

You will always wire for me, if you are ill.

I cannot say any more because I am too gloomy, I am glad to have that last letter from you because it matters so much to me that you care. But please believe I have come to this decision after a great deal of thinking and through caring for you. My fondest love my dear one.

Yr CIROD

PS Please don't write back I feel I can't bear any more thinking, or decisions.

[Gerald Brenan made the following entry in his diary dated November 1924.

'I was crossing Tottenham Court Road when I saw R[alph] and C.R.D. [CIROD] coming down the opposite pavement. Very large and tall and wearing a broad brimmed hat, he looked as though he came from the Colonies and was a tea-planter or a bull-fighter.

'Beside him, looking short and squat and dressed in ugly yellowish cloth, came C[arrington]. Her hair was a yellow mop: her face as it often does when she is alone, looked anxious and haggard. Her expression was disagreeable, her age might have been forty. As she walked, she turned her ankles inwards and she kept a pace behind him, as though she were an inferior. I could hear their voices as they passed without seeing me: they were arguing. His voice went up at every moment into a hoarse squeak: this was the effect of grafting on a man with a naturally deep voice L[ytton]'s peculiar treble. Hers was low and angry.

'I saw them perhaps for the first time in my life as strangers see them: a gypsy tinker and his squaw, striding through the London streets.

'They had for five years lived together and argued, he bullying her, she exasperating him. Though she always got her way, she had paid for it in the loss of her youth and beauty. At the same time they were inseparable. Bad habits attach people to one another as closely as good ones: they conserved the attachment when they had lost the sentiments of lovers and would no doubt continue to persecute and irritate and wear down one another until they were dead.

'Yet as she passed me I caught sight of her bare hand. It was the same hand on which I had so often fixed my eyes as though all the beauty in

the world and all my happiness were contained in it. Now at this
moment it seemed to me that nothing had altered, and that this middle-
aged, dull-looking married woman was in some way another 'myself',
since she carried about in her so large a part of my life. I felt for her as
one only feels for oneself, loved her as one only loves other people, and I
knew that no alteration in this would ever be possible.']

To Gerald Brenan

Wednesday [*December 17th, 1924*]   [*Ham Spray House, Hungerford*]

Dear Amigo, I send you this picture by Ralph. If you don't like it very
much I can easily do you another. I never have any feelings myself about
my pictures, they all seem after a few days equally dull. All is confusion
here getting ready for the party. Mercifully it is hot again and the sun
shines, so one does not feel that awful depression that the rain and cold
produce. I don't feel in a mood to write you a letter, partly because I
haven't heard from you, so I don't know what to say. I read 'War and
Peace' day after day, and live in another world, it is strangely beautiful
in so many varied ways. Late last night I heard a fox baying with short
barks at the moon in the field outside. The carter told Annie they are so
tame here they are not frightened of the men and the other day a fox
joined the workmen at lunch in a field and had to [be] driven away, he
was so anxious to join their feast. It is difficult to tell you when you ask
me, how I am still fond of you. I only know when I see you again, I am
overcome by a strange affection which is different from the love I have
for anybody else. Yesterday I thought of Spain. It was just a year ago
today we started for Yegen. Do you know I think there are very few
hours that I cannot remember every detail of at Yegen. You will never
know quite how much I loved staying with you. I can never forget, or
thank you enough for letting me share your life there and for showing
me so much. You know my life is almost entirely visual and no place
ever gave me such exquisite happiness as last winter with you. I hope
you will be happy, as far it is possible, at Edgeworth [Brenan's parents'
house] this Christmas. You asked me not to have a lover when you saw
me the other day. It is easy for me to promise. May I ask you for a
promise? Please avoid C[lare] B[ollard] as far as it is possible, because
I feel as certain, as spring follows winter, that only disasters to us all
will come of it.

I write purposely a little restrainedly, you understand why. Seeing
you again made me so happy. My fondest love

                                   Amigo mio, your CIROD
My dear one, I send you all my love.

1925

To Gerald Brenan

Thursday evening, 6.30 [January 22nd, 1925]				*Ham Spray House,*
										Hungerford

Amigo Mio, It was kind of you to write me two letters, especially the last one when you were ill with the headache. I am glad you liked the apple jelly. It was sent entirely for you, since R[alph][1] does not like it. I must write in pencil as my pen is in Lytton's room and he is working, so I must not bother him. In half an hour I shall have to fetch Ralph from the station. There is a howling gale outside, a Tiger of a wind, I wish I had not to go, as it is pleasant sitting over this blazing fire writing what ever comes into my head to you. Oh dear, I am sorry if I said anything to Helen [Anrep]. What could I have said? I thought I wrote very discreetly, I know I didn't say a thousand things that I wanted to say. Do if she hasn't gone already, give her my love and beg her forgiveness. Henry Lamb who came here on Monday and stayed till Tuesday, was very enraged with Boris and said it was appalling. He gave an awful description of Boris. He says Boris suffers from neurasthenia. I was interested at meeting Henry Lamb. Mostly because of Lytton's past relations with him and partly because of Helen. I longed to get him to talk of Helen, but somehow it wasn't possible. He looks like an Army doctor who has seen 'life' perhaps on the Tibet frontier or who has suffered from low fevers in Sierra Leone and also has a past murder, or crime, which makes him furtive and uneasy. He has a most unhappy face. But he is amusing and very charming sometimes. Did you ever meet him at Helen's house this winter? He promises to come over this spring with Dorelia to stay here. He is a most perverse man in his opinions. Almost as silly as Morgan [E. M. Forster] sometimes, but sometimes extremely intelligent and inventive. I made two glass pictures on Tuesday and Wednesday morning. Did you like them? I always want to know if *you* like them. Will it not be wonderful if I can at last and by such a

---

[1] Ralph, who had been lent Brenan's rooms while he was living at the Anreps' cottage, was still using them while in London.

delightful occupation, earn £2 a week? I fear Ralph will have licked the sugar off my biscuit-of-a-letter by telling you all the Ham Spray news.

This morning, as I didn't feel in a mood for drawing I cut out my green grass brocade dress, it's going to look very lovely Querido Mio. It is a copy of my Persian dress, only made with slight differences. I shall take some weeks to finish it, as I only do needlework in the evenings whilst Lytton reads to us. But in March, (after the Mystic Month of February is over) you and I will have a party together at Fitzroy Street, only with no guests and I will wear my Persian finery. It's going to be very elaborate, green silk stockings and scarlet shoes and an underdress of fine red silk. The clock flies too fast, a quarter of an hour has gone and in ten minutes I shall have to get the car out of the stable.

I will come up next Wednesday. I will try and stay Thursday night also. But I will not absolutely promise this. But I *do* promise all Wednesday and Thursday. There are pictures that I want to see, the toy shop at Hoxton and the London Library. But they are all occupations that I would like to pursue with a certain companion, if he will come with me. How can I tell you that I love more than all the ∼ something in you which I cannot explain? If you doubt this, you can easily prove it. We will spend our days in utter chastity, and I will still be happy.

I am glad you love Anastasia [Anrep] a little. I was very taken with her the last time we went together to Pond Street. I thought I had never seen her look so beautiful as she did, sitting up in bed, with that old stained handkerchief round her head. Then her character is so original and attractive. I can hardly bear to think of her changing, but perhaps she will retain her charm when she grows up. Helen obviously has not lost her quality which makes her so sympathetic.

Last night I read Defoe's Plague. Then before we went to bed Lytton and I had a long argument but I cannot be bothered to write it all out for you. Besides I was converted, so my arguments seem to me rather silly now. I hope your headaches will soon go.

Now I must go.

I will post this letter tonight, so you will get it very soon.

Lunch next *Wednesday* at 18 Fitzroy Street.

My love, dear one. Bless you   Yr Princess CIROD

To Frances Marshall

[*1925*]   *Ham Spray House, Hungerford*

Dearest Frances,
    You are an
    (which is an owl)
    also a
    (which is a noddle)
    also an
    (which is an idiot)
    When I say 'that depends'
it is by way of a joke. A joke
against Mr P[artridge] insinuating of course that 'it
depends' on nothing at all
and of course if she can
come and wants to come,
she must come and we shall
be delighted. You knew
this, owl, idiot, and noddle
and it's just because you
thought it would be gayer to
go off with Mr P.N. gallivant-
ing, that you excused yourself by pretending you didn't understand my
little (and rather feeble) humour.
PS If I hadn't wanted you I should hardly have dared to have said so
blatantly! PS Because my disease, 'that my prevalent of all complaints'
—causes me great torture, and produces a certain misery and despair,
you flatter yourself if you think this unhappiness is caused by your
presence! I ignore you Madame. I hardly notice your ghostly existence.
In truth I wish, speaking for myself, you weren't so ghostly. Oh but I
forgot you don't like advances from young, or to be exact middle aged,
women. We've just been reading Norman Douglas. He is superb! My
love dear lady. And please remember to come here when ever you want
to, for it will also be reciprocated by your   CARRINGTON

To Lytton Strachey

Monday morning, 7 o'ck in bed before breakfast, March 30th, 1925
Ham Spray House, Hungerford

Dearest Lytton, Such a weekend! Such orgies! Such conversations! Why
weren't you here? It was too dreadful. We arrived back on Saturday
after lunch. Found the house all secure but rather bleak. Two telegrams
pushed under the door, (or rather forms to say that telegrams existed
at Ham P.O. if we fetched them) I dashed off to fetch Olive, leaving
Ralph to light the fires, and Frances to go to sleep on her bed. I called
for letters and telegrams on the way, but the d–d post office was of
course shut. I thought you'd probably forgotten 1st B. Bands 2nd tooth-
brush, so didn't worry much about the telegrams. Olive sitting there all
spruce, with a large tin box. Reached H[am] S[pray] again in car. Ralph
said 'I think I'll go down at 4 o'ck and try and get the letters and the
wires'. So he went off and I started teaching Olive without a second's
pause, the ways of our world. Ralph came rushing back:—a wire from
Henry [Lamb] and D[orelia] to say they were arriving for tea. (Wire
from Tommy to say he couldn't come for weekend.) I just had time to
whisk a few rockeries into cupboards and they were upon us. D[orelia]
looking very lovely, and in high spirits. H[enry] a little older perhaps,
and a little balder, than last time! I soon gathered they had come to
spend the weekend. Mercifully we had some food in the house. They
were both very sad at not seeing you and Henry has taken your address
at Lyme and said he would like immensely to come over and see you. I
was completely knocked over by Dorelia and her beauty. She was very
talkative and gay.

We played the gramophone most of the time, drank mead and sloe
gin and bottles of wine, played ping pong and went to bed very late.
Yesterday we walked over after lunch to Sheepless Down. Poor Dorelia
got very exhausted, so I had to support her on my arm. She has a fearful cough the whole time. She goes in April to Isthictha (?), an island
near Capri, with John. It sounds perfect, a little cottage on the edge of
the sea, with a garden and an Italian cook and servant and a little sailing
boat. It was interesting to see Henry and Dorelia together. She fairly
raps him over the knuckles when he gets fussy and laughs at his absurd
conversations and rags him when he gets sententious. Olive is so far *perfect.* Far brisker than Annie, cleans and bustles about in a pair of

squeaking shoes, and beams with pleasure when one talks to her. I
think she will be alright in a few days. She is full of energy and com-
monsense. And already does a great many things on her own without
being told.

Henry of course couldn't resist making up to F[rances] M[arshall]
a little. But I fear his days of success with jeune filles are over. She
couldn't see *a trace* of that former dazzling beauty, in his battered face,
she confessed afterwards. Noel and Missie A[lexander] came over to tea
yesterday—we played poker after tea over the fire. [Five lines omitted]
Cream Brulé came off and created a very proper impression. They
[Henry Lamb and Dorelia John] go back this morning to Alderney.[1]
Henry brought me a most superb Mexican Lily, a great red lily on the
top of a thick purple stalk. I shall do a large painting of it today after
they have gone. Dorelia promises to come again. She was delighted with
our country, and properly enthusiastic over our beloved House. It was
sad not to have you here and I kept all the time wishing you were staying
at Ham Spray instead of at L[yme]R[egis]. [Twelve lines omitted]
We both miss you *very* much. I will try and find the cork of the hot
water bottle this morning.

Love from your MOPSA

To Lytton Strachey

Monday evening [March 30th, 1925]   *Ham Spray House, Hungerford*

Dearest Lytton, Here are some clothes from the wash and your bottle
stopper. I dimly hoped for a letter today, but perhaps you have been too
busy bathing with Sebastian to write any letters. D[orelia] and Henry
went off after breakfast this morning about 11 o'ck. Ralph was completely captivated by them both and enjoyed having them here, I think,
quite as much as I did. Olive is very charming, extremely naive, but
continues to work very hard. She came panting to me, saying 'Will those
same visitors come back next week?' 'I don't think so, why?' 'Because
they left something behind: they left 2 shillings in one room and half a
crown in the other.' She is only 15, I discover. Her father is a carpenter
at Hungerford and her brother works with the father. Mercifully she can
light fires so that dreadful morning crisis no longer exists. Unfortunately

---

[1] Alderney Manor, Augustus John's house in the country.

Henry's picture that fell off the nail, was never put up again! But the drawing of the boy was in his bedroom. I am going to do a large picture of the red Mexican Lily they gave me. It's really the most beautiful flower I've ever seen. I now feel rather alarmed at the thought of dining with Lord R. [Philip Ritchie] and the duke of Sackville West [the Hon. Eddy Sackville-West] tomorrow night. I should have preferred it to have been Mr Pockington, but I didn't dare say so. I hope you've been discreet about what I confided to you in my last letter. I think Dorelia is an admirable woman. Why doesn't she live near here, instead of at that outlandish place? Henry becomes a faded wall paper beside her.

My fondest love xxxxx   Yours D.C.
PS Lampshade made in sitting room quelle triumph! [PS of nineteen lines omitted]

To Lytton Strachey

Monday morning [April 27th, 1925]   *Ham Spray House, Hungerford*

Darling Lytton, It *was* good to hear your voice again last night I am glad you are recovering. [Twenty-three lines omitted]

The casks are at the station.[1] Tra la! Tra la! [Eight lines omitted]

I could write you a long letter on the modern French painters. Really they filled me with an unspeakable rage. They are fifty times worse, I think, than any other painters, English or German. Because they are morally wicked, being charlatans, cheats and imitators and outwardly they produce hideous, vulgar pictures. Really they have an exact parallel to those French women of 50, all made up to look beauties and underneath they are hags of iron. I shall be interested to hear what Roger and Clive have to say on these most modern monsters when they come back.

Will you write and tell us if you would like us to come up to London? Ralph is in any case coming up on Wednesday, I think. So if you don't feel strong enough to come down I will come up with him and see you. My very fondest love, dearest Lytton. My only pleasure is thinking that very soon you will be here with us again. I love you so very much.

Your CARRINGTON

Won't you, now that you are having Ellie [Rendel] as a doctor, broach the gland question?

[1] Casks of wine from France for bottling at home.

PS R[alph] has asked F[rances] M[arshall] next week end, but *not* the two weekends after that. So will you ask anyone you like for the future. [Six lines omitted]

'As it is Lent, puss has caught you a fish.' From a letter from Carrington to Lytton Strachey during Lent 1924.

[Carrington had persuaded Gerald Brenan to take lodgings at Shalbourne, the next village to Ham.]

To Gerald Brenan

Monday night, 12.30 [June 1st, 1925]

Amigo Mio, I hadn't read your letter when I passed you in the car. I couldn't read it till I got back here tonight. I am desperately unhappy and my head aches. Last night was awful. I cried in bed because of the sadness and dreariness of our day together. All today I was gloomy. Frances had a toothache so she and R[alph] wouldn't go to the MacCarthys'! So I had to go with Pippa Strachey. But it seemed a mere fly in my general gloom the dullness of this afternoon.

I felt last night you hadn't understood what I was trying to explain. I mean I told you all my worst moods crudely. I let you see the horror of my lowest days of gloom and nerves. But you are being unfair to both of us, if you don't see the other side. I mean you mustn't forget just as some days I feel removed and very distant physically, other days I feel the reverse. Only it is quite true it is awful for you who mind so much what my physical feelings are, never to know before hand, what mood I shall be in. I entirely sympathise with your feelings. That is the worst of it. I am in despair because I am against myself. I think about you until my head aches. But I do not know what to say or how to alter things.

You see when you came over yesterday morning I was transported with pleasure. I looked at you with the greatest happiness, filling the bottles and talking. Then suddenly in the greenhouse, I could hardly bear the difficulties and arguments which seemed to surround us. Just as I make you eccentric, you react on me by your noticing me in some peculiar way and make *me* disagreeable and nervous. I am *not* like that usually. Directly I am away from you, I hate myself for being so unfriendly. When I see you with Helen and other people I see all your charms, and love the humour and engagingness of your character. But when we are together, half the time seems to be spent in this friction and that instantly makes me intolerable not only to you, but far more to myself. I mean that scene over Sunday afternoon was quite irrational and pure nerves; I didn't really care a damn about what I was talking about.

Gerald you don't understand quite that it is only because you are so involved with my feelings that I feel all your moods so acutely. You can't think how miserable I shall be the moment you are gone. For you must know that all those things that I talked of yesterday vanish when I think of the loneliness of not seeing you next week.

The real thing that irritates you is my inability to have physical feelings when you have them. That sets up nerves in you which makes you restless, or depressed, which at once sets up nerves in me. You are dear to me. I have just read your second letter. I shall never have a friend like you again. Who would have been so forgiving but you? Do not have a grudge against me. I am more unhappy at being the cause of not only my own unhappiness, but yours also. It is awful to care so much for you, to love your character, to be excited by your mind and your writings and yet never to be in contact with these, because of these other complexes which suddenly without the slightest warning, appear. You cannot say I am incapable of physical feelings, yet the last 2 weeks I felt as if I was without a body. Will you please not bear me a grudge? Perhaps it's something which I will recover from. At the moment I seem impossible. I quite agree. Dear, it is awful, after bringing you to Shalbourne and getting what I had looked forward to for so long now, to see you unhappy and looking ill. Why is it we cannot strike a sort of every day relation that excludes these crises?

I showed R[alph] your letters, for I was in such despair. I did not know what to do, and couldn't bear not to talk to someone. Naturally since he knows, perhaps even better than you do, the tiresomeness of my character, he could say nothing.

Will you go to a doctor. Please go to Helen's doctor. I think he is

very good. Lytton goes to a doctor, a female, called Miss Rendel, 10 or
12 Connaught Sq. It is in the telephone book. Faith goes to her as well.
But perhaps you could not face a female. But will you promise to see a
doctor? What can I say to you Gerald? I feel so utterly gloomy because
I have made you unhappy. You will write to me? It's impossible for
me, even although it's so useless, not to go on caring very much for you.

My love   Yr CIROD

PS Please tell me exactly what the doctor says. Don't write anything too
depressing to me about myself. I've been in such despair these last two
days I couldn't bear you to reproach me. I cannot thank you for the
lilies. It simply makes me love you a little more. This letter is stupid but
I write very late at night and I am tired. So don't pay too much attention
to it.   Yr C.

Later, one o'ck
PS Don't let us make any decisions. Don't say you won't come back
here, or you won't see me again in London. For I am childish, I always
believe what you say. Now I must go to bed for I am so tired. Goodnight. I feel I've been so tiresome that I'll do exactly what you ask me.
Write, or not write. You mustn't go to London thinking I've turned
against you. It *isn't* against you. I wish I could explain. I care for you
as much as I ever did, Amigo Mio. You really mustn't think my distrait
moods are to do with you. I should be like that if I was surrounded by
beech trees and no men within a hundred miles. Bless you.

                                                                                     Yr C.
You shall have your birthday picture next week.
Tuesday morning
PS Please come over to talk to me today if you feel it will make things
any easier.

[On June 6th, 1925, Lytton delivered the Leslie Stephen Lecture at
Cambridge. For this Ralph and Carrington drove over from Ham Spray
and stayed the week-end with Ray and me at Hilton Hall, Huntingdon,
twelve miles from Cambridge. Lytton came for a short visit but stayed
the week-end in Cambridge in Maynard Keynes's rooms.]

To Gerald Brenan

Saturday [June 6th, 1925]   *Hilton Hall, Huntingdon*

Amigo Mio, We spent all yesterday travelling in the car to Hilton Hall.
It was terribly hot and very exasperating. I mean looking at the map and
mending punctures and taking wrong turnings. We had a lovely lunch
on Boxmoor Common under beech groves. Then I took R[alph] to
Ashridge House and showed him some frescoes I painted 12 years ago.
They are still intact, and haven't fallen down or changed colour which
just proves that frescoes can last in England, which everyone always
denies. It was strange driving through Ashridge park again where I
once spent a whole summer when I was painting there with Constance
Lane. Bunny lives in really a most exquisite house. One talks of Helen
having taste, and Dorelia, and Ham Spray and Duncan and Vanessa, but
really I think this house eclipses them all. Of course without Bunny it
would be a very lovely house, but he certainly has shown great discern-
ment and taste in his furnishing. We arrived about 6 o'ck last night
(Garrow [Tomlin] is also staying here!). It was very wonderful last night
wandering round the village green listening to the owls in the faint
evening moon light. We go off in half an hour to hear Lytton's lecture
at Cambridge. This evening we see a play. Tomorrow I lunch with
R[alph] and F[rances] M[arshall] in Cambridge with some other people
and then come back here to tea. On Monday I think we go to Norwich
for the day, but it depends on various other people's designs when we
come back to H[am] S[pray], probably Tuesday or Wednesday. I can't
write a long letter, as I've taken a dose and must dash downstairs. I
enjoy very much being away in some one else's house You ought to see
Bunny's house, it really is so very beautiful. My fondest love, dear
Amigo. Please go over to H[am] S[pray] whenever you like and sit in
the garden. Did you get your picture?   Yr loving CIROD

To Gerald Brenan

Tuesday [June 30th, 1925]   *Ham Spray House, Hungerford*

Amigo Mio, I can't help feeling everything is getting rather removed
from the point. I didn't show your PS to Ralph because you asked me

13 Samuel Carrington (Carrington's father). Painted 1915

14 Beach scene (probably
Brittany), 1919

15 Mountain church, Larrau,
Pyrenees, 1922

not to and I know really you would regret me showing it to him. Since
I really think that it showed feelings that you probably don't feel today.
I simply won't reply to your letter because it seems to me most of what
you say is absurd. May I come and see you on Thursday afternoon for
tea at 4 o'ck at Fitzroy Street? We will then talk sensibly about everything. Will you write and tell me, if you agree to this. I have to go to
Rylands' party, so in any case we shall meet there. You are trying to
press me into a position which I don't in the least hold. I had a great
deal to write to you today, but your letter has driven it all into the sea.
Sometimes when you send me such letters I feel I hardly know you. I am
sorry I can't feel quite the same as Helen does towards Boris or as
Vanessa does to Roger [Fry]. I don't believe you really think what you
write in your letters is true. Was it meant to annoy me? It didn't. Was
it meant to provoke me to come to tea on Thursday? Well it has.

    My love dear   Your loving CIROD

To Gerald Brenan

Sunday morning [*July 19th, 1925*]   *Ham Spray House, Hungerford*

Your letter came yesterday morning. I have thought about you for a
whole day. My detachment from us both seems complete. I shall always
believe you to be one of the most perfect, lovable characters I have ever
known. You contain more that attracts me in your character than I have
thought possible for one person to contain. Thinking of you I forget all
the difficulties and scenes and only remember other images of you.

    But looking at myself I feel only resentment at my character. Most
of your attacks are justified. I see *my* complexes only bring out your
worst features. Which probably if I didn't exist to torment them, would
be invisible. I am only sorry you never knew, or so seldom, my better
character. For somehow you also drag out something from me which I
myself do not ever feel except with you. The irony of it is that H[en-
rietta] (who is a person of no importance and lacks all the proper virtues,
for I can see even her, detachedly today) should have so completely
altered my physical feelings for everyone. It was seeing her again that
upset me so this spring. How feeble one is! To alter these things seems
the hardest thing in the world. Yet with one's head one is perfectly
logical, and sensible. Don't, Amigo Mio, turn on me and think it all a

waste of time. For my part I still care for you and I always shall I suppose, because one cannot forget anyone who has profoundly moved one
and with whom some of the most beautiful visions in one's life were seen
together. If this separation makes you no happier, if you find, nobody
else to make a more complete relation (you know we have never had any
pride between us and I [think] there is no reason why we ever should.)
You will always write, and ask me to see you when you feel inclined?
No one is quite happy. I know quite well, how much you really matter
to me, but I agree with you, after one has once had a sort of perfection
in a relation, one can't put up with something different. Actually,
although you do not mean to, I see your unhappiness and that at once
depresses me making me act unnaturally. Do not blame yourself that
anything was ever your fault. I hardly think it was mine. It was simply
an irony of fate, that drew out suddenly from a past bundle of suppres-
sions, these feelings of mine for H[enrietta]. Which are of course
perfectly futile and senseless. My secretiveness has always been my own
misery. But when I tell you I suffer literally physically sometimes, when
I hear my inside self discussed—but if you haven't these feelings it is
difficult to explain. Will you when you go to Edgeworth send me back
that diary I sent you. With you going away, my last contact with an
outside world probably vanishes. I shall now retreat back into my self
again. But I cannot bear to make you, (who in spite of all you say), I care
for in a way different from my feelings for anyone else, continually
unhappy. So I accept your letter. I will write to you no more and I will
not come to London for some time. If I do, I will do my best to avoid
any places where you may be. Dearest Amigo. You would forgive me if
you knew how unhappy I make myself in writing this. My fondest love
to you   Your CIROD x

Later

PS of course there is no reason why you should do what I ask you. But
if you could refrain from talking about me I would be so grateful. Even
Helen, I suspect, tells it all to R[alph] [and] F[rances] and then I suppose
to Gordon Square. If any of them cared, as Helen cares about your
feelings and mine, one would not mind. But if you knew what I know,
how ironical they are, and how in order to make it 'bien presenté' it is
quickly altered into gossip, you would think twice before you poured
out your heart to them. You hurt me more than you ever hurt me in any
way by once confiding to F[rances] M[arshall] that you had sent me 'an
ultimatum' (as she called it) and then begging *me* not to show the letter

you wrote me to anyone. When R[alph] said 'G[erald] told F[rances]
M[arshall] all about it and the letter he sent you,' I literally felt sick with
pain. You can never bind two intimates to secrecy. If I confided your
secrets and feelings as recklessly as you do mine, to R[alph] and
L[ytton] you would have soon felt the stings of publicity. I know it's an
obsession with me. But for a little I would beg you to remember it's
part of a person you care for: please don't write to me again; it simply
makes it harder to behave as one wishes to behave. My love again

Yr CIROD

Sunday evening 7 o'ck

I could not after all send my letter this afternoon because there were no
stamps in the house. I went a long walk with Alix this afternoon to
Shalbourne Hill. She talked a great deal to me. I think I admire her
more than any human being I have ever known. Her intellectual, and
moral honesty is so remarkable.

Gerald, I think I am unfitted as a human being to have a relation
with anyone. Sometimes I think my obsessions and fancies border on
insanity. As I haven't 2 gns a day to spare to be analysed I had better
put up with my complexes alone, by myself. In any case I think *you*
are too decent a human being to be dragged into my mire. The alternative is to try and be a serious artist. You once said I couldn't face being
alone. Don't you realize that unless one has intimate relations with a
person, one is really *alone* most of the time? I think you think I don't
understand your feelings. I understand them too well. Please do not
turn on me. I want your pity more than anything, because in agreeing
to separate I lose so much and gain nothing. It is always gloomy to be
defeated by one's own character. But you have no reason to be sad. You
have a great many friends and you aren't 'battu' in that sense of the
word. I'll ask R[alph] not to go and see you. Please be a little proud and
do not discuss me. After all there is nothing to say. I have written so
many letters to you in my head that now I can think of nothing to say.
My love again.   C.

To Gerald Brenan

Tuesday, July 21st, 1925   *Ham Spray House, Hungerford*

Amigo Mio, Your letter from Rodmell, came yesterday after I had
written to you. Oh my Amigo what an awful thing it is to be so divided,

so unhinged. How much easier it would be if one felt definite and positive feelings, like other people. If only our feelings for each coincided more often. You want perpetually something from me which it is not in my power to give you and I feel always a sense of guilt and depression because I cannot give it to you. Reasonably there is nothing to prevent me having a very intimate relation with you, except a feeling of secretiveness and an instinct to live away from the world which seems to drag me against all my reasonable inclinations, away into myself. I feel if only I mattered a little less to you, it would be less strained. But of course if I did, probably then you wouldn't want to see me. I torment myself with my own character. I envied Alix her independence from human beings and her concentrated interest in her work.

It is so difficult to explain, Amigo, and one knows that letters give such false impressions. But you do not know how different you are with me from other people and I feel the same is true probably about myself. With Helen you are gay animated and full of spirits. When I come to see you, I see you are depressed almost instantly and full of apprehensions. This of course reacts on me, making me depressed and dull. I think probably you want a very normal female who doesn't have moods, simply because you are so sensitive and easily depressed. I pray to God you will never have the misfortune to get involved with such a hopeless character as me again in your life. And yet do you know it is more difficult for me to agree not to see you than to do anything else? There is *so much* I love in you so entirely, that when one is removed here from the physical difficulties, one can only feel affections and (something which is almost) admiration for you.

I want so hard to try and be very exact. Because I know how easily you are depressed by misgivings. You know I have always hated being a woman. I think I mind much more than most women. The Fiend which most women hardly notice, fills me with such disgust and agitation every time, I cannot get reconciled to it. I am continually depressed by my effeminacy. It is true *au fond* I have a female inside which is proved by ∿ but afterwards a sort of rage fills me because of that very pleasure ∿. And I cannot literally bear to let my mind think of ∿ again, or of my femaleness. It is partly because R[alph] treats me not like a woman now that the strain has vanished between us. All this became clear really last summer with H[enrietta]. Really I had more ecstasy with her and no feelings of shame afterwards. You really pressed me out of myself into a hidden suppressed character. But when I returned, I turned against the other character that you had brought out and was filled with dread at meeting her again. I have been trying to make this clear, but perhaps it means nothing to you. (Suppose Seb. persuaded you to go to the furtherest point with him, can you not imagine although it was *also* part of yourself, you might be filled *afterwards* with feelings of terror?) It's really something nothing to do with *you*, but some struggle in myself between two characters. I think H[enrietta] although she gave me nothing else, gave a clue to my character. Probably if one was completely S[apphic] it would be much easier. I wouldn't then be interested in men at all, and wouldn't have these conflicts. It's not true to say I don't care for ∿ with you. Because you know I did. But at moments these other feelings come over me, and I dread facing that side in my character. (It's *not* a dread against you, but against myself, against my own femaleness.) Somehow it is always easier if I am treated negatively, a little as if I was *not* a female, then my day-dream character of not being a female, is somehow pacified. I have tried to make this clear. I have never completely told R[alph] this, or anyone. It is a confidence I make only to you. Merely thinking of this makes me so agitated I feel I can hardly bear any relations with anyone again. In the past everything I believe went wrong for this reason. Always this struggle with two insides, which makes one disjointed, unreliable and secretive. I find it as difficult as you do to bear the strain of making each other unhappy. I don't see how I can ever give you up. Because there is nobody who for me, can ever be quite what you are to me. Perhaps this internal combustion will one day cease, and my torments with it. I am going to try and lead a very regular life avoiding any personal agitations this summer and painting every day. I *don't* tell R[alph] about you and all our difficulties. You are wrong in writing this. I only talked to him this summer when you talked to him when you were at Shalbourne. I did not talk to him this weekend at all about you. Partly I confess because he wasn't interested. But mostly because somehow it is difficult to talk about one's inside feelings to anyone but the person concerned.

The pigeons arrived on Saturday. They were most lovely. This morning your mother sent me some plants; I am writing to thank her.

Let us calm down a little. If you want to write, or see me again, I shall not care less. You have been always so dear to me Amigo it's impossible to get over caring for you. Please don't answer this. I've simply tried to tell you something which I hadn't got clear until today.

My love dear one.   Your CIROD
PS Ralph will leave the Shalbourne books with you. But I'll ask him not to go and discuss it with you by staying at Fitzroy Street. I shall say

truly, that at present I've agreed, not to write, or see you. And that this is a mutual agreement on both sides.

To Julia Strachey

Sunday [Summer 1925]

Darling Julia, I am afraid you are a sad wretch. Because you go careering about in your Rolls Royce with a jeune homme of a Sunday and when asked to come here, don't come.

We all sat on tip toes [drawing omitted] waiting for the wheels of your new Royce up the gravel drive. But in vain, oh vain Julia. There were rows of young men on tip toes and yet you preferred to lie in the braken, or under the gorse bushes, instead of coming to see your old friend. Well, well.

I hope you will come next Saturday in your Rolls and stay the

promised week. I heard a great deal from poor Mr [drawing] about you.

You breaker of Lambs' fry, or tails. Oh I wish you were here to do all those 'little jobs about the house.' But I'll learn yer when yer comes down my sweet honey. I'd let you tidy my drawers, mend my socks, and polish the boots. Had I but known you loved and so excelled at those hundred and one little things, I would not have let you lie idle in bed reading Galsworthy (or Tchekov much the same) a sleeping draught. One draught of your sweet lips: now I am becoming both sentimental and in bad taste, so I must stop this letter and run and put the peas on to cook. For it's Sunday night and the maid, my dear! I always think it's best, don't you, to let them have one evening out, and Sunday you know, for church, a week. So you are having High Jinks with the Turk. I found out a good deal from Roger [Senhouse] about him yesterday. Ha! Ha! Roger *is* a charmer. I was very melted by him this weekend. [One line omitted]

    Darling Julia goodbye, my love   YOUR TANTE CARRINGTON

To Julia Strachey

[*1925*]   *Ham Spree House*
                        A Collins

Dearest Princess Julia, I can't help thanking you for being so charming
and so lovely every time I see you. I wish I was a young man with
 moustasches and a fine swaney neck so that I could dazzle
you. I told Mr. Lamb it wasn't any good his casting
sheep's eyes on Princesses unless he grew a fine yellow
moustasche and even then I wasn't sure if yellow would
count against black. But as he can't get a moustasche to grow on the top
of his head poor feller, I don't suppose he'll have much of a go.

 Ba! But this is not the
purpose of my letter, to make
sheepish jokes. The purpose
is to say unless you change
your mind you are to come on
August 14th for a week and
will you ask that Bird, the Tom Tit[1] to come for 2 or 3 days, *not* at the
weekend, middle of week better whilst you are here? If he can come
please write me a letter. I am afraid I shall not be in London for some
time now again. Thank you and Oliver *very* much for your kind

HOSPITALITY. My love dear lady from your admiring Mrs P.

To Gerald Brenan

Monday, September 21st, 1925   *Ham Spray House, Hungerford*

Dear Amigo, Thank you for your letter. It is simply another proof of our
fundamental difference of character. I wish to bury the past, you have
an infinite capacity for investigating it. I do not believe any particular
circumstances made our relation impossible. It was rather my predestined inability, (which whenever I think of my past life is forced upon

[1] Stephen Tomlin.

me), to have any 'intimate' relations with anyone. I believe I am a
perfect combination of a nymphomaniac and a wood-nymph! I hanker
after intimacies, which another side of my nature is perpetually at war
against. Lately, removed from *any* intimacies, causing no one unhappiness and having no sense of guilt I have felt more at peace inside myself
than I have ever felt before.

I am only sorry Amigo, that you have been made so unhappy by me.
At present I do my best not to think about you. So will you please not
write back again. It was kind of you to tell me you have got over some of
your resentment against me. Mine, against you, was always only for a
few days; the rest was against *myself* roused by you. I am glad you are
happier now. I beg you not to write again. I always shall think of you
with great affection. With my love   Your C.
PS It is quite alright about the diary. It doesn't seem to matter now, so
keep it if you like.

To Lytton Strachey

Saturday [September 26th, 1925]   *Ham Spray House, Hungerford*

Darling Lytton, Your letter has just come. I wrote you a long letter on
Thursday, and Friday, but didn't post it. So now I will write it all over
again. All Wednesday was very hot, and exquisite, I spent the entire
morning gossiping to Helen and inventing a dinner for our party. We
drove to Hungerford before lunch; otherwise the entire day seemed to
be spent in meandering conversations. The Japp world arrived at half
past seven. The dinner was indescribably grand. Epoch making; grape-
fruit, then a chicken covered with fennel and tomato sauce, a risotto
with almonds, onions, and pimentos, followed by sack cream, supported by Café Royal red wine, *perfectly* warmed. (The cradle took Mrs
Japp's breath away.) I shall repeat this grand dinner for our next weekend. We all became very boozed. You would hardly have recognized old
Japp. He became so flirtatious and talkative. Helen was a great support
and was very polite to the Japps. We tippled sherry over the fire till
after 11 o'ck. The next morning I manoeuvred and got Dorelia to
promise to come down, on her way to Alderney. She arrived at half past
six. Henry came over. We again had a *superb* dinner ending with crème
brulé and two bottles of champagne and more sherry afterwards!
Dorelia became completely boozed and very gay. Even Henry was less

gloomy and rather amusing. We played Haydn, made endless jokes and talked without stopping. Somehow I thought it was the most lovely evening I'd ever spent. I wished you could have been with us. It was partly the loveliness of that femme Dorelia. I got a good many embracades from her, and one passionate rencontre with Henry in the hall. But I preferred the former. Henry stayed the night. He has given me some of his pills for going to sleep, which alter my life, as I now sink off into a complete snooze the moment I get into bed, until the next morning. I will replenish the sherry section of the cellar next week, as I am afraid I made rather a hole in it. Poor Dorelia was rather ill the next morning after our debauch, but I didn't feel any the worse. They stayed to lunch and then went off to Alderney. Yesterday evening Helen's two children came down. Do not SHRIEK! They are very well behaved and they'll not be allowed to look at any of your books. Otherwise Helen would have to have gone back yesterday. Now she will be able to stay till Sunday evening. The weather is rather wobbling here. Last night the bulls broke loose and rushed roaring round the house and blew all the branches down. No interesting letters, only a post card from Ralph from Toledo. Will you tell me when you will be back? Do not hurry, if you are enjoying yourself, or want to go to London, as I am in very good spirits, and quite happy here. I've enjoyed having Helen here enormously. I like her children. Baba draws very good pictures and properly appreciated my bird book. Yesterday I started a new landscape of the downs from the garden. Helen got a black eye, the evening we had the Japps here. She was lurching to the W.C. in the dark and ran into a wall. I am sorry to hear about Judith's collar bone. But perhaps it wasn't very serious. How wonderful Charleston sounds. What lives they lead those people! Really Vanessa's behaviour is monstrous! I hope Virginia will be well enough to see you. I was delighted to hear all your news. My watch went two hours slow this morning, so I never got up till half past nine instead of half past seven. Today is lovely, so after lunch we are all going in the car to the deserted cottage, to pick sloes and have tea. The children are in raptures over the house and garden and seem very happy. Helen still talks to me under the verandah and is very charming. The carpenters have arrived, a lovely ship's carpenter in a sailor's shirt. He is a most amiable man. Rather plain, but full of humour. They are making a very neat job of a cupboard and floor. I have a lovely new cat. When I went to the Japps, they had ten exquisite cats of different sizes, tabbies, and blacks. So I chose a lovely dark tab, and brought it home. Poor Tiger had another fit this morning and rushed in circles frantically round and round the lawn, and then had seizures under the laurel hedge. I fear I shall have to get rid of her. For she seems very neurotic, and sad. The carpenter is going to do the windows next week. I long for a letter from Keynes Hall.[1]

The new cat is called Biddie. It's a most lovely creature. I shall go to London one day next week, perhaps on Monday for a day, and a night. The little Anrepinas look rather charming running about round the lawn with bamboo branches. Helen and I go to Japp's tonight to a return dinner. Apparently Mrs Japp is renowned for exquisite cuisine and was very agitated by our gorgeous display. So this is a rival supper party. I shall be glad to have you back again. Henry by the way made a long speech about you to me. So I assured him you weren't in the least hostile. He was pathetic in his curious way. He poured out a melancholy tale to me about Dorelia and John, and the lack of civilization at Alderney. Now dear I must go and attend to my duties. Helen has a most corrupting influence on one. One does nothing but sit under the verandah and talk. I love you so very much. My fondest love

your most loving MOPSA

[1] Lytton, who had been staying with Vanessa at Charleston, was going on for a visit to Maynard Keynes's house, Tilton, half a mile distant.

1926

[The following letter reveals an intrigue on Carrington's part to persuade Julia Strachey to get Frances Marshall to share her flat, instead of going to live with Ralph openly which she did in the spring of 1926. Until then Frances had lived in her mother's house, 27 Brunswick Square. Frances and Julia had been at Bedales School together. Julia had previously been living with Oliver and Ray (her father and step-mother) at 96 South Hill Park, Hampstead.]

To Julia Strachey

[Spring 1926]   *Ham Spray House, Hungerford*

[The first part of this letter is missing] But I see no reason, as it is in many ways the only obvious person [Frances Marshall] you could ask to share a flat with you and it certainly would probably make your difficulties of housekeeping easier. But I love you Julia for being so understanding and giving me a straw to cling to. I will come and see you again soon, and talk to you and then, when the weather is a little less grim, I will ask you here. You will come? *Don't write back to me*, as Ralph returns next Monday and please burn this letter. If only one's feelings weren't so involved there is a fascination in intrigue and plots that is unequalled. It is so interesting to have a part laid down with one's words to learn. But I've very little spirit left. For which reason I've rather taken to the other 'spirits'. Now I shall live for a little in my nunnery, drink glasses of hot water and lemon, go for long walks, and read Proust in the evenings. Did you like my decorations on Alix's walls. Honestly? You see I've rather an absurd opinion of your taste.

My love dear Julia   Your CARRINGTON

later Friday
PS Lytton has just had a conversation with me. He says a dentist has now entered the arena. But that you put up a brave fight. Most dear Julia. But of course if F[rances] *will* come there is no reason why *she* shouldn't take the lower floor instead of the dentist, or an upper floor, in

fact Gordon Square offers everything most suitable for the 'situation', general vagueness, tennis in the summer and company and nice rooms. However just because it would make life tolerable and prevent general disaster, I feel [it] won't happen. I shall always however love you for your kindness to me, even if it is of no avail. Meanwhile I hope the dentist will be prevented from actually taking the first floor until our fates are settled. My only hope rests with your diplomacy. I will write next Tuesday when I shall probably know from Ralph the result of your letter [three words omitted]. Please burn this letter.

My love again   Your CARRINGTON

To Frances Marshall

Wednesday [*early spring 1926*]   *Ham Spray House, Hungerford*

Dearest Frances, This is a difficult letter to write. If it wasn't that I have grown very fond of you I couldn't write it. You will understand that, also since you are as unhappy as I am, you will forgive me.

I wanted to see you to talk, but I now feel it's too hard, because our feelings are so involved.

We each know what we have all three been feeling these last months. Now it's more or less over. The Treaty has to be drawn up. I have to face that owing to a situation, which cannot be got over, I must give up living with Ralph. I simply now write quite frankly, to beg you to try, while these adjustments are being made, to see the position from my point of view and to try and see if it's not compatible with your happiness to still let me keep some of my friendship with Ralph. I can't get away from everything, because of Lytton. Even although the happiness of my relation with Lytton, ironically, is so bound up with Ralph, that that will be wrecked. I am obliged to accept this situation; you must see that. All I can do is to beg you to be, any rate at first, a little generous.

You see I've no pride, I write a letter which I suppose I oughtn't to write. You see, Frances, you can afford to be lenient because R[alph] is so completely yours in his affections. In spite of all your difficulties and unhappiness you are a gainer, we losers. And if you face it, the situation really is *that Ralph can only give me what you can spare to give*. My future does rest with you. I can't ask you to understand what I feel because it's really impossible ever to understand other people exactly. I can't really understand all your feelings. But by putting myself in your position I have been able to see the inevitability of this situation and to sympathise with your misery.

I do love Ralph, only in a different way, just as you love him. It isn't any easier for me to give him up than it would be for you. As he loves you, he must care for your feelings before those of anybody else. That is rather an important fact, but I have been facing it for some time. The bare truth from my point of view is that if Ralph leaves me completely, or to all practical purposes completely, it really means an end to this life. I can't ask *him* to go on seeing me down here, because he really feels it depends on whether *you* can bear it. If you can't, nothing can be done. If you can, you must know it would mean everything to Lytton and me.

I don't suppose you ever realized that it wasn't very easy for me a year ago, to give up what I did give up, to you.

In the next month a good deal will have to be settled. That is why I write to you. I am, you must see, rather outside everything. I can't alter anybody's happiness, or unhappiness. Ralph's position is much the hardest one to bear at present probably. Whatever happens, Frances, I would like to tell you, now, that I've never felt anything but fondness for you. I've no resentment because I regard it all beyond us, in an odd way. I send you my love and I hope you are happier. Forgive me if I should not have written; perhaps however you will understand. It would be kind if you burnt this letter, for it was rather difficult to write.

I send my love to you.   Yr CARRINGTON

Reading this over, I see I've expressed it very badly. And probably it's pointless. But I feel rather in despair, so forgive me and don't pay any attention to it, if you don't want to. There seems to be no answer, but perhaps you will write.

[Frances Marshall replied as follows:]

Frances Marshall to Carrington

Thursday [Spring 1926]   *Owley, Wittersham, Kent*[1]

Dearest Carrington, I was glad to get your letter, because for so long now we have only communicated indirectly through Ralph and it drives him to despair and yet we both long to go on talking. Perhaps if we

[1] The old farmhouse belonging to Colonel Dick Rendel, Lytton's nephew, who was married to Judy, Frances Marshall's elder sister.

talked or wrote to each other it would save him some unhappiness—so will you please write to me if you ever feel inclined. You have always been such an angel to me and I am so fond of you that it makes it all the more intolerable—this horrible knot in which our happinesses have got involved.

I know that I must seem a monster to you—I want just to explain how though sometimes in black moments you become an entity x and I have horrid feelings about you, always when I think of you as yourself I feel nothing but fondness for you. And I'm sure I am often to you an abstract monster—I explain it so badly.

I don't know now what the position is or what is going to happen. It is practically impossible to talk to R. about it—but whatever happens this is the main thing. I never never never feel that if R. should live with me I should want him not to see you very often and go on being fond of you. My greatest hope but I've feared an unreasonable one, was that living with me he should still be able to see you continually and eventually even that we should all be able to meet together without any of our present awful feelings—but R. pointed out to me what I see is only too true that it is not fair to you to count on your being able to bear that. I know how difficult it is to go on seeing people on the same terms when the circumstances have changed—and he seemed afraid that you might feel you couldn't bear to see him at all. Do believe that that is the most awful thought imaginable to me as well as to him.

Quite apart from everything it would be to my interest that he should see you a great deal—because it is to my interest that he should have to give up as little as possible of his happiness in order to live with me. I don't know why R. feels unwilling to believe that I really feel like this—or that I should go on feeling it if we lived together. I feel as certain as I feel of anything at all that I should. Perhaps it was because I raised objections to the half-and-half life theory proposed by Lytton in our conversation. I objected to that because it didn't seem to me a solution but simply a continuation of the present situation, that the strain on everyone's nerves would be as great if not greater than before, that particularly for R. it would be intolerable—and that it really is necessary (for practical reasons such as work incidentally as well) to have roots in one place and not two.

Because I love R. and want to live with him, and want him to share my life instead of being a visitor into it—I can't see how I could find this incompatible with his being fond of you and seeing you every day of his life.

It's terrible how difficult it is to say what one wants to, and very likely this all looks like nonsense—but do write again if there is anything you feel you would like to ask or say—One of the saddest results of this situation is the difficulties it puts between you and me—I send you my love if you feel you can bear a monster's love.   FRANCES

To Julia Strachey

Monday [1926]   *Ham Spray House, Hungerford*

Dearest Julia, I am going to Falmouth this week with Lytton. So I shall not see you for some weeks I am afraid. I wanted to tell you that things are rather better. By a miracle James and Alix have stepped into the arena and saved the situation. Frances is going to live at 41 G.S.,[1] so you will have her as a near neighbour to you. And a good deal of the horrors, will be mitigated for everyone I think by the new arrangement. It was so kind of you to be so friendly to me. I felt you hardly realized how grateful I felt to you.

I stay at Falmouth a week. Then I will probably come back here. Tell me about your mannequin job? Is it amusing? Does it help to gratify your passion for dressing up in grand gowns? I feel rather better in the head now. So next time I shall not be so boring I hope. May I come to your shop and buy something from you? Or have you nothing under 20 gns in your department? I will write again when I next come to London so that we can go on our jaunt to the Cinema. My love dear Julia.   Yr CARRINGTON

To Gerald Brenan

Thursday [May 1926]

[*Letter omitted*]

PS This letter didn't get posted yesterday. I shall get up to day after lunch, as my temperature is practically alright now. Lytton read Tamburlaine and Henry IV again to me yesterday.

I sit up in bed, and watch a curious world on a green stage. The loves

---

[1] 41 Gordon Square, James Strachey's house.

of cows, cats hunting rabbits in groves of laurels, gargantuan feasts
given by black birds on the lawn, the provincial life of the rooks in Ilex
tree and last night the great brown owl padded softly through the sky
past my window. The only thing that makes it a pleasure to be ill is the
beauty of the room when the fire casts great shadows from my bed
across the ceiling and Lytton sits on the little low Spanish chair framed
against the black Ilex in the window reading Tamburlaine. At these
moments I wish life would stay still and I could always be a little ill, cut
off from the world, listening to the wars of Persia, with the rain falling
through the black sky. Yes, it makes me happy also to think we are
friends again.   Your C.
PS Forgive the dullness of these letters. But one gets very stupid lying
in bed.

[The following letter was written during the General Strike.]

To Gerald Brenan

Thursday [May 6th, 1926]   *Ham Spray House, Hungerford*

Dearest Amigo, Thank you for your letter yesterday. I wrote rather a
stupid one, I am afraid when I was in bed. Now I am quite well and
sensible. I would like to thank you again for your kind presents and for
lending me your Mr Fisher.[1] The more I think of it, the better I think it
is. You have no idea how exactly it pleased all my tastes.

   We live marooned on a green island here, cut off from the world.
Except for a charming lady at Inkpen Post Office who rings up and gives
us 'the news' which she gleans from the wireless. You would fall completely in love with her, for she gives one such a perfect selection. 'The
Prince of Wales has just come back by aeroplane. It *is* nice to think of
having him back just *now* isn't it?' 'They say the hospitals will have
enough milk and that there were 150 volunteers in Bristol this morning,
before they were asked for. Oh yes, and the King is talking to Mr Bald-
win this afternoon and two warships have taken food to Liverpool. I
don't think there is anything else. No riots and everything much the
same in London. Oh yes, trains run every 15 mins on the Baker Street
railway.'

---

[1] An unfinished novel by Gerald Brenan.

My mother is ill with pneumonia at Cheltenham. But I hope I shall
not be forced to go over and see her. Lytton is reading Ford to me in the
evenings: 'The Broken Heart'. It is very good. This afternoon we have
just been an exquisite walk along the foot of the Downs. I found a wild
yellow auricula, a cross between a cowslip and a primrose. The woods
are filled with bluebells and all the birds sing great choruses in the little
copses. It's difficult looking at the green wheat fields and the pale green
woods to believe that anything unusual is happening in London.

I am sorry your journey is put off. But I expect the excitements of
innumerable tea parties and dinners will compensate you. I am painting
again, a still life of tulips.

I was delighted yesterday, as my friend Mr Pullin came over from
Ramsbury with a mirror for Lytton and saw my glass pictures and was so
pleased with them that he said he'd buy them. 'And the first one for
myself'. For some reason his warm praise, pleased me more than anything anyone has said for a long time. He is a charming character and
his taste (yes—because he admired your Spanish chairs, and the toasting
forks) is extraordinary.

I feel tired with the beauty of spring and too much internal enthu-
siasms. As the post takes 3 days to reach anyone this is probably the last
letter I'll write you. But I would like to send you my love before you
leave England.   Your AMIGA
PS Of course I will let you have the picture of Yegen back and that
[of] D. I meant to send it you but the uncertainty of the posts made me
change my mind. But you will have it on your return. Thank you for
being my friend.

To Julia Strachey

Thursday [*1926*]

Darling Julia, I shall be coming up next Wednesday so I hope I shall see
something of you—the marigolds are just coming out. I do wish you
were here to see my blue irises, Musa Coccinea is a perfect sight. The
Bacca Loculis have unfortunately died; the *drought* is terrible. My
little Bastard Satyrium is covered with blight, and my Bummonia
Uncanta[1] has the mildew badly. When *will* you come again? I do wish
you were here to help me in my garden.

[1] Those worried should consult *Sanders' Encyclopaedia of Gardening*.

Puss, puss, come out of the sun … Besides we are not amused. It was lovely, Julia darling having you here. I shall write a short story beginning with you tapping at my door, and ending with your departure! It will be called 'the BATHCHAIR'. I am almost sorry to be deprived of you convalescent here on the lawn under the beech tree! I've been laid low, thank God, for you began to sow the seeds of terror in my heart, since yesterday, so feel slightly feeble in the head. Did T[ommy] ever go to Oliver? Do write and tell me and remember to send to Chatto and Windus about that story. I think our vases look very swell. I completely took Ralph in over them! He said: 'It's quite clear which one *you* did. It simply shows it's done by a genius. Just look at the lack of subtlety of this (pointing to mine) and the beauty of the colours in this and LOOK at the repetition of this waving line and this delicate pink (pointing to yours). It's queer how *every* line of this could have been done by no one but you' etc etc. After 10 minutes I disillusioned him. In a fury he seized the vases and, or very nearly did. I'll bring you them if I can next

week. I hope you bear up. It is lovely again here today. Dearest Julia you can't think how much I love you and a little, your T. I shall be in and out of Gordon Square on Wednesday, so perdie and peradventure, I shall see you. When do you go to Dorset? I got an order through Lady Craig having seen my glass picture at Hester's House. So bless Hester [Chapman] from me. Please take care of yourself and don't under feed the system. My fondest love your adoring   TANTE C.

To Julia Strachey

Thursday [1926]   *The Owls' Retreat*

My dearest Julia, Here is your red pattern. I am afraid I can't find your spectacles. But perhaps the owl carried them off to his lair.

> 'Could I but vie
> That lady spry
> Underneath my aspens shaded
> Lying with that Tomlin jaded.'

Tommy and I have just been off to Dorset on a spree. Ma foi quelle spree! We visited Mr [✐] on Tuesday after tea. Went for a dismal walk along the sea shore with him. Had a lovely supper of broad beans and claret and rather revived. Then he and Tommy played music all the evening. The next morning we woke up very exhausted as the cats made such a noise one couldn't sleep. We had then more music till half-past 10. Then Tommy and I went off to another region of Dorset and visited his old friends Mr and Mrs Powys of Left Leg fame.[1] I found them wonderfully charming. Mr Powys seems without a fault. He was so beautiful good, and gracious. It was rather like travelling with some dethroned King of Bavaria, returning to his long lost country.[2] From every cottage old dames, and worthies, children and half witted hobbled out to kiss the hem of Tommy's corduroy trowsers. Tommy insisted on reading me Marvell's poems all last Monday. 'Laments on Julia'. 'To my fair Julia' etc. etc. so I gathered from the expression in his voice, and the sadness of his eye, that you have indented his young heart with your cold imprint. Fie Fie. However it's a great consolation for me to have another love sick bird to sing duets with on the loveliness of my Julia.

What about your disguise? What about this. P.T.O.

---

[1] *The Left Leg* was T. F. Powys's first book of fiction.
[2] Stephen Tomlin had lived at Chaldon Herring in 1921 and was beloved by its inhabitants.

I love having you here. I will ask you very soon
again. Most lovely Julia I send you my fondest love.

Your C

But I see after all it's hardly your style. In fact I
meant to draw something quite different. Only the
pen carried me away. In fact I had better stop this
letter. My love my most lovely Julia.

To Lytton Strachey

Sunday [September 19th, 1926]   *Ham Spray House, Hungerford*

My dearest Lytton, Quelle chaleur! Do you know one is forced to search
out, positively, one's old enemy the wind today. Even in the shade and
in the windiest corner of the lawn it is too hot. Faith [Henderson]
arrived yesterday at 4 *o'ck*. She seems in high spirits, and is very
charming. Japps came over the evening, without Henry [Lamb] who is
ill in bed. And we cadged a dinner off them for tonight so we won't have
to cook for ourselves any more meals. We didn't get breakfast till 10 o'ck
today and then went a walk along the Downs to the mushroom field and
didn't get back till half past two. It was twenty to four by the time
we finished lunch! Faith is very vague and doesn't mind spending a
weekend with beds unmade and no washing up. Which I have collected
into a great Silbury Hill in the kitchen for poor Madame Slater tomorrow! Do you know on the way to the mushrooms just at the top of Ham
Hill I heard a plaintive mewing, and there, peeping out of a rabbit hole
was a small cat, or rather half-cat half-rabbit. So I pulled it out, and

carried it on our walk, and brought it home. It is a curious little creature slightly like a monkey with a dark face feet and tail, and brownish fur standing up on end. It was terribly hungry. I shall try and find a home for it at the Lodge. Belle[1] is very happy in her field, I pay her visits and she comes up, and lets me pat her—It is exciting to see from the top of the Downs a little white horse walking across Huth's field and to know that it is Bellinda. We got a whole basket of mushrooms, but the heat was so great we only walked very slowly. Faith was completely exhausted by the time we got down to the bottom of the Downs and reached the Deserts of Sahara.

Write to me at 42, or 41, Gordon Square, as I am not certain how long I can stand Cheltenham and as Mrs C. is an arch-curiousitier I would not have a letter from you left in her clutches to forward. It is lovely here today, I wish you were here and not at Charleston. I spent a very quiet day after you left yesterday lying on the lawn reading and writing letters. Olive is better and got up yesterday afternoon and sat in a chair. Faith is a regular old gossip, but I am very wary and glean more than she reaps. You can't think Lytton darling how much I've loved being with you alone lately and how much I love you for being so kind to me always. It seems ridiculous after 10 years to still tell you that I care so much, but every time you go away it comes back to me, and I realize in spite of the beauties of the Ilex tree and the Downs, Ham Spray loses more than half its beauty robbed of its Fakir. My fondest love

Your most loving MOPSA XXX

To Lytton Strachey

[*September 23rd, 1926*]   *Littlebeck, Painswick Road, Cheltenham*

Darling Lytton, Here I am plunged in the middle of Benares brass life, and Japanese screens, while you lie on Firle Beacon with Tommy, or talk over fires with Duncan and Vanessa. I can hardly tell you the horror I was filled [with] coming back to this life of dead ghosts again. The gargoyle side-board and the small details, the inkstand, and the sugar spoon with arum lily handle, and chipcarved photograph frames. If only there was a confederate outside so one could make some jokes. My mother lives with a grey mouse of a lady-help, and the refinement, and

---

[1] Belle was a mare that Lytton had given to Carrington.

purity of life here is inconceivable! Home made lemonade, and cold blancmange and raspberry jam for supper last night. I went to bed at nine o'ck I was so depressed, with the endless conversation about aunt Ethel, the cousins and my mother's illnesses—However this afternoon I shall leap into a train, and escape to Alix and James, and glasses of sherry. But the folly of wasting an hour in such boredom seems madness on a lovely day. It will be lovely to see you in London again. As you live in a hothouse of steamers, and letter openers I'll not write you what I might write you. I shall go and look for a 1st edition of Wuthering Heights in Cheltenham this morning, and wander up and down the Promenade. I hope when I reach London this evening I may find a letter from you. I hope Mrs Slater has forwarded your letters, and that you got your parcel of dimities. Give Tommy my fondest love. I hope he will come and stay with us again.

I can't write you a letter, I am too depressed by the hideousness of this house, and the bric à bracs.

The awful thought is that one is tainted by the same blood, and perhaps my manias for treacle prints, and old tea pots is just as bad as Japanese vases, and Indian brasses! It's rather a charming little Georgian house, but the *inside* is now indistinguishable from every house we have ever lived in, so why my mother has moved so many times seems to me a mystery. I think however of Ham Spray, and our Downs and then this chimera vanishes. I love you so much, and think of you most of the time and wish I had you here this morning to do a little '—pavement tapping boy accosting'—You had forgotten that line?

My love Yr most loving   MOPSA XXX

[Brenan had been staying at Toulon but was returning to Paris.]

To Gerald Brenan

Sunday [November 7th, 1926]   *Ham Spray House, Hungerford*

Amigo Mio, The weather has recovered. Today is exquisite. I spent the morning riding on the Downs, with R[alph] and Frances who accompanied me, and also rode Belle part of the time. The beauty of the beech groves and woods is extraordinary just now and this morning it was so clear one could see Barbary Castle and Ludgershall in the south. Henry

[Lamb] came over to lunch, and stayed till after dinner. I went a walk with him to the top of the Downs before tea. He is very depressed as Dodo, and the children have gone to France. Do I really come to Paris in a week? It's ridiculous! Miss Moffat to be so daring! Impossible! Yet just to spite Miss Moffat D.G.[1] I think the Princess Cirod will come. Only you must meet the train at 5 o'ck as the Princess, not being a Governess, knows no French and would be lost if some [interpreter] or astrologer[2] does not meet her at the station. Then you must take a room at a hotel. And don't let it be, if you love your Princess, on the street side, as she has the ears of a hare and cannot sleep if there is a noise in the streets. I am worn out with the wind on the Downs, the autumnal sun, and too much red wine. I shall be dressed very neatly when I come to Paris for I have a theory one must not look like a Garden-Letchworth-city-Miss when one travels abroad. [Three lines omitted] Alix has just given [me] a new overcoat, and I am having a very spruce check coat and skirt from Bond Street made. You will not approve. [One line omitted] All this was just to tell you not to expect to see a familiar dishevelled figure on the platform, but a neat tailor made Princess in disguise.

Oh but it will certainly rain. So why do we go on talking of Paris? Seriously *if* there is a storm and the sea is rough, I shall not come. But if that is the case I will wire the hotel, which I hope you will tell me the name of, before next Saturday. If it's fine I come by the 11 o'ck train from Victoria and reach Paris at 5 o'ck. Is that clear? In case my other letter went astray. And I must come back on Wednesday evening. So you can easily see Miss B. Mrs B.P. Miss M. and Madame X. on Thursday as you arranged. I shall not tell anyone, except Ralph, that I go to Paris, so please don't tell Blair[3] to broadcast it on Monday evening. And if I am obliged to tell anyone, I go to see Phyllis De Janzé and not Mr Crusoe. It was charming of Ralph to lend me the money. For we are by no means well off at the moment.

Lytton gave me two superb books with pictures of birds on every page, the other day. They give me the greatest pleasure.

We had another great display of fireworks last night in the pitch-dark garden. I am too tired with riding and rustic activities to write a long letter to the King of astrologers but it will be nice to see him again and I pray the great God Thor will not send his thunders and rain, however if

---

[1] Dei Gratia—by the grace of God.

[2] Gerald had written *Dr Partridge's Almanack* (Chatto and Windus, 1934), a series of spoof astrological predictions.

[3] Blair Brenan, Gerald's younger brother, had a job in the B.B.C.

he does—please don't attach too much importance to it, as 'tomorrow is also a day' (old proverb) so Victoria is also a station. My love dear Amigo.

Your CIROD

Now don't ruin all by sending a letter unsealed. You see the Princess is also a Prophetess on occasions.

To Gerald Brenan

Monday evening, 11 o'ck [November 23rd, 1926]

I open my 'Ideal', is it a novel? a book of prophecies? or an advertisement for shaving soap? It is none of these. It is, but how could Mr Crusoe who never leaves his palm tree island tell what is in the 'Ideal' not any ideal, but THE IDEAL?

Thank you so much dearest Amigo for your letter.

I am sorry you are no longer I. L. ... with Miss Moffat this I take to be the import of your letter (sic). But I bear it well and bear you no grudge. I hope you enjoyed P. as much as I did. Patagonia? Yes. Patagonia. I felt rather ill, most of the time, but you realized that and forgave me for my (a) dullness (b) selfishness, I hope. D.V. I come up on Wednesday. Would you like to see your Miss M.? But where can we meet? at the B.M. under the shades of the Syrian horsemen and Arthur Waley? May we go to a cinema together? Suppose you say yes, then will you dine with me at my Chinese restaurant? I shall be at Alix's room about 6 o'ck onwards, if you cared to call for me. If you can't I shall spend the evening with Alix so you needn't feel you've deserted me. On Thursday we dine with Helen? That will be very nice. And shall we go to B minor Mass? I should like to. But do just as you like I mean, if you have a cold, and feel tired, do not trouble. Yesterday I went a lovely ride on my Belle to Gibbet Hill and saw a great storm driving over from the Chute Downs, lit up *from behind* by the setting sun. It drew nearer and nearer, and all the country was lit up by a strange electrified light. I sat on Belle watching the dark clouds coming across the plain and then suddenly the rain fell softly at first and then faster and faster and then the wind tore across the hills and blew till I felt Belle almost totter below me. There was no shelter so I sat still on my horse and watched the rain driving over the downs and the wind bending the red hawthorns and elderberry trees. Suddenly into Combe gorge a rainbow fell and it bent right over the top of the Downs into the Inkpen valley; then another echo of a rainbow joined it, till two great hoops stood before me barring my way. It was almost dark when I got back to the stable, and they had started tea. Desmond [MacCarthy] was here this weekend. Ralph on Sunday evening, showed him your Prophecies and the preface. He was full of praise for your writing. 'But he has style this writer, who ever he is. *This* is good writing you know, Lytton.' He liked some of the prophecies very much; others not at all. But he was *very* enthusiastic. I felt I confess, very proud. Was that absurd? It sounded very good when Desmond read it. He had an idea that you should only write prophecies on Saints' Days, so as to avoid having to write too many. I suggest, also, great men's birthdays and horse racing days. Aren't you rather pleased that Desmond (without knowing who it was by,) thought it so good? I always feel so strongly prejudiced in your favour simply because I like so much always, what you write, that I doubt, a little, my own judgements. Lytton agreed with Desmond that the preface was very well written and laughed a great deal. I've had a FROG in my throat all the weekend, so felt extra-stupid. Today I felt lumpish and rather despondent. I think I caught a cold in London perhaps. But I hope it will pass off tomorrow. I hope your cold, D. Amigo is better. I've been making your quilted dress this evening. It looks so lovely—Ralph was slightly furious with me for cutting it up and said I ought to have kept it as a bed quilt. Now I must go to bed as I am rather tired.

And do you ever think of Patagonia and Miss M? I doubt it. Already you are engulfed in a thousand intrigues and interviews and I am engulfed in clearing my stable and cutting up firewood. Only when I go to bed, I think, as I gaze on the Holy V.M. in her canopy of pearls, of a stranger, who once made me almost too happy. My love dear Mr Crusoe.

Your loving CIROD

To Gerald Brenan

[First half of letter omitted.]

Later Thursday evening, 6.30 [December 3rd, 1926]

My letters to you go on from one day to the next like an eight day clock
without winding. If I miss the postman, as I did today, I just open your
letter and write a few more pages. Tomorrow I really will try to post this.

I've just come back from a 15 mile ride. How I wish I could have had
you on a brown cob beside me. I have never seen the landscape so lovely.
I rode over Sheepless Down to Netherton Valley and then by familiar
lanes, known only to myself, to the back door of our old house Ibthorpe.
My sensations at seeing that house again and the little hill covered with
hawthorn and juniper bushes, was very great. How much one forgets of
the past. As I approached our village, a hundred memories crowded and
jostled, like humans getting on to a bus: the wooden Flying Fox, the
weather vane on the malting house, our kitchen garden with its high
wall and the pear tree, the sunk leads on the roof of the house where I
used to climb through a sky light and watch the village below me on hot
summer afternoons, my attic bedroom window, the garden, with the
variegated holly tree, and the Ilex tree in the corner, all the farm houses
and the particular trees along the road. I had lunch with the Scotch Mac-
Killigans. They had softened with time; it is 10 years since I saw them.
The dour son, now has white hair and was quite friendly. My mother
was there hopping about like a chaffinch full of bright meaningless remarks. I left at 2 o'ck and rode back the same way only in Sheepless
Down woods I met a game keeper with a face like a raven, otherwise not
a soul was to be seen. I rode most of the way across mossy valleys and
down narrow lanes. At one point where one turns up towards our
Downs, I saw by what used to be a deserted cottage, the hedge covered
with linen. I wondered who could live in this deserted place and thought
of the loneliness of their lives. When suddenly as I reached the hedge,
the washing took flight and it turned out to be a HUGE flock of pure white
turkeys. Who all set up a tremendous gobbling. The cottages were
empty. The woods were filled with tall withered loose-strife, hung with
white feathery seeds; the ground was palest green velvet and the brown
patches of dried heather made lovely patterns on it. I was intoxicated
with the sweet, wild, beauty of the woods and valleys.

Just as I reached Ham Hill which you know is very steep, I fell into a

slight trance, watching the little grey sheep, on the olive-green Downs;
the Downs melting away into the distance beyond Shalbourne. The sky
grey, flecked with a pinkish yellow, as the sun set beyond Pewsey.
Suddenly Belle stumbled and before I knew anything, I saw my brown
corduroy legs above my head from the corner of my eye. I saw Belle on
the ground and then a hard bump on my head. In a second I was full
length on the ground and Belle careering off down the ravine. I dashed
after her. Fortunately a labourer with a waggon stopped her in the road
for me. I wasn't hurt, only my head aches a little now. Belle must have
been tired. Now I have had tea, and sit in a dressing gown over the fire
waiting till a bath is hot. Olive and her mother have gone off for the
afternoon, so I am alone in the house. I see a review of the Adventures
of Johnny Walker by [W.H.] Davies in the Times Lit. Sup. today. It
sounds interesting. Margaret Waley has just sent me £8, so I feel in very
high spirits. She owed it me for a painted bird, that I did for her. But I
hardly hoped to get £5 for it. I'll preserve some of it, so we can have a
fine dinner together in London. Now my bath is hot, so I must leave, my
dear Amigo.

To live in such lovely country, and to have a gentle white horse
makes me very happy. L'agonie de Cayenne stands on my mantlepiece
looking very wise and fantastic. Forgive this rambling letter, but I send
it with much love to make up for its demerits.

Your loving CIROD

PS I see the first part of this letter is now almost as stale as the Boer War,
but I can't eradicate it, you must just skip it.

To Gerald Brenan

Friday evening [December 17th, 1926]

Dearest Amigo, Ralph has just come, and has brought the Christmas
tree decorations and the toys. I love the snake so much I can hardly
bear to give it away. The birds are exquisite. I now look forward to
nothing but decorating the tree. The party is to be on Monday afternoon. You were a very charming Amigo to take so much trouble. 'On
the contrary I just said to a girl, who by the way is coming to tea tomorrow, put me 5/-s worth of Christmas toys into a package, so don't
thank me, Miss Moffat.' Well even if you didn't put on your spectacles to
choose them, thank you very much. Helen writes to say she wants to

come here on Jan 1st but, for some reason, I have an intuition she won't come. So I shall not look forward to it, as I should, if I really thought she would come. Her letter was full of so many complications: Roger [Fry], children, Boris [Anrep] coming back, Mrs Maitland [her mother] that I can hardly believe she will get away. Two little pictures from Barbara this evening and a letter from Henry. No other news from the outside world, except what you must have already heard from Ralph. I gather you were 'the life of the party' last night and were 'very charming'. What is coming over grumpy Mr Crusoe? Senile decay, I fear.

> Hairy, old bear,
> Cried Lady Astare
> How can you dare,
> To pinch my arm bare
> Come give me a pear,
> Dear Lady Astare
> Cried, the old bear.

Lytton reads. What does Lytton read? Not what you expect or what the world (which is Gordon Square) expects, for Lytton sits over the fire, the firelight playing on his red beard, his lamb skin slippers ('oh, he treated Henry Lamb quite cruelly, I assure you') on his feet. The rug, (see Tate Gallery) thrown over his knees, surrounded by his library of books on every side (He collects mostly old books, especially 18th cent. French books) his three cats (Mr Strachey like Lord Kitchener and, or, Lord Roberts, cannot bear dogs) sitting on the hearth rug. His two companions Mr and Mrs Thrale in another corner of room, reading, as he sits over his fire; Lord Redincote, by Arnold Bennett. There! Mr Crusoe. What a surprise for you! You thought I was going to say, The Decline and Fall by Mr Gibbon!!!! Mr Thrale reads his Financial Times and makes calculations. Miss Moffat, for Mrs Thrale has suddenly left the room, sits in her blue overcoat with brass buttons and a pair of striped socks to keep her feet warm, writing a letter to a commercial traveller. 'And pray what *is* his commerce?' 'Oh, he's a coffee importer, my dear.' 'Is that the same as an imposter?' 'Now, Barbara my dear, really you must not be so stupid, or ask so many questions.' And it is time Aunt Moffat went to bed for she is almost asleep. My love dear Mr Crusoe. I am still and always will be your loving   Amiga C

                                                                    I
                                                                    R
                                                                    O
                                                                    D

To Gerald Brenan

Monday morning [December 27th, 1926]   Ham Spray House, Hungerford

Amigo Mio, I see from your letter that you go to Edgeworth next
weekend so you can't come here. When will you be going back to
London after the weekend? If you want to see me, ask me and I will
come up any day you like. I am tired and rather empty headed. I send
you a present. Is it what you still care for? I wish you had been here
this Christmas to put me in a good temper. For this morning I am in a
very cross patch mood. Simply because I couldn't sleep last night and
then, one gets so bored with looking after fires, coffee pots, and digging
vegetables and making beds. That['s] just what you like to hear: Miss
Moffat complaining, well, I will complain but only softly to my dear
Amigo! The Christmas tree looks exquisite. Those fairy balloons and
the birds of paradise are my favourites. Ottoline telephoned yesterday
to say she was coming over with Mark and the Turners today for tea.
But today she telephones to say their car has broken down so she will
not come. For which I am extremely glad, as I hate being responsible
for those crushed tea parties, with everyone talking at the tops of their
voices, or remaining gloomily silent. I haven't got your picture finished
but there has been no time since the invasion arrived on Friday. I love
having Julia here. She is a gay sympathetic character. Her turn of
humour is very fascinating. How did you survive Xmas? I suppose by
now your digestion is properly ruined and you are filled with gloomy
vapours and a dislike for the human race.

Tommy arrived last night and seems in high spirits. Marjorie Strachey
is very amusing and knits everyone together by her good temper and
perpetual jokes. So one may say it's been a very nice Xmas party and
everyone has enjoyed themselves.

Yes, I've been very happy except for this morning, when suddenly
finding the stove had gone out and the water in the bathroom was cold,
my neck was stiff and my head ached, I fell into a fine rage with life and
Christmas and anthracite stoves. But already I've recovered since I
started writing to you and now I feel very light hearted. This afternoon
I shall go for a ride on Belle directly after lunch. Marjorie Strachey gave
me the most beautiful Armenian boots and Julia a blue silk padded
dressing gown. Henry sent me some marsala and James gave me [a]

huge pot of caviare, so that for the first time in my life I've had the
pleasure of caviare for breakfast, and caviare for every meal. I want to
reform next year and do a great deal more serious painting and even
writing. Will one? Simply to spite oneself and one's traditional character
I think I will! You've been rather churlish writing me letters, but I forgive you on condition you write me a long one this week. Ralph gave me
a garbled and curious account of your affaires and conversations.

Dorelia sent me my most beautiful present. A box covered with
shells, only not ordinary shells, but the most fantastic rare-coloured
shells that you have ever seen and inside the box, were two charming
little figures of pottery.

Tonight we have a sort of dance, Japps, and Noel and Missie, I feel
rather apathetic about it. I prefer these amusing conversations with
Marjorie, Julia and Tommy over the fire to organized gaiety.

My love, dearest Amigo. Please write to me soon, if you are not too
busy working. (Have you any news of Helen?)

from your most loving CIROD xxxxxxx

1927

To Julia Strachey

Friday [about January 18th, 1927]   *Ham Spray House, Hungerford*

My dear Madame R——, May I congratulate you on your engagement, (next Saturday evening). I hear from all accounts that he is *ravishing*. How I envy you your fate! my dear. My emotions carry me away crushed against those moustaches, stifled under those aromatic southern scents, gazed at under those heavy silken eyelashes, what girl would not be envious? Here am I tied—or untied—oh Julia how I long for a Grecian embrace! Perhaps at your wedding, you will allow me one kiss from those be-bushed lips. It is indeed the day I dream of constantly. As for your rivals—Miss J. is a mass of lumps, more lumpy than Olympus, (not HIS favourite mountain. I gather he prefers the smooth straight shores of the Adriatic) and Miss R-g-r S-nh-use is, I gather, an already despoiled pomegranate. And who will revert to a half-sucked orange when a peach so rare and mysterious hangs untouched, with its bloom unimpaired, (painted as if by the artificer's hand) on the tree? In other words the Greek is yours.

I am sorry you can't come next weekend. But will you come the weekend after? Who shall I ask to satisfy your Hellenic passions? I still keep a warm place in the heart of that cold Lamb for you. I hear also the wild lion faced boy [Lionel Penrose] is under your Circean sway. And then Alexander the Great of St John's Wood [Alec Penrose]? or Lord Ritchie of Bayswater? I somehow feel it might not be politic to ask the 1880 lover without his hansom, and no greenhouse here with Maidens' Fern, and begonias. The roughness of this civilization might cast a damp on HIS exquisite gardenia tastes. Tell me who shall I ask with you? And will *you* come?

I feel slightly 'gone' in the head. So forgive my stupidity. If the Greek is of——persuasion I could wish his Gentile lady was of the other—— persuasion.

Do you follow me?

To Julia Strachey

[*January 1927*]

[First part of letter missing] to my sorrows on Wednesday at midnight, my other plague joined in the general internal avalanche. My brain has become very meteorological, I can only think in terms of the weather. Alix wrote me a letter yesterday [of] a world where icebergs evidently are non-existent, and all is an Indian summer. I am sorry my lovely Poppet you didn't have a nicer Xmas. But the truth was, I was sleeping rather badly and couldn't pull myself together, and everything seemed slightly disintegrated but perhaps when I wasn't in the room, the glasses clinked and all was in a roar. Well I only hope so. I will directly I get up send off your fashion books and Tommy's belt. Write me a letter when you have time please. You have no idea how much I enjoy lying in my bedroom watching the fire on the ceiling. After the crises of last week it is a paradise of peace. Today I shall write a story 'Mere imitation of me' Tommy. 'Isn't that just like Tante C.' No my dear, Rosamond [Lehmann] is the pattern on which I base my life. The style is to be an adroit mixture between Saint-Simon—and—Mr Gerhardie. And the title? Ha! But you will crib it. I shan't disclose the title, for therein lies the plot, the clue, and the mystery. Give Tommy my love, who I found, as I always do, the most sympathetic companion. Do let's

have a ball. Dress you as an Empire oriental beauty. At the moment I am
reigning Queen of Laplandia.

Your blue dressing gown is the comfort of my life.

My very fondest love   from your devoted old TANTE C.

To Gerald Brenan

Saturday [January 22nd, 1927]   *Ham Spray House, Hungerford*

Well, you're a nice one, indeed you are! I dragged myself, a partial
corpse to see you last Friday afternoon, when I would have far sooner
(or very nearly!) lain on a bed asleep at G. Square, and
then you pick a quarrel with me for no good reason
and don't write for a week. However Miss Moffat is far
too sensible to allow any such nonsensical mis-
understandings, and now having blown Mr Crusoe
sky high in spite of the snow and the fact he is in
his pyjamas sick with influenza and I daresay, yes I
daresay, in the middle of a conversation with Miss
A. from the next bed room, in spite of all this fine

blowing up he shall return to his bed, his mistresses, and his vomit. What a life we all lead to be sure. Influenzas, mistresses, colds, and now I have fallen off a toboggan and bruised my bottom black.

My week has actually been spent motoring twice a day backwards and forwards to Shalbourne[1] or entertaining Igor! I don't mind it at the time, but of course today, the day upon which one reflects what one has done during the week, I see I haven't even finished my picture and have done nothing but tidy my studio and motor a great many miles. I sent you a long letter by Helen to 48, Bernard Street, supposing you might be staying there. But I don't suppose you'll ever get it now. Poor amigo. I am sorry he is sick. I hope some kind person will look after you. Do not I beg get up too soon. Can I send you some delicacies? I would if you will only tell me how long you are going to live at your hotel. Helen comes back today, but I'll not drive to Shalbourne any more, as they go back to London next week.

Yesterday afternoon I went tobogganing with Olive on the Downs. It was a most lovely afternoon. The sun was just setting, and the sky was a most delicate green tinged with pink and little clouds rose up from behind the crest of the downs, like balloons liberated by some hidden hand and floated up into the pale opal sky.

The sun shone on the quarry, and lit up the snow along the ridge. I was so happy I could hardly bear to come back to tea. We had some lovely rushes down the hill. Olive had never been on a toboggan before. Unfortunately I took a ditch in my enthusiasm and bumped Olive's head and my bottom. But I feel better this morning. The country intoxicates me with its beauty, it fills me with the same sort of internal pleasure that one feels when the spring begins. Lytton read me 'the White Devil' by Webster last night over a fire. Just as I was getting into bed, I looked out for the last time on the moonlighted lawn and there was my enemy the rabbit, who all this week has eaten up my lettuces and cabbages, so I knelt at the open window and shot him. He died at once mercifully in one shot. This morning it is snowing again. To my mind this landscape is at its loveliest in the winter, covered with snow. How appalling about your aunt. For although one at first laughs at her extraordinary behaviour, one soon remembers it is the end of everyone and how miserable underneath all her confusion of mind she must be.

Lytton came into tea yesterday, and saw the two cats lying embraced

---

[1] Helen Anrep and her children were staying there.

JANUARY 1927   355

on his chair. 'Snakes in a sink, toads in a cistern' he said looking at the cats. For some reason with the expression on his face it was very amusing. There was irony in poor Fanny coming down to nurse Helen and her children, being bullied by Igor, crouching over cold fires and then Helen rushes off (to Roger [Fry]) and to take Igor back to school; the Japps come, and fetch Baba to stay in their house with their girl leaving Fanny alone at Shalbourne. I drove her to the station yesterday morning. I thought her resignment to her position which is one of 'crouching' and existing only to be of use to people was rather awful. 'I wish Helen had left Baba with me, as I get on so well with Baba and like her so much' she said just before the train left. And Helen had said to me, 'You see the children can't bear Fanny, she always says the wrong thing and gets on their nerves.'

Now I must have some breakfast—what given up her breakfast to write to Mr Crusoe? What a kind (or cruel) Miss Moffat. And on such a cold morning. I hope you will soon be well again. Tell me how you are. My fondest love dearest of Amigos. I am, in spite of all your prognostications your very loving   CIROD

To Julia Strachey

Thursday [about January 24th, 1927]   Ham Spray House, Hungerford

Dearest Julia, You are a fickle niece, find a comfortable bed and a kind uncle and poor tante C. is soon forgotten. Not so Tante C. She thinks perpetually of her Julia hence this letter. Well my dear you have no idea what an exciting time we have had here. Snow fights with lovely young men (or a man to be precise) with hair the colour of a canary bird[1] and the most heavenly blue eyes and Mr Peter Morris, his friend, with auburn hair and a 'quite lovely' nose. But his shoes were what won my heart. Under the excuse of examining the buckles, I gave them a delicate stroke, and the thrill that ran down my spine, my dear! I can hardly describe! I wish you were here to play the letter game with me and I would write you a description of the weekend with adjectival blanks. That wretch Ralph will have told you all our news so what can I tell you? All yesterday afternoon I cleaned my studio and this morning, true to my word (for I had made Tante C. who is rather a severe character, a promise to paint a picture today whatever happened) so I

[1] George Rylands.

sat in my bedroom and painted a landscape of the snow with some cows. MacWhirter instantly rushes to your mind, with Scotch firs and lochs and Highland cattle. Which just shows you know nothing, miss, about painting. Most of my week has been spent motoring over to Shalbourne to see poor Helen Anrep and her children, who have had influenza. Now they have gone away. So our hermitage life resumes its chilly course. Lytton is reading me the White Devil by Webster in the evenings. I can't ride Belle as the ground is covered with snow and very hard. When do you fly the country? Shall I ask Phyllis de Janzé to try and find rooms for you? Would you like a French maid to go with you to iron your frocks, and uncurl your hair? Unfortunately she don't speak French otherwise a most respectable woman.[1] Not a word has reached me from London. So I suppose you are all deeply engrossed in intrigues, or parties.

Give Thomas Stephen [Stephen Tomlin] my fondest love. When will my head of Alix come out of its shape?[2] The cold is intense, just as I was settling down to paint this morning looking like this blown out with

jerseys, overcoats, aprons, socks and fur shoes with a dribbling nose and unbrushed hair, who should arrive but the Japps, Mrs J. in a Paquin sports attire. Her female delight at seeing the exquisite Mrs P. in such deshabille or rather overhabille made her *most* cordial. Mr Japp who had always thought Mrs P. such a nice looking girl was frankly astonished! Which all goes to prove that it's very rash to think nobody calls at 12 o'ck in the country. Will you write me a letter? I hope you are happy, Julia. I have asked the cleaners to send your coat direct to 41 G.S. So you ought to get it by Monday next week. Lytton sits writing in the sitting room. The wind roars outside and the fire blazes up the chimney. Stump and Tinker lie in a lovers embrace asleep in the arm chair.

[1] Carrington herself.
[2] Stephen Tomlin was sculpting a head of Alix Strachey.

I long to paint a portrait of your Greek. Will you beg him to sit for me when the weather is warmer? Tell me what did he think of the party? Did you enjoy it? Last night I was chased by a huge black bull, in a dream. A tranquillity has settled on Ham Spray lately. Perhaps it is the snow. I feel incapable of anything but the very purest emotions. You have no idea how lovely the garden looks in the moonlight with the snow all glistening like diamonds. Tante C. is becoming romantic, that will never do. My love dearest Julia. You know I love you a great deal.

Your devoted C.

To Julia Strachey

Tuesday [February, 1927]   *Ham Spray House, Hungerford*

Well, you're a fine affectionate friend, a whole week in Paris and not one line just to say how you are to your old Tante. 'They are all alike these young girls now-a-days, give them a young man and a rope of pearls and you'll hear no more from them.' This from a letter in the Times yesterday on present day manners in our modern girls. Well it's all very sad, and I agree with every word that the Dowager Lady Nunholme writes. She was born in 1830. When I tell you my sad story surely the strings of your heart (or pearls) will be touched and you will vouchsafe me a line.

Last Thursday I went riding in Richmond Park with Mr

and Lady P[ansy] and came a flying crack on my back. I was picked up
for dead and carried by 10 stalwart men to a car and driven to the
hospital amidst a gaping crowd of admirers longing for death. 'Oh it
must hurt her *dreadfully*.' 'Poor thing she *must* be cold.' The mere expressions on their faces terrified me. Dr Lamb was as you would expect
very re-assuring. 'Chipped a bit off ... [the rest of this letter is illegible]

To Julia Strachey

Thursday [*February, 1927*]   *Ham Spray House, Hungerford*

My darling Julia, Your letter crossed mine, so now I must write again.
I still crouch in bed. Actually today for the first time for 2 weeks I have
tottered into a chair. How well you know this familiar picture of Madame
C. and her cats [drawing omitted] looking for all the world like a
picture of Queen Victoria in her bedroom at Balmoral. Last Tuesday
I had a great excitement for I went in an ambulance to Reading
and was X rayed in a hospital. The back chat of the stretcher
bearers and the nurse was very enlightening. The result was all
for the best. The pelvis is intact and there are no cracks or chips. So
back I was put in my four poster. It's what is called a sprained back.
'She'll never be the same girl again, I don't suppose. Can't lift a
kitten now; why I remember 'er and Mr Tomlin carrying that great
monument between 'em, and I believe Mrs P[artridge] carried the lion's
share.' Mere kitchen talk. Don't believe a word of it. The hospital
porter walked into the outpatients room where I laid stretched out
singing 'Fe Fi Fo Fum Tra La Tra La', then seeing the corpse said:
'Why what 'AVE we 'ere, and what's you been doing with yourself?'
Corpse in a melancholy voice 'Fallin' off a horse.' 'HO! You shouldn't
ride 'orses, mistake for you to ride 'orses' and then he walked out of the
room twirling his black moustaches. [The rest of this letter is missing]

To Gerald Brenan

Thursday, in bed [*February 27th, 1927*]   *Ham Spray House, Hungerford*

Dear Amigo, Thank you for your letter. It was like a cherry tart, one
continually had to be taking stones out of one's mouth. I am no duller I
assure you than I am usually. I enjoy reading enormously and I can do
that all day long. Then I lie for hours making up imaginary stories and

now that I cannot move I no longer wonder if the stove has gone out, or if Olive has remembered to put on the potatoes. In fact one is continually surprised that anyone ever brings one meals, or writes one letters. You wonder why I prefer my Wiltshire water closet to London? But where do you imagine I could lie in bed in London? I could not lie for ever in R[alph] and F[rances]'s sitting room and the alternative was a nursing home and I would literally rather die on a dung heap than be scolded and fussed over by nurses, who allow one to see visitors between 3 and 4 o'ck as a great favour and charge one 10 gns a week for boiled cod and corn-flour shape. 'How particular of Miss Moffat! Fancy wanting to miss the interesting experience of 2 weeks in a Welbeck Street nursing home.' You *are* a ridiculous bear. But I assure you I am not so stupid as you always think I am. The X raying was very interesting. I enjoyed enor-mously the excursion, the ambulance and listening to the nurses and watching the doctors doing the X raying. But I can only write letters to Amigos if I am encouraged. So I'll not bore you with a description of our adventures at Reading Hospital. You seem to have very little to com-plain of in your life. I can imagine nothing more enjoyable than kissing an exquisite Olive in a hansom cab. Lying in bed I've come to a great many conclusions: one is I shall paint all the wood work in my room pale-yellow-green, only so pale, it will be the colour of the calyx of a primrose and on the walls I shall frame, in pale yellow wood frames, my new pictures of birds that Margaret Waley sent me yesterday. I cannot conceive what green, cobalt blue and orange will look like, as you do not tell me the name of the green. But I expect *you* will make it look very lovely. I trust your taste a hundred times more than Roger's [Fry]. Lytton came back yesterday full of the most amusing gossip. I laughed for nearly 2 hours over his stories. Stump, my favourite cat, sits on my bed and drinks out of the saucer on my tray. It is very pleasant lying under this blue canopy hung round with the tapestries of Granada, with Stump for company and a grand concert of thrushes, blackbirds with a greek chorus of rooks outside. Yesterday for the first time I tottered three yards and sat in a chair over the fire. It's curious to feel so feeble. However Ellie [Rendel] when she examined me, gave me a very flat-tering account of my health. My blood pressure was only 118, and my physique was superb. She is a very charming doctor. She tells one very softly just what one most longs to hear. I have read all Gogol now. The 'Nose' pleased me as much as any story. And 'The Overcoat' and then the 'Diary of a Madman' is superb. But I can't write you a letter. It is a pity, for it used to be one of the greatest pleasures. Your philosophy of life sounds almost perfect. I have plenty of books to read thank you; and I want nothing to eat.

But you will find the new universally admired genius *will* turn out to be the same [Stephen] Tomlin and that all roads lead to Rome. That is one of the strangest phenomena of life. For a change, this year I will concentrate all my attention on my work and regard people as species of birds for my bird book which I am making. I hope you will like your new rooms. It was kind of you to write to me. Forgive my stupidity but any sense I had has been thrown down the Wiltshire water closet in the bed pans.   My love your C.

To Julia Strachey

Wednesday [March 1927]   *51 Ladbroke Grove, London*
                                                     write to Ham Spray next time

Dearest Julia, Now you are forgiven only unfortunately you have whetted an appetite that can only be satisfied by another letter and very quickly. I am glad you are so happy. It sounds much more pleasant, and economical than London.[1] I have been here for 10 days having my back massaged by a singularly unpleasant young woman with peroxide hair and the beauty of Phyllis Dare. She is terribly sadistic and hurts me very much. However I conceal my real character and lead her on to tell me all her innermost feelings. 'Don't you love Surrey Mrs P. I was down at Hindhead on Sunday giving my dog a run.' 'Don't you think dogs', violent slaps, 'much more', slaps, 'intelligent', bangs, 'and more capable of love', bangs, 'and affection than human beings', bangs. 'I think', slaps, 'something has been left out of human beings they are such miserable', bangs, 'mean', harder bangs, 'creatures', terrific bangs, 'compared to intelligent dogs'. Today being the last day shall I reveal my true character and shatter her? But that is probably impossible. She is made of iron. When one thinks of what might have happened, lying smoothed tenderly by gentle loving hands. But I suppose there wasn't much chance of Ellie sending one a sympathetic masseuse!! This is a vile pen. I haven't been able to do much frisking about in London as I get so tired in the back. So I've decorated Lytton's sitting room at Gordon Square for him: very chaste. In pale green, white, and cherry

<hr/>

[1] Julia Strachey had gone to live in Paris.

red, with decorations on the mantelpiece. Lytton bought a lovely still life by John B[anting] which is a joy to put over the mantelpiece.

Am I cutting my throat, I often wonder, making Lytton's room so elegant and lovely? Will he now fly to Gordon Square with R[oger] every Monday and leave me desoleé at Ham Spray? Then I've painted Gerald B[renan]'s new rooms in St James's Street, apple green and vermilion. And Alix has commissioned me to paint her gramophone with pictures all over it. Yes I know Pamela Fry. She used to be as lovely as an Uccello Page, but I believe now she has lost all her brilliance from living perpetually with a Diamond.[1] Poor Alix has been rather 'mouldy' with a sore throat this week. But we had a gay evening together on Saturday and went to a Chinese restaurant in Oxford Street and danced alone together. Tonight we go with John B[anting] and John S[trachey] to the Astoria. I live with the Hubert Waley's in the greatest comfort in Kensington, but I spend most of my days and nights with Alix and James. Henrietta [Bingham] has been out of town (or said she was on the telephone) so I've seen nothing of her. Yesterday afternoon Philip [Ritchie] took me to tea with Cynthia Noble at her shop in Hanover Square. Très elegant. The sort of place that would make Tommy sick! [The rest of this letter is missing]

To Gerald Brenan

Friday afternoon [May 13th, 1927]   *Ham Spray House, Hungerford*

Amigo Mio, I had written you a long letter on Wednesday but your two letters suddenly yesterday made it pointless to send it. I wrote you five letters yesterday, but finally I sent none of them. I only tell you this to account for my not answering your letters. May I lunch with you on Tuesday and talk to you? I cannot write you a letter or answer your letters. I would ask you here this weekend but I feel if you are against me, even slightly in spirit, Ham Spray isn't a very sympathetic back ground or conducive to a settlement. However if you'd like to come, you've only got to go round to Ralph, and come down with him after lunch. My head aches with thinking backwards and forwards about you, about myself. And I get more and more depressed. Yes, it's quite clear I am fit only to have relations with old plates and cats. I agree with

---

[1] Pamela, Roger Fry's daughter, married M. Diamond.

almost everything you say. Don't ask me to make any decisions, or more promises. For I am incapable of both. I only will try and reform and please you more and be less selfish. If you find me intolerable you had better give me up. I've such a poor opinion of myself. I can't argue about it. I am very sorry I have made you unhappy.

The poor cow is dead.[1]

My fondest love to you.   Your loving C.

To Gerald Brenan

Sunday [June 5th, 1927]   *Ham Spray House, Hungerford*

Well, well, let bye gones by gone byes. Finish your life of Mrs Robinson and begin one of Lady Grey tomorrow. I have already, dear amigo, forgotten all about it and I laughed so much over the last message of Lord Grey that I quickly loved you again.

Life is full of so many people and conversations my head is in a Buzzzzz. Tomorrow when the crush has thinned out, I will write you a long letter telling you all the events of the past week and when I shall see you again. I hope you enjoyed Whitsun. My fondest love to you and all my love and forgiveness.

Your very loving   Amiga CIROD

Sunday
Lady Grey sends her most amiable dove, Diskikins with a branch of peace to Mr Crusoe.

---

[1] Carrington had found a cow bogged in a pond and it had been rescued.

To Gerald Brenan

Tuesday [*June 7th, 1927*]

Dearest Amigo, I send this by Ralph as there are no stamps in the house
to post it. I've just broken my back gardening, planting out seedlings so
forgive my dull letter and bad writing. We went to a lovely fair yesterday at Hungerford and saw some horse races. It was a beautiful sight on
the big common, with the merry-go-rounds whirling and jockeys in
coloured blouses riding round in this absurdly rustic ring with a miniature grand stand with three flags flying! Belgium, England and France—
Belgium because Brett's aunts, who live at Hungerford Park, are
Belgians. I got a lovely silver vase by throwing darts. Julia was great
fun, and spent hours trying very slowly to throw rings on a nail to get a
silver candlestick. I went on a horse merry-go-round twice. There were
bicycle races and running races in the arena. And the most fascinating
crowd of strange rustics and Hardy females. Tommy was here for
Whitsun and Alix came suddenly and stayed till Sunday. There were so
many conversations that my head is dazed with the perpetual flow of
words. The quietness now seems funereal. I went a very long ride on
Friday with Tommy and Lytton along the Downs. And what did the
curious Dr Crusoe do? Or is that a secret? Faith says she likes her
decorated cottage which is a good thing. She rang me up on the telephone. I've been reading a book of short stories [*Rhapsody*] by a new
female writer, called Dorothy Edwards. I must say I thought they were
rather good. I would like your opinion on them. Lytton is writing away
at Elizabeth. I shall not come up this week. But probably next Tuesday,
I'll let you know later. Julia is a charming creature, like some strange
bird but with habits unlike any other birds. To see her, with her horn
spectacles and ropes and pearls, very gravely throwing rings on to hooks
yesterday at the fair, was fascinating. Forgive a dull letter but my head
is as heavy as lead this morning. There is a suspended thunder-storm
outside and my brain is held up waiting for it to descend. And I do no
painting, but dream away my time thinking of pictures and never
painting them. It's very deplorable. I hope you are working. Do you
know Alix said she admired your rooms very much and had enjoyed
your company?

   My love. I hope you are happy, and well, as it leaves, your very
faithful   MISS MOFFAT

To Gerald Brenan

Saturday [June 11th, 1927]   Ham Spray the House of Banging Doors

Dear Mr Crusoe, I should be glad if you could tell me, since you are a
seer, why doors bang instead of shutting, or keeping shut? Why everything is green in the summer? And why Mr Robinson does not write
letters? Phyllis [de Janzé] is coming to lunch today so you can just
imagine what a flutter Miss Moffat and her tuffet are in! Velouté sauce
to be made, rooms to be tidied, flowers for the mantelpieces, hair to be
cut by Olive, a sack possett to be brewed by Miss Moffat herself, and is
Olive to be trusted to make a French salad for a Vicomtesse? Better run
down and see and then, after all, the Vicomtesse will telephone to say
'Darling I'm terribly sorry I can't come after all.' Never mind, velouté
sauce and carrots are good in themselves, even without a Vicomtesse. No
visitors this weekend for a miracle, which is a mercy. For to tell you the
truth, much as Miss Moffat likes showing off her wilderness of green
leaves and her possetts of sack, even more does she prefer dawdling
away her time in her room and listening to Mansfield Park with Lytton
over the fire alone. Do I see you next Wednesday? That would be nice,
if you also thought it nice and I'll spend Thursday with you? No. Impossible! Yes. We'll spend *all* Thursday together, I'll not go back till
the evening train. Please finish the Tramp[1] so I can read it. Am I too old
for a spotted muslin? That's what occurs to me. Such a pretty Indian
muslin presents itself in a pattern book by post this morning, but I can't
help feeling it's too frail for my hulky-bulky decrepid frame. More
suitable for a nymph, Julia. [Twenty lines omitted] Perhaps I'll write
you a story. I thought of rather a good one yesterday. My love dearest
Amigo   From your amiable MISS MOFFAT
PS I've been reading a life of Sargent the painter. It is almost *un-*
believable that such people can exist.

Saturday evening
PS
My letter never got posted today. Phyllis came this morning looking very
dazzling like a grand Persian Wxxxe with a scarlet mouth. Really I

---

[1] MS of *Jack Robinson*, published by Brenan under the pen name of George Beaton
(Chatto and Windus, 1933).

could wish she didn't paint so violently. Lunch went off beautifully.
Velouté sauce and carrots, cold chicken and cream possett. Lytton was
very deign and friendly. After lunch we went off alone together and lay
in the grass and talked. Very amusing gossip and conversations about
lovers and lust. She had to go back at tea time. I must say she attracts me
very much but I can't quite tell you why. She loved Ham Spray and was
properly appreciative of everything. I wish she could have stayed longer,
as there was so much to talk about that I simply forgot to ask her.
Now I've finished painting my bedroom pale yellow and I've been a
walk with Lytton and discussed Phyllis's character with him. The day
is not very agreable, too sultry, and yet cold. I've got this pain in my
back again, so feel rather distrait. And exhausted after the agitations
of the Vicomtesse invasion. But it *will* be nice to see my sober Mr
Crusoe on Wednesday evening. I'll try and be as good as you deserve.

Your very loving C.

To Gerald Brenan

Tuesday [June 21st, 1927]   *Ham Spray House, Hungerford*

How to answer a magician's letter? Give me the rules, for that Mr
Crusoe? But I know why you do it, write magician's letters; just to put
me out of countenance. Turn me into a mere shadow, a counterfeit,
a moon, to your sun. But then I can always reply that Mr Crusoe takes
at least 4 hours writing and re-writing his letters whereas Miss M. takes
only 5 mins and never pauses to think for one second. 'Then why aren't
her letters 20 times as long? Can she only spare 5 mins of her day etc
etc.' Heavens, how the man trips one up. Now I shall never get any
peace again. Are you cold or hot, Mr Tap? Tell me that, and I will never
turn you on again, (or leave you running). I didn't tell you how much
I liked *Rhapsody* as I have no opinion of my judgement on literature and
thought also it might prejudice you against the book! I *am glad* you
liked it, for although I've re-read some of the stories twice, I like them
even better than I did at first. The curious thing is that not a single
review picked it out for praise and it was Topsy who wrote and told
Lytton about it. I like her (Miss Edwards') point of view so much. The
story of the elderly man who fell in love with the young girl in the
greenhouse was exquisite I thought. And the one about the electrical

engineer. The flag incident made me at once think of you. It was humour in your taste. [400 words omitted]

And when you do see my paintings you never notice them. I often observe Mr Crusoe your indifference to my masterpieces. There were two in Lytton's room. You peered at them, but because I didn't tell you who they were by, you thought them mere (Van Meer's?) and shrugged your shoulders. And had you asked to see any pictures at Ham Spray, or letters, you might have been shown them. But no. You preferred to stalk like Banquo's ghost your solitary way up and down the Downs. Although there are ballets and horse show at Olympia and a hundred fascinating lovers and loveresses calling me to London this week I must atone for my extravagances and work here. Next week I shall come dressed like a Francesca angel and be as angelic in my behaviour as Mademoiselle Ninon. And will you write this week, without the interruption of tiresome Miss M?

Mr C. My dear Miss M. do not flatter yourself *you* interrupt me, on the contrary when you are not here my rooms are crowded with all the rank and fashion of the town. Today Senorita De Zeuta [Beryl de Zoete] comes to tea and the wife of the Editor of the Nation [Faith Henderson]. I dine with the Chinese Ambassador Artie Waali [Arthur Waley], and then I daresay I shall visit a Woolf Tamer [Virginia Woolf], or Baron Penrose of Fen Stanton [Alec Penrose], or Serge Garrowitch [Garrow Tomlin], or my old friend the Astrologer [Ralph Partridge]. You are mistaken to think without you, my life is a blank.

Miss M. You are too verbose, your high faluting speeches cover half the page and it is all bragidero and about yourself.

Mr C. Well what shall we discuss? The reptile house at the Zoo? The situation in China? The weather?

Miss M. Thank you, but we have a wireless in the country and I do not like discussions on snakes.

Mr C. You are very difficult to please and thank goodness in another moment Miss Endive [Mrs Enfield] will be coming to tea.

Miss M. You'll find she's mere water cress when you come to examine her origin, believe me.

Mr C. I'll not believe you! (in anger)

Miss M. Mark my words. (sneers)

Mr C. You're green yourself, green with jealousy.

Miss M. I am not! I don't care a fig what you eat for tea.

Mr C. Then why get into such a raging state? Ha! Ha!

Miss M. Raging greenery yourself, you long tailed radish.

Come, this conversation is becoming rude, and the truth, which astrologer Partridge says is so vital to life is being obscured. The truth? That I wish to send you my fondest love (if you deserve it.) And pray God I will behave nicely next Wednesday.   Yr loving CIROD XXX

[The nautical fancy dress and bottle party described in the following letter was Madge Garland's idea, but as the party was too large for her house it took place in Mr Reitlinger's.]

To Saxon Sydney-Turner

July 15th, 1927   *Ham Spray House, Hungerford*

I think if I enjoyed the party more than other parties it was perhaps because of your friendly wave as I started off in my ship (or cab) on my voyage. There was a very mixed gathering of nautical beauties. Lytton predominated as an admiral. Duncan looked very exquisite as a comoradore(?). There was the usual contingent of male 'beauties', Douglas [Davidson], Dadie [Rylands], Angus [Davidson] and many others, all in white ducks. Julia was a 1890 middy. I meant to cut out the description in the Evening Standard which devoted two paragraphs to Lytton's appearance and the other notables. Miss Tallulah Bankhead the actress, Serge Lifar, Miss Todd etc. There was a professional cocktail shaker, who for 4 hours mixed 'side cars' and 'moon rakers' without stopping. I had a proposal from The Honourable Gathorne-Hardy, but unfortunately (or fortunately one never can tell) his original paramour a gentleman called Mr Ferriere, returned to the party, so he deserted me. And I ended up as I began with my old loves, Lytton and Alix and Dadie and returned with them to 41 Gordon Square. Alix moved me by giving me a passionate embracade half way up stairs at 4.30 and said after all old friends were best and these new adventures really ended in dust and ashes. The next day I woke up with a terrible headache, for I had drunk nothing but cocktails the night before. Still as a dream and a vision of beauty, it still gives me great pleasure to think of these lovely sailors and sailoresses, all so very amorous, and gay. Julia and Tommy are to be married next week I think. They seem very devoted and happy so I hope it will (at any rate for some time) turn out successful. Oliver was to entertain the Judge and Lady Tomlin at a formal dinner at the Oriental [Club] last night! Unfortunately Lady T. discovered about

Paris, so weeps all day and says if only it had been 'different' how
pleased she would have been to have welcomed Miss Strachey into the
Tomlin fold, but as things are, she can only receive her with icy drawn
back arms. The dreadful scandal has been kept from the Judge, so Lady
T. has to bear 'the burden of this great sorrow' alone. I bought them a
patch work quilt for a wedding present before I left London.

Lytton and I returned yesterday afternoon and at 4 o'ck the postman
brought me your letter. I regret I am not yet old enough to be insensible
to flattery. And I was *very* moved by your letter. But perhaps you also
had been drinking old brandy for dinner? Topsy and Peter Lucas
arrived yesterday and stay till tomorrow. Do you know them? Will you
write me a letter and tell me about Miss Selby. Poor Miss Selby, I think
she is rather a Dorothy Edwards heroine. After planning for months an
elopement with Sebastian ('who although he doesn't make love to me,
must be very fond of me to see me so often and tell me all his confidences')
to Finland, finds herself not with Sebastian but Mr Sydney-Turner. And
when she reaches Finland finds it not very different from being a
governess at Nottingham. But of course I have never seen her. Tomorrow
Olive goes to Brighton for the day. I feel slightly depressed as I can't do
any painting. There is no reason except that I feel I know what the
result will be before I start on a picture, and the result is so dull always,
it hardly seems worth while beginning. Lytton is getting on slowly with
'Elizabeth'. He hopes to get it finished by September and then perhaps
we may go away together for a fortnight. But I hardly like to look forward to it in case it doesn't come off. And in August perhaps you will
pay Ham Spray a visit? What are you reading on your voyage? I do hope
you will enjoy yourself and feel better. I am rather tired, so forgive a
rather dull letter. But if I don't write today I know I shall become
involved in the machinery of the estate. Do you grow happier or remain
in much the same mood from one year to another? Lately I feel as if for
the first time I've grasped what the general plan of one's life is, and will
be.

My fondest love to you.   Your CARRINGTON
A very notable black lily (the same variety as one Barbara had last year)
is just going to unroll itself into flower so I am very excited.

To Julia Strachey

Monday [mid-July 1927]

Darlingest Julia, You can imagine, Julia, the load that has been lifted
off my mind, and the hell I have been through and now all the loads are
lifted, and one can see daylight again, and I am *tremendously* glad
that you are so happy, for happy I know you *will be* with Stephen who is
a dear boy, and I am sure when you have both *found* yourselves as you
certainly will soon, you will understand what a *real* married life can be.
Oh Julia, I am very glad over your new born happiness.

Well well it's all very fine but exit Aunt C. I fear now that her bird of
a dove has found a nest.

I am glad seriously (exit Wogan for ever) you are going to marry
Tommy who if you didn't marry I should seriously think of marrying
myself, for he is such a charmer. I loved our last weekend together (sobs
and sighs) and I fear you'll incur a great many enemies, i.e. Lytton, by
snatching the lovely boy into your Swallow's nest.[1]

I am going to buy you a mirror for your blue spare room. I loved your
cottage really, it looks very lovely, although what with the children and
Barbara and one thing and another there was hardly time to look at it.
Burn this letter, or we shall be disgraced and don't tell T. as I am sure
he will disapprove! May I be your best aunt at your wedding? But I
suppose the crowd of sobbing, sighing lovers will be too thick and may I
come in August and see you? I will whether I may nor not. I wish I could
come up this week, but I am afraid I can't. Tell me if you want a
momentary loan of money to buy anything, a yard of brides-veiling for
the occasion. Darling Julia, nobody can be as glad as your most loving

TANTE C.

To Julia Strachey

Thursday [August 1927]   *H.S.H. Owlscliffe, Wiltshire*

Darling, I fairly exploded with laughter over your letter this morning in
bed much to the surprise of little Tiberius who was about to eat my

[1] Julia and Stephen Tomlin went to live at Swallowcliffe after their marriage. Hence
the address on Carrington's next letter.

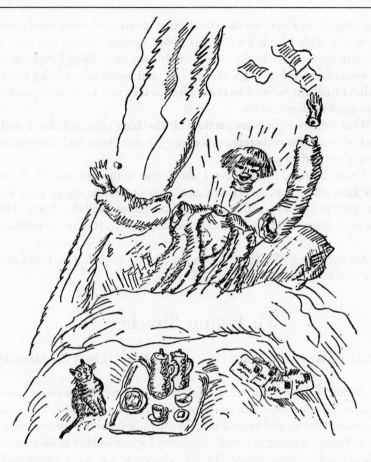

bread and butter (seeing it was a letter from you, and that my attention
was completely engrossed.) 'But who are all those other letters from,'
cries Mrs. Nosey Tomlin? Ha. Ha. If only you shared my double bed,
and left your Swallow's nest for my snuggery you would be able to read
all my letters, even those from the lovely R-s-m-on. Well, darling, if
you really liked the spotted dog which was I confess 'knocked off' in
two minutes to please a little boy of 4, I will do you a whole dinner
service of: Pussy Cats.

'Really Julia, I must protest. I simply can't face eating my boiled
sausage off a cat's back.'

'Believe me, Tommy, it is only one of her jokes. But what *shall* we
ask her to paint on our dinner service?'

There is a problem for you to solve and in two weeks please make up your answer, as I shall by then be starting on my new china enterprise. Oh dear I wish I hadn't a complex about earning money, and such a desire to have money at the same time. It's the same thing I suppose as my mania for wanting 'to go' to the W.C., and my dislike of being there, so that I rush out before I've even 'tried' as they say. I now take paraffin oil to assist madame nature.

What fun your birthday party, with the blue cake, will be. I shall think of some very recherchez gift to stagger and I hope melt the granite heart of my perfect paramour.

We are invested by rats also. I use Rodine with some success. But it only lasts about a week. Then a new army enters the house from the farm yard and starts nibbling the books, the papers, and the cheese. The cats catch some, but they obviously are too many … [the rest is missing]

[At the beginning of August Carrington visited Munich with James and Alix Strachey and Sebastian Sprott.]

To Lytton Strachey

Saturday [*August 6th, 1927*]   *Hotel* [*?Löwe*] *Loe* [*Munich*]

My darling Lytton, You can't think how delighted I was to get your letter on Wednesday with news of H[am] S[pray] and such a good account of Stump, and everything. I write in bed waiting for my breakfast so forgive it being in pencil. Thursday I spent looking at the picture galleries and the sculpture. In the afternoon we went to Munich Versailles. And then suddenly after 'tea' at our hotel (which is really mineral water) we telephoned Urfeld and ordered two rooms. We only just had time to catch the 7.30 train, and buy a sandwich. Our train was late so we didn't reach Kochel till it was quite dark, at 10 o'ck. No moon and only the light of the stars and glow worms to guide us up the dark mountain path, 5½ miles to Wifeld. It was I assure you very terrifying with a deep ravine and a torrent below us if we slipped off the path! However very bravely we climbed the mountain and reached Wifeld in one hour and a half. Although it was only half past eleven, everyone had gone to bed and as one couldn't tell in the pitch dark which was our hotel, we had to ring and knock at every one. After hours, a man got out of bed and let us in. A large wolf hound at the foot of the stairs was almost more terrifying than our precipices and ravines. No food or drink and no towels and no soap. However I had my brandy and dropped off to sleep very quickly. It was absurd waking up the next day and seeing the lake and conifer mountains covered with motor cars and tourists and looking so tame; even the fierce hound turned out to be stuffed!

We walked round the lake, abused conifers and tourists and then walked down the same path, covered now by steaming 'alpine climbers' in fancy dress, had lunch on the way overlooking Kochelsee, where I drew Sebastian a view. Ate the most lovely fresh baked trout, and reached Kochel in time to catch the 3 o'ck train. After a 'mineral tea' we rushed off to Cosi fan Tutte. It was a lovely performance, superbly done. In the audience I saw the greatest conductor in the world, Weingartner, also Frankenstein in a box and a great many other eminent German musicians. We were almost dead at 9.30, having eaten nothing since 12 o'ck, so went to a very grand restaurant (a converted Palace) and had a most beautiful dinner with the grandest Rhine wine, smoked eel and pâté and turbot. Today I shall spend shopping perhaps. Tomorrow give a final look at the galleries and on Monday start back. James, and Alix go off to their mountain on Monday. I've enjoyed myself tremendously the whole time. It is now my ambition to come to Munich and persuade Frankenstein to let me design the scenery for Cosi, and Don Giovanni. Breakfast comes so I will stop. The heat is still very intense, almost too much of a good thing in the middle of the day. I was glad we climbed our mountain in the cool night on Thursday. I shall start early on Monday for my homeward journey. So possibly I shall reach Ham Spray on Tuesday night! I will wire when I get to London. There are very few birds in the country. I only saw a German jay and a few chaffinches on our walk. And there are no cats in Munich. The inhabitants seem to me to be 'ohne Die lust,' but perhaps their appearances hardly inspire that sort of feeling. I quite agree with you about the propriety of night life. There seem as few 'birds' in the town as in the country. The inside has been rather a burden but the back is really much better. Thank you so much for forwarding my letters. Saxon wrote me a very characteristic Finnish account of his holiday. I've seen two charming German prints which I will try and get James to ask the price of this morning and a lovely plate of a stag contemplating a rabbit, but in an expensive shop. I hope you are having fine weather now. My very fondest love. I think, in spite of the fascination of this Munchen life, very often of you, and my Ilex tree. My love to S.   Votre MOPSA

To Gerald Brenan

Saturday [August 13th, 1927]   *Ham Spray House, Hungerford*

I haven't written to you because I have not known what to say. But I have been thinking a great deal about our relation.

The truth seems to be that I am almost diseased in the head over some matters and probably it's lunacy for me to try to have an intimate relation with anyone. Lately, I mean the last two months, I've had rather an obsession of the subject of copulation. The result is I sleep badly and get nerves about it. It seems out of my control. I mean when these feelings come, and go. However, I see it's maddening for you to have anything to do with me and the knowledge that my behaviour affects you so considerably and makes you bear me grudges only makes me feel disinclined to see you and depressed. I feel at the moment it's no good you seeing me. For I only irritate you. And I'm incapable of promising before hand what my moods will be, as I do not know about them myself. If however you want to see me again later on, when your irritation has passed and possibly my nerves left me, you must tell me. Apparently I only get on with people and behave 'decently' when they have no intimate relations with me. It's no good 'going into it', and seeking for explanations in our conduct. I am only sorry that I was wrong in thinking last autumn that I was capable of sustaining a lover-relation. But I assure you there is no pleasure to be got out of finding oneself impotent, which is what it amounts to, and you might instead of heaping abuse on my grey head, give me a little pity. You know I am devoted to you, but these barricades seem to make it impossible at the moment. I will send back your keys by Ralph next week, as I expect you would like them.

I feel rather depressed so I can't write very intelligently. But I send my love.   Your C.

To Julia Strachey

Monday [August 17th, 1927]   *Ham Spray House, Hungerford*

Written *in haste*

Darling Julia, Many happy returns of yesterday. The rain still pours down, and I sit and grumble indoors with my nose pressed against the

window pane. The cows think nothing of it. But I LONG to go out and walk in the hedgerows, and smell the sweet summer flowers, and ride my lovely white gee-gee. I can't FIND your blue pettie-coatie my sweetie. What's to be done? I am afraid Stump must have stolen it and seized it for Sunday wear. Oh dear, I've given her a tail! What's to be done? I send the other objects, the ruler and measure. I say do you mind, but I *think* I'd rather come next week for my visit and not this week. Because (a) the weather is so vile so I'm disinclined to start in our leaking old ship of a car. (b) There is a possible visitor descending on Wednesday to see me (ie) Margaret Waley, [three words omitted] and I'm painting a portrait of a rustic which I *very* much want to finish this week. So will you ask me next week instead, darling? [Remainder of letter missing]

To Julia Strachey

Tuesday
Ham Spray House, Hungerford

Darling Julia, I never saw anything
so beautiful as that skirt! I rather
think I shall take to a new style, a
weeping, trailing, sweeping lady style,
for ever picking roses, and trailing
my skirts in the dewy grass. You
were an angel to give me such a
beautiful present.

I am sorry you have turned leopard,
or spotty-dog-pudding. I hope you will soon recover. If I might recommend calamine lotion, used by your uncle the Right very Rev. Lytton
Strachey for your calamitous illness. The results in his case have been,
always, truly marvellous.

I am just dashing off to London, to try and get a servant, and see
about Lytton's new rooms. I shall be back tomorrow evening. Ralph
writes the strangest accounts of life in Yegen, very peculiar goings-on.
If London fails me, I might come to Salisbury registry office. In which
case I will send you a wire and drop in for tea one day. You can put on a
veil and receive me à la Persian.

It would be very nice as long as I was received one way, or another.
I write very quickly as we are just dashing off.

Here is a little apron that I bought for you in the market of Le Puy.
I hope you will sometimes
wear it and think of your
loving

TANTE C.

PS But if you think it hideous
give it to Agnes with my
fondest love!

To Lytton Strachey

Tuesday morning, 9 o'ck [September 20th, 1927]   *Ham Spray House*

Darling Lytton, I am lying in bed in my dressing gown whilst old Bowley 'grubs up' the stump on the lawn. It's rather like Lady Jane Grey hearing the executioner hewing her block. For the whole air is one of sombre bustle, arrangements for a departure strew the rooms and the hall. And as it is death to leave Ham Spray, soon I shall be a lifeless corpse on the lawn and old Bowley will reign King of Spray and Ham, with Stump and family, for subjects. Please tell Norman Douglas that your niece has an odd twist for birds and animals and would like very much a copy of his book. Sebastian wrote me a long letter this morning. He confessed (in secret) he suffered terribly in the misty mountains and was delighted to reach London again and the P.C. met him 'open armed open-mouthed open-legged. He is divine. It is odd being in love again.' I expect we should think so if we saw the P.C. Still I am glad he is so happy. Noel and Missie came to dinner with me last night and ate another chicken. Now I must get up and do my packing which isn't even started yet! It's a mercy not having a train to catch. R[alph] wrote yesterday from Barcelona. He will be in London next Monday evening so you will see him. Barcelona sounded rather grim and a little sordid. I think of you so much. I hope you are happier now you have seen Roger [Senhouse]. Perhaps you'll write to me at Swallowcliffe soon, as I think so much about you. And please do what you like about plans as I can quite easily come to London and leave the car in Hungerford if you want to go anywhere else, next week. You can never know how much you mean to me, I think it is only when you go away I realize how very much I care. I send you all my love.

Your very fond MXPSX

[The sudden death of Philip Ritchie had been a great blow to all his friends.]

To Lytton Strachey

[September 21st, 1927] with J. and T. *Swallowcliffe*

Darling Lytton, It was such a mercy to have your letter this morning. I am so glad you were able to comfort Roger [Senhouse]. I am sure it will

make such a difference to him now, having your affection in this crisis
to depend upon. I mean he has an excuse now for being natural and
showing that he isn't self supporting. He wrote me such a charming
letter this morning telling me all he had heard from Jennings about
P[hilip Ritchie]'s death. I thought of giving you that portrait of Philip
I painted this spring and doing Roger a copy of it, or if you don't think
you would like it, I'll give it to Roger. You can see it when you get back.
I am afraid you must be rather worn out after Monday. I do hope your
health keeps up. As I thought, it was half past 11 o'ck before I got off in
the car, laden with packages, and vegetables and black puss. I had a
good drive to Salisbury. As it was market day, I lingered about a little
and looked at the stalls, and farmers and bought some stockings. I
reached the Cliffe about half past two. Tommy was busy drawing out
plans of gates for Lincoln's Inn[1] and Julia making scones in the
kitchen. The cottage looks *very* nice inside. Really it's equal to Ham Spray
in elegance and comfort, only cleaner and tidier. Puss leapt out of her
basket and soon made herself at home in the kitchen, eating chickens'
bones and purring in front of the fire. I have a grand bedroom with the
new window that T[ommy] designed which proves I think that he has a
great architectural genius. Julia is in high spirits, and both of them seem
very happy.

After tea, I drove Julia to Tisbury, and did some shopping. We found
a marvellous postcard shop; I will send you a sample in a few days. Julia's
vagueness about ordering is only equalled by your ignorance! 'How
many potatoes shall we want?' in a whisper to me. In a commanding,
imperious voice to the man. 'Well send some potatoes, a good many.'
Man 'How many pounds 14, 28?' 'Oh no not so many as that, about
2 lbs would be enough I think.' (Two pounds being about 10 potatoes.)
It was great fun. We laughed so much and even the man could hardly
resist smiling. The cooking is really very good. Julia teaches the maid
herself with Mrs Beeton sitting like an immense goddess on the kitchen
table presiding. I am to paint a panel over a door, of the La Source a
goddess lying by the water's brink, over the sitting room door. John
B[anting] has done *an enormous* 9 foot high (rather awful, for Venus is
exactly like himself, I think, disguised as a female) Venus Rising out of
the Waves in the bathroom. What Judge and Lady T. must have thought
as they sat on the W.C.!! I looked at a natural history book last night and
T. and J. read, over a fine blazing log fire. I shall enjoy myself very much

---

[1] These gates were made by the blacksmith at Milton Ernest and presented to the
benchers of Lincoln's Inn by Lord Tomlin. They stand on the east side of New Square.

as it's exactly the sort of life I most love, talking and painting. The weather still looks very relentless. Your bed is a triumph of comfort they say and looks very sympathetic in their bedroom. The colours and curtains etc are all a great success. I do not know who is responsible. Julia seems infinitely better in health. Very energetic and brisked up. I think I shall probably go to Dorelia on Friday afternoon and come back here on Sunday. But I will see how I get on with my paintings here and when it's most convenient for Dorelia to have me.

Christ. Rain coming down again. The Cliffs, and swallows are all obscured by mountain mists. And what is the climate of Firle? Now I must get up. I've been writing to you in bed. Give my love to Vanessa and Duncan please and Virginia if you see her. I hear from Olive the new Ham rector is expected next week. He comes from Melksham, and has one son aged 20! I send you my fondest love.   Your loving M.

To Lytton Strachey

In haste, 1 o'ck [*October 6th, 1927*]   *Ham Spray House, Hungerford*

Darling Lytton, I've arrived more dead than alive with my cold and am now going to bed and hope to cure it. It's monstrous, for it's a divine lovely day but I feel good for nothing.—Finished the Beaver[1] before I left this morning however by getting up at 6.30! I send these in case you may find something rare in them. Please bring back the oriental catalogue. Oh, it is lovely to be back. The beauty of our house, and garden is unsurpassed—and you are unsurpassed as being the most charming and loving friend it is possible for a sneezing Mopsa to possess.

To Lytton Strachey

Monday morning, 12 o'ck [*October 24th, 1927*]
                              Ham Spray House, Hungerford
                              In the (sun) under the verandah

Darling Lytton, [Two lines omitted] The weekend passed very merrily.

[1]Part of a decoration Carrington painted at Fryern Court.

[Ten lines omitted] After lunch we all went riding. Coker's horse (really a miniature cart horse) was more comic than Belle. And the spectacle of them both trying to prance together was so funny, we simply became weak with laughing. Lionel looked exactly like a monkey in a circus on Belle and Margaret Leathes like nothing ever seen before. And when Huth's thoroughbred hunter pursued them across the second field it was like two walruses trying to escape from an antelope. We had some fine races on the top of the Downs.

The mouse ('quiet as a mouse' Mr Coker said to me) was egged on by Lionel into a gallop finally. There was a vast encampment of gypsies just near the Black wood. I have never seen such an exquisite girl. She had a thick silver necklace round her neck, and pale copper hair and a huge amazon figure. They all came running out of their ragged tents and begged for money. Dog gave her a shilling. In a field six children, very tattered, boys and girls of about 4 to 10 years old, were dancing the Charleston together! We talked and rode to the Gibbet. I think Lionel enjoyed his riding. The 'Robin' [Margaret Leathes] showed no feelings, only smiled brightly. In the evening we played the poetry game, Will's game and a drawing game. Dog came out of it rather better than one would expect. Lionel of course was frantic. The 'Robin' just what you would expect a Robin to write. [Twenty-five lines omitted]

My very fondest love to you most dear Lytton

Your devoted CENTAUR

PS Rosamond has sold 75,000 copies of her book in America! Love to Dadie.

To Dorelia John

[*Christmas 1927*]   *Ham Spray House, Hungerford*

Darling Dodo, What has prevented me writing to you is the vagueness
about your address. I had an idea it was Villa Lilac but Helen on the
telephone assures me it is St Anne. Well, we will see: or perhaps you are
so celebrated you can dispense with a house title? Ach! we have had an
awful time of it since you left. You were wise not to spend Christmas
at Fryern. I had 7 in this house for a week and then 2 for 4 days. And for
a whole week no cars could get from Hungerford, so we nibbled ham
and turkey bones like mice on siege. It was too cold to enjoy tobogganing
(or am I too old?) and I seemed to spend my whole day lighting fires,
thinking of new ways of cooking turkey bones and mincing ham and
fetching my horse through snow drifts. Then on Christmas day there
was a terrible scene. I rushed down in the ice cold morning in a dressing
gown and took a telegram on the telephone for 'Partridge, etc etc.
Dorelia'. I was in high feather and of course bragged to R.P. and he was
cross because he hadn't been sent a message on the telegram. The next
morning, 'a copy' came to confirm the telephone, addressed to 'Monsieur
Partridge'. Now if he'd been a nice sort of man he would have taken his
revenge silently and not mentioned the subject. For of course I read
the address on the wire and saw my, or rather the telephone girl's,
mistake. But the brute in front of everyone announces his triumph and
rubs in the ashes. So my nose was disjointed for days. However your
lovely postcard consoled me, and we are now on speaking terms again.
Julia and Tommy were here. J. very fat, and like a Veronese beauty.
James S[trachey], Frances Marshall, and Lytton. We had to fetch food
on sledges, and walk 6 miles across snow drifts to get to Hungerford.
On Monday everything thawed and we nearly lost the car for ever by
getting stuck in a raging icy torrent in our lane. Since Sunday I've been
in bed on and off with a chill and still feel pretty mouldery. But it's very
nice being here alone after the mob. Henry wrote me a letter with news
of you. He seemed very pleased with Toulon and terribly embarrassed
at having set foot in Cassis after all his protestations that he would never
go there!

Have you been keeping well? I was sorry to hear Vivien was in bed
through over eating. I've some pictures for your R.D.s [Ravishing

Daughters] but I can't get out to post them. I wish snow wasn't incompatible with pleasure, for the landscape looked exquisitely lovely.
Mountain gales travelling 150 miles an hour now tear past the house,
rattling all the windows to pieces. I feel very decayed in the head with
this blasted chill, forgive a dull letter and please write me one to
console me. And for what? For you having gone away. There'll never
be such a lovely evening as Chambertin until you come back. Give my
fondest love to Poppet and Vivien. Do you remember Raymond Mortimer? One of Lytton's Hoopoes, Henry called him. He is engaged to
Valerie Taylor. Ah but will he marry her? Quite another question.
What do you do? Stitch fine linen? Read Ethel M. Dell? But I shall
never know. Poppet I suppose is cutting out a new dress. Peeled pears
boiled in kirsch with a little sugar and then flambeau (?) as they come
on the table. Very good. But they must be Doyen[ne] de Comice.
Everyone is in London, so I sit alone with Black Puss over the fire,
covering the carpet with lettuce leaves, and salad oil. Tomorrow I shall
go up and see the circus, and give the poor overworked Olive a weekend
off. Now I must go to bed. I send you all my love but never dare if you
love me, send a telegram addressed to Monsieur Partridge in this house!

Your devoted most loving C.

[Lytton had gone to Brighton for a jaunt.]

To Lytton Strachey

Thursday, December 29th, 1927   *Ham Spray House, Hungerford*

Darling Lytton, I was glad to hear that you had arrived safely. Perhaps
it was rather a good thing to have a slight rest before starting off again.
I do hope Roger [Senhouse] will reach you this morning. It is *exactly*
the same this morning here, a howling wind and freezing so the con-
ditions would have been no better for the grand trek across Siberia. In
fact worse as the sun hasn't come out. Today we had a lovely lunch at
the Bear and I got completely boozed on a pint of xxxx beer, sherry,
and vermouth. Tommy and I walked back together and had such
fascinating conversations that I hardly noticed the distance. Just before
Prosperous Hill, the place I always call 'the frontier', was far the worst
drift.
We literally walked on the top of the hedges. I shall be surprised if

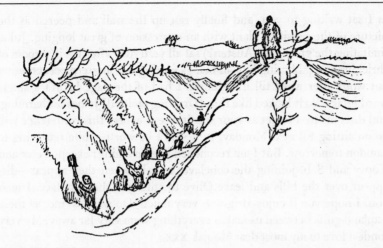

they clear it before another week. For it was really like digging out the Cheddar Cliffs in salt.

It was pretty bad along the rest of the road to Ham, very slippery and deep. On our return, James had kept in the fires, Thank God. We were all very exhausted. But I am frightfully glad we went, as one will certainly never see such a remarkable sight again. If there is a sun today I'll take some photographs for you. Saxon sent me a very lovely calendar yesterday of a hyena. I shalln't send this off till I get a wire from Brighton.

After breakfast.

The sun has come out. But nobody is down to breakfast and it's HALF PAST TEN storms the colonel, (or Mr MacDougal) and how can one have

a quiet discussion on the problems of life with the black cat at the breakfast table. The cat was seized with a creese des nérves this morning, what with the wind, the snow, and the birds on the window sill, and climbed up the chimney in my bedroom, and then climbed the four poster bed

as I sat writing to you, and finally ran up the wall and peered at the picture of the sensitive plant with an expression of great longing. Julia, (imitating the great Jane Austen?) sat all yesterday after tea in a room of shrieking and jabbering human beings writing her masterpiece, crossing out word after word till the glimpse I had of the page hadn't a single word intact! So it looked like this. [Drawing omitted] James is charming, and does his best to act as your subsititree. I expect this conference will go on sitting till next Monday, as it won't be worth while returning to London tomorrow. But I am reconciled to everything: except Peter and Topsy and Seb. joining the conclave. I shall, when they appear—disappear over the hills and leave Olive to entertain the populace. I miss you. I hope you'll enjoy Brighton very much. Do write to me, as these Lapland gulfs between us makes everything seem very far away. My very fondest love to my most dear Moujak xxx

Your loving MOPSA

1928

To Lytton Strachey

Tuesday [January 16th, 1928]   *The Pavilion [Cambridge]*

Dearest Toad in the Hole, It's lovely here today. I wish you could whisk
away and join me. A dazzling sun shines on the Pavilion. But where are
the ghosts in white flannel? Only a large black cat sits staring into eternity
on the window sill. Ach but I am in a rage! [Drawing omitted] That
odious old camel writes to say he *can't* go riding today, or tomorrow and so
there'll be no cantering along the Roman Road. I shall try and get Alec, or
Bunny to take me tomorrow if it's fine. A dreadful night of nightmares
leaves me rather dim in the head this morning, but I shall hope for a
cocktail when I get round to Dadie's to pull me together. Topsy is
charming and in very good spirits and Peter in very good spirits and
charming. And Stephen as solid, and predominant as ever. Now I must
whisk off to Dadie's room, and draw some plans. I shall console myself,
for my defrauded ride, by looking at the owl books this afternoon.
Please try and come back next Friday with us. Although I only tell you
in a whisper, but it does make a very great difference having a Ham
Spray without a fakir. When I reached here yesterday evening I discovered I had put Tuesday on my postcard so they were rather surprised
to see me on Monday.—Topsy was having a tête à tête with that mushroom growth Steven Runciman, when I arrived.

My love darling Lytton and please get quite well by Wednesday
evening. There is to be a very special concert on Wed. evening at James.

Your loving MRS SNIPE[1]

To Gerald Brenan

[February 9th, 1928]   *Ham Spray House, Hungerford*

I was lying in bed reading Swann's Way and two sentences made me
think of you. Olive at that moment tapped on the door, and brought me

[1] The signature of this letter is a jocular reference to her new attachment to Bernard
Penrose, 'Beakus'. Bécasse is actually a woodcock and not a snipe.

breakfast and my letters. That coincidence of course is in your favour. I have (as you probably have) TWO minds about seeing you again. I had *not* 'no doubt guessed' you had long ceased to have 'unfriendly feelings.' I imagined to tell you the truth, that I had ceased to exist. But perhaps you've said and felt rather more than is compatible with being friends again? And then I have found curious pleasures in my isolation, and being exempt from any responsibilities, or blame. But it's also true, I seldom can think of anything more 'amusing' (sic) than having tea or lunch with you. So I daresay I shall ring up one day. But not for some time, as I don't think I'll be in London this month.

Gerald—Well this is a nice encouraging sort of letter, and I wrote her such a friendly one.

But what can [one] do when one is a divided character? I still wonder of course what was your *real* reason for wanting to see me again. Curiosity? A desire to torment? Or had you also perhaps been reading Proust? Well, it's very nice to think that I can by putting 2 pennies in a slot and murmuring that mystic 8295 see you whenever I want to; very nice. I hope you are happy and working.   My love, your C.

[The fact that Carrington signed herself 'Mrs Snipe', and the following Valentine, reveal that she had met Bernard Penrose ('Beakus') and was greatly attracted. He was to become the last great passion of her life.

Beakus was the youngest of the four Penrose brothers and at the age of twenty-five (ten years younger than Carrington) had led an adventurous life at sea. He had served before the mast on the *Garthpool*, the last four-masted ship under the British flag, on her last voyage before she was wrecked, during which they rounded Cape Horn. He had also been one of the crew of the mission ship *Harmony*, in which he sailed to the Arctic and became acquainted with the Eskimos. Carrington consciously identified him with her sailor brother Teddy who had been reported missing in 1916.

Though reserved, often silent and slow of speech, Beakus Penrose already had his own strong aesthetic tastes and a clear sense of values. He was never at ease in Bloomsbury, but became one of Stephen Tomlin's closest friends and companions.]

A Valentine

A Dove brought back to me
My Love on a Wave of the sea,
A Dove brings my Love for you
Obscured in the Wool of a Ewe.

To Gerald Brenan

February 11th, 1928   *Ham Spray House, Hungerford*

I did not imagine there was any great mystery, or wedge work on foot.

And you ought to know by this time that I always disagree with Ralph in every discussion, even on that well worn theme 'Gerald's character'. One of the few pleasures resulting from having explored the bottom of the sea is that afterwards one has full liberty to break all rules and be as capricious as one likes. So there are no irrevocable endings, final letters, unforgivable insults, or closed doors.

To Sebastian Sprott

Dearest Sebastian, You are a snake of a man never to answer my letter.
But I shall endeavour to turn the other cheek and forgive you. I write as
Lytton's secretary, as he is rather ill, and worn, and unable to put pen
to paper. Oh yes, no doubt if *you* were his secretary bird you'd write a
much neater, better, more grammatical, and in every way superior
letter, but as you aren't here, I must do my best to imitate your inimi-
table style. 'Would you care,' says le grand maitre, 'to spend Easter chez
Ham Spray?' If you would will you fill up the enclosed card with Yes,
or No, in the space provided for the same; an early posting, surely you
can spare 3 mins to run to the post between Wilf, Will, and Edward?
Will oblige your late master and the present correspondent, his present
secretary. There have been sad shakings of heads over 'Poor Sebastian'
lately.—'Never hear a word of him, but I'm going to see him next weekend. Completely engulfed in his boot blacks and blackamoors. Alas if
only *I* could find consolation as easily for *my* broken heart.' Then this
morning by post. 'I take it rather ill that Sebastian who I wrote to at
Christmas, should never write to me, and neglect me so completely after
all that … etc.'
'But is she making all this up?'
'Who can tell? Nobody but your own conscience. I spent three days
at Cambridge last week, but the agony of painting Dadie's walls, (which
were a complete failure), ruined all my pleasures, except when I was
drunk with cocktails. Of course I like despondent rejected lovers, so
found Dadie very sympathetic and charming. The Pavilion[1] seemed to
me slightly 'strained' but I daresay it was nothing more than the 'end of
term' wearing them both down. I stayed one night with Penroses, in
their very superfine Queen Anne house.[2] Lytton has been over working,
and fell ill last Friday, and so couldn't go to Cambridge for the weekend
to see Coriolanus. (Who secretly I thought was lovely, very proud and
cruel with a tiger face.) I've masses of gossip for you, about Ramseys,
Penroses, Penwipers, etc etc but why should I cast my [drawing of pearls
before swine omitted] Why indeed? So you'll get no gossip till you come

[1] Peter and Topsy Lucas lived at the Pavilion.
[2] Alec Penrose was still living at Grove House, Fenstanton, Huntingdon.

here. I keep fairly well, rather worn down by nightmares and the difficulty of reconciling myself to the fact that my painting isn't any better
(if as good) as Douglas's [Davidson]. I hope you keep well, and enjoy
your low life with the blacks, and sweet Alice.

Morgan comes here next weekend. I still love my horse more than any
man, but less than some women. Lytton enjoyed Norman Douglas and
Paris enormously. But that's old cheese I expect to you, as I daresay
you've seen Roger [Senhouse].

Now I must run to the telephone and ring up the doctor in London
and ask for a tonic for Master and order some chops and feed the horse
and—you know the hundred and one little things that there are for a
busy housewife to do after breakfast on Wednesday morning. So I must
say goodbye to my dear [drawing of Saint Sebastian omitted] and rush
off. Be a dear and say if you can come for Easter.

Your most loving   C.
                                                     pp. Lytton Strachey

To Gerald Brenan

March 15th, 1928   *Ham Spray House, Hungerford*

I was sorry not to be able to come up to tea today. But there was only a
vague possibility that I should. If however you are in London next
Tuesday, I will be coming up and will have tea with you. But just as
you like. If you have by now changed your mind about the doubtful
pleasures of meeting me again, I shall understand. The cold here is too
intense to allow one's brain to creep even dimly near the surface.
Besides it is so long since I wrote a letter that I have forgotten how to
proceed. In case you thought it treachery my telling Ralph you had
written to me, I will point out that you should not leave my letters to
you lying on your table when you invite people to peer through your
telescopes at naked females (?) at night![1]

If you go to the country before Tuesday and if I fail to leave the
country, then we will meet later.   My love, your C.

[1] Gerald had invited Ralph, Frances and Alec Penrose excitedly by telephone to come
to his flat and look through a telescope at 'a beautiful girl having a bath' in a house opposite. They did, and saw an old man, and presumably also D.C.'s letter to G.B.

To Gerald Brenan

Good Friday, April 6th, 1928   *Ham Spray House, Hungerford*

From pure old fashioned sentiments I send you my love for your birth-day. For as you have so often observed fundamentally I am very con-ventional.

If I had not tetnuss (?) in my foot I should have written you one of my characteristic letters about the spring flowers, the birds, and my Ilex tree, but alas, striking an attitude this morning, as I surveyed my kingdom, I drove, in a triumphant gesture, my 4 pronged fork into the ground without observing my foot, in a white rubber boot, was below me. So typically, as Christ had 4 nails driven into his foot today 1928 years ago, or less, so I today crucified my flesh in memory of his death with four prongs. I go off tomorrow to that haven of fair women and Siamese cats.[1] If you were really at Broadchalke I might have dropped in on my way back and paid you a visit. But I expect you are already at Edgeworth's leafy glades.

Now it is time for tea, so I must go and wash my hands. There is a book called 'Scrutinies' which I would recommend to you. Roy Camp-bell has a review of poetry that is good and Lawrence is amusing with his tirades against Galsworthy. And our favourite, Dorothy Edwards is there. I hope you are able to work and that Tiz has subsided.

I send you my love for tomorrow.   Your C.

To Lytton Strachey

Tuesday [April 10th, 1928]   *Fryern Court, Fordingbridge, Hants.*

Darling Lytton, As you may surmise this isn't exactly a good house for writing letters, or posting them. I hope you are having lovely weather and feeling better for your change of life! The polished silver, and white bear skin rugs, and hot water cans before lunch in your bedroom. Life here is *very* pleasant and to my taste. I sleep with Vivien in that big room you had. She is a most amusing bedfellow. After breakfast every-

---

[1] The Johns' house, Fryern Court.

one sits on Dorelia's bed and talks. A strange spectacle the other
morning like a scene in an African harem, this mélange of recumbent
females. But you can't possibly imagine what it looked like and I cannot
draw it. This morning it was rather dull, but cleared up about 12 o'ck
and turned into an exquisite day later. I went into Fordingbridge with
Vivien in a gig. A charming old fashioned chariot very high, on two
wheels. We did some shopping for Dodo and then went a long ride
'exploring'. Finally we came to a charming lane which led to a farm.
Then it became very muddy and after going through two gates turned
into the merest track in a grass field. However it seemed feeble to turn
back, so we galloped on. Turning at the next gate we saw what we
thought was an enraged farmer crying 'stop' and rushing after us, so we
lashed up Topsy, and galloped on across field after field. Finally our
track turned under a railway bridge into terrible boggy ground then up
another grass field and ended in a little gravel pit! It was rather humiliating and then the farmer overtook us and told us we were trespassing
but he turned out on 'close up' to be an extremely attractive young man
in leather breeches. So it was rather a pity we didn't stop when he
called! We then had to retreat on our traces and undo all the 7 gates,
and return back through Fordingbridge the way we came. After lunch
today I went a marvellous long ride with Henry [Lamb] on the Cran-
borne Downs. He was very friendly. The country was looking exquisitely beautiful. Long stretches of pale olive green Downs covered with
little juniper bushes which look like misshapen black beasts bewitched
and rooted to the ground. We came back about 5 o'ck and then sat with
Dodo eating lovely honey and bread at that long table. Tomorrow
afternoon I shall drive over to J[ulia] and T[ommy] with Dorelia and
the children and have tea there and then bring J. and T. back here for
the night and go back with them the next day Thursday and either go
back to Ham Spray on the evening, or on Friday very early. Will you
tell me when you propose to come back to Ham Spray? I wish you could
be here and walk on these ravishing Downs with me. It is so very much
your style of country. There is such a perfect mixture of wildness, and
Wordsworthian loveliness here. The villages have little brooks with
daffodils growing at the water's edge and charming pink thatched
cottages. Tonight we go to cinema at Fordingbridge and see a Wild West
film!

Dodo sends you her love. She has given me a most lovely quilted
counterpane from Provence as a present. Everything here is so lovely,
the house, the garden, these females and the galloping horses. I am

happy all day long. In fact if it wasn't for a bearded El Greco saint living
in an Ilex bower, I think I could spend the rest of my days here, painting
pictures and riding. I made a Zambalione last night for dinner and just
as it was finished, Henry stepped backwards and knocked the bowl all
over the carpet into the fire place! I was making it by the fire in the
dining room. But fortunately there were masses of eggs, so I quickly
whisked up another one. The foot is much better. I was able to get a
shoe on today. Give Dadie and Topsy my fondest love please. I send
you all my love.   Your ever and always loving MOPSA

[The following poem is undated, but was perhaps written early in her
love for Beakus Penrose.]

Remembrance of Exmouth

He lay asleep on the cliffs high ridge
On the parched brown grass he lay
grass like fur on the wild hare's back
Which shines all silkily. Far deep below
Very far below, the grey sea flapped
as it ran unceasingly back and fro
And little white waves like a scalloped edge
of a petticoat, outlined the vast pewter pot
But he lay asleep in the brilling sun.
His hair bleached corn in the sun's hot rays
His face brick red and moist with sweat.
Eyelashes laying stuck fast to the cheeks
all tight and hot. The sensitive mouth
So proud, uncurled as if in contempt
as if in defiance of the sun. Far far
Below was rolling up the warm grey waves
And all above the hot blue sky
And yet he opened not his eyes for,
certainly make sure of life to him
Filled with that delicious joy of unexplored parts
Yet agonizing pain, because I knew not
What I longed to know.

What passed beneath those fast stuck eyelids
And what felt those proud curved lips
Surely not my enflamed gaze?
Or they could never rest so calmly thus
And so I fled breathless and panting
Down the cliff to the ever moving sea
With madness and despair, and left
the Proud curved lipped youth. Far
High up above me lying there.

To Gerald Brenan

Thursday, May 10th, 1928

Hôtel Nègre-Coste, Aix-en-Provence, France

Amigo Mio, I was sorry to hear that the wind blows at Combe Bisset and
disturbs your inside. Here a mistral blows which fills one's lungs with
dust and makes one's nose run. I reached here on Wednesday morning
with Lytton. We came in a marvellous train out of which one never
moved from Calais to Marseilles. I like Aix extremely. It is very beautiful and full of gay young men and women who parade up and down
the Boulevarde Mirabeau. Lytton has an infinite capacity for 'flanning'
and sitting in cafés. We looked at the market this morinng. Tomorrow
I am going to swim in the mineral baths. This is a very good hotel
with no Americans or English. And the boots is a nègre. I think we
stay here some little time, till next week and then go to Arles and Nimes
perhaps. I'd like to stay in the country and paint. It looked very
beautiful from the train before we reached Aix, high grey rocks, and
olive trees. Are you able to write in the country? I went to a party with
Alix the night before I left London and there I met Arthur [Waley] and
had a long chat with him. 'Do you think Gerald will ever finish anything? I ask because one would like to read his books, as he is by far the
most interesting writer I know.' It was rather a good party. I met the
lovely Kathleen Dillon again. (Now no longer lovely.) And danced a
passionate dance with Dorothy Varda. But it all seems very remote now
and I can't go back, and describe it to you. This is a fine town for cakes.
I expect in a few days I shall be very ill. What a pity English towns have
nothing like this life. One's head instantly becomes filled with a hundred

ideas for painting. And even if one doesn't paint it is pure pleasure to watch these curious black widows, old men with white moustaches, and portfolios, nuns herding petites peuples in white dresses to confirmations and the students of the Univeristy of Aix arguing with each other outside the cafés.

You were so charming the other evening. I enjoyed very much seeing you again. I was only sorry I had to go off so early. I expect we'll be back after Whitsun.

My love   Your C.

To Julia Strachey

Saturday morning [after return from Provence, 1928]
Ham Spray House, Hungerford

Dearest sweet [Thirteen lines omitted and a page missing] ... through the open window carrying a large rat which he lays at his master's feet. Master shrieks 'Horrid creature. Take it away.' Poor Tiber. Life was ever thus. Take it away. How often has one's offering of love laid at the toes of our beloved been greeted by those cutting words 'Take it away.' But Madame

Keep my counterpane
Let not in vain
My gift from Spain

or from Provence as the case may be.

So write to me again. My life is nothing but a whirl of carpenters, engineers and schemes for improvements. I'm getting quite a mechanic over the car now. But perhaps it would be better if I did a little less mechanicing and a little more: who can say? I wish I had a lover. Yes, just this morning I thought how nice it would be with the sun shining in my room and nothing to do, as it was 6 ock. But I read Borrow in bed and soon forgot and now breakfast is over and there are joints to supervise and raspberries to pick and no time for lovers.

To Sebastian Sprott

Saturday, Whitsun 1928   *Ham Spray House, Hungerford*

But 'any way my darling' it's very nice to get a letter from you. Even
although you can't come and stay. No you *will* get a photograph. Only it
just happened I was writing to Morgan and so he got it first. Two copies?
Well, that's asking. What pictures? My memory falls me, fails I mean.
Did you enjoy the Pavilion? Did you have 'heart-to-hearts'. I suppose
Peter was in high feather now that Topsy is alone on her beach once
more. What brutes men are! He-men I mean, my dear. I hope Arthur
[Waley] told you what a success he was with all of us here, and how
devoted I am to him now. He was rather crushing to my advances I
thought, actually! But as faint lady never won Chinese heart, I suppose
I mustn't complain. Lytton has just gone off to Sweden. It's queer how
much I miss him. He's a tremendous prop you know to my existence.
Ralph and Frances are here for Whitsun. No one else. Ralph came back
this morning from Brittany, in high spirits. But it's slightly like going
back to look at Tidmarsh. He brings back a sort of past life and makes
me see that I'm rather 'out' of the present. I slightly resent for some
reason, and obvious reason I suppose, feeling out of it and going off by
myself and being unable to be enthusiastic about Brittany. Suddenly in
the middle of tea this afternoon I felt cross I had no one to go to bed
with when I wanted to. But then, if I had, I should probably be cross
because it wasn't to my taste! I rather envy you your animal variety.
My life is rather too untouched by human hand at moments. Reading
Phèdre with Lytton of course is a very good substitute, curious as it
may seem. I mean I get tremendous pleasure you know by living here.
It's so lovely, and Lytton is such an angel to me. After Cambridge next
week I'm going to stay at Fryern with Dorelia and their exquisite little
sirens. That will be perfect. Then I come back here and probably linger
while the central heating is put in and paint 500 tiles for Margaret
Waley. Would you like a tile to stand your tea pot on? Then don't you
see, you preserve the French polish on your gate leg table—the photographs of Sidney Waterlow,[1] chief Boy Scout, were superb. I say you
mustn't go to Rome. Norman Douglas wrote to Lytton last week and
said it was *so* hot in Florence he had flown to the mountains. But of

[1] Sydney Waterlow, afterwards Ambassador to Greece and old friend of the Stracheys
and Stephens.

course it may have altered now. The cold here is icy, and one shivers in
one's drawers. How was Jim? Not know Jim, in his striped bathing
dress, what do you take me for? My new studio is going to be lovely. I
shall when it's finished, completely change my character and become a
very hardened recluse and paint pictures all day. Then all these spinster
ravings will no longer blast my letters to you. Now I must go and play
badminton, or it will look as if I'm sulky, which I'm not, or cooking the
dinner, which I'm not either. [Two lines omitted] I wish you were
available more often. Really that weekend was one of the nicest we have
had this year. I feel I never tell you quite how much I love seeing you
dear Sebastian. But in a whisper I do enormously. What is Oundle life
like? Any sprees? [Three lines omitted] Lytton read me Zadig last
night, very much to my taste. I go to the Cricket Hut [The Pavilion,
Cambridge] on Tuesday till Friday to paint Dadie's rooms. Oh why did
I ever embark on that foolish business, mere agony to me and mere
mumbo jumbo, as my father used to say, to Dadie. Do write to me and
tell me how you are. I hope the health bears up.

Your most loving CARRINGTON

To Lytton Strachey

Tuesday [August 7th, 1928]   *41 Gordon Square, London*
en route to Cambridge

My darling Lytton, I do hope the crossing wasn't too rough on Saturday
night. It blew rather fiercely at Ham Spray. Sunday was a bosky hot
today so I thought of you flanning on the deck in the grilling sun. We
had Noel and Missie on Saturday to supper. Rather dreary for some
reason. And I felt so tired, and sleepy I couldn't do anything to brisk it
up. On Sunday as it was so lovely, we went for the day to Fryern, Ralph
Frances and me. We has a superb lunch in the Dean Valley, (East of
Salisbury) in a little wood and reached Fryern about half past two. We
then went off and swam in their river. The girls, Romiley [John] and the
governess. Dorelia sat like a voluminous Sibyl in a flowing black dress
on the high bank watching us. Ralph looked so lovely naked, very
brown with the sun, swimming like an enormous Neptune amongst these
sirens. We had tea with Augustus and Trelawney Reed in Fanny's
[Fletcher] new tea shop. But in spite of all the attractions and notice
boards no cars stopped and no customers came. I bought you a lovely
Chinese blue sunshade from Fanny's Chinese department. In a moment

I must whisk off to Cambridge. The photographs of Arthur [Waley], Paul [Hyslop] and Janie [Bussy] are devastating in their realism! I hope you are keeping well and enjoying yourself very much.

We had to leave *before* the central heaters appeared. But Slater is in command and I shall drop in on Friday evening on my way to Fryern and see what the state of affairs is. My studio grows more and more beautiful. You are an angel to give me such a lovely present.

We had a strange party at Fryern on Sunday night, and I had the strangest of strange conversations with old Augustus.

A. 'Do you like Cxxxs Carrington?'
C. 'Um—yes—I do.'
A. 'So do I. I *adore* them.'

Then he confided in me all his love affairs. Dear, oh dear! I missed you very much at Ham Spray this weekend. My very fondest love

your devoted MOPSA

Love to Roger please

PS Saxon wrote me a very peculiar drunk letter from Bayreuth. James and Alix and Nancy come over in their Austin on Monday. Poor Tiber was terribly sad at being left behind today. But I feared Stephen's anger and did not bring him.

To Gerald Brenan

Wednesday [August 30th, 1928]   *Ham Spray House, Hungerford*

Dearest Amigo, It was nice to see you again. You always, you know, charm me rather. The pleasure of cooking mushrooms and meals with you is unique, if I may say so. And then you must know my life is conducted on a sort of fugue basis. I go forwards a few bars and then retreat and pick up the old theme. No, Ralph tells me little about your life; he was mostly concerned with a ravishing beauty at the swimming baths! So I heard very little about you, or Winnie.[1] Life here is one continuous banging with central-heating men and carpenters. I hope in *A Future*, life will be perfect. At present it is far from that. But by concentrating entirely on the mystic month of October, when these three hot pipe vandals will leave us, I manage to hardly notice their presence. My studio is a lovely room, like the bows of a ship with 4

[1] A girl who was sharing Gerald Brenan's flat. Hence he is Duke of Winniepeg.

windows and painted a lovely pale blue. But you will never come here and see it? You might one day, disguised as Lord Dufferin with red whiskers. [Drawing omitted] Helen asked, the other day, me to Ipswich but I'm afraid I can't go. It might have been rather nice if the Duke of Winniepeg had been there. I have 60 tiles to paint. And if I leave the house for more than a day, all the taps will be put in the wrong places. 'So you think.' And so it happens, I assure you.

Arthur wrote me a fine letter from Wales yesterday with a gloomy description of the inmates of his asylum. Give Helen my love when you see her. And do *not* tear my character to shreds! This morning at 7 o'ck I went on the Shalbourne Downs and picked mushrooms with Olive. It was an exquisite pale dewy morning. And I feel very purified inside now. If I come up again I will ring you up and we'll have a supper party together.

My letters are now written in such a different style that I've lost the old art of addressing crotchety amigos. Poppet and Vivien are my only correspondents. And the level I assure you is, although infinitely amorous, infinitely low.

My fondest love   Your C.

PS I did not even tell Ralph I had seen you twice! My life is so poor in secrets I was forced to turn you into one!

To Lytton Strachey

[*November 1st, 1928*]   *The Boot, Quainton, Aylesbury*

Darling Lytton, What do you think? You will never guess. I went to a hunt this morning. Not on a [drawing of horse omitted] but on [drawing of two walking omitted] with a small village girl as a companion. It was the greatest pleasure imaginable. We watched 'the meet' gather and then pursued them on foot where they found an old fox in a wood. But it was impossible to get the old fox on the run, so the horsemen galloped round and round the wood with the dogs baying inside. Twice we saw the fox quite close, but he always redoubled on his tracks and got back into the wood again. I talked to some strange foot retainers. A farmer, and a perfect Oiseaux of an old rustic. We stood and listened to the conversations of the huntsmen. I was pointed out 'Tom Gosling, the best steeplechase rider,' a very gay spark, who cracked jokes with the grooms. All the characters of the riders came out so vividly. Hardened old lined nut cracked men who rode without any expression on their faces. Fat Rowlandson ladies with grey buns of hair and veils, bouncing along on their fat horses. Farmers with elbows sticking out on nags not much better than Belle. By the end of an hour I knew every face. Rosamond lives in an absurd little cottage [drawing omitted] with roses, and arbours. She, and Wogan [Philipps] look like that picture of Alice in Wonderland enlarged. They can scarcely move in and out of rooms and their heads touch the ceilings. I shall come back tomorrow early to London. It's very nice here. So hot and the village looks exquisitely beautiful this morning, with shining thatched cottages in the sun and a great windmill dominating all the little houses like a broody hen, on the green. Wogan has done two very good pictures down here. There are three dogs but—the hearthrug style, that don't leap up on the lap. It's almost too agitating to think of the wardrobe![1] You must write *at once* to Cambridge, and put off the Victorian monster.

I broached our extravagances to the Prince[2] and he seemed rather in favour of the Normandy and *not* very severe!

I write with Ros. and Wogan talking to me, so I can't focus very well on this page.

Wogan looks much better. Ros. very charming. I had a fascinating long conversation with her last night. Oh, but I long for a hunter; I now see it would be perfect happiness to go galloping across a field with red huntsmen cracking whips and hounds baying. The wily old fox defeated them this morning, to my secret delight.

Now I must stop. Well I shall be at Gordon Square at quarter past 11 tomorrow morning. There doesn't seem much point in coming up to night and then we can go down by the lunch train, or afternoon train together. You were so charming yesterday. It was a *perfect* day. My very dear love to my very dear   Your loving MOPSA

To Augustus John

November 23rd, 1928   *Ham Spray House, Hungerford*

Dodo says you would like a letter so if you do not want one you must blame her. I hope you are enjoying Boston. Your Judge's country house looked to me slightly suburban if I may say so ...

[1] Carrington was always referring to Rosamond Lehmann's exquisite clothes.

[2] Ralph Partridge, originally 'our King' owing to his name, Rex, became 'the Prince of Economy' and finally 'the Prince'.

I stayed at Fryern about three weeks ago and had a lovely time riding on the Downs with your ravishing daughters. We had a fine evening tea party in the new forest under some Holly trees. Vivien was so particular about choosing a properly romantic spot that it was almost dark when we had our tea and chestnuts. I've hardly been to London this month so I've no gossip to tell you. I saw Phyllis de Janzé Boyd last week. She has left her Frog Prince, and now lives on her own in some mews in London, all for love of a Captain with no toes. He fell under a train rushing to see her one day and got all his toes cut off. He sounds a very dashing character with 6 hunters; the best steeplechase rider in England and spends £100 a year on hair oil.

Will you go to Clark House in Boston and look at some primitive 19th cent. wall paintings? I have a book on wall decorations in America and they look from the illustrations very good. And if you go to Westwood Massachusetts there are some very good ones there. [Twelve lines omitted]

Please bring back a lovely American beauty for me. But for me remember. Not to be shared. Dodo's little room is exquisite. I must go over soon and finish the cupboards.

I am, dear old chap your loving   CARRINGTON

To Julia Strachey

Saturday, late December 1928   *Ham Spray House, Hungerford*

Darling Julia, This is NO Collins but a pæan of praise for your lovely Christmas present. It arrived today, and really, saving my face, it looks enchanting! I have, of course, put it on, and will probably upset the ink over it at once, but I couldn't resist wearing it. Ralph and Frances think it very beautiful. But I wish *you* were here to admire it! Sweet Spilsbury [dressmaker] is a treasure; and I am going to put a bunch of yellow and pink feathers in the hat. I did love my visit to you. I am always only sorry that the time is so short. For some reason there is a strange enchantment about Swallowcliffe for where else could one find Larmen[1] groves, and dormitories, castellated ruins and swans? To say nothing of upstanding cockatoos and seagulls?[2] (Pardon my humour).

---

[1] A rare exotic tree growing on the Pitt-Rivers estate.

[2] Carrington's nickname for Beakus Penrose, more appropriate for a sailor than 'Snipe'.

I regret to say I behaved disgracefully after I left you for I was faithless to Dorelia and deserted her after lunch. I pretended I was going back to Ham Spray, but really I went off to—is it possible you can guess? We had a fine evening in Southampton together in the drizzling rain, buying a mattress and stores for the ship. Then in the slushing mud, we tramped through docks and saw great masts silhouetted against the night sky, and lights reflected across the harbour from Southampton, and presently found the Sans Pareil[1] with a black cat keeping watch on deck. It's an infinitely romantic ship, with brown varnished cupboards and cut glass handles and a little fire place with a brass mantelpiece. I don't think I've ever enjoyed an evening more in my life, the rain beating down on the deck above, sitting in the cabin lit by lamplight, cooking eggs and sausages over the fire and drinking rum. The Seagull is fascinating on board. He is so in love with his ship that he moons about in a trance opening cupboards and eulogizing over its beauties, in his slow voice. The only disadvantage is, if I may say so, that the bunks aren't built for two sailors alongside. The black puss is a great charmer and sat on the rails of the little balustrade that goes round the bunks peering with green eyes at the midnight feast. The next morning I washed up and cooked an omelette for breakfast and chatted to some sailors who were mending the cabin door.

The Seagull suffered a good deal from my un-nautical language. But was impressed by my lamp trimming. I dashed back to Ham Spray yesterday after lunch, in time to set the house in order, and meet Lytton at the station. I shall tell nobody but you of my romantic evening because nobody but you discerns the true beauty of varnished wood and [drawing omitted] silver suns behind lamps. This is a very tiresome letter I expect. As you can't possibly, without having seen the trawler, see how charming it is!

Tommy will love it I am sure. Molly MacCarthy is here this weekend. I asked her about Anthony Asquith and she says she will *certainly* ask you to dinner with him. But thinks that Mr Knoblock[2] is even better from a producer point of view. She would *love* to go to Swallowcliffe, so will you ask her and talk over your film and the play? I asked [name illegible] about David Herbert, and talked about Wilton. It's quite alright if you go over with him only ring up first, Fordingbridge 73, just to make certain she is there. Augustus was still writing his memoirs

---

[1] The *Sans Pareil* was Beakus Penrose's ship, a Brixham trawler, on which he was then living.

[2] A well-known dramatist.

in bed when I went to lunch. Edwin was just as strange and cryptic and Poppet still in her pyjamas, Vivien was tearing round the field on a horse jumping all the fallen trees. They all loved you, and Tommy. You were a great success. Lytton seems in very good spirits. He goes back to London all next week. I do not know when Lettice[1] comes down so I can make no plans about visiting your country next week until I hear from her. I hope you still keep well. Ralph met Lyn Irvine at a party at Helen Anrep's on Friday and said she was very intelligent but has a younger sister who is a crashing beauty. I gather Lyn is a rosebud, college girl style. Tell me how your Oliver Inez weekend went off. I am going to read the Tchekhov play tonight. Lytton must be shown our theatre. Molly was properly enthusiastic over the idea. You are both so charming NO words can express my love. Only Brand's Essence can (sic).

My love your TANTE C.

<hr />

[1] Wife of Frank Ramsey and old friend of Frances Marshall.

1929

To Julia Strachey

Saturday [*?January 1929*]

In haste

Darling Julia, Lytton says if you can't come on the 4th Feb weekend for
any reason, come on the 11th. Roger Senhouse will be here on the 11th
and would very much like to meet you. But if *you* feel otherwise, well,
mum's the word.

Ouff the rain and the wind. [Illustration of horse under oak too faint
for reproduction] The old horse shelters under the oak, but of what
avail are oaks in such a blast? The howling of a hundred woolves prowl
round the house night and day (which is as much as to say the wind
roareth like unto a woolf). I had two very striking letters from Poppet,
and Vivien John yesterday from France. No visitors this weekend, but
Ralph and Frances. We seem to live on stewed rabbit day after day, until
even the cats [drawing ommitted] turn up their noses. The truth is
the keeper caught 4 rabbits in the garden last week. And as 'Ecomonie'
is the watch word of our house, we must perforce mange lapin. I've been
reading the maxims of La Rochfoucauld, they made such an impression
on me that I intend to start a revival of the text habit over the beds

 ornamented with sprigs of forgetmenots. How do you bear up?

I heard from Helen that you 'looked so lovely like some mysterious
massive tolerant Italian lady of the 16th or 17 century, and she was
exquisitely kind to me'. I wish she'd be a little more exact about her
centuries! Do write soon and say when you can come. My love dear
Poppets xxxx   Your devoted C.

To Julia Strachey

Sunday [February 1929]   *Ham Spray House, Hungerford*

Darling Julia, [seven lines omitted] Oliver who is here with Inez, (and
Bunny) this weekend says you are now an honourable.[1] (I wish you
were 'Lady Julia'. But perhaps in a few years the Judge will be made
a Duke.) Do you like Honourable on your envelopes, or does it send up
the price of the milk? What do you think. I have at last seen Helen
T[omlin]. I went to London the week before last and when I was looking at the Dutch pictures came across little Barbara, Saxon and Helen.
I thought she was *charming*. Such a ravishing expression on her face.
[Twenty-five lines omitted]

To Sebastian Sprott

Sunday, 6.30 [early March 1929]   *Ham Spray House, Hungerford*

But what a horrid scene to see before one when one starts a letter to an
orderly young gentleman *of taste* in Nottingham. Breakfast, lunch and
tea mingled with fragments of Vita Wheat. Jam on the plates, whiskey
jostling with ink pots. You see to what a pass I am reduced and my
chamber pot is still unemptied and the beds NOT made, or is it merely

---

[1] Stephen Tomlin's father had been elevated to the Chancery Bench with the title of
Lord Tomlin.

an excuse for drawing a still-life après le grand maître Monsieur Fry?
Who can tell, who indeed? Olive is away in bed with lumbago, so
Lytton and I have to cook for ourselves. (Lytton is a first-class bed-
maker.) Darling, now my letter begins. You really are rather a [picture
of deer omitted] to give me such a beautiful present. Truly I have never
received anything that gave me half-so-much pleasure. What a
pity you aren't ... You might have added so much pleasure to my life,
dear boy. But there; 'its NO good REPINING over lost balls,' said the
Countess whilst playing croquet with the Archbishop of Canterbury.

'Do you know Sebastian?' said a gentleman at dinner the other night.
'You mean the Man of Taste who lives in Nottingham?'
'Precisely' answered he.

I simply love those prints. They are my favourite style. I wish I could
send you something you would like half-as-much. The ashtray? True.
I had forgotten. I will make it tomorrow, or the day after. Olive took ill
with lumbago 2 weeks ago, so after 10 days of cooking and chamber pots
Lytton and I went off to London last Wednesday, (or rather Lytton to
Cambridge) and I to London.

I had on Wednesday at [The] Etoile a lovely, but curious dinner party
with Morgan, Boy Joe [Ackerley], Gerald H[eard] and a drunkard called
Harold Monro (poet); the latter rather blighted the conversation, and the
evening as he was so boringly drunk. But it was in spite of him, a very
amusing evening. I liked Gerald quite a lot. Morgan wrote me practically
a proposal the next day. Couldn't make head or tail of it, half apologising
for the evening and the rest a bit incoherent. Is he rather unhappy? He
seemed as if he was trying to hide his feelings and to be gay in spite of an
ache in the heart. But I couldn't see him again, so I never had his confidence which he said he wanted to give me. He said you had influenza I am
sorry dearest. Are you better now? I had it in January and felt very
mouldy for quite a long time. Poor Puss was caught in a gin and for two
days and a night, at the height of the snow and blizzards, lay in a wood.

He is still rather ill, and I
fear, will never chase the
hare again. This has rather
upset me for you know how
deeply I love my cat and
what a beautiful creature
he was. Since Christmas all
our energies have gone to
beautifying the house and

making the library. At last it is nearly finished. Lytton seems tolerably pleased with it which means—very much so. He has been in very good spirits, in spite of this cruel devastating cold, frozen pipes, broken motor car and no cook. I think he was very set up by the success of Queen Elizabeth and the central heating certainly makes life far less grim in the winter here—sort of pads over the deficiencies of wayward lovers and cold hearted young men. I've no gossip. Everyone in London seems to be ill. Poor Alix has a septic eye and has to wear black spectacles. Frances has been ill, but mercifully has now recovered. Bunny's wife is ill. Raymond is poisoned with American drink, Lionel's wife is with child, Alec Penrose had to pay £500 damages to the wronged husband for his new mistress. Tommy is now an Honourable. (And Garrow hopes one day to become a Lord.) I have had lunch twice with Lord Wimborne, in his grand house next to the Ritz with footmen (very attractive) with white gloves. My Vicomtess took me there, she has now left her Frog Vicomte and lives in sin with a steeple chasing captain on her own in London. So I see a good deal of her. She's very much my style, very gay, and amusing. I go next Tuesday to Cambridge to see King Lear and stay 2 nights in the Pavilion. Lytton said they were both in better spirits. But the restless Peter was looking for a new mistress; Phyllis unable to stand him any longer. My future is terribly unsettled. I peer, and peer into the crystal but see nothing but a glass wall and a plain middle-aged-face. And how are your Nottingham intrigues? I hope you are enjoying yourself and your [drawing of man bicycling omitted] friend is king. Our new gardener is very kind. He washes up all the plates for me. We go away tomorrow and hope Olive will have recovered by the end of the week. Next term I am resolved to come and stay with you. This term it was too cold to move. Please write me a letter soon and tell me how you are. It was kind of you to think of me, and so tastefully. My very fondest love your fond

CARRINGTON XXX

Later, 9 o'ck, Sunday

PS But I have forgotten *the POINT* of this letter. The cock on the steeple as one might say—[Drawing of cock on steeple omitted] Lytton says will you come here for Easter as long as you like? and if you will (or will not) will you write to him at 37 Gordon Square, or to Mrs C.P. at 41 Gordon Square and say on which date you will arrive and for how long. (PS Please let it be for a long time.) As you keep a time table I am sure you

can have no difficulty in foretelling *your* future. As for me, I peer, and
peer, and stare, and stare and see nothing but the Pavilion on Tuesday
and shudder at the thought and peer and peer and see only Lear, and
again shudder at the thought. But should I peer and peer, and see my
Sebastian dear, then I'd no shud–dear, but order small-beer and—
apple turn-over.

New style of poetry in vogue at Cambridge. Really my dear the new
poetry numbers: 'The Venture' and 'Experiment'—you could hardly
believe it possible. Since I started this letter, the stove has gone out and
as usual I've drunk too much. Be a d–g and answer this PS as 'much'
HANGS ON your answer. [Drawing of a dog hanging on gallows omitted]

MY LOVE YOUR devoted C.

To Julia Strachey

[*End of March or early April 1929*]　　　*Ham Spray House, Hungerford*

Darling Julia, I write upside down under the spreading beech tree in the
sun. I was *delighted* to hear from you. '*Dowager* Doris Lady P.' if you

don't mind my dear. Tiber is much better. He has taken on a new character and is rather commanding and since he only has three legs, even Lytton is forced by Cat-Public-Opinion to get up and open the doors for him. When I was in France, Lytton stayed at the Old Rectory Hall with sweet Ros, and Wogan and their little doggies. But I was disappointed that he never once saw her in the cloud-green-chiffon tea gown writing her novel. [Five lines omitted] Lytton liked Wogan's pictures. I agree with every word you say about the Riviera. In fact I thought it the most hideous place I'd ever stayed at. Those dingy green pines and the villas, The Blue Bird, Bella Vista, Rest Dean, Kamjabee, Ma Retreat. But as Dorelia said it's rather a relief that all the rich odious inhabitants of the world should collect together in such an ugly place. For they leave the rest of France empty. I loved Dorelia. She is a most fascinating companion. I've had some grand pub crawls with old Augustus in the evenings. And went to some fashionable nightclubs in Monte Carlo with Poppet and Vivien and Kit Dunn. The Dunns are millionaire Canadians who owned the John's Villa. Kit was dimly like Henrietta, very bulky and strong, with school boy high spirits. Sir James D. who met our train at Dover with a Pullman was an appalling character 'vigorous at 50'. Practically Kruschen-Salts. Augustus had been painting portraits of the Dunn family for 2 months down there. Vivien was fascinating. Poppet slightly enfeebled in the head with falling 'in love' every day with a new young man. For a week it was perfect. Very hot and the most exquisite flowers in the garden. I think your Bibury idea is very good. Why on earth should you think I'd disapprove!! I'd go 50 miles any day to see a new house and its occupants. I always wish we knew more people in the country. I think there's NO greater pleasure than 'a visitor's bedroom' and new breakfasts. The Bibury country is lovely. I once paid Will Rothenstein a visit when he lived there. I've been rather in despair as Olive is still ill. I really went off for a holiday hoping to find her recovered when I came back, but unfortunately she is still in bed. The doctor says she is 'run down' but I have a sickening feeling it may be something worse so really most of my time lately has been spent cooking and emptying chamber pots. Ralph is bringing down his servant Mabel and her sister for Easter which will be a relief. Then I suppose I shall have to try and get a temporary, or a new girl. It's a frightful bore. I'm not a bit against Tommy's wall-decoration sculpture. It's only sometimes I get into a panic and wonder whether he will ever be able to make it stick on to the wall. (I get these panics when for no reason a great chunk of plaster suddenly falls off on to the lawn.)

Don't you think it's rather important to find out some one who has
stuck sculpture on to a concrete wall and discover the technique? But I
expect Tommy knows about it as much as anybody. Lytton, I think, had
a slight feeling that Tommy wasn't very keen on it perhaps. But if he
still is, I do hope he will come soon and stay with you and start it here
properly. For you must know, darling, that I am such an ardent admirer
of everything Tommy does, that I am always in favour of Ham Spray
gleaning as many of his works as possible. How is your short story?
When I was away in France I told the Slaters to paint the 'back sitting
room' cream. On my return I found my favourite blue front sitting
room painted out! For they call the 'back' of the house the 'front' and
vice versa. So I am rather bored with internal beautifying at the moment!
This weather is enchanting. Lytton and I go long walks and have all our
meals in the verandah. He has gone to London today to see the first
night of Cochran's Review with Lady Cunard. When will you come
here? You must suggest yourselves whenever you like. I've just tidied
up my studio and directly this servant crisis is over I shall draw up my
'plan' for your inspection and start on a new era of work and discipline.
The spelling seems rather drunk today. I am sorry. I love you so much
Julia. I hope Tommy is keeping well and happy.

All my love your C.

To Lytton Strachey

Tuesday evening, 7 o'ck May 21st 1929
Ham Spray House, Hungerford

My darling Lytton, [Seventeen lines omitted]
    It is such a lovely evening that my tranquillity and good humour have
returned. The poor rook is DEAD. I must make a little tombstone of
cowslips for him tomorrow. Puss is in high spirits. Nothing ever lowers
that cat. Dead rooks, dead cars, dead Mopsa's, it's nothing to him. I hope
you'll have a perfect time at Cambridge.
    I suppose we may assume that Peter Morris won't come. Missie
writes from Arles to say the weather is perfect, and they are enjoying
themselves very much. Noel didn't allow her to go to Aix, not time on
their programme, (secretly I am rather glad!). It was sad you couldn't come
last night. You would have loved the beauty of that dark yew wood with

its tunnels and nightingales. And Augustus playing melancholy Welsh airs on the mouth organ. Ralph is coming back on Friday evening. And what shall we drink for supper tonight??? What indeed. When the cat is away the mice will make hay.

You can't think how much I miss you. I would like you only to go away on wet gloomy days. It seems monstrous to waste a beautiful evening like this without you. I hear Dodo's car I must fly.

My fondest love   Your very very loving MOPSA
PS Love to Dadie.

To Lytton Strachey

Wednesday afternoon, May 22nd, 1929   Ham Spray House, Hungerford

Darling Lytton, I send you a budget of letters. I am rather boozed and befuddled with drink so forgive a poorish letter. Dorelia appeared yesterday, very late at 8 o'ck with the Earps[1] and Fanny Fletcher. We had a fine dinner with Moselle and burgundy, cold salmon and tartar sauce, followed by gammon and salad, followed by strawberries and kirsch, followed by brandies and coffee. The conversation *seemed* to me very brilliant and amusing, but perhaps it wasn't really. They stayed the night and went this afternoon after lunch. Dorelia sent you her love and Tommy sent his regards. I now lie in a drunken trance with darling Tiber on the sofa. Tiber came in for a tremendous amount of admiration from the cat-lovers. Everyone agreed he was the best cat that they had ever seen. Olive's little sister is better today. There seems a chance that she may recover. A cruel west wind rose up last night and now roars round the house. So basking days seem over. I hope it doesn't travel as far as Cambridge. Chatto have sent you a book on Gibbon. I

---

[1] Tommy Earp, art critic and subject of many anecdotes, and his wife.

send their letter. Dorelia loved your library and our botanical Dutch books. I wish she could have stayed, but she had Augustus and a tribe of visitors shrieking at Fryern today. In a moment I shall go to sleep but I must first order the wine bottles.[1] I shan't drink another drop now, till you return, and tomorrow I shall start a painting of tulips. Give Dadie my fondest love. I hope you are keeping well and enjoying yourself.

Your devoted loving intoxicated   MOPSA XXX

To Lytton Strachey

Monday, June 3rd, 1929   *Ham Spray House, Hungerford*

Darling Lytton, Thank you for the sumptuous dining room,[2] we had a fine party last night at Fryern. I drove over in Beackus' racing Bentley. He is a very careful driver, curiously efficient and on the spot. The Earps were there, a Christ-like artist called Lamborne, old Augustus in very good spirits, Mr. and Mrs. Keane of Tooth's Gallery and Dorelia dressed like a Chinese woman in spotted pink trouser and coat, looking divinely beautiful.

Beackus as I predicted thought it the most sympathetic house. 'One feels quite at home here and I've never seen so many beautiful women. And I like that table'. He got off with Mrs. Earp which absolutely enraged Alec, who thought her 'common' and unworthy of the noble Penrose taste. We got back at one o'ck. This morning I feel a little dim in the head with too much sherry. Everyone goes off at 11.30. [Two lines omitted] I had to pay £1.11.0 for tea-pot (which arrived broken so I have returned it with curses) and plates etc. etc. from Goods's on Saturday so it was just as well that you left me a little money! The weather seems querulous today. We bottled one cask of white on Saturday. I'll get Olive to help me do the red perhaps this week. It's really very simple with the new system. I've not heard from Iris [Tree] yet about the weekend. But I've written to Fitzroy Square in case she didn't get the other letter.

I wonder if you found any jewels at Bath?

I hope you'll enjoy London very much this week. Now I must stop.

My fondest love   Your devoted loving MOPSA

---

[1] They imported wine in barrels and bottled them at Ham Spray. See letter June 3rd, 1929.

[2] Lytton had sent her a postcard of the dining-room at the Pulteney Hotel, Bath.

To Julia Strachey

July 1st, 1929   *Den Haag*

Darling Julia, Thank you very much for your letter. We have been
ensconced in Holland since Saturday. The Dutch are extremely plain,
slow, and lacking in sensibility, (to my way of thinking). In their favour:
the coffee is good, some of the architecture very beautiful and lovely
pictures in the galleries.

We saw a fine zoo yesterday at Rotterdam mixed up with a botanical
garden, a great improvement on our rather sordid London Zoo. Lytton
says as far as he knows the first 2 weeks in August will be alright for a
visit and a 'sitting',[1] if this would suit you, or almost any time mid-
weeks in July. Will you tell Tommy?

I wish you were here for a chat. I must say I adore our conversations
together. I make a great many observations which I mean to tell you.
But now they have passed away. Perhaps after breakfast my wits will
return. Sebastian is very sympathetic company. Yesterday we went to a
lovely modern collection of pictures, mostly Van Goghs, but two divine
Seurats and a beautiful Renoir portrait of a clown, which I'd never seen
even in reproductions.

We've had one grand dinner so far, enormous varieties of hors
d'oeuvres: literally 20 dishes, turtle soup (too much peppered). Salmon.
Wild boar with 6 vegetables surrounding it on the dish and then roast
chicken and prune sauce and a slice of pineapple and a peach (really a
delightful mixture which I recommend.) Asparagus, ices, 6 fruits
strawberries to peaches. This was what was called the 'small dinner'.
The 'Larger menu' ended up on lobster. All the time a band of
Javanese coffee coloured musicians played passionate passages from the
greater Italian operas dressed in cherry red uniforms with gold frogs.

The Dutch under the influence of food and drink lapse back (even in
the grand restaurants) into amorous scenes by Rubens, loll in their chairs,
burst into coarse laughter and tinkle glasses together. So far I have seen no
interesting cats. This so called 'Dutch cleanliness' is rather a myth. The
streets are strewn with tram tickets and paper papers. An awful depression overtook me yesterday after looking at all these lovely pictures. My

---

[1] Stephen Tomlin was to model a head of Lytton. A cast is in the Tate Gallery,
another in the possession of the Editor.

life has been frittered away without producing anything worth looking at. You must at least learn by my sad example and finish your novel. Lytton continually asks whether you are writing. He was such an admirer of that letter. I'll give you a spare room when you come to stay with us and we will be a hive of bees buzzing from morning to night.

My fondest love   Your devoted C.

To Lytton Strachey

Saturday, August 17th, 1929   *Ham Spray House, Hungerford*

Darling Lytton, Not much news since you left. Ralph came yesterday and was very charming and full of incredible scandals and amazing stories.

We went a walk after a fine dinner (of stewed mushrooms and cold chicken) across the fields. It was a lovely evening. This morning we tried to find some mushrooms but they are over. Only a few dried bones to be found where last week they grew in hundreds. The photographs are very good. I have ordered another 1 dozen.

Monday, August 19th

Your letter came this morning. I was delighted to hear all your news. I can't write properly, as my head is completely exhausted by an unexpected weekend of endless activity and exhaustion. On Saturday morning little MacCarthys[1] and F[rances] arrived for lunch. Then Saxon for tea and suddenly as Saxon and I were walking in the park we saw a fifth apostle had joined the group in the distance. Even across the park there was no mistaking that fiery red face and short figure, not Norman Douglas, our old friend Beackus.

He had clearly dropped in for a weekend, very vaguely of course. All Saturday evening was spent planning a cinema performance as he had brought his camera. [Two lines omitted] Of course Ralph was very tiresome and destroyed every idea that was suggested until he had to be ignored!

On Sunday morning at 7 o'ck I started making 'dummies' and masks and finding properties. Arguments took up most of morning whilst the sun shone very brightly, almost 12 o'ck when the sun had completely retired, the company got under way. I must say it was great fun. Saxon in the leading role as Dr. Turner acted superbly. Rachael was a simple

---

[1] Rachel and Dermot, daughter and son of Desmond and Molly MacCarthy.

girl called Daisy, the rest of us were lunatics in Dr. Turner's mental home. (Of course I forgot that Saxon's father kept a 'Home'!! But I am sure Saxon didn't mind the coincidence.) We didn't have lunch till 2.30 and the whole afternoon was given over to drowning Rachael in the bath by the greenhouse.

This morning I've started before breakfast and at 11 o'ck the film was finished.

The doctor just had time to act his last scene before catching his train!

The mess and confusion left after all the acting is rather devastating and Ralph asked them to stay to lunch, which was rather a bore, as it was a great opportunity to let them go back with Beackus *before* lunch. At least the owl lunatic thought it was—puss played a large part in the film with great success. It is to be performed next Thursday at 41 Gordon Square. I suppose you won't be able to come up? [Three lines omitted]

I hope you enjoyed Horner Hall. Very interested about Siegfried [Sassoon] and Stephen [Tennant]. I *long* to visit the Snakerie. [Two lines omitted] I think the counsels of Tommy are more wise. (wiser?) I wish I'd taken more photographs of Roger [Senhouse] that day. I doubt if he'll ever look so lovely again. Isn't the Frog-Princess[1] a dream? I had a long letter from her this morning. Flowing over with gratitude and love. Please take care of yourself. I love you so much I can't bear you to be unhappy or ill. Now I must go and attend to the lunatics.

My very fondest love   Your loving MOPSA

To Lytton Strachey

Monday, August 19th, 1929   *Ham Spray House, Hungerford*

Darlingest Lytton, I forgot to give this to Ralph. I hope it will reach you safely.

I feel rather in the doldrums this afternoon. Partly because it seems a bit hollow and empty after the wild shrieks and gaiety of the weekend, and then one of those tiresome moods of craving for a little $\sim \sim \sim \sim$ came upon me. But I expect it will soon pass, only it's boring to feel so gloomy.

[1] Phyllis de Janzé.

Alix hasn't appeared or written yet. I hope she will this evening. But perhaps she'll get entrapped in the snares and gins of London. It's a lovely day here. Very hot and bosky. I am going myself to Fortnum and Mason on Thursday as Ralph didn't seem very anxious to go. My fondest love.

You are more to me than anybody else, you know. I don't know what I should do without you.

Your devoted MOPSA

PS The gamekeeper brought us a fine hare on Friday with Major Huth's compts!

[Lytton replied to this letter ending with the words: 'I hope your cheerfulness has returned and that Alix has appeared. I cannot try to say all you are to me. I feel that I am often as bad as Roger! But I hope not always! All my fondest love. Lytton.']

To Lytton Strachey

Wednesday, August 21st, 1929   *Ham Spray House, Hungerford*

Darling Lytton, It is the *most* beautiful bird I have ever seen. Even more lovely than the green parrot. You are an angel to give me such an exquisite present. Thank you a million times. I shall take it to London tomorrow to be framed at Pecks. Perhaps a silver wood frame would look best. Alix has restored my spirits and I am much happier.

Last night, before dinner, we walked past Walbury camp to the most distant downs further than I've ever walked before, where there are the most romantic groves of broom with black seed-pods that rattle in the wind. I am glad you got some curious pleasures out of Mells,[1] and found the Eton boys interesting. The rest of the company sounded rather drear. Did you spy any desks in the antiquaries of Bath?

James comes down this afternoon to Newbury at 4 o'ck. Fortnum and Mason say my prices are too expensive but ask for an interview at 3 o'ck tomorrow.

I foresee there is a fate against me ever making a fortune!

I shall see Ralph first at lunch tomorrow and ask his advice, before I visit that nest of caviare, and pâtés.

[1] Lytton had been staying with Lady Horner at her country house at Mells in Somerset.

I've asked Dodo here for the weekend alone with me. She's a little vague if she can come but I hope she will. If she can't I expect I could go over there instead. Inkpen Flower Show tomorrow. Batten sends some of our onions!

I go up by the 11.30, and leave the car at Newbury to get the door mended, and will probably come back on Friday evening here. I hope you had a lovely evening with the boys. Isn't it rather a good mark for Brian [Howard] taking to John Banting?

I suppose you didn't glean any information about swimming baths from la Horner?

I've had some fascinating conversations with Alix lying on the lawn in the sun. Really one is very fortunate to have such friends as Julia and Tommy, and Alix, and to have a Fakir, who with a wave of a wand, can send a golden parrot to his most loving and

[Lytton was staying with Jack and Mary Hutchinson at Eleanor. Carrington wrote from Henry and Pansy Lamb's house.]

To Lytton Strachey

Tuesday morning, August 27th, 1929   *Coombe Bissett, Salisbury*

Darling Lytton, Your wire came yesterday morning. I asked for your address by return wire because I thought you might like your letters sent on by Olive today to Chichester but I left Fryern before your reply came. So there may be a delay now. Well life has been a 'queer-snitch' or however the Germans spell that word (crosscut) since I left you. So frenzied that it seems more like a dream than reality. On Saturday morning I lay in bed late and recovered from the efforts of entertaining Mr. and

Mrs. Hubert H[enderson]. It was such an exquisite day I wandered about
the garden unable to make up my mind to do anything. About 2 o'ck I
set off in the car, left the washing and Lord Tiberius at Shalbourne, and
reached Salisbury soon after 3. Had my hair washed by a lovely female
with a Raphael face. But *not* a very good hair dresser unfortunately.
Reached Fryern for tea. After tea we sat in the fields in front of the
house and watched Poppet and Vivien jumping gates and hurdles.
Practising for the Romsey Horse Show on Wednesday.—I suppose you
won't be coming with Mary [Hutchinson]?—They looked so lovely with
bare legs and striped jersies. Kit Dunn was there too. She rides very
well, old Augustus said to me 'Must do a painting of Poppet jumping
those hurdles. Only don't you think it would look better it she hadn't
those breeches on?' The garden at Fryern is filled with ravishing flowers
in spite of droughts. Grapes fell into one's mouth and peaches lie upon
the walks.

There's no doubt green sand isn't green soil.[1] Oiseau Edwin [John]
more oiseauish than ever, appeared for dinner. On Sunday morning I
looked at Augustus' pictures, and had my usual proposal. He gave me a
very romantic poem, not indecent, curiously sad. Then Kit, and Poppet
and I went a long ride on the Downs. The horses were very fresh with
oats, and we went a terrifying speed. I wish you could walk across that
country. At this time of the year with yellow stubble fields, and great
dark yew woods it looks very amazing.

After lunch I painted a picture of a thorn apple tree in flower in the
garden on a huge canvas. The little Beackus turned up on his way to
Southampton at 4 o'ck. Followed in 5 mins by Sir James Dunn in a
Rolls Royce, and by Lois Sturt and her lover, a hideous bald headed man,
Capt. Fellows or Freeman? Dorelia then said she could bear it no longer,
so we fled to Fanny's cottage to tea, leaving Augustus to entertain Lois
and lover. But I've left out Col. Lawrence, or Shaw, who appeared in the
afternoon on his powerful bicycle. I met [him] in the garden going off to
Augustus' studio to be painted. He looked a measley little man, if I may
say so. Beackus came down with us to Fanny's. I chose some papers for
your bedroom in Gordon Square and she will print us some specimens.
We waited there till we saw Lois tearing along the road in her Mercedes,
and then retreated back to Fryern.

In half an hour another car, Naps Alington,[2] his cousin, Philip Yorke,
both half naked in vests and a ravishing female beauty a cousin of Nap's

---

[1] Carrington believed that Ham Spray was on the Greensand.
[2] Humphrey Napier Sturt, 2nd Lord Alington.

wife, (who is bulging with child so didn't come). They had been swimming at Kimmeridge. They lingered for [an] hour, carrying on a most extraordinary patois between themselves. Then we got rid of them and went off in three cars to the New Forest for a picnic. It was dark by the time we got there. The sun just setting. A beautiful dinner of cold chicken, and ham, and corton. We stayed there till the stars freckled the sky, and one could hardly see anything but the shapes of the trees. Fanny distinguished herself by singing in a cracked witch voice, songs. Beackus struck up some sea shanties. Old Augustus played hymns on a mouth organ and Edwin sang melancholy French songs. For some reason we had a fight with Edwin and got thrown into gorse bushes. So my legs are now a mass of prickles and thorns. We got back at half past 10 to Fryern, at 11 o'ck Naps and his cousin Yorke came reeling in, Naps looking very marvellous in a complete evening dress of black velvet. He is a very odd character, looks Jewish and Russian. He gave strange accounts of freaks at fairs. He has a passion for them. They stayed till about 2 o'ck, getting drunker and drunker. Naps has an appalling cough. I do not think he will live long. But I thought for pure S.A. he had more than almost any man I have met. Except for our friend of Boulestin's the Viennese count! Monday morning all the flowers looked very faded. Poor old Augustus as pale as a lily. [Twenty-four lines omitted]

I worked all Thursday at my painting. And in the afternoon came over here to tea. Mr. and Mrs. Francis Dodd[1] of Manchester appeared for tea, ghosts from Henry's past. A terrible couple! Lady Mary is here. So beautiful that I can do nothing, but gaze with rapture. I talked a good deal to her alone. She is very charming. Pansy and Henry seem very happy. Their garden *again*, is filled with flowers, and dropping with plums and apples. Really we are not under the star of Ceres, most assuredly. I hope you will have a lovely time with Mary [Hutchinson]. I shall go back on Thursday morning to Ham Spray. I post back to Fryern and my painting of the thorn apple this morning. This evening Dodo and I are going to Southampton to see the Macnamaras and visit Beackus' ship! I am enjoying myself very much. [One line omitted] Forgive such a straggling long letter.

My very fondest love,   Your devoted MOPSA XXX

---

[1] Francis Dodd was a painter.

To Lytton Strachey

Thursday, August 29th, 1929   *Fryern Court, Fordingbridge*

Darling Lyttoff, I couldn't post the letter I wrote to you yesterday till
rather late, (and even then I had to give it to an unknown female at the
horse show to post). So I don't know if you ever got it. I enjoyed the
Horse Show very much. Vivien with great courage entered every single
competition. But of course hadn't a chance as the other horses were very
grand, and much faster.—There was a charming assembly of rustics,
horsey-grooms. The hunting 'county', and aristocrats. It took place in
an enormous park just outside Romsey belonging to Col. Ashley (?).

We stayed till 7.30 o'ck and left three huge plough boys wrestling on
cart horses in the twilight. I was rather tired by the time we got back. It
is a lovely drive from here to Romsey across the moors of the New
Forest. Today Augustus and Dodo have gone up to London, and Edwin
goes back to France. I shall drive back after dropping Edwin at Southampton and looking at Beackus' ship. I've finished Dodo's little room,
so I leave with a quiet conscience. The weather is heavenly today. So
hot one can hardly walk across the garden without creeping into the
shade. Their great pond is nearly finished. It looks very beautiful
already although it's not yet filled with water. It *will* be lovely to see you
again on Friday, if only for a little. I still can't make out why Tommy
and Alix came to stay without a word! But I suppose the truth will leak
out one day.

My very fondest love   Your devoted MOPSA XXXX

[In one of her diaries (August 29th, 1929) Carrington wrote of that
evening:
'We looked at the ship. It was odd to see his bunk. So fuggy and dark.
Then we went to dinner and had fried soles. It was all very congenial.
Then E[dwin John] went off and we walked to the car in a square with a
church. As I drove down a street we kissed. Then we drove back across
the ferry to the shipyard. It reminded me of something years ago,
when one couldn't sit indoors. Hampstead Heath—and kissed with the
evening air on one's face. We said "we must go" and never went. Lurching sailors passed us, and a water cart with a lantern. "You must go
back." "Yes, I must" and still one didn't move, and then one moved and
sat still again. And I said to myself "Nothing can ever be as nice as this

again." The smell of decaying wood and sea weed, the lights in the distance and the feeling it was different from any other evening. At last about half past twelve, we parted and I drove across the ferry and he went back to his bunk.

' ... At two o'clock I dropped silently into Fryern and fell into "Caspar's bed". Not a sound in the house. I left before they were up.']

To Lytton Strachey

Wednesday, September 18th, 1929   *28 Mallord Street, Chelsea*

Darling Lytton, I sent you an address last night. So far as I can gather, we go straight to this 18 cent. chateau, and stay with these friends for 4 or 5 days. Then Augustus leaves Dodo, and me, and returns to England. He has to be back to paint the manager of Bank of England in a week. So it's certain he will go back.

Then Dodo and I will go off together choosing urns, and chests of drawers. I had rather a collapse last night. We went to dinner at the Tour, where I got very drunk on hock, in spite of all my intentions to keep a clean palate for Burgundy.

We had Sibyl Vincent (a niece of D'Abernon) rather a strange beauty, and Liam O'Flaherty with us. He is a very attractive Irish writer. What Gerald Heard ought to look like, same style. We also had Aleister Crowley at the end of dinner, a most impossible charlatan, looks like a north country pork manufacturer and speaks with a cockney-american accent.

A.C. 'Now where have I met you before? In a bar in Dublin?'

D.C. 'That's right, it was in Dublin!'

After dinner, we went, (*without* the High Priest fortunately) to a Russian restaurant in Piccadilly, a dreadful place with sham cossacks, where I regret to say, to my shame, I passed away insensible after drinking some glasses of vodka, and had to be removed home by Dodo, a sad ending to a charming evening. So this morning 3 very wobbly wobblers sail for France, accompanied by 2 Siamese cats!

I'll write an account of our travels. I hope you are enjoying Charleston.
I feel rather dim this morning with an aching head. So forgive my letter
being rather dreary. My love to any companions, you may have with
you.   Your loving adoring MOPSA

PS I don't expect we'll be away more than 2 weeks. So I shall be back
really very soon. Please if you aren't well, or want me, wire to the
Chateau, and I'll come straight home.

To Lytton Strachey

September 21st, 1929   *Château Missery, Côte D'Or (nr Saulieu)*

Darling Lytton, You have no idea what a marvellous chateau this is!!
It is difficult to believe it is not a strange dream. I lie at the moment in a
bedroom with walls 25 feet high. (The door is certainly 12 ft and it goes
more than twice in the walls). I will try and get a postcard to send you
today. The towers are 14 cent. there are four. The old chateau was
burnt down and this one was built in the late 17 century. It's a very
beautiful colour outside, pale pinkish cream, with a red tiled roof, and a
wide moat (30 feet across) with a most unusual balustrade of stone,
running right round the chateau. The old American, (who has lately
died) was an architect, so the inside is very carefully restored and
sympathetically furnished. He bought the place for £1000. Doesn't that
enrage one?!!! But Dodo told me in confidence, he spent £4000 repair-
ing *one* of the old towers and much more on the house. For when he found
it, [it] was inhabited by chickens and an abbé and two aged spinsters,
who lived in the kitchen and two rooms at the end of the house. The
American bought back all the old family portraits that used to be in the
hall. They found quantities of old MSS in an attic. Ach! Ach! Perhaps
today I'll be able to glean something about the family that used to live
here. Our host is a very dull young man about 30, a business man and a
great aviator in the war. He seems very amiable but stupid. His wife is a
dark beauty, very talkative and gay. She looks Spanish, I should say
about 25. What is queer is that with all her silliness, she plays the piano
extremely well and with great seriousness. The other inhabitants are 2
other business American friends. One is a bon viveur bachelor who
lives in Paris (great jokes last night about his being a bachelor but not
our style of joke). The other is a depressed young man who is married

to a French woman (not here). Then very late last night two more visitors arrived, the partner of our host and his wife, who also live in Paris. I gather they are all stock brokers. I am sure friends of Roger's [Senhouse] if only I asked! We drove over 160 miles from Reims yesterday and got here by 7 o'ck. Before we started we had a grand bottle of champagne and oysters at a bar. Very delicious at 10 o'ck in the morning I can assure you! Augustus and I inspected the cathedral of Reims which I think has been very much improved by being battered in the war. I fear they are now restoring it. Reims is a sympathetic town. But the modern buildings they are running up have almost ruined it.

We stopped for lunch at our old friend Troyes. Had most marvellous cooking and a bottle of Clos de Vougeot, of which I shall order at least a dozen it was so delicious. We passed Semur but didn't go through it. It looked very lovely in the evening light with its towers, and high walls. I was almost dead yesterday evening after our terrific drive. (There was a miniature mistral blowing all the time in our faces), and all this perpetual boozing and overeating. It was difficult to sparkle to thick headed Americans and eat a marvellous 8 course dinner, with hock and the grandest claret from the cellars. Augustus said the old father laid down a very grand collection of wines here. Today I believe we all go off to Beaune, wine tasting. I see I shall return a complete wreck! What is awful to think of, is that these imbecile Americans only live here for about 2 months in the year! I shall try and escape and do some drawings tomorrow. I have a grand bathroom adjoining my bedroom. The Siamese cats reached the end of their journey safely. They were very much admired by the French servants. One has just joined me in bed and is gnawing my fingers. I wish a thousand times a day that you were with me. The Demon Cat will jump on your letter and prevent me from writing. Dodo has been an angel to me all the time. So charming and amusing. Augustus made positively serious proposals at Reims, but received a rebuff very kindly. He fortunately doesn't seem to mind in the least! They say the vintage doesn't begin till the 1st week in October round here. 'A pussy cat's bite is not my delight.'

Unfortunately it seems my Demon companion's one pleasure. You have no idea the entertainment

they provided on the way. Frantic chases. An earthy bedpan which
accompanied us everywhere. Halts on the wayside for little 'busi-
nesses'. I think Augustus will go back on Monday by train and then
Dodo and I will have a week by ourselves pottering about. But I do
not know of any address. So I'm afraid it's hopeless to write. Please
give Roger my love. I can hear the carp splashing in the moat
below my window and the woodpecker shrieking across the orchard
and the fields. The landscape is covered in a white mist, so I hope it
will be a hot day. So far the weather has been distinctly autumnal, and
almost unpleasant. There was a hot sun yesterday but the wind
negafied it. I think of you very often.

My fondest love and a great many endearments.

Your devoted MOPSA

To Lytton Strachey

Friday, September 27th, 1929   *Martigues not Ham Spray*
[*Ham Spray crossed out*]

Darling Lytton, We travel so fast that my letters soon get out of date.
It is a perfect holiday only I wish you were sitting with us in the car.
[Twenty-five lines omitted] I think the Rhône valley is fascinating,
much better than it looks from the train. They are picking grapes in all
the vineyards and one passes continuously great waggons loaded with
barrels of glistening berries and as one meanders through villages,
buffets of wine come out of the courtyards. I am getting quite brave,
imitating Augustus, and yelling out 'Monsieur la route pour Nîmes?'
Typically when we resorted to a map yesterday we almost instantly got
lost and spent hours circling round the country in search of Beaucaire!

I have never seen this country look so beautiful as it does now,
everywhere these amiable wine activities. Viviers was a perfect town,
and quite a good hotel, although very small. We climbed through the
town after breakfast and saw the cathedral and peered down on a vast
vista stretching up the Rhône valley. Whilst we were watching at some
pressing, the owner came out, and begged us to taste his grapes, and
with incredibly dirty fingers fished about in huge tub of shining wet
grapes, (also covered with wasps, and flies) for a special bunch of
muscatels for the Princess Dorelia. At last he found a worthy bunch!

I must say they were delicious. He then showed us over his house which was 16 cent covered with curious Renaissance stone carvings. Perhaps I sent you a card. There were old Renaissance frescoes on the walls. But the whole place was incredibly dirty and only used for wine pressing. 'My brother he is cook in England at the Langham Hotel' he told us in French. You would marvel at my long conversations in that language! Dodo is the most perfect companion. I shall never forget the dreamy way she said in Dijon, 'Lets go down to Provence. I am sure it would be very nice down there. I've a hankering to see some olives'. She is longing to buy an old Roman villa in this country, outside Martigues. We passed it yesterday, a divine old ruin, with cypresses, and pines and old columns at the gate way. But invested by mosquitoes, which rather damped Dorelia's enthusiasm. Martigues is an extraordinary place. Filled with fishermen, I have never seen such beauties of both sexes. Paul Cross would look positively plain here. They are enormously strong and brown and, in the evening, flane up and down under the plane trees, the men walking in threes and fours arm in arm and the girls walking in threes and fours separately. Just laughing and talking and then walking on again. The cafés are filled; Arabs, Spaniards, and fishermen. So far on our whole journey, we haven't heard a single word of English spoken, or seen any English or Americans. Rather a triumph. I drove the car the whole day yesterday till we reached Salon. So I shall come back a very proficient French driver. I hope there may be a letter from you today. It was with great difficulty I managed to pin Dodo down to admitting she intended to come to Martigues!—We drink half a bottle for lunch every day with cheese, and a salad at some small inn. Then another half bottle and a brioche for tea and a whole bottle of very grand wine for dinner. This letter was interrupted by an expedition yesterday to our darling Aix. It was a lovely drive round the edge of the lake and across great red ochre hills with burnt Roman pines on them. When we reached Nègre coste what do you think? A charming Negro in buttons rushed out, and piloted our car to the side of the road. 'Tout c'est changé ici!' Indeed you would hardly recognize the hotel without our old friend, the waiter. The new waiter is a brisk little Italian, with two under waiters. Lunch served outside under the planes. Old Madame recognized me and was charming and asked after 'Monsieur' and the lunch! Hare pâté, grilled red mullet, a marvellous salad and delicious coffee, and Château des Papes Telegraphe, a whole bottle; our resolutions for a cheese and salad lunch faded away! Inside it is still as charming as ever, only this marvellous change in the cooking. We then visited

the library, which Dorelia admired in the proper spirit. Tried to find
our old rag and bone shop, where I bought the counterpane. But they
had left the town, so that odd female and her stable of furniture are
never to be seen again. Found a new antiquité. But not much good.
Visited our old ones; Madame was away, so we could get nothing out of
the shop, as there was an old man imbecile, in charge. Visited the artist
antiquité, sweet boy was there and remembered me. I rather wanted to
buy two small arm chairs for you, 100 francs each. But we didn't decide
definitely. There is a lovely writing desk at Madame's shop (the courtyard one) which I think it's worth going back to ask the price. We had
tea in our old tea shop. Just the same and went to the picture gallery,
and saw the Rembrandt, and Ingres. Aix was looking very beautiful. It
was an absolutely still day with a hot sun. I drove the car all the way
back, and we reached Martigues about 7 o'ck, and had a grand dinner at
Pascals, an Italian place where Dorelia is adored, on the each [? edge]
of the quay. It was pleasant sipping Marsala in a little bamboo hut over
hanging the water, listening to the lapping water, and watching the sky
grow dark, and dark fishing boats moving across the water with ripples
after them. Pascal is a terrific character with a huge wife who does all
the cooking. A golden pheasant, 3 doves, some pigeons, 4 cats and 2
guinea pigs walked about on the floor. We had langouste and mushrooms and cheese sauce, and a very delicious white wine. Graniche (?)[1]
But I forget—I hope you are quite well, and happy. I feel slightly
depressed at not having heard yet from you. I'll send a wire, if there
isn't a letter today.

The noise in this town at night is rather awful. Motor cars shrieking
their vile hooters, and dogs yowling. But one gets accustomed
to never sleeping! We both keep very well, on Monday we will start
back. I shall aim at reaching Ham Spray on Saturday or Friday if
possible. Now I must stop as we are going off to Marseilles for the day
to peer about for antiquities, and look at the ships.

My love très chère   votre devoutée MOPSA

---

[1] Grenache, a 'vin doux naturel du Roussillon', on the sweet side.

To Julia Strachey

Monday, October 7th, 1929   *Ham Spray House, Hungerford*

Darling Julia, Thank you so much for your letter. It was lovely to see your pussycat handwriting surmounting a mountain of bills and drearies, on my return to Ham Spray last Saturday afternoon. What fun your holiday sounds with these exotic people, and the wind-up in Paris with the gallant Scots-Kilt and the cossacks. I am glad your old stock will turn out pleasantly odd. I long positively to see you and skim the cream off your Italian-Paris milk jug before you turn it into owl cheese. I mean before you forget the subtlest details. So we MUST, sweetest Julia, meet before long. I had a really very perfect holiday with Dorelia, who is a paragon of a character. Exactly to my taste. We had no Baedeker or maps, or plans, and simply peered down alleys, sat in workman's cafes, peered at markets and drank endlessly, perpetually, the grandest wines of France. The chateau in Burgundy with the Americans was indeed strange, almost impossible to describe I fear. We got drenched the last two days, as it rained without a pause and the roof of the car leaked, and there were no side curtains.

I am sending you your Chinese present. Rather late and rather chilly. But you might wear it sometimes to dazzle the rats.

I've had an awful blow. [Fifteen lines omitted]

Olive leaves me, for ever, the end of this month. She has to go into a family business, a bakery. It's mostly I am very fond of her. But then I dread starting all over again teaching someone to cook, and our habits. My mind wavers between getting a Swede or Finn, two sisters, a Chinese boy, an elderly housekeeper, a country girl. But whatever nationality they are, or sex, or age, they are bound to be terrible. It's a bad moment for I must do some glass pictures for a commission, and earn a little money this week. Then there are Lytton's rooms in London which *must* be painted and at once—he is in despair about them—and between all this I have three weeks to find a servant. [End of letter is missing]

To Julia Strachey

A Collins

My dearest Julia, You have no idea how much I enjoyed staying with
you. You are a charmer to be so kind to votre tante. Oh dear I see I am
all wrong I care *far* too much for Ham Spray. I am weak in body, and
soul because ever since lunch I have been in ecstasies over the beauty of
the fields, the sunlight on the top of the stairs, the beech grove, faded
and already tinged with brown, and my family of cats.

rabbit cat   Stump   Black Major Domo & minor Domos

They were dreadfully hungry and pleased to see me so I am glad I came
back. My lovely Belle recognized me across the field, and came to be
patted, so I feel very happy to be back in my animal kingdom. I ran
about the garden looking at all the trees and flowers. I found I had forgotten the extraordinary beauty of the Downs, and the garden. Lytton
has just sent a wire to say he has been seduced by Dadie and isn't coming
back tonight. It makes me a little melancholy to be here alone in this
paradise of beauty with no body but the dumb animal kingdom to share
it with. Olive is still ill with a cold, so there isn't even her to discuss the
beauties of nature with, only my 7 dumb cats and the talking horse.
Julia I wish I was a young man and not a hybrid monster, so that I could
please you a little in some way, with my affection. You know you move
me strangely. I remember for some reason every thing you say and do,
you charm me so much. This letter is rather distrait, but I am worn out
with going into too many internal ecstasies—and then I was too excited
all day to eat anything but some lettuce. I hope you will come on Sunday.
Lytton would be delighted to see your beaux I am sure, and I should be
to see my Belle.

Forgive me for being one evening, rather ponderous. But you are very long suffering. Now I shall go over all my conversations, the plays, the dances, the proposals, sitting with my cats over the log fire.

My love darling Julia

Yr most loving CARRINGTON

To Julia Strachey

Tuesday, October 29th, 1929   *Ham Spray House, Hungerford*

Darling Julia, I meant to write before to thank you for your kind visit to Ham Spray, but for some reason ever since we parted over the tea cups, and candles, life has been one incessant whirl of a whirly-gig. It was sad leaving you. Because I grow a little fonder every time we meet. Often of course I am aware what a bore I must be with my perpetual conversations.

Lady Julia. Not at all. Don't mention it 'mam.

But the truth is I have so few cronies to Gazaway—(Brian Howard's real name incidentally) to. Lytton is not, as you may have noticed, quite the crony to listen to the out pourings of a virgin's heart. But I've strayed away from the bore, and reached nowhere in this letter. Fatal. Have you 'gone on' with your play? I can't help thinking about it very often, and longing to see it performed. Lytton you must know, was in rapture over your brilliance and wit. Life in London was spent amidst the paint pots most of the time.

I only saw Dorelia, outside the Gordon Square family. She took me to tea one pouring wet afternoon with Romilly and Cathy, on their barge at Hammersmith. It seemed to me a very snug romantic life for 25/- a week, furnished and complete. The barge rocks very slightly as the tugs go by, and one peers out of little windows and sees the lapping waves of Thames. Cathy is a very suspicious self contented little puss. Romilly

charming but infinitely conceited and vague. Slightly in the same genre
as Dick Strachey perhaps. In the evening we had dinner with old
Augustus at the Eiffel Tour. Rather fun. Very late, at 9.30. Such a
delicious meal. Snails. Wild duck and orange salad, and real iced raspberries and cream and two bottle of Burgundy. Augustus was in very
good form, most amusing.

We bought some very cheap furniture at the Caledonian Market for
Lytton's rooms, a sofa for 30/- and a table for the same price, and 2
Victorian chairs £2/-.

I came back here on Saturday. Saw a man cheated of £5 by a shark in
the train, a racing crowd with a cheater, and confederates. If I had had
any money I shouldn't have been able to resist trying to outwit the
cheater. But Lytton says one never can.

Olive left us on Saturday and Kitty an ice cold maid reigns in the
kitchen. She is much more orderly than Olive. She reminds me of
Squeaker for some reason, every time I see her. On the 15 Nov. the new
servant comes. I got rather an odd reference from her mistress saying
she was good in every respect but that she 'didn't mend her clothes, or
keep her aprons reasonably clean' 'But that was some time ago. So she
may have improved.' I hope so.

Now I must go off and see if Kitty has made a sauce for the fish.

Lytton has been in bed ever since Saturday with a bad cold in his
head. So I've been nursing him most of this week. Today he seems to
have recovered.

Would you like this rather peculiar jersey? I bought it, but never
wore it, as it didn't as they say, suit my style. If you think it hideous,
without a word give it sweet Agnes with my love. You might cut it up
in some way I thought. I've just been through my drawers, and cupboards. Vogue would be horrified! Such a mishmash of old linen dresses
old waistcoats, old velveteens. Not a single shee-shee dress amongst
them. I've made up one horrid parcel for the poor, and divided the rest,
in 'dresses to be altered' or 'to be made use of in other ways', and
'dresses to be worn again'. The difficulty was, deciding which class they
fell into! Hateful Rosamond to have drawers of clean new silk stockings,
and crêpe-de-chine underclothes! At last we are one, dear Madame, in
our hatreds.

I had a sweet letter on pink notepaper from my sailor friend last week.
He seemed sadly bored with a sailor's lot and thick captain Biscuits.

James seemed still rather distracted, and aloof last week, and Alix
pre-occupied with Esther and Heather, and Nancy. So I felt slightly lost

between them. Next weekend Morgan comes, boy Tennant, and Siegfried Sassoon on Sunday to lunch and Ralph and Frances.

Have you seen the Pitmans lately? I thought your house was looking
so beautiful. You are a genius to create out of 6d such a lovely bedroom.

Pansy wrote me a letter the other day. She still seemed rather vague
about Henry's diseases. I gathered from Dorelia she had been rather
ill also.

Give Tommy my love. Tell him to call at 51 [Gordon Square] if he has
time for a chat. I wish I could paint you a wallpaper strewn with con-
volvuluses. I would if only I was[n't] so harassed for time.

Cat catching flies, a million flies buzz in and out of
our heads making life intolerable. 'But cats can't eat
flies', Lytton shrieks. Puss replies with a crackley
crunch.

My fondest love darling Julia

                 Your devoted TANTE C.

Alas photographs never came out, all blurry, we
must try again. I am sorry.

PS The enclosed for Tommy

To Julia Strachey

Saturday [end of October or early November 1929]   *Ham Spray House,*
                                           Hungerford

Darling Julia, I'd love above everything to see the Three Sisters on
Thursday afternoon. Will you call for me at 51 Gordon Square (and *I*
will ask you to come with me and have lunch first) will Tommy be with
us? or will it be a tête à tête? I wasn't going to London NEXT week, but
your letter so stirred my heart, I at once broke up all my economical
resolutions for a quiet week in the country and fly to your arms.

The scene is laid in the Grand National Hotel—I am thrilled at your new Pansy-Lely style. It looks very alluring. Well, London was

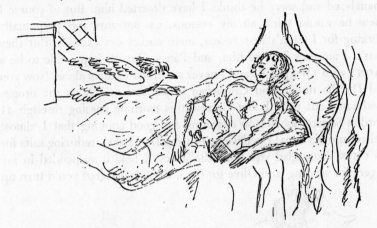

crammed with notables and news (I went up for 2 days on Thursday) this week although I was painting sham marble fireplaces all the time. This morning Alec [Penrose] married Frances and Lionel and Margaret drove off to Cardiff. Alix and James telephone very day to a motor firm and order a new car and then during the night get seized with panic and cancel the order. Then by lunch time gain courage and order it again. I think in the end Alix's recklessness will predominate. I was poisoned by a cheap dinner [one word omitted] on Thursday and was ill most of Friday. I saw Oliver at 41 on Thursday night and he confided to me that Madame XXXX is to be delivered of a child in April. He is *not* the father. Paul Cross and Angus Wilson[1] are going round the world together. There is a rumour (which will cut you, I fear, to the HEART) that Douglas is engaged to a Scotch heiress with '£700 a year' and prospects. But this is not confirmed yet.

I went to Chelsea, and saw Dorelia and Augustus one evening and then took little Vivien to a fascinating cinema. 'Bull Dog Drummond', very well acted with a fine pussy cat vamp in it. Lytton's rooms are nearly finished now and begin to look slightly more human. I got up at 7 o'ck and start work before breakfast. This weekend we have Morgan and Ralph and Frances and Lytton here. Tomorrow there is a prospect of an invasion from Stephen Tennant, Willy Walton and Arthur [Waley] over here for lunch OR we must go over to lunch there and see the new

---

[1] A friend of Paul Cross and one of the 'Tidcombe boys'—not the author.

snakes. I really can't decide which is the worst! I hope to evade both. Your life sounds very gay and varied. I am sorry old Lamb is still ill and unanalysed and sorry he thinks I have deserted him. But of course I knew he would think all my reasons, i.e. servants and perpetually working for Lytton's new rooms, mere cockey-eye excuses. But they aren't, I am *very* fond of him, and Pansy. But it's impossible to be a CRONY with TWO people and I never see either of them alone. Now you and Dorelia understand Cronieism to perfection. I hope the bronze head came out well. I saw Garrow this morning passing through 41 Gordon Square, looking so charming and good LOOKing that I almost melted into his arms! I believe he is using Dr Clarke's reducing salts for his CHIN. I *am* glad you liked the jersey. I held it suspended in my fingers for sending it to Olive for days. Because I feared you'd turn up

your 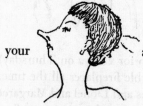 at it. Sorry Tommy didn't like my joke. Write

to me at Hamspray if you want to change plans. I'll go to London probably on Thursday morning.

My fondest love to T. and very much to you darling.

Your devoted C.

[Carrington thought (rightly) that she was pregnant. The following three letters show how much she depended on Lytton for sympathy in any crisis. The pregnancy was later terminated.]

To Lytton Strachey

Wednesday, November 4th, 1929   *Ham Spray House, Hungerford*

Darling Lytton, I feel rather tongue tied always about telling you how much I love you, and incapable of thanking you for all you do for me. But it does you know, make all the difference, in the world. You give me a standard of sensible behaviour which makes it much easier to be reasonable. R[alph] has been so kind also, (I really don't see why such foolishness should be rewarded!). I've been working in my studio all this morning. The rain beats down outside in a most dismal fashion. It's a pity you weren't an actor. I couldn't secretly help watching (split infin.) your ivory hands last night, and thought no movements ever conveyed as much feeling as yours did, on any stage. The rain has washed my brains away I can't write a letter this afternoon! Truly, I am quite happy here. If I feel gloomy I will motor over to Julia, and Tommy for a visit.

I hope you will enjoy London this week. Do ask Dorelia to your Bust Cocktail Party. She would like to see the head. I love you so much, and I shall never forget your kindness lately to me.

Your devoted, loving C.

To Lytton Strachey

Tuesday, November 5th, 1929   *Ham Spray House, Hungerford*
Lytton Strachey Esq., 51, Gordon Square, London

Darling Lytton, Nothing has happened since you left so this letter must be more or less imaginary. Brews of quince cheese scent the whole house. The wind roars round and round, bending the poor pampas to the ground and all the time a hundred chaotic sounds and foreign voices lie chained in the back room like sleeping dogs.

I am just going to have lunch. Then I go for a 'jog' on Belle and then I shall sit down and listen to the wireless and twiddle my thumbs, and repeat old proverbs about stable doors and steeds. I hope you will enjoy London this week. Do not do anything rash! But please look out for a Rococo looking glass. Never neglect to peer into the darkest recesses in case you may find one. D.V. I will appear on Thursday for lunch at 41 G.S. Really your understanding is magnificent. Nobody can be so reassuring, or so endearing. I pin all my faith on the jog-trot!

My love, your devoted C.

To Lytton Strachey

Wednesday, November 6th, 1929   *Ham Spray House, Hungerford*
Lytton Strachey Esq., 51, Gordon Square, London

Darling Lytton, The rain pours down and the Downs are obliterated by
clouds. Je pense je suis perdu. I took a very violent ride on Belle all
yesterday afternoon along the top of the Downs, mais, sans effect. It is a
little difficult to keep one's spirits up, and preserve a sense of humour.
Especially with thick grey clouds hanging over one's head and oblitera-
ting all the light! I say, I have just been inspecting the cellar and putting
away my 1929 sloe gin and I see there is *no whiskey*, or *light sherry, or
brandy* in the spirit department. I thought perhaps you would like to
order some.

Puss came clambering in my bedroom window last night mewing
piteously in the rain. He has learnt a new trick of climbing up the
verandah ironwork. No interesting letters this morning; I send you
yours. I sat, listening to the wireless, sewing last night, and felt very
middle class and suburban. London was so boring, I was reduced to
trying to get foreign stations in the end. I read George Moore in bed last
night, The Celibates, I found it rather too old fashioned. I think
Virginia is fascinating.[1] But I still don't agree that poverty and a room
of one's own, is the explanation why women didn't write poetry. If the
Brontës could write in their Rectory, with cooking and housework, why
not other clergyman's daughters? Have you read it yet? I'll bring the
curtains tomorrow with me. Perhaps you'll be in after lunch? Ach. But
I am in rather a rage with myself! Better buzz this letter away. Tiber
sends his love and so does his mistress dismal-eye erray erray.

[1] *A Room of One's Own*, by Virginia Woolf (Hogarth Press, 1929).

To Lytton Strachey

December 3rd, 1929   *Ham Spray House, Hungerford*
Lytton Strachey Esq., 51, Gordon Square, London

Darling Lytton, Thank you for the nicest letter that a Mopsa has ever
received. I am glad Rose admired the handkerchief. I bought it in a
curious little shop just outside Vichy. Don't you think perhaps we ought
to ask Clive [Bell] next weekend.
His two pheasants sit in the larder,
and will be fit for consumption
next Sunday. Just as you like. It
doesn't make any difference to me.
Today it 'positively isn't raining and the sun shines. Perhaps
tomorrow if it's fine I might drive
over and see Tommy and Julia but

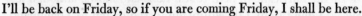

I'll be back on Friday, so if you are coming Friday, I shall be here.

Kitty, (the ice cold maid) has just sent another pair of socks for you.
I hope the Horner's dinner party will be amusing and did you enjoy
Brocas at the Ivy? The birds of the air have tongues! Dodo telephones
that the doctor's address is at the moment lost, but she hopes to find it
in London and will write to me.

Phyllis wrote me an amusing letter from a house party in Nottingham-
shire. Jack was there and Diana etc. Phyllis was suffering terribly from
his Lordship's nerves. The sneak-guest letters are becoming a farce. I
listened to the Berlin orchestra last night. It was marvellously clear. Flo
had a lesson in making an omelette last night, for lunch she is making a
'soupe à la bonne femme'. Tiber sits on the kitchen table giving her
instructions. Batten is in the garden rabbitting with the gamekeeper.
R[alph] was charming all yesterday, we went a walk before lunch along
the terrace and in the afternoon had a great argument for, and against,
constancy! I denied the existence of such a quality. Ralph upheld it, as
being the foundation of true love. The Philip review[1] seems to me
rather a problem, of course they'll accuse you of envy and hatred, even
if you write a discreet 'dim' article. No, I really can*not* buy a 'set of
books showing God's mission to men and the circulation of bible in
foreign lands' from a sweet faced christian female. So after a painful five

---

[1] Lytton had to write a review of Philip Morrell's book on Greville.

minutes the grey lady departed with her little bag of books from the front door.

Cheeselets (Peak and Freane) stuffed olives, and 2 bottles of sherry; really you exaggerate the difficulties.[1]

My fondest love   Your very loving C.

PS Really, I foresee I shall stay here and won't move, out of sheer laziness this week.

To Lytton Strachey

Thursday, December 5th, 1929   *Ham Spray House, Hungerford*

Darling Lytton, Really, the gale last night! I've just been up under the roof with the bats, putting down pails to catch the drippings, for the water was oozing through the library ceiling. This morning the whole house was running with water. The south wind lashed the rain through every crack and crevice. I feel rather wan, and worn after being battered to death by the hurricane in bed. It still rains and blows, although less furiously, so I don't think I'd venture out, certainly not to Tomlinland. Elephant Flo has just had a lesson with the vacuum cleaner and your library, and bedroom have been beautifully burnished up. Tell me how many visitors I am to expect? I feel quite strong, so don't mind asking anyone you want to, except, except Paul [Cross] and Angus [Wilson]. I do not feel quite strong enough for them. So Peter [Lucas] gets a 2nd consolation prize for his historical novel! But we won't have to read it even if it is published, will we? No news here. Telephone broken, so I am forced to live on tinned herrings. The 'park' is a mass of blue lakes this morning and the lawn looks like a battlefield with broken lances. I read Tchekhov in bed and perhaps compared to 'Russia' we lead very sheltered lives.

Mr Gibbs comes to mend the slates, and the roof, next Monday. If there is any roof left to mend by then.

My fondest love, darling Lytton,   Your devoted loving C.

[1] Of the cocktail party given to exhibit Stephen Tomlin's bust of Lytton.

1930

To Julia Strachey

Sunday [January 1930]   *Ham Spray House, Hungerford*

My darling Julia, Too old for kisses am I? Well, well every cat her day I
suppose. Tell Tommy, without reading another WORD, that directly the
frost stops I will climb up the ladder. But since he came here the
carpenter has been ill in bed with lumbago and I've not dared scale the
ladder alone to take the measurements of his triangle. Pippa isn't really
well enough for a winter drive. If only it came warm I think it would be
alright. She would love to see you and was delighted at your suggestion.
I do like her very much. There is a harmony about her temperament
that seems good. (If you understand what I mean.) Lytton is ill in bed
with a cold so I have my work cut out rushing up stairs to my two
invalids and downstairs to my weekend visitors, (or rather Lytton's)
Dadie, and Topsy. I shall be rather glad when the loneliness of Ham
Spray descends once more and I can lie in bed and idle away the hours.
I gather from Ralph, Frances is still rather ill. They have been staying
with Dick and Esmé [Strachey] who keep a grand establishment with
neat maids, dogs in kennels, and everything in its place, lists of books
read, lists of books to be read. Please give Hester [Chapman] this letter.
I would love to come over but I'm afraid in this frost it's not possible.
Have you seen the Lambs again? I am sending you a New Year's present.
There is a pretty poem 'to Julia'. (Silly tosh, some might say.) I can't
find the improper John drawing and I can hardly hope Pippa will pass
another day without finding it, a good Freudian example of Lytton
wanting to suppress his lust for females and forgetting even the name of
the book he put it into. Pippa said this morning in bed that Topsy has a
'Rouault' face. Now I can think of nothing else when I see her! Do
write and tell me about Bobbie Hale[1] and her husband. Barbara tells me
little Tim is going to pose for our cupids on the wall, cold work. She

[1] Mrs Douglas McClean, author of Orlando The Marmalade Cat books.

seems much happier in her new house. I long to hear about the Connolly week and I still laugh over our Christmas Noserie. The spectacle of you with that little hat, and Ralph. I thought it was a perfect evening. Give Tommy my fondest love. I hope he is not held up for the measurements.

My love darling Julia,   Your C.

To Lytton Strachey

Thursday [*January 23rd, 1930*]
                              The Mill Cottage, Swallowcliffe, Wiltshire

Darling Lytton, No time for a letter, as life is so rushed and whirling— as you rightly guessed we dash about the country to Fryern, and Combe Bissett and drink and talk like magpies without a pause. I painted a picture for the Lambs, in a panel in their passage, which seemed to please them. Julia and Tommy are in very good spirits and we have had a lovely time together. I paid two visits to my rustic dressmaker in her little thatched farm. My new dress is very grand. I loved your letter, thank you so much for writing to me. I will see you tomorrow at 6.20 at Hungerford. I go back early tomorrow morning. Tommy and Julia send their fondest love. And so does your very loving

                                                                 C.

To Lytton Strachey

6, o'ck [*March 6th, 1930*]   *P.O. Hungerford*

Darling Lytton, We had the strangest of drives, with old Lady Tree, Iris and Pansy Rayner. Lady Tree is fascinating. I got tired with laughing she was so amusing. We lunched at the Bear and then drove to Tidcombe. They loved the house. But it's clear the old yeoman farmer won't sell or let. Tea at Ham Spray. Now they have just gone. It was very gay, and I enjoyed myself tremendously. Love from puss, and

                                                          MOPSA XX

To Lytton Strachey

Friday [March 7th, 1930]   *Ham Spray House, Hungerford*

Darling Lytton, I suppose Lady Tree's 'style' is 'old cheese' to you, but I was completely bowled over by her punning humour and high spirits. No wonder Iris is such an amusing good humoured character, living with such a steel to sharpen her wits upon. And again I am not surprised she prefers Lady Tree's company to any husband. I was sad after they left. It was such a delightful expedition. In half an hour I must drive Flo off to Newbury to have a tooth drawn. The insurance won't pay for her teeth this year. Typical of the brutes. I've finished Ros's novel. But I'll not commit to paper my thoughts yet, as I am still rather muddled as to what I really think about it. The Blue Bells horrified me! It's a lovely day here. (If one ever again dares to describe nature.) Misty and warm, with the sun shining on our beautiful park. I hope you'll enjoy Cambridge very much. I am so glad you are so happy, I hope the weekend will be as nice as Thursday evening. Now I must go off and get ready for Newbury. My very fondest love darling Lytton.

Your devoted MOPSA

PS Pansy Rayner turned out to be rather a charming character but I suspect he has NO heart, and is ambitious.

[Lytton went for a visit to Rome with George Rylands, leaving on April 4th after spending the night with Carrington. He returned on the 21st. During his absence they wrote to each other almost every day, Lytton confessing that he was homesick and wished that Carrington was with them.]

To Julia Strachey

[n.d.] Monday evening, 10 o'ck   *Ham Spray House, Hungerford*

THIS letter never got posted

Darling Julia, I am just off to London tomorrow morning. But I shall probably come back in the evening, almost certainly, if not, on Wednesday morning for lunch.—Do please come over if you would like to,

either with T[ommy] and Gilbert [Debenham] or alone. I would so love
your company. Just send a wire, or ring up from Swallowcliffe. There
was so much I wanted to talk to you about the other day that I feel
breathless to see you soon again! I painted 150 tiles. The weight of
them in a box nearly kills me. But they are now all packed up ready to
start off tomorrow. I feel rather lonely this evening. There is so much
beauty strewn about, hay fields, birds singing and the warm evening
breeze stirring in the oak tree and nobody but a mad cuckoo to talk to,
except the cat, who has gone off chasing moles.

> 'To have a craving
> For a bird[1]
> Is but raving
> I'm afear'd.'

And now I must go to bed. I only felt I didn't tell you, darling, properly
this afternoon how much I'd like to see you again.

Your loving   TANTE C. XXXX

[In a diary Carrington wrote of an evening at Ham Spray. (Whitsun or
June 10th, 1930.)]

The Reverse of the Medal

Directly he arrived I saw he was changed. I thought I would leave him
to see how long it would be before he joined me. He was only occupied by
the lateness of the time he went to bed the night before, that he did not
get any sleep till 3 o'ck. I knew with my gypsy's warning that he had
really been to B., with B., and was exhausted and was starting to explain
his indifference by sleepiness. We played Badminton, after that ping-
pong after dinner. There was a wireless. I hoped he would sit alone with
me or go for a walk, but he insisted on listening. I couldn't listen. I
watched him half asleep in his chair, and thought he was probably after all
a figure head. I remembered how all day I'd been looking forward to his
coming and now how bored and flat it seemed. And I felt not the
slightest interest in me. After the wireless, I suggested going to bed and
left the room. F[rances] with what I call the 'frustration of lover's
movement,' at once put on the wireless. I told R[alph] that Lytton was
longing to go to bed and begged him to put off the wireless. He was
cross, in the engine house. I saw Lytton wandering disconsolately in the

[1] A Seagull.

sitting-room; it was half past ten. I saw F[rances] was determined to play the wireless dance music. Then Roger [Senhouse] and B[eakus] started ping pong. I suddenly saw the similarity between Lytton and my position. Both unable to do anything because we longed for our bed companions who were equally indifferent, to put it bluntly, about coming to bed. I couldn't bear to see Lytton unhappy, so I went out and sat in the moonlight on a stump under the Ilex with Tiber who was prowling about on our lawn. I watched Lytton flapping the pages of the Nation restlessly on his chair in the sitting room. I could hear the dim strains of the wireless and hear the ping of the ping pong balls. After half an hour Ralph passed through the dining room and went, I knew by instinct, into the kitchen for ice to make drinks. He seemed to take a long time. I got colder and colder. Suddenly Lytton got up, and went to see if Ralph was R[oger] perhaps I thought, then went back to his paper in the chair. At last Ralph went back with drinks. Then Lytton got up and went upstairs to his library. I was afraid he'd see me under the tree, so I went round to the beech tree and lay on the motor mower cover. Puss running after me and lay on my lap; I could see Frances playing ping pong and B[eakus] sitting in a chair staring in front of him. I looked at the moon through the beech leaves which had a fine grey edge against the sky. And listening to the sad pee-wee cats got very cold. I thought B[eakus] has never once wondered where I have gone to. At last the light was put out. I went and lay under the Ilex and watched Ralph look for me in the bedroom, undress and put out the light, Lytton go to bed. Two lights down the passage windows. Roger undressing. B[eakus] very slowly standing by his bed, finally pulling off his shirt and putting on blue striped pyjamas. Lytton evidently came to Roger's room for suddenly Roger pulled his curtains. B[eakus] put out his light. I heard the door in the lavatory shut. No light turned up in my empty eyed windows. He had gone however for after ten minutes there was a light turned up in his bedroom. But I was not, after that, going to go to his room. It was after half past twelve. Lying in the cold grass I suddenly realized that he was completely indifferent to my sensations, incapable of any love. Only quite ready to go to bed if there was anyone ready to go to bed. Probably thought it was expected of him by me. [Twenty lines omitted]

It was interesting viewing the world, so to speak, from a lighted Dolls' house seen from outside. [Fifty lines omitted]

To Julia Strachey

Wednesday morning [about June 10th, 1930]   *Ham Spray House,*
                                                             nr Marlborough, Wilts.

Darling Julia, Thank you for your very charming letter. It considerably
set me ⟨heart⟩ on its legs again. It's difficult to describe my feelings
because they are so illogical. It's partly the effect of having laid two
years in the coffin untouched, so as to speak, that these last months of
animal affection rather ruined my moral. It's difficult to go back to
coffin life again and with my numerous complexes not very easy even if
one wanted to, to get a transfer ticket onto some one else. Fortunately
it's mostly a matter of bodily lusts I have to deal with in other respects.

> 'You are always first, in spite
> of strange birds of flight
> One, whilst flying o'er the sea
> dropt a "something" on to me
> "something" can be wiped away,
> But FRIENDSHIP lasts till crack of day.'

His Mrs B.B. [initials substituted] (which it didn't want the eyesight of
an owl to see, was occupying really all his attention this weekend)
unless I grossly underrate the girl, is a gold digger taken by his Bentley
and his good looks. (No blame to her). But she finds it tough work
digging! To tell you the truth when the Gull said ages ago 'I wish you'd
wear black silk stockings, or dark brown, they show off a leg, so much
better than those awful white ones you always wear' I realized our
PATHS lay differently. I shall mourn in secret this week, painting my
tiles and then go back to my coffin and enjoy the company of my friends
again. Actually I gave up a good deal of my time which I might have
spent at Swallowcliffe and Fryern, washing up dishes on board for this
unworthy Gull!! So now I'll wash dishes, and bake pies for my darling
Julia, who *doesn't* crab my white stockings! [Forty-two lines omitted]

To Lytton Strachey

Wednesday morning [*June 11th, 1930*]
                                          Ham Spray House, Hungerford

Dearest Lytton, No news since I wrote last night, a grilling hot day with
thunder claps and downpours of rain, interspersed with the hottest sun
and not a breath of wind. However nothing exhausts the blue bottles,
and bumble bees *they* rush about like Vikings. Poor puss feels the heat
dreadfully in his astracat fur coat.

'Then why not take it off dear Puss?' and what do you think the
ridiculous conservative Puss replied.

'The birds would laugh at me.'

The abigails are off to Littlecote to look at the gardens and enjoy a
tobacco profiteer's fete this afternoon. I must toil and boil away at the
tiles. I tried to lure Tommy and Julia over to dinner, but they were
adamant. I *hope*, because they are working at our china figures. It was
lovely seeing you yesterday. I enjoyed myself so much. This in haste,
but my fondest love   Your MOPSA

To Julia Strachey

Wednesday morning [*about June 11th, 1930*]   *Ham Spray House,*
                                                      Hungerford

Darling Julia,   I sent you a wire,
                        Filled with fire
                        Of love quite silly
                        But receiv'd, answer chilly.

As a matter of fact I ought *not* to have asked you over as I ought to be
working from cock crow to hoot of owl—yet I sinned, so God, in the
shape of Tommy, rebuked me. I only hope that you also are all working
so hard you had to give up the delights of a visit to Littlecote gardens
with me and a picnic afterwards by the river's edge. If it is was for any
other reason I shall never darken your doors again, Madame! I went to
London yesterday, Tuesday with my tiles. Had lunch with Lytton and
Ralph. Looked at the National Portrait Gallery and the National Gallery.

Saw Alix in Gordon Square and chatted to her under the trees, And had a babies' tea party with Alec and Frances [Penrose]. Lionel and Margaret were there. Lionel and Margaret are simply potty over their baby. Alec and Frances very restrained in comparison. But I foresee the beginnings of a dreadful drama between the infant Penroses. They were very

engaging in their different styles. Frances made a most beautiful picture with her enormous naked arms intertwined with her sprawling half naked son on her lap. My train was struck by lighting so we sat for $\frac{1}{2}$ an hr in an appalling thunderstorm just outside Paddington. Today I start on another fireplace. Oh, dear I am so bored with these dreary tiles! Perhaps it's just as well you aren't coming over, as deluges of rain descend driving indoors millions of blue bottles, bumblebees and queenie wasps and thunder claps resound from down to down. There are two lobsters to eat by myself. Rather a gloomy thought! When will you come over in your car? Please do sometime if you can. My love darlings,   Your TANTE C.

To David Garnett

Tuesday [June, 1930]   *Ham Spray House, Hungerford*

Dearest Bunny, There is nothing I would like better.[1] I think Sebastian comes here on the 25th weekend. I somehow feel he wouldn't get on very

---

[1] Carrington wanted to meet Dorothy Edwards, the author of *Rhapsody*, and I had suggested bringing her to Ham Spray.

well with Dorothy. What do you think? So I rather advocate the Tuesday
and Wednesday scheme. I am afraid Lytton goes to London on Monday
for the Camargo. Will you mind if he isn't here?

But you must do as you like about the weekend. It's only I'd like it to
be as perfect as possible and I think Sebastian's Nottingham chatter
might not be to her taste.

Julian Bell came over yesterday with his hoyden in a car to fetch
Peter Lucas who was here. I rode Belle on the downs on Sunday and saw
two beautiful Swedish Princesses (they were twins) with yellow curls
and Fra Angelico faces walking on the downs with an austere father.
They were so beautiful that I thought of nothing else for the rest of the
day. Life is almost too varied. It seems to have no G.C.M. But perhaps
you have forgotten your mathematics? On Friday I lay in the sun under
a large sunshade, on a double bed, with a pale pink fur coverlet with
Stephen Tennant. Green lizards ran on the paths and tropical parrots
and African birds flew in an aviary. On the table mixed up with lunch
were marvellous orchids and yesterday morning in the dark Three
Plumes at Hungerford, I found Paul Cross, Lett Haynes and Angus
Wilson all very drunk at 12 o'ck, cracking curious jokes. And then at
3 o'ck lying in a haystack with Peter [Lucas] and Helen [Anrep]
listening to Cambridge gossip. And late last night James and Alix
dropped in and we were back again over the fire talking about old days
at Hartland Point, as if Stephen Tennant and such strange fish were
mere phantasmires. Do come on Tues or Wed. After that weekend will
Ray be able to come? It would be lovely if she could. Thank you for
second page of love. For really it means a great deal to your

devoted DORIC

To Lytton Strachey

Friday, 3.30 [June 13th, 1930]   *Ham Spray House, Hungerford*

Darling Lytton, A terrible thunderstorm is crashing overhead as I write
this letter. So it may be the LAST you will ever get.

Dodo rang up at lunch, to say she was coming over with Augustus
and Poppet and Fanny for a moonlight picnic this afternoon! It will be
delightful munching sardines on the downs in mackintoshes. I have
painted 120 tiles, and feel as if the brain was about to give way, so do

not expect a very brilliant letter. [Fourteen lines omitted] What shall I
do if this cohort of Bohemians arrive, and we have to sit hour after hour
in this deafening thunder storm? Old Augustus is deaf enough already!
What did you think of Romilly's poems? I thought they were rather
moving, but the last one rather obscure? Do you see the sales of that
odious female's Edwardian book? The Woolverines will soon be the
richest couple in Europe.[1] I think Maynard's article was very good. Now
I must go on with my tiles. I love you so much, and think of you half the
day. D.V. I expect I shall come up in the Sunbeam on Monday with a
crate load of tiles to be baked. I'll let you know if I do.

My very dear love to D.L.   from MOPSA

June 19th, 1930

The Faded Passion Flower

The Passion Flower hangs over the door,
But oh! it's an idle mockerie
For where is the love of my Paramoor?
The sea thyme is dead on the rockerie.
The Passion Flower with its ashen face
Hangs against the evening sky
It droops as if in some disgrace
My day has run, so droop I.
He to another mistress flies.
I listen to the owl's sad cry,
And wish tomorrow would not rise
And I in my grave might lie.

June 20th, 1930

On a Picture of a Ship

A cross stitch ship in a frame of wood
Could life be once again as good,
As the day he gave me that picture rare
And I rumpled my hand in his wind-swept hair.
But good days are past, and before me lies
An eternity of dull blank skies.

[1] *The Edwardians* by Victoria Sackville West had been published by the Hogarth
Press in 1930.

To Julia Strachey

Friday morning [*? June 1930*]   *Ham Spray House, Hungerford*

Darling Julia, I wish a hundred times you were here today. Just to weep
tears on your shoulders? No but to drive away the melancholy of the
drizzling Scotch mists that envelope the downs and the bitter west wind
that batters against the window panes. It's all very well aiming at being
a stoic, but a different matter carrying out one's philosophy. I woke up
in an ecstasy of love this morning very early to find my mouth full of
sheets which I was biting passionately. Tomorrow 'company' as the
servants say, will arrive and I'll get over my despairs. I feel it dreadfully
ignominious to mind living alone. But the difficulty is not to let one's
mind wander off into abysses of gloom that lead but to munching
sheets by moonlight in bed. I can't tell you how much I loved our
bathing tea party. After the blinking tiles are finished I am going to
paint a picture of the little child at the lodge. I saw her sitting in a little
[word illegible] the other [word illegible] in her [word illegible] with a
doll: if it comes off, fatal words again, you shall have it for your birthday
sweetie. [word illegible] day, I expect. I'll tell you on Monday or
Tuesday about the chances of a visit with Lytton one week.

Your very loving   TANTE C.

To Sebastian Sprott

Sunday [*July 1930*]   *Ham Spray House, Hungerford*

All too true.
Darling Sebastian, Can you forgive me. It was a terrible example of the
state of my brain. You see we always go to Short's for sherry and so a
complex against the word 'Short'; a complex in favour of 'sherry', and
poor you and Bob spend an hour wandering in the rain. Please forgive
me. Our vessel didn't arrive till 7 o'ck at Hythe, so it was too late to go
to Southampton and I motored straight back to London without
touching Southampton. But your letter was fascinating. I *long* to know
what came of the Labour Exchange companion. (The 'Horse and Groom'
is the best pub in Southampton. I've just remembered the name for you.)

Your washing debt I hope will wash away my sins, a present for you.
I am sorry the food was such cold comfort at the weekend. I'm afraid
Flo isn't very bright in the head. But Lytton said the conversation was
so amusing and brilliant that the cold repast wasn't much noticed. I hope
so. I've never been so happy in my life as on our voyage. The Seagull
was particularly charming and I may say that I am so badly gone on that
boy that one 'night' sets me up for days afterwards. We had a lovely
time in London last Friday evening: a cinema and sipping sherry in the
little bed room at Gordon Square out of a tooth glass. Madame Penrose
has had a stroke and is very ill so that Alec has become head of the
family and is in a terrible state of fuss and agitation. Consequently
wants to dominate Sea Gull and has been very tiresome. So there's a
very complicated family feud brewing up. Rather tedious. However it
means the Sea Gull will be in London more often, which suits my interests. [Two lines omitted]

This weekend we have Dadie, Dorothy and Janie. Dadie in his
highest high brow mood. 'I don't think I can agree. You find in Shakespear's sonnets ... ' comes through the window, from Dadie on the
verandah. 'It is essential that the poet, as indeed all writers, should use
words etc. etc.' However the ladies are delighted and very impressed.
Only one pussy cat on the sofa writes to another pussy cat and miaows!

'There is a great deal of very serious moral idea in the poem as a
whole etc.'

Please write me a letter with all your adventures. *Nothing* to be left
out. I wish I wasn't so mashed on this sea captain. I can hardly think of
anything else and I can't bear to make any plans in case I might see him.
[Two lines omitted] I hope Toulon will come up to your expectations!
I did love your visit here. More than any of your visits. Now I must go
and see about lunch. (Dadie is now dissecting Gray's Elegy for the
ladies.) Next week I go to London to draw designs for Phyllis de Janzé's
library. She says 'I hope it will lead to great things for you.' So do I.

Falmouth was a fascinating town. But I don't think quite your style.
I have a notion the Devonshire and Cornwall inhabitants are not au fait
with that taste. Is it possible? I didn't see a single queerie. ('Listen to
this:

'The expedition of my careless love outran the etc. Then there is a
very good commodity passage in King John. Listen to this ... ' etc.)

All this at 11 o'ck in the morning and it's been going on for 2 hours!

I loved your post card to Lytton. Now really I must dash off and
compose a lunch. I love you so much, for being so sweet and listening to

my tedious confidences but I love you also for better reasons for—but
perhaps you will never know.   Your loving C. xxx

To Lytton Strachey

Saturday 2 o'ck [*August 9th, 1930*]   Back at *Ham Spray House,*
                                                             Hungerford

Darling Lytton, I hope you had a peaceful journey. Now you are in the
thick of horse shows, and Irish intrigues. I give you a month! Really
there is nothing to tell you, as I've hardly done anything since you left.
I painted 18 tiles. But will have to go back next week and do another 20
in order to finish it. They are mostly of old Peckover[1] country seats,
interspersed with flowers. I hope Alec will like them. He is rather
critical—it's very comfortable at Inverness Terrace and peaceful. So
quiet after Gordon Square and Mrs England. I saw Gull on and off,
fairly often. When I'm not with him I am quite immune but face to face
I become like treacle! Ralph came and had tea with me over my tiles
yesterday. He was very sweet. He thought letting Ham Spray to Penroses quite a good idea. I gathered Alec was very keen to have it. What
do you think he had better pay? Last night I spent with James, we saw
a lovely film together and at last I've seen a Mickey Mouse. I thought it
was almost a work of genius! We laughed tremendously (aloud!) over it.
Afterwards we went to Rules and got very drunk on brandy and saw
Mr Cochran and a great many curious people at the next table. When I
got back to Inverness Terrace I nearly went mad trying to get in, as the
latch key didn't fit the door. So I said in my rage 'How *typical* of Gull to
have given me the wrong key. How I *hate* these muddlers.' I hesitated
about ringing up the servants as I couldn't find a night bell. I then
looked up and saw it was *87* Inverness Terrace, not *85*!

This morning after 3 more tiles were painted, I caught the 10.45. A
terribly crowded journey, with hundreds of Boy Scouts and Girl Scouts.

Puss is in very high spirits delighted to see me again. Dodo has just
rung up and asked me to Fryern, so after seeing my mother I shall go
over there. My adorable oiseau Edwin is there! Ham Spray looks so
peaceful and beautiful, with our white pigeons dancing a quadrille on
the lawn.

---

[1] The Penroses' grandfather was Lord Peckover.

The sky of course is grey with rain, so there's really nothing to do but sit in doors, and admire the view. Now it's crashing down. [Drawing of rain omitted] I hope Ireland doesn't suffer from the same depression. Ralph has a secret: that Gerald is engaged to be married!! To an American lady authoress [Gamel Woolsey] that he met in the Powys world. But [it] is a deadly secret so you're not to tell anyone! She sounds a little too 'Lolly Willowes'[1] but nobody has been allowed to see her yet!

Now I must go and wash my hair and start off again on my travels. It's very sad to be here without you. To see so many lovely dahlias blooming unseen.

My fondest love your most loving   MOPSA XXX
Love to the [drawing of Lambs omitted][2]

To Lytton Strachey

Monday [August 11th, 1930]   *Ham Spray House, Hungerford*

Darling Lytton, It was lovely getting your letter tonight when I got back. What wizards we are to have guessed there would be a Vice Regal Ball with white shirts! I am glad Henry is such a support. I hope you will get to the Wicklow Mountains. Have you seen sweet George Thompson yet? I spent a curious weekend at Fryern. Drove Edwin [John] to Hythe on Sunday afternoon to a tea party on Gull's ship, where we found Frank Birch and a brother Birch and a sister-in-law Gage and another female on board. Frank Birch having chartered the ship was, so as to speak, the Captain. We had a very dull tea party. Old Frank isn't what [you] could call life-enhancing. Then Edwin and Gull and I escaped and sank into Lord Nelson's Arms where we drank gin after gin and talked to a lovely bar-lady. Beackus (quite erroneously) thought I wasn't capable of driving back to Fryern so drove back with us. Typically Fryern had NO key to the cellar, so we had a drinkless meal at 10.30 and then at 11.30 drove back to Hythe where Edwin and I dropped Beackus. Today I left, and dropped in on the Tomlins where I found Lady Tomlin and Janie! Rather a strain keeping up a conversation with Lady Tomlin at lunch. But I had a lovely long talk with Julia walking across the fields in the afternoon and another private talk with Tommy. Tommy has done a really lovely head of Gilbert Debenham quite the

[1] A novel by Sylvia Townsend Warner.
[2] Lytton was staying with Henry and Lady Pansy Lamb in Ireland.

best thing he has ever done. Tea at the Pitman's. They have a very beautiful house. But tainted with Chelsea, and [George] Kennedy.

Back here at 7.30. Dorelia has given me a sweet little sandy puss called 'George'!! Oh dear! 'Fondu' was Welsh rabbit (what would the archbishop have said?) so I had to give Florence a terrible lecture and a general blowing up. As usual I feel quite ill after it.

Mr Walters (the cowman) wants me to drive Mrs Walters to Savernake Hospital tomorrow to have all her teeth pulled out, oh dear! oh dear! I shall go to London on Wednesday to finish Alec's tiles in Bayswater and hope to see you on Friday, darling, in London. I shall ring up Gordon Square on Friday evening.

I've been asked to a Scotch castle on an island off Scotland by Dorelia for September and to go as ship's cook to France and to stay with the Tomlins. But where, oh where, is the time for all these pleasures? where indeed. I loved your letter more than I can say. You were a dear to write so quickly.   Yr very loving fond   MOPSA XXXX

To Julia Strachey

Wednesday [1930]   *Ham Spray House*

Darling Julia, Do tell me how your chart progresses? and your general state of health? Dorelia told me that they paid you a visit last week and were very upset to find you away. They took several hours circling round the swallows nest like vultures, so were sad after going some 100 miles up and down narrow lanes, to find no prey. Do ask them to dinner, or tea, one day. Augustus would be delighted and Dorelia longs to taste your Wiltshire-renowned-pasties. We had Sea-gull with us last weekend so I feel rather flattened at the moment. High jinks may be alright for girls in their teens but old Harridans ought to be pushed by old sea salts in Bath-chairs on the sea front instead of being pushed—fill up at your pleasure. Lettice [Ramsey] has measles so will not come here this week. Secretly I am slightly relieved. Tiber is looking very lovely today and sits in pensive vein, staring into eternity.— puzzling out some obstruse problem by Whitehead.

I did enjoy our jaunt together tremendously. Nobody of course had ever heard of Johnny Fields,[1] our lovely young man. I asked Raymond [Mortimer] casually the next morning and he of course hadn't even seen the show. I've got rather a thick throat today so don't feel very bright in the head. Forgive a dullish letter. Sweet Flo makes marmalade in the kitchen to the strains of the gramophone.

I must write to sweet Spilsbury.[2] She made a lovely overcoat out of Hester's tweed and the neatest little velvet jacket. Your present I may say is universally admired. I hope you have been able to do some writing this week. When shall I see you again?

My love to T. and very much to you.   Your devoted TANTE C. Lytton and Ralph are up in London so tomorrow I am going to do a day's painting as my record is deplorable this year so far.

To Lytton Strachey

Sunday [*September 14th, 1930*]
The Mill Cottage, Swallowcliffe, Wilts

Darling Lytton, I will write you a letter telling you my news since I last wrote on Friday. I hope you are having better weather than we have had. For a cold Watendlath[3] wind blows here, and it poured with rain yesterday and last night. I left Fryern on Friday morning, and went to Lambland for lunch. Henry was very charming, and out to be agreeable. I heard a great deal about Ireland. 'Lytton came rushing in as a fast bowler and completely took them by storm.' Another sister of Pansy's was there—a cross-eyed very fat little school girl, the same beautiful Renoir appearance with enormous legs and arms. In spite of steering on my side, directly anything approaching 'roses', 'portraits', 'novels' or even 'wagonettes', or anything *dimly* leading to Ipsden[4] appeared on the horizon, I heard the whole story again and was forcibly drawn into it. I failed both parties! By taking no sides! In the end I became so bored, I very nearly said: 'Now you've got your money why can't you let the subject drop?' The Guinnesses[5] so far haven't bought any portraits and

---

[1] The comedian.

[2] Dressmaker.

[3] A wind like that at Watendlath in the Lake District.

[4] Puns and references to Rosamond Lehmann and Wogan Philipps, who lived at Ipsden.

[5] Bryan and Diana Guinness. The dog was their Irish wolfhound.

Henry has embarked on a life size enormous family group with a dog the size of a grey cow, which if he doesn't sell, I should think would cost a fortune in paint, and canvas. I thought one of Bryan very pretty. But surely if it wasn't of a lovely young man, not a very good picture? And I completely agree about Diana's portrait. It gave one no impression of that Moon Goddess effect. I failed I fear to confide anything and I could see by their expressions as I left they were saying I was cold and reserved. Oh dear! oh dear! I found Gilbert Debenham here and—five minutes after I arrived, little Barbara came clattering up all smiles in her horrid little motor car, just 'dropping in' on the way from Cornwall to Kent. But she was rather severely drowned by us all, and subsided like the dormouse into her soup basin. Yesterday morning was spent walking to the dressmaker with Julia, endless confidence, trying on a beautiful black velvet dress (I shall look like a Renaissance widow) glasses of cider after trying on dresses, then on my return here talks with Barbara about little Tim,[1] a visit to Mrs Powell who lies ill in bed with some awful internal disease. In the evening Tommy, Gilbert, Julia and I drove off to the Haunch of Venison where we had some sausages and chips and then went to the theatre. It was a *marvellous* performance. Indescribably English. Two very good comedians, the Wilkie Bard school, very 1890'ish. A leading lady who was practically Beryl de Zoete. A chorus of fat little girls with cockney voices, in the style of Annie and elephant Flo. Two acrobats dressed as mechanics, one the double of Henry [Lamb] till in the end we all found it hard to believe it wasn't Henry. The audience was mostly soldiers and Salisbury yokels and they rocked backwards and forwards with shouts of laughter at the jokes about illegitimate babies and coming home with the milk. It was so perfect we could hardly bear it to end. When we got back here the wet evening had changed into a lovely moon light night. I went for a long walk with Tommy alone and enjoyed his conversation very much. Afterwards we lay in the orchard under the apple trees.

—Today I go back to Fryern.—

I hope the weather will recover for sailing next week. I rang up Ham Spray twice; they said everything was perfect, and they were extremely happy. Give darling Rosamond, and Wogan my fondest love and Dadie. I do hope you are enjoying yourself tremendously. I think of you so often and love you more than I can say.

Your very fond   MOPSA
XXXXXXXXXXXX

[1] Barbara's younger son, Tim Bagenal.

To Lytton Strachey

Wednesday [September 24th, 1930]   *Fryern Court, Fordingbridge*

Darling Lytton, Thank you so much for your letter. Today is exquisitely
fine quite hot for a wonder. I shall go back to Ham Spray tomorrow and
start preparing the way for the advent of Count Lyttof. Last night John
Strachey[1] and I went into Southampton and discovered some fine pubs.
The 'Horse and Groom' was a masterpiece. The Cathedral of public
houses. And sitting in the centre was a venerable archbishop of pro-
prietresses. We lingered there for some time. Then we went to a grill
room where to my amazement I saw Horace de Vere Cole and his consort Mavis, having dinner. Mavis left to go to the New Forest and old
Horace joined us after our dinner. We didn't part till 1.30 at his South
Western Hotel. Poor John was very ill all today and complained bitterly
that 'it was Horace Cole's exaggerated stories and LIES that made him
sick not the drink.' There is no pleasing this younger generation. After
all an evening with Cole is an experience. But he showed no gratitude,
partly because he didn't get a chance of telling his own exaggerated
stories. After tea today I am going to ride with Poppet. This evening
perhaps Dodo and I will go down to Hythe.

Vivien insists on becoming a dancer and has today gone up to London
to interview Dolin, about joining his school. Ralph is enjoying his
holiday enormously in spite of Mr Pollock's odious company! He says he
will be back next Sunday.

Julia rang up today. She, and Tommy are better, and in more cheerful spirits. I bought 6 very pretty plates in the Salisbury market yesterday, and a Claude reproduction for you as a present. [Two lines
omitted] I hope you keep well. All my love Yr very fond   MOPSA

From Carrington's Diary

[October 30th, 1930]

And I said to myself, 'Was this really the character that I have thought
about these last three weeks night and day? Can this be the nose, the
mouth, that I craved for? Can this be the evening that I was frustrated

---

[1] Lytton's nephew.

of, this the body that I longed for?' And as we talked of Dürer etchings, motor engines, Alec's character, I thought how dim all this is from what has obsessed me all these weeks. How completely uninterested he is. I am dressed in black tonight, a sudden reversion from colour. Mercifully what was revealed wasn't endearing. I didn't love *more* tonight like some nights. I am sinking back into that previous state of *not* being a female. Hating undressing, hating getting into bed, after hours of thinking about an evening, it is curious how completely uneventful it can be. I mean without any emotion in my feelings, how already the past has become the past and I am a crony, a crony who never knew more than conversations about motor engines and Dürer etchings. I accepted the 'convention' and our conversation and behaviour was detached as a detached house. As we passed the British Museum I seized a sham opportunity of becoming semi-detached until we reached Woolf's garage. But I was fore-armed prepared. So when the blow fell, I had on my armour and felt very little. Looking of course in the looking glass on my return I felt no surprise. Candidly the surprise is that this bedroom should have 4 months ago have witnessed a different scene. Yet I confess even as I write, I am half in tears with disappointment. I still care so much. However it; 'You will never know,' holds good, then 'He must never know,' and I flatter myself I didn't betray any feelings tonight.

Ham Spray House,
Hungerford. Berks.

> I cannot thee with loving bind
> For love you do despise,
> Oh why, in sea birds did I find
> My anchor and demise?

I cannot keep you with a tear,
Brine water's naught to thee,
And in thy eyes I must appear
A wave upon the sea.

But if I cannot tie thee dear
Or live beneath thy deck,
Yet I shall always know you wear
My *tie* around your neck.

December 30th, 1930

To Lytton Strachey

End of the year, December 31st, 1930

Ham Spray House, Hungerford

Darling Lytton, I am ensconced in your snug library, as it's so much
warmer than down stairs. I hope you don't mind. I am doing nothing but
write letters. No chapaties on the floor![1] Oh, what a day to end a year.
What a finale! The wind and rain lash the window panes, and it's as
cold as the north pole. I've had tremendous talks with Julia. Rather
agitating, and very melancholy. But I suppose it's impossible to alter

[1] A Strachey family story was that Lady Strachey's brother Trevor Grant had an
Indian wife who had been found eating curry off the carpet.

the situation now. Yesterday we drove down to Southampton, and met the Sea Gull and old Macnamara and Witch Edie. We had tea and went to some lovely pubs. I had one amazing conversation with the Queen of the Horse and Groom. I wish I could draw her for you. [Drawing omitted] And yet this is a mere insult for she was far more royal and *immense*.

'There isn't anything I am frightened of, oh, nothing you could say, except, (and she narrowed her eyes and looked very confidential) except—SPIDERS. I can't *stand* a spider. My mother before I was born was frightened by my father, who brought a spider home from the West Indies and put it on her arm. A cru*ee*l thing to DO.' 'Oh, they're terrible creatures. Terrible. Now my husband there, he don't mind anything but snakes. Funny, isn't it, what some people can't stand?'

It's a marvellous pub, with stuffed bears, canaries and a band that plays old fashioned tunes and gay barmaids who run about singing as they serve the sailors and Sebastians.

We went to another a very different style, Edwardian, with a little old lady behind the bar and 1880 photographs of the war and ferns and flowers hanging from the ceiling. After dinner we went to the Musical Hall and saw George Robey and Marie Lloyd's sister, Rosie Lloyd. She had some of Marie's old tricks and songs. It was lovely sitting in a box and examining them very closely. I do love Music Halls.

As the lights of the car weren't working very well, for some reason Julia and I stayed on Beackus's ship. It was very romantic waking up in the shiny mahogany cabin this morning. We left early as Julia had to catch the 11.30 from Hungerford to London. Of course she nearly missed it, by powdering her nose in the bathroom, when we ought to have started! I threw her into the train just as it moved off! Gull went off to London from Hythe. I don't think I'll go up this week. As duty really demands that I finish some work and it would be nicer to be up next week when you are there. I send you James's letters so you can read all *his news*. [Fifteen lines omitted]

I wish I wasn't such a mass of mixed feelings. I feel absolutely exhausted now just by having felt so much, so intensely, these last 12 hours. Gull was rather gloomy and preoccupied, worrying over something I suppose, so was rather unapproachable. Although I know it's absurd, I mind so much, (partly because I see him so little) if when I do see him, he isn't happy. And yet really of course the whole thing is a chimera, a mirage of my own making. He is quite incapable of understanding my odd cravings and feelings about him.

Yet in spite of my miseries I would not have had anything different. Would you? For, one perfect evening seems to me, even in memory, to make days of gloom worth putting up with. But this letter is getting as involved as a mooncalf's labyrinth. So I will stop. Olive, and Phyllis have gone out for the evening, so I shall be able to eat chapaties on the floor. (Downstairs, *not* in your library) to my heart's content tonight, with Tiber—'Lady into Cat.' A fascinating photograph of Gilbert Spencer and his bride in the Mirror today.

My love to Pippa and you darling yr very fondest   C.

1931

To Stephen Tomlin

Tuesday [? *January 1931*]   *Ham Spray House, Hungerford*

Darling, If only you didn't hate reading letters, I would write you a long one. For I crave to have a chat with you. It was sad last week not seeing you alone. I hope you enjoyed your weekend. We stayed with Bryan, instead of here, as Olive was ill and away and Bryan alone at Biddesden. I had a lovely ride on Goldielocks and went some grand gallops. Poor Ralph was rather shattered by Bronc and Bryan exhausted by Belinda. I finished my cook at the window[1]—Bryan enquired very anxiously about his statue.[2] I said you were working very hard I thought. So I hope you are. It's a lovely day here. Drizzling (untrue) straight rain, rooks cawing in the beech groves. No wind and so warm I sit with the windows open, my favourite sort of day. I am living upstairs in my bedroom, eating meals on the carpet with puss. Just to annoy you.

I hope you will enjoy the party *very* much. I don't feel I can face London this week somehow. Too moody. This letter is getting too long and your attention is wandering off. So I will say goodbye, darling.

Your fondest C.

There is an interesting article by E. V. Lucas in this Life and Letters. Do you like Lamb as much as I do as a character?

[1] Carrington painted a *trompe-l'oeil* picture on the outside wall of Biddesden House.
[2] Stephen Tomlin made a large statue for the garden at Biddesden.

From Carrington's Diary

March 20th, 1931

As I stuck the book plates in with Lytton I suddenly thought of Sothebys and the book plates in some books I had looked at, when Lytton was bidding for a book and I thought: These books will one day be looked at by those gloomy faced booksellers and buyers. And suddenly a premonition of a day when these labels will no longer [be] in this library came over me. I longed to ask Lytton not to stick in any more.

To Lytton Strachey

May 12th, 1931   *Sans Pareil, Falmouth*

Darling Lytton, As far as I can make out we shall not reach Hythe till *Sunday*, as we may not get off from here till Wednesday and some things must be picked up at *Brixham*. So that rather alters plans about the weekend. Could you write to me at Brixham, c/o Globe Hotel, Brixham,

Devon, where we shall be till Friday and tell me your plans instead of to Hythe.

The car is at Martin and Chillingworth Newbury. So if you decided to use it you could ask them to drive it to Newbury Station, or any other station. If you want to spend the weekend at Ham Spray will you ask Olive to order you a joint and some FISH and vegetables, or order anything you like from Colebrooks yourself on a P.C. from London. I am sorry I didn't know before, but it wasn't my fault. Falmouth looks so sympathetic in spite of the rain and mist. We sit in the harbour not very far from the Green Bank Hotel. George is cooking dinner in the galley and I sit over a little fire with a grey tabby cat. I hope it will be fine tomorrow. The old salt 'William' says it is going to be hot. Please tell Olive I shan't be back on Thursday, and tell her you'll let her know about the weekend if you haven't decided before you go to London. I will go back on Monday to Ham Spray tell her. Could you possibly send me from the bottom drawer in my wardrobe a red silk dress, with a red belt and a black and green check silk blouse and from the bathroom cupboard a pair of pyjamas either blue or blue checked? It would be *extremely* kind of you if you could, as thinking we would only be away 3 or 4 days, I didn't put in any clothes. Olive would pack them for you. I hope you'll be very happy with puss and your fire. You've no idea how much I loved last weekend alone with you and our excursion to the forest of Savernake. I feel I've been rather dull lately darling but the truth is ma coeur était cracqué—comme le dos, you told me about and I've been trying to rivet it together again, which was rather painful and I felt made me often self absorbed and tiresome. Your friendliness means more than I can ever express. Coming in the train (it was too shaky to read Proust all the way) I thought of you and how happy you made me by living at Ham Spray. I wish you were here to prowl up the little streets with although I confess tonight it's hardly an evening for flanning.

Proust is fascinating, but the end of Charlus is almost too terrible. It has the appalling horror of Lear, in quite a different way. I wish I could write properly. The emotions and curious visions, that come back to one sitting in this little cabin and seeing Falmouth again. It seems rather a waste often to have so much material and to be able to make nothing of it. Now I must go and show George how to make our fried bread and sugar sweet. Perhaps a dentist and his wife [will] come to dinner or perhaps Warnford! Beakus has just gone ashore in the little boat. I shall hope for a letter at Brixham from you. I hope you'll have lovely weather for next weekend and enjoy yourself very much.

My very fondest love,   Yr most loving MOPSA

PS Don't leave this for the abigails to read please!

To Lytton Strachey

Tuesday evening, May 12th, 1931   *Sans Pareil to Brixham en route*

Darling Lytton, Had a curious dinner with Mr Tressiller dentist of Falmouth last night. He was a great friend of Tuke.[1] But not at all what you might imagine from that. He gave one a curious vision of Falmouth life. He was a great admirer of Warnford who dominates low life in that port, in very much the same way as Augustus does in Chelsea. But he was one of those characters who perpetually surprise one by the great originality and equal stupidity of their remarks. I think if he was a food he would be beef steak. We left Falmouth at 7.30, a cold misty morning and have been steaming and sailing ever since. Passed alongside one trawler and had some mystical nautical conversation, otherwise no adventures. A grey dull sea. I went to sleep on deck this afternoon when the sun came out. Poor George is ill, so I was cook.

We will get into Brixham at 7.0 o'ck when I will contrive to post this. I hope you are happy and that Olive is looking after you properly. Don't forget to give Sibbie[2] a ratting for her heinous crime.

My love to Roger.   Yr very loving MOPSA

[There is no date to this poem which I insert here as Carrington had been sailing in the *Sans Pareil*.]

> The heavy sea carved in grey still
> Raced round the ship
> Making one's wrists ache holding
> the tiller with clenching grip
> The drying dish cloths shone white
> In the moon's cold light
> And I thought of ducks on murky pools

[1] The R.A. who painted many pictures of boys bathing naked in Cornwall.
[2] Lady Colefax.

In Woolston's yard
Under December moon
And wished this night
Would never pass,
Sing again body and soul.

To Lytton Strachey

Wednesday, June 3rd, 1931   *Ham Spray House, Hungerford*

Darling Lytton, I am rather unhappy at not seeing you today—I had looked forward to it all yesterday. But it seemed rather beastly to turn poor Gull out, and send him to Oxhey, and the doctor was against London. He is still rather ill[1] and has a headache and feels rather depressed.

Dog Roland [Penrose] was rather charming in a dim way, (not so dim as he used to be perhaps). We went a long walk yesterday evening to the Gibbet and down by the left terrace and through the little wood which was filled with very beautiful flowers and blue bells and got in to dinner at 8 *o'ck*. He has just bought a house in France near Pau, it looked very lovely from the photographs. Rather an oppressive day here, the air thick as cheese and no proper sun. I expect it will end in crashes and bashes and thunder.

As I couldn't find out any brewery who would give us clean bottles, I set the girls to work (2/- each!) to wash the white wine bottles. They have started to work. So all will be ready by the weekend.

I must say the Lambs rang up and proposed themselves to dinner next *Sunday*. I thought I'd just warn you! Have you asked any cohorts?

I gather from a letter from Alix that she has gone to Brighton to recuperate, or is just going. I couldn't quite make out. I hope you bear up with all your activities and junketings. Is [Janko] Varda's show over yet? Or do you still go, every day, just to look once more at your picture!!

The birdies are a positive nuisance, they make such a noise in the garden. Tiber is better. He is taking a course of liver pills. Now I must stop, as I have a hundred and one things to do.

Yr very loving fondest   C. xxxx

---

[1] Bernard Penrose's illness turned to jaundice. Oxhey was the Penroses' family house.

To Rosamond Lehmann

Thursday [early June 1931]   *Ham Spray House, Hungerford*

Darling, How very kind of you to write. It was a beautiful surprise this morning after a terrible night of thunderstorms, nightmares, and glooms. You couldn't have been as disappointed as I was. I was really so savage, Wogan will tell you, I started cutting off the innocent heads of the verbena on the verandah with a kitchen knife. Beakus is better this morning. So I feel it was probably worth while giving up London and staying here. I suppose you wonder sometimes why I am so fond of him. It's really very little to do with him actually, but because he is so like my brother who was killed. I couldn't say this to anyone. Please don't show my letter to Wogan, as I am awfully self conscious of being a romantic, and rather stupid. My brother was very silent and removed. I hardly ever was allowed to be intimate with him and I always put it off, thinking one day I'd be able to show him how much I cared and then it was too late. And partly because he wasn't reported killed, it took me ages to ever believe consciously he was dead. I don't know why I shouldn't say this to you. Only you were so nice to write about your feelings and glooms. I don't agree about your being 'stuck'. I think Wogan puts almost too much emphasis on 'movement' and 'adventure'. Well that's not quite what I mean to say, really I think it's NO good being anything but what you are and the great thing is never to do anything one doesn't feel genuinely inside oneself. (This is Lytton's creed, not *my* invention!) And actually one can be very tame inside in spite of all one's dashing about. People like Sandy and Bryan aren't truly progressive characters I am sure. James Strachey is more advanced, although he hardly ever budges from his gas fire. I think your writing is what is really important and if you found the house and domestic things hampered *that*, I would agree with you about it being bad for you. I always see Rebecca West when literary women are mentioned! I am sure really everyone has to find their adventure in different ways. Wogan clearly finds stimulation in parties and excitable people, but I don't see why you shouldn't get, in other directions, quite as intensely. I am sure you do. I pass over your cauliflower moan. It's just the result of all your horrors and lying in bed. I am eight (?) years older than you are darling, so if one's going to start talking in the cabbage vein, you must condole with my later winter broccoli. Ralph is always blowing *me* up for not settling down to a purple sprouting old age and hates me going off to parties and boozing! —and holds up Beryl de Zoete as a warning! I will try and get hold of Brett. Perhaps she will be in England this year. She could, if she would, tell you far more about Katherine M[ansfield] than I could. Another person who could is Koteliansky and Gertler, but you'd have a job sifting the evidence.

I am so glad you liked the tulips. Yesterday Paul Cross and an aunt (?) (a dreadful old lady with a white nose—truly like a cauliflower and clothes that gave one the creeps. She was quite friendly, but so lacking in some quality of charm that is rather essential to spidery ladies of 56, if you understand) and Angus Wilson and another young man, came over after tea. Ham Spray was looking beautiful, untidy and dusty. I am afraid they were rather appalled. And then the old aunt said: 'And you live here all alone Mrs Partridge, *how* romantic, and after we go you'll go on weeding the garden? and you don't mind the loneliness, No? of course not, not with this view.' I was half longing when I was showing them the mosaic[1] that Beackus would appear in his pyjamas wandering to the W.C. Now I must go and see about lunch. I read 'Dr. Moreau's Island'[2] to Beackus all yesterday afternoon. Have you read Vita's book? Very *un*original I thought. James said Alix was getting on much better now and will soon be well. Lytton has asked T[ommy] and Julia for the weekend. I do hope they'll be able to come. Your reproaches towards yourself for not writing more, make my cheeks *burn* with shame. For really I used every excuse not to do any proper painting. It's partly I have such high standards that I can't bear going on with pictures when I can see they are amateurish and dull. This is a tediously long letter darling and it was meant to be a bright ray of sunshine to cheer your invalid cell instead of which it's as heavy as a suet pudding. I am sorry. I'll ring Wogan up tomorrow. All my love darling.

Yr very fondest loving C.

---

[1] By Boris Anrep in Lytton's room.
[2] By H. G. Wells.

To Lytton Strachey

Tuesday, Summer 1931   *Ham Spray House, Hungerford*

Darling Lytton, [Ten lines omitted] It's a heavy lugubrious day. Fit
for no better 'pursuit than weeding. The brain curdles and not a leaf
moves. The blackamoors however bound and tear about like lunatics. I
wish cats could be trained to weed gardens.

I say who *shall* we get to lighten load with old Saxon next weekend?
Do consult the Prince. What about Tommy and Julia (except you must
lend them their fares, I suppose) or Morgan? or Pippa? I hope you
enjoyed your lunch … and even more your dinner.

I've sent off that book to Riley[1] with some marbled paper to rebind
it with. So that there can be NO mistake. Now it is time for lunch so I
must go off. You are everything to me. I don't know how I should face
life without you. Thank you so much for putting up with my befogged
melancholies lately. I hope I shall have recovered by the end of this
week.

All my love.   Your very fondest most adoring C.

[Carrington went in for a competition set in the *Weekend Review* to
write an obituary of one of a list of writers, one of whom was Lytton, in
his own style.

She won it with the following entry.]

[1] A bookbinder with a shop in an alley off Tavistock Square.

FIRST PRIZE

Crouching under the ilex tree in his chaise longue, remote, aloof, self-occupied, and mysteriously contented, lay the venerable biographer. Muffled in a sealskin coat (for although it was July he felt the cold) he knitted with elongated fingers a coatee for his favourite cat, Tiberius. He was in his 99th year. He did not know it was his last day on earth.

A constable called for a subscription for the local sports. 'Trop tard, trop tard; mes jeux sont finis.' He gazed at the distant downs; he did not mind—not mind in the very least the thought that this was probably his last summer; after all, summers were now infinitely cold and dismal. One might as well be a mole. He did not particularly care that he was no longer thought the greatest biographer, or that the Countess no longer —or did he? Had he been a woman he would not have shone as a writer, but as a dissipated mistress of infinite intrigues.

But—lying on the grass lay a loose button, a peculiarly revolting specimen; it was an intolerable, an unspeakable catastrophe. He stooped from his chaise longue to pick it up, murmuring to his cat 'Mais quelle horreur!' for once stooped too far—and passed away for ever. MOPSA

[Lytton, who knew nothing of her venture, saw the entry and informed Carrington in a telegram.]

To Lytton Strachey

Saturday, July 18th, 1931   *Ham Spray House, Hungerford*

Darling Lytton, My most venerable Biographer, knitter of coatees, most dissipated of masters, do you know your wire gave me more pleasure than anything in the world? You were kind to think of sending it me. Terrible to think I nearly lost my two guineas through cruelty! Ralph is really more delighted than I am, I believe! But of course they will all say you wrote it for me. In fact I am terrified when I send my address the editor will refuse me my prize. I hope you enjoyed Thursday evening, and that the buffet wasn't too much of a cold collation, and that your 'savoury' was warm afterwards. How do you like Sparrow Pie? Give Dadie my love.

I went over to Fryern on Thursday evening as Dodo rang up and begged me to go over as she was alone. Untrue as a matter of fact, as sweet Edwin was there and Fanny witch. Dodo was exceptionally charming. I sat in bed and had breakfast with her and had a lovely talk on Friday morning.

She was rather shattered by that awful accident. It was a miracle Augustus and the two others escaped their deaths.

Edwin is looking very romantic. He has grown into a huge creature, very strong. He is now a professional boxer, with a 'manager'.

We went to tea with Rom and Cathy on Friday afternoon in their beautiful little cottage on the edge of the New Forest. Strange creatures. Romilly is trying to find a job as a 'coach in mathematics' at a boys' school as his poetry doesn't bring in enough money! May I give Fanny a copy of your American Miniatures?[1] She would so love one and so would Romilly, I think, if you sent him a copy. Of course I didn't say I'd give Fanny one. But she asked me if I could lend it her to read. It's bitterly cold here; fires and furs. [Thirteen lines omitted] A mad hatter's tea party this weekend. I wonder how it will go off! I rather dread the lady poetess, Madame Gamal Brenan.[2] Tomorrow Earp sends very enthusiastic wires 'Looking forward very much to weekend. Arriving 4.10 with happy anticipation' I hope he won't be furious to find you not here.

The cats all send you their loves and pussykisses. Tiber is very proud to at last be immortalized in print. What about our chaise-longue now?

Did you hear that Bunny was sent for by Sir Philip Sassoon and has been asked to Lympne for a weekend, to fly in an aeroplane!

I send on all your letters, which seem pretty dreary. I shall miss you very much. I rather favour the curly mirror. But have not quite made up my mind yet. [Illustration omitted] Again it is the expense, which is rather serious.

I hope you'll have a lovely time at Cambridge, and enjoy yourself very much darling.

I shall stay here, and paint next week, and try and improve the house a little, and the garden, before your return.

Dodo's garden was looking very beautiful. She gave me some rare cactuses for my greenhouse.

Poppet, and Derek,[3] are coming to dinner tomorrow to complete the congress of mad hatters!

[1] A copy of the American edition of Lytton's *Portraits in Miniature*.
[2] Gerald Brenan had married Gamel Woolsey.
[3] Derek Jackson was to marry Poppet John.

I love you so much, and think of you very often. Please write to me, as I shall miss you very much.

All my love   Your devoted and most loving MOPSA xxxx
PS Mrs. MacNamara has a 'Candide' 1st edition, original boards, which she wants to sell privately and asked if you wanted to buy a copy. She will send it on approval. Shall I ask her to send it to you at Cambridge or wait till you come back?

To Lytton Strachey

Sunday, July 19th, 1931   *Ham Spray House, Hungerford*

Darling Lytton, I had a lovely ride with Bryan [Guinness] on Friday evening, and a nice chat with Diana over the fire after dinner alone. She told me a great deal about Tom [Mosley's] character. Rather interesting. I stayed too late—but it is the disease of my old age I foresee, lingering on till everyone falls unconscious with sleep. But what do you think! On the way home I met a badger on the road. And what did the badger say to Mopsa? You will never know. But really it was rather exciting. I could see it very clearly as it ran along in front of the headlights of the car and finally climbed up a bank and went through the hedge. A quiet weekend here. Julia has gone to sleep most of the time. Tommy, Eddie [Gathorne-Hardy] and I sat up till about 2 *o'ck* arguing and boozing last night. Today Woggies[1] come to lunch and we tea at Fryern. Julia wants to stay on with me next weekend for some days. Will that be alright?

All the covers have been washed in the sitting room. It looks quite smart. 20 bottles of gooseberries for the winter and some pots of redcurrant jelly for you and your mutton pies.

Pansy has sent me her essay for you to read. I hope you are happy darling.

All my love and love from the cats.   Your fondest MOPSA
Olive made some really *delicious bread* for us, this weekend.

---

[1] Rosamond and Wogan Philipps.

To Sebastian Sprott

Monday [July 1931]   *Ham Spray House, Hungerford*

Darling Sebastian, I was just on the point of writing to you. Really I meant to write yesterday but was so busy entertaining Toppers[1] that there wasn't time. I've been through the MILL rather severely lately, or I'd have written before. Now it's all over and I will resume my proper life, and hope my friends will forgive me for being so curmudgeonly. Well darling I doubt if I'll be able to get the Dook of Marlborough here for you on the 6th. But I'll try to raise up a Lord. I take it, reading between the lines, that you want to come here on the 8th Wednesday. Well, Lytton says he'll be in London probably that week. But would love to have you here for the weekend till the Monday. *But* why not come and stay with Mopsa and her cat alone on the Thursday before the weekend? (I have an idea there's some'at on on the Wednesday.) Please do, and we'll go on a jaunt together if it's fine. The blasted Captain has gone off to Spain for the summer so that's all off and you'll have *all* my attention dearie. I had him here to nurse for 3 weeks with jaundice this month. Rather ironical to realize one's mission in life is Florence Nightingale! However I learnt everything there was to know about him and in some ways cured my illgotten passion.

I am glad Les is everything to you still. And what were you doing with old Bunny pray?

I have put down the 9th in my diary with a S. after it. So do not fail me. All my love   Your most loving C.

To Dorelia John

Thursday [July 1931]   *Ham Spray House, Hungerford*

Darling Dodo, Here is rather a mangy tribute of my love. I did enjoy yesterday evening, although I was rather overpowered by the Chambertin. When you come back in the spring I shall take you out again, only we must think of a better Harmony than that gloomy cave[2] to end our

---

[1] Topsy Lucas.
[2] The Cave of Harmony, a nightclub started by Elsa Lanchester.

symphony upon. It's a relief to get back here. I got rather bored by the perpetual pinning, and unpinning of the dusty blue brocade.

When I told Lytton of all the marrying and giving-in-marriages[1] he said 'well it's about time I got married. I think I shall marry Dorelia. I've often thought about it, only (groans) I suppose there'd have to be a duel with John.' Well all I can say and did say, is, that it would be very nice if you did. I should like nothing better.

Will you really go to France? If you don't, please tell me and come here instead. I promise you we have a special sun that shines here every day, log fires in visitors bedrooms, Chambertin for every meal. As I drove back in my solitary taxi last night I thought what a pity [it] was we hadn't had a great many more evenings together. For me it was completely perfect. Please give my love to lovely Poppet and Vivien.

In February I shall send you a telegram.

'Good God, here's that woman coming down. We fly to Spain.'

But I daresay Spain will prove no refuge. On the other hand god tells me we shall unfortunately not meet until May 7th at Fryern. I am boozed with Tarragona and sleep. But I wanted before you passed away to tell you how much I loved our dinner, the brandy, and more especially you.

Your devoted C. x

To Stephen Tomlin

Monday [*July 1931*]   *Ham Spray House, Hungerford*

Dearest Tommy, This is a *very* private letter and I shall MURDER you if you show anyone my scenario, or pictures. You must read Goblin Market to understand, I expect, the gist of my ballet—

Do you think

(a) There is anything in it?

(b) If there was would you combine with me over the dresses and masks, and scenery?

(c) If there isn't any of (a) will you say so and say no more.

I am too impatient to draw it out nicely, also I've a terrible cold and a temperature so can't concentrate. The dairymaids would be dressed in my favourite rustic china-figure-1840-style. You would have to make my masks and help with the inventions, please. I then thought, supposing you thought it possible, we might draw it out neatly, with colours,

[1] See previous letter of July 18th.

and ask Lydia [Lopokova] and Constant Lambert to give us a £100 and put it on the stage. Or shall we ask Mr Cochran and get £1000 and sink art and ambition?

But all this depends on your coperation. (Excuse me Dr Jones, for hesitating over that word.) When shall I see you again? Derek and Poppet have just left us, a *strange* pair of turtle doves.

My fondest love   Your devoted C.

PS I am going to suggest to Derek that he has a head done of Poppet, by you. Don't you think it would be a good idea??

PS The moral I confess of this ballet seems a little obscure. The triumph of Lesbianism?

To Julia Strachey

Monday, 1931   *Ham Spray House, Hungerford*

Darling Julia, It was so lovely seeing you yesterday but rather agonizing as the time was so short and I felt rather dazed by all the conversations and fallings off horses. I don't think I can quite face London this week. But next week perhaps I'll be up. I hope the headache got better yesterday evening. Please give Tommy my love. I'll start your cover tomorrow, and send you a proof by the end of the week. Your hat was lovely, and suited you to perfection.

All my love darling.   Your very loving old TANTE C.

To Lytton Strachey

Tuesday, July 28th, 1931   *Ham Spray House, Hungerford*

Darling Lytton, What do you say to these examples? will you look at them, and give me your opinion.

I went with Julia to lunch with Diana [Guinness] today. There we found 3 sisters and Mama Redesdale. The little sisters were ravishingly beautiful, and another of 16 very marvellous, and grecian. I thought the mother was rather remarkable, very sensible and no upper classes graces.

We were half an hour late having spent nearly an hour wandering about the byways and footpaths of Glanville. Julia as you might guess wasn't much good with the map! Mercifully lunch was late as they had only just come back from Stonehenge.

The little sister was a great botanist, and completely won me by her high spirits and charm.

Now I must send this to the post.

I talk with Julia all day, on rather painful topics and get rather gloomy. I do not know what to advise, for I have very little faith in there being any happiness for human beings on this earth.

I shall not come to London, as there will be preparations to make for the weekend and I think Julia stays with me till Friday probably. I miss you more than I can say.

The Sans Pareil has just reached Lisbon. I had a post card yesterday. Fanny asked me to thank you very much for her present of P. in M.[1]

All my love to you darling   Your fondest MOPSA

To Frances Marshall

Monday, v. early in bed [*September 1931*]   *Ham Spray House,*
                                                        Hungerford

Dearest Frances, I am so glad you are so well set up in jobs. I shall expect a commission out of Alec's job occasionally! 'Should a Typist Tell?' 'The Secrets of Inverness Terrace'! 'The Quaker's Slave'—a

---

[1] Lytton had sent a copy of *Portraits in Miniature* to Fanny Fletcher.

new film with you as the heroine. Life here seems very hectic lately. But so beautiful because it is blazing hot all day, that the hecticness is almost pleasant.

Every day the telephone buzzes, or a man appears at the door asking for Major Partridge; a gardener from Ham Rectory or a Labour leader from Devizes. Then there are dinners at Fryern, dinners at Biddesden, and last Saturday, excursions to Tidcombe with Alix, and a fair at Marlborough, a drive back to Tidcombe afterwards in the mist and fog for eggs and bacon (we didn't get back here till 2 o'clock.) The fair was lovely. I hit the hammer but couldn't sound the bell. Went on swing merry-go-rounds with Paul [Cross], and shot at bulls and bottles. Alix went quite mad in those little electric motor cars and charged everyone to pieces. Yesterday Alix and I walked almost to the Three Legged Inn, along the downs and got back for lunch. It was amazingly beautiful on Walbury Camp. In the afternoon Ros. and Woggie turned up from Marlow, and we all went on a picnic in Savernake Forest. Alix, James and George Hervey went back by the new 6 o'clock train from Savernake station, and Wogan and Rosamond came back here to dinner. They were *both* very charming. Wogan has a picture in the London Group.

Have you read Virginia's novel yet?[1] I've been working very hard at little Bryan's dummy window. I might get it finished today. Phillis is 'sitting' for the ghostly cook, and Tiber for the ghostly cat.

The shells are found! So I am transported with happiness this morning. Did you laugh over little Hampden, and the hole? I thought it amazingly funny, and longed to know what was left out by the J.C. Squires. I am sorry poor Flopsy has been so ill. I hope she is better. D.V. I may come up on Wednesday evening. I'll ring up when I do arrive. When do you go bird shooting with the convict?[2] This letter is for Ralph also. I give him my love with love to you.   Yr. C.

There is a grand Mop fair at Marlborough *next* Saturday!

---

[1] *The Waves*, (Hogarth Press, 1931).
[2] Ralph Partridge had made the acquaintance of Mr Hayley Morris who had been convicted of a sexual offence with a young woman.

To Lytton Strachey

October 29th, 1931   *Ham Spray House, Hungerford*

Darling Lytton, Oh dear! Inanimate objects are very animated down here! I can pay no attention to elections and tariffs when motorcars refuse to start, scissors disappear and gloves walk off and hide themselves. I got up at half past 7 this morning in order to start my picture at Biddesden early.[1] Bryan had asked me to breakfast. The car refuses to operate and it was 10 *o'ck* before I got to Biddesden. Then, typically as you would say, the moment I started to paint it came on to rain. So all my paints got mixed with water. My hair dripped into my eyes and my feet became icy cold. Diana was delighted. Bryan kept it a complete surprise from her till 3 *o'ck*. May joined in the joke, and kept my presence dark all this morning and pretended I had walked over from Ham Spray as my car had to be hidden. Diana, of course, thought nothing of my walking over in the rain and merely said 'But Carrington you *ought* to have let me send the car for you.' I had tea there and then came back. Diana is sweet. She was looking very lovely today, in a curious dark bottle green jersey with a white frill round her neck. Bryan ate 2 huge slices of his birthday cake for lunch! It was his birthday yesterday. Diana gave a very amusing account of an excursion to see Miss Mona Wilson and Mr. Young[2] at Oare. 'Oh Carrington I cannot *tell* you how *dreadful* they were.'

Bryan—'Carrington you mustn't believe it. It was a *fascinating* afternoon.'

'Ough, she smoked a pipe and Mr. Young talked about the middle classes and had a blob at the end of his nose' etc. etc. etc.

Diana says 'Will you tell *Mr* oh indeed to remember the christening on Monday'.

I got back here at half past five and had a hot bath for nearly an hour. This evening I have been painting china. I have nearly finished one breakfast set. I wonder what adventures you have had? This from Sibbie, hypocritical old puss! Adrian D[aintry] wrote a very charming collins thanking us for giving him such a nice weekend.

Hugo and Reine [Pitman] say they are coming to tea tomorrow. But

---

[1] The *trompe-l'oeil* painting of the housemaid looking out of the kitchen window on the west wall of Biddesden House.

[2] G. M. Young, reactionary essayist and biographer.

I rather doubt if they will. Don't come back too exhausted; remember our literary weekend! *You* are responsible for the dazzling conversations. I shall just put opium in the pies to mitigate Aldous's brilliance. Puss sends you his love and a kiss. I must go to bed now as I am half asleep. I take the car into Newbury tomorrow. Really it is too much to BEAR. Biddesden was looking ravishing today. The afternoon was beautiful and hot. It's rather a relief to know nothing of elections. Ham was quiet as a dead mouse.   My love darling *Mr*. Oh indeed   Yr loving C.

To Lytton Strachey

Sunday [*November 15th, 1931*]
                              Ham Spray House, nr Marlborough, Wilts.

Darling, I am coming up on Tuesday with Ralph so will see you then and hear all your news. I do hope you are better, and enjoyed Brighton very much. We went over to Biddesden to tea yesterday and saw Diana and Bryan and the ghostly housemaid. Diana longs to see you again. Eddie [Gathorne-Hardy] and Julia are here this weekend. The house seems alright, no calamities, puss very glad to see us again. So you were detected at the Ivy!!!

I have dinner with Bryan and Diana on Wednesday and little Clutton-Brocks on Thursday and Dorelia (who is up in London) on Tuesday night.

Angus Wilson knows René Clair, 'Le Million' film producer, and is going to ask him to Tidcombe. So perhaps after all I shall end up by being a film-produceress. Really, Philip Stegmann's pictures! I saw some in the Graphic. Pretty so-so. Eddie is charming, very bawdy and amusing. We go to Tidcombe to look at the film today for tea. Ralph is frightfully excited because he has triumphed over America! He can hardly get over it! He now longs for Strickland's scalp to add to his laurels.

It will be lovely to see you on Tuesday. Perhaps we could lunch together? I will call at 1 o'ck in case you are free. Otherwise will you leave a note for me at 41 G.S. I saw a Duncan Grant in a curious shop in Wardour Street for £7. 10. It's a shop that sells coloured prints nearly next to Clarkson's the wig shop. You might look at it if you were passing. The man is very agreeable.

All my love. Your very fondest most loving   MOPSA

PS We might go and see Dobson's[1] after lunch; they are rather lovely, particularly the heads.

To Julia Strachey

Thursday, 6 o'ck   *Ham Spray House, Hungerford*

Darling Julia, Virginia, and Leonard have just been down here for the day. They are a fascinating couple. I found Virginia's conversation irresistible. She is *very* enthusiastic about your story,[2] and so was Leonard. They gave you a tremendous high praise, your old Tante was delighted. She has been struggling with a cover, but how not to look like Mr Whistler (Rex). That is the problem. How to cram in the socks, penknives, ferns, inkpots, wedding cakes and jellies. All very difficult. I suggested to Virginia that she should get *you* to illustrate your own masterpiece (C. 'her drawings, only of course she never lets anyone see them and always crosses them out, are equal to her writing'), I regret to say Virginia refused to be lured away from her horrid intentions. But seriously my dear why don't you do them? Then, ah then, no fault could be found by the author with the illustrator.

I am mad about my grove and spend all my time weeding, and carrying nettles on to bonfires. When the heavenly grove is finished poor Tante C. will, I fear, be so bent double she won't be able to look about her and appreciate the darker shades. It's been very pleasant here this week, such lovely quiet weather. No winds. Olive is ill, so a nice person calls Mrs Walters from the lodge waits on me. She is a sweet character. How are you? You never write now, Piggie. What am I to imagine? Your doggie picture is at 16 Great James's Street so go and see it if you want it. It is literally 16 years old. Almost as old as Vivien. Is the 'cook and the pussy cat'[3] an improvement? If you'd tell me that, I should then know whether to go on with my painting, or take to poker-work. But nobody speaks the truth. So it's all no use.

My love to Tommy and you darling.   Yr fondest old TANTE C.

---

[1] A show of Frank Dobson's sculpture.

[2] *Cheerful Weather for the Wedding* (Hogarth Press, 1932).

[3] The painting on the window at Biddesden.

[On November 5th, 1931, Lytton had been taken seriously ill. The symptoms were high temperature and dysentery, or colitis. The doctors diagnosed typhoid fever, though no typhoid germs could be found. In spite of this they persisted in believing it to be typhoid and it was not until a post mortem that it was shown to be cancer of the intestine which in any case was inoperable.]

To Rosamond Lehmann

Thursday [November 1931]   *Ham Spray House, Hungerford*

Darling, I'll write tonight because tomorrow may be rather a busy day. Lytton is really a little better today, temperature lower, and no haemorrhages, but he feels rather worse, I suppose because of the low temperature and exhaustion. I feel so relieved when each day is over, as I gathered from the specialist that if there is a turn for the worse it will be in the next few days probably. I sat all this afternoon with Lytton, sponging his face, and hands with scent and water. There is practically nothing one can do. The nurses are very kind and let Pippa and me go in and out of his room when we like. Lytton is so good. He lies without moving day after day and never complains. They still can't find the germ in any of the blood cultures, but apparently it is undoubtedly typhoid from temperatures and other symptoms. Pippa is such a remarkable character, she adores Lytton and yet never betrays her grief, or thinks of herself. Oliver came down yesterday and stays at the Bear and comes up for meals and spends the day with us. James is coming this weekend I think. Lytton is too weak to talk much, so one sits in his room by the fire without talking. He sends you and Wogan his love. He was so touched by your enquiries, and letters.

I feel dreadfully upset about Garrow.[1] I felt I'd been so stingy not caring for him, when probably quite a little affection might have made him happier. Julia said Tommy was terribly upset in her letter to me yesterday.

I met Mrs Hammersley at the Guiness[es'] last Saturday evening and was fascinated by her. She talked a *great* deal about you. She is so beautiful in a romantic Russian style. I couldn't take my eyes off her. Bryan longs to visit Wales. 'Do you thing they would mind if we all made an

---

[1] Garrow Tomlin had been killed practising spins in an aeroplane.

expedition and visited them? and Diana we could look at *all* the cathedrals on the way!'

'Oh Bryan, *must* we, I do hate cathedrals ... '

Mrs Hammersley said she'd join the party so about the 6th Jan. you must expect the invasion! Ralph went up to London today but he will be back tomorrow. The owls have come out of their hiding, and hoot round the house tonight and the lawn is white with frost. I'll write when there is more news. I gather the climb down hill for Lytton will be very slow. You are dear to write such cheering letters. I've been feeling in a black dungeon all this week. Nightmarish day and night.

Your most fond DORIC

To Sebastian Sprott

Sunday [*December 1931*]   *Ham Spray House, Hungerford*

Darling Sebastian, Thank you so much for the lovely handkerchief and even more for your letter. Another specialist today! Dudgeon, of St Thomas's. He said Lytton's state was remarkable considering what he had been through. That he was 'holding his own' very well. But of course there must be danger whilst the temperatures continue, and the poison goes on. I feel rather unreal. Can't feel very much now, after last Wednesday, which was the worst possible day as they all gave up hope. Now nothing can be as bad I feel.

Tommy has come here to stay with us which is a great support to me. There are all the Stracheys at 'the Bear' and Alix and Saxon who strolled in without a word. So really nothing more can be done in the way of human kindness. James lives in the house and Pippa of course. Lytton sends you his love. He is marvellously brave and the doctors are all astonished by his courage and spirits. I am sad darling, that you have had so much trouble, very sorry.

I'll write again soon. Today he is a fraction better, but really there is no very great change. I can't write a proper letter as there isn't any time. But I know you care most, so I'll try and write often

Yr loving C.

To Diana and Bryan Guinness

Christmas Day, 1931   *Ham Spray House, nr Marlborough, Wilts.*

Darling Diana and Bryan, You can't think how I loved all your presents.
You are geniuses to know the colour of my stockings, my socks and my
favourite necklace. Please don't be cross if your surprise isn't quite
ready by the time you get back. I hope it will be, but there never seems
any time now for ...

I can't write today as I feel rather crushed and flattened by horrors.
I gather now the worst is over, at least they hope it is. Yesterday was a
terrible day. You can't think how I look forward to seeing you both
again.

Lytton asked after you today and sent you his love. Your letters were
very supporting. Your fondest, with a great deal of love, CARRINGTON
10 o'clk. PS The nurse has just told me that the temperature is lower
tonight.

To Sebastian Sprott

Tuesday evening [December 1931]   *Ham Spray House*

Darling Sebastian, Lytton was pleased this morning when I told him of
your present. He said: 'How sweet of Sebastian. Do send him my love.
I knew Du Maurier he was a traitor' and gave me a long account of him.
It always astonishes the grand doctors how clear his brain is and how
good his spirits. We had Dudgeon the grandest pathologist in the world
here on Sunday. He confirmed Cassidy's opinion about the ulcerated
colitis, but gave a new treatment, more drastic washing outs and pills.
So far there is no visible result but I suppose it's too soon to expect it
yet. The temperatures are still high, they go up to 102 and 103, but
pulse is better which is the important thing. The local doctor seems
pleased at the way Lytton is holding his own and hopes the bugs and
abscesses are being held in check. Your love means so much. I'll write
when there is any change and when it's possible to have you here
darling. I hope you are a little happier now. And next year will be
better. Did you see 'an elderly respectable stockbroker' got pinched, in
yesterday's paper, for buying female underclothes in D.L. draper's shop.
It is a scandal.

My fondest love.   Your loving C.

1932

[Lytton died in his sleep on Thursday, January 21st, at half past two in the afternoon, without pain.]

From Carrington's Diary

On Wednesday afternoon the 20th Jan. at a quarter to three, there was a change in his face. I suddenly noticed his breathing was different although he did not wake up. And I thought of the Goya painting of a dead man with the high light on the cheek bones. I ran and called nurse MacCabe, as he had a slight attack of hiccups, she at once asked me to ring up Dr. S. S[mith] and ask how much strychnine she could give him. I saw Pippa and James at the top of the stairs just going out. Pippa said 'what is it?' I didn't tell her. I ran back after telephoning and held his arm bare while nurse MacCabe injected 30 grains. Then his breathing became less short. I ran and told James and asked Pippa to come—at that moment it became clear to me he could not live. Ralph returned from a picnic with Gerald at quarter to four. Dr. S.S. arrived and gave another injection. I saw from his face he had no hope. He slept without any discomfort or pain. A hatred for nurse Phillips came on me. I cannot remember now anything except watching Lytton's pale face and his close shut eyes lying on the pillows and Pippa standing by his bed. Sleeping with his mouth open. Ray arrived. Cars came backwards and forwards on the gravel. 'There must be nightwatches. Pippa will stay with him till 12 o'clock. Then I till 3 o'clock. Ralph till 6 o'clock and then you after 6 o'clock.' At 3 o'clock I saw James outside on the landing. I had not slept. I went in and asked nurse Mooney if there was any chance of his living, she said: 'Oh no, I don't think so now.' I gave him a kiss on his cold forehead, it was damp and cold. I gave Ralph a kiss and asked him not to come and wake me. I saw him sit by the fire, and sip some tea in Lytton's room. James went downstairs. I walked very quietly down the passage and down the back stairs. It was half past three. The house was quiet and outside the moon shone in the yard, through the elms across the barns. The garage door was stuck open I could hardly move it. Every movement seemed to screech through the still night air. At last I got the doors closed. Then sitting in the car I touched the horn, and my heart stood still, for I felt R[alph] must have heard, as the landing window was open. I stood in the yard watching for a light to go on in the passages. After some time I crept back again and made every preparation, all ready that I could start up the car directly the milking engine started in the farm yard. But not a sound outside. It was very cold in my dressing gown, I thought the milkers started at 4.30. It was 4.30 by the car clock and still nobody stirred. I longed to go round the garden but I feared to be too far from the garage to run back, so I stood under the beech tree by the back door. On the edge of the gutter on the roof, perched 6 pigeons asleep silhouetted against the pale dawn sky. The moon sunk lower. The faint noise of a wind blowing up came across from the trees in the garden. I thought how different one feels everything to what one usually does. As if one was almost trans-parent, so without any emotion. I was only terrified the cowmen had overslept and that it would be 6 o'clock before they would start. The moon disappeared behind a cloud. I went indoors and drank a whiskey in a tea cup in the dining room. The house was very warm after outside. I went back to my watch under the trees. Suddenly I heard sounds across the yard and movements in the milking shed. I ran to the garage and shut the doors. I got in the car. I started it up one minute after the milking machine which was half past five by the car clock, but that is ten minutes fast. I was terrified by the noise. Once it nearly stopped so I had to turn on the petrol more. There seemed no smell. I got over in the back of the car and lay down and listened to the sound of the crying below me, and the noise of the milking machine puffing way outside. At last I smelt it was beginning to get rather thick. I turned on the light in the side of the car and looked at the clock. Only ten minutes had gone. However Ralph would probably not come exactly at 6 o'clock. The windows of the car looked foggy and a bit misty. I turned out the light again, and lay down. Gradually I felt rather sleepy, and the buzzing noise grew fainter and further off. Rather like fainting I remember thinking. And not what Ellie had told me about a pain in one's throat. I thought of Lytton, and was glad to think I shouldn't know any more. Then I remember a sort of dream which faded away.

Suddenly, long after, waking up in my bed with a buzzing in my ears, and Dr. Starkey Smith holding my arm and injecting a syringe. I cried: 'No, no, go away,' and pushed him and his hand away and saw him vanish like the Cheshire cat. Then I looked and saw my bedroom window and it was daylight, and Ralph was there. Ralph held me in his arms and

kissed me and said: 'How could you do it?' I felt *angry* at being back
after being in a very happy dream. Sorry to be awake again. A buzzing in
my ears and something wrong with my eyes. I couldn't see my hands, or
focus on anything. Ralph asked me if I'd have some tea. I asked for some
water. He was very upset and I felt he was angry with me at first; perhaps he wasn't. I had no idea of the time. Then Tommy came in, but
perhaps that was much later and talked to me. I felt rather far away and
my eyes were still queer. James came and talked to me. I felt no remorse,
I must confess I felt defrauded and angry that fate had cheated me in
such a way and brought me back again. I got up at 12 o'clock and went
into Lytton's room. He was still sleeping, breathing very deeply and
fast. Pippa sat in a chair. I went and sat in the chair and watched him.
'So this is death,' I kept saying to myself. The two nurses moved about
behind the screen. Ralph came and sat on the floor I felt completely
calm. His face was very pale like ivory. Everything seemed to be transfixed. The pale face of nurse MacCabe standing by his bed, in her white
clothes. Pippa watching with those sweet brown eyes, all tear stained
and her face mottled. The noise of the electric light machine outside. I
sat there thinking of all the other mornings in Lytton's room and there
was 'Pride and Prejudice', that I had been reading the afternoon before
still on the table. It seemed as if time had lost all its properties. As if
everything was marked by Lytton's [heart] beating, not by the ticks of
the clock. Suddenly I felt very sick, and ran out to my bedroom and was
violently sick into the chamberpot. I remember watching the yellow
water pour out of my mouth and thought it is the same as what is in the
pot already. Then Ralph came with a basin but I had finished being sick
by then. I saw as I walked down the passage, Tommy talking to James in
the library. I went back to Lytton's room and sat on the chair. About 2
o'clock or 1.30 Lytton grew worse and his breathing became shorter. I
stood holding Pippa round the waist. Lytton never opened his eyes. I
could not cry. I felt if he woke up we must be there not depressing or
melancholy. James came in and stood behind us with Ralph. I felt like
a Russian soldier holding Pippa against my body. Nurse MacCabe stood
against the wall, alternately watching us and Lytton, sometimes taking
his pulse. Nurse Philipps suddenly came forwards and said: 'I think you
ladies had better go, and sit down, you can do no good here.' I was
furious and hated her. Ralph brought me some glasses of brandy and
some sal volatile to drink. A blackbird sung outside in the sun on the
aspen. We stood there. I do not know for how long. Sometimes his
breathing almost stopped. But then he breathed again fainter. Suddenly

he breathed no more and nurse MacCabe put her hand on his heart under the clothes and felt it. I looked at his face: it was pale as ivory. I went forward and kissed his eyes, and his forehead. They were cold. Pippa was crying. I took her to the library. James kissed me. Outside on the lawn in the sunshine Tommy walked backwards and forwards picking up dead sticks off the lawn. There was nothing to say. I held Pippa's hand on the sofa. Ralph brought us some tea. Nurse Philipps looked in and said: 'That's right, drinking a cup of tea. Don't come in the room now will you. That will do you good.' I hated her.

'I hope they will all go I can't bear the sight of them' Pippa said.

I felt very far away without any sensations. I do not know what the time was. The glass of the window distorted Tommy on the lawn in the sun. Pippa said 'Is that Tommy. He looks so like Garrow.'

I said 'It is the glass.'

She said 'I couldn't think who it was till you told me, what is he doing.'

People walked up and down stairs. I felt I couldn't bear to move, or for anything to happen. I wanted to be transfixed sitting there with Pippa. The sun outside and the birds singing in the laurels. We opened the window and I knelt on the floor. The fresh air was very cool on one's face.

'Will you go and lie down Pippa, if I do.' I will have some tea in my bedroom I think. I went to my bedroom. Presently James came and lay on the bed with me. I heard voices below. Gerald was talking to Ralph. Tommy came and talked to me. There was a noise of cars outside. At six o'clock the nurses all went and the house was still. I could only think of that pale face in the other room. I went in and kissed him. Ralph came with me. He was colder than when I kissed him before. Cold as stone. An electric light was burning. Ralph said 'they leave a light on all night.' The room looked so lonely. The fire had gone out, and everything had been removed. I burst into tears when I got back to my room. For suddenly I felt terribly sorry for darling Lytton lying there so cold by himself alone.

On Friday morning early I woke from a terrible dream. But now I cannot remember it. It was about Lytton and terrible, deformed faces cut in half. I burst into tears. Pippa came, and saw me. She went to London with Marjorie and James. Ray stays till the evening they say. Tommy came and sat with me. It was a beautiful day outside. I felt different. Nothing inside me felt the same. Ralph brought me some bay leaves, and I made a wreath. I tried it on my head, it was a little large. I went in and put it round Lytton's head. He looked so beautiful. The olive green leaves against his ivory skin. I kissed his eyes, and his ice cold lips. The sun shone through the open window. Ralph went into the town with Ray after lunch. I asked Tommy if I could go in again to Lytton. He went in first and then I went in for the last time and kissed his lips, and his forehead and the tears dropped from my eyes on his face. Outside Tommy stood waiting on the landing. Then I went back to my bed.

At 4 o'clock we went in the car for a drive to Savernake. I knew while we were away men would come with the coffin and take Lytton away. That was what I could not bear. We left Ray behind. All the time I thought of Lytton with his pale face lying on the white pillow with the green leaves. How strange to drive 'this way' to Savernake. We talked ordinarily. I sat in front with R[alph], T[ommy] and Frances behind. In the forest we saw little deer and one big stag and quite near to us; further off some other stags. The forest was deserted and the sun had set. We walked under the beech avenue together. I could only think of Lytton and other times and then too painfully retreated from my thoughts. We went to Marlborough and bought some cakes. The last time it was the Fair. We drove back through the forest. It was half past six when we got back. The house was quite deserted. I went up to bed and Tommy came and sat and talked to me and read me poetry after supper. Ralph told me that Lytton could never have lived. It makes a difference. For I had been thinking of that medicine he took on Monday all the week. He wasn't defeated by any ordinary disease. And my premonition when I listened to Pippa talking to James was right.

It is ironical that Lytton by that early attack at 6 o'clock saved my life. When I gave my life for his, he should give it back.

To Stephen Tomlin

Saturday evening [written shortly after Lytton's death]
Ham Spray House, Hungerford

Darling, I miss you very much. I wish you had not gone. This afternoon
I made a bonfire and laid some grass under the yews. I hope you had a
lovely ride with Diana on the downs. Julia seems better. I can't write
a letter you see, so I had better stop. You made this last week bearable
which nobody else could have done. Those endless conversations were
not quite pointless. Today has been a great improvement in one direction. Ralph seems much calmer and more natural. I think of what you
said to me very often. Forgive me for going to bed yesterday, but you
had no idea how bad my headache was. It really was cracking my skull.
I didn't want to complain and fuss. Now you are gone I can! But I had
had it all the morning. I hope you had a lovely evening with sweet H.[1]

All my love my darling supporter   Your very loving C. x
I am sending you some ties, and handkerchiefs belonging to Lytton just
to keep. Later if there's anything else you would like, you must tell me.
He loved you so much that I'd like to give you some of his books for you
to keep always but you must choose.

To Sebastian Sprott

Sunday   *Ham Spray House, Hungerford*

Darling Sebastian, I wanted to give you these ties and the belt to keep.
Later you must tell James if there is anything of Lytton's you want.
Something you remembered here. You understand more than anyone
what it means. I long to be here alone. But everyone seems to be my
enemy and insists on treating me like an imbecile invalid. They want
me to go to Dorelia for a week but I hope I shall persuade her to let me
return if I can't bear it. Forgive this letter and don't write back. Later
come here and stay with me alone and talk to me of Lytton and yourself.
Your very loving CARRINGTON

[1] A man friend of Stephen Tomlin's, always referred to as H.

To Rosamond Lehmann

Tuesday   *Ham Spray House, Hungerford*

Darling Rosamond, I am so sorry you are still ill in bed. This is just to send you all my love and to thank Wogan for writing to me. Next week perhaps I'll be able to face London, if I do, I will come and see you. Ralph says he will go and see you for me. I am alone at last, it is for some reason a relief. I feel a happiness in just wandering in the garden and being able to sit by myself in the library. I find Ralph's grief almost too much to bear. He has been so kind to me, but I feel we only make it harder for each other in some ways. Please give Wogan my love. Do take great care of yourself and don't get up too soon. I've been planting daffodils and snowdrops under the yew trees, making a little grove. It begins to look rather beautiful. James and Alix come next weekend and Ralph and Frances.

My love darling   Your fondest D.

To Rosamond Lehmann

Sunday   *Ham Spray House, Hungerford*

Darling Rosamond, Will you do the greatest thing I can ask of anyone, help me to bear something that is a little too much? Ralph's grief? I think he would be happy with you, and Wogan. It was the only place he thought of going to. I thought if he had the car he could go off with Frances sometimes if you had people to lunch, or if you had to go out. For a little I shall stay here. I can't bear going away. Tommy and Julia will be with me. Nothing Rosamond will ever be the same again. He was more completely all my life than it is possible for any person to be. By being kind to Ralph you will be helping me more than I can say. Your love for Lytton and me meant so much these last two months. I will write soon to you darling. My love to Wogan and you   Yr. D.

To Rosamond Lehmann

Saturday evening   *Ham Spray House, Hungerford*

Darling, Thank you so much for being so kind to Ralph. He came back
looking so much better and so did Frances. I long to see you. But I
don't think I can face London for some time. Will you come here later
on? I really want to stay here alone for a bit, but Ralph seems rather
opposed to the idea, and insists on my going to stay with Dorelia next
week. So I suppose I shall have to. I expect I shall be there for some days
after next Tuesday, a week perhaps. I am not facing things. I can't for a
bit. The impossibility of it happening, a possibility I never believed in
my worse moments of despair, still makes it seem a nightmare. I find it
difficult to go on with ordinary life and I almost hate anybody else who
can, although I know it's unreasonable to expect the world to stand still.
I dread leaving here. Forgive me if I can't write, but you know I love
you. Later you must tell James or Ralph if there is anything of Lytton's
you would like as a keepsake. Anything here that you loved particularly.
Ralph told me you weren't looking well. Please take care of yourself in
London, and DO darling, go to a specialist about the glands. I am so glad
the book is finished.

My love to Wogan, and very much to you.   Your loving DORIC

From Carrington's Diary

February 11th

No one will ever know the special perfectness of Lytton. The jokes
when he was gay. 'The queen of the East has vanished.' I believe you
eat my nail scissors and then at lunch pretending to play a grand fugue
before we got up. And the jokes about the coffee never coming because
I stayed so long eating cheese. Sometimes I thought how wasteful to let
these jokes fly like swallows across the sky. But one couldn't write them
down. We couldn't have been happier together. For every mood of his
instantly made me feel in the same mood. All gone. And I never told
him or showed him how utterly I loved him. And now there is nobody,
darling Lytton, to make jokes with about Tiber and the horse of the
ocean, no one to read me Pope in the evenings, no one to walk on the
terrace. No one to write letters to, oh my very darling Lytton.

Fryern, Friday

G[erald] B[renan] writes. 'If you had loved Lytton less absolutely and completely your recovery would be more difficult. For death is a thing that in itself is absolutely incomprehensible.' 'To be happy you won't have to forget him, only to think of him without pain and that I really believe may be easier than you can now imagine.'

Death is unfortunately *not* incomprehensible. It is all too easy to understand. There is no pain in thinking of Lytton now, different from it can ever be. It is only the advice of a person who has not ever loved a person more than himself, and who does not know what it is to live everyday in utter and complete intimacy, even if separated from the other person. What point is there now in what I see every day, in conversations, jokes, beautiful visions, pains, even nightmares? Who can I tell them to, who will understand? One cannot find such another character as Lytton and curious as it may seem to G.B. these friends that he talks of as consolers and [? substitutes] for Lytton cannot be the same, and it is *exactly* what Lytton meant to me that matters.

One cannot live on memories when the point of one's whole life was the interchange of love, ideas, and conversation.

Everyday is the same. 'When D[orelia] says shall we go to the Lambs.' I know it does not really matter. I shall *not* write a letter tonight describing Henry and everything that only Lytton would understand because of our past conversations about Henry. There is no interest in Peter Spencer's conversation, or speculations about his character, now I shall have no one to describe him to. And when the Lambs say: 'Will you come here next week', a misery comes over me when I know there is no reason now why I should not stay weeks away from Hamspray. Nobody now to 'consult' about plans. And when Reine [Pitman] said 'I think one always gets, if one wants it enough, whatever one longs for' I felt like saying, 'You are utterly wrong, for you have forgotten death.' I just feel I must get through these days, and pray they won't be very many more. I have been reading Lytton's diary. I remember how interminably long those two weeks seemed if no consequence just because of that. And the happiness when I got his telegram saying he would be back a day earlier than I thought. And my pleasure in dealing with his letters when he was away. The bookshops which used to be my secret pleasure because I might find him a present and write and tell him of a book to buy. I just think now of getting back to Hamspray next Monday because there I can think of him undisturbed, alone.

[The two paragraphs which follow are quoted from David Hume's *Essay on Suicide*, first published anonymously in 1777. Carrington picked out the sentences which seemed to her most important. Thus there is an omission after the word 'ineligible' of two pages and another omission of six lines after the words 'ceases to do good'. The second paragraph, which occurs on the page following, is quoted entire. The choice of sentences indicates that Carrington had re-read Hume's essay and thought closely about it, finding it more convincing than Alix Strachey's and Stephen Tomlin's arguments. Note also in her letter to Sebastian Sprott, on p. 498, she asks: 'Can you refute Mr Hume?']

'I am only convinced as a matter of fact which you yourself acknowledge possible, that human life may be unhappy and that my existence if further prolonged, would become ineligible. A man who retires from life does no harm to society. He only ceases to do good. I am not obliged to do a small good to society at the expense of a great harm to myself. Why then should I prolong a miserable existence. Because of some frivolous advantage which the public may perhaps receive from me?'

'I believe that no man ever threw away life, while it was worth keeping ... and though perhaps the situation of a man's health or fortune did not seem to require this remedy, we may at least be assured that anyone, who, without apparent reason, has had recourse to it was cursed with such an incurable depraving or gloominess of temper as must poison all enjoyment and render him equally miserable as if he had been loaded with the most grievous misfortunes.'

I remember L. reading to me this Essay. And we both agreed on the sense and truth of the arguments. Tommy with all his reasoning against death did not really alter my mind. He persuaded me that after a serious operation or fever, a man's mind would not be in a good state to decide on such an important step. I agreed. So I will defer my decision for a month or two until the result of the operation is less acute.

Tommy says that if death was accidental through illness it would be a different matter, and I should not be to blame.

'When I fall upon my own sword therefore I receive my death equally from the hands of the Deity as if it had proceeded from a lion, a precipice, *or a fever* and why may I not employ one remedy as well as another?'

Human beings seem to me divided in[to] those who can say 'I live for only myself alone' and those who know that 'without this person or this thing I could not live.'

I agree one may have delusions, but when it comes to the test it may be proved.

By not allowing myself to think of the reality of the situation I can bear life. But then it is not life. It is a contradiction. I pretend to myself this week at Fryern that I am on holiday. I avoid allowing my thoughts to even approach Lytton. If for a moment they break through my fences I at once feel so utterly miserable that it is only by thinking there will be only a few more weeks, I can bear the pain. That there is nobody any longer to serve and love completely and entirely makes everything pointless.

Really I have decided. And if I bring myself to think of reality for a few hours how could I bear the emptiness and loneliness of life without Lytton? For our separations were for me enforced. I was never in all these 16 years happy [when] I was without him. It was only I knew he disliked me to be dependent that I forced myself to make other attachments. Everything was enjoyed to be with him. He was, and this is why he was everything to me, the only person to whom I never needed to lie, because he never expected me to be anything different to what I was. And he never was curious if I did not tell him things. And he could do no wrong. No one will ever know the utter happiness of our life together. The absurd and fantastic jokes at meals, and on our walks, and over our friends and his marvellous descriptions of the parties in London and his love affairs and then all his thoughts he shared with me. And I knew he loved me and would always comfort me when I was sad and be pleased with my success.

When he was very ill, it was on the Tuesday, he suddenly said: 'Carrington, why isn't she here? I want her. Darling Carrington. I love her. I always wanted to marry Carrington and I never did.'

He could never have said anything more consoling. Not that I would have, even if he had asked me. But it was happiness to know he secretly had loved me so much and told me before he died. There is nothing I regret except perhaps that I didn't go away with him this summer. I couldn't ever have loved him more. This August when I wrote that essay for the Weekend Review, I cried as I read it because I suddenly felt a premonition that it might be true, and thought that there might be a day when Lytton would die. And often when he was asleep when his mouth was open I used to watch with terror at my heart and think if Lytton died, I could not live. He was so good to me. No one will ever know how kind and dear, or that he could have ever had to bear such pain. I can hardly bear to think those long weeks of torturous discom-

fort and all for no end. And I could never say a word because I could
not bear to let myself think there might be [The passage is unfinished]

To Virginia Woolf

Thursday [*February 1932*]   *Fryern Court, Fordingbridge*

Darling Virginia, Thank you so much for your letter. There are only a
few letters that have been any use. Yours most of all because you understand. I've just been reading a diary Lytton kept in Nancy this September, again. It is a comfort because he was so happy, sometime James will
give it you to read. His emotional troubles were over and it was a perfect
holiday by himself, enjoying all the accumulated pleasures of his lifetime.

Do ask Ralph to see you some time. He is so lonely and I think it
would make him happier to talk about Lytton with you. I can't quite
bear to face things, or people. But you are the first person I'd like to see
when I come to London. Please give my love to Leonard. All my love
darling Virginia.

Your very fond CARRINGTON

From Carrington's Diary

February 12th

I can think of nothing but the past, everything reminds me of Lytton.
There is no one to tell one's thought to now. And the loneliness is un-
bearable. No one can be what Lytton was. He had the power of altering
me. So that I was never unhappy as long as he was with me. I keep on
trying to forget it is true. At Fryern I almost pretended it was a holiday
and things weren't all altered but the pressure to keep these thoughts
out of my head is almost as much of a strain, as the pain of thinking of
Lytton dead. Then I have a longing to enmesh myself in his relics. That
craving for death which I know he disapproved of and would have disliked. If I could sit here alone just holding his clothes in my arms on the
sofa with that handkerchief over my face I feel I would get comfort, but
I know these feelings are bad. And if I became bad then I should feel

he would disapprove and all would be worse. So I must and cannot go backwards to his grave. Tommy made that clear to me on Monday night when we discussed it. What can I do. For no future interests me. I do not care about anything now. R[alph]'s love is a reproach to me. For I feel so cold and melancholy. I can do nothing for him. Oh why did I not know, not believe the warning premonitions that I sometimes had, that I did not spend every hour of every day with him. Oh Lytton darling, you are dead. The impossible terrible thing has happened. And all is utterly cold and grey on his earth now. All our plans for this year are laid in dust. What is Venice now without you and Rome? All your books in the library that we loved together so fondly and arranged evening after evening. They are desolate. This house and garden which was beautiful for you and me, stands empty and forlorn. Those friends who we loved to see, they have vanished now. I read their letters but they all cease to be real. Except Tommy and James and Pippa. But they were with us both when you were ill. And Ralph but he is too near, he understands so much I can hardly bear his sorrow added to mine.

All our jokes even when you were ill about 'Nursiana' and Dr. Starkey. We shall never have them now. They say one must keep your standards and your values of life alive. But how can I, when I only kept them for you? Everything was for you. I loved life just because you made it so perfect, and now there is no one left to make jokes with, or to talk about Racine and Molière and talk of plans and work and people.

Everything I look at brings back a memory of you. Your brown writing case that I bought you in Aix. Your clothes that I chose with you at Carpentier and Packer. All our pictures and furniture that we chose together. Oh darling did you know how I adored you. I feared often to tell you because I thought you might feel encumbered by your 'incubus'. I knew you didn't want to feel me dependent on you. I pretended so often I didn't mind staying alone. When I was utterly miserable as the train went out and your face vanished. You were the kindest dearest man who ever lived on this earth. No one can ever be your equal for wit and gaiety. And you transported me by your magical conversations and teaching into a world which no one could have dreamt of; it was so fantastically happy and amusing. What does anything mean to me now without you. I see my paints and think it is no use, for Lytton will never see my pictures now, and I cry. And our happiness was getting so much more. This year there would have been no troubles, no disturbing loves. Oh if only we would have gone to Malaga alone, and talked and read together. Everything was designed for this year. Last year we recovered

from our emotions, and this autumn we were closer than we have ever
been before. Oh darling Lytton you are dead. I can tell you nothing.

Tuesday, February 16th, 1932

At last I am alone. At last there is nothing between us. I have been
reading my letters to you in the library this evening. You are so en-
graved on my brain that I think of nothing else. Everything I look at is
part of you. And there seems no point in life now you are gone. I used
to say: 'I must eat my meals properly as Lytton wouldn't like me to
behave badly when he was away.' But now there is no coming back. No
point in 'improvements'. Nobody to write letters to. Only the terminable
long days which never seem to end and the nights which end all too
soon and turn to dawns. All the gaiety has gone out of my life and I
feel old and melancholy. All I can do is to plant snow drops and daffodils
in my graveyard! Frankie [Birrell] sent me some old letters to read. I
read them at tea. Now there is nothing left. All your papers have been
taken away. Your clothes have gone. Your room is bare. In a few months
no traces will be left. Just a few book plates in some books and never
again, however long I look out of the window, will I see your tall thin
figure walking across the park past the dwarf pine past the stumps, and
then climb the ha-ha and come across the lawn. Our jokes have gone for
ever. There is nobody now to make 'disçerattas' with, to laugh over
our particular words. To discuss the difficulties of love, to read Ibsen
in the evening. And to play cards when we were too 'dim' for reading.
These mourning sentinels that we arranged so carefully. The shiftings
to get the new rose Corneille in the best position. They will go, and the
beauty of our library 'will be over.' —I feel as if I was in a dream almost
unconscious, so much of me was in you.

February 16th, 1932

And I thought as I threw the rubbish on the bonfire 'So that's the
end of his spectacles. Those spectacles that have been his companions
all these years. Burnt in a heap of leaves.' And those vests the 'bodily
companions' of his days now are worn by a carter in the fields. In a
few years what will be left of him? A few books on some shelves, but the
intimate things that I loved, all gone.

And soon even the people who knew his pale thin hands and the
texture of his thick shiny hair, and grisly beard, they will be dead and

all remembrance of him will vanish. I watched the gap close over others but for Lytton one couldn't have believed (because one did not believe it was ever possible) that the world would go on the same.

February 17th. In the Library

I dreamt of you again last night. And when I woke up it was as if you had died afresh. Every day I find it *harder* to bear. For what point is there in life now? I read all your letters this afternoon. Because I could not bear the utter loneliness here without you. If only I had believed my fears and had never left you for a day. But that would have meant 'encroaching' on your liberty, and breaking the 'laws'. What is the use of anything now without you? I keep on consulting you. But for what purpose? For I can no longer please you. I look at our favourites I try and read them, but without you they give me no pleasure. I only remember the evenings when you read them to me aloud and then I cry. I feel as if we had collected all our wheat into a barn to make bread and beer for the rest of our lives and now our barn has been burnt down and we stand on a cold winter morning looking at the charred ruins. For this little room was the gleanings of our life together. All our happiness was over this fire and with these books. With Voltaire blessing us with up-raised hand on the wall. It was all for you; I loved you so utterly and now there is nothing left to look forward to. You made me so absolutely happy. Every year had grown happier with you. It is impossible to think that I shall never sit with you again and hear your laugh. *That everyday for the rest of my life you will be away.* No one to talk to about my pleasures. No one to call me for walks to go 'to the terrace'. I write in an empty book. I cry in an empty room. And there can never be any comfort again. 'You can't get away from the fact that Lytton is dead', he said.

Monday 19th

Yesterday at Biddesden suddenly I came face to face with Death. For the horse bolted down the road and I could not pull him up, as my wrists were so weak with trying to hold him in. I saw the long road with the bend and the chicken huts and the logs on the bank and the horse tearing along the tarred road towards the bend. He swerved round the corner, and I came off and just missed the logs and the road and fell on the bank. I was completely unhurt. Only winded by the sudden fall. I thought of the irony of fate. That I, who long for death, find it so hard to meet him. I wrote R[alph] a letter this evening. The picture of the cook on the wall is perhaps one of the only pictures I have ever 'brought off'. I am glad Lytton saw it and liked it.

Thursday

Dodo and Helen came to lunch today. Dodo is the most beautiful perfect woman in the world. I longed to keep her here with me.

Looked through all my old pictures to find some of Lytton to give James. Tidmarsh all came back. How much I love places. I remembered suddenly my 'passion' for a certain tree in Burgess's back field. And the beauty of the mill at the back of the house and how once a king-fisher dived from the roof into the stream. Although I seem, looking back, to have been in a very vague state of mind about 'situations' in those days. An inability to face looking into one's motives, or facing the outside world. I had a terror, I remember, of believing: 'if people knew what I wanted they'd prevent me,' and I could very seldom face thinking, in consequence, of what I wanted myself in case I betrayed myself. In ten years perhaps I'll be just as prosy and wise about myself now!

To Margaret Waley

Wednesday [? February 1932]   *Ham Spray House, Hungerford*

Dearest Margaret, I found that poem I wanted. *You* sent it me. The 'Long Low Rambling' house was the last line, so how could you have remembered it? It's too far away, right away in my studio, to get now, but you sent it me with some others years ago and I have put them in a book and only found them yesterday.

Yes, I've been reading Cowper. I love his poems and his letters. They are just my style of poetry. I am reading 'Sense and Sensibility' at meals and in bed at night I read poetry. Shakespeare's Sonnets at the moment and odd Elizabethan lyrics.

The grove is getting quite presentable. I wish I could find some urns to put under the yews. Perhaps I might when I go to Hungerford on Friday. The Ramsbury man is so expensive now.

Ralph went up to London yesterday. I feel more peaceful alone. One feels less conscious of one's disagreeable, melancholy state of mind. Misery makes people very selfish, except really 'good' character[s] like Pippa Strachey. They become saints.

I hope the children keep well, and you all avoid the plague of London. Please give Hubert my love and my fondest love to you, and thank you so much for your very kind letter.

Your loving C.

To Bryan Guinness

March 1932   *Ham Spray House, nr Marlborough, Wilts.*

Darling Bryan, If 'Collins' are to be written, it is *I* who should have written to you not you to me. You never realise how much I love my visits to Biddesden, and those gallops, even if they do end by falling off. I must admit I thought our picnic was an *especially* good one this time and our kitchen party delightful. David Garnett and Ralph and Frances, enjoyed themselves enormously and loved you.

I hope you have a lovely time tonight. I can hardly bear not to see you both in your dresses ... But I have enjoyed so many parties at the Johns' that I couldn't face sitting out watching or feeling gloomy.

The country is so lovely. Yesterday was a beautiful drizzling spring day. Very sympathetic. Give darling Diana all my love and a hundred kisses and all my love to you and one kiss.

Your loving C.

To Sebastian Sprott

[March 1932]

[A fragment; the rest of this letter is missing] You see I'm not a modern cynical character really, I mind terribly the changes. And nothing seems to me worth anything in comparison with that perfection of jokes and intelligence. It breaks my heart every night I sit in the library to think of all the hours Lytton spent arranging his books and putting in book plates and cleaning them, all to see them within a few months dispersed and probably sold. I know these things are bound to happen and are always happening. But if one person really flavours all life for one it is difficult to see how to set about starting a new one. Yes, that is what I should ask you this evening. Alix says one's object must be to maintain and live up to, those standards of good and intelligence that he believed in. But for whom? You see my weakness is that I only led, or tried to lead, a 'good' life to please Lytton, left to myself I lapse (secretly) into superstition, drink and mooning about. Come, write me on your typewriter a discourse on 'the object of life.' You must know the preliminary lecture by now. Can you refute Mr Hume? But unless you write before Thursday afternoon Ralph will be back, and will read your letter. So perhaps you had better leave me alone to my mooning meditations.

[I include four poems that Carrington wrote after Lytton's death. From the letter to Margaret Waley it is evident that she adapted the line
            'I saw no beauty in our long low house'
from the last line
            'the long low rambling house'
of a poem which Mrs Waley had failed to trace.
    She may have used other remembered lines in the same way.]

Mourning your loss involuntary

The ilex tree droops against the sky
For never again in the Park will I see
That thin familiar figure stalk,
As I sit waiting for winter tea.
No more will he call me for our walk
'Across the fields to the Russian Wood'
Life never again can be so good
For I sit alone in his empty room
Filled with melancholy thoughts and gloom
These books we arranged with infinite care
Oh, darling Lytton, now you're not here
Stand funeral sentinels with ashen faces
They too must follow and leave empty places
Oh why was I left on this wretched earth
For you have left me quite bereft.

A Field Mouse's Lament

I did not realize till now, that you
Made lovely all my fields and view;
Walking across our Park, the sun
Sank down behind the beechen-grove,
I saw no beauty in our long low house
So pink and trim, that we standing still
Often upon the crest of Downey Hill
Paused to admire and pride ourselves upon.
We vied each other in our love of Spray
Your presence here made perfect every day,
Back to an empty nest goes the field mouse
No more in Russian Woods she'll roam
No more bake pies, and delicacies to sup on
For all is drear and dead, in this small world
Tho' spring is here, and brightly shines the sun.

This is all our world
We shall know nothing here but one another
Hear nothing but the clock that tells our woes
The vine shall grow but we shall never see it?
But dead cold winter must inhabit here still.

Advice to Oneself

Turn down the wick!
Your night is done
There rises up another sun
Another day is now begun
Turn down your wick.

Turn down the lamp!
Time to expire
'Body and soul' end your tune
Retreat my pale moon,
And turn out your lamp.

[The following lines are copied in Carrington's handwriting.]

He first deceased, she for a little tried
To live without him, liked it not and died.
[Sir Henry Wotton. 1627. 'Upon the death of Sir Albert Morton's Wife'.]

[Carrington had borrowed a shot gun saying that she wished to shoot rabbits out of the window.

On March 11th, 1932, she shot herself, but the wound was not immediately fatal. She was found by the gardener who called the doctor and telephoned to Ralph.

I was sleeping in the same house in Great James Street and fortunately had my car in London, and drove Ralph and Frances to Ham Spray.

Carrington died not long after our arrival.]

Carrington's Early Life
by
Noel Carrington

The early life of my sister up to the time when she left school for the Slade was uneventful and certainly not unhappy. Her family was middle class and thoroughly imbued with the Victorian ideal of respectability.

Dora de Houghton Carrington was born at Hereford on March 29th, 1893, and was the fourth child in a family of five. She came to dislike the name Dora and never used it after she had gone to the Slade, where surnames were the rule. Still less did she like the second name, embodying our mother's vague aspirations to a mythical nobility. Our father, Samuel Carrington, was born in 1832, five years before Victoria came to the throne, the eldest son of another Samuel, a Liverpool merchant who had retired to Penrith. Thus when Carrington came into the world her father was over sixty and she could only know him in his old age. As a young man he had gone to India to build railways for the East India Company. He landed when the Indian Mutiny was at its height and, though he took no military part in the affair, was close enough to the fighting and butchery to be affected for life. He became by conviction and religion a man of peace. This may well have had some influence on Carrington's pacifism, which in the First World War was to be an article of passionate faith. He was a devout Christian, his beliefs ¦were based largely on the Bible; he had no interest in either dogmas or rituals. In this he differed from his own relations and from our mother, who had strong inclinations towards High Church, genuflexions and pious observances.

His periods of long leave from India were spent mostly in travel to the farther East or back through America. From these journeys he brought back case after case of works of art and curios, chosen without too much discrimination, so that our home, especially that holy of holies the drawing-room, was for ever after an oriental museum. After thirty years out East it was time for him to retire, partially deaf through dosing malaria with quinine, but otherwise active and energetic. His two sisters had married at the age of sixteen and had each bred a round dozen of children, now mostly grown up and with families of their own. With one of the sisters lived Charlotte Houghton as a governess, already connected with the family by her brother's marriage. Samuel Carrington—the rich bachelor uncle from India—surprised and almost certainly disappointed his own relations by marrying the governess. At any rate it was perceptible later that the Carrington connection felt itself a cut above the Houghtons, who came from Erith in Kent and from a less affluent stratum of the middle class. The aunts and cousins on the Carrington side were cheerful, easy-going and spendthrift. 'How jolly for the dear girls,' was the refrain. Invariably they dispensed gifts to us from readily opened purses which had almost certainly just been replenished by loans from our father. Our mother's relations were forbidding and finders of fault, perpetually in mourning, perpetually suffering from colds, and apprehensive of draughts. Our year was punctuated by visits from all these relations, who came by custom rather than invitation and always outstayed their welcome because they knew that our father had an oriental code of hospitality. Except for a rare summer holiday, year followed year with virtually no other inter-ruption to this ordered pattern.

In summer we were encouraged to be out of doors—bicycling expeditions led by our father on his tricycle, games with school friends in the park, or fishing on the river. In winter a Victorian family had long hours of leisure which children were required to occupy use-fully: boys at carpentry or hobbies, girls at needlework or 'practice', as music was usually called. Only Carrington escaped the ordeal by music. It was tacitly accepted that, with her talent for drawing, musical accom-plishment could be dispensed with. I hardly remember a time when she was not drawing, mostly from life. All of us, including my school friends, were cajoled into sitting as models.

We were educated at Bedford, where the family moved in 1902 and did not leave until twelve years later when our schooling was finished. Only two subjects at the High School engaged Carrington's interest: drawing and natural history. Thus her general education tended to languish, and as soon as she went to the Slade, at sixteen, lapsed altogether.

About 1908 our father suffered a stroke and was thereafter partially paralysed. As a result he was cut off from us, often in pain, nursed devotedly by our mother, but guarded, too, and interpreted. He had always been unconventional in dress: equally in the friends he made and the standards he set. He was charitable and uninterested in gossip. We could not help noticing that those few old Anglo-Indian friends who visited him spoke of him with glowing admiration. One of them told us how in a famine he had fed a whole district from his own resources. And this was not entirely a myth, as I recently discovered from his letters. He in his turn was so loyal to his friends that for many years an old Welsh doctor lived with us, our father declaring that the man who had once saved his life should never lack a home.

Our mother, on the other hand, was cast in a different mould, and her virtues seemed less and less commendable as we grew older. She was obsessed at all times with 'what people would think'. She was lame and rheumatic but indefatigable in doing what she conceived to be her duty, which was to oversee what her children and the servants were doing. On the occasion of the slightest lapse we would be reminded that she had given up everything to bring us up in a God-fearing way. That children must grow up, become individuals in their own right, form their own friendships and way of life, was a thought that she could never bring herself to accept. Keeping secrets from one's parents was almost the ultimate sin. Even before she went to London Carrington's friendships and letter-writing became a source of disturbance, especially as she was incurably careless in leaving letters insecurely hidden. As the older members of the family left home to take up careers, so our mother's determination to keep the family together became concentrated on the two last and youngest, Carrington and myself.

The art mistress of her school at Bedford had suggested that the Slade was the only proper place for Carrington's talents to develop. Family pride induced our mother to fall for this notion, which she afterwards professed to regret. To guard against the notorious dangers of London life, Carrington was placed at Byng House in Gordon Square, a hostel with a reputation for respectability and discipline. After a year she was able to persuade the family that the food was unhealthy—a sure argument for parents—with the result that she and her elder sister, now a nurse at a London hospital, were allowed to share a little house off Regent's Park. She never had much in common with her sister, but a convenient neutrality was observed.

The Slade at that time was probably at its peak as a teaching school, with Steer, Brown and Tonks on the staff; Tonks in particular was a dominating and even intimidating figure. Carrington's conversation was soon full of this trinity, with the names of John and McEvoy also spoken with reverence. To our mother's circle the only Mecca for artists was still the Royal Academy which, of course, Carrington treated with disdain. She might try, she said, for the London Group or perhaps the New English, institutions of which Bedford had never heard. Amongst the men students were Stanley and Gilbert Spencer, the Nash brothers, Bomberg, Nevinson and Gertler. Amongst the girls her particular friends were Ruth Humphries, daughter of a Bradford printer, Brett, the daughter of Lord Esher, Lynton and Barbara Hiles.

What irked her most each time she came home were conventions she no longer believed in and to which she felt reasonable people elsewhere no longer conformed. To conform under such circumstances was hypocritical. There were two principal conventions which our mother had inherited. The first was extreme prudishness. Any mention of sex or the common bodily functions was unthinkable. We were not even expected to know that a woman was pregnant. Even a word like 'confined' was kept to a whisper. The second was church-going and behaviour on Sunday. We all came to hate the whole atmosphere of a Sunday morning. The special clothes, the carrying of prayer books, the kneeling, standing and murmuring of litanies. Yet to lead her family up the aisle, especially on Easter Sunday for communion, was to our mother the true reward of righteousness. I believe Carrington would have refused point-blank to bend the knee had it not been that it would have bitterly grieved our father.

Apart from her disgust with what Gilbert Cannan described as the 'meaningless tradition of gentility', new friendships were effecting another change which was to be probably of greater importance in her future: this was a desire to educate herself in those areas of knowledge —literature and history in particular—which she had hitherto neglected. I found that my text books were being borrowed and not always returned. When sitting as a model, my brains were picked over for any useful information. It was not all 'take': in return I was forcibly educated in Art, according to the creeds then held at the Slade. For this I should have been grateful. An essay on the all-embracing virtue of 'Significant Form' was decisive in gaining me an open scholarship in History, my examiners being unaware that it was virtually lifted from a recent work of Clive Bell. If Carrington was tireless herself in the quest of knowledge at this time, she also never wearied of improving her brothers' too-conventional minds.

After each term in London the disparity between her home life and what was opening before her became more frustrating. Gradually she devised a makeshift system of alibis, based on painting commissions or visits to approved friends. All this led to a complicated calendar of

deceptions which became a second habit even when no longer necessary. Quite apart from our father's feelings, she was economically
dependent on the family, so that evasion was preferable to defiance.

There was one occasion when deception could not be practised. This
was when she arrived home with her hair cut short or bobbed. She said
she had needed to have it cut to fit her costume at a fancy-dress party,
but it may have been for other reasons, perhaps psychological. Short
hair for girls was then virtually unknown and unheard of at Bedford.
Thus it was read as a declaration of audacity and independence and one,
alas, which could not be concealed. For a long while our mother continued to lament the loss of 'such beautiful hair' as if it were a family
rather than a personal possession. I think it impressed on us that something had happened to mark her off as different from the rest, an unmis-
takable assertion of personality. From that moment her mother began
to treat her with a trace of caution in her reprimands, even though she
could not restrain her inquisitiveness or gestures of pained disapproval.

By nature Carrington was warm-hearted and affectionate. These feelings were denied expression with her parents once she had left home. With
her mother, who survived her by some ten years, neither understanding
nor reconciliation was possible. Her father may be supposed to have
understood her more than he was able to show in life, for in his Will
he left her a modest but independent income. One further consequence
of the conflict was that she developed a repugnance for family life as
such. As her own friends in turn came to marry she was apt to treat it
as a lapse from grace, with maternity an inevitable but none the less
deplorable sequel for a person of intelligence.

Bibliography

Brenan, Gerald, *A Life of One's Own* (Hamish Hamilton, 1962)

Cannan, Gilbert, *Mendel* (Fisher Unwin, 1916)

Carrington, Noel (ed.), *Mark Gertler,* Selected Letters (Hart-Davis, 1965)

Devas, Nicolette, *Two Flamboyant Fathers* (Collins, 1966)

Garnett, David, *Flowers of the Forest* (Chatto and Windus, 1955)

Garnett, David, *The Familiar Faces* (Chatto and Windus, 1962)

Hardy, Robert Gathorne-, *Ottoline, the Early Memoirs of Lady Ottoline Morrell* (Faber and Faber, 1963)

Holroyd, Michael, *Lytton Strachey, a Critical Biography*, 2 vols (Heinemann, 1968)

Huxley, Aldous, *Crome Yellow* (Chatto and Windus, 1921)

Sanders, Charles R., *The Strachey Family* 1588–1932 (Duke University Press, 1953)

Smith, Grover (ed.), *The Letters of Aldous Huxley* (Chatto and Windus, 1969)

Woolf, Leonard, *Downhill All the Way* (Hogarth Press, 1967)

Index

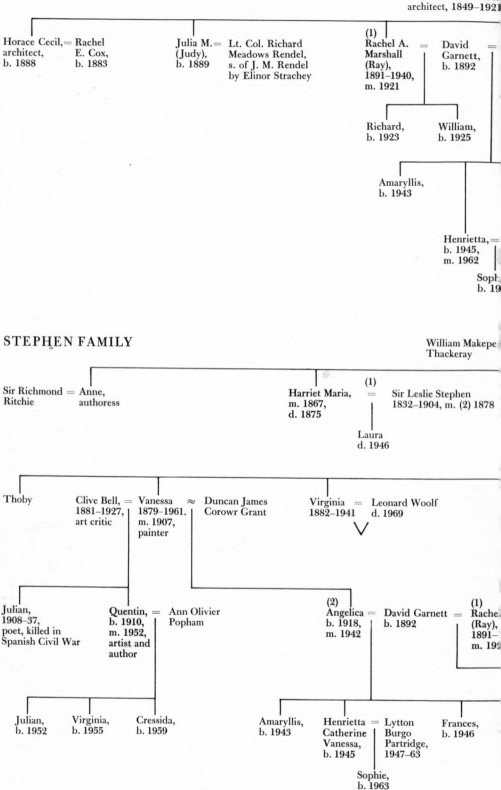

MARSHALL FAMILY

William Cecil Marsh[...]
architect, 1849–1921[...]

Horace Cecil, = Rachel   Julia M. = Lt. Col. Richard   **(1)**
architect,   E. Cox,   (Judy),   Meadows Rendel,   Rachel A.   =   David   =
b. 1888   b. 1883   b. 1889   s. of J. M. Rendel   Marshall   Garnett,
   by Elinor Strachey   (Ray),   b. 1892
   1891–1940,
   m. 1921

Richard,   William,
b. 1923   b. 1925

Amaryllis,
b. 1943

Henrietta, =
b. 1945,
m. 1962

Sop[...]
b. 19[...]

STEPHEN FAMILY

William Makepe[...]
Thackeray

Sir Richmond = Anne,   Harriet Maria,   **(1)**
Ritchie   authoress   m. 1867,   =   Sir Leslie Stephen
   d. 1875   1832–1904, m. (2) 1878

Laura
d. 1946

Thoby   Clive Bell, = Vanessa ≈ Duncan James   Virginia = Leonard Woolf
   1881–1927,   1879–1961.   Corowr Grant   1882–1941   d. 1969
   art critic   m. 1907,   ∨
   painter

Julian,   Quentin, = Ann Olivier   **(2)**   **(1)**
1908–37,   b. 1910,   Popham   Angelica = David Garnett = Rache[...]
poet, killed in   m. 1952,   b. 1918,   b. 1892   (Ray),
Spanish Civil War   artist and   m. 1942   1891–[...]
   author   m. 19[...]

Julian,   Virginia,   Cressida,   Amaryllis,   Henrietta = Lytton   Frances,
b. 1952   b. 1955   b. 1959   b. 1943   Catherine   Burgo   b. 1946
   Vanessa,   Partridge,
   b. 1945   1947–63

Sophie,
b. 1963